Tunisia

David Willett

D1324334

LONELY PLANET PUBLICATIONS
Melbourne • Oakland • London • Paris

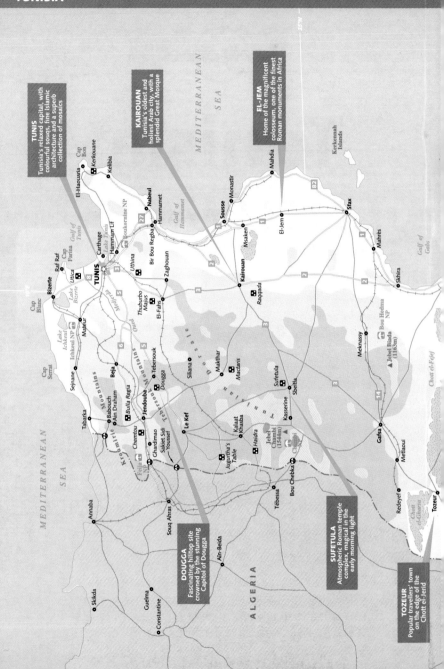

TUNIS
Tunisia's relaxed capital, with colourful souqs, fine Islamic architecture and a superb collection of mosaics

KAIROUAN
Tunisia's oldest and holiest Arab city, with a splendid Great Mosque

EL-JEM
Home of the magnificent colosseum, one of the finest Roman monuments in Africa

DOUGGA
Fascinating hilltop site crowned by the stunning Capitol of Dougga

SUFETULA
Atmospheric Roman temple complex, magical in the early morning light

TOZEUR
Popular travellers' town on the edge of the Chott el-Jerid

MEDITERRANEAN SEA

ALGERIA

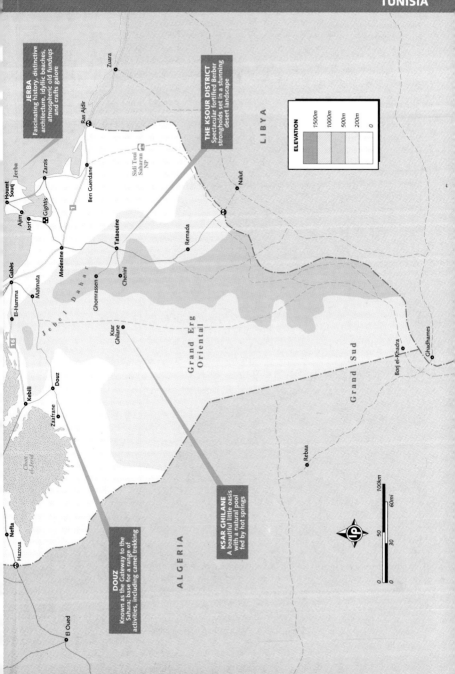

JERBA
Fascinating history, distinctive architecture, idyllic beaches, atmospheric old *funduqs* and crafts galore

THE KSOUR DISTRICT
Spectacular fortified Berber strongholds set in a stunning desert landscape

ELEVATION

1500m
1000m
500m
200m
0

DOUZ
Known as the Gateway to the Sahara; base for a range of activities, including camel trekking

KSAR GHILANE
A beautiful little oasis with a natural pool fed by hot springs

LIBYA

ALGERIA

Zuara

Ras Ajdir

Zarzis

Hount Souq

Jerba

Ajim

Jorf

Gights

Ben Guerdane

Sidi Toui
Saharan
NP

Nalut

Gabes

El-Hamma

Matmata

Medenine

Ghomrassen

Tataouine

Chenni

Remada

Jebel Dahar

Ksar
Ghilane

Kebili

Douz

Zaafrane

Nefta

Hazoua

*Chott
el-Jerid*

El Oued

**Grand Erg
Oriental**

Grand Sud

Borj el-Khadra

Ghadhames

Rebaa

16

100km

60mi

50

30

0

0

Tunisia
2nd edition – February 2001
First published – July 1998

Published by
Lonely Planet Publications Pty Ltd ABN 36 005 607 983
90 Maribyrnong St, Footscray, Victoria 3011, Australia

Lonely Planet Offices
Australia Locked Bag 1, Footscray, Victoria 3011
USA 150 Linden St, Oakland, CA 94607
UK 10a Spring Place, London NW5 3BH
France 1 rue du Dahomey, 75011 Paris

Photographs
Many of the images in this guide are available for licensing from
Lonely Planet Images.
email: lpi@lonelyplanet.com.au

Front cover photograph
Man leading camel across desert dune, Tunisia (Pete Seaward, Stone)

ISBN 1 86450 185 5

text & maps © Lonely Planet 2001
photos © photographers as indicated 2001

Printed by Craft Print International Ltd, Singapore

**Although the authors
and Lonely Planet try
to make the informa-
tion as accurate as
possible, we accept
no responsibility for
any loss, injury or
inconvenience sus-
tained by anyone
using this book.**

Contents – Text

1

2 Contents – Text

Contents – Maps

The Author

David Willett

David is a freelance journalist based near Bellingen on the mid-north coast of New South Wales, Australia. He grew up in Hampshire, England, and wound up in Australia in 1980 after stints working on newspapers in Iran and Bahrain. David spent two years working as a subeditor on the *Melbourne Sun* before trading a steady job for a warmer climate. Between jobs, he has travelled extensively in Europe, the Middle East and Asia.

David also works on Lonely Planet's guide to Greece, and has contributed to various other guides, including *Africa on a shoestring, Australia, Indonesia, South-East Asia, Mediterranean Europe* and *Western Europe.*

FROM DAVID

I'd like to thank all my friends in Tunisia, who have contributed so much to my understanding of the country over the years. They include Kamel ben Brahim, from the ONTT office in Tunis; Zaied ben Zaied, from Zaied Travel in Douz; Amel Djait-Belkaid, from Visit Tunisia in Hammamet; the Grar family (Larbi, Nejia, Kamel, Lamia, Anis and Bassem); Chokri ben Nessir; and Henda Salhi. Thanks also to Jacqui Gilchrist from the ONTT office in London.

Last but not least, I'd like to thank my partner, Rowan, and our son, Tom, for holding the fort at home during my frequent trips to Tunisia.

This Book

From the Publisher

This 2nd edition of *Tunisia* was edited in Lonely Planet's Melbourne office by Bethune Carmichael with the assistance of Justin Flynn. Heath Comrie led the mapping and design team, and was assisted by Sonya Brooke, Sarah Sloane, Jacqui Saunders, Kieran Grogan, Corinne Waddell, Hunor Csutoros and Rodney Zandbergs. Jenny Jones designed the cover and Emma Koch edited the Language chapter.

Acknowledgments

Many thanks to the following travellers who used the first edition of Tunisia and wrote to us with helpful hints, useful advice and interesting anecdotes:

DL Baker, Sandra & Wendy Bebbington, Lisa Blair, Han Blankstein, Hatem Bouattour, J Butcher, Karen Carlsen, Heidi Clemmenson, Renee Cole, Luis Costa, Malgorzata Dera, PA Edney, Galasso Elisabetta, Vanessa Elliott-Smith, Richard N Frye, Ann Graham, Linda Gregory, Emmy Hahurji, Solange Hando, Haider Haraghi, Sally Jennings, David Krivanek, Robb Lawton, Chung-Chu Leung, Alessandro Liverani, A Magnus, Nissim Mizrahi, EP Mycroft, Imogen C Myers, R & J Naiman, André Paillard, David Petrie, Lori Plotkin, Rosemarie Richards, Tony Robinson, Nathalie Schmelz, Jennifer Smith, Sally Smith, Alison Sterling, Kurt Stevens, Kris Terauds, Marius Throndsen, Rene van Havene, Lieven Van Keer, Frank Watson.

Foreword

ABOUT LONELY PLANET GUIDEBOOKS

The story begins with a classic travel adventure: Tony and Maureen Wheeler's 1972 journey across Europe and Asia to Australia. Useful information about the overland trail did not exist at that time, so Tony and Maureen published the first Lonely Planet guidebook to meet a growing need.

From a kitchen table, then from a tiny office in Melbourne (Australia), Lonely Planet has become the largest independent travel publisher in the world, an international company with offices in Melbourne, Oakland (USA), London (UK) and Paris (France).

Today Lonely Planet guidebooks cover the globe. There is an ever-growing list of books and there's information in a variety of forms and media. Some things haven't changed. The main aim is still to help make it possible for adventurous travellers to get out there – to explore and better understand the world.

At Lonely Planet we believe travellers can make a positive contribution to the countries they visit – if they respect their host communities and spend their money wisely. Since 1986 a percentage of the income from each book has been donated to aid projects and human rights campaigns.

Updates Lonely Planet thoroughly updates each guidebook as often as possible. This usually means there are around two years between editions, although for more unusual or more stable destinations the gap can be longer. Check the imprint page (following the colour map at the beginning of the book) for publication dates.

Between editions up-to-date information is available in two free newsletters – the paper *Planet Talk* and email *Comet* (to subscribe, contact any Lonely Planet office) – and on our Web site at www.lonelyplanet.com. The *Upgrades* section of the Web site covers a number of important and volatile destinations and is regularly updated by Lonely Planet authors. *Scoop* covers news and current affairs relevant to travellers. And, lastly, the *Thorn Tree* bulletin board and *Postcards* section of the site carry unverified, but fascinating, reports from travellers.

Correspondence The process of creating new editions begins with the letters, postcards and emails received from travellers. This correspondence often includes suggestions, criticisms and comments about the current editions. Interesting excerpts are immediately passed on via newsletters and the Web site, and everything goes to our authors to be verified when they're researching on the road. We're keen to get more feedback from organisations or individuals who represent communities visited by travellers.

Lonely Planet gathers information for everyone who's curious about the planet – and especially for those who explore it first-hand. Through guidebooks, phrasebooks, activity guides, maps, literature, newsletters, image library, TV series and Web site we act as an information exchange for a worldwide community of travellers.

Research Authors aim to gather sufficient practical information to enable travellers to make informed choices and to make the mechanics of a journey run smoothly. They also research historical and cultural background to help enrich the travel experience and allow travellers to understand and respond appropriately to cultural and environmental issues.

Authors don't stay in every hotel because that would mean spending a couple of months in each medium-sized city and, no, they don't eat at every restaurant because that would mean stretching belts beyond capacity. They do visit hotels and restaurants to check standards and prices, but feedback based on readers' direct experiences can be very helpful.

Many of our authors work undercover, others aren't so secretive. None of them accept freebies in exchange for positive write-ups. And none of our guidebooks contain any advertising.

Production Authors submit their raw manuscripts and maps to offices in Australia, USA, UK or France. Editors and cartographers – all experienced travellers themselves – then begin the process of assembling the pieces. When the book finally hits the shops, some things are already out of date, we start getting feedback from readers and the process begins again …

WARNING & REQUEST

Things change – prices go up, schedules change, good places go bad and bad places go bankrupt – nothing stays the same. So, if you find things better or worse, recently opened or long since closed, please tell us and help make the next edition even more accurate and useful. We genuinely value all the feedback we receive. A well travelled team reads and acknowledges every letter, postcard and email and ensures that every morsel of information finds its way to the appropriate authors, editors and cartographers for verification.

Everyone who writes to us will find their name in the next edition of the appropriate guidebook. They will also receive the latest issue of *Planet Talk*, our quarterly printed newsletter, or *Comet*, our monthly email newsletter. Subscriptions to both newsletters are free. The very best contributions will be rewarded with a free guidebook.

Excerpts from your correspondence may appear in new editions of Lonely Planet guidebooks, the Lonely Planet Web site, *Planet Talk* or *Comet*, so please let us know if you *don't* want your letter published or your name acknowledged.

Send all correspondence to the Lonely Planet office closest to you:

Australia: Locked Bag 1, Footscray, Victoria 3011
USA: 150 Linden St, Oakland, CA 94607
UK: 10A Spring Place, London NW5 3BH
France: 1 rue du Dahomey, 75011 Paris

Or email us at: talk2us@lonelyplanet.com.au

For news, views and updates see our Web site: www.lonelyplanet.com

HOW TO USE A LONELY PLANET GUIDEBOOK

The best way to use a Lonely Planet guidebook is any way you choose. At Lonely Planet we believe the most memorable travel experiences are often those that are unexpected, and the finest discoveries are those you make yourself. Guidebooks are not intended to be used as if they provide a detailed set of infallible instructions!

Contents All Lonely Planet guidebooks follow roughly the same format. The Facts about the Destination chapters or sections give background information ranging from history to weather. Facts for the Visitor gives practical information on issues like visas and health. Getting There & Away gives a brief starting point for researching travel to and from the destination. Getting Around gives an overview of the transport options when you arrive.

The peculiar demands of each destination determine how subsequent chapters are broken up, but some things remain constant. We always start with background, then proceed to sights, places to stay, places to eat, entertainment, getting there and away, and getting around information – in that order.

Heading Hierarchy Lonely Planet headings are used in a strict hierarchical structure that can be visualised as a set of Russian dolls. Each heading (and its following text) is encompassed by any preceding heading that is higher on the hierarchical ladder.

Entry Points We do not assume guidebooks will be read from beginning to end, but that people will dip into them. The traditional entry points are the list of contents and the index. In addition, however, some books have a complete list of maps and an index map illustrating map coverage.

There may also be a colour map that shows highlights. These highlights are dealt with in greater detail in the Facts for the Visitor chapter, along with planning questions and suggested itineraries. Each chapter covering a geographical region usually begins with a locator map and another list of highlights. Once you find something of interest in a list of highlights, turn to the index.

Maps Maps play a crucial role in Lonely Planet guidebooks and include a huge amount of information. A legend is printed on the back page. We seek to have complete consistency between maps and text, and to have every important place in the text captured on a map. Map key numbers usually start in the top left corner.

Although inclusion in a guidebook usually implies a recommendation we cannot list every good place. Exclusion does not necessarily imply criticism. In fact there are a number of reasons why we might exclude a place – sometimes it is simply inappropriate to encourage an influx of travellers.

Introduction

Tunisia has a list of attractions that would do justice to a country many times its size – superb beaches, spectacular desert scenery and a wealth of historical sites dating back 2500 years to the days when the ancient city of Carthage dominated the entire western Mediterranean.

Beaches are the country's major drawcard and the cornerstone of its well-developed tourism industry. The coastal resorts of Hammamet, Monastir and Jerba have long been favourite destinations for holiday-makers seeking to escape the grey skies of Northern Europe for a week or two of guaranteed sunshine. They are the places to go if you want to spend your days lazing on the beach and your nights wining, dining and dancing.

For many travellers, though, the major attraction is the opportunity to venture south into the wilds of the world's greatest desert, the Sahara. Tourism has boomed here in recent years; however, there is still plenty of scope to get right off the beaten track. There's no better way to get a feel for

desert life than to go on a camel trek, which can be easily organised from the village of Zaafrane, near Douz.

The regions on the fringe of the Sahara are every bit as remarkable as the desert itself: the spectacular hilltop villages of the Ksour district around Tataouine, the troglodyte village of Matmata, the glimmering salt flats of the Chott el-Jerid and the beautiful old oasis towns of Nefta and Tozeur.

Tourism remains very low-key along the north coast, although it is one of the prettiest parts of the country. The contrast with the arid south couldn't be greater – the densely forested Kroumirie Mountains overlook a narrow, fertile coastal plain. There are some fine beaches around the small resort town of Tabarka, and the hill town of Ain Draham makes a good base for walks through the surrounding forests.

Tunisia's extremely colourful past has left it rich in historical sites, starting with Carthage itself, now surrounded by the plush northern suburbs of the capital, Tunis.

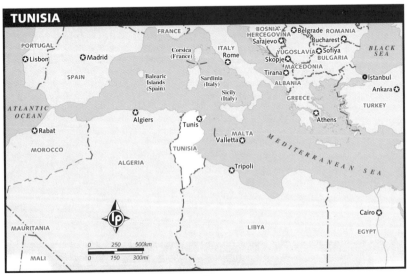

Elsewhere there are some magnificent Roman ruins. The colosseum at El-Jem rates among the finest Roman monuments in Africa, and the ruins of Bulla Regia and Dougga follow close behind. The Bardo Museum in Tunis houses a fantastic collection of Roman mosaics – one of the best in the world.

Tunisia's Islamic heritage has produced architecture that is every bit as impressive, including the mighty ramparts that surround the ancient medina cities of Sfax and Sousse, and the medina of Tunis, which is a treasure trove of Islamic architecture dating back more than 1000 years.

Tunisia is an easy place to get around. Distances are short and public transport cheap, and efficient. You'll find a good choice of accommodation in all the major towns, whether you're looking for a clean budget room or for the latest in star-studded luxury.

Tunisia is also a safe place to travel. Street crime is rare and political stability has become a feature of the country, which has had just one change of government in the 44 years since independence.

Facts about Tunisia

HISTORY

Tunisia is the smallest nation in North Africa, but its strategic position has ensured it an eventful history. The Phoenicians, Romans, Vandals, Byzantines, Arabs, Ottomans and French have all come and gone in this part of the world.

The name that looms largest in Tunisian history is Carthage, arch enemy of Rome in the 3rd and 2nd centuries BC. Now a well-heeled northern suburb of Tunis, Carthage was once a Phoenician trading post that emerged to dominate the western Mediterranean in the 6th century BC. Excluding the Saharan south, the boundaries of Modern Tunisia are virtually identical to those of the area controlled by the ancient city state 2500 years ago.

Prehistory

The earliest humans to set foot in Tunisia were probably a group of *Homo erectus*, who stumbled upon the place a few hundred thousand years ago as they joined a general migration north-west across the Sahara from East Africa. In those days, the Sahara enjoyed a very different climate to today, with regular rainfall. The massive swathe of desert that now isolates the fertile north coast of Africa from the rest of the continent is believed to have been covered in forest, scrub and savanna grasses, much like the plains of Kenya and Tanzania today.

The earliest hard evidence of human activity in Tunisia dates back about 200,000 years, which is the age archaeologists have put on primitive stone tools discovered near the southern oasis town of Kebili. Migration from the south became less viable as the Sahara began to dry out at the end of the last Ice Age. The regular rains that watered the region are thought to have finally ceased in around 6000 BC.

By this time, people had begun to arrive from other directions. The most significant new arrivals were people of the Capsian culture, proto-Mediterranean stock who had travelled across North Africa from the near east. Named after finds uncovered near the city of Gafsa (ancient Capsa), the Capsian people lived in southern Tunisia from about 8000 to 4500 BC. The finely sculpted stone and bone implements found point to a relatively sophisticated society.

Settlement of the north followed a different pattern, with waves of migration from southern Europe between 6000 and 2500 BC.

It is from these Neolithic peoples that the Berbers (the indigenous people of North Africa, including Tunisia) are thought to be descended. Allowing for regional variations and the lack of hard evidence, they appear to have been predominantly nomadic pastoralists. By the time the Phoenicians arrived in 1100 BC, these local tribes were well established.

Carthaginian Dominance

The Phoenicians were drawn to the Tunisian coast in search of staging posts along the trade route between their mother city of Tyre (in modern Lebanon) and the silver mines of southern Spain. The first of these staging posts was established at Utica, about 35km north of Tunis, in 1100 BC. By the time Carthage was founded at the end of the 9th century BC, this lone outpost had expanded into a chain of port settlements that stretched along the North African coast. They included Hadrumètum (Sousse), Hippo Diarrhytus (Bizerte) and Thrabaka (Tabarka).

From the outset, Carthage appeared to have been planned as something more than a mere port of call. Its name, which derives from the Phoenician *qart dasht* (new city), and elaborate foundation myth (see the boxed text 'Elissa the Wanderer' in the Tunis chapter) indicate that it was intended as the start of a more permanent Phoenician presence in the western Mediterranean. The timing of its establishment and its strategic location suggests that this move was prompted by the growing Greek presence in the western Mediterranean.

Carthage quickly established itself as the leader of the western Phoenician world. While Tyre suffered at the hands of the Assyrians in the 7th and 6th centuries BC, Carthage went from strength to strength. By the end of 6th century BC, it had become the main power in the western Mediterranean. It controlled a stretch of the North African coast from Tripolitania (western Libya) to the Atlantic and had established colonies in the Balearic Islands, Corsica, Malta, Sardinia and Sicily.

Carthage itself rapidly grew into the metropolis of the Phoenician world, recording a population of about 500,000 at its peak. Its wealth derived from its control of trade, enforced by a powerful navy. During the 5th and 4th centuries BC, Carthage turned its attentions to expanding its empire in Africa, carving out a territory that ran from Tabarka in the north-west to Sfax in the south-east. It was supposedly defined by a defensive ditch, although no trace has been found. This new territory included the fertile lands of the Cap Bon Peninsula and the Medjerda Valley, supplying Carthage with a large agricultural surplus to export.

It was inevitable that this regional primacy would lead to conflict with the other great powers of the Mediterranean, first Greece and then Rome. Sicily, just 80km north-east of Carthage, was the main bone of contention. Carthage fought numerous wars with the Greeks over the island and suffered its share of setbacks along the way. The most notable was in 310 BC when Greek raiders led by Agathocles landed in North Africa, starting a trail of destruction which lasted for three years. When the Carthaginians finally took control of the island in the middle of the 3rd century BC, they found themselves squaring off against an expansionist Rome that had just completed the conquest of southern Italy.

The scene was set for the first of the so-called Punic Wars that were to preoccupy the two powers for the next 100 years. Rome launched the first war in 263 BC with a campaign to win control of Sicily. In spite of a couple of early Roman successes on land, the supremacy of Carthage's navy resulted in a stalemate that dragged on for the next 20 years. An attempt by the Romans to carry the battle to Carthage resulted in the defeat and capture of the Roman general Regulus.

Rome finally got the break it wanted when its fledgling navy destroyed the Carthaginian fleet off Trapani (eastern Sicily) in 242 BC. Navyless and close to broke, Carthage was forced to accept Roman terms and abandon Sicily, followed by Sardinia and Corsica in 238 BC. Trouble at home grew as unpaid mercenaries revolted, sparking a bitter conflict that dragged on for around three years before the mercenaries were finally trapped and annihilated near Zaghouan. The savagery of the war later inspired Gustave Flaubert's over-the-top novel *Salammbô*.

Carthage then turned its attention to consolidating its position in Africa, and established itself in the former Phoenician settlements of southern Spain under the leadership of Hamilcar. It wasn't long before Carthage felt strong enough to take on the Romans again. In 218 BC, Hamilcar's son Hannibal set off from Spain at the head of an army of 90,000 troops backed by 37 war elephants. He crossed the Alps into Italy and inflicted crushing defeats at Lake Trasimene (217 BC) and Cannae (216 BC) in what came to be known as the Second Punic War. Rome seemed powerless and only after Hannibal had been stranded in southern Italy for some seven years waiting for reinforcements were the Romans able to forget about the threat of being overrun.

The Roman general Scipio retook Spain and landed in Africa at Utica in 204 BC. Carthage was teetering; Hannibal was recalled from Italy in 203 BC in an attempt to halt the Romans, but was resoundingly beaten at Zama (near Siliana) in 202 BC. Carthage capitulated and paid an enormous price, giving up its fleet and all its overseas territories. Hannibal fled to Asia Minor, where he eventually committed suicide to avoid capture by the Romans in 182 BC.

Hannibal Barca

Acclaimed by some as the finest military leader in history, the great Carthaginian general Hannibal Barca came within a whisker of erasing the emerging Roman Empire from the history books in the course of the Second Punic War (218–202 BC).

He was born in 247 BC, the son of Hamilcar Barca, Carthage's leading general during the First Punic War. The Carthaginian surrender that ended the war followed a disastrous naval setback that, nevertheless, left Hamilcar unconquered and thirsting for revenge.

Frustrated by Carthage's powerful merchant lobby, which preferred trade to war, Hamilcar set about establishing an alternative power base in Spain. According to legend, he made the nine-year-old Hannibal swear an oath of eternal enmity to Rome at the altar of Carthage's great Temple of Baal before setting out in 237 BC. By the time Hannibal took over, in 221 BC, southern and eastern Spain had become the virtually autonomous Barcid Kingdom.

He spent the next three years preparing to take on the Romans, setting off in 218 BC at the head an army of 90,000 infantry backed by 12,000 cavalry and 37 elephants. Hannibal's journey took him across hostile Gaul before an epic crossing of the Alps that saw him descend into the plains of northern Italy in the spring of 217 BC. Only 17 elephants survived the crossing, and his army had shrunk to just 23,000, but he proceeded to inflict a series of crushing defeats on numerically superior Roman forces.

His finest hour came the following year at the Battle of Cannae, where Hannibal virtually annihilated a Roman army of 80,000 despite being vastly outnumbered. His tactic of employing a 'soft centre' to his line, which lured the Romans forward into a trap, makes this one of the most studied battles in history.

Despite his success on the battlefield, he was unable to break Rome. More than a decade of hide and seek followed as Rome sought to contain Hannibal without engaging him in battle. Finally Rome sent Scipio Africanus to attack Carthage, forcing the recall of Hannibal from Italy. They met at the Battle of Zama in 202 BC, Hannibal's only defeat. The outcome was largely decided by the defection of his crack Numidian cavalry.

After the war Hannibal moved briefly into politics before he was forced by a plot to flee. He spent the last years of his life touting his skills as a military adviser around the eastern fringes of the Roman Empire before finally committing suicide in 183 BC when betrayed to the Romans.

Hannibal remains a popular figure in Tunisian lore, and his rugged features adorn the Tunisian TD5 note.

Carthage wasn't finished though, and over the next 50 years it re-established itself as a commercial centre in spite of losing much of its former territory to the Numidian king Massinissa, whose cavalry had fought alongside Scipio at Zama. The city's continued revival began to create increasing unease in Rome, where there were many who thought that Carthage remained a threat as long as it existed. Whipped up by men like Cato the Elder, an eminent statesman and writer, who became well known for his vehement opposition to Carthage, Rome launched the Third Punic War with the intention of settling the issue once and for all. In 149 BC, the Roman army again landed in Utica and laid siege to Carthage for three years. When it finally fell in 146 BC, the Romans showed no mercy. The city was utterly destroyed, the people sold into slavery and the site symbolically sprinkled with salt and damned forever.

The Carthaginians had been great traders and merchants, but they were ruthless rulers who managed to alienate the indigenous Berber peoples around them. It is often claimed that the Berbers learnt advanced agricultural methods from the Carthaginians but many were simply forced into the desert and mountain hinterland. It is unlikely that many mourned Carthage's demise.

The Romans

Carthage's territory became the Roman province of Africa. At first Rome showed little interest in its new acquisition. The Empire was expanding fast and Africa was fairly low on the priority list. It was happy to leave most of the country to the Numidians. Under Massinissa, the Numidians had established a kingdom that stretched from western Algeria to Libya. Its major towns included Sicca Veneria (Le Kef), Thugga (Dougga) and Vaga (Beja). On Massinissa's death in 148 BC, Rome attempted to cut the kingdom down to size by dividing it up between his three sons. The tactic worked well until the kingdom was reunited by Massinissa's grandson Jugurtha, who then

incurred the wrath of Rome by massacring a Roman company sent to Cirta Regia (present day Constantine in Algeria), sparking a war that lasted from 112 to 105 BC. Jugurtha was eventually betrayed by his father-in-law, King Bocchus I of Mauretania, and captured.

Rome was prepared to give the Numidians another chance, splitting the kingdom into a western half centred on Cirta Regia and an eastern half based at Zama, near Siliana. The last of the Zama kings, Juba I, backed the wrong side in the Roman civil war (based on the power struggle between Julius Caesar and Pompey) and was trounced by Julius Caesar at the Battle of Thapsus in 46 BC, along with the remnants of Pompey's army.

The battle left Rome firmly in control of its African outpost and it was time for settlement to begin in earnest. Julius Caesar re-established Carthage as a Roman city in 44 BC and it became the capital of the expanded colony of Africa Proconsularis.

The Origins of 'Africa'

Once the Romans had completed their destruction of Carthage, they looked around for a name for the swathe of new territory they had acquired.

The search ended about 50km to the west, in the band of low hills running north from the Medjerda River between the towns of Membressa (modern Mejez el-Bab) and Matar (Mateur). This was the homeland of the Afri, a Berber tribe whose loyalty the Romans were keen to cultivate in their efforts to create a buffer against the Numidian kingdom further to the west.

The new province of Africa occupied the north-eastern third of modern Tunisia, and was reputedly enclosed by a ditch – although no trace of any ditch has ever been found. The name spread as the boundaries of Roman control were extended east and west along the north coast, until eventually the name became synonymous with the entire continent.

Agriculture was all important. By the 1st century AD, the wheat-growing plains of the Medjerda Valley and the Tell Plateau were supplying more than 60% of the Roman Empire's grain requirements. The great cities built by the Romans on these plains are now among Tunisia's principal tourist attractions. Africa also supplied the majority of the wild animals used in amphitheatre shows, as well as gold, olive oil, slaves, ivory, ostrich plumes and *garum* (a fish-paste delicacy).

The Romans were also the first people to recognise the attractions of the Tunisian coastline, establishing a string of coastal colonies for army veterans that assisted the spread of urbanisation and Roman ways. Berber communities also prospered and some Berbers were granted Roman citizenship. It was these wealthy citizens who donated the monumental public buildings that graced the Roman cities of the region. Africa even provided an emperor, Septimius Severus, a Libyan from Leptis Magna who took power in AD 193 and died in Yorkshire, of all places.

Christianity

Roman rule also brought the first appearance of Christianity in North Africa at the end of the 2nd century AD. Despite early persecution, Christianity continued to spread throughout the 3rd century. Many of the early converts were native Berbers, who saw the new faith as a way of rebelling against Roman authority. Its spread was aided by the collapse of central government that followed an ill-fated tax revolt against Rome led by the African pro-consul Gordian in AD 238.

The Council of Carthage, held in AD 256, was attended by almost 100 bishops. They included the bishop of Carthage, St Cyprien, who was put to death by the Romans two years later. Thousands more were put to death in the amphitheatres of Carthage, El-Jem and elsewhere during the persecutions ordered by the Emperor Diocletian in AD 305–7.

Constantine's adoption of Christianity in AD 312 may have ended the conflict elsewhere in the empire, but in Tunisia it marked the beginning of the Donatist schism. Led by Bishop Donatus, the donatists refused to recognise the authority of church leaders who had cooperated with Rome during the persecutions. They excommunicated all members of the Roman church, and built their own rival churches – which is why so many of Tunisia's Roman sites have at least two churches.

St Augustine was among those who argued strongly for a return to the orthodox church at the Council of Carthage in AD 411, which outlawed Donatism. Diehard followers ignored this ruling, and were accused of assisting the subsequent arrival of the Vandals.

The Vandals & the Byzantines

By the beginning of the 5th century AD, Roman power was in terminal decline and the Vandal king Gaeseric (or Genseric), who had been busy marauding in southern Spain, decided that Rome's North African colonies were there for the taking. He set off across the Straits of Gibraltar in AD 429, bringing the entire Vandal people (about 80,000 men, women and children) with him. Within 10 years, the Vandals had fought their way across to Carthage, which they made the capital of a short-lived empire that also controlled most of the islands of the western Mediterranean.

The Vandals appear to have lived up to their reputation. They did little more than help themselves to what they found. They built no great monuments and left virtually no trace of their rule. The Vandals confiscated large amounts of property and their exploitative policies accelerated North Africa's economic decline. The Berbers became increasingly rebellious and, as the Vandals recoiled, small local kingdoms sprang up.

The Byzantine emperor Justinian, based in Constantinople (modern İstanbul), had in the meantime revived the eastern half of the Roman Empire and had similar plans for the lost western territories. His general Belisarius defeated the Vandals in AD 533, ushering in 150 years of Byzantine rule. Like the

Vandals before them, the Byzantines found themselves living in a state of constant siege, with Berber chiefs controlling the bulk of the country. They built with their customary zeal, however, and many of Tunisia's Roman sites feature later Byzantine modifications, in particular, churches and forts.

The Coming of Islam

No-one could have guessed that the emergence of an obscure new religion in the distant peninsula of Arabia in the early 7th century AD was about to completely change the face of North Africa. Islam's green banner was flying over Egypt by AD 640 (see also Religion later in this chapter), and soon after Tripoli was in Muslim hands, too.

In AD 646, with the Arab armies on his doorstep, the Prefect Gregory added a farcical footnote to the Byzantine era by declaring himself the ruler of an independent state based at Sufetula (modern Sbeitla). It lasted less than a year before the Arabs attacked Sufetula, defeating and killing Gregory. The Arabs withdrew with their spoils, allowing the Byzantines to hold on to their possessions in the north for a while longer.

It was not until Okba ibn Nafaa al-Fihri began his campaign of conquest that the full military force of Islam was brought to bear on North Africa. For three years, beginning in AD 669, he swept across the top of the continent, stopping on the way to establish Qayrawan (Kairouan), Islam's first great city in the Maghreb. With his army of Arab cavalry and Islamised Berber infantry from Libya, he marched until he reached the Atlantic.

The Berbers adopted the religion of the invaders readily enough but not Arab rule, and in AD 683 the Arabs were forced to abandon North Africa after Okba was defeated and killed by a combined Berber-Byzantine army at the Battle of Tahuda, near Biskra in modern Algeria. The victors were led by the Berber chieftain Qusayla, who then established his own Islamic kingdom based at Kairouan.

The Arab's withdrawal was only temporary. They retook Kairouan in AD 689 and dislodged the Byzantines from Carthage in AD 698, but continued to encounter spirited resistance from Berbers who had rallied behind the legendary princess Al-Kahina (see the boxed texts 'The Berbers' later in this chapter, and 'The Colosseum of El-Jem' in the Central Tunisia chapter). She defeated the Arabs at Tébessa (Algeria) in AD 696, but was eventually cornered and killed after a legendary last stand at El-Jem in AD 701.

North Africa, with Kairouan as its capital, became a province of the rapidly expanding Islamic empire controlled by the Umayyad caliphs, based in Damascus. Under the command of Musa bin Nusayr, the Arab armies now turned their attentions to the conquest of Spain (AD 711–19). In AD 732, Musa advanced as far as Poitiers in France before being turned back.

Meanwhile, the tyrannical behaviour of Arab troops stationed in North Africa had pushed the Berbers to the brink of yet another rebellion. The Berbers were inspired by the teachings of Kharijites, a puritanical Islamic sect whose egalitarian beliefs contrasted sharply with the arrogant and worldly ways of the Umayyad elite. A local uprising in Morocco in AD 740 quickly spread across North Africa. Although it was suppressed in AD 743, regional problems continued to flare.

By the time the caliphate shifted to the Abbasids in Baghdad in AD 761, Spain and much of North Africa had effectively broken away from the eastern part of the empire. Morocco became the stronghold of the Idrissids, who had fled Abbasid persecution in Baghdad and established their own kingdom in northern Morocco, and most of Algeria was ruled by the Kharijite Rustamids from Tahart.

Ifriqiyya (Tunisia and parts of Libya) looked like breaking away too, until the appointment of Ibrahim Ibn al-Aghlab as governor in AD 797. Operating from Kairouan, he soon secured control of an area covering western Algeria, Tunisia and the Libyan province of Tripolitania. He was rewarded for his efforts by being made hereditary emir and was the founder of the successful Aghlabid dynasty that ruled until the arrival

CHRIS WOOD

DAVID WILLETT

DAVID WILLETT

Traditional Tunisian dress: a Berber woman with a red *bakhnoug* (shawl; top left); Marazig tribesman with keffiyeh (top right); and Berber women with *assaba* (headbands) at a wedding (bottom)

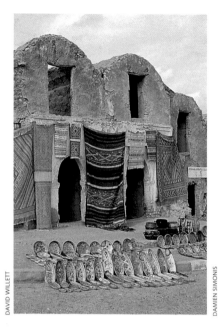

Tunisia offers a diverse range of crafts and produce, from Berber kilims (top left), tiles (top right) and Sejnane ware (bottom right), to a multitude of market goods (middle and bottom left).

of the Fatimids in AD 909. The Great Mosque in Kairouan and the *ribats* (monastic forts) at Sousse and Monastir were all built during the Aghlabid period.

The Fatimids

The Fatimids were a group of Berber Shiites (see Religion later in this chapter) from the Kabylie region of central Algeria on a mission from God – to depose the Abbasid caliphate and declare their leader, Obeid Allah, as the new caliph. Obeid was known to his followers as El-Madhi (The Saviour).

Through alliances with disaffected Berber tribes, the Fatimids quickly conquered North Africa. The Aghlabids were defeated in AD 909, and a year later Obeid Allah was declared the true caliph at Raqqada, south of Kairouan. Anticipating reprisals, the Fatimids built a new capital, Mahdia, on a small, easily defended headland on the coast and set about plotting the capture of Egypt. Their plans almost came unstuck in the face of a Kharijite uprising in AD 944 led by Abu Yazid, who captured Kairouan and laid siege to Mahdia before being driven off by Berber tribesmen led by Ziri ibn Manad. When the Fatimid caliph Amir al-Moez defeated the Egyptians and moved the capital to Cairo in AD 969, the Zirids were rewarded by being left in charge of the Maghreb.

They held the reins capably enough for a while, but with the Fatimids off the scene pressure began to mount for a return to religious orthodoxy. In 1045, the Zirids caved in and officially returned to the Sunni mainstream in open defiance of the Fatimids. The reply from Cairo was devastating: The Beni Hilal and Beni Sulaim tribes of upper Egypt were encouraged to invade the Maghreb, and over the following century North Africa was slowly reduced to ruins.

The Normans, led by Roger II of Sicily, took advantage of the chaos to occupy a number of towns along the Tunisian coast, including Mahdia, Sfax and Sousse.

Berber Empires

The power vacuum was eventually filled by the Almohads, who came to power in Morocco at the beginning of the 12th century. They completed their conquest of North Africa with the capture of Mahdia in 1160, but the empire immediately began to crumble. As it caved in, the Maghreb split into three parts: Ifriqiyya came under the Hafsids; Algeria under the Banu Abd al-Wad; and Morocco under the Merenids. Although borders have changed and rulers have come and gone, this division remains more or less intact today.

The Hafsids managed to hang on until the middle of the 16th century, when they found themselves caught in the middle of the rivalry between Spain and the Ottoman Empire that followed the Christian reconquest of Spain.

The Ottoman Turks

The Spanish had early successes, capturing a number of ports along the North African coast, including Algiers. Their opponents in the early days were Muslim corsairs, or pirates, who were drawn to the fight by religious conviction as well as the profit motive. The most famous of these corsairs were the Barbarossa brothers, Aruj and Khair ed-Din, sons of a Turk from the Greek island of Lesbos, who had established themselves on the island of Jerba. Aruj captured Algiers from the Spanish but was killed when they retook the city in 1518. Khair ed-Din turned to the Turks for help, who jumped at the chance. He was given the title of *beylerbey* (governor) and supplied with troops. In 1529 he managed to boot the Spaniards out of Algiers once again and five years later was in control of Tunis as well.

Tunis was to change hands four more times in the next 45 years before Sinan Pasha finally claimed it for the Turks in 1574, forcing the last of the Hafsids into exile. Tunis became a *sanjak* (province) of the Ottoman Empire. It was ruled by a pasha, whose authority was backed by a force of 4000 janissaries. These troops were divided into units led by *deys*, who were the Ottoman army's equivalent of sergeants. The deys were in turn commanded by *obasdashis* (lieutenants), *bulukbashis* (captains) and an *agha* (chief), those who made up the *diwan* or assembly.

This model Ottoman province didn't last long. In 1591, the deys staged a coup, massacring their senior officers and taking control of the military. They took the process a stage further in 1598 when Othman Dey seized power, downgrading the pasha to a figurehead. The dey ruled Tunis, Kairouan and the major coastal towns, but control of the interior was put in the hands of a provincial governor, called the *bey*. The bey was given his own army with which to tame the Berber tribes, defend borders and – most importantly – collect taxes.

So successful were the beys that their power soon surpassed that of the deys, leading to the accession of the Muradite beys. After a period of great prosperity under Hamuda Bey (AD 1631–59), the Muradites slowly self-destructed over the course of 40 years of internecine warfare. The line came to a violent end in 1702 when Ibraham Sherif, commander of the bey's cavalry, seized power. The last Muradite ruler, Murad III, was captured and executed along with all of his family. Ibrahim Sherif survived until 1705, when he was captured by an army sent by the dey of Algiers to attack Tunis.

He was succeeded as bey by Hussein ben Ali, the son of a Turkish janissary from Crete who had followed Ibrahim Sherif's career path as commander of the beylical cavalry. He turned back the Algerians and founded the Husseinite line of beys, who survived until Tunisia became a republic in 1957.

The French Protectorate

Ottoman power was in serious decline by the beginning of the 19th century. France was the new power in the western Mediterranean, and the beys in Tunis came under increasing pressure to fall into line with European ways. Privateering was outlawed in 1816, slavery was abolished in 1846 and a *destour* (constitution) – the first in the Arab world – was proclaimed in 1861.

These Western reforms, however, exacted a heavy toll on the country's limited finances, necessitating heavy borrowing in the form of high-interest loans from European banks. Proposed higher taxes led to internal revolt, and by 1869 the country was in such a shambles financially that control of its finances was handed over to an international commission.

A final attempt to hold off European control was made by a short-lived ministry led by the reformer Khaireddin (1873–7), but he was forced from office and his plans were scuttled. At the Congress of Berlin in 1878, the major European powers divided up the southern Mediterranean region, and the only challenge to French dominance in Tunisia came from the Italians.

In 1881, in order to consolidate their position, the French sent 30,000 troops into Tunisia on the pretext of countering border raids by Tunisian tribesmen into French occupied Algeria. They quickly occupied Le Kef and Tunis, and the bey was forced to sign the Treaty of Kassar Saïd. The treaty acknowledged the sovereignty of the bey, but effectively put power in the hands of a French resident-general.

The French took the arrangement a step further in 1883 with the signing of the Convention of La Marsa, which established co-sovereignty and parallel justice systems. Under this arrangement, Europeans were judged under French law and locals under a modified form of Islamic law. The protectorate prospered under French rule, although most of the benefits went to the European population.

The French went about the business of land acquisition more discreetly than in neighbouring Algeria, where land was sequestered on a massive scale. In Tunisia, the French managed to get their hands on the best of the fertile land without confiscating property from individuals; they simply took over the large tracts of the Cap Bon Peninsula and the Medjerda Valley that had previously been controlled by the bey or used by nomads for grazing their animals. The citrus groves of Cap Bon are a legacy of this time, as are the vineyards that provide the bulk of the country's wine grapes.

The south was too arid for agriculture and was left largely alone – until the beginning of the 20th century when it was discovered that the hills west of Gafsa were made of phosphate. The massive mining operation begun by the French remains an important export earner for the modern Tunisian economy.

In 1920 the first nationalist political party, the Destour Party (named after the short-lived constitution of 1861), was formed. The party's demands for democratic government, though supported by the bey, were ignored by the French, and the nationalist movement lost its way for some years.

In 1934 a young, charismatic Sorbonne-educated Tunisian lawyer, Habib Bourguiba, led a breakaway movement from the Destour Party. He founded the Neo-Destour Party, which soon replaced the old guard of the Destour. Support for the party soon spread. On 9 April 1938, dozens of people were reported killed when the French turned their guns on demonstrators in Tunis. The party was banned, and Bourguiba was arrested and removed to France.

Wartime Tunisia

With the fall of France during WWII, the Neo-Destour leaders, who had been imprisoned there, were handed over to the Italians by the occupying Germans. Although they were well treated in Rome, they refused to support Italy.

In 1942 the Germans landed in Tunis in the hope that they could turn back the Allied advances from East and West: The Americans were on their way from Algeria and the British forces, led by Field Marshal Montgomery, were driving back Rommel's Afrika Korps in Egypt and Libya. The campaign in Tunisia raged for six months and the Allies lost more than 15,000 men before they captured Bizerte on 7 May 1943.

In the same year, the Neo-Destour leaders were finally allowed to return to Tunisia, where a government with Neo-Destour sympathies was formed by Moncef Bey.

Towards Independence

When the French resumed control after the war, they were as uncompromising as ever: The bey was deposed and Bourguiba was forced to flee to Cairo to avoid capture. In the next few years he organised a propaganda campaign aimed at bringing Tunisia's position into the international limelight. He was extremely successful in this, and by 1951 the French were ready to make concessions. A nationalist government was set up and Bourguiba was allowed to return. No sooner had this been accomplished than the French had a change of mind – Bourguiba was exiled and most of the ministers were arrested. Violence followed, and the country was soon in a state of total disarray.

In July 1954, with few alternatives, the French president finally announced plans for negotiations for Tunisian autonomy. In June 1955 an agreement was reached, and Bourguiba returned to Tunis to a hero's welcome. The agreement reached was restrictive in the fields of foreign policy and finance, and was condemned by Salah ben Youssef, former secretary of the Neo-Destour. He attempted to lead an armed insurrection, but without popular support he was soon forced to flee the country.

Tunisia was formally granted independence on 20 March 1956, with Bourguiba as prime minister. In the course of the following year, the last bey was deposed, the country became a republic and Bourguiba was declared Tunisia's first president.

Independent Tunisia

Bourguiba was quick to introduce sweeping political and social changes, looking to Westernisation as the way to modernise. His ideals were socialist and secular, and he regarded Islam as a force that was holding the country back.

He set about reducing the role of religion in society by removing religious leaders from their traditional areas of influence, such as education and the law. Probably the most significant step was the abolition of religious schools. This deprived religious leaders of their grass-roots educational role in shaping society. The religious school at the Zitouna Mosque in Tunis, a centre of Islamic learning, suffered the indignity of being incorporated into the Western-style University of Tunis.

The sharia'a (Quranic law) courts were also abolished, and more than 60,000 hectares of land that had financed mosques and religious institutions were confiscated.

Bourguiba also introduced major changes to the role of women in society. His 1956 Personal Status Code banned polygamy and ended the practice of divorce by renunciation. He called the veil an 'odious rag' and banned it from schools as part of an intensive campaign to end the wearing of a garment he regarded as demeaning. (See also Women in Tunisia in the Society & Conduct section later in this chapter.)

However, when Bourguiba began urging workers to ignore the Ramadan fast in 1960 he met serious opposition from religious leaders. He regarded the dawn-to-dusk fast as economically damaging because of its effect on productivity. He mounted an ingenious argument against the fast, declaring that Tunisians were exempted because they were waging a *jihad* (holy war) against poverty – and that the Prophet Mohammed himself had excused warriors engaged in a jihad from fasting so that they could be at full strength to tackle the enemy.

Not surprisingly, religious leaders didn't swallow the argument. Trouble broke out in Kairouan following the removal of a senior religious figure who had denounced the government. However, the fighting that resulted took only 24 hours to subdue.

Opposition

Despite his autocratic style and frequent prolonged absences through ill health, Bourguiba managed to keep the bulk of the population on his side, and in 1974 the National Assembly made him president for life.

The 1970s were significant, however, for the gradual emergence of an Islamic opposition in the form of the Islamic Association, led by popular preacher Rashid Ghannouchi. Disillusionment with Bourguiba and his Parti Socialiste Destourien (PSD) – as the Neo-Destour Party became known in 1964 – increased dramatically following the use of the military to crush a general strike called by the UGTT (Tunisia's first trade union federation) in January 1978.

After promising more political freedoms, the government persuaded Bourguiba to call the first multiparty elections in 1981. The Islamic Association became the Islamic Tendency Movement (MTI), which advocated a return to Islamic values. Bourguiba, who didn't have much time for opposition of any sort, was certainly not prepared to tolerate an Islamic party and refused to license the MTI.

The elections were a total letdown for the new opposition parties. The National Front (an alliance formed between the PSD and the UGTT) took all 136 seats on offer, drawing cries of foul play.

After the elections, Bourguiba cracked down hard on the MTI. Ghannouchi and its other leaders were jailed and remained so until 1984, when riots were sparked by the withdrawal of a bread subsidy. The rioting lasted six days and stopped only when Bourguiba resumed the subsidy. The riots were notable for the shouting of slogans such as 'God is Great' and 'Down with America', and eventually the MTI leaders were freed to ease tensions.

Bourguiba's Final Years

As the 1980s progressed, Bourguiba was seen to be more and more out of touch both with Tunisians and with Tunisia's position in the Arab world. An example of his erratic behaviour was his sudden decision in 1986 to sack Prime Minister Mohammed Mzali, just weeks after naming Mzali as his successor. Mzali's replacement, Rachid Sfar, lasted only a year before making way for Zine el-Abidine ben Ali, the tough minister for the interior and former army general who would eventually orchestrate the ousting of the ageing Bourguiba.

As minister for the interior, Ben Ali had presided over yet another crackdown on the Islamic opposition, which had produced more than 1000 arrests. In September 1987, 90 of those held, including Ghannouchi, were put on trial on charges ranging from planting bombs to conspiring to overthrow the regime. The bombings were a curious affair. Twelve tourists were injured in blasts at hotels in Sousse and Monastir, and responsibility was claimed by the pro-Iranian Islamic Jihad organisation. The government, however, held the MTI to blame, even though most of those charged had been in jail at the time.

The trial produced seven death sentences, while Ghannouchi was given hard labour for life. Bourguiba demanded the death sentence for all the accused and was furious at the outcome, insisting on retrials and that Ghannouchi and 15 others be executed by 16 November 1987.

It was against this backdrop that Ben Ali made his move. The arrest of Ghannouchi had sparked street battles, and there were fears that executions could lead to a popular uprising. On 7 November 1987, Ben Ali seized power in a palace coup. He assembled a group of doctors who were asked to examine the 83-year-old president, who, predictably, was declared unfit to carry out his duties. It seems that, despite a heart condition, his physical health was not too bad for a man of his age; it was his mental health that was causing the concern.

Bourguiba was held for some time in detention in his palace in Carthage before being shunted off to 'retirement' in another palace outside Monastir, where he remained until his death in April 2000.

Bourguiba's greatest achievements were the fostering of a strong national identity and the development of a standard of living which puts Tunisia at the top of the pile in the developing world.

President Ben Ali

Ben Ali moved quickly to appease the Islamic opposition. He headed off on a heavily publicised pilgrimage to Mecca to establish his own credentials as a good Muslim, and ordered that the Ramadan fast be observed. He also promised a multiparty political system, although he baulked at legalising the MTI – which by now had changed its name to Hizb al-Nahda (Renaissance Party).

Political prisoners were released, the State Security Court was abolished and police powers of detention were limited. Political exiles were invited to return, and many decided that it was safe to do so.

However, the general elections held in April 1989 didn't exactly reflect a new liberalism. Ben Ali's Rassemblement Constitutionel Democratique (RCD), as the PSD had become, won all the seats amid charges of vote rigging. In the presidential elections, Ben Ali was re-elected with 99.27% of the vote.

Hizb al-Nahda was not allowed to contest the poll, but many of its candidates stood as independents. Estimates of their share of the vote varied from 13% up to 40% in some urban areas.

This result, coupled with the successes of the Islamic Salvation Front (FIS) in municipal elections in Algeria, prompted Ben Ali to rule out official recognition of the Hizb al-Nahda.

However, no major move was made against the party until after the 1991 Gulf War. Tunisia officially supported the USA-led alliance, but popular sentiment was very much behind Iraq's Saddam Hussein. In May 1991, the government announced that it had uncovered a Hizb al-Nahda plot to establish an Islamic state by force. A sizeable number of those arrested were members of the military.

The Islamic threat, real or otherwise, remained the government's major concern throughout the 1990s. Its fears were reinforced by the brutal civil war in neighbouring Algeria. The resulting security crackdown drew some unwelcome criticism from Amnesty International, which accused the government of heavy-handedness in its suppression of all forms of dissent.

Ben Ali, meanwhile, confirmed his hold on power at elections staged in 1994 and 1999. His most uncomfortable moment in 13 years at the helm came with the funeral of his charismatic predecessor, Habib Bourguiba, in April 2000. Official attempts to play down the occasion inflamed crowds, who responded with taunts of 'Long live Bourguiba'.

There is no suggestion, however, that the government is anything other than in complete control. Politics is not a popular (or advisable) topic of conversation, but many Tunisians express what appears to be a genuine admiration for Ben Ali's leadership.

Foreign Policy

Much of the esteem in which Ben Ali is held stems from Tunisia's high standing in the Arab world. The country has developed a reputation for stability in a volatile region. Tunisia was home to the Arab League for most of the 1980s. The league returned to Cairo in the late 1980s because Egypt had by now re-entered the Arab fold after years on the outside for having made peace with Israel in 1979.

The Palestine Liberation Organisation (PLO) was based at Hammam Plage, just south of Tunis, after it was forced out of Lebanon by the Israelis in the early 1980s. The headquarters were badly damaged by an Israeli bombing raid in 1985 in retaliation for the killing of three Israelis in Cyprus. In mid-1994, Yasser Arafat and the PLO returned to the Israeli-controlled occupied territories to set up a local autonomous government.

Relations with France have been generally good since independence, despite a few major hiccups in the late 1950s and early 1960s. In 1958, France bombed the Tunisian border village of Sakiet Sidi Youssef, claiming that Algerian rebels had crossed into Tunisian territory and that France had the right to pursue them. The Tunisians demanded that France evacuate the military base at Bizerte, which it had retained after independence. Tunisian troops opened fire on the French, prompting a bloody retaliation in which more than 1000 Tunisians died. The French finally withdrew in 1963.

Another incident flared in 1964, when Tunisia suddenly nationalised land owned by foreigners. France responded by cutting off all aid, a situation that was not remedied until 1966.

Under Ben Ali's leadership, Tunisia's foreign policy has become steadily more pro-Western. The Americans are the major supplier of equipment to the Tunisian army and Tunisia officially supported the USA-led Western alliance during the Gulf War.

Foreign policy through the 1990s was dominated by the desire to cultivate closer ties with the European Union in the hope of opening up new markets for Tunisian produce.

Relations with Libya have been fraught with difficulties over the years, but Tunisia provided the Gaddafi government with a vital lifeline to the outside world during the years of the international air embargo imposed over Libya's alleged involvement in the Lockerbie jumbo-jet bombing.

GEOGRAPHY

Tunisia occupies the northernmost point of the African continent, at the centre of the north coast. Sicily is the closest European landfall, just 80km to the north-east across the Straits of Sicily. Tunisia borders Algeria to the west and Libya to the south-east. The ragged and irregular 1400km Mediterranean coastline forms the eastern and northern boundaries.

With an area of 164,000 sq km, Tunisia is by far the smallest country in North Africa. Tunisia measures 750km from north to south but only 150km from east to west. Put into perspective, it's a fraction larger than England and Wales combined, or about the same size as Washington state in the USA or Victoria in Australia.

Topographically, the country divides fairly neatly into the mountainous northern one-third and the flat southern two-thirds.

The main mountain range is the Tunisian Dorsale, which represents the eastern extension of Algeria's Saharan Atlas and the High Atlas Mountains of Morocco. The Dorsale runs north-east from Tébessa, just across the Algerian border, to Zaghouan, just south of Tunis. It includes the highest mountain in the country, Jebel Chambi (1544m), west of Kasserine. After Zaghouan, the mountains taper off to form the Cap Bon Peninsula.

The majority of the country's viable arable land lies north of this line – the region referred to in history books as the granary of ancient Rome. It covers the high plains of the Tunisian Dorsale, known as the Tell, and the fertile valley of the Oued Medjerda. The Medjerda, which rises near Souq Ahras in eastern Algeria, is the country's only permanent river. Its waters are used for irrigation and the generation of hydroelectricity. To the north of the Medjerda are the Kroumirie Mountains, stretching along most of the north coast from the Algerian border. This range gives way to a narrow coastal plain.

Directly south of the Dorsale is a treeless plain, 200 to 400m above sea level, which drops down to a series of *chotts* (salt lakes) before giving way completely to desert in the south. Abundant artesian water makes cultivation possible in places and from these green oases come some of the finest dates in the world.

The *erg* (sand sea) that completely covers the southern tip of Tunisia is the eastern extremity of the Grand Erg Oriental (Great Eastern Erg), which also covers a large area of Algeria.

CLIMATE
Northern Tunisia has a typical Mediterranean climate, with hot, dry summers and mild, wet winters. The mountains of the north-west occasionally get snow. The further south you go, the hotter and drier it gets. Annual rainfall ranges from 1000mm in the north down to 150mm in the south, although some Saharan areas go for years without rain.

ECOLOGY & ENVIRONMENT
The country suffers from a long list of environmental problems, balanced by a few positives.

Water, or the shortage thereof, is a favourite topic of conversation. In most places, though, water is not a real problem – except in the south where the huge water requirements of the tourist industry have depleted artesian water levels and dried up springs in the oasis towns of the Saharan fringe. A far-sighted policy of dam construction in the north has assured that most places have adequate supply.

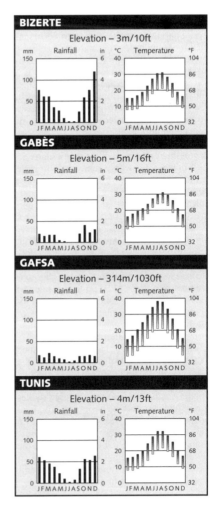

The most serious problem is a combination of desertification and erosion. More than 2500 years of deforestation and overgrazing have taken a heavy toll, and the country loses an estimated 23,000 hectares of arable land to erosion every year. The problem is most acute in the wheat-growing regions of the Tell, which are scarred by massive erosion gullies. The clearing of forests for timber and agriculture has reduced forest cover from an estimated 30% in pre-Roman times to less than 2%. Deforestation has been accompanied by a similar loss of biodiversity.

Another major problem is pollution, in all its many forms. Industrial pollution is a serious issue in the cities of Gabès and Sfax, and around Menzel Bourguiba in the north. The nationwide problem of human-waste disposal is exacerbated by the number of unplanned buildings.

Westerners are sure to be affronted by the depressing amount of litter, particularly in the countryside, where many people have yet to come to terms with the fact that most 20th-century packaging is not biodegradable. Discarded cans and plastic junk spoil many a beautiful setting.

Government campaigns appear to be having some success in educating people about responsible garbage disposal, but it's a slow process. Tunisia's cities are surprisingly clean, especially in resort areas. The government has also woken up to the value of the nation's beaches, and has invested a lot of money in clearing them of the overlay of plastic bottles and general detritus found throughout the Mediterranean.

Environmental problems aren't confined to the land. Industrial pollution from the Gannouche petrochemical plant outside Gabès and from phosphate-fertiliser production south of Sfax has caused widespread damage to the marine environment of the shallow Gulf of Gabès. The gulf's rich fishing grounds are also under threat from the destructive fishing practices of the country's 400-strong trawler fleet, which has depleted stocks and put many traditional fishermen out of business.

FLORA & FAUNA
Flora
Rainfall dictates what grows where. The Kroumirie Mountains of the north-west receive the lion's share of the country's rainfall and are densely forested. These forests mainly consist of the handsome evergreen holm oak and the cork oak. Another common species is the strawberry tree, so-called for the striking reddish fruit that ripen in November/December. The fruit is edible, if somewhat tasteless, and you'll see small boys offering punnets of them for sale on roadsides. Just as striking as the fruit are the dense panicles of fragrant, white, urn-shaped flowers that cover the tree in autumn.

The plains of the Tell were once covered in forests of Aleppo pine, but only small pockets remain. The largest remaining stand is between Siliana and Makthar. Further south, the *Acacia raddiana* forest of Bou Hedma National Park, east of Gafsa, is the last remnant of the old pre-Saharan savanna.

The semiarid Sahel region in the central east is dominated by the olive tree, cultivated on a large scale since before Roman times. Passing through the area by road or rail, the rows upon rows of olive trees seem to stretch forever. If you fly between Jerba and Tunis in daylight, you get an even better idea of the enormous area under olive cultivation. Another feature of this area is *Opuntia tomentosa*, better known as the prickly pear. This cactus species can grow to a height of 7m and is used as a hedging plant as well as for its fruit.

The treeless plains of the south support large areas of esparto grass, which is gathered for use in the production of high-quality paper. It is also woven into bags, hats and a range of tourist paraphernalia.

Further south, the vegetation gives way altogether to desert, and, apart from the occasional oasis, there is barely a bush or blade of grass to be seen. One curiosity of this area is a plant called the Jericho rose. It rolls around the desert, carried by the wind, with its branches curled up in a tight ball that encloses its seeds. It opens only on contact with moisture. In the oases, towering date palms provide shelter for a surprising variety of fruit trees, which in turn provide protection for vegetable crops.

Fauna
Tunisia was once home to an exotic range of wildlife that included elephants and big cats such as lions and cheetahs. The war elephants employed by Hannibal were North African forest elephants, smaller cousins of

the modern African elephants. They disappeared along with the trees when the Carthaginians and the Romans began clearing the forests of the interior to grow wheat.

Christians thrown to the lions at the colosseum in Rome had every chance of being mauled by a Tunisian specimen. Thousands of big cats were shipped off to provide entertainment for the citizens of Rome. Lions survived in limited numbers until the mid-19th century, when the last was shot near Haidra.

The only large mammal that exists in large numbers is the wild boar, but this shy animal is seldom seen. Sightings of mongooses, porcupines and genets (a spectacular arboreal, cat-like carnivore) are even rarer. All live in the forests of the north. Jackals are more widely distributed and striped hyenas are found in the south.

The desert regions are home to camels. There are no wild camels – all the animals you see in the desert, even in what appears to be the middle of nowhere, are owned by somebody.

The wild animals of the south include gerbils, foxes, hares and the cute, squirrel-like suslik.

There's more chance of spotting some of the region's reptiles, including the desert varanid (lizard) – a smaller member of the family that includes Australia's goanna and Indonesia's Komodo dragon.

The south has lots of snakes, including horned vipers, and also scorpions. The presence of these creatures means that you should wear solid shoes when walking in rocky areas.

Birds More than 200 species have been recorded in Tunisia across habitats ranging from coastal wetlands to mountains and desert. They include some spectacular, unusual and colourful birds: storks, hawks and eagles in spring and autumn; colourful bee-eaters and rollers; and a host of wading birds and waterfowls.

Although the number of resident species is comparatively small, bird numbers are swollen by millions of migrants using the country as a route between Europe and sub-Saharan Africa in spring and autumn. As they head north in spring they must cross the formidable barrier of the Sahara, and on their southward journey in autumn they run the gauntlet of hunters' guns in Sicily and Malta as they cross the Mediterranean. Either way, landfall in Tunisia provides a welcome respite for exhausted and hungry birds.

See the Activities section in the Facts for the Visitor chapter for information about bird-watching, as well as the boxed text 'Lake Ichkeul Birdlife' in the Northern Tunisia chapter.

Endangered Species

French hunters shot several species to the brink of extinction. These include the shy Barbary deer and a couple of species of gazelle, all now recovering under government protection in the country's national parks.

Two antelope species, the addax and the oryx, were wiped out, but have now been reintroduced to Bou Hedma National Park. The addax sports a set of impressive spiral horns. Other species that are being reintroduced at Bou Hedma are ostriches and maned mouflon (a wild sheep).

The fennec, a nocturnal desert fox with enormous, radar-like ears, was once quite common but now survives only in very small numbers in the south.

National Parks

The government has attempted to do something to protect the country's disappearing environmental heritage by declaring a number of national parks, each protecting a surviving remnant of a typical ecosystem. There were seven at the time of writing and a further two are planned.

The only park with facilities for visitors is Ichkeul National Park, 30km south-west of Bizerte, which protects Lake Ichkeul and adjoining Jebel Ichkeul. See the Northern Tunisia chapter for more information on the park.

Unfortunately the other parks are not particularly user-friendly. Most are very difficult to get to, and a couple double as military areas – which rules out any possibility of a visit. The other national parks are as follows:

Bou Hedma National Park 85km east of Gafsa near the small town of Meknassy, has great potential, but no attempt has yet been made to exploit it. The park protects some 16,000 hectares of acacia forest, representing the last pocket of the extensive savanna forest that once covered the region. The park is being used to reintroduce a number of species previously extinct in Tunisia, including addax, maned mouflon, oryx and ostrich.

Boukornine National Park Just 18km south of Tunis at Hammam Lif, Boukornine is a tiny park of 1900 hectares surrounding Jebel Boukornine (576m). The park is home to wild boars, jackals, porcupines – and the military.

Chambi National Park Located 15km west of Kasserine, the park protects 6700 hectares of forest surrounding Tunisia's highest mountain, Jebel Chambi. Most of the forest is Aleppo pine, but the moister eastern flank of Jebel Chambi supports a pocket of cork oak and juniper. Animals include mountain gazelles and striped hyenas.

Feija National Park Near the Algerian border, 20km north-west of Ghardimao, this park covers 2600 hectares of oak forest. Animals include Barbary deers, wild boars and jackals.

Sidi Toui Saharan National Park Located near the Libyan border, 50km south of Ben Guerdane, Sidi Toui covers 6300 hectares of arid plains and dune country. It's home to a sizeable population of gazelles, as well as jackals and wild cats. The rare nocturnal desert fox, the fennec, has been successfully reintroduced to the park.

Zembra-Zembretta National Park The islands of Zembra and Zembretta are situated in the Gulf of Tunis about 15km west of Cap Bon. Military personnel are the only people who get to see what's there. The official species list includes three types of algae!

GOVERNMENT & POLITICS

The 1959 constitution of the Republic of Tunisia gives legislative power to a chamber of deputies, which consists of 185 members elected directly by universal suffrage for a five-year term.

The president, who is elected separately, has executive power and is the head of both the state and the government. The constitu-

tion states that the president must be a Muslim. The original version also stated that the president can serve for no more than three consecutive terms, but this was amended in 1974 to allow the first president of independent Tunisia, Habib Bourguiba, to become president for life (until he was ousted in 1987).

The current president, Ben Ali, is now in the his fourth term following elections held in October 1999. Ben Ali is the dominant political figure – his smiling face features on posters everywhere. The only other figures who get a mention occasionally are Prime Minister Hamed Karoui, who was appointed by the president, and the president's wife, Madame Leila.

The Opposition

After decades of holding all the seats in the National Assembly, the rules were changed for the 1994 elections to ensure the presence of a few token opposition members.

The 1999 elections left the ruling Rassemblement Constitutionel Democratique (RCD) with 150 seats. The official opposition is the Mouvement des Democratiques Socialistes (MDS), which was awarded 13 seats. Four other parties share the remaining 22 seats.

Ben Ali retained the presidency with 99.44% of the vote. For the record, the remaining 0.56% was split between Mohammed Belhadj Amor of the Parti de l'Unité Populaire (0.31%) and Abdelrahmane Tlili of the Union Democratique Unioniste (0.25%).

The Ben Ali government's main concern, however, continues to be the outlawed Islamic opposition.

ECONOMY

The mixed Tunisian economy, in which both the public and the private sectors participate, relies heavily on tourism and on remittances from nationals working abroad, primarily in France, Italy and the Gulf States.

Petrol and petroleum products account for about 25% of exports, but Tunisia's lack of a refinery means that most of the country's heavy petroleum needs have to be met with imports. Other important exports include textiles and leather, fertilisers and chemicals, with the main destinations being France, Italy, Germany and the USA. Imports consist chiefly of food, raw materials and capital goods such as cars, buses and industrial machinery.

The agricultural sector has become smaller in the last 20 years and now provides work for less than 25% of the workforce; almost 40% of food has to be imported. Despite the fact that large areas of the south of the country are desert, almost 50% of the land is cultivated. The main crops are wheat, barley, maize, sorghum, dates, olives and oranges.

Major industries are the processing of agricultural produce and minerals, including olive oil, textiles, foodstuffs, cement, steel and phosphate. The importance of Tunisia's mining industry is reflected in the fact that Tunisia is the world's sixth-largest producer of phosphate.

Once a socialist economy, Tunisia is now privatising many state-owned industries. Tax and employment laws have been changed to favour the private sector and the country is being marketed abroad as an investment opportunity. The transition has not been easy, however. Unemployment is widespread and the situation is exacerbated by the fact that most manufacturing is small scale and most businesses employ no more than five people. In 1995, Tunisia signed an association agreement with the European Union (EU), ushering in a new era of trade relations with Europe. Under the terms of the agreement, all customs tariffs will be dropped over a 12-year period, leading eventually to full free trade between the EU and Tunisia. The government hopes that this will open new markets for Tunisian goods and encourage the inflow of investment capital, although in the short term it is likely to have a negative impact on the economy.

Socio-Economic Conditions

Unemployment, currently around 13%, is the main social issue, as it seems to be almost everywhere in the world. As a visitor, one of the first questions you will be asked is what the unemployment rate is in your country, closely followed by a question about the chances of finding a job.

While the social security system provides old age and disability pensions, and compensation for sickness and injury, the unemployed get nothing. They survive thanks to the closeness of the family network; often one working adult has to support four or five other adult family members. In spite of this, living standards are generally good and are considered high by developing-world standards. Per capita GDP is around US$5200.

Health care is free, and low-income earners are eligible for extra benefits such as free milk for newborn babies and free school lunches. Although there are still shortages of trained personnel and modern facilities, general health conditions have improved dramatically in the last 20 years. The government claims it has 96% coverage for its immunisation program, which is the most comprehensive in the developing world.

POPULATION & PEOPLE

The population of Tunisia is estimated to be 9.5 million. The vast majority (98%) are Arab-Berber, with Europeans and Jews making up the remaining 2%.

The government's family planning program has slowed the population growth rate to 1.4%, but almost half the population is under the age of 15, which places a great strain on social services. Another problem is population distribution, which varies from more than 2000 per sq km in Tunis to less than 10 per sq km in the south.

The Berbers (see the boxed text 'The Berbers') were the original inhabitants of the area, but waves of immigrants over the centuries have brought Phoenicians, Jews, Romans, Vandals and Arabs. There was a major influx of Spanish Muslims in the 17th century. The Ottoman Turks have also added their bit to the great ethnic mix.

EDUCATION

Education is free and, thanks to the high government spending (typically 25% of

The Berbers

The Berbers are the native people of North Africa.

The name was bestowed on them by the Arabs when they arrived at the end of the 7th century. The Arabs distinguished between the people who had adopted Roman/Byzantine culture and those who had not. The former were called Roum Afrik (African people), and the latter were called Berbers – from the Greek *barbarikos* (foreign). The ancient Egyptians knew them as the Libou (nomads); the Greeks called them Libyans, as did the Phoenicians; and the Romans called them Africans (see the boxed text 'The Origins of "Africa"' in the History section earlier).

Ethnically, the Berbers represent something of a cultural melting pot – the result of successive waves of immigration from the Near East, sub-Saharan Africa and southern Europe. By the time the Phoenicians arrived in the 10th century BC, these diverse peoples had adopted a uniform language and culture.

Territory was divided up into tribal confederations. Northern Tunisia was the territory of the Numidians, founders of the cities of Bulla Regia, Sicca (El-Kef) and Thugga (Dougga). Other tribes had settled in the major oases of the south, while others lived a semi-nomadic pastoral existence.

Although conquered many times through history, the Berbers proved hard to repress. Military resistance to Roman rule continued until 24 AD, and later resurfaced in the form of the Donatist movement, which split the African church in the 4th century.

They benefited from 250 years of increasingly ineffectual Vandal and Byzantine rule, and were probably at the peak of their political and military power when the Arabs arrived. Early Arab successes against Byzantine forces were reversed by the Berbers at Tahuda (in Algeria) in 683. This was followed by the capture of Kairouan – which became the base for a short-lived Berber kingdom until 689.

The next wave of rebellion was led by Al-Kahena, a legendary figure in Berber lore. The widow of a tribal chief from the Aures Mountains in Algeria, she defeated the Hassan bin Nooman at Tebessa in 695 and pushed back the Arab armies as far as Gabès. She was finally defeated after a defiant last stand at El-Jem in 701.

More trouble was to follow in the form of the Berber-led Kharijite rebellions that flared intermittently over the following 250 years, but effective resistance to Arab rule ended with the Hilalian invasions at the end of the 10th century.

Algeria still has a sizeable Berber population, based in the mountains east of Algiers, but Tunisia's Berbers have become all but totally assimilated with the Arab population over the centuries.

Berber customs, however, continue to survive – particularly in rural areas. Many women still wear the traditional *bakhnoug* (shawl) and *assaba* (headband) and tattoo their faces with ancient tribal symbols; men still favour the *burnous*, a hooded woollen cape.

Brightly-coloured kilim and *mergoum* rugs decorated with Berber motifs make excellent souvenirs, as does the primitive moulded pottery known as Sejnane ware (see the Sejnane section in the Northern Tunisia chapter for details on Berber pottery).

The most striking reminder of Tunisia's Berber heritage, however, is the dazzling architecture of Jerba and the villages of the Ksour district around Tataouine. See the Jerba & the South-East Coast chapter and the Ksour section of the Southern Tunisia chapter for details.

total expenditure), there has been a rapid increase in the number of schools since independence. As a result of this, literacy is fairly high at 66.6% (78.6% for males; 54.6% for females).

ARTS
Dance

Performances of traditional Berber dancing are a popular form of entertainment at the country's resort hotels. These dances

Malouf

Malouf, which means 'normal', is the name given to the form of traditional Arab-style music that has become a national institution in Tunisia. Introduced into Tunisia in the 15th century by Andalusian refugees, this distinctive Hispano-Arabic style of music rapidly became so popular that it replaced the existing forms of Arab-Muslim music. It consists of instrumental pieces, which serve as preludes and breaks, and vocal works performed in a set sequence, called a *nouba*. Traditionally, malouf was performed by small ensembles using a *rbab* (a kind of two-stringed violin), *oud* (lute) and *darbuka* (drum, usually made of terracotta with a goatskin cover on one side), with a solo vocalist. Today, ensembles are more likely to be made up of large instrumental and choral groups, playing a mixture of western and traditional Arabic instruments. The repetitive melodies and lack of tonal variation can be a challenge for Western listeners.

Malouf was adopted by the Sufi religious brotherhoods to play at their ceremonies (see also the boxed text 'Sufism' under Religion later in this chapter). It gradually declined in popularity as it was superseded by a new, lighter style of music introduced from Egypt in the mid 1920s. Malouf underwent a revival in the 1930s when Baron Erlangen, a musicologist living in the Tunis suburb of Sidi Bou Saïd, founded the Rachidia Ensemble. The Baron's six volumes on the history and rules of malouf are testament to his passionate involvement with the art form. Although purists might question the authenticity of the ensemble, the Rachidia became the official centre for malouf music and is where most of Tunisia's leading musicians have trained.

After independence, malouf was adopted as a symbol of national identity. Since then, with the dissolution of the Sufi brotherhoods, it has become institutionalised to a great extent, with the government offering courses in malouf at the National Conservatory of Music in Tunis and an annual cycle of festivals and competitions culminating in the International Festival of Malouf held in July in Testour. It has also become an established form of tourist entertainment.

Stars of the malouf scene include the El-Azifet Ensemble (an exclusively female orchestra – a rarity in this part of the world) and the oud player Anouar Brahem. Tourist restaurants often put on live performances of traditional music; the Restaurant M'Rabet in the Tunis medina is a good place to try – see the Entertainment section in the Tunis chapter for more details.

date back to pre-Islamic times. They include the dramatic Dance of the Vases, performed by dancers with vases balanced on their heads. This is also a highlight of the Festival of the Ksour, held around Tataouine in November.

Many visitors arrive expecting to see Egyptian-style belly dancing, which is much harder to locate. Belly dancing is officially frowned upon as un-Islamic, but is tolerated at some of the more risqué nightclubs in Sousse and Tunis. For more details, see the Entertainment section of the Tunis chapter and under Entertainment in the Sousse section of the Central Tunisia chapter.

Music

Western ears will need to adjust in order to appreciate the range of musical offerings available. While Western music is based on the octave, Arabic music uses the shorter, five-note pentatomic scale.

Most of the music you'll hear as you travel around is classical Arabic, usually love songs performed by some raven-haired songstress from Cairo. Tunisia's speciality is *malouf*, which was introduced by Andalusian migrants fleeing Spain in the 15th century (see the boxed text 'Malouf').

The Algerian dance music known as *rai* was all the rage at the time of research, especially with the nation's louage drivers – a good barometer of popular taste! The style was popularised in the West by the Sting song *Desert Rose* – performed in conjunction with Algerian rai artist Cheb Mami.

Western popular music is a favourite with many young Tunisians – especially techno.

Western classical music is rare, although the floodlit colosseum at El-Jem becomes the setting for the spectacular El-Jem Symphonic Music Festival in late July.

Literature

There are countless streets in Tunisian towns named after Tunisia's national poet, Abu el-Kacem el-Chabbi, whose poem *Will to Live* is taught to every schoolchild.

Few Tunisian writers have been translated into English. One who has and whose work is available internationally is Mustapha Tlili, whose novel *Lion Mountain* tells the story of the disasters wrought upon a remote village by progress and tourism. You won't find it in bookshops in Tunisia.

Acclaimed author Albert Memmi qualifies as Tunisian by birth, but he lives in Paris and writes in French about the identity crisis faced by North African Jews like himself. His books include the *Pillar of Salt* and *Jews and Arabs. Sleepless Nights* by Ali Duaji is a collection of short stories and sketches about life in and around Tunis during the first half of the 20th century. It's available only in Tunisia.

Architecture

Tunisia boasts a wide range of architectural styles covering more than 2500 years of

Modern Art in Tunisia

Introduced by the French, painting is a well-established contemporary-art form in Tunisia. It ranges from the highly geometric forms of Hédi Turki and from intricate free-flowing Arabic calligraphy, such as the work of artist Nja Mahdaoui, to traditional western styles that aim to encapsulate the essence of Tunisian daily life and culture, including scenes of cafes, *hammams* and music and dance performances. The work of Yahia Turki and Ammar Farhat, in particular, falls into this last category.

Under the French, the ambient lifestyle of Tunisia attracted European artists who, were entranced by the North African light and architecture. Perhaps most famously, Tunisia was a source of inspiration to the Swiss expressionist painter Paul Klee, who first visited the country in 1914.

A Tunisian Salon, heavily dependent on colonial styles and set up by European painters, was established in 1894 in Tunis. In the 1940s, a collection of professional and amateur artists broke away from the Salon to establish the more nationalist École de Tunis. It welcomed Tunisian members and was responsible for popularising Tunisian life as a subject matter for painting. Early members of this school include Yahia Turki who is widely considered to be the father of Tunisian painting. Other well-known names (within Tunisia, at any rate) include Ammar Farhat, Jellal Ben Abdallah, Zoubeir Turki, Hédi Turki and Abdelaziz Gorgi. Sérès Productions publishes a series, available from art bookshops in Tunisia, on the life and works of the most prominent members. If you can't afford to buy a print, you could just settle for a postage stamp – the philatelic-sales section of the main post office in Tunis sells stamps depicting the work of some of the more celebrated national artists.

Modern art galleries in Tunisia are mainly confined to Tunis and its wealthy suburbs, especially the traditional artist's haven of Sidi Bou Saïd. The inside back page of the English-language weekly *Tunisia News* has a list of exhibitions. Galerie Alif, behind the French Embassy in Tunis, is a gem. It has a vast collection of art books, including ones it publishes itself. It usually has an art exhibition, in the basement, that changes every couple of months – photography, painting, prints and installations. Espace Diwan 9, in the Tunis Medina at 9 Rue Sidi ben Arous, also has a good collection of art books focusing on Tunisia and the Maghreb.

Other places in Tunis that may be worth checking out include Galerie Yahia, in the Complex Palmarium, 64 Ave Habib Bourguiba; Galerie Artémis at 30 Rue 7232, El-Menzah IX; Galerie des Arts at 42 Complex Jamil, El-Menzah VI; and Galerie Gorgi at 31 Rue Jugurtha, Le Belvédère.

Roger Sheen

history. Top of the list is Islamic architecture, which itself covers a multitude of styles ranging from the austere, functional buildings of the early Aghlabids to the exuberant work of the later Andalusians and Ottomans. All are discussed in the special Islamic Architecture section included in this chapter.

Other architectural styles are discussed throughout this book, and these include the following:

Berber Architecture The finest examples of Berber architecture to be found in the south, particularly the troglodyte pit houses of the Matmata region and the wonderfully idiosyncratic *ksour* (fortified granaries) around Tataouine. Both found international fame as settings in the *Star Wars* films, and are discussed in more detail in The Ksour section in the Southern Tunisia chapter.

Another highlight is the traditional relief brickwork found in Tozeur and Nefta, which uses protruding bricks to create intricate geometric patterns. See the Southern Tunisia chapter for more details.

Jerban Architecture Although also of Berber origin, Jerba's highly distinctive fortress architecture reflects the island's long history as a stronghold of the fiercely autonomous Kharijite sect. The buildings were all designed with defence in mind, and the landscape is dotted with what looks like fortresses and air-raid shelters, all painted a brilliant white. See the Jerban Architecture special section in the Jerba & the South-East Coast chapter for more information.

Punic Architecture Punic is the name given to the architectural style that emerged after several hundred years of assimilation between the Phoenicians, who arrived in Tunisia around the beginning of the 1st millennium BC, and the native Berbers. Unfortunately, the Romans did such a good job of destroying Punic Carthage that only a few scattered sites remain (see the Carthage section in the Tunis chapter for more information). Other Punic

cities remain buried beneath centuries of subsequent development.

The exception is the remote coastal site of Kerkouane, which was sacked by a Roman army in 256 BC and never re-occupied. This World Heritage-listed site is the subject of a special section in the Cap Bon Peninsula chapter.

Roman Architecture Roman architects have provided the country with many of its leading tourist attractions, including the stunning Capitol of Dougga – covered in the Dougga special section of the Northern Tunisia chapter. Other highlights include the colosseum at El-Jem and the temples of ancient Sufetula (Sbeitla) – both are covered in the Central Tunisia chapter.

European Architecture The *villes nouvelles* of Tunisia's major cities are graced with many fine buildings dating from the period when Tunisia was a French protectorate. Their dimensions are European in form, but adapted to the climate and culture of Tunisia with generous balconies and courtyards. They feature some wonderfully extravagant neo-classical facades, particularly in Tunis. See the Ville Nouvelle section in the Tunis chapter for more information.

Calligraphy

Calligraphy is an art form with a long history in the Islamic world, stemming from the belief that Arabic is a holy language revealed by Allah (God) to the Prophet Mohammed in the form of the Q'uran.

Derived from the Greek words *kala* (beautiful) and *graphos* (writing), calligraphy was a way of glorifying the word of God. In a culture that regarded representation of the human form as a heresy, calligraphy was a popular form of decoration. Early calligraphers used an angular script called Kufic that was perfect for stone carving. There are some superb examples of Kufic script on the eastern wall and minaret of the Great Mosque in Sfax, and above the entrance to the Mosque of the Three Doors in Kairouan.

[Continued on page 44]

ISLAMIC ARCHITECTURE

History

From the 7th century onwards, Tunisia – like the rest of North Africa, the Middle East, northern India and Spain – came under the control of Islam. The impact on the country's culture was enormous and Tunisia's architecture, like its arts, was heavily influenced by Islamic styles.

With the course of time, however, Tunisia developed its own style. The climate, history, social structure and natural resources all played their part, as did its situation at the crossroads of the Mediterranean – which brought it into contact with other foreign influences. The angular, austere style of early Aghlabid mosques, for example, is in stark contrast to the opulent buildings of the Ottoman Turks and the Andalusians.

Nevertheless, much of the philosophy and basic principles of construction remain constant throughout the Islamic world, including Tunisia.

Religious Architecture

Mosques The mosque, or *masjid*, embodies the Islamic faith and represents one of its predominant architectural features.

In Tunisia, mosque design is based on the layout of the Mosque of Sidi Okba (Great Mosque) in Kairouan, founded at the end of the 7th century – the first mosque to be built in the country after the Arab conquest. Like all mosques, however, the Great Mosque of Kairouan itself is based on the layout of the house belonging to the Prophet Mohammed in Medina. The original setting was an enclosed, oblong courtyard with huts (housing Mohammed's wives) along one side wall and a rough portico, or *zulla*, providing shade at one end for the poorer worshippers.

This plan can be seen in almost all mosques. The courtyard has become the *sahn*, the portico the arcaded *riwaqs* and the houses the *haram* or prayer hall. Divided into a series of aisles that segregate the sexes, the prayer hall can reach immense proportions in the larger mosques. Running down the middle is a broad aisle which leads to the mihrab, a vaulted niche at the centre of the qibla wall. Built to face Mecca, this wall indicates the direction of prayer.

It is also the site of the minbar, a kind of pulpit raised above a narrow staircase. As a rule, only the main community mosque, or *jomaa*, contains a minbar. In grander mosques, the minbar is often ornately and beautifully decorated. They are less commonly found in the smaller local mosques.

On Friday, the minbar is the place from where the *khutba* (weekly sermon) is

VERITY CAMPBELL

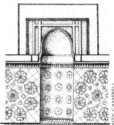

VERITY CAMPBELL

Inset: The prayer-hall arcade of the Mosque of Sidi Okba, Kairouan. (Photo by Chris Wood)

Middle: A minbar – the pulpit from which the sermon is delivered in a mosque.

Bottom: A mihrab – a niche in the wall of a mosque that indicates the direction of Mecca.

The minaret of Kairouan's Great Mosque (top left) and the watchtower of Monastir's ribat (top right) display an austerity unique to Tunisian Islamic architecture. Equally imposing are the crenellated walls of the Sfax medina (bottom). A doorway in the Tunis medina (middle right) conveys strength and elegance.

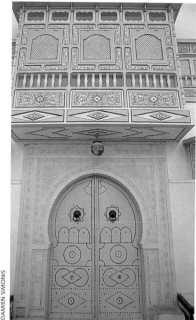

Though they did not invent it, Islamic architects took the horseshoe arch to new stylistic heights: merchant houses, Kairouan (top left & right); the Great Mosque of Kairouan (middle left); and the polychrome marble arches of the Zaouia of Sidi Abdel Kador, Kairouan (bottom).

TYPICAL MOSQUE PLAN

1 Qibla Wall	5 Fountain for
2 Mihrab	Ritual Ablution
3 Haram	6 Sahn
4 Riwaq	7 Minaret

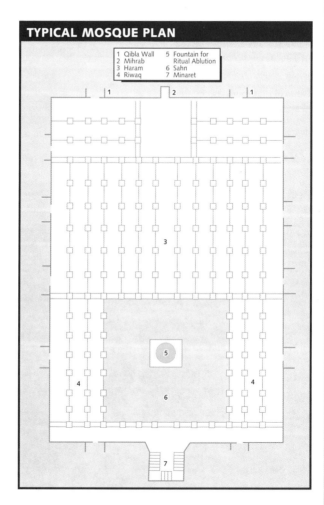

delivered to the congregation. Islam does not recognise priests as such, but the closest equivalent is the imam, a learned man schooled in Islam and Islamic law. Often he doubles as the mosque's muezzin, who calls the faithful to prayer five times a day.

Before entering the haram and participating in communal worship, Muslims must perform a ritual washing at the mosque's fountain or basin. This is placed in the middle of the courtyard and is usually carved from marble; in the older mosques, it's often worn from centuries of use.

Beyond its obvious religious function, the mosque also serves as a kind of community centre, school, and point of social contact.

Many mosques are open to non-Muslims, but in some they may not be allowed beyond the courtyard.

Minarets The minaret (from the word *menara*, meaning lighthouse) is the tower at one corner of the mosque. They come in all shapes and sizes, usually built on a square base. The dominant style in Tunisia is square-based all the way to the top, which was the style favoured by the early Aghlabids, as well as by the Andalusians.

Most minarets have internal staircases for the muezzins to climb; the advent of the microphone saves them the effort now.

Medersas Medersas served as residential colleges where theology and Muslim law were taught. Some also functioned as early universities.

GEOFF STRINGER

Left: The minaret of the Mosque of Youssef Day, the first Ottoman-style mosque to be built in Tunis.

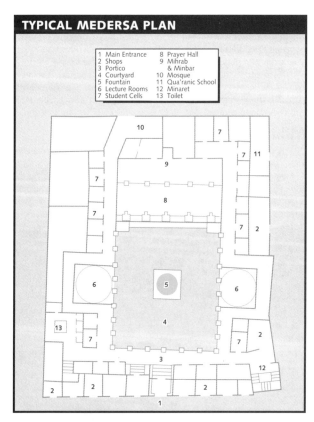

TYPICAL MEDERSA PLAN

1 Main Entrance
2 Shops
3 Portico
4 Courtyard
5 Fountain
6 Lecture Rooms
7 Student Cells
8 Prayer Hall
9 Mihrab
  & Minbar
10 Mosque
11 Qua'ranic School
12 Minaret
13 Toilet

They comprise an open-air courtyard, with an ablution fountain in the centre and a main prayer hall at the far end, surrounded by an upper gallery of student cells.

The medersas are remarkable not so much for their architecture, but for their incredibly elaborate decoration, which includes detailed carving, tile work, kufic script and muqarnas (stalactite-like stone carvings). There are some good examples of medersas in the Tunis medina, including the three near the Zitouna Mosque on Souq des Libraires. The Medersa of the Palm Tree still serves as a Quranic school and is closed to the public, but the Medersa Bachia and Medersa Slimania can both be visited.

Marabouts The countryside is dotted with the small, white-washed domes that mark the tombs of marabouts, Muslim holy men. You'll find them everywhere, from the medinas of the big cities to the remotest desert locations.

Zaouia A *zaouia* is an expanded version of a marabout, usually found where the cult of a marabout has developed to the point where additional facilities are required to handle visiting pilgrims. A typical zaouia thus includes a prayer hall and accommodation for visitors.

Widespread as they are, the zaouias play a very important role in the lives of the local communities. They serve not just as sites for pilgrimages (for those in search of *baraka*, a blessing), but also as charitable and community centres.

Military Architecture

Islamic military architecture is characterised by three major features: walls, gates and fortresses.

From the late 9th century until they were rendered useless by artillery, vast fortified walls, mighty towers, and elaborate gates became a crucial feature of almost every city and town. While many of these fortifications have disappeared, some outstanding examples remain.

Left: Late afternoon sun on the city gates of old Sousse.

Walls & Towers Walls were designed to daunt rather than to dazzle. Undistinguished architecturally, they were impressive more for their size than for their intricate touches.

Typically, they were constructed of rock set in clay, and also served as barracks, granaries, and arsenals. Towers, or small turrets, were placed at regular intervals around the perimeter, while the top of the wall featured crenellations to provide shelter for defenders.

The best examples are the walls surrounding the medinas of Sfax and Sousse, both built by the Aghlabids in the 9th century.

Gates The Islamic gate, or *bab*, was designed above all to impress. It was a symbol of power, security and riches, as well as a fortified entrance to the city.

In general, two crenellated, stone-block towers flank the central bay in which the gate is set. The arch itself most frequently takes the horseshoe form and encloses or is enclosed by multifoil curves. The gates are usually highly decorated with friezes, using geometric, flower and foliage or shell motifs.

Favourites include the 9th century Bab Jedid in Sfax. The medinas of Kairouan and Monastir are other good places to look.

Another form of gate is the *skifa*. The name usually refers to the entrance lobby of a private home, through which all visitors must pass. When used in the context of a city gate, the skifa becomes a fortification – such as the formidable Skifa el-Kahla at Mahdia, which features a long, vaulted passageway protected by a series of gates.

Fortresses There are three main types of fortress to be found, classified according to their size and their role.

In Tunisia, a kasbah is not a market. It's the name given to the principle fortress guarding a medina. Usually the kasbah was built astride the city's walls, or positioned in a commanding corner.

The kasbah at Monastir has been hailed as the finest piece of military architecture in North Africa, but it is just one of many fine examples. No kasbah occupies a position as commanding as the one that towers over the ancient fortress city of Le Kef, while the kasbah at Kairouan has been converted into a hotel.

Next in line in terms of size comes the *borj*. The term is used to describe the smaller forts that were sometimes added to bolster a medina's defences at key points, such as the Borj Ennour in Sfax, and for free-standing forts like the Borj Ghazi Mustapha on Jerba.

A *ribat* was a cross between a fort and a monastery. The Aghlabids built a series of them around the coast of the Sahel to safeguard the frontiers of Islam from Christian attack. They were occupied by Islamic warriors, who divided their time between fighting and quiet contemplation of the Quran. Most have now disappeared, with the notable exceptions of the ribats of Sousse and Monastir.

Medina Architecture

Named after the birthplace of the Prophet Mohammed, medinas are the Islamic equivalent of the old walled cities of medieval Europe. Dating from the early days of the Arab conquest, they remained the principle form of urban settlement in Tunisia until the arrival of the French.

Despite their chaotic appearance, these medinas were laid out according to strict Islamic principles, thought to have originated in 8th century Baghdad. Their layout is carefully adapted to the rigours of the climate. The deep, narrow streets of the medina keep the sun's rays from the centre during the day, and draw in the cool, dense evening air during the night.

The massing of structures sharing walls also reduces the total surface area exposed to the sun. Traditional building materials such as earth, stone and wood absorb water, which then evaporates from their surfaces and cools the surrounding air.

The heart of any medina is the city's main mosque, normally known as the jami-e-kebir or Great Mosque. This should be located at the exact centre of the medina, as is the case in Sfax and Tunis. There are plenty of exceptions to this rule, usually as a result of subsequent changes to the shape of the medina (Kairouan, Sousse).

Souqs Traditionally, the Great Mosque is surrounded by *souqs* – areas of shops specialising in particular products or services. These are located in strict hierarchy, starting with the so-called 'noble trades' occupying the area of covered souqs immediately around the mosque.

DAMIEN SIMONIS

First come the vendors of candles, incense and other objects used in the rites of worship, whose shops line the mosque walls, effectively masking the mosque from view. Next to them are the booksellers, long venerated by Muslim cultures, and the vendors of small leather goods. These are followed by the clothing and textile stalls, long the domain of the richest and most powerful merchants.

The hierarchy then descends through furnishings, domestic goods and utensils, until, with the most ordinary wares, the walls and gates of the city are reached.

Left: Built to impress and daunt – the formidable walls of Sousse's medina.

Here, on the city perimeters, where the caravans used to assemble, are the ironmongers, blacksmiths and the other craftsmen and vendors serving the caravan trade.

Furthest afield are the potteries and the tanneries, usually exiled to beyond the city walls because of the noxious odours and smoke they produce. There was no place in the medina for markets. They were to be found outside the city's gates.

Funduqs Muslim civilisations have always been mobile. Arab conquerors were originally nomadic; huge Muslim armies were constantly on the move, and students and scholars undertook long journeys to sit at the feet of famous masters. From the earliest days of Islam, pilgrims travelled long distances for the hajj (pilgrimage) to Mecca. Above all, there was a strong tradition of trade, with merchants travelling vast distances to buy and sell goods. This led to the creation of caravanserais, known in Tunisia as *funduqs*, which sprang up at regular intervals along the major trade routes of the entire Islamic world.

Their function was similar to that of modern-day motels or motorway cafes, providing food and accommodation for both traveller and their transport, usually camels, mules or horses.

In general, they were unremarkable architecturally. An unadorned facade provided a doorway wide enough to allow camels or heavily laden beasts to enter. The central courtyard was usually open to the sky and was surrounded by a number of similar stalls, bays or niches, usually arranged over two floors. The ground floor housed shops, warehouses, tea shops and stabling for the animals, and the 2nd floor accommodated the travellers.

Funduqs were once found in all of Tunisia's major towns. At Houmt Souq, on the island of Jerba, four of the town's old funduqs have been converted into tourist accommodation and are well worth seeking out.

Residential Quarters

Hammams Another essential feature of Islamic towns and societies is the hammam or public bath. Although serving a mundane function, the hammam can be a surprisingly impressive architectural structure. Most commonly, however, they are identifiable only by the smoking chimney and low, glass-studded dome.

The Muslim hammam is directly descended from the baths of classical times, although with time the emphasis shifted from social and sporting purposes to the Muslim concern with cleanliness.

The entrance to a hammam is through a *skifa* (hallway), which leads to a spacious, domed *mahress* (disrobing room) surrounded by wide benches covered with matting. A doorway leads from here to a succession of humid rooms, starting with the *bit el-bered* (cold room), an elongated room with facilities for the ritual ablutions to be performed before bathing. Next comes the *bit el-taïeb* (warm room), larger and more elaborately constructed and decorated than the cold room, with benches where the bather can recline or be massaged.

Last of all is *bir el-skhun* (steam room), where bathers sweat it out before returning to the warm room to be cleansed and massaged, soaped, shampooed and rinsed by bath attendants.

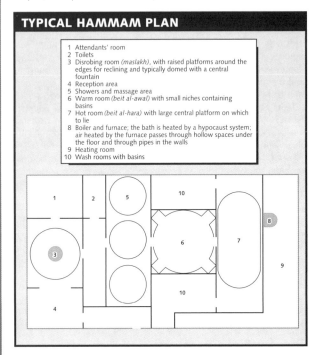

TYPICAL HAMMAM PLAN

1 Attendants' room
2 Toilets
3 Disrobing room *(maslakh)*, with raised platforms around the edges for reclining and typically domed with a central fountain
4 Reception area
5 Showers and massage area
6 Warm room *(beit al-awal)* with small niches containing basins
7 Hot room *(beit al-hara)* with large central platform on which to lie
8 Boiler and furnace; the bath is heated by a hypocaust system; air heated by the furnace passes through hollow spaces under the floor and through pipes in the walls
9 Heating room
10 Wash rooms with basins

Domestic Architecture

The Tunisian town house has remained largely unaltered for 3000 years. Known as the *dar* or interior courtyard house, it is typical of the Islamic dwellings of the Middle East and Mediterranean.

The principal feature is a central courtyard, around which are grouped suites of rooms in a symmetrical pattern. In the wealthier houses, service areas are often tacked on to one side, and these in turn might have their own courtyard as necessity and means dictate.

The interior courtyard serves a very important function as a modifier of the climate in hot, dry regions. With very few exterior windows, the courtyard functions as a kind of 'light well' into which the light penetrates during the day, and an 'air well', into which the cool, dense air of evening sinks at night.

One of the great advantages of this set-up is that it permits outdoor activities, with protection from the wind, dust and sun. The system also allows natural ventilation. Because the house is surrounded by tall walls, the sun's rays cannot reach the courtyard until later in the afternoon. When they do reach the courtyard, and heated air rises, convection currents set up a flow of air that ventilates the house and keeps it cool.

While rooms in European houses are usually allotted a specific function, the rooms in Muslim houses are more multipurpose. Rooms can be used interchangeably for eating, relaxing and sleeping.

The function of interiors can also change with the time of day. In summer, the hottest part of the day is spent in the cool of the courtyard, and at night, the roof terrace can be used as a sleeping area.

Again, reflecting the Islamic architectural concern with the interior space of a building, decoration is reserved for the internal elements such as the courtyard, and not, as is the European style, the external elements. The street facade is usually just a plain wall, and the only opening is the entrance door. Any other openings are small, grilled and above the line of vision of passers-by. This reflects the strict demarcation of public and private life in Islamic society.

Sometimes the doors of houses can be elaborately decorated, marking the symbolic importance of the house entrance – the vulnerable threshold between private and public worlds. Auspicious symbols, designs and colours are often used, such as the stylised design of the hand of Fatima.

The importance of privacy is also extended into the interior of the house. The word for women, *harim,* is related to the word harem, 'sacred area', which, far removed from its Western connotations, denotes the family living quarters.

The harem, or domestic area of the house, is primarily the women's domain. The husband usually has his own room just outside this area. In the interiors of some houses, *mashrabiyya,* or perforated wooden screens, are sometimes erected in front of a harem which opens onto the reception room. This allows women to observe men's gatherings and festivities without being observed themselves.

Forming an essential part of the wealthier town houses are the interior gardens. These can be elaborately paved with ceramic tiles, and richly planted. Paths, often raised above ground level, divide the flowerbeds. Usually the centre of the garden is dominated by a fountain or pool – even the poorer houses may contain some focal point such as a tree, shrub or ornamental object. This design again is closely connected to the climate: The evaporation of water and the presence of plants both raise the humidity and keep the air cool.

The garden also has a strongly symbolic function too. To the Muslim, the beauty of creation and of the garden is held to be a reflection of God. Within the dusty wilderness of the city, and hidden behind a small door, lies a sudden paradise of vegetation and tranquillity.

Mosaics

An astonishing number of floor mosaics has been discovered in Tunisia and it's likely that many more remain undiscovered. Reasons for this abundance of mosaics include: the wealth of Africa Proconsularis in the 2nd and 3rd centuries AD (based on trade in wheat and olive oil); the availability of coloured stones, including marble; and influences from the Romans in Italy via Sicily and the eastern Mediterranean. In addition, Tunisia's warm, dry climate has meant that the mosaics have generally been well preserved.

A depiction of September from a mosaic of the months of the year. One of the many fine mosaics now in the Museum at El-Jem.

Mosaic is an ancient technique which flourished from the 4th century BC to the 14th century AD and was particularly popular during the time of the Roman Empire. The mosaics found in Tunisia date mainly from the 2nd to 6th centuries AD, although a simple early type of floor mosaic, *opus siginum* (cement with a sprinkling of marble fragments), has been found in Punic houses, leading to the suggestion that mosaic art originated in Carthage in the 4th and 3rd centuries BC. It's more generally accepted, however, that mosaics were introduced to Tunisia from Sicily, which was at the edge of the Carthaginian Empire.

The early mosaics, dating from the 1st and 2nd centuries AD, show evidence of Italian and Alexandrian influence, but by the middle of the 2nd century, distinct schools of mosaicists were established and working in Tunisia, mostly in the El-Jem/Sousse region. By the end of the 2nd century most cities of any size in Tunisia had a local workshop, and from this time on mosaics were a standard form of floor decoration and possibly also of wall decoration, although few wall mosaics have survived. Tunisian mosaics from the 3rd century onwards show a distinctive African style, characterised by larger dramatic compositions with vigorous colour and realistic subjects such as amphitheatre games, hunting and scenes of life on the African estates. They appear to have been primarily decorative in function, unlike elsewhere in the Roman Empire where they were used for a variety of purposes, including shop signs and advertising.

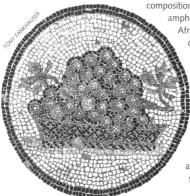

Basket of grapes – detail of a mosaic from the House of Africa (El-Jem Museum).

Most of the mosaics to be seen in Tunisia are the type known as *opus tessellatum*, in which patterns are formed out of little squares or pieces of stone called tesserae (from the Latin, meaning cubes or dice). The technique involved laying out a setting bed of mortar in which the tesserae were placed. Underpaintings discovered in floor and wall mosaics indicate that preparatory sketches served as a guide for the placement and colour of the tesserae. Not much is known about the artisans who produced the mosaics, although a few have signed their names on their work.

Mosaics

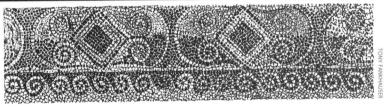

TONY FANKHAUSER

The decorative frameworks around the mosaics are often as stunning as the pictures themselves.

The majority of the mosaics found in Tunisia come from private houses; the second major source is public baths. The houses were usually the property of wealthy merchants and landowners. The mosaics were distributed throughout the houses, with the most elaborate mosaics being found in the main reception rooms, to impress visitors and clients. A certain amount of 'keeping up with the Joneses' was presumably responsible for the extraordinary quality and quantity of mosaics found in these houses.

The themes depicted reflect the preoccupations and interests of the commissioning house owners and include banquets, amphitheatre games, mythology, the sea and daily life on the great estates. In Tunisian mosaics, the depiction of time (eg, personifications of the seasons) is a common theme, denoting the harmony and permanence of the universe. Good examples include the *Seasons and the Months* mosaic in the El-Jem Museum and the *La Chebba* mosaic in the Bardo Museum in Tunis. Dionysus, the god of fruitfulness and wine, who had the gift of being able to free the spirit of worries, was another very popular subject. At El-Jem more than 20 mosaics depicting Dionysian themes have been found, including the *Triumph of Dionysus* (now at the Bardo Museum). Another common theme was the sea, with the emphasis being on its inexhaustible riches, seen especially on mosaics from the Sousse region. The *Fishing Scenes* mosaic at the Sousse Museum shows four boats floating on a sea filled with fish and shellfish. Mosaics with sea themes are also found in houses further inland, perhaps reflecting both the house owners' love of the Mediterranean and the contribution shipping made to their wealth.

The mosaics that depict life on the great African estates in the 3rd and 4th centuries AD are among the most impressive in Tunisia and are distinctively African. They are both narrative and descriptive and portray the life of the rich landowners who commissioned the works. The *Lord Julius* mosaic at the Bardo Museum, shows one such landowner, with his wife, in four scenes corresponding to the four seasons.

In the 4th to 6th centuries AD, mosaics were influenced by early Christian beliefs and themes, such as the mosaic of Daniel in the Lion's Den in the Bardo Museum. They were commissioned for the pavements of basilicas and tombs, such as those found at Tabarka. The tomb mosaics depict either a conventional image of the deceased in an attitude of prayer or just an epitaph. By the 7th century, with the Arab invasion, mosaic art fell into a decline, although mosaic pavements have been discovered in the ruins of the Aghlabite palaces at Raqqada, perhaps dating from the 9th century AD, and 10th century Arab mosaics have been found at Mahdia.

Marine themes were very popular in Tunisian mosiacs.

TONY FANKHAUSER

Isabelle Young

[Continued from page 31]

Modern calligraphy uses a flowing cursive style, more suited to working with pen and ink.

Film

Tunisia is often used as a setting for international film makers, but it also has a busy – and surprisingly daring – film industry of its own. Few locally produced films make it beyond the Arab world, although a couple of directors have won critical acclaim in Europe in recent years.

They include Ferid Boughedir, whose *Halfaouine* featured at the Cannes Film Festival in 1990. It tells a humorous tale of sexual awakening in the suburbs of Tunis. Female director Moutfida Tlatli won a special prize at the 1994 festival for her film *Silence of the Palace*.

The biennial Carthage International Film Festival offers a good opportunity to view the latest work from Tunisian and regional directors. The next festival will be held in October 2001.

Crafts

Tunisia produces a huge range of handicrafts. They include some beautiful pieces – carpets, pottery and copperwork – that are genuine works of art. Most of the stuff, though, is mass produced to meet the souvenir requirements of the tourist industry, see the Shopping section in the Facts for the Visitor chapter for further details.

SOCIETY & CONDUCT
Traditional Culture

Tunisian society has changed beyond all recognition in the course of last century. There are now two parallel societies: the modern, Western-leaning, cosmopolitan society of big cities like Tunis and Sousse, and the traditional society of the smaller towns and villages. The further you stray from the big cities, the more traditional the lifestyle becomes.

Traditional society is based on the family. In rural areas, it is still common to find three generations living under one roof, and social life (especially for women) is restricted largely to the extended family. Traditionally, people married young and had lots of children.

The other main force shaping traditional society is religion. Religious observance is generally much higher in poorer rural areas than among the urban elite.

In the west and south of the country, small groups of Berber nomads continue to live a lifestyle that has barely changed in centuries, moving around the countryside with their flocks of sheep and goats. Their black goat-hair tents are a feature of the landscape between Kasserine and Le Kef, and the women still wear traditional Berber dress and tattoo their faces with tribal symbols.

Dos & Don'ts

Despite Tunisia's liberal reputation, it is a Muslim country and most people are conservative about dress. Although dress codes vary quite widely from the chic resorts and cities to the conservative countryside, you can save yourself trouble and embarrassment by erring on the side of modesty in what you wear.

Women, in particular, are well advised to keep shoulders and upper arms covered and to opt for long skirts or trousers. Stricter Muslims consider an excessive display of flesh, whether in a man or a woman, offensive. Women disregarding such considerations risk not only arousing the ire of the genuinely offended but also the unwanted interest of the lecherous. Men wearing shorts (away from the coast at any rate) are considered to be in their underwear and can occasionally arouse indignation too. A little common sense goes a long way. You can get away with a lot more on the beaches of Hammamet and Sousse than in the villages of the interior.

Public displays of affection are frowned upon. See the Responsible Tourism section in the Facts for the Visitor chapter for information on how to minimise the impact of your presence in Tunisia.

Women in Tunisia

Thanks largely to the efforts of their secular, socialist former president, Habib Bourguiba, conditions for women in Tunisia are better than just about anywhere in the Islamic world – to Western eyes, at least. Bourguiba, whose first wife was French, was a staunch supporter of women's rights, and it was one of the first issues on the agenda after independence. His 1956 Personal Status Code banned polygamy and ended divorce by renunciation. It also placed restrictions on the tradition of arranged marriages, setting a minimum marriage age of 17 for girls and giving them the right to refuse a proposed marriage.

Bourguiba was outspoken in his criticism of the *hijab* (the veil worn by Muslim women), which he regarded as demeaning. He called it an 'odious rag', and banned it from schools as part of a campaign to phase it out. He didn't quite succeed, although it is now very unusual to find a woman under 30 wearing one. You may see some interesting mother/daughter combinations wandering around, with mother wearing a hijab and daughter wearing the latest Western fashions.

The Tunisian government is fond of trumpeting its record on women's issues, which helps to deflect criticism of its treatment of political opposition. It likes to point out that life expectancy for women has increased from 58 to 70 years since 1985; that girls now have equal access to educational opportunities; and that women now make up 21% of the workforce.

The government is less keen to discuss the social impact of these reforms, the most serious of which is an extremely high divorce rate. No statistics are available, but the government acknowledged the extent of the problem in 1992 by setting up a special fund guaranteeing alimony payments for divorced women and their children. Men, it seems, are having trouble coming to terms with the expectations of modern Tunisian women. While not advocating a return to the pre-Bourguiba days, many men complain that the pendulum has now swung too far the other way.

RELIGION

Islam is the state religion in Tunisia. While there has been a definite resurgence of religious adherence, particularly among the young and unemployed, Tunisia remains a fairly liberal society. There is a small Jewish community, living mainly in Tunis and on the island of Jerba (see the boxed text 'The Jews of Jerba' in the Jerba section in the Southern Tunisia chapter), as well as about 20,000 Roman Catholics.

Islam

The first slivers of dawn are flickering on the horizon, and the deep quiet of a city asleep is pierced by the cries of the muezzin exhorting the faithful to the first of the day's prayers:

Allahu akbar, Allahu akbar
Ashhadu an la Ilah ila Allah
Ashhadu an Mohammed rasul Allah
Haya ala as-sala
Haya ala as-sala

Of all the sounds that assault the ears of the first-time visitor to Tunisia, it is possibly the call to prayer that leaves the most indelible impression. Five times a day, Muslims are called, if not actually to enter a mosque to pray, at least to take the time to do so where they are. The midday prayers on Friday, when the sheikh of the mosque delivers his weekly sermon, or *khutba*, are considered the most important. The mosque also serves as a kind of community centre, and often you'll find groups of children or adults receiving lessons (usually in the Quran or Muslim holy book), people in quiet prayer and others simply sheltering in the tranquil peace of the mosque.

Islam shares its roots with the great monotheistic faiths that sprang from the harsh land of the Middle East – Judaism and Christianity – but it is considerably younger than these religions. The holy book of Islam is the Quran. Its pages carry many references to the earlier prophets of both the older religions – Adam, Abraham, Noah, Moses and others are recognised as prophets – but there the similarities begin to end. Jesus is seen merely as another in a long line of prophets that ends definitively with the Prophet Mohammed.

What makes Mohammed different from the rest is that the Quran, unlike either the Torah of the Jews or the Christian Gospels, is the word of God, directly communicated to Mohammed in a series of revelations. For Muslims, Islam can only be the apogee of the monotheistic faiths from which it derives so much. Muslims traditionally attribute a place of great respect to Christians and Jews as *ahl al-kitab*, the people of the book. However, the more strident will claim Christianity was a new and improved version of the teachings of the Torah, and that Islam was the next logical step and therefore superior. Don't be surprised if you occasionally run into someone wanting you to convert!

Mohammed, born into one of the trading families of the Arabian city of Mecca (in present-day Saudi Arabia) in AD 570, began to receive revelations in AD 610, and after a time started imparting the content of Allah's message to the Meccans. Its essence was a call to submit to God's will ('Islam' means submission), but not all Meccans were impressed.

Mohammed gathered quite a following in his campaign against Meccan idolaters, but the powerful families of the city became so hostile that he felt forced to flee to Medina in AD 622. Mohammed's flight from Mecca, or *hijra* (migration), marks the beginning of the Muslim calendar. In Medina he continued to preach, while increasing his power base. Soon he and his supporters began to clash with the Meccans, led by powerful elements of the Quraysh tribe, possibly over trade routes.

By AD 632, Mohammed had revisited Mecca and many of the tribes in the surrounding area had sworn allegiance to him and the new faith. Mecca became the symbolic centre of the faith, containing as it did the Kaaba, which housed the black stone supposedly given to Ibrahim (Abraham) by the Angel Gabriel. Mohammed determined that Muslims should face Mecca when praying outside the city.

On his death in AD 632, the Arabs exploded into the Syrian desert, quickly conquering the areas that make up modern Syria, Iraq, Lebanon, Israel and the Palestinian Territories. This was accomplished under Mohammed's successors, the caliphs (or Companions of Mohammed), of whom there were four. They in turn were succeeded by the Umayyad dynasty (AD 661–750) in Damascus, followed by the Abbasid line (749–1258) in the newly built city of Baghdad.

Islam quickly spread west, first taking in Egypt and then fanning out across North Africa. By the end of the 7th century, the Muslims had reached the Atlantic and thought themselves sufficiently in control of the Gezirat al-Maghreb (Island of the West, or North Africa beyond Egypt) to consider marching on Spain in AD 710.

Five Pillars of Islam Islam is now the religion of almost all the inhabitants of the Maghreb. In order to live a devout life, Muslims are expected at least to carry out the Five Pillars of Islam:

Shahada This is the profession of faith, Islam's basic tenet: 'There is no god but Allah, and Mohammed is the Prophet of Allah' *(Allahu akbar, Ashhadu an la Ilah ila Allah, Ashhadu an Mohammed rasul Allah...)*. It is a phrase commonly heard as part of the call to prayer and at many other events, such as births and deaths. The first part has virtually become an exclamation good for any time of life or situation. People can often be heard muttering it to themselves, as if seeking a little strength to get through the trials of the day.

Sala Sometimes written 'salat', this is the obligation of prayer, ideally five times a day, when muezzins call the faithful to pray. Although Muslims can pray anywhere, it is considered more laudable to do so together in a mosque (*masjid* or *jami*). The important midday prayers on Friday (the loose equivalent of Sunday Mass for Catholics) are usually held in the jami, which is the main district mosque.

Zakat Giving of alms to the poor was from the beginning an essential part of the social teaching of Islam, and was later developed in some parts of the Muslim world into various forms of tax to redistribute funds to the needy. The moral obligation towards one's poorer neighbours continues to be emphasised at a personal level, and there are often exhortations to give posted up outside mosques.

Sawm Ramadan, the ninth month of the Muslim calendar, commemorates the revelation of the

Quran to Mohammed. In a demonstration of the Muslims' renewal of faith, they are asked not to let *anything* pass their lips from dawn to dusk and to refrain from sex every day of the month. For more information on the month of fasting, see Islamic Holidays later in this section.

Hajj The pinnacle of a devout Muslim's life is the pilgrimage to the holy sites in and around Mecca. Ideally, the pilgrim should go to Mecca in the last month of the year, Zuul Hijja, to join Muslims from all over the world in the pilgrimage and the subsequent feast. The returned pilgrim can be addressed as *hajji* and, in simpler villages at least, it is still quite common to see the word *al-hajj* and simple scenes painted on the walls of houses showing that their inhabitants have made the pilgrimage. For more details, see Islamic Holidays later in this section.

Sunnis & Shiites The power struggle between Ali ibn Abi Talib, Mohammed's son-in-law and the last of the four caliphs, and the emerging Umayyad dynasty in Damascus caused a great schism at the heart of the new religion. The succession to the caliphate had been marked by considerable intrigue and bloodshed. Ali, the father of Mohammed's male heirs, lost the struggle, and the Umayyad leader was recognised as the legitimate successor to the caliphate.

Those who favoured the Umayyad caliph became known as Sunnis. The majority of Muslims are Sunnis, considered to be the orthodox mainstream of Islam. The Shiites, on the other hand, recognise only the successors of Ali.

The Sunnis have divided into four schools of religious thought, each lending varying degrees of importance to different aspects of doctrine. In Tunisia, where the population is almost entirely Sunni, it is the Malekite school that predominates. The Malekites, along with the Hanafite school, are somewhat less rigid in their application and interpretation of the Quran than the other schools.

This liberal trend had already emerged by the 15th century, when *qadis* (community judges) are recorded as having applied sharia'a in accordance with local custom rather than to the letter.

Saints & Mysticism From an early point in the life of Islam, certain practitioners sought to move closer to God through individual effort and spiritual devotion, rather than simply living by God's laws. These people came to be known as Sufis (from *suf* meaning wool and referring to the simple cord they tended to wear as a belt), and various orders emerged throughout the lands where Islam held sway.

Orthodox Muslims have always regarded such manifestations with suspicion, particularly as the orders tend to gather in the name of a holy man (or *wali*, a term loosely translated as 'saint', although saints in the Christian sense play no role in Islam). Public gatherings take many forms, from the dances of the whirling dervishes to more ecstatic and extreme demonstrations of self-mutilation (participants may, for instance, push skewers into their cheeks, apparently without feeling pain).

The orders generally gather at the mosque or tomb of their saint and follow a particular *tariqa* (path), or way of worshipping. Various orders have acquired permanence over the centuries, and 'membership' can run through generations of the same families, tracing their lineage back to the original saint or spiritual master and through him to the Prophet (the veracity of such links is of secondary importance).

For orthodox Muslims, veneration of the saint is tantamount to worship of an idol, although Sufis would not see it that way. The wali is a 'friend' (the more literal meaning of the word) of God and so an intermediary, and all marabouts (or holy men) are regarded in a similar fashion. The great *moussems* or pilgrimages to the tombs of such saints are as much a celebration of the triumph of the spirit as an act of worship of a particular saint.

Islamic Customs When a baby is born, the first words uttered to it are the call to prayer. A week later this is followed by a ceremony in which the baby's head is shaved and an animal is sacrificed.

The major event of a boy's childhood is circumcision, which normally takes place sometime between the ages of seven and 12.

Sufism

The Islamic sect of Sufism was formed by ascetics who wished to achieve a mystical communion with God through spiritual development rather than through the study of the Quran. This brought them into conflict with the religious orthodoxy, but because they were prepared to make concessions to local rites and superstitions, they were able to attract large numbers of people who had not embraced Islam and were therefore tolerated. The Sufis also believed in the miraculous powers of saints, and saints' tombs became places of worship. A particular aspect of Berber Sufism in North Africa is maraboutism – the worship of a holy man endowed with magical powers.

Literally hundreds of different Sufi orders sprang up throughout the Islamic world. The differences between them lay largely in the rituals they performed and how far they deviated from the Quran. They were regarded with a good deal of suspicion, which was exacerbated by some of their peculiar devotional practices such as eating glass and walking on coals (which they did in order to come closer to God).

The Sufis held positions of power in Tunisia, particularly in rural areas, following the breakdown of Almohad rule in the 13th century.

Marriage ceremonies are colourful and noisy affairs and usually take place in summer. One custom is for all the males to get in their cars and drive around the streets in a convoy making as much noise as possible. The vows are made some time prior to the ceremony, which usually takes place in the home of the bride or groom. The partying goes on until the early hours of the morning, often until sunrise.

The death ceremony is simple: A burial service is held at the mosque and the body is then buried with the feet facing Mecca.

When Muslims pray, they must follow certain rituals. First they must wash their hands, arms, feet, head and neck in running water before praying; all mosques have an area set aside for this purpose. If they are not in a mosque and there is no water available, clean sand suffices; and where there is no sand, they must just go through the motions of washing.

Then they must face Mecca (all mosques are oriented so that the mihrab, or prayer niche, faces the correct direction) and follow a set pattern of gestures – photos of rows of Muslims kneeling in the direction of Mecca with their heads touching the ground are legion. You regularly see Muslims praying by the side of the road as well as in mosques. In everyday life, Muslims are prohibited from drinking alcohol and eating pork (considered unclean).

Islamic Holidays The principal religious holidays in Muslim countries are tied to the lunar Hijra calendar. The word *hijra* refers to the flight of the Prophet Mohammed from Mecca to Medina in AD 622, which marks the first year of the calendar (the year AD 622 is the year 1 AH). The calendar is about 11 days shorter than the Gregorian (Western) calendar, meaning that in Western terms the holidays fall at different times each year. See under Public Holidays in the Facts for the Visitor chapter for a table of dates of Islamic holidays. The principal religious holidays are:

Ras as-Sana This means New Year's day, and is celebrated on the first day of the Hijra calendar year, 1 Moharram.
Achoura This is a day of public mourning observed by Shiites on 10 Moharram. It commemorates the assassination of Hussain ibn Ali, grandson of the Prophet Mohammed and pretender to the caliphate, which led to the schism between Sunnis and Shiites.
Mawlid an-Nabi This is a lesser feast celebrating the birth of the Prophet Mohammed on 12 Rabi' al-Awal. For a long time it was not celebrated at all in the Islamic world. In the Maghreb this is generally known as Mouloud.
Ramadan & Eid al-Fitr Most Muslims, albeit not all with equal rigour, take part in the fasting that characterises the month of Ramadan, a time when the faithful are called upon as a community to renew their relationship with God. Ramadan is the month in which the Quran was first revealed. From dawn to dusk, a Muslim is expected to refrain from eating, drinking, smoking

and sex. This can be a difficult discipline, and only people in good health are asked to participate. Those engaged in exacting physical work or travelling are considered exempt. In a sense, every evening during Ramadan is a celebration. *Iftar* or *ftur*, the breaking of the day's fast, is a time of animated activity, when the people of the local community come together not only to eat and drink but also to pray. Non-Muslims are not expected to participate, even if more pious Muslims suggest you do. Restaurants and cafes that are open during the day may be harder to come by, and at any rate you should try to avoid openly flouting the fast – there's nothing worse for the strung-out and hungry smoker than seeing non-Muslims cheerfully wandering about, cigarettes in hand and munching away. The end of Ramadan, or more accurately the first days of the following month of Shawwal, mark the Eid al-Fitr, the Festival of Breaking of the Fast (also known as the Eid as-Sagheer, the Small Feast), which generally lasts for four or five days, during which time just about everything grinds to a halt. This is not a good time to travel, but can be a great experience if you are invited to share in some of the festivities with a family. It is a very family-oriented feast, much as Christmas is to Christians.

Hajj & Eid al-Adha The fifth pillar of Islam, a sacred duty of all who can afford it, is to make the pilgrimage to Mecca – the hajj. It can be done at any time, but at least one should be accomplished in Zuul Hijja, the 12th month of the Muslim year. At this time, thousands of Muslims from all over the world converge on Islam's most holy city. The high point is the visit to the Kaaba, the construction housing the stone of Ibrahim in the centre of the haram, the sacred area into which non-Muslims are forbidden to enter. The faithful, dressed only in a white robe, circle the Kaaba seven times and kiss the black stone. This is one of a series of acts of devotion carried out by pilgrims. The hajj culminates in the ritual slaughter of a lamb (in commemoration of Ibrahim's sacrifice) at Mina. This marks the end of the pilgrimage and the beginning of the Eid al-Adha, or Feast of the Sacrifice (aka the Grand Feast, or Eid al-Kabir). Throughout the Muslim world the act of sacrifice is repeated, and the streets of towns and cities seem to run with the blood of slaughtered sheep. The holiday runs from 10 to 13 Zuul-Hijja.

LANGUAGE

Tunisia is virtually bilingual. Arabic is the language of education and government, but almost everyone speaks some French. You are unlikely to come across many English, German or Italian speakers outside the main tourist centres.

Tunisians speak a dialect that differs slightly from the Arabic found elsewhere in North Africa, although speakers of classical or Moroccan Arabic will have no trouble communicating.

See the Language chapter at the back of this book for a pronunciation guide and useful words and phrases in Arabic and French.

Facts for the Visitor

The Best & Worst

Top 10

Choosing just 10 highlights from a country as diverse as Tunisia is a difficult job, but here are some of the author's nominations:

1 The friendly people you meet
2 Early morning visits to the *ksour* (fortified granaries) around Tataouine
3 Oasis greenery
4 The mountain oases west of Gafsa
5 Islamic architecture in Kairouan, Sfax and Tunis
6 The colosseum at El-Jem
7 Exploring the Roman ruins at Dougga in spring
8 Walking in the forest around Ain Draham
9 Spicy *chorba* (soup)
10 Vieux Magon (red wine)

Bottom 10

Every destination has its downsides too. Here are some of the author's pet hates:

1 High-season crowds at ancient sites
2 Boring food at resort hotels
3 Inadequate labelling at museums
4 Tour groups dressed up in mock Arab costume
5 Rusting beer cans on beaches
6 Polluted waterways in Gabès
7 The toilets at Ksar Ghilane
8 4WDs tearing up the desert
9 The beaches of the Kerkennah Islands
10 Persistent touts in Kairouan

SUGGESTED ITINERARIES

The following itineraries are designed to help travellers make the most of their time in Tunisia. They start with a one-week whistle-stop tour designed to take in as many highlights as possible without spending 24 hours a day on a bus. The two-week tour allows time to settle in and explore a couple of the most interesting regions, while the four-week grand tour circumnavigates the country, taking in all the major sites – and a few lesser ones.

All the tours are designed for travellers using public transport, but it's worth hiring a car for a couple of days – particularly in the south, where public transport is more limited. Having your own vehicle greatly increases your options, and won't cost much more than chartering taxis.

One Week Start in Tunis and spend a day visiting the medina and the Bardo Museum (one day); catch an early train south to El-Jem, check out the colosseum and continue to Sfax (one day); allow enough time to explore Sfax's medina before heading south-west to Douz (one day); arrange an overnight camel trek into the Sahara (one day); travel across Chott el-Jerid to Tozeur, then spend the afternoon strolling through the palmeraie (oasis) or exploring the old Ouled el-Hadef quarter (one day); catch an early bus north to Kairouan and spend the remainder of the day exploring the sites of the holy city (one day); return to Tunis and spend the day visiting Carthage before finishing your stay with a slap-up meal at one of the restaurants in the capital's medina.

Two Weeks Start in Tunis (one day); then stop in Sousse (one day) on the way south to El-Jem and Sfax (one day); continue south to Jerba and spend a couple of days relaxing in Houmt Souq and exploring the island (two days); head west to Tataouine and use it as a base to visit Ksar Ouled Soltane and/or Douiret (one day); travel to Douz (one day) and organise a camel trek (one day); travel across the Chott-el Jerid to Tozeur and spend a couple of days exploring the town and the region (two days); spend a day travelling north through Gafsa and Kasserine to Le Kef (one day); use Le Kef as a base to visit Dougga (one day); head north across the Kroumirie Mountains to Tabarka (one day); return to Tunis (one day).

Four Weeks Start in Tunis (two days); then travel along the north-west coast of Cap Bon to El-Haouaria (one day); call at Kerkouane and Kelibia on the way south to Nabeul or Hammamet (one day); continue to Sousse (three days) and use it as a base for trips to Kairouan and to Monastir/Mahdia; visit El-Jem and Sfax (one day); continue south to Jerba and spend a few days relaxing and exploring the island (three days); head west to Tataouine and use it as a base for visits to Ksar Ouled Soltane, Douiret and other surrounding villages; some rest and recuperation (three days); stop at Matmata (one day) on the way to Douz (two days) and Tozeur (two days); include Sbeitla (one day) on the way north to Le Kef (one day) and Dougga (one day); stop at Bulla Regia on the way to Ain Draham (one day); hang out in Tabarka (two days); then head east along the north coast to Bizerte (one day); return to Tunis (one day).

PLANNING
When to Go
Tunisia's tourism year peaks in July and August when about two million northern European holiday-makers descend on the country in search of guaranteed sunshine. This is a good time to stay away. Hotel prices go up, rooms can be hard to find and public transport gets packed out. It's also too hot for serious activity between 10 am and 6 pm, which places considerable restrictions on activities like visits to ancient sites.

The best time to visit is between mid-March and mid-May. The spring days are pleasantly warm and the countryside is at its prettiest after the winter rains. By the middle of May, the summer heat has arrived, and it doesn't relent until the middle of September. From mid-September until the beginning of December, conditions are again ideal for touring.

Winter is wet and dreary in the north, but it is the best time to see the migratory birds at Lake Ichkeul. It's also the perfect time to visit the Saharan south.

What Kind of Trip
How Long? Most people find that one month is long enough to take in all the major places of interest without rushing themselves off their feet. Tunisia is also a perfect place to go for a short break from Europe, perhaps as an impulse holiday to get away from whatever the latest weather atrocity might be. The country's huge package tourism industry means that cheap tickets are always available with charter airlines.

Package Tours Unless you want to stay on the coast in the high season, accommodation is readily available and you need do no more than turn up. Some first-time visitors opt to buy a flight/accommodation package with the idea of using the hotel as a base, but it's not worth it. Such accommodation is always in some giant resort hotel on one of the many tourist strips. You're better off avoiding them and looking for your own accommodation in the local towns; all the major towns have a range of places to choose from. If you want to establish a base, most hotels will be happy to store baggage for you while you tour around. It's not particularly important where you fly to – nowhere is more than nine hours by bus from Tunis.

Travelling Companions Travelling alone is much easier for single men than for single women (see also the Women Travellers section later in this chapter). Travelling with a friend or a group of friends has the advantage of enabling you to share the cost of a hire car, which then opens up a whole new range of possibilities for exploring off the beaten track.

If you decide to travel with others, bear in mind that travel can put relationships to the test in a way that few other experiences can. Many a long-term friendship has collapsed under the strain of constant negotiations on where to stay and eat, what to do and where to go next. Other friendships become much closer than before – there's no way of knowing until you try it. It's a good idea to agree on a rough itinerary before you go, and to be operating with similar budgets. Above all, you need to be flexible.

Maps
The government-run Office National du Tourisme Tunisien (ONTT) hands out a reasonable, free 1:1,000,000 road map of the country. It includes a fair amount of

information in English and French, about places of interest, but it is a long time since it was updated. A lot of new roads have been built in the interim, and many roads in the south that previously could be tackled only by 4WD have been upgraded or sealed. These maps are available from ONTT offices both in Tunisia and abroad (see Tourist Offices later in this chapter). Most local ONTT offices also hand out free town maps. They range from the excellent (Tunis) to the barely comprehensible (Gabès).

The best maps are produced by the Tunisian Office de la Topographie et de la Cartographie (OTC). Its *Carte Touristique et Routiére* (1:750,000) is the most up-to-date road map around, although even it can't keep up with the pace of change in the south. The OTC also produces a series of street maps of major cities. It includes Tunis, Sfax and Sousse (all 1:10,000); Kairouan (1:8000); and Hammamet and Nabeul (1:5000). Unfortunately, the only places you can buy these maps are the OTC offices in Tunis and Sousse. See the Information section in the Tunis chapter and the Sousse section in the Central Tunisia chapter for details of these offices.

If you want to buy a map before you go, Freytag & Berndt's 1:800,000 map of Tunisia is the most comprehensive.

What to Bring

Bring the minimum. When you have gathered all the stuff you think you're going to need, throw half of it out and you'll probably be close to a sensible amount. There is nothing worse than having to lug loads of excess stuff around. Unless it's essential, leave it at home!

A backpack is far more practical than an overnight bag and more likely to stand up to the rigours of travel. It is worth paying for a good one.

Your clothing needs will depend on the time of year you visit and where you are going. In summer, you need little more than light cotton clothes on the coast, but you will need to pack a light sweater if you are planning on venturing into the interior. The nights are cool in the mountains even in summer, and it gets surprisingly cold in the Sahara. In winter, you need to pack for all climates; rainproof clothing is a good idea as it can get quite wet.

Also bear in mind the clothing guidelines outlined in Dos & Don'ts under Society & Conduct in the Facts about Tunisia chapter.

For most of the year, a hat, sunglasses and sunscreen are useful, and they are indispensable in the desert. Other handy items include a Swiss Army knife, compass (especially in the desert and mountains), a torch (flashlight), a universal sink plug, a few metres of nylon cord (in case you need to rig up a washing line), a small sewing kit and a medical kit (see the Health section later in this chapter for more details).

Most toiletries – soap, shampoo, toothpaste, toilet paper, washing powder – are available all over Tunisia, although tampons are usually only found in supermarkets. Condoms are cheap and readily available over the counter at pharmacies.

RESPONSIBLE TOURISM

In a country as dependent on mass tourism as Tunisia, responsible tourism is a difficult topic.

Ideally, being a responsible tourist entails an effort to minimise the detrimental effects of tourism – and maximise the benefits. This starts with such fundamental decisions as choosing between buying a cheap holiday package from an agency in your home country or travelling independently. The cheap package may save you money, but much of the money stays at home and is of no benefit to Tunisian operators. Travelling independently places money directly into the tills of local hotels, restaurants and other small businesses. It is, of course, possible to steer a middle path between these options. Lots of European operators offer excellent special interest tours for small groups. These tours employ local operators and include some interesting destinations.

Responsible tourism also involves an element of cultural exchange, and there's no better way to achieve this than travelling around on public transport. Many ordinary

Tunisians look on package groups like visitors from another planet.

Fortunately, there are simpler ways of being a responsible tourist – such as taking heed of the signs urging tourists to *économisez sur l'eau* (save water), and not buying environmentally unsound souvenirs like scorpions and snakes preserved in jars.

See the Society & Conduct section in the Facts about Tunisia chapter for tips about dress and how to avoid causing offence.

TOURIST OFFICES

The government-run Office National du Tourisme Tunisien (ONTT) handles tourist information. It has a network of offices throughout Tunisia as well as overseas.

Most of the information available from these offices can also be found on the ONTT Web site (www.tourismtunisia.com).

Local Tourist Offices

The standard of service varies from super efficient to totally apathetic. Most offices can supply no more than glossy brochures in half a dozen languages and a map. Some can supply a list of hotels and prices, and one or two have transport information. ONTT offices in Tunisia include the following:

Bizerte (☎ 02-432 897) 1 Rue de Constantinople
Douz (☎ 05-470 351) Place des Martyrs
Gabès (☎ 05-270 254) Ave Hedi Chaker
Gafsa (☎ 06-221 664) Place des Piscines Romaines
Hammamet (☎ 02-280 423) Ave Habib Bourguiba
Jerba (☎ 05-650 016) Blvd de l'Environment, Houmt Souq
Kairouan (☎ 07-231 897) Ave de la République
Mahdia (☎ 03-681 098) Rue el-Moez
Monastir (☎ 03-461 960) Rue de l'Indépendance
Nabeul (☎ 02-286 800) Ave Taieb Mehiri
Sfax (☎ 03-211 040) Ave Mohammed Hedi Khefecha
Sousse (☎ 03-225 157) 1 Ave Habib Bourguiba
Tabarka (☎ 08-673 496) 2 Rue de Bizerte
Tataouine (☎ 05-850 686) Ave Habib Bourguiba
Tozeur (☎ 06-454 088) Ave Abdulkacem Chebbi
Tunis (☎ 01-341 077) 1 Ave Mohammed V

Some towns have municipal tourist offices, called *syndicats d'initiative*, which tend to open only in the high season.

Tourist Offices Abroad

ONTT's foreign representatives tend to be much better equipped, and more enthusiastic, than their domestic counterparts. They include the following:

Austria (☎ 1-585 34 80) 1-Stiege R, Tûr 109 Vienna
Belgium (☎ 2-511 11 42) Galerie Ravenstein 60, 1000 Brussels
Canada (☎ 514-397 1182) 1253 McGill College, Montreal, Quebec H3 B2 Y5
France
  Paris: (☎ 01 47 42 72 67) 32, Ave de l'Opéra, 75002
  Lyon: (☎ 04 78 52 35 86) 12, rue de Séze, 69006
Germany
  Berlin: (☎ 30-885 0457) Kurfuerstendamm 171, 10707
  Düsseldorf: (☎ 211-880 0644) Flingerstrasse 66, 40213
  Frankfurt am Main: (☎ 69-297 0640) Goethplatz, 60313
Italy
  Rome: (☎ 06-42 01 01 49) Via Calabria 25, 0018
  Milan: (☎ 02-86 45 30-44) Via Baracchini 10, 20123
Netherlands (☎ 20-622 4971) Muntplein 2, 1012 WR Amsterdam
UK (☎ 020-7224 5561) 77A Wigmore St, London W1H GLJ

VISAS & DOCUMENTS
Passport

Your most important travel document is your passport. Before you go, make sure that it is valid until well after your planned return. If there's any danger that it might expire while you're away, renew it before you go. Renewing a passport overseas can be a hassle and involve days of waiting. Even at home it can be a slow business, so don't leave it until the last minute. You can usually speed the process up by doing things in person rather than relying on the mail or on agents.

Once you start travelling, carry your passport with you at all times and guard it carefully. Hotels sometimes want to hold onto your passport for the duration of your stay, which can be inconvenient. You can usually get around this by simply paying for your room in advance or by offering your driving licence as an alternative.

Visas

A visa is a stamp in your passport (or sometimes a separate piece of paper) that permits you to enter the issuing country for a specified period of time. Fortunately, visas are not a problem for most visitors to Tunisia. Nationals of most Western European countries can stay for up to three months without a visa – you just roll up and collect a stamp in your passport. Americans, Canadians, Germans and Japanese can stay for up to four months.

The situation is a bit more complicated for other nationalities, but most visitors do not require a visa if arriving on an organised tour. Australians and South Africans can get a visa at the airport for TD6. New Zealanders need to get their visas in advance – available wherever Tunisia has diplomatic representation.

Israeli nationals are not allowed into the country.

Visa Extensions It is unlikely that you will need to extend your visa, because one month in Tunisia is ample time for most people. If you do, applications can be made only at the Interior Ministry on Ave Habib Bourguiba in Tunis. They cost TD3, are payable only in revenue stamps (available from post offices), take up to 10 days to issue and require two photographs, bank receipts and a *facture* (receipt) from your hotel. It may sound simple, but the process is more hassle than it's worth.

Travel Insurance

It is sensible to take out travel insurance. This not only covers you for medical expenses and luggage theft or loss, but also for cancellation or delays in your travel arrangements (eg, you could fall seriously ill a few days before departure). Cover depends on the type of insurance and the type

Visas for Algeria & Libya

The Algerian and Libyan embassies in Tunis do not issue visas. If you want to visit either of these countries from Tunisia, you must get your visas before you arrive. Prospective travellers should apply to the Algerian or Libyan embassy/consulate in their home country. Australians and New Zealanders can apply in London. Don't leave it until the last minute because it can be a lengthy process.

of airline ticket, so ask both your insurer and your ticket-issuing agency to explain exactly where you stand and check the small print. Ticket loss is also covered by travel insurance. Some policies specifically exclude 'dangerous activities', which can include scuba diving, motorcycling and even trekking. A locally acquired motorcycle licence is not valid under some policies.

You may prefer a policy that pays doctors or hospitals directly rather than you having to pay on the spot and claim later. If you have to claim later make sure you keep all documentation. Some policies ask you to call back reverse charges (collect) to a centre in your home country where an immediate assessment of your problem is made. Check that the policy covers ambulances or an emergency flight home.

Buy travel insurance as early as possible. You may find that if you buy it at the last minute you are not covered for problems caused by strikes or other industrial action that started, or had been threatened, before you took out the insurance.

The best places to seek good insurance deals are travel agents specialising in youth or student travel, but make sure that the package you buy meets your needs. Ask, for example, about refund limits for special items like cameras and computers.

Paying for your airline ticket with a credit card sometimes provides limited travel insurance, and you may be able to reclaim the payment if the flight operator doesn't deliver. In the UK, institutions issuing credit cards are required by law to re-imburse consumers if a company goes into liquidation and the amount in contention is more than UK£100. Ask your credit-card company what it covers.

Driving Licence & Permits
If you plan to hire a car or motorcycle of more than 50cc, you will need to bring your national driving licence, which you must have held for at least one year. International driving permits are also acceptable.

Hostel Cards
You need to be a member of Hostelling International (HI) if you want to stay at any of Tunisia's four affiliated hostels (see Hostels under Accommodation later in this chapter for more details). You can join on the spot at the hostel in Tunis (☎ 01-567 850), 25 Rue Saida Ajoula, Tunis Medina.

Student & Youth Cards
There are no advertised discounts for student cards – although it never hurts to ask. One traveller reported being given free admission to some of the ancient sites on flashing a student card – probably because the site guardian mistook the card for some sort of official document.

Seniors Cards
There are no special discounts for senior travellers in Tunisia – holders of seniors cards have as much chance of finding a discount as holders of student cards. See also the Senior Travellers section later in this chapter.

Vaccination Certificates
You'll need this little yellow booklet only if you're coming from parts of Africa where yellow fever has been reported. See the Health section later in this chapter for further details.

Copies
All important documents (passport data page and visa page, credit cards, travel insurance policy, air/bus/train tickets, driving licence etc) should be photocopied before you leave home. Leave one copy with someone at home and keep another with you, separate from the originals.

It's also a good idea to store details of your vital travel documents in Lonely Planet's free online Travel Vault in case you lose the photocopies. Your password-protected Travel Vault is accessible online anywhere in the world – you can create it at www.ekno.lonelyplanet.com.

EMBASSIES & CONSULATES
As a tourist, it's important to realise what your own embassy – the embassy of the country of which you are a citizen – can and can't do. Generally speaking, it won't help much in emergencies if the trouble you're in is remotely your own fault. Remember that you are bound by the laws of the country you're in. Embassies will not be sympathetic if you end up in jail after committing a crime locally, even if such actions are legal in your own country. In genuine emergencies you might get some assistance, but only if other channels have been exhausted. For example, if you need to get home urgently, a free ticket home is exceedingly unlikely – the embassy would expect you to have insurance. If you have all your money and documents stolen, it might assist with getting a new passport, but a loan for onward travel is out of the question.

Embassies used to keep letters for travellers or have a small reading room with home newspapers, but these days the mail-holding service has been stopped, and even newspapers tend to be out of date.

On the more positive side, if you are heading into very remote or politically volatile areas, you might consider registering with your embassy so it knows where you are, but make sure you tell it when you come back, too. Some embassies post useful warning notices about local dangers or potential problems. The US embassies are particularly good for providing this information and it's worth scanning their notice-boards for 'travellers advisories' about security, local epidemics and dangers to lone travellers.

Tunisian Embassies & Consulates

Following is a list of Tunisian embassies and consulates abroad:

Algeria (☎ 2-69 20 857) Rue Ammar Rahmani, El-Biar, 16000 Algiers
Australia
Honorary Consulate in Sydney: (☎ 02-9363 5588) GPO Box 801, Double Bay, NSW 2028
Belgium (☎ 2-771 7395) 278 Ave De Tervueren, 1150 Brussels
Canada (☎ 613-237 0330/2) 515 O'Connor St, Ottawa, Ontario K1S 3P8
Egypt (☎ 2-340 4940) 26 Rue el-Jazirah, Zamalek, 11211 Cairo
France (☎ 01 45 53 50 94) 17–19 Rue de Lubeck, 75016 Paris
Consulate in Lyon: (☎ 04 78 93 42 87) 14 Ave du Maréchal Foch, 69412
Consulate in Marseilles: (☎ 04 91 50 28 68) 8 Blvd d'Athènes, 13001
Consulate in Nice: (☎ 04 93 96 81 81) 18 Ave des Fleurs, 66000
Consulate in Toulouse: (☎ 05 61 63 61 61) 19 Allé Jean Jaurès, 3100
Germany (☎ 30-4 72 20 64/7) 110 Esplanade 12, 1100 Berlin
Consulate in Düsseldorf: (☎ 211-37 10 07) 7–9 Graf Adolf Platz, 4000
Consulate in Hamburg: (☎ 40-2 20 17 56) Overbeckstrasse 19, 2000, 76
Consulate in Munich: (☎ 89-55 45 51) Adimstrasse 4, 8000, 19
Italy (☎ 06-860 42 82) Via Asmara 5, 00199 Rome
Consulate in Palermo: (☎ 091-32 89 26) 24 Piazza Ignazio Florio, 90100
Japan (☎ 3-3353 4111) 1-18-8 Wakaba Cho, Shinjuku-Ku, 160 Tokyo
Libya (☎ 21-607161) Ave Jehara, Sharia Bin Ashur, 3160 Tripoli
Morocco (☎ 7-730 576) 6 Rue de Fès, Rabat
Netherlands (☎ 7-351 22 51) Gentestraat 98, 2587 HX, The Hague
South Africa (☎ 12-342 6283) 850 Church St, Arcadia, 0007 Pretoria
Spain (☎ 1-447 35 08) Plaza Alonzo Martinez 3, 28004 Madrid
UK (☎ 020-7584 8117) 29 Prince's Gate, London SW7 1QG
USA (☎ 202-862 1850) 1515 Massachusetts Ave NW, Washington DC 20005

Embassies & Consulates in Tunisia

There is a large selection of foreign embassies concentrated in the capital, Tunis

(telephone area code ☎ 01), these include the following:

Algeria (☎ 780 055, fax 790 852) 18 Rue du Niger, 1002 Tunis
Consulate: (☎ 287 139) 83 Ave Jugurtha, 1002 Tunis
Australia The Canadian embassy in Tunis handles consular affairs in Tunisia for the Australian government.
Austria (☎ 751 091, fax 751 094) 6 Rue Ibn Hamdiss, 1004 El-Menzah
Belgium (☎ 781 655, fax 792 797) 47 Rue du 1 Juin, 1002 Tunis
Canada (☎ 796 577, fax 792 371) 3 Rue du Sénégal, 1002 Tunis
Denmark (☎ 792 600, fax 793 804) 5 Rue de Mauritanie, 1002 Tunis
Egypt (☎ 791 181, fax 792 233) Ave Mohammed V, 1002 Tunis
France (☎ 347 838, fax 354 388) Place de l'Indépendance, Ave Habib Bourguiba, 1000 Tunis
Consulate: (☎ 333 027, fax 351 967) 1 Rue de Hollande, 1000 Tunis
Germany (☎ 786 455, fax 788 242) 1 Rue el-Hamra, 1002 Tunis
Italy (☎ 341 811, fax 354 155) 3 Rue de Russie, 1000 Tunis
Japan (☎ 791 251, fax 792 363) 10 Rue Mahmoud el-Matri, 1002 Tunis
Libya (☎ 781 913, fax 780 866) 48 Rue du 1er Juin, 1002 Tunis
Consulate: (☎ 285 402, fax 280 586) 74 Ave Mohammed V, 1002 Tunis
Morocco (☎ 782 775, fax 787 103) 39 Rue du 1er Juin, 1002 Tunis
Consulate: (☎ 784 442, fax 783 627) 26 Rue Ibn Mandhour, Notre Dame, 1002 Tunis
Netherlands (☎ 799 442, fax 785 557) 8 Rue de Meycen, 1002 Tunis
Spain (☎ 782 217, fax 786 267) 22 Rue Dr Ernest Conseil, 1002 Tunis
South Africa (☎ 798 449, fax 796 742) 7 Rue Achtart, 1002 Tunis
UK (☎ 341 444, fax 354 877) 5 Place de la Victoire, 1000 Tunis
Consulate: (☎ 793 322, fax 792 644) 141–143 Ave de la Liberté, 1002 Tunis
USA (☎ 782 566, fax 789 719) 144 Ave de la Liberté, 1002 Tunis

CUSTOMS

The duty-free allowance is 400 cigarettes, 2L of wine, 1L of spirits and 250ml of perfume. It is advisable to declare valuable items (such as cameras) on arrival to ensure a smooth departure.

MONEY
Currency
The unit of currency is the Tunisian dinar (TD), which is divided into 1000 millimes (mills). There are five, 10, 20, 50, 100 and 500 mills coins and one-dinar coins. Dinar notes come in denominations of five, 10, 20 and 30. Changing the larger notes is not a problem.

Exchange Rates
Exchange rates for the major currencies are:

country	unit		dinar
Australia	A$1	=	TD0.719
Canada	C$1	=	TD0.892
euro	€1	=	TD1.244
France	10FF	=	TD1.900
Germany	DM1	=	TD0.636
Italy	L1000	=	TD0.642
Japan	¥100	=	TD1.236
New Zealand	NZ$1	=	TD0.561
UK	UK£1	=	TD2.072
USA	US$1	=	TD1.230

These exchange rates were correct at the time of writing, but check with your bank for the latest rates.

Exchanging Money
The TD is a soft currency, which means that exchange rates are fixed artificially by the government. The dinar cannot be traded on currency markets and it's illegal to import or export it, so you won't be able to equip yourself with any local currency before you arrive. It is not necessary to declare your foreign currency on arrival.

Within the country, all the major European currencies are readily exchangeable, as well as US and Canadian dollars and Japanese yen. Australian and New Zealand dollars and South Afrisan rand are not accepted. Exchange rates are regulated, so the rate is the same everywhere. Banks charge a standard 351 mills commission per travellers cheque and the larger hotels take slightly more. Post offices will change cash only. When leaving the country, you can re-exchange up to 30% of the amount you changed into dinars, up to a limit of TD100. You need to produce bank receipts to prove you changed the money in the first place.

Cash Nothing beats cash for convenience – or for risk. If you lose it, it's gone for good and very few travel insurers will come to your rescue. Those who do will normally limit the amount to about US$300. It's best not to carry too much cash on you at any one time – use travellers cheques or your automated teller machine (ATM) card to withdraw as much cash as you think you'll need for a few days at a time. It's also a good idea to set aside a small amount of cash, say US$50, as an emergency stash.

Travellers Cheques The main reason for carrying your funds as travellers cheques rather than cash is the protection they offer against theft. They are, however, losing popularity as more and more travellers opt to leave their money in a bank at home and withdraw it at ATMs as they travel.

American Express (AmEx), Visa and Thomas Cook cheques are all widely accepted and have efficient replacement policies. Maintaining a record of the cheque numbers and when you use them is vital when it comes to replacing lost cheques. Keep this record separate from the cheques themselves. US dollars are a good currency to use, since US$1 is about TD1.

Tunisian banks will want to see your passport when you change money. The Banque Nationale Agricole (BNA) also insists on being shown the customer purchase record.

ATMs ATMs are found in almost every town large enough to support a bank – and certainly in all the tourist areas. If you've got MasterCard or Visa, there are plenty of places to withdraw money.

Automatic foreign exchange machines (AFEMs) are starting to make an appearance. They take all the major European currencies, US dollars and Japanese yen.

Credit Cards Credit cards are an accepted part of the commercial scene in Tunisia, especially in major towns and tourist areas. They can be used to pay for a wide range of goods and services such as upmarket meals and accommodation, car hire and souvenir shopping.

If you are not familiar with the card options, ask your bank to explain the workings and relative merits of the various schemes: cash cards, charge cards and credit/debit cards. You should explain what you want to do with the card and push for a credit limit that meets your needs. Ask whether the card can be replaced in Tunisia if it gets stolen, and ask what happens if a card issued in Europe gets swallowed by a Tunisian ATM.

The main credit cards are MasterCard and Visa (Access in the UK), both of which are widely accepted in Tunisia. They can also be used as cash cards to draw Tunisian dinars from the ATMs of affiliated Tunisian banks in the same way as at home. Daily withdrawal limits are set by the issuing bank. Cash advances are given in local currency only. Both companies say they can replace a lost card in Tunisia within 24 hours, and will supply you with a phone number in your home country that you can call, reverse charges, in an emergency.

The main charge cards are AmEx and Diners Club, which are widely accepted in tourist areas, but unheard of elsewhere.

Black Market There is no black market in Tunisia.

Security
Tunisia is a relatively safe place to travel with very low levels of street crime. Still, it pays to take precautions, particularly in busy areas like the medinas of Tunis and Sousse.

The safest way to carry cash and valuables (passport, travellers cheques, credit cards etc) is a favourite topic of travel conversation. The simple answer is that there is no foolproof method. The general principle is to keep things out of sight. The front pouch, for example, presents an obvious target for a would-be thief – it's only mar-

ginally less inviting than a fat wallet bulging in your back pocket.

The best place to keep your valuables is under your clothes in contact with your skin where, hopefully, you will be aware of an alien hand before it's too late. Most people opt for a moneybelt, while others prefer a leather pouch hung around the neck. Another option is to sew a secret stash pocket into the inside of your clothes. Whichever method you choose, put your valuables in a plastic bag first – otherwise they will get soaked in sweat as you wander around in the heat of the day and after a few days they'll end up looking like they've been through a washing machine.

Costs
Tunisia is an inexpensive country to travel in, especially for Western visitors.

If you're desperate to keep costs down, you can get by on TD20 a day. This would involve staying in hostels or budget hotels, eating at local restaurants, restricting travel and abstaining from alcohol. In other words, more of a survival exercise than a holiday.

A more realistic budget is about TD40 a day. This is enough to get a comfortable room (with private bathroom), travel around and enjoy a glass of wine with your evening meal. Allow TD60 a day and you'll have enough in reserve for the occasional blow-out.

It is, of course, possible to spend TD200 on a single night's luxury accommodation. If you're that way inclined towards luxury hotels, it's much cheaper to buy a flight and accommodation package in advance.

Tipping & Bargaining
Tipping is not a requirement. Cafes and local restaurants put out a saucer for customers to throw their small change into, but this is seldom more than 50 mills. Waiters in tourist restaurants are accustomed to tips: 10% is plenty. Taxi drivers do not usually expect tips from locals, but often round up the fare for travellers.

Handicrafts are about the only items you may have to bargain for in Tunisia. To be good at bargaining, you need to enjoy the banter. If you don't, you're better off buying your souvenirs from the Société de Commercialisation des Produits de l'Artisanats (SOCOPA) stores. It's a good idea to go there anyway just to get an idea of prices.

POST & COMMUNICATIONS
Post Offices
Post offices are known as PTTs. Opening hours are a little confusing. They differ between city and country areas – most places you are likely to visit will be keeping city hours – and the hours change again in summer (July and August) and during Ramadan (see Public Holidays later in this chapter).

Most of the year, city post offices are open from 8 am to 6 pm Monday to Saturday and from 9 to 11 am Sunday; in summer, they open from 7.30 am to 1.30 pm Monday to Saturday while Sunday hours are unchanged. Country offices usually open from 8 am to noon and 3 to 6 pm Monday to Thursday and from 7.30 am to 1.30 pm Friday and Saturday; in summer, they open from 7.30 am to 1.30 pm Monday to Saturday.

During Ramadan, post offices are usually open from 7.30 am to 1.30 pm Monday to Saturday.

Postal Rates
Air-mail letters cost 650 mills to Europe and 700 mills to Australia and the Americas; postcards are 100 mills cheaper. You can buy stamps at post offices, major hotels and some general stores and newsstands.

Sending Mail
The Tunisian postal service is slow but reliable. Letters from Europe generally take about a week to arrive; letters from further afield take about two weeks. Delivery times are similar in the other direction. If you want to ensure that your mail gets through quickly, the Rapide Poste service guarantees to deliver anywhere in Europe within two working days (TD22), or within four working days to the Americas, Asia and Oceania (TD25). The service is available from all post offices.

Parcels weighing less than 2kg can be sent by ordinary mail. Larger parcels should be taken, unwrapped for inspection, to the special parcel counter. There you will be required to indicate clearly if you want to send something surface mail.

Receiving Mail
Mail can be received poste restante at any post office in the country. It should be addressed clearly, with your family name in capitals. Ask the clerks to check under your given name as well if you think you are missing mail. There is a collection fee of 180 mills per letter.

Telephone
Local Calls The Tunisian telephone system is modern and efficient. Public telephones, known as Taxiphones, are everywhere and it's rare to find one that doesn't work. Most places have Taxiphone offices, readily identified by their yellow signs, with several booths and attendants to give change. Some shops have public phones, usually indicated by a blue sign, and you'll normally find a public phone at post offices. Many households do not have a phone, so public phones are always busy.

Phones are equipped to take 100 mills, 500 mills and TD1 coins. Local calls cost 100 mills for two minutes, so you'll need a few to have a conversation.

Taxiphone offices keep a copy of the recently updated national telephone directory, published in both Arabic and French, as well as having information on international area codes and charges. The number for directory information is ☎ 120.

Area Codes	
Bizert, Hammamet & Nabeul	☎ 02
Gabès & Jerba	☎ 05
Kairouan	☎ 07
Sfax	☎ 04
Sousse & Monastir	☎ 03
Tabarka & Le Kef	☎ 08
Tozeur & Gafsa	☎ 06
Tunis region	☎ 01

International Calls Making an international call is straightforward, but expensive. Almost all public phones are equipped for international direct dialling. You just feed them dinar coins instead of 100 mills coins. To dial out, phone the international access code (☎ 00), followed by the country code, then the local code and number. If you're calling Tunisia from abroad, the country code is ☎ 216. International codes and charges per minute are listed in the table below. Rates are 10% cheaper between 8 pm and 6 am.

International Codes & Charges

country	code (☎)	cost (TD)
Algeria	213	.540
Australia	61	1.080
France	33	.900
Germany	49	.900
Italy	39	.900
Morocco	212	.540
New Zealand	64	1.080
UK	44	.900
USA/Canada	01	1.080

Fax
Faxes are all the rage in Tunisia, and almost every classified hotel has a fax machine. Most major hotels also offer telex facilities. It will cost you less to use the public facilities available at the telephone offices in major towns. Telegrams can be sent from any post office.

Email & Internet Access
The Internet is still quite new in Tunisia. Few hotels and businesses have email, although the number is growing fast. Addresses are listed throughout this book, where available.

Public access to the Internet is handled by Publinet. There are about 50 offices around the country, and new ones are opening all the time. There are addresses listed throughout this book. Check out the Web site: www.tunisie.com/internet/index.html for the latest additions.

INTERNET RESOURCES
The World Wide Web is a rich resource for travellers. You can research your trip, hunt down bargain air fares, book hotels, check on weather conditions or chat with locals and other travellers about the best places to visit (or avoid!).

There's no better place to start your Web explorations than the Lonely Planet Web site (www.lonelyplanet.com). Here you'll find succinct summaries on travelling to most places on earth, postcards from other travellers and the Thorn Tree bulletin board, where you can ask questions before you go or dispense advice when you get back. You can also find travel news and updates to many of our most popular guidebooks, and the subWWWay section links you to the most useful travel resources elsewhere on the Web.

Of course, the amount of specific information on Tunisia that can be gleaned from the Web is still fairly limited. Many sites turn out to be little more than rehashes of official information.

However, one site worth checking out is Miftah Shamali's Tunisia at http://i-cias .com/m.s/tunisia/index.htm. It has lots of photos.

The best links are found at http://members .tripod.com/Djebbana/links.html.

A more interesting site to explore is www .tunisiaonline.com, where you can read the Tunisian newspapers. You'll find *La Presse* and *Le Temps* in French, and the Arabic dailies *Essahafa* and *Assabah*, all available on the day of publication.

A bit of searching around on the Web turns up all sorts of oddities, such as the home page of soccer club Sportif Sfaxien (www.geocities.com).

The main service provider is Planet Tunisie (www.planet.tn). The Tunisian Internet Agency's site (www.ati.tn) has general information about the Internet.

BOOKS
Unless you want your literary diet to consist of nothing but expensive English newspapers, bring enough books to keep yourself busy. Bookshops, although common, do not stock anything in English. There are a couple of exceptions to this rule, see under Children later in this section, but they're

not worth hanging out for. The best solution is to look out for fellow travellers with books to swap.

Books that deal solely with Tunisia are few and far between. If your French is up to book standard you have a far better chance of finding something. See also Literature under Arts in the Facts about Tunisia chapter.

Most books are published in different editions by different publishers in different countries. As a result, a book might be a hardcover rarity in one country while it's readily available in paperback in another. Fortunately, bookshops and libraries search by title or author, so your local bookshop or library is best placed to advise you on the availability of the recommendations listed following.

Lonely Planet

For travellers on wider-reaching trips, Lonely Planet publishes *Mediterranean Europe*, which has chapters on the countries around the Mediterranean, and *Africa on a shoestring*, which covers the entire continent. It also publishes a wide range of language guides, including *French* and *Egyptian Arabic* phrasebooks.

Travel

Many of the early European travellers were stiff-upper-lip colonialist types who wrote about the 'natives' with barely disguised contempt. About the most bigoted of the lot was Norman Douglas, who passed through southwestern Tunisia in 1912 and wrote about his experiences in *Fountains in the Sand*. His account is entertaining enough – as long as you can ignore his intolerance of Arabs in general and everything Tunisian in particular.

Paul Theroux visited Tunisia during his grand tour of the Mediterranean in the early 1990s, which resulted in *The Pillars of Hercules*. The chapter on Tunisia includes an amusing account of an encounter with a carpet tout in Tunis as well as descriptions of his visit to Sfax and the Kerkennah Islands.

History & Politics

Carthage, A History by French scholar Serge Lancel is a detailed history and analy-

sis of the Punic state from its foundation to its ultimate destruction by Rome in 146 BC.

Nigel Bagnall provides a very readable account of the prolonged conflict between Carthage and Rome in *The Punic Wars*. Most military historians prefer to concentrate on the exploits of Carthage's most famous son, Hannibal Barca, and his exploits in carrying the fight to Italy during the Second Punic War. Theodore Ayrault Dodge, writing back in 1891, covers the campaign in minute detail with plans of all the main battles.

Susan Raven's *Rome in Africa* provides a good account of Rome's tussle with Carthage and the subsequent conquest of North Africa.

The Sultan's Admiral by Ernie Bradford is a lively biography of the famous 16th-century pirate Khair ed-Din, who terrorised Christian shipping in the western Mediterranean and paved the way for the Ottoman conquest of North Africa.

Peter Mansfield offers an excellent insight into the Arab psyche in *The Arabs*, widely regarded as providing the best available explanation of the many forces at work in this complicated part of the world. It includes a section on Tunisia. *Crossroads* by David Pryce-Jones is a good introduction to the modern Islamic world in general.

Novels

Salammbô by Gustave Flaubert is an historical epic set at the time of the mercenaries' rebellion against Carthage in the 3rd century BC. Flaubert was known for his painstaking research, and the book paints an interesting picture of Carthaginian life at the time. You'll need a strong stomach though to cope with the overlay of blood and gore.

Aldous Huxley fans will be disappointed by the patronising tone of *In a Tunisia Oasis*, set around Nefta in the 1930s. It features in a collection of his short stories entitled *The Olive Tree*.

Bird-Watching

The best guides to European birds also cover Tunisia. The popularity of bird-watching has inspired a number of excellent illustrated titles to suit all budgets and levels of interest. *Birds of the Middle East and North Africa* by Hollom, Porter, Christensen and Willis is the definitive guide to the region. *Birds of Europe with North Africa and the Middle East* by Lars Jonsson is superbly illustrated and covers all species likely to be found in Tunisia. The *Collins Pocket Guide to Birds of Britain & Europe with North Africa & the Middle East* by Heinzel, Fitter and Parslow is an excellent little book and fits into a large pocket.

FILMS

Tunisia's dramatic landscapes and unique architecture have made the country a firm favourite with movie makers.

George Lucas decided that the south was perfect for his *Star Wars* series, and the Saharan fringes are dotted with reminders of Luke Skywalker et al. Some companies offer special tours for aficionados, calling at the set of the planet Tatooine, north-west of Tozeur; Ksar Haddada, just north of the real Tataouine; and the Hôtel Sidi Driss at Matmata.

The English Patient features some stunning footage of the open desert south of the Chott el-Jerid, and of the gorge country between Tamerza and Mides. The same film uses the medina of Sfax as the Cairo bazaar, and the docks at Mahdia as the seafront at Benghazi.

The ribat/kasbah complex at Monastir became part of the Holy Land for the Monty Python crew in *Life of Brian*, while the green hills passed as Japan in *Madame Butterfly*.

NEWSPAPERS & MAGAZINES

La Presse and *Le Temps* are the main French-language newspapers. They offer very similar fare, although *Le Temps* has better international coverage. Both put a heavy emphasis on sport, particularly football (soccer). They also have local service information such as train, bus and flight times; both cost 350 mills. Arabic daily newspapers include *Assabah* and *Al-Houria*. All these papers produce on-line Internet editions, which can be accessed through the TunisieInfo Web site (www .tunisieinfo.com/).

The weekly *Tunisian News* is the only locally produced publication in English. It costs TD1 and usually includes a few interesting feature articles about Tunisia together with some very unexciting local news stories that read like ministerial press releases.

You can buy two-day-old English, German, Italian and French newspapers in all the major centres. International current-affairs magazines such as *Time* and *Newsweek* are also readily available.

RADIO & TV

There is a French-language radio station broadcasting on (or around) FM 98. It broadcasts in English from 2 to 3 pm, in German from 3 to 4 pm and in Italian from 4 to 5 pm. A much better source of English-language radio is the BBC World Service, which can be picked up on short wave at 15.070MHz and 12.095MHz.

The French-language TV station has 30 minutes of news, with lots of foreign news and sport, at 8 pm every night. Most of the regular TV programs are mindless game shows (which you end up watching in cheap restaurants), although sometimes there are decent movies on Friday night. Some of the more upmarket hotels offer satellite TV, allowing guests to tune in to CNN news.

VIDEO SYSTEMS

If you want to record or buy video tapes to play back home, you won't get a picture unless the image registration systems are the same. Like Europe and Australia, Tunisia uses PAL, which is incompatible with the North American and Japanese NTSC system.

PHOTOGRAPHY
Film & Equipment

Name-brand film such as Kodak and Fuji is widely available and reasonably priced. Expect to pay about TD4.500 for 24-exposure 100 ASA film, and TD5.500 for 36 exposures. It is hard to find slides and film of other speeds outside the main tourist areas.

Processing is relatively cheap, and there are quick-processing labs in all the main tourist areas. Expect to pay about TD8 for 36 standard prints.

Technical Tips

The main problem facing the photographer is the brilliant sunlight. If you don't take suitable precautions, your holiday snaps will all end up over-exposed – pale and washed out. You can get around the problem either by using a polarising filter or by restricting your photography sessions to the times of the day when the light is best, generally early morning and late evening.

For detailed technical advice, get a copy of Lonely Planet's *Travel Photography: A Guide to Taking Better Pictures*, written by internationally renowned travel photographer, Richard I'Anson. It's full colour throughout and designed to take on the road.

Restrictions

It is forbidden to take photographs of airfields, military installations, police stations and government buildings.

Photographing People

You should always ask permission before taking photographs of people. While Tunisians expect every tourist to carry a camera, most do not like to have the lens turned on them. This applies particularly to Tunisian women and to people in rural areas.

VIDEO

Properly used, a video camera can give a fascinating record of your holiday. As well as videoing the obvious things, remember to record some of the ordinary everyday details of life in the country. Often the most interesting things occur when you're actually intent on filming something else. Remember too that, unlike still photography, video 'flows' – so, for example, you can shoot scenes of countryside rolling past the train window, which gives an overall impression that isn't possible with ordinary photos.

Video cameras these days have amazingly sensitive microphones, and you might be surprised how much sound will be picked up. This can also be a problem if there is a lot of ambient noise – filming by the side of a busy road might seem OK when you do it, but viewing it back home might simply give you a deafening cacophony of traffic noise.

One good rule to follow for beginners is to try to film in long takes, and don't move the camera around too much. Otherwise, your video could well make your viewers seasick! If your camera has a stabiliser, you can use it to obtain good footage while travelling on various means of transport, even on bumpy roads. And remember, you're on holiday – don't let the video take over your life and turn your trip into a Cecil B de Mille production.

Make sure you keep the batteries charged and have the necessary charger, plugs and transformer for the country you are visiting. In most countries, it is possible to obtain video cartridges easily in large towns and cities, but make sure you buy the correct format. It is usually worth buying at least a few cartridges duty free to begin your trip.

Finally, remember to follow the same rules regarding people's sensitivities as for still photography – having a video camera shoved in their face is probably even more annoying and offensive for locals than a still camera. Always ask permission first.

TIME

Tunisia is one hour ahead of GMT/UTC from October to April, and two hours ahead of GMT/UTC from May to September.

ELECTRICITY

You'll find mains electricity in all but the remotest villages. The supply is 220V and generally reliable and uninterrupted. As in Europe, wall plugs have two round pins.

WEIGHTS & MEASURES

Tunisia uses the metric system, with weights expressed in kilograms and distances in metres. Basic conversion charts are given on the inside back cover of this book.

LAUNDRY

The only laundrette in the entire country is in Tunis (see the Tunis chapter), which means that the only options for most travellers is to hand wash or to use hotel laundry services. Some budget hotels can provide buckets for hand washing.

There are, however, dozens of dry-cleaning shops. Some typical prices include the following: shirt TD1, silk shirt TD1.300, trousers TD1.200, jeans TD1.700, cloth jacket TD1.800, and women's skirt and jacket TD2.800.

TOILETS

You will still come across the occasional squat toilet, but most places frequented by tourists have Western-style, sit-down toilets – as do most modern Tunisian homes.

Public toilets are almost unheard of, except in places like airports and major bus and train stations. If you're caught short, the best bet is to go to a cafe, but you will be expected to buy something for the privilege of using their facilities.

HEALTH

Travel health depends on your predeparture preparations, your daily health care while travelling and how you handle any medical problem that does develop. While the potential dangers can seem quite frightening, in reality few travellers experience anything more than an upset stomach.

Predeparture planning

Immunisations Plan ahead for getting your vaccinations: Some vaccinations require more than one injection, while some should not be given together. It is recommended you seek medical advice at least six weeks before travel. Note that some vaccinations should not be given during pregnancy or to people with allergies – discuss with your doctor. Also be aware that there is often a greater risk of disease with children and during pregnancy.

Discuss your requirements with your doctor, but vaccinations you should consider for your trip to Tunisia include the following (for more details about the diseases themselves, see the individual disease entries later in this section). Carry proof of your vaccinations, especially yellow fever, as this is sometimes needed to enter some countries.

Diphtheria & Tetanus Vaccinations for these two diseases are usually combined and are recommended for everyone. After an initial course of three injections (usually given in childhood), boosters are necessary every 10 years.

Polio Everyone should keep up to date with this vaccination, which is normally given in childhood. A booster every 10 years maintains immunity.

Hepatitis A Hepatitis A vaccine (eg, Avaxim, Havrix 1440 or VAQTA) provides long-term immunity (possibly more than 10 years) after an initial injection and a booster at six to 12 months. Alternatively, an injection of gamma globulin can provide short-term protection against hepatitis A – two to six months, depending on the dose given. It is not a vaccine, but is ready-made antibody collected from blood donations. It is reasonably effective and, unlike the vaccine, it is protective immediately, but because it is a blood product, there are current concerns about its long-term safety. Hepatitis A vaccine is also available in a combined form, Twinrix, with hepatitis B vaccine. Three injections over a six-month period are required, the first two providing substantial protection against hepatitis A.

Typhoid Vaccination against typhoid may be required if you are travelling for more than a couple of weeks. It is now available either as an injection or as capsules to be taken orally.

Hepatitis B Travellers who should consider vaccination against hepatitis B include those on a long trip, as well as those visiting countries where there are high levels of hepatitis B infection, where blood transfusions may not be adequately screened or where sexual contact or needle sharing is a possibility. Vaccination involves three injections, with a booster at 12 months. More rapid courses are available if necessary.

Rabies Vaccination should be considered by those who will spend a month or longer in a country where rabies is common, especially if they are cycling, handling animals, caving or travelling to remote areas, and for children (who may not report a bite). Pretravel rabies vaccination involves having three injections over 21 to 28 days. If someone who has been vaccinated is bitten or scratched by an animal, they will require two booster injections of vaccine; those not vaccinated require more.

Tuberculosis The risk of TB to travellers is usually very low, unless you will be living with or closely associated with local people in high-risk areas such as Asia, Africa and some parts of the Americas and Pacific. Vaccination against TB (BCG) is recommended for children and young adults living in these areas for three months or more.

Health Insurance Make sure that you have adequate health insurance. See Travel Insurance under Visas & Documents in the Facts for the Visitor chapter for details.

Travel Health Guides Lonely Planet's *Healthy Travel Africa* is a handy pocket size and packed with useful information including pretrip planning, emergency first aid, immunisation and disease information, and what to do if you get sick on the road. *Travel with Children* from Lonely Planet also includes advice on travel health for younger children.

There are also a number of excellent travel health sites on the Internet. From the Lonely Planet home page (www.lonelyplanet.com/weblinks/wlheal.htm) there are links to the World Health Organization and the US Centers for Disease Control & Prevention.

Other Preparations Make sure you're healthy before you start travelling. If you are going on a long trip make sure your teeth are OK. If you wear glasses take a spare pair and your prescription.

If you require a particular medication take an adequate supply, as it may not be available locally. Take part of the packaging showing the generic name rather than the brand, which will make getting replacements easier. It's a good idea to have a legible prescription or letter from your doctor to show that you legally use the medication to avoid any problems.

Basic Rules

Food There is an old colonial adage which says: 'If you can cook it, boil it or peel it you can eat it...otherwise forget it'. Vegetables and fruit should be washed with purified water or peeled where possible. Beware of ice cream which is sold in the street or anywhere it might have been melted and refrozen; if there's any doubt (eg, a power cut in the last day or two), steer well clear. Shellfish such as mussels, oysters and clams should be avoided as well as undercooked meat, particularly in the form of mince. Steaming does not make shellfish safe for eating.

If a place looks clean and well run and the vendor also looks clean and healthy, then the food is probably safe. In general, places that are packed with travellers or locals will be fine, while empty restaurants are questionable. The food in busy restaurants is cooked and eaten quite quickly with little standing around and is probably not reheated.

Water The tap water is safe to drink everywhere in Tunisia, although it often doesn't taste too good because of the high chlorine levels in some regions. Bottled mineral water is cheap and widely available if you prefer it.

Water Purification The simplest way of purifying water is to boil it thoroughly. Vigorous boiling should be satisfactory; however, at high altitude water boils at a lower temperature, so germs are less likely to be killed. Boil it for longer in these environments.

Consider purchasing a water filter for a long trip. There are two main kinds of filter. Total filters take out all parasites, bacteria and viruses and make water safe to drink. They are often expensive, but they can be more cost effective than buying bottled water. Simple filters (which can even be a nylon mesh bag) take out dirt and larger foreign bodies from the water so that chemical solutions work much more effectively; if water is dirty, chemical solutions may not work at all. It's very important when buying a filter to read the specifications, so that you know exactly what it removes from the water and what it doesn't. Simple filtering will not remove all dangerous organisms, so if you cannot boil water it should be treated chemically. Chlorine tablets will kill many pathogens, but not some parasites like giardiasis and amoebic cysts. Iodine is more effective in purifying water and is available in tablet form. Follow the directions carefully and remember that too much iodine can be harmful.

Medical Problems & Treatment

Self-diagnosis and treatment can be risky, so you should always seek medical help. An embassy, consulate or five-star hotel can usually recommend a local doctor or clinic.

Everyday Health

Normal body temperature is up to 37°C (98.6°F); more than 2°C (4°F) higher indicates a high fever. The normal adult pulse rate is 60 to 100 per minute (children 80 to 100, babies 100 to 140). As a general rule the pulse increases about 20 beats per minute for each 1°C (2°F) rise in fever.

Respiration (breathing) rate is also an indicator of illness. Count the number of breaths per minute: between 12 and 20 is normal for adults and older children (up to 30 for younger children, 40 for babies). People with a high fever or serious respiratory illness breathe more quickly than normal. More than 40 shallow breaths a minute may indicate pneumonia.

Although we do give drug dosages in this section, they are for emergency use only. Correct diagnosis is vital. In this section we have used the generic names for medications – check with a pharmacist for brands available locally.

Note that antibiotics should ideally be administered only under medical supervision. Take only the recommended dose at the prescribed intervals and use the whole course, even if the illness seems to be cured earlier. Stop immediately if there are any serious reactions and don't use the antibiotic at all if you are unsure that you have the correct one. Some people are allergic to commonly prescribed antibiotics such as penicillin; carry this information (eg, on a bracelet) when travelling.

Environmental Hazards

Heat Exhaustion Dehydration and salt deficiency can cause heat exhaustion. Take time to acclimatise to high temperatures, drink sufficient liquids and do not do anything too physically demanding.

Salt deficiency is characterised by fatigue, lethargy, headaches, giddiness and muscle cramps; salt tablets may help, but adding extra salt to your food is better.

Anhydrotic heat exhaustion is a rare form of heat exhaustion that is caused by an inability to sweat. It tends to affect people who

have been in a hot climate for some time, rather than newcomers. It can progress to heatstroke. Treatment involves removal to a cooler climate.

Heatstroke This serious, occasionally fatal, condition can occur if the body's heat-regulating mechanism breaks down and the body temperature rises to dangerous levels. Long, continuous periods of exposure to high temperatures and insufficient fluids can leave you vulnerable to heatstroke.

The symptoms are feeling unwell, not sweating very much (or at all) and a high body temperature (39°C to 41°C or 102°F to 106°F). Where sweating has ceased, the skin becomes flushed and red. Severe, throbbing headaches and lack of coordination will also occur, and the sufferer may be confused or aggressive. Eventually the victim will become delirious or convulse. Hospitalisation is essential, but in the interim get victims out of the sun, remove their clothing, cover them with a wet sheet or towel and then fan continually. Give fluids if they are conscious.

Hypothermia Too much cold can be just as dangerous as too much heat. Although most people usually associate Tunisia with heat and sunshine, it gets very cold in the winter in the north and nights in the desert can get surprisingly chilly, even in summer.

Hypothermia occurs when the body loses heat faster than it can produce it and the core temperature of the body falls. It is surprisingly easy to progress from very cold to dangerously cold due to a combination of wind, wet clothing, fatigue and hunger, even if the air temperature is above freezing.

It is best to dress in layers; Silk, wool and some of the new artificial fibres are all good insulating materials. A hat is important, as a lot of heat is lost through the head. A strong, waterproof outer layer (and a 'space' blanket for emergencies) is essential. Carry basic supplies, including food containing simple sugars, to generate heat quickly, and fluid to drink.

Symptoms of hypothermia are exhaustion, numb skin (particularly toes and fingers), shivering, slurred speech, irrational or violent behaviour, lethargy, stumbling, dizzy spells, muscle cramps and violent bursts of energy. Irrationality may take the form of sufferers claiming they are warm and trying to take off their clothes.

To treat mild hypothermia, first get the person out of the wind and/or rain, remove their clothing if it's wet and replace it with dry, warm clothing. Give them hot liquids – not alcohol – and some high-kilojoule, easily digestible food. Do not rub victims: instead, allow them to slowly warm themselves. This should be enough to treat the early stages of hypothermia. The early recognition and treatment of mild hypothermia is the only way to prevent severe hypothermia, which is a critical condition.

Jet Lag Jet lag is experienced when a person travels by air across more than three time zones (each time zone usually represents a one-hour time difference). It occurs because many of the functions of the human body (such as temperature, pulse rate and emptying of the bladder and bowels) are regulated by internal 24-hour cycles. When we travel long distances rapidly, our bodies take time to adjust to the 'new time' of our destination, and we may experience fatigue, disorientation, insomnia, anxiety, impaired concentration and loss of appetite. These effects will usually be gone within three days of arrival, but to minimise the impact of jet lag:

- Rest for a couple of days prior to departure.
- Try to select flight schedules that minimise sleep deprivation; arriving late in the day means you can go to sleep soon after you arrive. For very long flights, try to organise a stopover.
- Avoid excessive eating (which bloats the stomach) and alcohol (which causes dehydration) during the flight. Instead, drink plenty of non-carbonated, nonalcoholic drinks such as fruit juice or water.
- Avoid smoking.
- Make yourself comfortable by wearing loose-fitting clothes and perhaps bringing an eye mask and ear plugs to help you sleep.
- Try to sleep at the appropriate time for the time zone you are travelling to.

Motion Sickness Eating lightly before and during a trip will reduce the chances of motion sickness. If you are prone to motion sickness try to find a place that minimises movement – near the wing on aircraft, close to midships on boats, near the centre on buses. Fresh air usually helps; reading and cigarette smoke don't. Commercial motion-sickness preparations, which can cause drowsiness, have to be taken before the trip commences. Ginger (available in capsule form) and peppermint (including mint-flavoured sweets) are natural preventatives.

Prickly Heat Prickly heat is an itchy rash caused by excessive perspiration trapped under the skin. It usually strikes people who have just arrived in a hot climate. Keeping cool, bathing often, drying the skin and using a mild talcum or prickly heat powder or resorting to air-conditioning may help.

Sunburn The intensity of the sun is by far the biggest risk in Tunisia. You can get sunburnt surprisingly quickly, even through cloud. Use a sunscreen, a hat, and a barrier cream for your nose and lips. Calamine lotion or a commercial after-sun preparation are good for mild sunburn. Protect your eyes with good quality sunglasses, particularly if you will be near water, sand or snow.

Infectious Diseases

Diarrhoea Simple things like a change of water, food or climate can all cause a mild bout of diarrhoea, but a few rushed toilet trips with no other symptoms is not indicative of a major problem.

Dehydration is the main danger with any diarrhoea, particularly in children or the elderly as dehydration can occur quite quickly. Under all circumstances fluid replacement (at least equal to the volume being lost) is the most important thing to remember. Weak black tea with a little sugar, soda water, or soft drinks allowed to go flat and diluted 50% with clean water are all good. With severe diarrhoea a rehydrating solution is preferable to replace minerals and salts lost. Commercially available oral

Medical Kit Check List

Following is a list of items you should consider including in your medical kit – consult your pharmacist for brands available in your country.

- ☐ **Aspirin** or **paracetamol** (acetaminophen in the USA) – for pain or fever
- ☐ **Antihistamine** – for allergies, eg, hay fever; to ease the itch from insect bites or stings; and to prevent motion sickness
- ☐ **Cold** and **flu tablets, throat lozenges** and **nasal decongestant**
- ☐ **Multivitamins** – consider for long trips, when dietary vitamin intake may be inadequate
- ☐ **Antibiotics** – consider including these if you're travelling well off the beaten track; see your doctor, as they must be prescribed, and carry the prescription with you
- ☐ **Loperamide** or **diphenoxylate** –'blockers' for diarrhoea
- ☐ **Prochlorperazine** or **metaclopramide** – for nausea and vomiting
- ☐ **Rehydration mixture** – to prevent dehydration, which may occur, for example, during bouts of diarrhoea; particularly important when travelling with children
- ☐ **Insect repellent, sunscreen, lip balm** and **eye drops**
- ☐ **Calamine lotion, sting relief spray** or **aloe vera** – to ease irritation from sunburn and insect bites or stings
- ☐ **Antifungal cream** or **powder** – for fungal skin infections and thrush
- ☐ **Antiseptic** (such as povidone-iodine) – for cuts and grazes
- ☐ **Bandages, Band-Aids** (plasters) and other wound dressings
- ☐ **Water purification tablets** or **iodine**
- ☐ **Scissors, tweezers** and a **thermometer** – note that mercury thermometers are prohibited by airlines
- ☐ **Sterile kit** – in case you need injections in a country with medical hygiene problems; discuss with your doctor

rehydration salts (ORS) are very useful; add them to boiled or bottled water. In an emergency you can make up a solution of six teaspoons of sugar and a half teaspoon of salt to 1L of boiled or bottled water. You need to drink at least the same volume of fluid that you are losing in bowel movements and vomiting. Urine is the best guide to the adequacy of replacement – if you have small amounts of concentrated urine, you need to drink more. Keep drinking small amounts often. Stick to a bland diet.

Gut-paralysing drugs such as loperamide or diphenoxylate can be used to bring relief from the symptoms, although they do not actually cure the problem. Only use these drugs if you do not have access to toilets (eg, if you *must* travel). Note that these drugs are not recommended for children under 12 years.

In certain situations antibiotics may be required: diarrhoea with blood or mucus (dysentery), any diarrhoea with fever, profuse watery diarrhoea, persistent diarrhoea not improving after 48 hours and severe diarrhoea. These suggest a more serious cause of diarrhoea and in these situations gut-paralysing drugs should be avoided.

In these situations, a stool test may be necessary to diagnose what bug is causing your diarrhoea, so you should seek medical help urgently. Where this is not possible the recommended drugs for bacterial diarrhoea (the most likely cause of severe diarrhoea in travellers) are norfloxacin 400mg twice daily for three days or ciprofloxacin 500mg twice daily for five days. These are not recommended for children or pregnant women. The drug of choice for children would be co-trimoxazole with dosage dependent on weight. A five-day course is given. Ampicillin or amoxycillin may be given in pregnancy, but medical care is necessary.

Two other causes of persistent diarrhoea in travellers are giardiasis and amoebic dysentery.

Giardiasis is caused by a common parasite, *Giardia lamblia*. Symptoms include stomach cramps, nausea, a bloated stomach, watery, foul-smelling diarrhoea and frequent gas. Giardiasis can appear several weeks after you have been exposed to the parasite. The symptoms may disappear for a few days and then return; this can go on for several weeks.

Amoebic dysentery This is caused by the protozoan *Entamoeba histolytica*, and is characterised by a gradual onset of low-grade diarrhoea, often with blood and mucus. Cramping abdominal pain and vomiting are less likely than in other types of diarrhoea, and fever may not be present. It will persist until treated and can recur and cause other health problems.

You should seek medical advice if you think you have giardiasis or amoebic dysentery, but where this is not possible, tinidazole or metronidazole are the recommended drugs. Treatment is a 2g single dose of tinidazole or 250mg of metronidazole three times daily for five to 10 days.

Fungal Infections Fungal infections occur more commonly in hot weather and are usually found on the scalp, between the toes (athlete's foot) or fingers, in the groin and on the body (ringworm). You get ringworm (which is a fungal infection, not a worm) from infected animals or other people. Moisture encourages these infections.

To prevent fungal infections wear loose, comfortable clothes, avoid artificial fibres, wash frequently and dry yourself carefully. If you do get an infection, wash the infected area at least daily with a disinfectant or medicated soap and water, and rinse and dry well. Apply an antifungal cream or powder like tolnaftate. Try to expose the infected area to air or sunlight as much as possible and wash all towels and underwear in hot water, change them often and let them dry in the sun.

Hepatitis Hepatitis is a general term for inflammation of the liver. It is a common disease worldwide. There are several different viruses that cause hepatitis, and they differ in the way that they are transmitted. The symptoms are similar in all forms of the illness, and include fever, chills, headache, fatigue, feelings of weakness and aches and pains, followed by loss of appetite, nausea, vomiting, abdominal pain, dark urine, light-coloured faeces, jaundiced (yellow) skin and yellowing of the whites of the eyes. People who have had hepatitis should avoid

Nutrition

If your diet is poor or limited in variety, if you're travelling hard and fast and therefore missing meals or if you simply lose your appetite, you can soon start to lose weight and place your health at risk.

Make sure your diet is well balanced. Cooked eggs, tofu, beans, lentils and nuts are all safe ways to get protein. Fruit you can peel (eg, bananas, oranges or mandarins) is usually safe (melons can harbour bacteria in their flesh and are best avoided) and a good source of vitamins. Try to eat plenty of grains (including rice) and bread. Remember that although food is generally safer if it is cooked well, overcooked food loses much of its nutritional value. If your diet isn't well balanced or if your food intake is insufficient, it's a good idea to take vitamin and iron pills.

In hot climates make sure you drink enough – don't rely on feeling thirsty to indicate when you should drink. Not needing to urinate or small amounts of very dark yellow urine is a danger sign. Always carry a water bottle with you on long trips. Excessive sweating can lead to loss of salt and therefore muscle cramping. Salt tablets are not a good idea as a preventative, but in places where salt is not used much, adding salt to food can help.

alcohol for some time after the illness, as the liver needs time to recover.

Hepatitis A is transmitted by contaminated food and drinking water. You should seek medical advice, but there is not much you can do apart from resting, drinking lots of fluids, eating lightly and avoiding fatty foods. Hepatitis E is transmitted in the same way as hepatitis A; it can be particularly serious in pregnant women.

There are almost 300 million chronic carriers of hepatitis B in the world. It is spread through contact with infected blood, blood products or body fluids (eg, through sexual contact, unsterilised needles and blood transfusions, or contact with blood via small breaks in the skin). Other risk situations include shaving, tattoo or body piercing with contaminated equipment. The symptoms of hepatitis B may be more severe than type A and the disease can lead to long-term problems such as chronic liver damage, liver cancer or a long term carrier state. Hepatitis C and D are spread in the same way as hepatitis B and can also lead to long-term complications.

There are vaccines against hepatitis A and B, but there are currently no vaccines against the other types of hepatitis. Following the basic rules about food and water (hepatitis A and E) and avoiding risk situations (hepatitis B, C and D) are important preventative measures.

HIV & AIDS Infection with the human immunodeficiency virus (HIV) may lead to acquired immune deficiency syndrome (AIDS), which is a fatal disease. HIV is a major problem in many countries and Tunisia (where AIDS is known by its French acronym SIDA) is no exception. Any exposure to blood, blood products or body fluids may put the individual at risk. The disease is often transmitted through sexual contact or dirty needles – vaccinations, acupuncture, tattooing and body piercing can be potentially as dangerous as intravenous drug use. HIV/AIDS can also be spread through infected blood transfusions; some developing countries cannot afford to screen blood used for transfusions.

If you do need an injection, ask to see the syringe unwrapped in front of you, or take a needle and syringe pack with you.

Fear of HIV infection should never preclude treatment for serious medical conditions.

Intestinal Worms These parasites are most common in rural, tropical areas. The different worms have different ways of infecting people. Some may be ingested on food such as undercooked meat (eg, tapeworms) and some enter through your skin (eg, hookworms). Infestations may not show up for some time, and although they are generally not serious, if left untreated some can cause severe health problems later. Consider having a stool test when you

return home to check for these and determine the appropriate treatment.

Sexually Transmitted Diseases Hepatitis B and HIV/AIDS can be transmitted through sexual contact – see the relevant sections earlier for more details. Other STDs include gonorrhoea, herpes and syphilis; sores, blisters or rashes around the genitals and discharges or pain when urinating are common symptoms. In some STDs, such as wart virus or chlamydia, symptoms may be less marked or not observed at all, especially in women. Chlamydia infection can cause infertility in men and women before any symptoms have been noticed. Syphilis symptoms eventually disappear completely but the disease continues and can cause severe problems in later years. While abstinence from sexual contact is the only 100% effective prevention, using condoms is also effective. The treatment of gonorrhoea and syphilis is with antibiotics. The different sexually transmitted diseases each require specific antibiotics.

Typhoid Typhoid fever is a dangerous gut infection caused by contaminated water and food. Medical help must be sought.

In its early stages sufferers may feel they have a bad cold or flu on the way, as early symptoms are a headache, body aches and a fever which rises a little each day until it is around 40°C (104°F) or more. The victim's pulse is often slow relative to the degree of fever present – unlike a normal fever where the pulse increases. There may also be vomiting, abdominal pain, diarrhoea or constipation.

In the second week the high fever and slow pulse continue and a few pink spots may appear on the body; trembling, delirium, weakness, weight loss and dehydration may occur. Complications such as pneumonia, perforated bowel or meningitis may occur.

Insect-Borne Diseases

Chagas' disease, filariasis, leishmaniasis, Lyme disease, sleeping sickness, typhus and yellow fever are all insect-borne diseases, but they do not pose a great risk to travellers.

For more information see Less-Common Diseases at the end of this Health section.

Cuts, Bites & Stings

See Less-Common Diseases for details of rabies, which is passed through animal bites.

Cuts & Scratches Wash well and treat any cut with antiseptic such as povidone-iodine. Where possible avoid bandages and Band-Aids, which can keep wounds wet. Coral cuts are notoriously slow to heal and if they are not adequately cleaned, small pieces of coral can become embedded in the wound.

Bedbugs & Lice Bedbugs live in various places, but particularly in dirty mattresses and bedding, evidenced by spots of blood on bedclothes or on the wall. Bedbugs leave itchy bites in neat rows. Calamine lotion or a sting relief spray may help.

All lice cause itching and discomfort. They make themselves at home in your hair (head lice), your clothing (body lice) or in your pubic hair (crabs). You catch lice through direct contact with infected people or by sharing combs, clothing and the like. Powder or shampoo treatment will kill the lice and infected clothing should then be washed in very hot, soapy water and left in the sun to dry.

Bites & Stings Although there are lots of bees and wasps in Tunisia, their stings are usually painful rather than dangerous. However, in people who are allergic to them severe breathing difficulties may occur and require urgent medical care. Calamine lotion or a sting-relief spray will give relief and ice packs will reduce the pain and swelling. There are some spiders with dangerous bites, but antivenins are usually available.

Scorpions are common in southern Tunisia. Scorpion stings are notoriously painful and can sometimes be fatal. Scorpions often shelter in shoes or clothing.

There are various fish and other sea creatures that can sting or bite dangerously or which are dangerous to eat – seek local advice.

Sea Urchins & Jellyfish Watch out for sea urchins around rocky beaches; if you get their needles embedded in your skin, olive oil will help to loosen them. If they are not removed they will become infected. Be wary also of jellyfish, particularly during September and October. Although they are not lethal, their stings can be very painful. A dousing in vinegar will deactivate any stingers that have not 'fired'. Calamine lotion, antihistamines and analgesics may reduce the reaction and relieve the pain.

Snakes There are lots of snakes, including the poisonous horned viper, in Tunisia, especially in the south. To minimise your chances of being bitten always wear boots, socks and long trousers when walking through undergrowth where snakes may be present. Don't put your hands into holes and crevices, and be careful when collecting firewood.

Snake bites do not cause instantaneous death and antivenins are usually available. Immediately wrap the bitten limb tightly, as you would for a sprained ankle, and then attach a splint to immobilise it. Keep the victim totally still and as calm as possible while you seek medical help. Tourniquets and sucking out the poison are now comprehensively discredited.

Women's Health

Gynaecological Problems Antibiotic use, synthetic underwear, sweating and contraceptive pills can lead to fungal vaginal infections, especially when travelling in hot climates. Fungal infections are characterised by a rash, itch and discharge and can be treated with a vinegar or lemon-juice douche, or with yoghurt. Nystatin, miconazole or clotrimazole pessaries or vaginal cream are the usual treatment. Maintaining good personal hygiene and wearing loose-fitting clothes and cotton underwear may help prevent these infections.

Sexually transmitted diseases are a major cause of vaginal problems. Symptoms include a smelly discharge, painful intercourse and sometimes a burning sensation when urinating. Medical attention should be sought and male sexual partners must also be treated. For more details see the section on Sexually Transmitted Diseases earlier. Besides abstinence, the best thing is to practise safer sex using condoms.

Pregnancy It is not advisable to travel to some places while pregnant as some vaccinations normally used to prevent serious diseases are not advisable during pregnancy (eg, yellow fever). In addition, some diseases are much more serious for the mother (and may increase the risk of a stillborn child) in pregnancy (eg, malaria).

Most miscarriages occur during the first three months of pregnancy. Miscarriage is not uncommon and can occasionally lead to severe bleeding. The last three months should also be spent within reasonable distance of good medical care. A baby born as early as 24 weeks stands a chance of survival, but only in a good modern hospital. Pregnant women should avoid all unnecessary medication, although vaccinations and malarial prophylactics should still be taken where needed.

Less-Common Diseases
The following diseases pose a small risk to travellers, and so are only mentioned in passing. Seek medical advice if you think you may have any of these diseases.

Cholera This is the worst of the watery diarrhoeas and medical help should be sought. Outbreaks of cholera are generally widely reported, so you can avoid such problem areas. *Fluid replacement is the most vital treatment* – the risk of dehydration is severe as you may lose up to 20L a day. If there is a delay in getting to hospital, then begin taking tetracycline. The adult dose is 250mg four times daily. It is not recommended for children under nine years nor for pregnant women. Tetracycline may help shorten the illness, but adequate fluids are required to save lives.

Rabies This fatal viral infection is found in many countries. Many animals can be infected (such as dogs, cats, bats and monkeys) and it is their saliva that is infectious. Any bite, scratch or even lick from an animal should be cleaned immediately and thoroughly. Scrub with soap and running water, and then apply alcohol or iodine solution. Medical help should be sought promptly to receive a course of injections to prevent the onset of symptoms and death.

Tetanus This disease is caused by a germ that lives in soil and in the faeces of horses and other animals. It enters the body via breaks in the skin. The first symptom may be discomfort in swallowing, or stiffening of the jaw and neck; this is followed by painful convulsions of the jaw and whole body. The disease can be fatal. It can be prevented by vaccination.

Tuberculosis (TB) TB is a bacterial infection usually transmitted from person to person by coughing, but which may be transmitted through consumption of unpasteurised milk. Milk that has been boiled is safe to drink, and the souring of milk to make yoghurt or cheese also kills the bacilli. Travellers are usually not at great risk as close household contact with the infected person is usually required before the disease is passed on.

WOMEN TRAVELLERS
Women travellers face an additional problem that is unlikely to be encountered by male travellers – the threat of sexual harassment. Fortunately, the situation in Tunisia is not as bad as in other North African and Middle Eastern countries. The harassment is more likely to take the form of being stared at, harmless banter or proposals of marriage and declarations of undying love (or considerably less noble suggestions). Physical harassment is very rare; it may happen in a crowded medina, but it's unlikely to occur elsewhere. Most women report no problems at all.

Prior to marriage, Tunisian men have very little opportunity to meet and get to know women. Western women exist outside the Tunisian social structure and are seen as almost a different species – not bound by the laws of Islam, excitingly independent, somewhat exotic and possibly even available. Be warned that the country's beach resorts are the territory of casanovas, who spend their summers attempting to charm their way into the bedrooms of female tourists.

Women can reduce their chances of being hassled by taking a few basic precautions. Modest dress is the first and most obvious thing, particularly in more conservative rural areas. Even in the height of summer keep shoulders, upper arms and legs covered – and not with skin-tight apparel. Women who feel threatened should seek help from an older person or another woman. Some travellers have reported that a headscarf can come in handy in remote areas as proof of modesty. A wedding ring can also be a useful accessory for discouraging unwelcome attention. If you are not married but are travelling in male company, say you are married rather than girlfriend/boyfriend. If you are travelling alone or in female company, a photo of some unsuspecting boyfriend or male friend also helps. Women should seek out seats next to other women in buses and louages, and sit in the back seat of taxis.

Women travelling alone are strongly advised not to hitchhike. They should also avoid the cheap medina hotels. On a more mundane level, toiletries, cosmetics, tampons etc are widely available from shops and supermarkets.

GAY & LESBIAN TRAVELLERS

While the lifestyle in Tunisia is liberal by Islamic standards, society has yet to come to terms with overt homosexuality. Homosexuality is illegal under Tunisian law.

DISABLED TRAVELLERS

If mobility is a problem and you wish to visit Tunisia, the hard fact is that most hotels, museums and sites are not wheelchair accessible. If you are determined, then take heart in the knowledge that disabled people do come to Tunisia. The trip will need careful planning, so get as much information as you can before you go. The British-based Royal Association for Disability and Rehabilitation

(RADAR) publishes a useful guide called *Holidays & Travel Abroad: A Guide for Disabled People.* It's available from RADAR (☎ 020-7637 5400) at 25 Mortimer St, London W1N 8AB.

SENIOR TRAVELLERS

Tunisia is a popular destination for older travellers, and Tunisian tourist operators are used to catering for their needs. Travellers who are reasonably fit should have no problems in Tunisia, as most of the sites do not involve strenuous exertion. Avoiding the heat of the summer is advice that holds good for any age. There are no special discounts available for older travellers in Tunisia.

There are several UK tour operators which arrange accommodation and flight packages for the over-50s. These include Cadogan (☎ 01703-332661), Airtours (☎ 01706-260000) and Thomson (☎ 0990-502554). Panorama Holidays (☎ 01273-206531), 29 Queens Road, Brighton BN1 3YN, also offer bridge, painting, golf and sequence-dancing holidays. Several companies offer special interest archaeology, desert safari and bird-watching tours that are suitable for older travellers.

See also the Organised Tours section in the main Getting There & Away chapter for more information on tours to Tunisia.

TRAVEL WITH CHILDREN

With war-torn Algeria next door, it's hardly surprising that Tunisia puts a lot of effort into promoting itself as a safe family holiday destination – which it definitely is. Most families stick to the beach resorts, probably because most children prefer playing on the beach to touring Roman ruins, but travellers who have struck out on their own have nothing but good things to report. Tunisians seem to love making a fuss of children. Baby food, nappies (diapers) and other requirements are available at supermarkets everywhere.

Planet's *Travel with Children* is full of useful tips for parents.

DANGERS & ANNOYANCES

Probably the worst hassles you will encounter are the carpet touts of Kairouan, but they are persistent rather than threatening. There have been reports of beach thefts, but they are normally the result of carelessness. Crimes such as mugging are rare.

EMERGENCIES
The police emergency number is ☎ 197, and the ambulance number is ☎ 190. There is a poisons centre (☎ 01-245 075) in Tunis.

LEGAL MATTERS
Tunisian drug laws are very strict: Possession of even the smallest amount of cannabis resin is punishable by one year in jail and/or a hefty fine.

Otherwise, travellers are unlikely to get into trouble with the Tunisian police, who routinely turn a blind eye to minor indiscretions by tourists.

BUSINESS HOURS
Banks
From July to September, opening times for banks are 7.30 to 11 am weekdays; for the rest of the year, the hours are 8 to 11 am and 2 to 4.15 pm Monday to Thursday and from 8 to 11 am and 1 to 3.15 pm Friday. In tourist areas, one bank is rostered to open on Saturday morning. Ask at the local tourist office.

Offices
These are open from 8.30 am to 1 pm and 3 to 5.45 pm Monday to Thursday, and from 8.30 am to 1.30 pm Friday and Saturday. In summer, offices do not open in the afternoon at all.

Shops
Generally, shops are open from 8 am to 12.30 pm and 2.30 to 6 pm weekdays, and from 8 am to noon Saturday. Summer hours are usually 7.30 am to 1 pm. These hours vary slightly from place to place, especially in the south, where the weather is more extreme in summer. Souvenir shops tend to stay open as long as there are tourists around.

PUBLIC HOLIDAYS & SPECIAL EVENTS
Public holidays are primarily religious celebrations or festivities, which mark the anniversary of various events in the creation of the modern state. Some of these holidays, such as Women's Day and Evacuation Day (see the boxed text 'Holidays'), pass without notice. On others, everything comes to a halt and absolutely nothing happens (although transport still runs). On some long weekends, such as the Eid al-Fitr (celebrating the

---

Holidays

Islamic Holidays

Hejira Year	New Year	Prophet's Birthday	Ramadan Begins	Eid al-Fitr	Eid al-Adha
1421	06.04.00	14.06.00	27.11.00	27.12.00	06.03.01
1422	26.03.01	03.06.01	16.11.01	16.12.01	23.02.02
1423	15.03.02	23.05.02	05.11.02	05.12.02	12.02.03
1424	04.03.03	12.05.03	25.10.03	24.11.03	01.02.04
1425	22.02.04	01.05.04	14.10.04	13.11.04	21.01.05
1426	11.02.05	20.04.05	03.10.05	02.11.05	10.01.06

Other Public Holidays

New Year's Day	1 Jan	Republic Day	25 July
Independence Day	20 March	Public Holiday	3 Aug
Youth Day	21 March	WomensDay	13 Aug
Martyrs' Day	9 April	Evacuation Day	15 Oct
Labour Day	1 May	Anniversary of Ben Ali's Accession	7 Nov

end of Ramadan), public transport gets strained to the limit as everyone tries to get home for the festival.

As the Gregorian (Western) and Islamic calendars are of different lengths, the Islamic holidays fall 10 days earlier every Western calendar year. For more details on the Islamic calendar and holidays, see Religion in the Facts about Tunisia chapter. Ramadan is the main holiday to watch out for, because for a month the opening hours of everything are disrupted.

ACTIVITIES
Beaches

Tunisia's tourist industry is built around its beaches. The best known are those of the big resorts. Hammamet's prime attraction is a glorious curve of golden sand, which begins in the shadow of a picturesque old kasbah (fort) and stretches away as far as the eye can see. There are more good beaches north of Sousse and around Monastir.

The beaches further south look attractive enough in the glossy tourist brochures, but are not much good for swimming. The sea is so shallow around the Kerkennah Islands and Gabès that you have to walk out hundreds of metres just to get your knees wet. The best beach in the south is Sidi Mahres on Jerba.

There are also some fine spots in the north of the country. The beaches at Raf Raf and Sidi Ali el-Mekki, between Tunis and Bizerte, are very popular with Tunisian holidaymakers. Cap Serrat, at the centre of the rugged north coast, shelters a glorious sandy bay that is all but deserted for most of the year. More accessible is Montezah Beach at Tabarka, set against the backdrop of the densely forested Kroumirie Mountains.

Diving & Water Sports

The best place to go diving is Tabarka on the north coast. The Club de Plongée (☎ 08-644 478), at the marina, organises trips, rents equipment and runs courses for beginners.

The beaches of the big tourist resorts (Hammamet, Sousse, Monastir and Jerba) are the places to go for water sports. You'll

Festivals

Tunisia's calendar is chock full of festivals, celebrating everything from octopus fishing to the wheat harvest.

The high point in the festival year comes in July and August with the opportunity to see performances of classical music and drama at some of the country's best-known ancient sites. The El-Jem International Symphonic Music Festival uses the town's magnificent floodlit colosseum to great effect, while the International Festival of Carthage features classical drama at the Roman theatres of Carthage and Dougga.

The Tabarka International Jazz Festival, staged in early July, is an event that has grown considerably in stature in recent years.

Another festival to seek out is the Sahara Festival in Douz, held at the beginning of November. It features camel racing and displays of traditional desert skills as well as music, parades and poetry reading.

Other festivals include:

March
Octopus Festival, Kerkennah – features people dressed up in octopus costumes

June
Falconry Festival, El-Haouaria – features displays of falconry by local enthusiasts

July
Festival of Malouf (Testour) – performances of Tunisia's musical emblem, malouf

October
Carthage International Film Festival – biennial, even-numbered years, every other year it is held in Ouagadougou (Burkina Faso); two weeks of films from around the world, with an emphasis on Arab and African cinema

November
Festival of the Ksour (Tataouine) – includes performances of Berber dance at nearby Ksar Ouled Soltane.

You'll find a full list of festivals, complete with dates, on the ONTT's Web site: www .tourismtunisia.com/culture/festivals.

Hammams

Hammams (public bathhouses) are one of the focal points of life in every Tunisian town, as they are just about everywhere in the Middle East and North Africa. They are much more than just a place to go and clean up. In the Roman fashion, they are places to go to unwind and socialise. Every town has at least one hammam, with separate admission times for men and women, while the bigger towns have separate ones for each sex. Some resort towns have unisex hammams for the benefit of tourists. Hammams are recommended as a good way to get a glimpse of Tunisian life.

Men don't need to take anything along. The standard TD1.500 charge includes a *fouta* (cotton bath towel), which is worn around the waist while you move about the hammam (don't walk around naked). The charge also includes a rubdown with a *kassa*, a coarse mitten that is used to remove the grime and dead skin after your stint in the steam room. It is usually possible to have a massage as well.

Women are not issued with a fouta and so will need to bring along a towel. The idea is to wear a pair of underpants while washing, so you'll need to bring a dry pair to change into. Be warned: A rubdown with the kassa is not for the faint-hearted – it can be quite rough.

find a whole range of activities such as windsurfing, water-skiing and parasailing.

Camel Trekking

The Saharan town of Douz is the place to go camel trekking. You can organise anything from a one-hour ride (TD2.500) to an eight-day, oasis-hopping trek to Ksar Ghilane and back (from TD35 per day).

Bird-Watching

Tunisia is a good place to see an interesting variety of birds, ranging from rarities such as Audouin's gull to local specialities such as Levaillant's woodpecker and Moussier's redstart.

Although Tunisia doesn't have many resident species, it is an important stopover for migratory birds. Spring and autumn are therefore the best times to see a wide range of birds. In winter, the wetlands of the World Heritage-listed Ichkeul National Park, in the north, are home to more than 200,000 migratory waterfowl from all over Europe. They include the park's emblem, the rare greylag goose.

For more information about birds, see the Fauna section in the Facts about Tunisia chapter.

Golf

Many people come to Tunisia especially to play golf, particularly in winter when the fairways of northern Europe are either waterlogged or covered in snow.

Hammamet is the best served, with two beautifully manicured courses to choose from. There are also good lay-outs at Jerba, Port el-Kantaoui (Sousse), Tabarka and Tunis. Green fees average about TD45 for 18 holes. Golfers of any standard are welcome at Tabarka, but elsewhere players need to show proof of their handicap.

It's very rare to encounter a Tunisian who has played golf, which is looked on as a game for wealthy foreigners.

Trekking

Tunisia is only just starting to wake up to the possibilities for trekking. The forests of the Kroumirie Mountains around Ain Draham have enormous potential as a trekking destination. The region is stunningly beautiful and conditions are perfect for walking in spring and autumn. The potential is limited by the absence of the sort of detailed local maps you need in order to venture off the beaten track by yourself.

See the Ain Draham and Tabarka sections in the Northern Tunisia chapter for information about organised treks.

Ballooning

Tozeur-based AerOasis (☎ 06-454 577) is the only company in Tunisia offering balloon flights. It operates year-round and charges TD100 for a one-hour flight.

Dune Skiing

The Hôtel Faouar (☎ 05-460 531, fax 460 576), 30km south-west of Douz at the tiny oasis village of El-Faouar, includes dune skiing on its list of activities.

Scenic Flights

The only place offering flights is Jerba, where Air Tropic (☎ 05-606 996) charges TD30 for a 30-minute ride in one of its tiny Petrel hydroplanes. It operates from the sand flats south of Aghir on the east coast of the island.

Yachting

Tourist authorities have taken to promoting the country as a destination for yachting. The main attraction seems to be the price of winter berthing compared with prices in the trendy northern Mediterranean. The largest yachting marinas are at Monastir, Port el-Kantaoui, Sidi Bou Saïd, Tabarka and Zarzis.

COURSES
Language

The Institut Bourguiba des Langues Vivantes (☎ 01-282 418, fax 780 398), 47 Ave de la Liberté, 1002 Tunis Belvedere, offers summer and year-long courses in standard Arabic and Tunisian Arabic (see the Language chapter for information about these two forms of Arabic).

WORK

Work is not really an option in a country with high unemployment and low wages.

English teaching jobs are occasionally advertised in the British press, but are rare.

Another possibility is seasonal work minding tour groups as a representative of one of the many European tour operators.

Either way, you'll need a work permit – issued only when the job can't be done by a local.

ACCOMMODATION
Camping

Camping has not caught on in the same way as it has in other parts of the Mediterranean. There are few official camp sites, and facilities tend to be pretty basic. Most charge about TD2.500 per person.

Camp sites apart, it should be possible to camp anywhere as long as you get the permission of the landowner. We have not heard of any readers having problems camping.

Sleeping out on the beach is the accepted thing in the north at Raf Raf and Ghar el-Melh, near Bizerte, and the same applies to the remote beaches of the north coast. The same does not apply, however, to the beaches in the resort areas of the Cap Bon Peninsula, Jerba and Sousse.

Hostels

Hostels fall into two categories. There are the *auberges de jeunesse*, affiliated to Hostelling International, and there are the government-run *maisons des jeunes*. They couldn't be more different.

The auberges de jeunesse are thoroughly recommended. Most have prime locations, such as a converted palace in the Tunis medina and a fascinating old *funduq* (caravanserai) in Houmt Souq on Jerba. Others are located at Remel Plage outside Bizerte and at the beach in Nabeul. See the Places to Stay sections under individual town entries for more details.

They generally charge about TD3.500 per night, with breakfast available for TD1 and other meals for TD3 each. Their popularity means that they impose a three-night limit during the high season.

There's no reason for anyone to introduce any time limits at the maisons des jeunes. Almost without exception (see the one at Ain Draham), they are characterless concrete boxes with all the charm of an army barracks. They are run along the same lines. Almost every town has one, normally stuck way out in the middle of nowhere and hard to get to without private transport. They are used mainly for holiday camps for school kids, or to accommodate visiting sporting teams. The only reason to mention them is that in some towns they are the only budget accommodation option. They all charge TD4 for a dorm bed.

There are a couple of places where the maison des jeunes concept has evolved into a grander scheme called *centre des stages et vacances*, which are holiday camps that combine hostel and camp site. These are located on the beach at Aghir on Jerba, in the oasis at Gabès and north of Kelibia on Cap Bon (see the relevant chapters for more details). Camping charges are TD2 per person and 500 mills per tent. Power and hot showers are available.

Hotels
Tunisian hotels fall into two main categories: classified hotels, which have been awarded between one and five stars under the government's rating system; and nonclassified hotels, which haven't. The latter are indicated by the initials NC *(nonclassifié)* on the accommodation lists handed out by tourist offices.

The fact that a hotel has not been classified does not mean it is no good – the majority of the budget places recommended in this book are nonclassified. You can normally find reasonable singles/doubles with shared bathroom for around TD8/14, sometimes less. Hot showers normally cost extra.

The cheapest rooms are found at the nonclassified hotels in the medinas of the major cities. They are basic, often with no showers, and you pay for a bed in a shared room. The price ranges from TD2.500 to TD5 per person, depending on the level of facilities. If you want the room to yourself, you will normally be asked to pay for all the beds. Note that these hotels are not generally recommended for westerners and they are totally unsuitable for women travellers.

The majority of hotels are classified. The one- and two-star hotels tend to be smaller, older hotels, often built in colonial times. They are generally clean, if a little shabby, and are popular with local business travellers and tourists who want a decent double room with private bathroom and hot water. A three-star rating usually indicates a hotel built to cater for tour groups. Four- and five-star hotels are of international standard with all the usual facilities.

Prices are normally listed according to three seasons – *haute* (high), *moyenne* (middle) and *basse* (low). The high season runs from 1 July to 15 September, low season is from 1 November to 15 March, and the rest is middle season. Typical high-season charges for single/double rooms in these categories are: one star – TD21/35; two star – TD30/45; three star – TD50/75; four star – TD65/90; and five star – TD100/130. There can be huge price differences between seasons, especially in resort areas. In Hammamet, for example, prices for singles/doubles at the four star Sheraton Hôtel fall from TD66.500/92 in high season to TD52/76 in middle season and a bargain TD26/39 in low season.

Nonclassified hotels normally charge the same all year. The prices are the maximum that the hotel can charge: it never hurts to ask for a discount, especially if you're staying a few days.

Most hotels serve breakfast. At classified hotels, the room rates include breakfast; at nonclassified hotels, breakfast is often quoted separately, so ask. A typical hotel breakfast consists of coffee, French bread, butter and jam. Occasionally, you may be lucky enough to be offered a croissant instead of the French bread. Hotels that cater for package groups normally offer a buffet breakfast.

FOOD
Tunisian food ranks among the world's spicier cuisines. The prime ingredient is *harissa*, a fiery chilli paste that is used to add zip to a range of stews and sauces. Locals enjoy their harissa so much that is it served, drizzled with olive oil, as an appetiser to be mopped up with fresh bread.

While couscous (see the boxed text 'Couscous') is the country's national dish, bread is the staple. Bread features in every meal: served with jam for breakfast, and eaten as an accompaniment with lunch and dinner. The cost of bread is a sensitive political issue. Prices are heavily subsidised and strictly controlled; past attempts to raise prices have sparked riots. The main form of bread is the *baguette*, the long, crusty

Couscous

Tunisia's national dish is *couscous* (semolina granules). There are said to be more than 300 ways of preparing it – sweet as well as savoury.

Couscous is not a separate grain, as is often thought, but is derived from durum wheat. It's thought to have been originally created by the Berbers, and primitive couscous steamers have been found in tombs in the Maghreb dating back to 200 BC.

Couscous is sold everywhere in a pre-cooked or instant form that takes a couple of minutes to prepare. This is quite a recent invention; traditionally, all couscous was made by hand by the women of the household. Pre-cooked couscous, with its political implications for the emancipation of women, is claimed as a Tunisian invention.

Couscous, home-made or pre-cooked, is steamed in a special *couscoussier*. This quintessentially North African piece of equipment consists of a large vessel (made of tin, aluminium, stainless steel or earthenware) with two parts: a lower part in which the accompanying stew is cooked and an upper part which holds the couscous. The removable upper part has a perforated base, allowing steam from below to permeate and flavour the couscous.

Couscous is usually served in a large bowl with the spicy stew poured over. A bowl served with stew costs from TD2.500 in local restaurants.

French loaf. A standard loaf sells for 140 mills. Look out for *tabouna*, the traditional flat Berber bread.

Tunisian Specialities

Salads Tunisia produces a good range of salad vegetables all year round, and salads feature prominently in the local diet.

The favourite is *salade tunisienne*, which is a mix of finely diced salad vegetables served with a dressing of lemon juice and olive oil. *Salade mechouia* is a spicy mixture of mashed grilled vegetables. It's served alone as an appetiser, or as an accompaniment to dishes such as roast chicken.

You'll find both on just about every restaurant menu.

Soups Soups are also popular. *Lablabi* is a spicy chickpea broth, which is doled out on a bed of broken bread – a cheap, sustaining meal that is a great favourite with Tunisian labourers. It's normally eaten early in the day; it's rare to find lablabi on the menu after noon. Restaurants that serve it are identifiable by the stacks of large earthenware soup bowls in their windows.

Chorba is a spicy soup that takes its name from the special rice-shaped pasta with which it is made. A variation is *chorba fric*, which is made with barley granules. This produces a thicker soup that is superb on cold winter days. Usually, these soups are made on a lamb or chicken stock. Fish chorba is a speciality of the Sfax region.

Sfax is also the place to seek out *tchich*, a thick soup made from dried octopus. It's a speciality of the nearby Kerkennah Islands.

Egg Dishes Tunisian cooks have come up with some unusual ways of serving eggs.

Foremost among them is the curiously named *briq*. The standard briq is the *briq à l'oeuf*, which is a whole egg deep-fried in a triangle of wafer-thin *malsouqa* pastry – served with a wedge of lemon. It should be eaten with the fingers: hold the corners and munch away at the middle until the soft yolk runs down your chin! There are dozens of varieties, including *briq au thon* (with tuna) and *briq aux crevettes* (with prawns). It is normally eaten as an appetiser.

Another great favourite is *ojja*, which is eggs poached in a spicy, harissa-based tomato sauce. Sometimes the eggs are stirred into the sauce. The basic form is known as *ojja nature*. It can be expanded to *ojja aux crevettes* with the addition of a few prawns, or *ojja merguez* with chunks of spicy sausage.

Main Courses You'll find couscous on the menu of just about every restaurant in the country. Other dishes include:

Shakshuka This is a thick vegetable soup based on onions and green peppers; unfortunately for vegetarians, it's normally made with a meat stock.

Kammounia Meat stew made with lots of cumin.

Mloukhia This is similar to kammounia, except that it's made with the powdered leaf of the local mloukhia plant. Cuts of lamb or beef are simmered until they almost disappear into the rich, green sauce.

Tajine The Tunisian version of Tajine is no relation to its Moroccan namesake; it's similar to an Italian frittata and is normally served cold with chips and salad.

Seafood Tunisia has a large variety of seafood. Unfortunately, as everywhere, it's not cheap. The bulk of the catch is bought up by the big hotels and restaurants, who have plenty of customers willing to pay top dollar.

Cheaper fish like sardines and *rouget* (red mullet) are still good value at around TD3.500 for a decent serve. Prime species like *dorade* (sea bream) and *loup de mer* (sea perch) are priced by weight, normally at between TD4 and TD6 per 100g – depending on the category of restaurant. More expensive still are *crevettes royales* (king prawns) and *langouste* (crayfish) at around TD8 per 100g.

A local seafood speciality is *spaghetti aux fruits de mer*, which is a spicy version of spaghetti marinara loaded with prawns and octopus.

Grilled Food Many restaurants also offer a selection of grilled food, including *cotelettes* (lamb cutlets) and *brochettes*. One delicacy not to be missed is *merguez*, a spicy lamb sausage similar to the Mexican *chorizo*. Grilled food is normally served with chips and salad.

Turkey Locals like to joke that every day is Christmas in Tunisia, such is the popularity of turkey in the diet. Tunisians are the world's largest per capita consumers of turkey meat. The breast meat is sliced thin and served grilled as *escallope de dinde* or crumbed and fried as *escallope panée*, while the red meat is cooked in stews or made into *merguez de dinde* (turkey sausages).

Where to Eat

If you want to sample real Tunisian food, you'll have to eat in local restaurants – or, better still, make friends with a Tunisian family.

Gargottes *Gargottes* are the cheapest form of local restaurant, usually small places with old formica-topped tables, plastic chairs and a blackboard menu with three or four daily specials. Main courses seldom cost more than TD2.500.

Local Restaurants Other local restaurants are more upmarket, with tablecloths, printed menus and a wider choice of dishes, often including grilled foods. It's generally possible to get a good meal for less than TD5. It's very rare, but not unheard of, to find a cheap, local restaurant that serves alcohol.

Bars/Restaurants Some towns have local bars that also serve simple meals like chicken, chips and salad for around TD3.

Tourist Restaurants If you want to enjoy a glass of wine with your meal in comfortable surroundings, you will need to go to a *restaurant touristique*. This doesn't mean the restaurant is exclusively for tourists; it means that the restaurant has been inspected by the country's tourist authorities and awarded between one and three forks. Many of these places serve what they like to call Franco-Tunisienne cuisine, and boast menus heavy with seafood. If you can avoid lobster, most meals cost less than TD15.

Hotels Hotels that cater for package groups serve what they usually call 'international food', which is normally tailored to the particular nationality that stays there. Local dishes are also modified to suit local tastes, which usually means leaving out chilli.

Fast Food

Almost every town has a shop selling casse-croûtes, half a French loaf stuffed with a choice of fillings – fried egg, chips and harissa is a favourite, known as khaftegi. Western-style fast food is also becoming popular. Pizza parlours and burger joints can be found in most of the major towns. Pizza is very popular. It is normally made in large trays, then cut up and sold by weight (from TD6 per kg). After a couple of days in Tunisia it will come as no surprise to discover that tuna is the most popular topping.

Vegetarian

Vegetarians are in for a hard time. Although many people eat vegetarian food regularly at home, they do so because of the price of meat not for philosophical reasons. Tunisians love their meat and can't understand why anyone would want to give it up – if they can afford it. There are very few dishes that don't contain meat in some form. Even seemingly safe dishes such as salade tunisienne and salade mechaouia normally come garnished with tuna, while soups and stews use a meat stock.

The result is that vegetarians will need to do a fair amount of self-catering (see also under Self-Catering later in this section). If you eat dairy products, these can be a good fallback. You'll find a good range of local cheeses at supermarkets, and yoghurt is available everywhere. Fruit is also plentiful and cheap.

Sweets & Pastries

Sweet-toothed travellers have quite a line-up of treats to look forward to. The French left their mark with their patisseries. The best are on Ave Habib Bourguiba in Tunis, where you'll find shop after shop selling delicious chocolate and almond croissants and a colourful assortment of cakes overloaded with chocolate.

The Turks brought their range of goodies, too. Favourites include baklava (layers of pastry filled with crushed nuts and honey) and loukoum (Turkish delight). The best loukoum comes from Kairouan, which is also famous for its makhroud – small cakes made from semolina and dates.

The corne de gazelle, a pastry horn filled with chopped nuts and drowned in honey, is a speciality of southern Tunisia.

Fruit

Tunisia is a great place for fruit eaters. There's always fresh, locally grown fruit of some description to be found at the markets.

Spring is the only time of year when the pickings are a bit slim, but you'll still find fresh oranges. The first fruit of the new season are medlars (also known as loquats). They are closely followed by cherries, apricots, plums and other stone fruit, melons and watermelons.

Grapes make their first appearance on the scene in late June, but the best eating varieties don't reach the markets until the end of August. Look out for the delicious white muscats from around Kelibia and razzegoui, a large white grape that ripens to a pink blush. August is also the month for figs and peaches.

Prickly pears, also known as barbary figs or cactus fruit, are very popular. Their season is from October until December, when you'll see street vendors pushing around barrows of the plump, orange/red fruit. The vendors will peel them for you, so you don't have to contend with the prickles. You should never touch the unpeeled fruit with bare hands. The prickles are so fine as to be virtually invisible – but you'll soon know all about them if you pick one up. It's a mistake that most people only make once.

October is the time of year when pomegranates start to make their appearance. These beautiful ruby-red fruit are a colourful addition to the marketplace – and they taste as good as they look. November is the start of the date season. The best variety is deglat ennour (finger of light), so called because of the delicate, translucent quality of the flesh. Tunisia also produces a lot of citrus fruit, particularly oranges and mandarins. The season starts in December and extends through until March.

Bananas are available all year round. Most are imported from South America, but some are grown locally. The bananas from around El-Haouaria (Cap Bon) and the southern oases are smaller and sweeter than the imported varieties and worth seeking out.

Self-Catering

Self-caterers will find supermarkets in all the major towns and resort areas, although Tunisian supermarkets are very poorly stocked by Western standards. In fact, they are more like budget department stores and often have very little space devoted to food. What they do normally have, however, is a good dairy-produce section with cheese, yoghurt and (occasionally) fresh milk. The country's biggest supermarket chain is Monoprix, which has branches in all the major towns. Monoprix supermarkets also stock a good range of local wines.

Supermarkets don't sell fruit and vegetables, which are readily available from shops and stalls. Major towns have special produce markets.

DRINKS
Nonalcoholic Drinks

Tunisians are big coffee drinkers, and great coffee is only as far away as the nearest cafe. Most cafes have an espresso machine and offer a choice of styles. The most popular is *exprès*, which equates to a short black. A *capucin* bears absolutely no resemblance to a cappucino; it's a short black with a barely detectable dash of milk. The closest thing to a cappucino is a *café direct*, which is served with milk foamed in the espresso machine. They also serve Turkish coffee, called *café turc*. Upmarket cafes in tourist areas also sell filtered coffee.

Tea is also popular, but most westerners have trouble with the Tunisian way of drinking it. All types of tea – black, green and mint – are treated in the same way: Almost equal quantities of tea leaves, sugar and water are boiled up to produce something with a viscosity similar to tar. It is then sipped from very small cups. Mint tea comes served with a sprig of fresh mint, which makes it look attractive at least.

English-style tea is known as an *infusion du thé au lait* and is available only from tourist cafes and hotels. Unfortunately UHT milk is used. You'll occasionally find fresh milk in supermarkets, but don't count on it. UHT milk is available everywhere.

Bottled mineral water is cheap and available everywhere. Safia is the most popular brand. Coca-Cola and all the others are here in force. They are known collectively as *boissons gazeuses* (carbonated drinks). Freshly squeezed orange juice is readily available in season. You can find packaged juices in supermarkets, but they are expensive.

Alcoholic Drinks

Drinking alcohol is forbidden by Islam, but that doesn't stop a lot of Tunisians from indulging in the odd tipple. Alcohol is readily available. It is sold at bars and some restaurants as well as from supermarkets. Supermarkets sell alcohol from noon to 6.30 pm only, and not on Friday. Alcohol you have bought from a supermarket should be carried discreetly, preferably in a closed bag.

Celtia is the most popular beer. A 330ml bottle sells for TD1.400 at bars in Tunis, and for as little as TD1.200 outside the capital. Supermarkets stock only 300ml cans, which sell for 800 mills. Stella Artois and Lowenbrau are also brewed locally under licence, but can be difficult to find away from resort areas.

Thibarine is a local curiosity produced in the village of Thibar (in the Tebersouk Mountains near Dougga). It's made according to a secret recipe dreamt up last century by French monks from the order of the White Fathers. Supposedly a digestive, it tastes like herbal cough mixture. *Boukha* is a fiery white spirit made from figs. It is generally consumed with a mixer. If you are curious, a small bottle costs TD2.800.

ENTERTAINMENT
Cinemas

Cinemas are everywhere in Tunisia and are a popular form of entertainment. Many of the films are Bollywood-style action blockbusters in Arabic, but you'll also find the latest international films, dubbed in French. A ticket costs between TD1.200 and TD2.

Cafes

Cafes are an integral part of Tunisian life. They are much more than a place to stop for a coffee. It is here that the menfolk gather in the evening to smoke their *chichas* (water pipes), exchange gossip and play cards. It has been estimated that 60% of the male population smoke the traditional chicha. Cafes provide the chicha free, charging only for a plug of tobacco.

The main card games are rummy and *quarante*, a game with no Western equivalent that is played with such speed and enthusiasm that it's impossible to figure out the rules. Watching the animated participants is entertainment enough.

Bars

Bars can be found in all the major towns. They are generally hard-drinking, smoke-filled, male preserves. Travellers, particularly women, may feel more comfortable drinking at the resort hotels.

Discos

Discos exist basically for the benefit of tourists and are virtually always associated with big hotels in the main tourist areas.

SPECTATOR SPORTS
Football

Football (soccer) is the country's most popular sport. After school, every side street and patch of wasteland is taken over by kids kicking a ball around.

Tunisia fields one of the strongest teams in Africa. It is hoping to qualify for its third World Cup finals in 2002, following appearances in Argentina (1978) and France (1998). The 1978 team failed to advance beyond the group stage despite defeating Mexico 3-1 and holding West Germany to a nil-all draw.

Tunisia's club teams are also among the best on the continent, with representatives in the finals of all three major African competitions in 1999. Etoile Sportif du Sahel (Sousse) led the way, taking out the Cup Winners' Cup, while Espérance Sportive de Tunisie (Tunis) went down narrowly in the final of the Champions' League.

These two clubs dominated the 1999–2000 domestic season, with Espérance winning its third consecutive championship. Etoile Sportif finished second, 18 points clear of third-placed Club Sfaxien.

The competition runs from early October until the end of March, with matches played on Saturday and Sunday afternoon starting at 3 pm. You'll find fixtures and results in the local papers. Teams are usually referred to by their initials.

The top clubs are joined by teams from the lower divisions to contest the Tunisian Cup, a knock-out competition, which is played midweek.

Athletics

Like its North African neighbours, Algeria and Morocco, Tunisia has a history of producing good middle- and long-distance runners. You'll see plenty of budding young athletes out pounding the streets in the early hours of the day, no doubt dreaming of emulating the feats of the country's greatest runner, Mohammed Gammoudi, who won medals at three Olympic Games. Gammoudi started by winning silver in the 10,000m at Tokyo. He struck gold over 5000m in Mexico City in 1968 and then collected another silver over the same distance in Munich in 1972.

Volleyball

Volleyball is also popular. At the time of writing, the national team was ranked No 16 in the world after winning the 1997 African Championships in Lagos, defeating Cameroon 3-0 in the final. The papers indicate that this is also the most popular women's sport, although they don't give any details of when or where matches are played. There are national volleyball competitions for both men and women.

Handball

While something of a curiosity to many westerners, handball is taken very seriously in Tunisia. The national men's team is ranked among the best in the world, and the national competition gets a lot of press coverage.

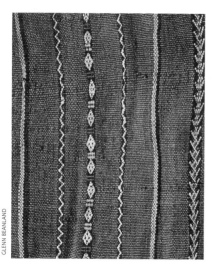

GLENN BEANLAND

Flatwoven Berber rug, with traditional motifs

SHOPPING
Rugs & Carpets

These are among the most readily available souvenirs and, although they are not cheap, there are some really beautiful ones for sale. The main carpet-selling centres are Tunis, Kairouan, Tozeur and Jerba.

There are two basic types of carpet: knotted and woven. The traditional (pre-Islamic conquest) carpet industry was based on the weaving of *mergoums* and kilims. Mergoums feature very bright, geometric designs, with bold use of reds, purples, blues and other vivid colours. Kilims use traditional Berber motifs on a woven background. Both are reasonably cheap to buy – you can reckon on paying about TD60 per sq metre.

Allouchas are a type of thick-pile Berber woven rug, spun by hand in wool. They feature natural tones and are decorated with simple traditional Berber motifs. Look for them in Ain Draham, where they are produced by a small women's cooperative called Les Tapis de Kroumirie. (See the boxed text 'Les Tapis de Kroumirie' in the Ain Draham section in the Northern Tunisia chapter for more details.) They are also sold in Tunis at Main des Femmes,

above the Banque de l'Habitat in Ave Habib Bourguiba.

The best known of the knotted carpets are the classical (Persian-style) Kairouan carpets. This style of carpet-making was first introduced to Tunisia by the Turks. Legend has it that the first knotted carpet to be made in Tunisia was by the daughter of the Turkish governor of Kairouan. Whatever the truth might be, today Kairouan is the carpet capital of the country.

Knotted carpets are priced according to the number of knots per sq metre. A carpet with 40,000 knots per sq metre costs about TD130 per sq metre, while an exceptionally fine carpet with 250,000 knots per sq metre can cost up to TD1500 per sq metre. The Berber *guetiffa* is a another type of knotted carpet. It is a thick-pile carpet, normally cream coloured, with Berber motifs.

All these types of carpets are sold at the government-run SOCOPA emporiums found in all the major tourist centres. They have been inspected by Organisation National de l'Artisanat (ONAT) and classified according to type and number of knots. They come with an affixed label giving this information.

The different qualities are ordinary *(deuxième choix)* – up to 40,000 knots per sq metre; fine *(premier choix)* – up to 90,000 knots per sq metre; and superfine *(qualité supérieure)* – up to 250,000 knots per sq metre.

See under Where to Shop later in this section for more information about SOCOPA.

Pottery & Ceramics

Tunisia has long been associated with the art of pottery. The main centres of production are Nabeul and the town of Guellala on the island of Jerba is another. The workshops in these places turn out a variety of styles from simple terracotta ware to elegant Andalusian-style vases and dinner settings. See the Nabeul section in the Cap Bon Peninsula chapter, and the Guellela section in the Jerba & the South-East Coast chapter for more information.

The Berber villages around the small northern town of Sejnane are famous for a primitive style of pottery known as Sejnane ware, producing unusual moulded bowls and animal figures decorated with traditional motifs. See the Sejnane section in the Northern Tunisia chapter for more information.

Leather
Kairouan is the country's leading producer of leather goods, supplying the nation's souvenir shops with belts, wallets, purses and handbags embossed with camels and palm trees.

Other articles for sale include traditional pieces such as camel and donkey saddles, water skins and cartridge pouches, as well as more mundane objects like wallets and belts.

Copper & Brass
Beaten copper and brass items are also popular and are widely available. Beaten plates, which range in size from a saucer to a coffee table, make good souvenirs, although transporting the larger ones can be a problem.

Jewellery
Arabic jewellery (and particularly gold jewellery) is often too gaudy and ornate for western tastes. The Hand of Fatima (daughter of the Prophet) or *khomsa* is a traditional

The Hand of Fatima is a popular motif in jewellery.

Arabic motif. It is used in many different forms and in varying sizes, from small earrings to large neck pendants, and is usually made of silver. In pre-Islamic times this same design represented Baal, the protector of the Carthaginians.

Other traditional pieces of jewellery include the *hedeyed*, which are finely engraved, wide bracelets made of gold or silver, and *kholkal*, which are similar, but worn around the ankle. In Carthaginian times kholkal were commonly worn to signify chastity; today they are still a symbol of fidelity and are often part of a bride's dowry.

The quality of pure silver and gold jewellery can be established by the official stamps used to grade all work. The quality of unstamped items is immediately suspect. The stamps in use are: the horse's head (the Carthaginian symbol for money) – used to mark all 18 carat gold jewellery; the scorpion – used on all nine carat gold jewellery; grape clusters – used on silver graded at 900 mills per gram; and the Negro head – used on poorer-quality silver graded at 800 mills per gram.

Esparto Goods
Rectangular, woven esparto baskets are practical and cheap. Some are pretty awful, with pictures of camels and 'typical desert scenes' woven into them, but there are plenty of other more simple designs. Hats and fans are other popular goods. Most of the esparto items come from Gabès and Jerba in the south of the country.

Chechias
Chechias are the small, red felt hats worn by older Tunisian men. The chechia souq in Tunis is the obvious place to look for them. Quality varies, but an average price is around TD6.

Oils & Perfume
The Cap Bon Peninsula is famous for the production of essential oils, especially orange blossom and geranium. Most of the output goes to the international perfume

market, but some is kept and used to make the cheap scented oils that are sold in tourist shops everywhere. Prices start at TD1.500 for 5ml.

Sand Roses
Sand roses are the speciality of southern Tunisia, although they are sold all over the country. They are formed of gypsum, which has dissolved from the sand and then crystallised into spectacular patterns that resemble flower petals.

They range from about 5cm in diameter up to the size of a large watermelon. They do make good cheap souvenirs, but carting around a great chunk of gypsum for weeks on end isn't much fun.

Chichas
The ubiquitous water pipes come in all shapes and sizes and are readily available from souqs and tourist shops. They range in price from around TD4 for a small, cheap one up to TD70 for a good quality, full-size version.

Where to Shop
You'll find that all the items previously listed are available from souvenir shops everywhere in the country.

The problem is finding the right price. The tourist shops in the big medinas are probably the worst place to start, especially if you have no idea what you should be paying. First prices are sometimes 10 times higher than the real price.

The best place to start is at one of the government-run SOCOPA emporiums found in all the major tourist centres. Expert bargainers may be able to find cheaper prices elsewhere, but not the guarantee of quality that SOCOPA provides. Sales staff in these shops are paid to assist shoppers, not to apply hard-sell techniques. Even if you don't buy, it's a good idea to visit a SOCOPA shop just to get an idea of what constitutes a reasonable price before heading to the medina.

If you do opt to shop in the medina, be careful: Many a TD100 carpet has been sold for TD500 on the strength of a complimentary cup of mint tea.

Markets
Town and village life often revolves around the weekly markets. Market day is a good day to be in a town, as it will be far more lively than usual and, apart from the itinerant merchants selling fairly mundane household goods, there will be other local people who have travelled in from outlying districts.

Some markets have become real tourist traps; nevertheless, it is on market days that there is the best selection of stuff for sale. For the dates of the main market days in Tunisia's main towns, see the boxed text 'Market Days'.

Market Days	
day	**location**
Monday	Ain Draham, El-Jem, Houmt Souq, Kairouan, Kelibia, Matmata and Tataouine
Tuesday	Ghardimao, Kasserine and Kebili
Wednesday	Gafsa, Jendouba and Sbeitla
Thursday	Douz, El-Haouaria, Hammamet, Nefta, Remla (Kerkennah), Sejnane and Tebersouk
Friday	Mahdia, Mateur, Midoun, Nabeul, Sfax, Tabarka, Tamerza, Zaghouan and Zarzis
Saturday	Ben Guerdane, El-Fahs, Gabés and Monastir
Sunday	Hammam Lif, Le Kef, Sousse and Tozeur

Gifts for Children
Stuffed Camels If in Arabic desert countries you can tell how well developed the tourist industry is by the number of stuffed camels for sale then Tunisia is way out in front. Every souvenir shop has them, ranging from pocket size right up to about one-third full size. Prices start at TD1.500.

Books Local publisher Editions Alif does an excellent series of pop-up books about Tunisian and regional life. The series includes only one title in English, *A Walk Through an Arab City: the Tunis Medina*, which is also published in German and French. The other books in the series are in French, and they look at oasis life, ancient Carthage and Mediterranean life in 1492. The books have two levels of appeal: Children like them for their pop-up features, and adults will find a wealth of information that is hard to find elsewhere.

These books can be hard to find. They are sold at the National Museum in Carthage, Tunis airport, the Dar Charait Museum in Tozeur and at the ancient site in Sbeitla – as well as at the Editions Alif shop, 115 Souq de l'Artisanat, Nabeul.

Jigsaws Editions Alif also produces a range of jigsaws that is suitable for various age groups. It includes 100-piece maps of both Tunis and the Tunis Medina (TD6), a 50-piece puzzle of a mosaic of two fighting cocks (TD4.800) as well as several minipuzzles (TD1.500).

More widely on sale are 200-piece jigsaws of Sidi Bou Saïd, Carthage, Jerba and the Kerkennah Islands. Monoprix supermarkets stock the full range.

Getting There & Away

AIR
Airports & Airlines

Most of the four million tourists who travel to Tunisia each year arrive by air. The three main airports for international flights are Tunis-Carthage, Monastir and Jerba. The airports at Sfax, Tozeur and Tabarka also handle a few international flights.

Tunisia's national airline is Tunis Air, which operates a fleet of European Airbuses (A320 and A300) and Boeing 737s to a wide range of destinations in Europe, the Middle East and North Africa. It normally shares the route with the national airline of the country concerned. There are no direct flights between Tunisia and North or South America, Asia or Oceania.

Buying Tickets

An air ticket alone can gouge a great slice out of anyone's budget, but you can reduce the cost by finding discounted fares. Stiff competition has resulted in widespread discounting – good news for travellers! The only people likely to be paying full fare these days are travellers flying in 1st or business class. Passengers flying in economy can usually manage some sort of discount. But unless you buy carefully and flexibly, it is still possible to end up paying exorbitant amounts for a journey.

For long-term travel, there are plenty of discount tickets valid for 12 months, allowing multiple stopovers with open dates. For short-term travel, cheaper fares are available by travelling midweek, staying away at least one Saturday night or taking advantage of short-lived promotional offers.

When you're looking for bargain air fares, go to a travel agent rather than directly to the airline. From time to time, airlines have promotional fares and special offers, but generally they only sell fares at the official listed price. One exception to this rule is the expanding number of 'no-frills' carriers operating in the USA and north-west Europe, which mostly sell direct to travellers. Unlike the 'full service' airlines, no-frills carriers often make one-way tickets available at around half the return fare, meaning that it is easy to put together a return ticket when you fly to one place but leave from another.

The other exception is booking on the Internet. Many airlines, full-service and no-frills, offer some excellent fares to Web surfers. They may sell seats by auction or simply cut prices to reflect the reduced cost of electronic selling. Many travel agents around the world have Web sites, which can make the Internet a quick and easy way to compare prices. It's a good start for when you're ready to start negotiating with your favourite travel agency. Online ticket sales work well if you are doing a simple one-way or return trip on specified dates. However, on-line super-fast fare generators are no substitute for a travel agent who knows all about special deals, has strategies for avoiding layovers and can offer advice on everything from which airline has the best vegetarian food to the best travel insurance to bundle with your ticket.

The days when some travel agents would routinely fleece travellers by running off with their money are, happily, almost over. Paying by credit card generally offers protection, as most card issuers provide refunds if you can prove you didn't get what you paid for. Similar protection can be obtained by buying a ticket from a bonded agent, such as one covered by the Air Transport Operators License (ATOL) scheme in the UK. Agents who only accept cash should hand over the tickets immediately and not tell you to 'come back tomorrow'. After you've made a booking or paid a deposit, call the airline and confirm that the booking was made. It's generally not advisable to send money (even cheques) through the post unless the agent is very well established – some travellers have reported being ripped off by fly-by-night mail-order ticket agents.

Air Travel Glossary

Cancellation Penalties If you have to cancel or change a discounted ticket, there are often heavy penalties involved; insurance can sometimes be taken out against these penalties. Some airlines impose penalties on regular tickets as well, particularly against 'no-show' passengers.

Courier Fares Businesses often need to send urgent documents or freight securely and quickly. Courier companies hire people to accompany the package through customs and, in return, offer a discount ticket which is sometimes a phenomenal bargain. However, you may have to surrender all your baggage allowance and take only carry-on luggage.

Full Fares Airlines traditionally offer 1st class (coded F), business class (coded J) and economy class (coded Y) tickets. These days there are so many promotional and discounted fares available that few passengers pay full economy fare.

Lost Tickets If you lose your airline ticket an airline will usually treat it like a travellers cheque and, after inquiries, issue you with another one. Legally, however, an airline is entitled to treat it like cash and if you lose it then it's gone forever. Take good care of your tickets.

Onward Tickets An entry requirement for many countries is that you have a ticket out of the country. If you're unsure of your next move, the easiest solution is to buy the cheapest onward ticket to a neighbouring country or a ticket from a reliable airline which can later be refunded if you do not use it.

Open-Jaw Tickets These are return tickets where you fly out to one place but return from another. If available, this can save you backtracking to your arrival point.

Overbooking Since every flight has some passengers who fail to show up, airlines often book more passengers than they have seats. Usually excess passengers make up for the no-shows, but occasionally somebody gets 'bumped' onto the next available flight. Guess who it is most likely to be? The passengers who check in late.

Promotional Fares These are officially discounted fares, available from travel agencies or direct from the airline.

Reconfirmation If you don't reconfirm your flight at least 72 hours prior to departure, the airline may delete your name from the passenger list. Ring to find out if your airline requires reconfirmation.

Restrictions Discounted tickets often have various restrictions on them – such as needing to be paid for in advance and incurring a penalty to be altered. Others are restrictions on the minimum and maximum period you must be away.

Round-the-World Tickets RTW tickets give you a limited period (usually a year) in which to circumnavigate the globe. You can go anywhere the carrying airlines go, as long as you don't backtrack. The number of stopovers or total number of separate flights is decided before you set off and they usually cost a bit more than a basic return flight.

Transferred Tickets Airline tickets cannot be transferred from one person to another. Travellers sometimes try to sell the return half of their ticket, but officials can ask you to prove that you are the person named on the ticket. On an international flight tickets are compared with passports.

Travel Periods Ticket prices vary with the time of year. There is a low (off-peak) season and a high (peak) season, and often a low-shoulder season and a high-shoulder season as well. Usually the fare depends on your outward flight – if you depart in the high season and return in the low season, you pay the high-season fare.

You may decide to pay more than the rock-bottom fare by opting for the safety of a better-known travel agent. Firms such as STA Travel, which has offices worldwide, Council Travel in the USA and Usit Campus (formerly Campus Travel) in the UK is not going to disappear overnight and it offers good prices to most destinations.

If you purchase a ticket and later want to make changes to your route or get a refund, you need to contact the original travel agent. Airlines only issue refunds to the purchaser of a ticket – usually the travel agent who bought the ticket on your behalf. Many travellers change their routes halfway through their trips, so think carefully before you buy a ticket which is not easily refunded.

Student & Youth Fares Full-time students and people under 26 have access to better deals than other travellers. The better deals may not always be cheaper fares but can include more flexibility to change flights and/or routes. You have to show a document proving your date of birth or a valid International Student Identity Card (ISIC) when buying your ticket and boarding the plane. There are plenty of places around the world where nonstudents can get fake student cards, but if you get caught using a fake card you could have your ticket confiscated.

Frequent Flyers Most airlines offer frequent flyer deals that can earn you a free air ticket or other goodies. To qualify, you have to accumulate sufficient mileage with the same airline or airline alliance. Many airlines have 'blackout periods', or times when you cannot fly for free on your frequent-flyer points (eg, Christmas and Chinese New Year). The worst thing about frequent-flyer programs is that they tend to lock you into one airline, and that airline may not always have the cheapest fares or most convenient flight schedule.

Courier Flights Courier flights are a great bargain if you're lucky enough to find one. Air-freight companies expedite delivery of urgent items by sending them with you as your baggage allowance. You are permitted to bring along a carry-on bag, but that's all. In return, you get a steeply discounted ticket.

There are other restrictions: Courier tickets are sold for a fixed date and schedule changes can be difficult to make. If you buy a return ticket, your schedule will be even more rigid. You need to clarify before you fly what restrictions apply to your ticket, and don't expect a refund once you've paid.

Booking a courier ticket takes some effort. They are not readily available and arrangements have to be made one month or more in advance. You won't find courier flights on all routes either – just on the major air routes.

Courier flights are occasionally advertised in the newspapers, or you could contact air-freight companies listed in the phone book. You may even have to go to the air-freight company to get an answer – the companies aren't always keen to give out information over the phone. *Travel Unlimited* (PO Box 1058, Allston, MA 02134, USA) is a monthly travel newsletter that publishes many courier flight deals from destinations worldwide. A 12-month subscription to the newsletter costs US$25, or US$35 for readers outside the USA. Another possibility (at least for USA residents) is to join the International Association of Air Travel Couriers (IAATC). The membership fee of US$45 gets members a bimonthly update of air-courier offerings, access to a fax-on-demand service with daily updates of last-minute specials and the bimonthly newsletter the *Shoestring Traveler.* For more information, contact IAATC (☎ 561-582 8320) or visit its Web site: www.courier.org. However, be aware that joining this organisation does not guarantee that you'll get a courier flight.

Second-Hand Tickets You'll occasionally see advertisements on youth-hostel bulletin boards and sometimes in newspapers for 'second-hand tickets'. That is, somebody purchased a return ticket or a ticket with multiple stopovers and now wants to sell the unused portion of the ticket.

The prices offered look very attractive indeed. Unfortunately, these tickets, if used for international travel, are usually worthless, as the name on the ticket must match the name on the passport of the person checking in. Some people reason that the seller of the ticket can check you in with his or her passport, and then give you the boarding pass – wrong again! Usually the immigration people want to see your boarding pass, and if it doesn't match the name in your passport, then you won't be able to board your flight.

What happens if you purchase a ticket and then change your name? It can happen – some people change their name when they get married or divorced and some people change their name because they feel like it. If the name on the ticket doesn't match the name in your passport, you could have problems. In this case, be sure you have documents such as your old passport to prove that the old you and the new you are the same person.

Ticketless Travel Ticketless travel, whereby your reservation details are contained within an airline computer, is becoming more common. On simple return trips the absence of a ticket can be a benefit – it's one less thing to worry about; however, if you are planning a complicated itinerary, which you may wish to amend en route, there is no substitute for the good old paper version.

Travellers with Special Needs

Most international airlines can cater to people with special needs – travellers with disabilities, people with young children and even children travelling alone.

Travellers with special dietary preferences (vegetarian, kosher etc) can request appropriate meals with advance notice. If you are travelling in a wheelchair, most international airports can provide an escort from check-in desk to plane where needed, and ramps, lifts, toilets and phones are generally available.

Airlines usually allow babies up to two years of age to fly for 10% of the adult fare, although a few may allow them to fly free of charge. Reputable international airlines usually provide nappies (diapers), tissues, talcum and all the other paraphernalia needed to keep babies clean, dry and half-happy. For children between the ages of two and 12, the fare on international flights is usually 50% of the regular fare or 67% of a discounted fare.

Departure Tax

There is no departure tax to be paid when leaving Tunisia. A TD8 airport tax is included in the price of an air ticket.

The USA

There are no direct flights between the USA and Tunisia, but other options are as follows.

Scheduled Flights New York has both the cheapest air fares and the largest choice of airlines. At the time of research, British Airways was offering Tunis via London for as little as US$502 return in February, rising to around US$980 in July/August. From the west coast, the fares range from US$752 in February to US$1230 in July/August. Student and youth fares are about 30% cheaper.

Cheap Flights There are cheaper ways of getting to Tunisia from the USA, but they involve considerably more time and effort. The cheapest option is to buy a discount ticket to Europe and then to shop around, but there's not much point in doing this unless you want to spend a few days hanging around. London is the best place to head for.

The North Atlantic is the world's busiest long-haul air corridor, and the flight options to Europe are bewildering. Microsoft's popular Expedia Web site (www.msn.com) gives a good idea of the possibilities. Other sites worth checking out are ITN (www.itn.net) and Travelocity (www.travelocity.com).

Discount travel agents in the USA are known as consolidators (although you won't see a sign on the door saying 'Consolidator'). San Francisco is the ticket-consolidator capital of the USA, although some good deals can be found in Los Angeles, New York and other big cities. Consolidators can be found through the *Yellow Pages* or the major daily newspapers.

The *New York Times*, *Los Angeles Times*, *Chicago Tribune* and *San Francisco Examiner* all produce weekly travel sections in which you will find a number of travel agency advertisements. Ticket Planet is a leading ticket consolidator in the USA and is recommended. Check out its Web site: www.ticketplanet.com.

Council Travel, North America's largest student travel organisation, has around 60 offices in the USA; its head office (☎ 800-226 8624) is at 205 E 42 St, New York, NY 10017. Call the head office number for the office nearest you or visit its Web site: www.ciee.org.

STA Travel (☎ 800-777 0112) has offices in Boston, Chicago, Miami, New York, Philadelphia, San Francisco and other major cities. Call the toll-free 800 number for office locations or visit its Web site: www.statravel.com.

Canada
There are no direct flights to or from Canada to Tunisia, which means that Canadians are faced with a similar range of alternatives to Americans. You can either use one of the major European airlines and take a connecting flight to Tunis, or fly to Europe as cheaply as possible and then shop around.

Canadian discount air-ticket sellers are commonly referred to as consolidators and their air fares tend to be around about 10% higher than those sold in the USA. The *Globe & Mail*, *Toronto Star*, *Montreal Gazette* and *Vancouver Sun* carry travel-agent ads and are a good place to look for cheap fares.

Travel CUTS (☎ 800-667 2887) is Canada's national student-travel agency and has offices in all major cities. Its Web address is www.travelcuts.com. You should be able to get to Tunis from Toronto and Montreal for about C$1150 or from Vancouver for C$1500 return.

For courier flights originating in Canada, contact FB On Board Courier Services, which is based in Montreal (☎ 514-631 2677). This company can get you to London for C$575 return.

Australia
There are no direct flights between Australia and Tunisia. The easiest option is to travel to Europe with one of the major European airlines with good connections to Tunisia, and then fly to Tunis as a side trip. The possibilities include Alitalia and KLM, while Air France and Lufthansa have good deals using Singapore Airlines or Thai Airways International between Australia and South-East Asia.

For flights from Europe or North America to Australia, there are a lot of competing airlines and a wide variety of air fares. Round-the-World (RTW) tickets are often real bargains and since Australia is pretty much on the other side of the world from Europe or North America, it can sometimes work out cheaper to keep going around the world on a RTW ticket than do a U-turn on a return ticket.

Cheap flights from Australia to Europe generally travel via South-East Asian capitals, involving stopovers at Kuala Lumpur, Bangkok or Singapore. If a long stopover between connections is necessary, transit accommodation is sometimes included in the price of the ticket. If it's at your own expense, it may be worth considering a more expensive ticket.

Quite a few travel agencies specialise in discount air tickets. Some travel agents, particularly smaller ones, advertise cheap air fares in the travel sections of weekend newspapers, such as the *Age* in Melbourne and the *Sydney Morning Herald*.

Two well-known agents for cheap fares are STA Travel and Flight Centre. STA Travel (☎ 03-9349 2411) has its main office at 224 Faraday St, Carlton, Vic 3053, and offices in all major cities and on many university campuses. Call ☎131 776 Australia-wide for the location of your nearest branch or visit its Web site (www.statravel.com.au). The Flight Centre (☎ 131 600 Australia-wide) has a central office at 82 Elizabeth St, Sydney, and there are dozens of offices throughout Australia or visit its Web site: www.flightcentre.com.au.

The cheapest fares cost from A$1700 in low season to A$2100 in high season.

New Zealand

The situation is much the same as from Australia. There are no direct flights from New Zealand to Tunisia, and STA Travel and Flight Centre are good places to check ticket prices.

The quickest way to get to Tunis is to fly Thai Airways International/Lufthansa to Frankfurt and connect with the daily Lufthansa flight to Tunis.

The *New Zealand Herald* has a travel section in which travel agents advertise fares. Flight Centre (☎ 09-309 6171) has a large central office in Auckland at National Bank Towers (corner of Queen and Darby Sts) and many branches throughout the country. STA Travel (☎ 09-309 0458) has its main office at 10 High St, Auckland, and has other offices in Auckland as well as in Hamilton, Palmerston North, Wellington, Christchurch and Dunedin. Check out its Web site: www.sta.travel.com.au.

The UK

Airline ticket discounters are known as bucket shops in the UK. Despite the somewhat disreputable name, there is nothing under-the-counter about them. Discount air travel is big business in London. Advertisements for many travel agents appear in the travel pages of the weekend broadsheets, such as the *Independent* on Saturday and the *Sunday Times*. Look out for the free magazines, such as *TNT*, which are widely available in London – start by looking outside the main train and underground stations.

For students or travellers under 26, popular travel agencies in the UK include STA Travel (☎ 020-7361 6144), which has an office at 86 Old Brompton Rd, London SW7 3LQ, and other offices in London and Manchester (Web site: www.statravel.co.uk). Usit Campus (☎ 0870-240 1010), 52 Grosvenor Gardens, London SW1W 0AG, has branches throughout the UK (Web site: www.usitcampus.com). Both of these agencies sell tickets to all travellers, but cater especially to young people and students. Charter flights can work out as a cheaper alternative to scheduled flights, especially if you do not qualify for the under-26 and student discounts.

Other recommended travel agencies include: Trailfinders (☎ 020-7938 3939), 194 Kensington High St, London W8 7RG (Web site: www.trailfinders.com); Bridge the World (☎ 020-7734 7447), 4 Regent Place, London W1R 5FB; and Flightbookers (☎ 020-7757 2000), 177–178 Tottenham Court Rd, London W1P 9LF.

Scheduled Flights GB Airways, a subsidiary of British Airways, and Tunis Air both operate scheduled flights from London to Tunis. You'll find the best deals with GB Airways (☎ 0990-444 000), which flies from Gatwick four times a week. The cheapest advance-purchase return fares range from UK£169 in February to UK£178 in July and August. GB Airways also has same-day connecting flights from Manchester and Glasgow. The equivalent low/high season fares from Manchester are UK£228/261 and from Glasgow it's UK£238/271. The airline also offers special deals, which are usually announced between four and six weeks before departure and advertised in the press and at travel agents.

Tunis Air (☎ 020-7734 7644) flies from Heathrow four times a week. Return fares range from UK£178 to UK£211. Tunis Air doesn't offer special deals.

Charter Flights Contrary to popular perception, charter flights are not much cheaper than special deals on scheduled flights, unless you are prepared to hunt around for a last minute deal. One advantage of using charter flights is that they offer a much wider choice of departure points. The options include departures from Belfast, Bristol, Birmingham, East Midlands, Gatwick, Glasgow, Luton, Manchester, Newcastle and Stansted. The biggest disadvantage is the restriction on the length of time you can stay away, which ranges from one to three weeks. Most tickets are for a two-week stay. Two of the biggest British charter operators are Thomson Holidays (☎ 0990-502555) and Thomas Cook (☎ 0990-666222). The Tunisian National Tourist Office (☎ 020-7224 5561, fax 7224 4053), 77A Wigmore St, London W1H 9LJ, has a list of all the operators.

Typical high-season return fares include Gatwick to Monastir for UK£209, dropping to UK£179 in low season, but you should be able to pick up a discount ticket for half that if you shop around.

Continental Europe

Though London is the travel discount capital of Europe, there are several other cities in which you will find a range of good deals. Generally, there is not much variation in air fares for departures from the main European cities. All the major airlines are usually offering some sort of deal, and travel agents generally have a number of deals on offer, so shop around.

Across Europe many travel agencies have ties with STA Travel, where cheap tickets can be purchased and STA-issued tickets can be altered (usually for a US$25 fee). Outlets in major cities include: Voyages Wasteels (☎ 08 03 88 70 04, fax 01 43 25 46 25), 11 rue Dupuytren, 756006 Paris; STA Travel (☎ 030-311 0950, fax 313 0948), Goethestrasse 73, 10625 Berlin; Passaggi (☎ 06-474 0923, fax 482 7436), Stazione Termini FS, Galleria Di Tesla, Rome; and ISYTS (☎ 01-322 1267, fax 323 3767), 11 Nikis St, Upper floor, Syntagma Square, Athens.

France Not surprisingly, France has better flight connections to Tunisia than anywhere else in Europe. Air France and Tunis Air both have at least two flights daily from Paris to Tunis. Advance-purchase fares start at around 2500FF return. Tunis Air has weekly flights from Paris to Sfax and Tozeur. There are also daily flights to Tunis from Lyon, Marseille and Nice, and two flights weekly from Bordeaux.

Charter flights are much cheaper. You'll pay around 1700FF in high season for a return flight from Paris to Tunis or Jerba, and 2500FF to Tozeur. In low season, return fares to Tunis fall below 1000FF; the corresponding fares to Jerba and Tozeur are 1350FF and 1650FF, respectively. Return flights from Marseille to Tunis range from 1400FF in high season to 1200FF in low season.

Reliable travel agents include: OTU Voyages (☎ 01 44 41 38 50), which has a central Paris office at 39 Ave Georges Bernanos (5e) and another 42 offices around the country (Web site: www.otu.fr); Acceuil des Jeunes en France (☎ 01 42 77 87 80), 119 rue Saint Martin (4e); Nouvelles Frontières (☎ 08 03 33 33 33), 5 Ave de l'Opéra (1er; Web site: www.nouvelles-frontieres.com); and Voyageurs du Monde (☎ 01 42 86 16 00), 55 rue Sainte Anne (2e).

Germany For cheap air fares in Frankfurt, try SRID Reisen (☎ 069-43 01 91), Berger Strasse 118. In Berlin, Alternativ Tours (☎ 030-881 2089), Wilmersdorfer Strasse 94 (U-Bahn: Adenauerplatz), specialises in discounted fares to just about anywhere in the world. SRS Studenten Reise Service (☎ 030-283 3094), at Marienstrasse 23, near Friedrichstrasse station, offers discounted student (aged 34 or less) or youth (aged 25 or less) fares. Travel agents offering cheap flights advertise in *Zitty*, Berlin's fortnightly entertainment magazine.

Greece Tunis Air flies from Athens to Tunis on Tuesday and Thursday. A one-month excursion fare costs about 85,000 dr. In Athens, check the many travel agencies in the backstreets between Syntagma and Omonia Squares. For student and non-concessionary fares, try Magic Bus (☎ 01-323 7471, fax 322 0219).

Belgium & Switzerland In Belgium, Acotra Student Travel Agency (☎ 02-512 8607) at rue de la Madeline, Brussels, and WATS Reizen (☎ 03-226 1626) at de Keyserlei 44, Antwerp, are both well-known agencies.

In Switzerland, SSR Voyages (☎ 01-297 1111) specialises in student, youth and budget fares. In Zurich, there is a branch at Leonhardstrasse 10 and there are others in most major Swiss cities (Web site: www.ssr.ch).

The Netherlands In the Netherlands, NBBS Reizen is the official student-travel agency. You can find it in Amsterdam (☎ 020-624 0989) at Rokin 66 and there are several other agencies around the city. Another recommended travel agent in Amsterdam is Malibu Travel (☎ 020-626 3230) at Prinsengracht 230.

Africa

Egypt EgyptAir and Tunis Air both operate between Cairo and Tunis. The one-month excursion fare is TD425.

Morocco Royal Air Maroc and Tunis Air share the route between Tunis and Casablanca. The one-month excursion fare from Tunis is TD360.500.

LAND

Although you are unlikely, for the foreseeable future anyway, to be taking your own vehicle into Tunisia from either Libya or Algeria, crossing by ferry from Italy or France is a popular option (see the Sea section later in this chapter for details of ferry timetables and fares). Drivers of cars and riders of motorcycles will need the vehicle's registration papers, liability insurance and an international drivers' permit in addition to their domestic licence. Beware: There are two kinds of international permits, one of which is needed mostly for former British colonies. There is no need for a *carnet de passage en douane* (which is effectively a passport for the vehicle and acts as a temporary waiver of import duty) when taking your car into Tunisia. However, this document is required in many other African countries and would be worth getting if you think you'll be driving on beyond Tunisia, Algeria or Morocco. Contact your local automobile association for details about all documentation required.

Liability insurance is not available in advance for many out-of-the-way countries, but has to be bought when crossing the border. The cost and quality of such local insurance varies wildly, and you will find in some countries that you are effectively travelling uninsured.

Anyone who is planning to take their own vehicle needs to check the likely availability of spares – good for French marques, but not so good for others. See also Car & Motorcycle in the Getting Around chapter.

Algeria

Algeria has been effectively out of bounds to travellers since the start of the civil war in early 1993. The conflict has forced the cancellation of all bus and train services between the two countries, including the Trans Maghreb Express train, *Al-Maghreb al-Arabi*, which once linked Tunisia with Morocco via Algiers.

Border Crossings For the record, the main crossing points between Tunisia and Algeria are at Babouch (between Ain Draham and Annaba), Ghardimao (Jendouba and Souq Ahras), Sakiet Sidi Youssef (Le Kef and Souq Ahras), Bou Chebka (Kasserine and Tébessa) and the desert crossing at Hazoua between Nefta and El-Oued. This was once a popular crossing with travellers heading south-west to the Algerian Sahara.

Louage *Louages* (shared taxis) are the only form of public transport still operating between the two countries. They operate from Place Sidi Bou Mendil in the Tunis medina to Annaba (TD18) and Constantine (TD25).

Libya

Tunisia was Libya's lifeline to the outside world during the air embargo imposed on Libya over the 1992 Lockerbie bombing. The embargo may be over, but the road from Tunis to Tripoli remains as busy as ever.

For a tourist, the main obstacle is obtaining a visa. It's difficult for an individual to get a visa; the best approach is to use a tour company specialising in trips to Libya.

Border Crossings The main crossing point is at Ras Ajdir, on the coast 33km east of Ben Guerdane. There's another border crossing in the south between Dehiba (Tunisia) and Wazin, but Libyan immigration officials have a habit of sending people back up to Ras Ajdir.

Bus There are daily buses to Tripoli from the southern bus station in Tunis, departing at 5 pm. The trip costs TD26.420 and takes from 14 to 16 hours. There are also daily services from Sfax (TD16.130, 10 to 12 hours).

Louage Louages are faster and more convenient than the buses. There are regular services to Tripoli from many Tunisian towns, including Tunis, Sfax, Gabès, Medenine, Houmt Souq and Ben Guerdane. The louages that work these routes are yellow with a white stripe.

SEA
Departure Tax
There is no departure tax when leaving the country. A TD2 port tax is included in the price of ferry tickets.

France
Both CTN and French company SNCM operate all year round between Marseille and Tunis. Between them there are at least two ferries a week, even in the middle of winter. There are sailings almost every day between late June and the middle of November. The boats are usually packed, so you will need to book well ahead if you want to take a vehicle across. The trip costs 900FF one way and 1620FF return and takes 24 hours. Small vehicles cost 1980FF one way and 3160FF return.

SNCM also operates a weekly service from Bastia, on the island of Corsica, between late May and mid-September.

For more information about these services and bookings, contact the following shipping agents:

Compagnie Tunisienne de Navigation
Tunis: (☎ 01-322 775/802, fax 354 855) 122 Rue de Yougoslavie, Tunis
Marseille: (☎ 04 91 56 32 00, fax 04 91 56 36 36) 61 Blvd des Dames, Marseille
SNCM
(☎ 01-330 636) 47 Ave Farhat Hached, Tunis
Southern Ferries
(☎ 020-7491 4968) 5th floor, 179 Piccadilly, London W1V 9DB

Italy
There are year-round ferry connections between Tunis and the Italian ports of Genoa, La Spezia, Naples and Trapani (in Sicily). The ferries are heavily booked in summer, so it is essential to book well in advance if you want to take a car or camper van across

to Tunisia. Unless otherwise stated, the fares that are quoted here are for one-way travel in economy class, which gets you an aircraft-type reclining seat. There are all sorts of discounts available, starting from about 15% on return tickets. Children aged under four travel free, and children aged four to 15 are charged half. Students (with cards) aged 15 to 25 also qualify for discounts of up to 50%.

For more information about these services and bookings, contact the following shipping agents:

Compagnie Tunisienne de Navigation
(☎ 01-322 775/802, fax 354 855) 122 Rue de Yougoslavie, Tunis 1000
Lauro Lines
Tunis: (☎ 01-347 015, fax 330 902,
ⓔ carthage.tours@gnet.tn) Carthage Tours, 59 Ave Habib Bourguiba, Tunis 1001
La Spezia: (0187-507 031, fax 509 255) Ufficio Imbarco, Molo 48
Naples: (☎ 081-551 3352, fax 552 4329,
ⓔ prenotazioni@lauro.it) Piazza Municipio 88, *Trapani:* (☎/fax 0923-24073) Ufficio Imbarco, Statione Marittima, Trapani
Tirrenia Navigazione
Trapani: (☎ 0923-21896) Salvo Viaggi, Corso Italia 48
Genoa: (☎ 010-275 8041, fax 269 82 55) Stazione Marittima Ponte Colombo
Southern Ferries
(☎ 020-7491 4968) 5th floor, 179 Piccadilly, London W1V 9DB
Viamare Travel
(☎ 020-7431 4560) Graphic House, 2 Sumatra Road, London NW6 1PU

Trapani-Tunis Both Lauro Lines and Tirrenia Navigazione operate between Trapani and Tunis.

Lauro Lines sails at least once a week, although the day varies. The trip costs from L60,000 in low season to L100,000 in high season and takes 10 hours. Small cars cost from L150,000 to L180,000.

The trip costs from L80,500 to L94,500 and takes eight hours with Tirrenia. The boat leaves Trapani at 10 am on Monday morning and Tunis at 9 pm the same day.

Naples-Tunis Lauro Lines operates at least one boat a week on this route. The trip costs from L120,000 to L180,000 and takes 17 hours.

Genoa-Tunis The route between Tunis and the northern Italian port of Genoa is operated by CTN. The frequency of services ranges from four a month in winter to 13 a month in July and August. The trip costs L230,000 one way and takes between 22 and 24 hours.

La Spezia-Tunis Lauro runs a weekly service between Tunis and La Spezia, about 100km south-east of Genoa. One-way fares range from L130,000 to L190,000.

ORGANISED TOURS

Nearly every European country has travel companies specialising in hotel and air fare packages to Tunisia. British operators have some of the cheapest deals.

In addition to the standard package tours, a number of operators run specialist tours, ranging from archaeology tours of the ancient sites to bird-watching, golfing and even thalassotherapy tours. They tend to be at the upper end of the price range and itineraries are quite tight, leaving little time for roaming around on your own. But if your time is short and purse deep, they may be the deal for you.

The following information is intended as a guide only and is not a recommendation of these operators over others. Examples of specialist tours from the UK to Tunisia include:

Archaeology
Andante Travels (☎ 01980-610 555) The Old Telephone Exchange, Winterbourne Dauntsey, Salisbury SP4 6EH. Offers an eight-day accompanied archaeological tour of Carthage and northern Tunisia and a 14-day tour that includes the south.
Martin Randall Travel (☎ 020-8742 3355) 10 Barley Mow Passage, Chiswick, London W4 4PH. Has eight-day accompanied tours of the main Roman sites.
Prospect Music and Art Tours (☎ 020-8995 2151) 454–458 Chiswick High Rd, London W4 5TT. Does an eight-day accompanied cultural tour, including the main Roman sites as well as Tunis and Monastir, for UK£995.

The British Museum Traveller (☎ 020-7436 7575) 46 Bloomsbury St, London WC1 3QQ. Offers an eight-day Christmas tour.

Bird-Watching
Branta Travel (☎ 020-7635 5812) 7 Wingfield St, London SE15 4LN. Runs bird-watching tours to Lake Ichkeul and the south.

Camel Trekking
Explore Worldwide (☎ 01252-319 448, 344 161) 1 Frederick St, Aldershot, Hants GU11 1LQ. Offers a 15-day tour combining camel trekking with visits to a selection of ancient sites.

Diving
Aquatours (☎ 020-8398 0505) Shelletts House, Angel Rd, Ditton, Surrey KT7 0AU. Organises diving trips to Tabarka.

Golf
Club Golf (☎ 01293-723 134) British Airways Holidays, Astral Towers, Betts Way, London Rd, Crawley, West Sussex RH10 2XA. This company offers a choice of golfing destinations: Hammamet, Jerba and Port el-Kantaoui (Sousse).
Longshot Golf Holidays (☎ 01730-230 370) Meon House, College St, Petersfield, Hants GU32 3JN. Specialises in packages to Hammamet.

Warning

The information in this chapter is particularly vulnerable to change: Prices for international travel are volatile, routes are introduced and cancelled, schedules change, special deals come and go, and rules and visa requirements are amended. Airlines and governments seem to take a perverse pleasure in making price structures and regulations as complicated as possible. You should check directly with the airline or a travel agent to make sure you understand how a fare (and ticket you may buy) works. In addition, the travel industry is highly competitive, there are many lurks and perks.

The upshot of this is that you should get opinions, quotes and advice from as many airlines and travel agents as possible before you part with your hard-earned cash. The details given in this chapter should be regarded as pointers and are not a substitute for your own careful, up-to-date research.

Thalassotherapy
Aspects of Tunisia (☎ 020-7836 4999) 9 Kingsway, London WC2B 6YF. Has a choice of holidays based on spa hotel accommodation.

The London office of the Tunisian National Tourist Office (☎ 020-7224 5561, fax 224 4053), 77A Wigmore St, maintains an extensive list of all UK companies offering holidays in Tunisia. The office can assist in a variety of other ways, too. See the Tourist Offices section in the Facts for the Visitor chapter for a list of addresses.

Getting Around

Tunisia has a well-developed transport network. It's a small country, and just about every town of any consequence has daily connections with the capital, Tunis.

For most of the year public transport copes easily with the demand, but things get pretty hectic during the school holidays in August and September and on public holidays. At these times, book ahead if possible.

AIR

Tunisia's domestic air network is fairly limited – there just aren't many places that are far enough from Tunis to warrant catching a plane.

Domestic flights are operated by Tunis Air subsidiary Tuninter, which uses the strangely inappropriate flight code UG. It operates to a summer timetable from April to October, and to a slightly curtailed winter schedule for the rest of the year. Four airports service domestic routes: Tunis, Jerba, Sfax and Tozeur. There are no domestic flights to either Monastir or Tabarka.

By far the most popular route is between Tunis and Jerba, with seven flights a day each way in summer and six in winter. There are also five flights a week between Tunis and Tozeur, stopping at Gafsa on the way, and four a week between Tunis and Sfax. See the table 'Domestic Flight Routes & Fares' for details.

BUS
National Buses

The national bus company, the Société Nationale du Transport Rural et Interurbain, is always referred to as SNTRI – pronounced 'sintry'. It operates daily air-conditioned buses from Tunis to just about every town in the country. The frequency of services ranges from one bus a day to small towns to 10 a day to major cities like Sousse and Sfax. The green-and-white buses run pretty much to schedule, and they're fast, comfortable and not too expensive. Sample one-way fares from Tunis include TD6.220 to Sousse, TD10.810 to Sfax and TD17.420 to Tozeur.

In summer, many of the long-distance departures are at night to avoid the heat of the day, which means you don't get to see any of the country you are travelling through. It's a good idea to book in advance at this time, especially if you are planning to leave from Tunis.

All buses originating or terminating in Tunis stop en route to pick up and set down passengers, so you don't have to be going all the way to or from Tunis to use them. If you pick one up en route, however, there is no guarantee that seats will be available.

For details of intercity bus services, see the Getting There & Away sections for individual towns and cities.

Regional Buses

In addition to the national company, SNTRI, there are regional bus companies operating services within a particular region and to nearby cities outside the region. They often also operate services to Tunis.

These buses are reliable enough, but most are getting on a bit; they are also slow and are never air-conditioned. Coverage of routes is good and services are frequent enough to meet demand most of the time.

Domestic Flight Routes & Fares

route	frequency	duration	fares (TD; one way/return)
Tunis to Jerba	daily (summer)	1 hour	51.200/100.700
Tunis to Tozeur	5/week	1 hour	49.200/93.200
Tunis to Sfax	4/week	45 minutes	43.200/84.200
Tunis to Gafsa	2/week	40 minutes	42.700/85.200

Booking in advance is both impossible and unnecessary. The only way to be sure of bus schedules is to go to the bus station and ask. Most depots do not have timetables displayed; those that do, have them in Arabic only – with the exception of Houmt Souq on Jerba. The bulk of departures tend to be early in the day. If seeking directions to the bus station, ask for the *gare routière*.

One catch to be aware of is that some towns are served by two or three regional companies. They generally share depots, but in some places (eg, Tabarka) each company has its own, so always ask if there is more than one company in town. Officials from one company never know about the schedules of another.

LOUAGE

Louages are long-distance taxis offering a parallel service to buses. Whereas buses leave to a timetable, louages leave when they're full. Drivers stand by their vehicles and call out their destinations. They seldom take long to fill up. Louages are the fastest way to get around, and the fares are only slightly higher than bus fares. In most towns, the louage 'station' is close to, or combined with, the bus station, enabling you to choose between the services.

Most of the vehicles are Peugeot or Renault station wagons with an extra bench seat in the back. They are licensed to carry five passengers. There are also a growing number of 'people mover' vans operating on the busiest routes. These vans are licensed to carry eight passengers. These limits are strictly adhered to. Fares are quoted *par place* (per person). There are no discounts for children.

There are two types of louage. The majority of louages are white with a red stripe, which means they are licensed to operate nationwide. Some are white with a blue stripe, which means they are licensed to operate only within their local government area. The town name on the roof of each louage indicates where it's licensed, which is not necessarily where it's going.

At larger louage stations, there's always someone calling out destinations and di-

recting people to louages. A foreigner is sure to be asked their destination and given assistance. It's often a good idea to ask the fare before you get in. If you think you are being ripped off, ask to see the list of tariffs (set by the government) that all drivers are required to carry.

At certain times, particularly during summer, public transport is in high demand and competition for seats in louages can be fierce. You may find it necessary to be fairly ruthless when it comes to the battle for a seat or you will simply not get a ride. The tactic is to grab onto a door handle as the louage arrives. Fortunately, this situation does not arise very often.

CAMIONNETTE

Between small towns, *camionnettes*, or pick-ups, are the usual means of transport. You will normally be expected to pay the equivalent of the bus fare. Try to establish what the locals are paying before you pay.

TRAIN

Trains are run by the Société Nationale des Chemins de Fer Tunisiens (SNCFT). The rail network is a long way short of comprehensive. What there is, however, is modern and efficient – and the trains run on time.

The main train line runs north–south between Tunis and Gabès, via Sousse and Sfax. There are at least eight trains a day as far as Sousse, six to Sfax and three to Gabès. One train per day branches off at Mahrès, south of Sfax, to Gafsa and Metlaoui. There are also lines to Bizerte, via Mateur; Ghardimao (near the Algerian border), via Jendouba; and Kalaat Khasba (halfway between Le Kef and Kasserine).

Cap Bon is serviced by a branch line between Bir Bou Regba and Nabeul, while the Metro du Sahel network operates south from Sousse to Monastir and Mahdia. Both these lines are linked to the main north–south line and offer at least one direct train to Tunis daily. Other rail lines shown on maps are for freight only.

Passenger trains offer three classes: 2nd, 1st and *confort*. Second class costs about the same as a bus, and is normally packed – with everything from people and produce to livestock. It's a circus that can be fun to experience for a short journey. Unless you get on at the point of origin, there's little chance of finding a seat.

You're better off travelling 1st class, which costs about 40% more than 2nd class. There are reclining, upholstered seats, and every chance of actually sitting in one. Confort costs a bit more again, but doesn't offer much more than 1st class apart from a smaller, slightly more exclusive compartment. Most mainline trains have a restaurant car, which sends out a regular supply of sandwiches, soft drinks and coffee.

See the Getting There & Away sections for more details of fares and timetables for cities and towns.

For train enthusiasts, the *Lezard Rouge* (Red Lizard) is a restored beylical train that runs between Metlaoui and Redeyef daily, offering great views of the Seldja Gorge. For more details, see the Around Gafsa section in the Southern Tunisia chapter.

CAR & MOTORCYCLE

Tunisia has an excellent road network. All but the most minor roads are tar sealed and

well maintained. Potholes are almost unheard of. Many of the roads which are marked as unsealed on maps have now been sealed, particularly in the south where the army has heavily involved itself in the road-building effort.

There is one *péage* (toll road) in Tunisia – the new A1 expressway between Tunis and Msaken, south of Sousse. The trip costs TD2.200 by car. At the time of writing, there were plans to extend the system north to Bizerte and south to Sfax and Gabès.

There are still a lot of unsealed roads in the south, but these are graded regularly and can usually be negotiated easily enough with a conventional 2WD vehicle.

Tunisian drivers are generally well behaved, and drive fairly predictably and safely. For someone used to driving in Western Europe, the worst thing is not the cars but the moped riders, who weave suicidally in and out of traffic, and pedestrians, who think they have an inalienable right to walk on the road regardless of traffic conditions.

There are police and National Guard checkpoints all over the country. Officials are not normally too bothered with checking foreigners, but it's best to make sure you have your passport handy at all times.

Road Distances (km)

	Bizerte	Gabès	Gafsa	Houmt Souq	Kairouan	Nabeul	Sfax	Sousse	Tabarka	Tataouine	Tozeur	Tunis
Bizerte	---											
Gabès	375	---										
Gafsa	409	149	---									
Houmt Souq	547	106	255	---								
Kairouan	220	215	209	321	---							
Nabeul	130	357	323	463	114	---						
Sfax	332	137	197	243	136	220	---					
Sousse	208	264	277	132	68	96	127	---				
Tabarka	147	496	347	602	277	239	441	317	---			
Tataouine	563	122	271	118	337	479	259	259	672	---		
Tozeur	502	242	93	348	302	416	290	370	440	364	---	
Tunis	66	375	343	481	154	64	266	142	175	497	436	---

Road Rules

The road rules in Tunisia are much the same as in continental Europe. You drive on the right and overtake on the left. The speed limits are 50km/h in built-up areas and 90km/h on the open road. The only exception is on the toll road from Tunis to Sousse, where the speed limit is 110km/h.

The regulation that causes the most problems for tourists is the one giving priority to traffic coming from the right in built-up areas. This also extends to roundabouts, where you are obliged to give way to traffic approaching from the right even if you are already at the roundabout.

The special intersections for turning left off major roads are another curiosity of Tunisian driving. Instead of using a turning lane in the centre of the road, the Tunisian system involves a special lane leading off to the right which loops back and crosses the main road at right angles. It can be very confusing if you're driving along looking for a sign pointing to the left – and then find a sign telling you to turn right!

Tunisia seems to have a lot of traffic police, and the road rules are strictly enforced – for locals anyway. It's almost unheard of for a tourist to be booked – unless the infringement causes an accident, when the police are obliged to act. The rest of the time they are unlikely to do more than check your driving licence and passport, which you should carry with you at all times.

Rental

Hire cars can be a great way to see the country in more detail, but they are so expensive that they're not a realistic option unless you have a fat wallet or are travelling in a small group.

Typical rental charges for the smallest cars (Renault Express or Citroen C15) start at about TD25 per day plus 250 mills per kilometre. It is cheaper to take one of the unlimited kilometre deals, which start at about TD350 per week. On top of these rates you'll have to pay 17% tax, insurance at about TD10 per day, contract fees etc. Medium-sized cars (Renault Clio or VW Polo) cost about TD35 per day plus 350 mills per kilometre, or TD420 per week with unlimited kilometres.

Some companies also have 4WDs. Reckon on TD75 per day plus 750 mills per kilometre for a Toyota Land Cruiser, or TD1200 per week.

You'll have little option but to pay these prices in summer when demand is at its highest, but there's plenty of scope for bargaining at other times. You'll find the best deals at local companies, which have more scope for negotiation. In winter, it should be possible to find someone willing to hire a Renault Clio for less than TD300 per week. Tunis and Houmt Souq on Jerba, are the best places to look for bargains.

All the major international operators have offices in the larger towns – see under individual town entries for addresses of local and international car-rental companies. Rental conditions are fairly straightforward. If you are paying by cash, a deposit of roughly the equivalent of the rental is required. Credit cards don't have the same restriction.

Rental companies require that drivers be aged over 21 and hold a driving licence that has been valid for at least a year.

When you hire the car, make sure that an accident report form has been included with the car's papers. If you have an accident while driving a hire car, both parties involved must complete the form. If the form is not completed, you may be liable for the costs, regardless of whether you have paid for insurance or not.

Fuel Prices

Fuel is inexpensive by European standards and prices are the same everywhere: 395 mills per litre for diesel, 670 mills per litre for super (high octane), 635 mills per litre for regular (low octane) and 650 mills per litre for two-stroke mix. Unleaded fuel (690 mills per litre) is still something of a rarity outside the major towns.

Licence Requirements

To drive a car or motorcycle of more than 50cc, you must be over 21 and hold a valid licence in your country of residence or an international driving permit.

Automobile Clubs

The Touring Club de Tunisie (☎ 01-323 114, fax 324 834), 15 Rue d'Allemagne, Tunis 1000, has a reciprocal rights arrangement with many European automobile clubs, including the UK's Automobile Association. If your car conks out, they can direct you to an affiliated breakdown service.

Motorcycle Rental

The short distances and good road conditions make motorcycles an ideal mode of transport. Unfortunately, there is only one motorcycle rental agency in the country – Raïs Rentals in Houmt Souq on Jerba – and it handles nothing bigger than 80cc scooters. No licence or insurance is required for a moped, but to rent a machine of more than 50cc you need to be over 21 and to have held a valid motorcycle licence for more than one year.

If you are bringing your own motorcycle, make sure you carry some basic spare parts. These are virtually impossible to find within the country; few people in Tunisia own motorcycles.

BICYCLE

Cycling is an inexpensive, healthy, environmentally sound and, above all, fun way of travelling – and Tunisia is a country that is developing a good reputation as a destination for cycling fans.

Cycling can be an excellent way to see the country, providing you pick the right time of year. It's too hot in summer and it can get very cold in winter in the north, but for the rest of the year conditions are ideal.

It's possible to put a bike on the train if you want to skip a long stretch or get yourself back to Tunis. All louages are equipped with roof racks and can also carry bikes.

If you want a decent touring bike, you should bring your own. Bicycles pose few problems for airlines. You can take it to pieces and put it in a bike bag or box, but it's much easier simply to wheel your bike to the check-in desk, where it should be treated as a piece of baggage. You may have to remove the pedals and turn the handlebars sideways so that it takes up less space in the aircraft's hold; check all this with the airline well in advance.

One note of caution: Before you leave home, go over your bike with a fine-toothed comb and fill your repair kit with every imaginable spare. As with cars and motorcycles, you won't necessarily be able to buy spares for your machine if it breaks down in the middle of nowhere.

There are a few places which rent bicycles, but they are expensive by Tunisian standards. Most charge between TD8 and TD10 per day, and a lot of the bikes are horrible old rattlers that leave you tired and sore at the end of the day. Where possible, check through the bikes to find the best one – and make sure that the brakes work. Hire places seem to be concerned only about whether the bike goes or not and aren't too bothered about how to stop it!

HITCHING

The following information is intended solely as an explanation of how hitching works in Tunisia, not as a recommendation. Although many people do hitch, it is not an entirely safe method of transport and you do so at your own risk. It is strongly recommended that women do not attempt to hitch without a male companion.

Conditions for hitching vary throughout the country. The south is easiest as there is a great deal more tourist traffic – either people who hire cars on Jerba or overlanders heading for Tozeur and the Sahara. You shouldn't have to wait more than a couple of hours for a lift. In the north, people seem less inclined to pick up hitchers, particularly in summer when there are so many tourists in the country.

BOAT

There are two regular scheduled ferry services in the country. The first connects Sfax with the Kerkennah Islands, about 25km off the coast. In summer, there are up to eight crossings daily, dropping to four in winter. The trip takes 1½ hours and costs 570 mills one way for passengers without vehicles. It costs TD4 to take a car across, and you need to get in the queue well before the first departure at 7.30 am to be assured of getting across that morning.

The second service runs from Jorf on the mainland to Ajim on the island of Jerba. The crossing takes 15 minutes and ferries run throughout the day and night. The fare is 600 mills one way for a car. Passengers travel free. See the Jerba section in the Southern Tunisia chapter for more details.

LOCAL TRANSPORT
Most towns are compact enough to get around on foot. The problem comes in summer, when it is too hot to walk far during the day.

Taxis are the best alternative. They can be found in all but the smallest towns and are cheap by European standards. The day rate (tariff A or tariff 1) applies from 5 am to 8 pm; flag fall is 310 mills, and fares work out at about 500 mills per kilometre. At night the flag fall is 480 mills and fares are 50% higher.

Towns without taxis will normally have a camionnette working a specific route or available for charter.

Major towns like Sousse, Sfax and Tunis have local bus networks. Tunis also has a modern (tram) network as well as a suburban train line (TGM) connecting the city centre with the northern suburbs.

Some towns, including Gabès, Houmt Souq, Nabeul and Tozeur, have *calèches* (horse-drawn carriages) for hire. All charge TD10 per hour.

See the Getting Around sections in individual town entries for more details of local transport options.

ORGANISED TOURS
Organised tours are usually a good option if you're short of time. Tours are big business in Tunisia, and locating a tour operator is not difficult. In resort areas, every hotel in the country advertises tours, ranging from half-day local excursions to seven-day nationwide marathons that take

in all the major sites. You can expect to pay about TD30 to TD35 for a half-day tour, TD45 to TD60 for a full-day tour and TD60 to TD80 per day for tours that include accommodation

You won't find tours in Tunis, which apparently doesn't have enough resident tourists. However, the capital city's main attractions – the Bardo Museum, Carthage and the medina – feature prominently among the itineraries offered by tour operators in Cap Bon and Sousse/Monastir.

Tabarka, on the north coast, is the best base for organised tours to the Roman sites of Bulla Regia, Chemtou and Dougga – all of which are difficult to get to by public transport.

Operators in Tozeur specialise in tours to the nearby mountain oases of Chebika, Midès and Tamerza, while the ksour district around Tataouine is easily visited on a day trip from Jerba.

Saharan 4WD safaris are the name of the game everywhere in the south, but the main players are from Douz. They can take you into the Sahara for any length of time, from eight hours to a week. Many of the tours include camel riding and camping in the desert.

These tours take you to some spectacular and otherwise inaccessible (except to about 100 other 4WDs) places, but they generally involve hours bouncing around in the desert crammed in a vehicle with 10 other tourists. See under Douz in the Southern Tunisia chapter for more details.

Ecotours Ecotourism is a relatively new concept in a country where environmental awareness in general remains depressingly low, and guides with a good understanding of ecology are hard to find.

One man to seek out is Tarek Nefzi, whose company Becasse (π 01-960 314, fax 960 249, @ becasse@planet.tn) specialises in small group tours to areas of outstanding natural interest. Tarek is a great bird-watching enthusiast.

See Organised Tours in the Getting There & Away chapter for details of companies operating organised tours to Tunisia.

Tunis

☎ 01 • pop 1.5 million

Tunisia's capital comes as a pleasant surprise to most Western visitors. Compared with the mega-cities found elsewhere in the world, Tunis is little more than a large country town.

The city centre is compact and easy to negotiate, and there are enough attractions to warrant stopping for a few days. The World Heritage–listed *medina* (Arab quarter) is a treasure trove of Islamic architecture dating back more than one thousand years, while the Bardo Museum has a superb collection of Roman mosaics. The ruins of ancient Carthage are situated just a few kilometres north-east of the city, across Lake Tunis.

Tunis is a very liberal city by Islamic standards, and it's an easy place to make the adjustment from west to east. Wandering around the new city, it is hard to tell that you are in a Muslim country, let alone in Africa.

History

Tunis (ancient Tynes) has existed since the earliest days of Carthaginian expansion into the hinterland. The name features on maps of the region dating from the 5th century BC, and the Roman general Regulus camped there in 255 BC during the First Punic War.

The Romans ignored Tunis after the defeat of Carthage, and the name all but disappears from the record books until the arrival of the Arabs at the end of the 7th century AD. After ousting the Byzantines from Carthage in AD 695, the victorious Hassan bin Nooman decided against moving in. He preferred to build again at Tunis, which he deemed to have a better defensive position. The medina was sited on what was then a narrow band of high ground flanked by the Sebkhet Sejoumi (salt lake) to the south-west and Lake Tunis to the east. A special deep-water channel was dug across shallow Lake Tunis to give the city proper access to the sea.

Highlights

- Marvelling at the world's finest collection of Roman mosaics at the Bardo Museum
- Browsing through the colourful *souqs* and studying the fine Islamic architecture of the *medina*
- Admiring the views over the site of ancient Carthage from the top of the Byrsa Hill
- Exploring Sidi Bou Saïd's cobbled streets, white-washed houses and blue-painted window grills

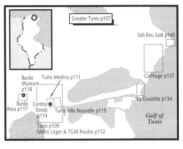

The birth of the city can be dated to the building of the Zitouna (Great) Mosque in AD 732, although it wasn't until the 9th century, when Aghlabid ruler Ibrahim ibn Ahmed II moved his court to Tunis, that it became the seat of power.

It fell from favour under the Fatimids, who chose Mahdia as their capital in the 10th century, but escaped the subsequent ravages of the Hilalian invasion in the 11th century. It emerged once again as the capital following the conquest of North Africa by the Almohads in 1160.

The city flourished under the Hafsids, who ruled from 1229 to 1574 – a period regarded as the city's golden age. The population more than tripled (to about 60,000) during this time. *Souqs* (markets), mosques and *medersas* (Quranic schools) were built, trade with

Louis IX & the Eighth Crusade

The arrival of the eighth and final Crusade at Tunis on 18 July 1270 was one of the stranger episodes in Tunisian history. The Crusades had been going on for the best part of 200 years by this time, and people had become increasingly cynical about the motivation behind them. The noblemen who led these assaults on the Holy Land appeared to be more interested in getting rich than in religion.

This was confirmed once and for all by the Tunis venture, which was basically a scam organised by Charles of Anjou, younger brother of the French saint-king, Louis IX. Charles was King of Sicily, and thought that North Africa would make a nice little addition to his domains. Louis, for his part, had long been planning to send another Crusade to atone for the disasters of the Seventh Crusade, which had been all but wiped out by the Mamluk armies in Egypt. Charles managed to persuade him that Tunis was a better target than Jerusalem. He explained that the Hafsid ruler of Tunis, El-Mustansir, was prepared, given a nudge, to convert to the cross, and painted a picture of a Christian North Africa harking back to the days of St Augustine.

The Crusade was a fiasco from start to finish. Everything was ready to roll by the beginning of 1270, but Louis spent so long stopping at monasteries to pray that his troops started fighting among themselves. It was July before the fleet finally set out from France. The Crusaders landed without much trouble, but soon discovered that it's too hot to do anything in Tunisia in summer – let alone dress up in armour and fight. The residents of Tunis simply withdrew behind their walls and watched as the crazy foreigners wilted in the heat. By the end of August, the crusading army was in tatters, enfeebled by the sun, lack of water and the effects of poor sanitation. By the time Charles showed up with reinforcements, Louis IX was on his deathbed. Charles succeeded in making his troops look sufficiently threatening to extract a payment of 94,500kg of gold from El-Mustansir and headed home, running into a crashing storm on the way.

Europe flourished and one of the great Islamic universities was established in the heart of the medina at the Zitouna Mosque.

Tunis suffered badly during a power struggle between the Ottoman Turks and Spain that gave rise to the unseating of the Hafsids. Much of the city was destroyed and the population fled as the city changed hands repeatedly. Tunis was finally secured for the Ottomans by Sinan Pasha in 1574, and the population began to return. Their number was swollen by the arrival of large numbers of Andalusian refugees fleeing religious persecution in Spain, and a similar exodus of Jews from Livorno in Italy. The newcomers included many fine artisans, who played an important role in the rebuilding of the city.

The medina remained very much the centre of things until the arrival of the French in 1881. The French wasted no time in stamping their influence on the place, building their Ville Nouvelle (new town) directly to the east of the medina on land reclaimed from Lake Tunis.

This new city, laid out on a grid, is very much the heart of modern Tunis; it has a distinctly European feel, with its wide main boulevard, street cafes and some fine examples of 1920s colonial architecture.

Orientation

Few cities in the world are as easy to negotiate as Tunis. Almost everything of importance to travellers is within the compact Ville Nouvelle, and the straight-forward grid layout makes it hard to get lost.

The main thoroughfare of the Ville Nouvelle is Ave Habib Bourguiba, which runs east-west from Lake Tunis to Place de l'Indépendance. Ave Habib Bourguiba is lined with an assortment of banks, cinemas, hotels, travel agencies, restaurants, patisseries and fast-food joints, and the shady, tree-filled central strip is a favourite spot for well-dressed Tunisians to strut their stuff.

The western extension of Ave Habib Bourguiba between Place de l'Indépendance and the medina is Ave de France. It terminates in front of the Bab Bhar, also known as the Porte de France. This huge freestanding arch was once the eastern gateway to the medina – until the surrounding walls were demolished to create Place de la Victoire. The two main streets of the medina lead off the western side of this square: Rue de la Kasbah cuts straight through the medina to Place du Gouvernement, while Rue Jemaa Zitouna leads to the Zitouna Mosque.

A causeway at the eastern end of Ave Habib Bourguiba carries road and light-rail traffic east across Lake Tunis to the port suburb of La Goulette, and then north along the coast to the affluent beach suburbs of Carthage, Sidi Bou Saïd and La Marsa. The lake itself is not a thing of beauty, although in November and December there are often small flocks of pink flamingos on the edge of the causeway.

The main north-south thoroughfare of the Ville Nouvelle is the street known as Ave de Carthage to the south of Ave Habib Bour-

guiba and as Ave de Paris to the north. Ave de Carthage runs east to Place Barcelone, hub of the city's excellent *métro léger* (tram network). The train station is on the southern side of the square. Ave de Paris leads to a chaotic five-way intersection known as Place de la République. République station, on the northern side of this intersection, is another important stop on the métro léger network (see Getting Around later in this chapter).

Maps The tourist office hands out a good, free map of Tunis. The best maps are produced by the Office de la Topographie et de la Cartographie (☎ 891 477, fax 797 539). Its titles include *Tunis – Ariana/Bardo*, which covers the city centre, and *La Marsa, Sidi Bou Saïd, Carthage & La Goulette*, which covers the coastal suburbs. Both are on a scale of 1:10,000 and cost TD6.

These maps can be hard to track down in bookshops. You'll find the full series at the OTC office on Ave Mohammed Ali Akid,

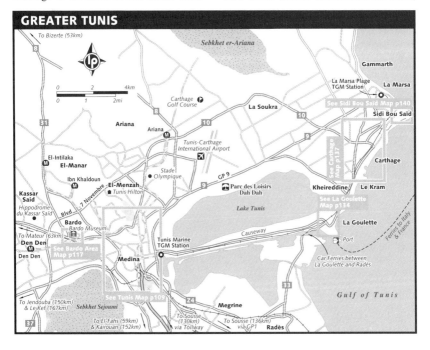

about 5km north of the city centre near the junction of Ave du Grand Maghreb. The sales office is open from 8.30 am to noon and 2 to 4 pm weekdays.

Information

Tourist Offices The tourist office (☎ 341 077) is on the corner of Ave Habib Bourguiba and Ave Mohammed V, just north of Place du 7 Novembre 1987, with its large roundabout and clock tower. This is the head office of the tourist authority, but the service is largely restricted to handing out glossy brochures full of flowery descriptions of places of interest. The office does, however, hand out a good map of Tunis and useful brochures on the medina and Carthage. The staff speak English, German and Italian – as well as French and Arabic.

The office is open from 8 am to 1.30 pm in summer and from 8 am to noon and 3 to 6 pm in winter Monday to Saturday. It's closed Sunday and public holidays.

There is another branch of the tourist office at the train station; it hands out train timetables, among other things. Yet another branch can be found on the mezzanine level at the airport.

Money There are branches of all the major banks on Ave Habib Bourguiba. The branch of the STB next to the Hôtel Africa Méridien is open to 6 pm daily, including weekends, for foreign exchange.

Most banks have ATMs. Some also have automatic exchange machines for banknotes; these include the branch of the UIB on the corner of Ave Habib Bourguiba and Rue de Hollande and the Banque de l'Habitat on the corner of Ave Habib Bourguiba and Ave de Paris.

There are also banks and ATMs at the airport, including a branch of the STB inside the arrivals hall before customs. It is supposed to be open to meet all incoming flights, but if you arrive late at night you will probably have to wait for someone to come and open it up.

American Express (AmEx) is represented by Carthage Tours (☎ 347 015, fax 352 740), 59 Ave Habib Bourguiba.

Post & Communications The main post office (PTT) is the cavernous old building on Rue Charles de Gaulle, between Rue d'Espagne and Rue d'Angleterre. The poste restante counter is well organised, but it will hold mail for two weeks only. There is a charge of 200 mills for each letter.

For most of the year, the post office is open from 8 am to 6 pm Monday to Saturday and from 9 to 11 am Sunday. The exception is during July and August, when it's open from 7.30 am to 1.30 pm Monday to Saturday and closed Sunday. There are plenty of Taxiphone offices around town.

Email & Internet Access There are Publinet offices opposite the tourist office at 28 Ave Habib Bourguiba, and next to République métro léger station at 70 Ave Jean Jaurès.

Travel Agencies There are lots of travel agencies around the city centre. Carthage Tours (☎ 347 015, fax 352 740) and Transtours (☎ 346 035, fax 347 782), at 14 Ave de Carthage, are two of the biggest.

Bookshops There are very few places that stock English-language books. For novels, try Librairie Claire Fontaine, just off Ave Habib Bourguiba at 14 Rue d'Alger. It has a small English-language section that includes the Penguin Classics. Espace Diwan 9, 9 Rue Sidi ben Arous, has a good selection of books about Tunisia. Rue Sidi ben Arous runs north from the Zitouna Mosque in the centre of the medina.

The second-hand bookshop on Rue d'Angleterre, opposite the main post office, has some books in English. Most of them are trash, but there's the odd decent novel among them. The owner also buys books.

International Newspapers & Magazines The stalls in the middle of Ave Habib Bourguiba stock English newspapers (such as the *Times*, the *Guardian*, the *Sun* and the *Sunday Times)* as well as the *International Herald Tribune*, *USA Today*, *Time* and *Newsweek*. They also sell Italian, German and French newspapers.

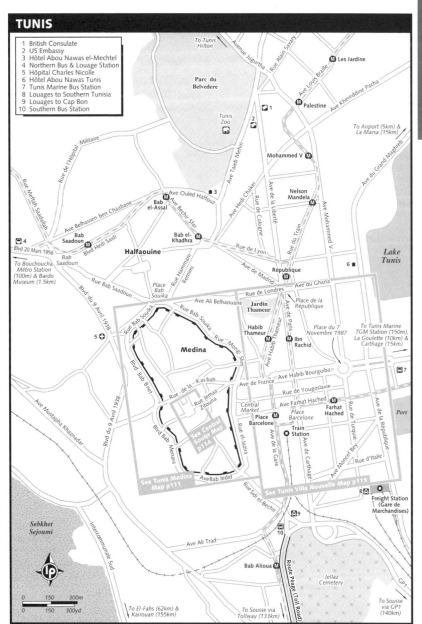

TUNIS

1 British Consulate
2 US Embassy
3 Hôtel Abou Nawas el-Mechtel
4 Northern Bus & Louage Station
5 Hôpital Charles Nicolle
6 Hôtel Abou Nawas Tunis
7 Tunis Marine Bus Station
8 Louages to Southern Tunisia
9 Louages to Cap Bon
10 Southern Bus Station

To Tunis Hilton

Avenue Jugurtha

Rue Alain Savary

Les Jardine

Ave Louis Braille

Ave Khereddine Pacha

Parc du Belvedere

Palestine

Ave Hedi Chaker

Tunis Zoo

Ave Taieb Mehiri

To Airport (5km) & La Marsa (15km)

Mohammed V

Ave du Grand Maghreb

Ave Ouled Haffouz

Bab el-Assal

Ave Bechir Sfar

Rue de la Liberté

Rue de Cologne

Nelson Mandela

Ave Mohammed V.

Rue de l'Hôpital Militaire

Rue Metlah Saadallah

Ave Belhassen ben Chaabane

Bab Saadoun

Bab el-Khadhra

Blvd Hedi Saïdi

Rue du Train

Lake Tunis

Blvd 20 Mars 1956

Bab Saadoun

Halfaouine

Rue de Lyon

To Bouchoucha Métro Station (100m) & Bardo Museum (1.5km)

Rue Bab Saadoun

Rue Hammam Remmi

Place Bab Souika

Ave de Madrid

République

Ave de Ghana

Blvd du 9 Avril 1938

Ave Ali Belhaouane

Rue de Londres

Jardin Thameur

Place de la République

Rue Bab Souika

Rue Bab Souika

Habib Thameur

Ave de Paris

Place du 7 Novembre 1987

To Tunis Marine TGM Station (150m), La Goulette (10km) & Carthage (15km)

Medina

Rue Monji Slim

Ave Habib Thameur

Ibn Rachid

Rue de la Kasbah

Ave Habib Bourguiba

Blvd Bab Bnet

Ave de France

Rue de Yougoslavie

Ave Mustapha Khaznadar

Rue Jemaa Zitouna

Central Market

Ave Farhat Hached

Farhat Hached

Port

Ave de la République

Blvd du 9 Avril 1938

Place Barcelone

Place Barcelone

Rue de Turquie

Blvd Bab Menara

Rue el-Jazira

Train Station

Ave de la Gare

Ave de Carthage

Ave Moncef Bey

Rue d'Italie

See Central Souqs Map p114

See Tunis Medina Map p111

Ave Bab Jedid

Rue Sidi el-Bechir

See Tunis Ville Nouvelle Map p115

Freight Station (Gare de Marchandises)

Sebkhet Sejoumi

Intercommunale Sud

Ave Ali Trad

Bab Alioua

Route Peage (Toll Road)

Jellaz Cemetery

0   150   300m
0   150   300yd

To El-Fahs (62km) & Kairouan (155km)

To Sousse via Tollway (133km)

To Sousse via GP1 (140km)

GP1

Cultural Centres The British Council, next to the British embassy on Place de la Victoire, has a good library. Visitors can go in and browse, but you need to become a member before you can borrow books. It's not worth the trouble unless you're a resident in Tunis.

The US Cultural Center, at 14 Rue Yahia Ibn Omar, requires visitors to become a member before they can come in and browse. You'll need your passport and a couple of passport photos. The Goethe Institut (☎ 799 131) is at 14 Rue Ibn Jazzar and the Centre Culturel Français (☎ 783 355) is at 87 Ave de la Liberté. Both host exhibitions and cultural events, which are advertised in the French-language newspapers.

Laundry The Lavarie Tahar, 15 Rue d'Allemagne, charges TD5.500 to wash and dry 5kg of clothes, which are returned neatly folded.

Film & Photography There are numerous shops in the city centre that sell and process print film. Typical prices are TD2 for developing plus 80 mills for each 10cm x 15cm print.

Emergency The following phone numbers may be useful in case of emergency:

Ambulance & Doctor	☎ 341 250
Hôpital Charles Nicolle	☎ 662 275
Poisons Centre	☎ 245 075
Police & Fire Brigade	☎ 197

The inside back pages of the local papers, *La Presse*, *Le Temps* and *Tunisia News*, all have the addresses and phone numbers of late-night chemists.

Lost passports and travellers cheques etc should be reported to the police as soon as possible. The nearest police station to the central hotel district is on Rue Jamel Abdelnasser, just south of the PTT building. A couple of the officers speak English. Be sure to ask for a copy of the police report. You should report the loss of your passport to your embassy. Lost travellers cheques should be reported to the company con-

cerned – see Money earlier in this section for information about AmEx.

Dangers & Annoyances Tunis is a very safe city. The only annoyance worth mentioning is the touts working for some of the carpet dealers in the medina. They have some ingenious lines to lure potential customers into their employers' clutches. The touts who hang around the Zitouna Mosque, for example, will ask if you would like a roof-top view of the mosque. It sounds innocent enough – until you realise that getting to the rooftop entails walking through a carpet shop! Travel writer Paul Theroux came away very impressed by his encounter with a Tunis carpet tout, and wrote about it at length in *The Pillars of Hercules*.

It's easy enough to turn down the touts, who are normally polite and (apparently) helpful, but the carpet dealers can be very hard to shake once you step through their doors.

Medina

The medina is the historical and cultural heart of the modern city of Tunis and is the ideal place to get a feel for the Tunisian way of life.

It was founded at the end of the 7th century AD (shortly after the Arab conquest), and was the focal point of the city for more than one thousand years – until the arrival of the French in 1881.

The development of the Ville Nouvelle deprived the medina of its role as a commercial centre and it slipped into steady decline. Less than 15,000 people live in the medina today, and souvenir shops provide the main commercial activity – catering for the thousands of tourists who pour through here each summer.

Large parts of the northern section of the medina were demolished in the 1930s and 1940s under a program of slum demolition that was designed to create vehicle access to the medina. Fortunately, the demolition days are over and conservation is now the order of the day. The conservation effort is led by the Association de Sauvegarde de la Medina (☎ 560 896, fax 560 965), based at the Dar

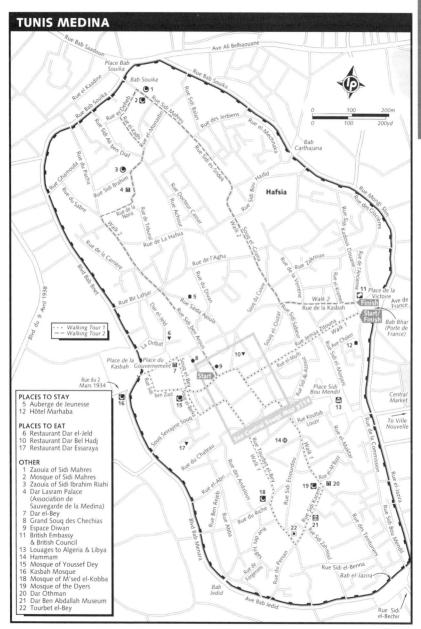

TUNIS MEDINA

PLACES TO STAY
5 Auberge de Jeunesse
12 Hôtel Marhaba

PLACES TO EAT
6 Restaurant Dar el-Jeld
10 Restaurant Dar Bel Hadj
17 Restaurant Dar Essaraya

OTHER
1 Zaouia of Sidi Mahres
2 Mosque of Sidi Mahres
3 Zaouia of Sidi Ibrahim Riahi
4 Dar Lasram Palace
    (Association de
    Sauvegarde de la Medina)
7 Dar el-Bey
8 Grand Souq des Chechias
9 Espace Diwan
11 British Embassy
    & British Council
13 Louages to Algeria & Libya
14 Hammam
15 Mosque of Youssef Dey
16 Kasbah Mosque
18 Mosque of M'sed el-Kobba
19 Mosque of the Dyers
20 Dar Othman
21 Dar Ben Abdallah Museum
22 Tourbet el-Bey

··· Walking Tour 1
--- Walking Tour 2

Lasram Palace, 24 Rue du Tribunal, in the northern part of the medina. As a result of the association's efforts, the medina was added to the UN's World Heritage List in 1981.

The southern part of the medina remains pretty much in its original condition and houses the majority of the attractions described in this section. Only three sites charge for admission: the Zitouna Mosque, the Dar Ben Abdallah Museum and the Tourbet el-Bey. Admission to each is TD1.600.

Walking Tour One This walk starts and finishes at the Bab Bhar, on the eastern side of the medina, and follows a route designed by the Association de Sauvegarde de la Medina to include the cream of the medina's attractions. The route is indicated with faded orange arrows along the way and is also marked on the free medina map available from the tourist office on Ave Habib Bourguiba in the Ville Nouvelle. The walk itself takes about 45 minutes, but this can easily stretch to four hours by the time you've checked out the various attractions along the way. It's best to start early – both to beat the heat and to ensure you reach the Zitouna Mosque before it closes at noon.

From the Bab Bhar, head into the medina along Rue Jemaa Zitouna, which is packed solid with tourist shops selling everything from tacky T-shirts and stuffed camels to high-quality handicrafts. The storekeepers can be very persistent. If you're tempted to buy, bargain hard as the prices quoted here are some of the highest in Tunisia.

Rue Jemaa Zitouna eventually emerges at the main entrance of the **Zitouna Mosque** (Mosque of the Olive Tree), also known as the Great Mosque. The first mosque to occupy this site was built in AD 698, at the time the medina was founded, but it was completely rebuilt in the 9th century by the Aghlabid ruler Ibrahim ibn Ahmed (AD 856–63) – in typically austere Aghlabid fashion. The builders recycled 200 columns salvaged from the ruins of Roman Carthage for the central prayer hall.

The mosque's theological faculty was an important centre of Islamic learning until it was closed down by Bourguiba shortly after

independence as part of a campaign to reduce the influence of religion on society. The faculty, known as Zitouna University, was re-opened in 1987. Non-Muslims are allowed in as far as the courtyard of the mosque between 8 am and noon daily except Friday; modest dress is compulsory.

Turn right at the Zitouna Mosque, and then left into the covered **Souq el-Attarine**. Your nose will tell you before your eyes that this is the Perfume Makers' Souq. The shops here sell a range of essential oils, some blended to imitate well-known brands of perfume.

Souq el-Attarine leads into the **Souq el-Trouk**, the Turkish Sailors' Souq. The main point of interest here is an old Turkish cafe, Café M'Rabet, that has been maintained in authentic condition. It's a good excuse to stop for a coffee.

Continuing west from the Café M'Rabet, Souq el-Trouk finishes in front of the **Mosque of Youssef Dey**. Built in 1616, this was the first Ottoman-style mosque built in Tunis. It was designed by the Andalusian architect Ibn Ghalib and is a colourful combination of styles. Look out for the octagonal minaret crowned with a miniature green-tiled pyramid for a roof.

Turn right at the end of Souq el-Trouk and walk along Souq el-Bey until you come out at Place du Gouvernement, a shady square on the western edge of the medina. The **Dar el-Bey**, on the southern side of the square, is a former palace guesthouse that now houses the prime minister's office. The guards are quite a sight in their red uniforms, but photographs are not permitted.

West of the Dar el-Bey is the **Place de la Kasbah**. Now an enormous open square, beautifully paved with local granite, it was once overlooked by the old kasbah (citadel), which was destroyed by the French in 1883. The **Kasbah Mosque**, to the south-west, dates from the 13th century. The call to prayer is signalled by a white flag hung from the pole on the minaret. You have to be quick to spot it as it is only displayed for a minute or two.

From here, head back to the Mosque of Youssef Dey via Rue Sidi ben Ziad, and turn right into the **Souq el-Berka**. In Ottoman times, this was the slave souq where prisoners, taken at sea by the Muslim corsairs, were brought to be sold into slavery.

Keep going south through the Souq el-Berka and turn left into Souq el-Leffa, which runs downhill to the Souq des Étoffes, on the western side of the Zitouna Mosque. Behind the ornately studded door of No 37 is the **Medersa Mouradia**, a former Islamic college built in 1673 on the ruins of a Turkish barracks destroyed during a rebellion. Today, it is used to train apprentices in traditional crafts and is open from 9 am to 4.30 pm Monday to Saturday.

The tour now heads for the southern section of the medina via the Souq des Femmes, which leads into Rue Tourbet el-Bey – one of the main thoroughfares. The discreet little mosque on the right at No 41 is the **Mosque of M'sed el-Kobba**. The famous historian Ibn Khaldun (1332–1406) was born just along the street at No 33 and taught briefly at the mosque before leaving Tunis to further his career in Cairo. Accordingly, the mosque is also known as the Kouttab Ibn Khaldoun (a *kouttab* is a Quranic primary school).

Keep heading south along Rue Tourbet el-Bey for another 100m and you'll come to the building that gives the street its name, the **Tourbet el-Bey**. This huge mausoleum was built during the reign of Ali Pasha II (1758–82) and became the final resting place of many of the subsequent Husseinite beys, together with various princesses, ministers and trusted advisers. It was closed for repairs at the time of research. Normally, it's open from 9.30 am to 4.30 pm Monday to Saturday. Admission is TD1.600.

Turn left after the Tourbet el-Bey onto Rue Sidi Kacem, cross Rue Sidi Zahmoul and you'll see a sign on the right pointing to the **Dar Ben Abdallah Museum**, on Impasse Ben Abdallah.

Built in 1796, this former palace now houses the Centre for Popular Arts and Traditions. Four of the rooms have been used to create scenes of bourgeois life in 19th-century Tunis, using dummies dressed in traditional costumes. Another room has a very detailed map of the medina showing all the *hammams* (public bathhouses), mosques, souqs and other points of interest.

The building itself is probably of more interest than the museum: It has an unusual, highly ornate entrance leading to a marble courtyard complete with fountains and sculptures. The museum is open from 9.30 am to 4.30 pm Tuesday to Saturday. Admission is TD1.600.

Continue to the end of Rue Sidi Kacem and turn left onto Rue des Teinturiers (the Street of the Dyers). The octagonal minaret on the corner marks the extravagant **Mosque of the Dyers**, built in 1716 by Hussein ben Ali, founder of the Husseinite line of beys.

Opposite the mosque, an archway leads to Rue el-M'Bazz and the **Dar Othman**. Built by Othman Dey at the beginning of the 17th century, the palace is an excellent example of period architecture, distinguished by its magnificent facade. Some of the rooms have been converted into offices, but visitors are welcome to look around the courtyards.

Return to Rue des Teinturiers and keep heading north for about 150m, then turn left into Rue de la Medersa es-Simania and take the first right into the Souq des Libraires (the Booksellers' Souq). The western side of the souq is lined with a series of medersas formerly linked to the theological faculty of the Zitouna Mosque. The **Medersa Slimania**, on the corner of Souq des Libraires and Souq el-Kachachine, was also built by Ali Pasha. It was constructed in 1754 in memory of Ali Pasha's son Suleiman, who was poisoned by his brother. Some of the rooms are now occupied by the Tunisian Medical Association, but the remainder is open to the public. The **Medersa Bachia**, at No 19, is identifiable by the small public fountain beside the entrance. It was built in 1752 by the Husseinite bey Ali Pasha and now houses a school for apprentice artisans. The oldest medersa is the **Medersa of the Palm Tree**, at No 11, which was built in 1714 on the site of a former *funduq* (travellers' inn) and is named after a palm tree that once occupied its central courtyard. It still serves as a Quranic school and is closed to the public.

TUNIS

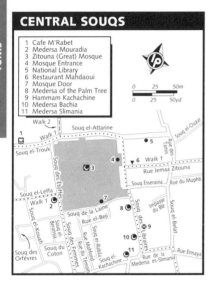

CENTRAL SOUQS

1 Cafe M'Rabet
2 Medersa Mouradia
3 Zitouna (Great) Mosque
4 Mosque Entrance
5 National Library
6 Restaurant Mahdaoui
7 Mosque Door
8 Medersa of the Palm Tree
9 Hammam Kachachine
10 Medersa Bachia
11 Medersa Slimania

The Souq des Libraires continues north and emerges in front of the Zitouna Mosque. The Restaurant Mahdaoui, on Rue Jemaa Zitouna near the mosque, claims to be the oldest restaurant in Tunis. A bowl of couscous here is the perfect way to finish your tour before heading back along Rue Jemaa Zitouna to the Bab Bhar.

Walking Tour Two This walk also begins at the Bab Bhar. It follows Walking Tour One as far as the **Great Mosque** and **Souq el-Attarine**, but then heads north to take in the main points of interest of the northern medina. The walk itself takes about 30 minutes, but allow at least two hours.

Follow Walking Tour One as far as the western end of the Souq el-Attarine, then turn right onto Rue Sidi ben Arous and follow it north across Rue de la Kasbah. Rue Sidi ben Arous is part of the medina's main north-south thoroughfare. After 200m, and after the intersection with Rue Saida Ajoula, it becomes **Rue du Pacha**. Look out for the many grand doorways along here. The size and decoration of a doorway is a direct reflection of the dwelling behind. The bigger and grander the door, the grander the

dwelling – and the higher the social standing of its occupant. Rue du Pacha was the smartest address in town during Ottoman times, and home to the town's ruling elite. Check out the fabulous studded doors at No 29, beneath the vaulted skifa that marks the entrance to this exclusive district, and at No 34. The number of door knockers, by the way, indicates the number of families living within.

Keep heading north along Rue du Pacha for about 200m, and then turn right into Rue de la Noria. At the end of Rue de la Noria, veer left into Rue du Tribunal. The **Dar Lasram Palace**, at No 24, rates as one of the finest buildings in the medina as well as being the home of the Association de Sauvegarde de la Medina. Visitors are welcome to look around the beautifully restored interior. There's a standing display with maps, plans and photographs as well as a library. The Dar Lasram is open during standard office hours.

From Dar Lasram, continue north along Rue du Tribunal, turn right onto Rue Sidi Brahim and then left onto Rue Achour. Take the right fork (Rue el-Monastir) at the northern end of Rue Achour, and then turn left onto Rue el-Kadhi. Turn right at the top of Rue el-Kadhi and you'll be on Rue el-Deheb, walking past the **Mosque of Sidi Mahres**.

Built in 1675, it is named after the patron saint of Tunis, who saved the city after it was captured by Abu Yazd during a rebellion against Fatimid rule in AD 944. His tomb lies opposite the entrance to the mosque, in the **Zaouia of Sidi Mahres**. The mosque is ranked as one of the city's finest Ottoman buildings. Unfortunately, it's now closed to non-Muslims, so most tourists can do no more than admire the fine collection of cupolas and half-cupolas surrounding the central dome.

Rue el-Deheb ends at Rue Sidi Mahres. This busy street starts just north of the junction with Rue el-Deheb amid the markets surrounding the **Bab Souika**, the main northern entrance to the medina. The tour heads south, following Rue Sidi Mahres to the **Hafsia** district. This was once the Jewish quarter, but the original inhabitants vacated the medina

TUNIS VILLE NOUVELLE

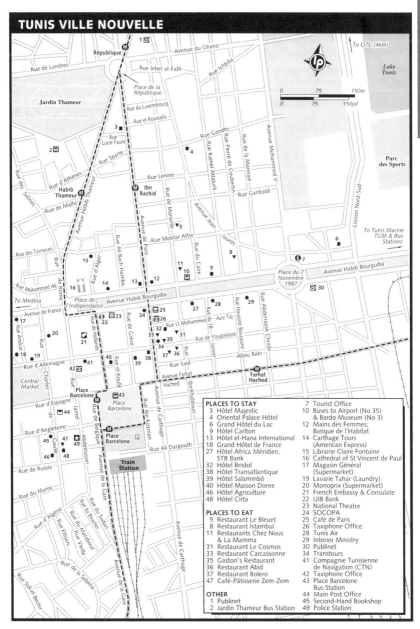

PLACES TO STAY
3 Hôtel Majestic
4 Oriental Palace Hôtel
6 Grand Hôtel du Lac
9 Hôtel Carlton
13 Hôtel el-Hana International
18 Grand Hôtel de France
27 Hôtel Africa Méridien;
    STB Bank
32 Hôtel Bristol
38 Hôtel Transatlantique
39 Hôtel Salammbô
40 Hôtel Maison Doree
46 Hôtel Agriculture
48 Hôtel Cirta

PLACES TO EAT
5 Restaurant Le Bleuet
8 Restaurant Istambul
11 Restaurants Chez Nous
    & La Mamma
31 Restaurant Le Cosmos
33 Restaurant Carcassonne
35 Gaston's Restaurant
36 Restaurant Abid
37 Restaurant Bolero
47 Café-Pâtisserie Zem-Zem

OTHER
1 Publinet
2 Jardin Thameur Bus Station

7 Tourist Office
10 Buses to Airport (No 35)
    & Bardo Museum (No 3)
12 Mains des Femmes;
    Banque de l'Habitat
14 Carthage Tours
    (American Express)
15 Librairie Claire Fontaine
16 Cathedral of St Vincent de Paul
17 Magasin Général
    (Supermarket)
19 Lavarie Tahar (Laundry)
20 Monoprix (Supermarket)
21 French Embassy & Consulate
22 UIB Bank
23 National Theatre
24 SOCOPA
25 Café de Paris
26 Taxiphone Office
28 Tunis Air
29 Interior Ministry
30 Publinet
34 Transtours
41 Compagnie Tunisienne
    de Navigation (CTN)
42 Taxiphone Office
43 Place Barcelone
    Bus Station
44 Main Post Office
45 Second-Hand Bookshop
49 Police Station

for the Ville Nouvelle at the end of the 19th century. It then became known as one of the roughest parts of town, and was demolished in the 1950s. A plan to rehabilitate the area won the Aga Khan Prize for Architecture in 1995, but the work itself has barely begun.

Follow Rue Sidi Mahres and Rue Sidi es-Sridek south through the Hafsia district, veering right at the square, until you reach for the junction with Rue Sidi Bou Hamid. The route south now enters the covered **Souq el-Grana**, always packed with women hunting for bargains among the endless clothing and footwear stalls. It can be slow going. Souq el-Grana finishes 200m to the south at Rue de la Kasbah. Turn left here and follow Rue de la Kasbah downhill until it emerges back at the starting point, the Bab Bhar.

Ville Nouvelle
The streets of the Ville Nouvelle are lined with old French buildings with louvred windows and balconies with wrought-iron railings. This gives the entire place a very European feel, which is heightened by the pavement cafes and the numerous patisseries selling all manner of both sweet and savoury pastries.

There are few points of interest apart from some fine examples of colonial architecture. You'll find a selection of styles, ranging from the exuberant to the bizarre.

Bizarre is the only way to describe the **Cathedral of St Vincent de Paul**, which faces the French embassy on Place de l'Indépendance. Built in 1883, the cathedral incorporates an extraordinary collection of clashing styles – part-Gothic, part-Byzantine and part-North African. The main doors are normally locked, but there is a side entrance on Rue d'Alger. The **statue** opposite the cathedral is of Ibn Khaldun, the great Islamic teacher and philosopher, who was born in Tunis.

There are some fabulously ornate facades around. The **Hôtel Majestic**, at 36 Ave de Paris, was in need of a coat of paint at the time of research, but was still very impressive. There are several more good examples elsewhere on Ave de Paris and further north on Ave de la Liberté, as well as south of Ave Habib Bourguiba on Rue de Yougoslavie.

The formidable **Interior Ministry building**, which occupies an entire block at the eastern end of Ave Habib Bourguiba, was clearly designed to intimidate. It's best if you don't spend too much time searching for architectural nuances – the building is heavily guarded 24 hours a day, and is barricaded to prevent pedestrians wandering past. Other grand structures like the **post office** and the **French embassy** were designed to impress through their size and grandeur.

Hammams
If you are staying in a hotel without washing facilities, or if you just feel like a hot sauna and massage, there are numerous hammams in the medina. One of the best is the Hammam Kachachine, at 30 Souq des Libraires, but it's for men only.

The hammam at 11 Rue el-Methira, west of Rue des Teinturiers, is reserved for women between noon and 6 pm.

Beaches
The beaches of Tunis are all accessible by TGM suburban train from Tunis Marine station at the eastern end of Ave Habib Bourguiba (see the Getting Around section and the Tunis Metro & TGM Routes map later in this chapter). La Marsa, at the end of the line, is the best of them and less crowded than those at Carthage and La Goulette.

Activities for Children
The top spot for children is the Parc des Loisirs Dah Dah, a modern entertainment park near the airport on the northern shore of Lake Tunis. It has a good choice of rides, including bumper cars and a big wheel, and activities for smaller children. It's open from 6 to 10 pm weekdays, and from 10 am to 10 pm weekends. Most rides cost between 300 and 500 mills. A taxi ride from the city centre costs about TD2.500.

Another possibility is the Tunis Zoo, located in the south-eastern corner of the Parc du Belvedere. It's open from 9 am to 6 pm Tuesday to Sunday. Admission is 400 mills for adults and 200 mills for children.

[Continued on page 124]

BARDO MUSEUM

The Bardo is the finest museum in Tunisia, housing the most important finds from the country's many ancient sites. It's famous for its superb collection of mosaics, commissioned between the 2nd and 4th centuries AD to adorn the sumptuous villas of Roman Africa's many wealthy citizens.

The Bardo would be worth a visit even without its exhibits. Located in the suburb of Bardo, about 4km west of the city centre, it occupies the former Bardo Palace – official residence of the Husseinite beys. The first palace to be built on the site was commissioned by the Hafsid sultan El-Mustansir (1249–77). He was responsible for restoring and diverting the Zaghouan-to-Carthage aqueduct to supply the palace and the medina with water. The present palace was built at the end of the 17th century, and was steadily enlarged by a succession of Husseinite occupants. It became a museum in 1888.

Exhibits are organised into sections covering the Punic, Roman, early Christian and Islamic periods.

Practicalities

The museum is open daily except Monday. Opening hours are from 9 am to 5 pm in summer (1 April to 15 September) and from 9.30 am to 4.30 pm for the rest of the year. It's open on all public holidays except for Eid al-Fitr, at the end of Ramadan, and Eid al-Adha (see Public Holidays & Special Events in the Facts for the Visitor chapter for a table of dates). Entry is TD3.150, plus a further TD1 if you want to take photos.

The simplest way to get there is by taxi – about TD2.500 from the city centre. It's also possible to get there by *métro léger* (Tunis' tram network). The museum is a short walk from Le Bardo station, three stops west of Bab Saadoun on line 4. The museum entrance is on the northern side of the museum on Rue Mongi Slim, while the station is on the southern side of the museum on Blvd du 20 Mars 1956.

A third option is to catch the yellow city bus No 3 from Tunis Marine, which terminates just around the corner from the museum

Inset: The eye of Neptune, god of the sea and giver of mercy. (Illustration by Tony Fankhauser)

Bottom: Interior of the Bardo Museum. Housed in what was once the official residence of the Husseinite beys, the Bardo's palatial setting alone makes it worthy of a visit.

SCOTT DARSNEY

BARDO AREA

0   100   200m
0   100   200yd

1 Mosque
2 Museum
3 Esso Petrol Station
4 Police Station
5 Buses from Tunis
6 Buses to Tunis
7 National Assembly

Rue Moussa ibn Noussair
Rue de Securite
Ave de l'Union
Ave Mongi Slim
Ave Moussa ibn Noussair
Ave Habib Thameur
Ave Maghreb Arabe
Le Bardo Train Station
Ave de Independance
Metro Station

BARDO MUSEUM

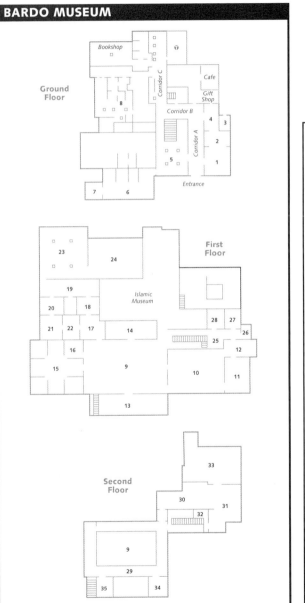

Ground Floor

1 Prehistoric
2 Baal Hammon
3 Ticket Office
4 Punic
5 Early Christian
6 Bulla Regia
7 Busts of Roman
   Emperors
8 Islamic Museum

First Floor

9   Carthage
10 Sousse
11 Dougga
12 El-Jem
13 Althiburos
14 Uthina
15 Virgil
16 Punic Jewellery
17 Mahdia Wreck
18 Mahdia Wreck
19 Mahdia Wreck
20 Mahdia Wreck
21 Mahdia Wreck
22 Mahdia Wreck
23 Marine Mosaics
24 Mausoleum
25 Mosaics
26 Bacchus & Ariadne
27 Ulysses
28 Mosaics

Second Floor

29 Bronze &
    Terracotta Figurines
30 Mosaics
31 Mosaics
32 Mosaics
33 Acholla
34 Frescos
35 Frescos

entrance on Ave de l'Union de Maghreb Arabe. You can catch this service from the bus stop opposite the Hôtel Africa Méridien.

It's best to arrive early to get in ahead of the tour groups travelling up from Hammamet and Sousse. In summer, it's a good idea to start on the 2nd floor, which gets very hot later in the day.

Unfortunately for English speakers, most of the explanations are in Arabic and French only. The same problem extends to the museum bookshop, which sells guides to the museum in French and German – but not English. The only publication about the museum in English is *Mosaics of the Bardo* (TD9), which features the pick of mosaics. It's available at the museum bookshop.

Highlights

Following is a brief summary of the museum's highlights, viewed room-by-room.

Ground Floor

Room 1, Prehistoric This is the latest addition to the museum's line-up. It traces the country's history from early-Palaeolithic times (200,000 to 100,000 BC) to Neolithic times. Displays include a re-creation of the Hermaion d'El Guettar, a religious monument discovered near Gafsa. It is thought to be 40,000 years old.

Room 2, Baal Hammon This room is named after a small terra-cotta statue of the lord of the Punic pantheon seated on a throne. It also houses an extraordinary lion-headed representation of the goddess Tanit. Both were found at Thinissut, near Bir Bou Regba, and date from the 1st century AD – proof that Punic religious practices continued long after the Roman conquest. The room also houses the famous priest stele from the Tophet at Carthage: The inscription shows a priest preparing to sacrifice a child.

Room 4, Punic Most visitors head straight for the collection of clay funeral masks from Carthage. These bizarre, contorted faces were intended to keep bad spirits away from the dead; the collection includes both male and female masks. Other features include a statue from the 1st century AD of a horned god from Makthar, and an unusual primitive carving of a face on a ball of rock – dated to the 5th century BC.

Right: A Punic grave stele inscribed with the sign of Tanit.

Corridor C The Punic theme continues with a delightful collection of pottery lamps in the shape of assorted

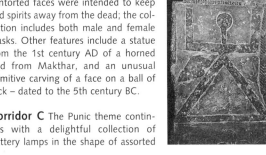
DAVID WILLETT

animals, including a mouse, a pig and a ram. The finest piece is a lamp in the shape of a man's head, with the flame emerging from the man's beard.

Corridor B This corridor is lined with a collection of elaborately decorated stelae unearthed at the minor site of Macota, near Makthar. They are accompanied by one of the few explanations in English in the museum, explaining the composition of the decorations.

Corridor A Most of the sarcophagi and statuary that once adorned this corridor were missing at the time of research, possibly because of construction work in the adjacent Islamic rooms. The only statue remaining is of a ghostly caped figure with a dog at his feet, dating from the 3rd century AD.

Room 5, Early Christian The centrepiece is an unusual 6th-century cruciform baptismal font from El-Kantara, surrounded by several impressively large stone sarcophagi. The walls are covered with funeral mosaics from early churches. Among them is a vivid representation of Daniel and the Lion's Den, and a schematic mosaic from Tabarka showing the layout of an early church. The short corridor leading to Room 6 has a collection of terracotta tiles used to decorate early churches. Look out for the depiction of Eve handing an apple to Adam.

Room 6, Bulla Regia The star attraction is a collection of Roman statues discovered at Bulla Regia's Temple of Apollo, which occupy the alcoves along the northern wall. At the centre is a magnificent statue of Apollo, god of light and music, holding a lyre. He is flanked by Aesculapius, the god of healing, and Ceres, goddess of the earth, who had an important role to play in the Tunisian wheat belt. Much of the facing wall is taken up by a mosaic of Perseus rescuing Andromeda from a sea monster.

Room 7, Roman Emperors The walls are lined with busts of Roman emperors found at sites around the country. They include a cherubic Augustus, known as the father of Roman Tunisia. Septimus Severus, the only African-born emperor, has been given very Roman features, while the octogenarian Gordian sports a two-day growth and has the look of a man about to commit suicide.

Islamic Museum This section of the Islamic Museum was closed for re-organisation at the time of research. It features displays of calligraphy, ceramics and glassware.

1st Floor
The stairway leading up to the 1st floor from Room 5 is lined with more Christian funerary mosaics.

Islamic Museum A right turn at the top of the stairs leads to an older section of the palace that houses the second part of the Islamic Museum. The rooms are spread around a central courtyard, once open to the sky, and are furnished in the 19th-century Husseinite style.

Room 9, Carthage On the left at the top of the stairs, this grand, colonnaded palace reception room is devoted to statuary from Roman Carthage. The statues are arranged around a couple of large floor mosaics from Uthina, including a wonderful portrait of 3rd-century farm life in Roman Africa.

Room 10, Sousse Pride of place belongs to an enormous floor mosaic recovered from the reception hall of the villa of a wealthy horse breeder from Sousse. It covers nearly 140 sq metres, surrounding a central medallion representing the Triumph of Neptune (see Room 11), riding in a chariot drawn by sea horses.

The giant sandalled foot and head by the doorway leading to the Dougga room belong to a statue of Jupiter from the Capitol of Thuburbo Majus. The size of the fragments suggest the statue stood 7.5m high.

Room 11, Dougga This room contains several fine mosaics from Dougga, including the celebrated cyclops from the site's Cyclops Bathes. However, the highlight comes from the seaside town of La Chebba – an incredibly fine piece, again depicting the Triumph of Neptune. Neptune was god of the sea and the giver of mercy, and his triumph (over adversity at sea) was a popular theme in coastal towns. He is surrounded by the four seasons, represented by rushes, vines, ears of wheat and olive branches.

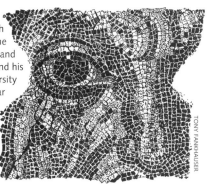

TONY FANKHAUSER

Right: Detail from the magnificent mosaic *The Triumph of Neptune*, discovered in the seaside town of La Chebba.

Room 12, El-Jem This small collection of mosaics is centred on a suitably decadent depiction of the Triumph of Bacchus, god of wine, riding a chariot pulled by two tigresses. The corners are filled with vines sprouting forth from vases. The walls are lined with some charming small pieces: a hare, a fish, and a bunch of grapes.

Room 13, Althiburos The remote site of Althiburos, on the high plains about 30km south of Le Kef, yielded one of the museum's more extraordinary finds – a mosaic featuring 25 different types of boat, crewed by an assortment of cupids. The room also features an interesting fishing scene found near Menzel Bourguiba. Look out for the unfortunate swimmer being devoured by a sea monster.

Room 14, Uthina The centrepiece is a large 4th-century mosaic of Orpheus charming the beasts with his lyre. Although parts are badly damaged, the artistry of the surviving detail is quite astonishing. Next to it is a small mosaic fragment with a rare depiction of a Carthaginian war elephant. The room also features several finds uncovered at the site's House of the Laberii, including the depiction of the moon goddess Selene gazing on the sleeping figure of Endymion – a handsome shepherd boy granted eternal youth by Jupiter.

Room 15, Virgil Room 15 is something in its own right. It was formerly the palace harem, and the four smaller corner rooms were occupied by the ruler's favourite wives. The star piece is a 3rd-century mosaic of Virgil unearthed in Sousse. Virgil is seated holding a copy of his Aeniad, flanked by the two Muses who inspired his endeavour – Clio (history) and Melpomene (tragedy). One of the bedrooms is given over to an exquisite collection of Punic jewellery. The northern part of the anteroom contains a collection of coins: Punic, Numidian, Roman, Vandal, Byzantine, Arab, Spanish and Ottoman.

Rooms 17 to 22, Mahdia Wreck These rooms are devoted to finds from the wreck of a ship that went down off Mahdia in the 1st century AD with a cargo of Greek marble and bronze statuary. The rooms were closed at the time of research, also barring the way to Rooms 23 and 24.

Room 25, Various Mosaics More of a corridor than a room, the main feature is an elaborate floral composition of acanthus flowers surrounding peacocks and other birds.

Room 26, Hall of Bacchus and Ariadne The main feature is a large mosaic of the same name from Thuburbo Majus, which covers one wall. This room also holds one of the museum's smallest pieces, found at Gightis. The mosaic features two naked wrestlers.

Room 27, Ulysses The room is named after a famous mosaic of Ulysses from the House of Ulysses at Dougga. The wandering hero is tied to the mast of his ship to save him from the Sirens, who are lined up stage right. Another feature to look out for is the beautiful fountain from Thuburbo Majus.

Room 28, Various Mosaics The star here is a large mosaic of Venus, with perfect orbs for breasts, flanked by two female centaurs from Elles, near Makthar.

2nd Floor

Room 29, Bronze & Terracotta Figurines This room takes the form of a gallery overlooking Room 9. The glass cases that line the walls feature funerary pottery and statuettes, mainly from the ancient necropolises of Carthage and Sousse. Look out for the wonderful bronze statue of a drunken Hercules relieving himself. It's one of several unusual pieces on the left as you enter from the stairs.

Room 30, Various Mosaics Wild beasts feature prominently among the offerings, with ostriches from Le Kef and a pair of ferocious bears from Korba. Looking somewhat lost among them is the so-called tragic poet of Thuburbo Majus, staring dolefully at the ground.

Room 31, Various Mosaics The theme is hard to pick. The main attraction is a portrayal of Diana, goddess of hunting, riding a stag – again from Thuburbo Majus. There are some beautiful geometric floral designs on the walls leading to Room 32, no more than a tiny gallery off Room 31.

Room 33, Acholla The minor Roman port of Acholla, just north of Sfax, yielded some particularly fine mosaics. Many of the pieces displayed here come from the Trajan baths. The finest depicts a sea centaur carrying off a nymph.

Rooms 34 & 35, Frescos Both rooms were closed at the time of research.

Right: Ulysses, the wandering hero, tied to the mast of his ship in order to resist the songs of the Sirens. This exceptionally fine mosaic was discovered in Dougga.

DAVID WILLETT

[Continued from page 116]

Organised Tours

Although lots of tour companies offer tours to Tunis, there are no organised tours available from Tunis. If you want to be taken on a guided tour of Tunis, you'll need to arrange a tour from one of the major resorts, like Hammamet or Sousse.

Special Events

The main event on the Tunis cultural calendar is the Carthage International Festival in July and August – two months of music, dance and theatre held at Carthage's Roman theatre.

The biennial Carthage International Film Festival concentrates on Middle Eastern and African cinema. The two-week festival is next due in October 2001. It's held at major cinemas throughout Tunis.

You'll find information about both these festivals in the local French-language newspapers. Tickets are sold at the door.

Places to Stay

Tunis has a good choice of accommodation for all budgets. The options range from youth hostel accommodation in an old palace to the latest in five-star luxury.

Places to Stay – Budget

Hostels The *Auberge de Jeunesse (☎ 567 850, 25 Rue Saida Ajoula)* occupies the 150-year-old Dar Saida Ajoula Palace, in the heart of the medina north-west of the Zitouna Mosque. The hostel is signposted off Rue de la Kasbah. The dorms are quite good, if a little crowded, and cost TD4.500 per person, including a free hot shower. Breakfast costs TD1. Half board is available for TD7.500; full board is TD10.500. The hostel is affiliated to Hostelling International (HI) and you have to be a member to stay. It's possible to join on the spot for TD12. The hostel imposes a three-night limit during busy times.

Hotels Tunis has dozens of cheap hotels. The cheapest are the medina hotels, which are found either within the medina or in the streets immediately surrounding it. Most of them are set up with visiting labourers in mind, not Western tourists, and are best avoided.

The only medina place worth considering is the *Hôtel Marhaba (☎ 354 006, 5 Rue de la Commission)*, just off Place de la Victoire. It has clean singles/doubles for TD8/12. Hot showers cost an extra TD1.

Most travellers opt to stay outside the medina in the area south of Ave Habib Bourguiba. The *Hôtel Cirta (☎ 321 584, 42 Rue Charles de Gaulle)* looks a bit shabby from the outside, but the rooms are clean enough and the management friendly. It also charges TD8/12 and an extra TD1 for hot showers.

If these prices are too steep, try the *Hôtel Bristol (☎ 254 835, 30 Rue Lt Mohammed Aziz Taj)*, off Ave de Carthage. It charges TD5/8, but noise is a problem.

Places to Stay – Mid-Range

Most of the hotels that fall into this category are old-style French hotels that date back to the 1930s and 1940s. In their prime, they ranked as the best hotels in town. They include some good places and generally have much more character than their modern counterparts. The streets south of Ave Habib Bourguiba are where to start looking. All prices in this section include breakfast.

The pick of the bunch is the two star *Hôtel Maison Doree (☎ 240 632, fax 332 401, 3 Rue el-Koufa)*, just north of Place Barcelone and east of Rue de Hollande. Opened in 1940, it has been maintained in tip-top condition by the French family which runs it. Comfortable singles/doubles cost TD26/29 with shower and toilet, or TD33.500/37 with bath and toilet. All rooms have central heating in winter, and air-con is available in summer.

Another excellent choice is the *Hôtel Salammbô (☎ 334 252, fax 337 498, [e] hotel .salammbo@gnet.tn, 6 Rue de Grèce)*, a block to the east of the Maison Doree. It's a one-star version of the Maison Doree. The staff are friendly and efficient, and the entire place is kept spotlessly clean. It has rooms with shower for TD17/28, or TD18/29 with bath and toilet.

Other possibilities include the nearby **Hôtel Transatlantique** (☎ 240 680, 106 Rue de Yougoslavie), its name emblazoned in a mosaic on the corner of Ave de Carthage, and the **Grand Hôtel de France** (☎ 326 244, fax 323 314, 8 Rue Mustapha Mbarek). Both have similar rates to the Salammbô.

The **Hôtel Agriculture** (☎ 326 394, fax 321 685, 25 Rue Charles de Gaulle) has been transformed from a run-down cheapie into a comfortable mid-range hotel. Rooms with bathroom are TD15.200/26.400.

The **Hôtel Majestic** (☎ 332 848, fax 332 666, e majestic@gnet.tn, 36 Ave de Paris) is a splendid piece of fading grandeur with one of the finest French colonial facades in town. Rooms cost TD35/50 with breakfast. Air-con is available for an extra TD3.500 in summer.

Places to Stay – Top End

For those with the money and the inclination, Tunis has its full quota of expensive hotels. At the last count, there were at least 20 hotels in town rated with three stars or more – and there were a dozen more by the beach at Gammarth, north of Carthage (see the Around Tunis section later in this chapter for details).

The **Hôtel Carlton** (☎ 330 664, fax 338 168, e carlton@planet.tn, 31 Ave Habib Bourguiba) represents one of the best deals around. Situated in the heart of town, this small, immaculately maintained three-star hotel has all the comforts (including satellite TV and air-con) you could want at a price that won't break the bank. It charges TD47/74, including a generous buffet breakfast, for singles/doubles.

The bizarre, inverted pyramid behind the tourist office at the eastern end of Ave Habib Bourguiba is the **Grand Hôtel du Lac** (☎ 336 100, fax 342 759), the city's leading architectural curiosity. You're better off looking at it from the outside. Rooms cost TD60/90 with breakfast.

You won't have any trouble locating the five star **Hôtel Africa Méridien** (☎ 347 477, fax 347 432, e africa.com@planet.tn) – it's the tallest building in the city centre. Natu-

rally enough, the rooms have great views over the city. It charges TD120/150 or you can lash out TD480 on the presidential suite.

Rather more discreet is the stylish **Oriental Palace Hôtel** (☎ 342 500, fax 330 471, e oriental.palace@planet.tn, 29 Ave Jean Jaurès). Five-star treatment here costs TD105/115.

The smartest rooms in town are at the swanky **Hôtel Abou Nawas Tunis** (☎ 350 355, fax 352 882, e abounawas.tunis@ abounawas.com.tn, Place des Droits de l'Homme), overlooking Lake Tunis between Ave Mohammed V and Ave du Grand Maghreb. Prices start at TD200/210 for predicably plush singles/doubles, including breakfast.

The Abou Nawas group has a second hotel, the **Abou Nawas el-Mechtel** (☎ 783 200, fax 781 973, Ave Ouled Haffouz), south of Parc du Belvedere. It charges a more modest TD110/125.

Places to Eat

The city centre is dotted with dozens of restaurants, cafes and fast-food joints. Although at first glance there appears to be plenty of variety, they have remarkably similar menus, with about a dozen standard dishes. Service, prices and decor are the major variables.

Restaurants – Budget There's no shortage of cheap places serving good local food. The best deal around is to be found at the long-time favourite, the **Restaurant Carcassonne** (8 Ave de Carthage). The value offered by its TD3.800 four-course menu is little short of remarkable, even if the meat dishes are not exactly enormous. The creme caramel is a nice touch. The place also has welcome ceiling fans and fast, friendly service. It's not hard to understand why it's popular with tourists and locals alike.

The Carcassonne is not the cheapest place around. That title goes to the **Restaurant Istambul** (3 Rue Pierre de Coubertin), north of Ave Habib Bourguiba. It charges just TD3 for four courses.

The main problem with these set menus is that the choice is limited to dishes that are cheap and easy to prepare. You'll find a much better range of dishes at the *Restaurant Abid* (98 Rue de Yougoslavie). It has a selection of daily specials, each for TD3 or less.

The *Restaurant Mahdaoui* (3 Rue Jemaa Zitouna), near the Zitouna Mosque, claims to be the oldest restaurant in Tunis. It's the perfect place for medina visitors to stop for lunch. It has a daily menu of traditional dishes, each for about TD3.500, and specialises in couscous. The restaurant is closed in the evening.

Restaurants – Mid-Range There are stacks of upmarket restaurants around the Ville Nouvelle. The main concentrations are south of Ave Habib Bourguiba around the junction of Rue de Yougoslavie and Rue Ibn Khaldoun, and on the southern reaches of Ave de Paris and Rue de Marseille. Many restaurants in this category have live entertainment, and are covered in the Entertainment section later in this chapter; all the restaurants listed in this section serve alcohol.

The *Restaurant Le Cosmos* (☎ 241 610, 7 Rue Ibn Khaldoun) is a place that has built up a solid reputation for good French-style food and reasonable prices. You can amuse yourself by studying the awful paint job of the universe on the ceiling and the collection of kitsch around the walls.

The French connection at the Hôtel Maison Doree (see Places to Stay – Mid-Range earlier in this chapter) extends to the hotel's excellent *Restaurant Margaritas* (☎ 240 632). The three-course menu is very good value at TD5.500. The restaurant entrance is at 6 Rue de Hollande.

The *Restaurant Bolero* (☎ 245 928, 6 Passage el-Guattar) is a great favourite with Tunis businessmen, who retreat here for long lunches. It specialises in grilled meats and seafood, and boasts an extensive wine list. A hearty meal for two with wine costs from TD25. Passage el-Guattar is a small side street running south off Rue de Yougoslavie between Ave de Carthage and Rue Ibn Khaldoun.

Rue de Marseille is another good area to look. *Restaurant La Mamma* (☎ 241 256, 11 Rue de Marseille) is at the cheaper end of the price range and is popular with younger couples looking for somewhere discrete to share a bottle of wine. It has pizzas and pasta as well as dishes like spicy barbecued octopus (TD5.500).

The menu is more sophisticated at *Chez Nous* (☎ 243 043, 5 Rue de Marseille). The walls are decked with photos of the likes of Michael York and Mohammed Ali having a good time. Most people ignore the overpriced a la carte menu, opting instead for the TD12 three-course menu.

Restaurants – Top End If you're looking for a real dining experience, head for one of the excellent 'Dar' restaurants in the medina. There are four, all occupying palatial homes built by the city's bourgeois elite at the end of the 18th century.

The best known of these is the long-running *Restaurant Dar el-Jeld* (☎ 560 916, fax 567 845, 5 Rue Dar el-Jeld). It's an experience from the moment you knock at the grand arched entrance doorway. The house's former reception rooms have been retained in that role, with the addition of a bar. These rooms lead to a covered central courtyard, which has been converted into a sumptuous main dining room, decorated in traditional style – with table settings to match. If you'd like more privacy, ask for a table in one of the smaller surrounding rooms.

The menu is typically Tunisian, specialising in traditional pastries and appetisers. The names will mean nothing to many people, so you may as well order a selection (TD8 per person). Whatever you choose for a main course (from TD15), make sure you leave room for the array of delicious traditional cakes and sweets on the dessert menu. Again, the selection (TD6 per person) is the way to go. All told, you can expect to pay about TD30 per person, plus wine.

It's popularity has prompted the owner to open a second restaurant, the *Diwan Dar el-Jeld*, just down the street at 10 Rue Dar el-Jeld. Rue Dar el-Jeld is on the western side of the medina off Place du Governement.

The success of the Dar el-Jeld has also encouraged a couple of competitors, the *Dar*

Essaraya (☎ 560 310, fax 571 465, 6 Rue Ben Mahmoud), south-west of the Great Mosque, and the *Dar Bel Hadj (☎ 336 910, fax 339 549, 17 Rue des Tamis)*, north of the Zitouna Mosque.

All of these restaurants are open Monday to Saturday for lunch and dinner. Bookings are advisable at all four, essential on Friday and Saturday evenings.

Cafes Cafes are an essential part of life in Tunis. Most of them are small, neighbourhood places, but a couple have achieved celebrity status.

The *Café de Paris*, on the corner of Ave Habib Bourguiba and Ave de Carthage, is the trendy spot to be seen. It's expensive – prices start at TD1.200 for an expresso coffee – but it's a convenient meeting place and a good spot for people-watching. It's one of the few cafes in the country that serves beer.

The *Café M'Rabet*, in the heart of the medina in the Souq el-Trouk, is an old Ottoman cafe that has been maintained in authentic condition. The restaurant upstairs is used for performances of Tunisian music and dance in the evenings (see the Entertainment section, following). The entrance to the cafe is hard to spot; look for the old wrought-iron street lamp outside.

Fast Food At the bottom of the cheap-eats scale and found all over the city are the *rôtisseries*. They specialise in grilled chicken with chips, either to eat in or to take away. Most of them charge around TD1.800 for a quarter chicken with chips, which comes with a handful of salad and a chunk of bread.

Pizza parlours are the most popular Western-food outlets. There are several places on Ave Habib Bourguiba, opposite the Hôtel Africa Méridien, that sell a range of pizzas by the slice. Prices start at 800 mills for 100g – you can just point to a slice, which is then weighed and priced accordingly.

Patisseries The French left their mark in the shape of the many patisseries in the Ville Nouvelle. These stock an array of mouth-watering sweet cakes and croissants, as well as small pizzas, savoury pastries and

crepes (pancakes) – perfect for breakfast or lunch. There is nearly always a cafe at the back of these places, where you can get a coffee to have with your snack.

You'll find the best selection of goodies at the big patisseries opposite the Hôtel Africa Méridien on the northern side of Ave Habib Bourguiba. There are more places on Rue Charles de Gaulle, including the excellent *Café-Patisserie Zem-Zem*, two doors north of the Hôtel Cirta. Fresh is the operative word here: It has freshly squeezed orange juice (500 mills), freshly ground coffee and a good range of cakes, croissants and other pastries.

Self-Catering The *central market* on Rue Charles de Gaulle is the best place to stock up on food. You'll find a wide selection of local cheeses and yoghurts, cold meats, fresh bread, olives and pickles as well as fresh fruit and vegetables. The fish section is on the northern side of the market.

The main supermarkets in the city centre are *Monoprix*, on Rue Charles de Gaulle, and the *Magasin Général* on Ave de France. Both stock a good range of local wines as well as food, toiletries etc.

Entertainment
Cinemas Tunis residents are obviously keen cinema-goers, given the large number of cinemas around town. Many of them show Bollywood-style action movies in Arabic, but you'll also find the latest Hollywood box-office hits, dubbed into French.

You'll find the cinema listings in the entertainment pages of the French-language papers. Admission prices are TD1.200 at smaller cinemas, rising to TD2.500 at plush, modern, air-con cinema centres like *La Parnasse*, inside the arcade on Ave Habib Bourguiba between Rue d'Alger and Rue Ali Bach Hamba, and *Le Capitole*, next to the Café de Paris on Ave Habib Bourguiba.

Discos Discos don't feature prominently on the local entertainment scene. They are found in the big hotels, and exist primarily for the benefit of tourists and the Tunisian jet set. The main ones in the city centre are the Jockey Club, at the *Hôtel el-Hana International*, and Club Shehrazade, at the *Hôtel Abou Nawas*.

Traditional Music & Dance The best-known venue is the *Restaurant M'Rabet* (☎ 261 729), in the medina's Souq el-Trouk, above the Café M'Rabet. There is a range of set meals for TD7 to TD24, plus an extra TD5 per person for the show. It features traditional folk music, displays of Berber dance and a brief appearance by a belly-dancer. The place is open every night and is very popular with tour groups.

Locals prefer to head for Rue de Marseille in the Ville Nouvelle, where several of the restaurants have live music. The action continues until the small hours at *Restaurant Le Bleuet* (☎ 349 280, 23 Rue de Marseille). There's no cover charge for the show in these places, but most customers give generously when the hat is passed around. Not surprisingly, Le Bleuet isn't particularly cheap – allow at least TD30 for two, plus wine. *Restaurant Gaston's* (73 Rue de Yougoslavie) has music on Tuesday, Friday and Saturday evenings.

Bars The bars in Tunis are serious drinking dens. The *Bar Coquille*, next to the Restaurant Carcassonne on Ave de Carthage, is typical. It charges TD1.450 for a beer, the most popular drink. These bars are not suitable for women travellers, who will feel more comfortable at the bars of the bigger hotels. The best is the bar at the *Hôtel Abou Nawas*.

Spectator Sports
Horse Racing There's horse racing every Sunday afternoon at L'Hippodrome de Kassar Saïd, about 10km west of the city centre. The six-race card normally starts at about 1 pm, and includes events for Arab horses as well as for imported thoroughbreds. There is computerised betting, both on local races and on racing from France. Entry is 500 mills. Buses to Kassar Saïd (720 mills) leave from the Jardin Thameur bus station. A taxi from the city centre costs about TD5.

Football (Soccer) Five of the 14 teams in the Tunisian first division are from Tunis, including arch rivals Club Africain and Espérance Sportive de Tunisie. Both use the Stade Olympique in El-Menzah as a home ground, and play there on alternate weeks. Matches are played at 2 pm Sunday. Admission prices start at TD5 for the cheapest terrace tickets. To get there, take métro léger line 2 from République and get off at the Cité Sportive stop.

You'll find details of fixtures in the Saturday French-language papers. The teams are usually referred to by their initials – CA for Club Africain, and EST for Espérance Sportive de Tunisie. The other clubs from around Tunis are Stade Tunisien (ST) and Club Olympique de Transports (COT) from the western suburbs; Avenir Sportif de La Marsa (ASM) from La Marsa; and Club Sportif de Hammam Lif (CSHL), from the southern suburbs.

Shopping
Although Tunis is not noted for its handicraft production, the shops of the Tunis medina offer everything the souvenir hunter could desire.

Rue Jemaa Zitouna is packed solid with shops selling everything from tacky T-shirts adorned with cartoons of copulating camels to top-quality handicrafts. There are more souvenir shops on Rue de la Kasbah and in the souqs around the Zitouna Mosque. Prices start high, so be prepared to haggle like hell if you want to buy anything.

If you don't enjoy bargaining, you're better off heading for the new Société de Commercialisation des Produits de l'Artisanats (SOCOPA) store on the corner of Ave Habib Bourguiba and Ave de Carthage. It has a huge selection of crafts from all over the country, the quality is good and prices are clearly marked. Even if you don't buy here, you can get a good idea of the quality and price of the best stuff available before you start bargaining with the shop owners in the medina.

Another good place to buy handicrafts is Mains des Femmes, above the Banque de l'Habitat at 47 Ave Habib Bourguiba. The shop is the sales outlet for handicrafts produced by a variety of women's cooperatives in poor rural areas.

It has a good selection of carpets, woven rugs, including kilims and *mergoums* (woven carpets with geometric designs), embroidered blankets, wooden toys, dolls and jewellery. Prices are very reasonable, and be aware that the money goes to a good cause. The shop is open from 9.30 am to 1 pm and 3 to 6.30 pm Monday to Saturday.

Getting There & Away

Air Tuninter flies at least six times a day to Jerba and less frequently to Tozeur and Sfax. Getting a booking in the middle of summer can be hard. See the Air section of the Getting Around chapter for details.

Tuninter tickets can be bought from the Tunis Air office (☎ 330 100) at 48 Ave Habib Bourguiba, or from any travel agent. Tuninter also has a special reservations service: call ☎ 701 111.

For details of international flights to and from Tunis, see the main Getting There & Away chapter. International airline offices in Tunis include the following:

Air France (☎ 341 578) 1 Rue d'Athènes
Alitalia (☎ 331 377) 17 Ave Habib Thameur
EgyptAir (☎ 341 182) 1st floor, Complexe el-Hana International, 49 Ave Habib Bourguiba
GB Airways (☎ 330 046) 17 Ave Habib Bourguiba
KLM (Transavia) (☎ 341 309) 6 Rue Lucie Faure
Lufthansa Airlines (☎ 793 515) Complexe el-Mechtel, Ave Ouled Haffouz
Middle East Airlines (☎ 341 206) Hôtel Africa Méridien, 50 Ave Habib Bourguiba
Royal Air Maroc (☎ 351 377) 16 Ave Habib Bourguiba
Tunis Air (☎ 330 100) 48 Ave Habib Bourguiba

Bus Tunis has two intercity bus stations – one for departures to the south of Tunis and another for departures to the north. The two are linked by yellow city bus No 50.

The French-language papers, *La Presse* and *Le Temps*, carry details of SNTRI departures from both bus stations every day. It should be noted that these schedules list only final destinations and not the places passed through en route. Thus Sousse and Kairouan

seldom get a mention, even though all buses heading south pass through one of them.

Southern Bus Station Buses to the south leave from the Gare Routière Sud de Bab el-Fellah (☎ 495 255), situated just south of the city centre opposite the huge Jellaz Cemetery. It's a 10-minute walk south of Place Barcelone, beyond the overpass at the end of Ave de la Gare. Alternatively, you can catch métro léger line 1 heading south and get off at the first stop, Bab Alioua, which is 200m beyond the bus station.

The bus station is well organised and easy to work out. Arrival and departure times are clearly indicated on large information boards. The staff at the information kiosk speak minimal English, but are friendly and will do their best to help.

The table 'Southern Bus Services' below lists the journey times, one-way fares (in TD) and frequency of services to selected destinations:

Southern Bus Services

destination	duration (hours)	fare (TD)	frequency (per day)
Ben Guerdane	8½	20.81	1
Douz	9	20.67	1
El-Haouaria	1¾	4.20	7
El-Jem	3	8.59	5
Gabès	6½	14.48	10
Gafsa	5½	14.17	10
Hammamet	1½	3	hourly
Jerba	7–8	18.70	4
Kairouan	2¼	6.80	hourly
Makthar	3	7.04	3
Matmata	7½	16.97	3
Medenine	7½	16.76	6
Nabeul	1½	2.80	hourly
Nefta	7½	18.22	2
Sbeitla	3¾	9.88	3
Sfax	4½	10.81	11
Sousse	4¼	6.22	10
Tamerza	8	19.32	2
Tataouine	8½	20.39	2
Tozeur	7	17.42	5
Zaghouan	1¼	2.37	9

TUNIS

Northern Bus Station Buses to the north leave from the Gare Routière Nord de Bab Saadoun (☎ 562 299), about 2km north-west of the city centre.

The easiest way to get there is by métro léger line 4 to Bouchoucha station (320 mills) from Place Barcelone or République stations. The métro léger station is about 150m west of the bus station on Blvd 20 Mars 1956. Alternatively, take a No 3 bus from Tunis Marine bus station or from Ave Habib Bourguiba opposite the Hôtel Africa Méridien, and get off at the first stop after Bab Saadoun (which you can't miss – it's a massive, triple-arched gate in the middle of a roundabout), also on Blvd 20 Mars 1956.

The table 'Northern Bus Services' lists the journey times, one-way fares (in TD) and frequency of services to selected destinations:

Northern Bus Services

destination	duration (hours)	fare (TD)	frequency (per day)
Ain Draham	3¾	7.28	3
Bizerte	1¾	3.07	half-hourly
Jendouba	3	6.05	5
Kalaat Kasba	4½	8.15	2
Le Kef	3½	7.23	9
Tabarka	3¼	7.14	9
Tebersouk	2¼	3.90	9

Train The trains are a good way to travel, although the number of destinations is limited. The train station is on Place Barcelone, conveniently close to the hotels of the Ville Nouvelle.

Scheduled departures and arrivals are displayed on a huge electronic board in the terminal building. The staff at the small information kiosk can help with queries – provided you can speak enough Arabic or French to ask.

The most useful route is the main line south to Sousse, Sfax and beyond. There are at least eight trains a day to Sousse (two hours), leaving between 7.10 am and 9.20 pm. Four of these services continue to El-Jem (three hours) and Sfax (four hours).

Three then continue down the coast from Sfax to Gabès (6½ hours), while the fourth branches inland to Gafsa (7½ hours) and Metlaoui (8¼ hours).

There are at least two trains a day to Monastir (2¾ hours), and one to Mahdia; otherwise change at Sousse.

There are also at least 10 trains a day to Hammamet (one hour) and Nabeul (1¼ hours). There is one through service daily but the other services involve changing trains at Bir Bou Regba.

Other services from Tunis include five trains a day to Bizerte (1½ hours); five to Jendouba (2¾ hours) and Ghardimao (3¼ hours); and one a day to Kalaat Kasba (five hours).

The trains can get very crowded in summer, especially on the main line south. If you want a guaranteed seat, it's a good idea to make a reservation at the station the day before you travel. Be aware also that there's a discount of 15% on return tickets.

The following table lists one-way fares (in TD) from Tunis to various destinations:

Train Services

destination	2nd class	1st class	confort
Bizerte	3.35	3.90	4.20
El-Jem	7.35	9.80	10.40
Gabès	12.75	17.20	18.30
Gafsa	11.85	15.95	17.00
Hammamet	2.95	3.70	-
Jendouba	5.60	7.05	7.55
Kalaat Kasba	7.80	9.15	9.80
Mahdia	7.35	9.80	10.40
Nabeul	2.95	3.70	-
Sfax	8.75	11.75	12.55
Sousse	5.35	7.20	7.65

Louage Tunis has three main *louage* (shared long-distance taxi) stations. Louages to Cap Bon leave from opposite the southern bus station (see Bus earlier in this section), and services to other southern destinations leave from the station at the eastern end of Rue al Aid el-Jebbari, off Ave Moncef Bey.

Louages to the north leave from outside the northern bus station.

The louage station located at Place Sidi Bou Mendil in the medina is for services to Algeria and Libya.

Car All the major car rental companies have offices at the airport and in town. These include:

Avis (☎ 782 017) 90 Ave de la Liberté;
   (☎ 782 112) Tunis Hilton lobby
Azur (☎ 782 224) 59 Ave Hedi Chaker
Europcar (☎ 340 303) 17 Ave Habib
   Bourguiba
Express (☎ 259 954) 39 Ave Farhat Hached
Garage Lafayette (☎ 287 284) 84 Ave
   de la Liberté
Hertz (☎ 248 559) 29 Ave Habib Bourguiba
Topcar (☎ 285 003) 7 Rue de Mahdia

Boat The ferries from Europe arrive at the port of La Goulette, at the eastern end of the causeway across Lake Tunis. A taxi from here to the city centre costs about TD6 – a good investment compared with the strenuous effort involved in walking all the way to La Goulette Vieille station and then catching a TGM train to Tunis (see the following Getting Around section for details).

Getting a booking on a ferry out of Tunis can be a problem in summer, so make reservations as early as possible, especially if you want to take a vehicle.

The Compagnie Tunisienne de Navigation (CTN; ☎ 322 775/802, fax 354 855) office, which can be found at 122 Rue de Yougoslavie handles tickets for ferries operated by CTN and its French partner SNCM. It also handles tickets for Tirrenia Navigazione services to Sicily. Carthage Tours handles tickets for Lauro Lines.

See the Getting There & Away chapter earlier in this book for full details on the range of ferry services to and from France (Marseilles) and Italy (Genoa, Naples and Trapani).

Getting Around
To/From the Airport Tunis-Carthage International Airport is 8km north-east of the city centre. Yellow city bus No 35 runs there from the Tunis Marine terminus every 30 minutes or so from 6 am to 9 pm. You can also pick it up at the stop opposite the Hôtel Africa Méridien. The trip takes about 25 minutes and costs 650 mills. Coming from the airport, the bus stop is on the right just outside the terminal.

A taxi to the city centre from the airport costs about TD5.

Warning L'Aeroport station, on the TGM line from Tunis Marine to La Marsa, is nowhere near the airport.

Bus Yellow city buses operate to all parts of the city, but you should have little cause to use them other than for getting to the airport, the Bardo Museum or the northern bus station. The destination, point of origin and route number are displayed in Arabic on a board by the entry door at the rear of the vehicle.

Routes of possible interest to tourists have the destination marked in Latin script as well. The number is also displayed in the front window. The basic fare is 260 mills on most routes. You should buy your ticket on the bus.

There are three main terminuses for the buses: Tunis Marine, which is near the TGM station at the causeway end of Ave Habib Bourguiba; Place Barcelone; and Jardin Thameur, just off Ave Habib Thameur. Tunis Marine is the starting point for the No 3 bus to the Bardo Museum via the northern bus and louage stations, and for the No 35 bus to the airport.

Métro Léger The smart new métro léger tram network is much easier to use than the buses. There are five main routes running to various parts of the city – see the Métro Léger & TGM Routes map for details of stations. There are route maps in both Arabic and French inside the trams which show the order of the stations.

Tickets are sold at the small kiosks at the entrance to each station. They must be bought before you travel. The basic fare is 260 mills.

TUNIS

MÉTRO LÉGER & TGM ROUTES

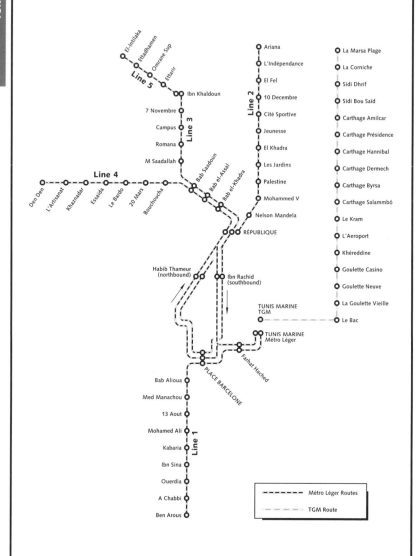

Line 5
El-Intilaka
Ettadhamen
Omrane Sup
Ettarir
Ibn Khaldoun

7 Novembre
Campus
Romana
M Saadallah

Line 3

Line 4
Den Den
L'Artisanat
Khaznadar
Essaida
Le Bardo
20 Mars
Bouchoucha

Bab Saadoun
Bab el-Assal
Bab el-Khadra

Line 2
Ariana
L'Indépendance
El Fel
10 Decembre
Cité Sportive
Jeunesse
El Khadra
Les Jardins
Palestine
Mohammed V
Nelson Mandela
RÉPUBLIQUE

La Marsa Plage
La Corniche
Sidi Dhrif
Sidi Bou Saïd
Carthage Amilcar
Carthage Présidence
Carthage Hannibal
Carthage Dermech
Carthage Byrsa
Carthage Salammbô
Le Kram
L'Aeroport
Khéreddine
Goulette Casino
Goulette Neuve
La Goulette Vieille
Le Bac

Habib Thameur
(northbound)

Ibn Rachid
(southbound)

TUNIS MARINE
TGM

TUNIS MARINE
Métro Léger

Farhat Hached

PLACE BARCELONE

Bab Alioua
Med Manachou
13 Aout
Mohamed Ali
Kabaria
Ibn Sina
Ouerdia
A Chabbi
Ben Arous

Line 1

- - - - - Métro Léger Routes

· – · – · – TGM Route

Line 1 runs from Tunis Marine to Ben Arous via Place Barcelone. Bab Alioua, one stop south of Place Barcelone, is the closest stop to the southern bus and louage stations.

Line 2 runs from République to the northern suburb of Ariana. Useful stops include Palestine (US embassy and the British consulate) and Cité Sportive (El-Menzah football stadium).

Line 3 runs from Place Barcelone to Ibn Khaldoun via République. This line services the Tunis University campus north-west of the city centre.

Line 4 runs from Tunis Marine to the western suburb of Den Den via République. Useful stops include Bouchoucha (northern bus and louage stations) and Le Bardo (Bardo Museum).

Line 5 runs from Ibn Khaldoun to El-Intilaka. This line is no more than an extension of line 3.

Services using lines 3, 4 and 5 between République and Place Barcelone travel south along Ave de Paris and Ave de Carthage and north on Rue de Hollande and Ave Habib Thameur.

TGM The TGM is a suburban train line that connects central Tunis with the beachside suburbs of La Goulette, Carthage, Sidi Bou Saïd and La Marsa. It is fast, cheap and convenient, although it can get very crowded; avoid the rush hours from 7.30 to 8.30 am and 5 to 6.30 pm. The first train leaves Tunis Marine at 3.42 am, and the last train at 12.30 am. The last train back from La Marsa leaves at midnight. Departures range from every 12 minutes during peak hours to every 40 minutes at the beginning and end of the day. First class is well worth the extra cost. It costs 630 mills to La Goulette (20 minutes); and 930 mills to Carthage (30 minutes), Sidi Bou Saïd (35 minutes) and La Marsa Plage (45 minutes).

Taxi Taxis are cheap by European standards. All taxis are fitted with meters. On day rate, shown as Tariff 1 on the meter, flag fall is 310 mills and the meter ticks over at about 500 mills per kilometre. Tariff 2 applies from 9 pm to 5 am: flag fall is 480 mills, followed by approximately 750 mills per km. Even on Tariff 2, it's difficult to run up a fare of more than TD10. Other than at the airport, where some drivers are intent on negotiating a set fare, drivers always use the meter. Taxis are especially good if you are visiting embassies, as the drivers always know where the embassies are and can save you a good deal of foot slogging. The only problem with taxis is that there aren't enough of them. During peak hours this is a real problem; you just have to be patient and lucky. Taxis can also be booked by phone – very handy when you're trying to get to the airport with a mountain of baggage. Ask at your hotel reception.

Around Tunis

La Goulette, Carthage, Sidi Bou Saïd and La Marsa have become coastal suburbs of Tunis these days. Until the arrival of the French at the end of the 19th century, these settlements remained quite isolated from the capital. This changed with the building of the causeway across Lake Tunis, providing easy rail and road access to the city centre.

They remain, however, quite different. Each has an atmosphere of its own – from the lively fish restaurants of La Goulette to the charming cobbled streets of Sidi Bou Saïd and the luxury villas of La Marsa.

Foremost among them though is the World Heritage–listed site of ancient Carthage, the Phoenician settlement that grew into the greatest city in the western Mediterranean – and was later reborn as one of the finest cities in the Roman Empire.

LA GOULETTE
☎ 01

The old port settlement of La Goulette, 10km from the city centre, is the first stop east of the causeway across Lake Tunis. The name, which means 'the gullet' in French, refers to its position on the narrow channel connecting Lake Tunis to the open sea.

It remains a major port, handling cargo as well as passenger ferries from Europe. It's also very popular with Tunis residents, who flock here on summer evenings to enjoy the sea breezes and eat at one of the many fish restaurants.

La Goulette's principle monument is its Ottoman kasbah. Sadly, it's closed to the public.

History

La Goulette was developed as a port by the Arabs after their capture of Tunis at the end of the 7th century, and it became a strategic outpost guarding the maritime approach to Tunis. Its importance can be gauged from the dimensions of the massive Borj el-Karrak, built by the Ottomans at the end of the 16th century on the ruins of an earlier Spanish fort constructed in 1535.

The eventual Ottoman victory heralded a golden age for La Goulette, which became home to one of the state-approved corsair (pirate) fleets which preyed on Christian shipping in the Mediterranean. The kasbah was used to house the hundreds of slaves needed to row corsair galleys. The riches they brought back led to the emergence of a small, walled town west of the kasbah. It housed a substantial Jewish community.

In colonial times, it attracted a sizeable Italian community, which developed the area known as Little Sicily to the north of the old town. Today, both the Jewish and Italian communities have moved on and, away from the coast, much of La Goulette has a rather run-down feel.

Places to Stay

The *Hôtel La Jetée* (☎ *736 000, fax 738 396, 2 Rue de la Grand Mosquée*) is a brand new three-star hotel with singles/doubles for TD55/85. It overlooks the beach.

Places to Eat

There are more than a dozen restaurants to choose from around Place 7 Novembre and on the southern reaches of Ave Franklin Roosevelt.

The only cheap place among them is the basic *Restaurant Stamboula*, opposite the fish markets on Ave Franklin Roosevelt. It's always full of workers tucking into bowls of *lablabi* (type of soup; 900 mills), but also serves grilled fish, chips and salad (TD5).

All the other restaurants specialise in seafood, so none are particularly cheap. Most price their fish between TD4 and TD6 per 100g. Most also offer very similar menus.

If you opt for the popular *Restaurant La Victoire* (☎ *735 398, 1 Ave Franklin Roo-*

LA GOULETTE

To Carthage (4.5km)
& Sidi Bou Saïd (7km)

Gulf of Tunis

1 Restaurant le Monte Carlo
2 Restaurant Stamboula
3 Restaurant La Cordoue
4 Police
5 Post Office
6 Banque de Tunisie
7 Restaurant la Victoire
8 UIB Bank
9 Hôtel La Jetée
10 Borj el-Karraka
11 Mosque
12 BNA Bank
13 Sports Hall

Port

To Arch (50m) & Tunis (10km)

Place 7 Novembre

To Ticket Office (50m), Customs (100m) & Embarkation Hall (400m)

To Fishing Port (300m)

sevelt), don't miss the delicious *calamares et crevettes à la creme* (TD8). Other places with good reputations include *Restaurant La Cordoue* (☎ *735 476, 13 Ave Franklin Roosevelt*) and *Restaurant Le Monte Carlo* (☎ *735 338, 14 Ave Franklin Roosevelt*). A meal at any of these places costs about TD20 per person, plus drinks.

Getting There & Away

Train is the easiest way to travel. The journey from Tunis Marine to La Goulette Vieille costs 630 mills in 1st class and takes about 15 minutes. A taxi to the city centre costs from TD6 to TD10, depending on the time of day.

CARTHAGE

☎ 01

Once one of the great cities of the ancient world, Carthage has been reduced to a dozen or so sites scattered among the villas of the affluent north-eastern suburbs. Some visitors are disappointed by the meagre remains, but students of history still relish the opportunity to climb the Byrsa Hill, gaze out over the Punic ports and contemplate how life must once have been.

The site was added to the World Heritage List in 1981.

History
Archaeologists and historians continue to debate the origins of Carthage, the former Phoenician colony that rose to become the dominant power of the western Mediterranean in the 5th century BC, and arch rival of Rome in the 3rd and 2nd centuries BC. Attempts to date the city vary widely. The Greek writer Euripides reckoned that Carthage was already in existence at the time of the Trojan War in the 12th century BC. This is somewhat at odds with the evidence provided by pottery remains, the earliest of which date to around 750 BC.

It seems likely that the legendary foundation date of 814 BC (see the boxed text 'Elissa the Wanderer') is not far off the mark. Phoenician power, based in the city of Tyre in modern Lebanon, was at its peak at this time, and the Phoenicians appeared to have founded Carthage with the aim of consolidating their hold on North Africa established by smaller, earlier settlements.

Its Phoenician name of Qart Hadasht (meaning 'new city') suggests that from the very outset it was intended to be more than just another trading post. The location was ideal for a seafaring people – a narrow, hilly promontory flanked by the sea on three sides (the Sebkhet er-Ariana, the salt lake to the north of Tunis, was connected to the sea at this time).

The first settlement was limited to the coastal strip now occupied by the modern suburb of Dermech and the lower slopes of the Byrsa Hill. The summit of the Byrsa is thought to have been a temple district, all evidence of which was later destroyed when the Romans cut the top off the hill to create a suitable space for their own temples.

Tyre came under increasing threat from the Assyrians in the course of the 7th century BC, and Carthage took over as the major city of the Phoenician world. Its de-

velopment as the main power of the western Mediterranean and its epic conflict with Rome are covered in the History section in the Facts about Tunisia chapter at the beginning of this book.

Despite the colourful legend surrounding the demise of the Punic city, which relates that the site was levelled and symbolically sprinkled with salt, it wasn't long before the Romans began to show an interest in the site. Julius Caesar re-established the city in 44 BC, and it became a provincial capital in 29 BC. Within 200 years, it had grown to be the third-largest city in the empire behind Rome and Alexandria. It was also an important early centre of Christianity. The Vandals and Byzantines ruled from Carthage, but the city slipped back into obscurity following its capture by the Arabs in AD 695.

Things to See
There are six main sites: Byrsa Hill and the Musée de Cartage; the Roman amphitheatre; the Roman theatre and villas; the Antonine Baths; the Sanctuary of Tophet; and the Punic ports.

The biggest problem for the visitor is that they are spread over a wide area. It's 2km from the Sanctuary of Tophet in the south to the Antonine Baths in the north, and getting around all the sites entails a lot of walking – and time. You need to allow at least an hour for each site. If you have only a few hours, your best bet is to limit yourself to the museum and the surrounding Punic ruins on the slopes of the Byrsa Hill.

Unless otherwise mentioned, all the sites described following are covered by a single multiple-entry ticket, available everywhere. It costs TD5.200, plus TD1 to take photos. All sites are open from 8 am to 7 pm daily from April 1 to September 15 and 8.30 am to 5.30 pm daily for the rest of the year.

Byrsa Hill The Byrsa is the best place to start any visit to Carthage. It dominates the area and the entire site is visible from the summit.

The hill was the spiritual heart of the ancient city. In Punic times, it was occupied by a temple to the Carthaginian god

Elissa the Wanderer

The legend surrounding the founding of Carthage in 814 BC evolved from the efforts of Greek and Roman writers to come up with a suitably aristocratic background for one of the great cities of the ancient Mediterranean world. They based the story on the few facts known to them about Carthage's Phoenician origins, and emphasised the blue-blooded nature of the link. The best-known version features in Virgil's epic poem *The Aeneid*.

The story begins in the Phoenician capital of Tyre in the time of King Pygmalion. According to Virgil, Pygmalion coveted the wealth of the high priest Sichaeus, who was married to his sister, Princess Elissa. Pygmalion arranged for Sichaeus to be murdered and, concealing his involvement from Elissa, attempted to lay his hands on the loot. The ghost of Sichaeus, however, told Elissa what had happened and advised her to flee – as well as revealing the location of his treasure. Elissa decided to take his advice, and tricked Pygmalion into providing her with ships on the pretext of moving to a new palace down the coast, away from the memory of her husband. Thus she was able to load up all her belongings without raising Pygmalion's suspicions. At the last moment, she was joined by 80 noblemen, including her brother Barca.

They fled first to Cyprus, where they were joined by 80 suitable wives and the island's high priest, before setting sail for North Africa. By now Elissa had become Elissa Didon, meaning 'the wanderer' in Phoenician. On arriving in North Africa, Elissa set about the job of acquiring land on which to found the city that would become Carthage. She struck a deal with the locals whereby she could have as much land as could be covered with an ox hide. The wily Elissa cut the hide into thin strips, which she used to surround the hill that became the Byrsa. (This final part of the legend is seen by many as a snide Roman dig at the Carthaginians' reputation for sharp business practices.)

Eschmoun; the Romans levelled off the top to create a space large enough to hold their capitol and forum. All have long since gone. These days the setting in dominated by the Gothic spires of the **Cathedral of St Louis**. Built by the French in 1890, it was dedicated to the 13th-century French saint-king who died on the beach at Carthage in 1270 during the ill-fated Eighth Crusade (see the boxed text 'Louis IX & the Eighth Crusade' earlier in this chapter). The cathedral has been restored and is open to the public, but it's not covered by the multiple-entry ticket. Admission is TD2.

The entrance to the **Musée de Carthage** is next to cathedral on the western side of the hill. The Punic displays are especially good, and there is a fine collection of Roman statuary. Some of the explanations are in English following US/Canadian assistance in revamping the museum, but most are in Arabic and French.

The museum's grounds also contain the celebrated **Byrsa Quarter**, a small section of the Punic city that was buried – and preserved – during Roman levelling operations. It was uncovered during excavation of the Byrsa's south-eastern slopes, and the finds are described in the museum.

Amphitheatre The Roman amphitheatre is on the western side of the Byrsa, about a 15-minute walk from the museum. It was supposedly one of the largest in the Roman Empire, but not much remains today. Most of its stones were stolen for other building projects in later centuries. The outer circle is difficult to distinguish, and the limited excavations and reconstructions date from 1919.

La Malga Cisterns The 15 huge cisterns north-east of the amphitheatre were the main water supply for Carthage in Roman times. The cisterns were fed by an aqueduct, which carried mountain spring water from Zaghouan, 55km to the south. They are impressively big, but hardly worth the effort involved in getting there.

Tunis, old and new: the ancient Roman aqueduct connecting Tunis and Zaghouan (top); the 19th century Ville Nouvelle (middle); and the extraordinary Grand Hôtel du Lac (bottom)

The Cathedral of Saint Vincent, Tunis, displays a bizarre collection of clashing styles.

The labyrinthine Tunis medina

The minaret of the Mosque of Sisi el-Bechir, Tunis

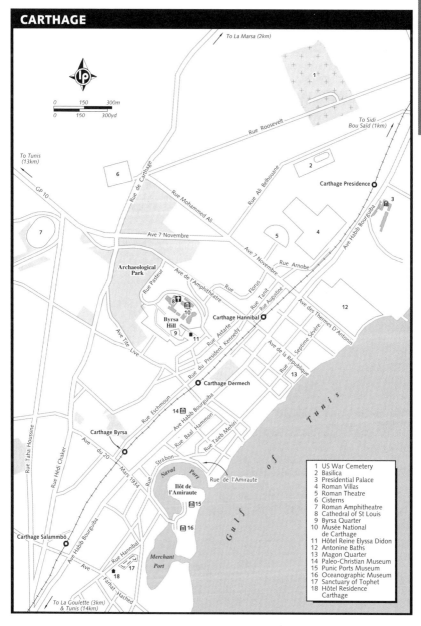

CARTHAGE

To La Marsa (2km)

Rue Roosevelt

To Sidi
Bou Saïd (1km)

Carthage Presidence

To Tunis
(13km)

GP 10

6

Rue de Carthage

Rue Mohammed Ali

Rue Ali Belhouane

2

1

3

Ave 7 Novembre

7

5

4

Ave Habib Bourguiba

Archaeological
Park

Rue Pasteur

Ave de l'Amphithéâtre

Ave 7 Novembre

Rue Arnobe

Rue Florus

12

8

10

Byrsa
Hill

9

11

Carthage Hannibal

Rue Astarte

Rue du Président Kennedy

Rue Tanit

Rue Augustine

Ave des Thermes D'Antonin

Septime Sévère

Ave Tite-Live

Carthage Dermech

Rue Eschmoun

Ave de la République

Rue

13

Gulf

14

Ave Habib Bourguiba

Carthage Byrsa

Rue Baal Hammon

Rue Taïeb Mehiri

of

Ave du 20

Strabon

Mars 1934

Rue Hédi Chaker

Rue Taha Houssine

Naval
Port

Port

Îlot de
l'Amirauté

Rue de l'Amirauté

Tunis

15

16

Carthage Salammbô

Ave Habib Bourguiba

Ave

Rue Hannibal

Merchant
Port

17

18

Farhat Hached

To La Goulette (3km)
& Tunis (14km)

1 US War Cemetery
2 Basilica
3 Presidential Palace
4 Roman Villas
5 Roman Theatre
6 Cisterns
7 Roman Amphitheatre
8 Cathedral of St Louis
9 Byrsa Quarter
10 Musée National
   de Carthage
11 Hôtel Reine Elyssa Didon
12 Antonine Baths
13 Magon Quarter
14 Paleo-Christian Museum
15 Punic Ports Museum
16 Oceanographic Museum
17 Sanctuary of Tophet
18 Hôtel Residence
   Carthage

0 150 300m
0 150 300yd

Roman Theatre & Villas The theatre has been completely covered in concrete and obscured with lighting towers and equipment for the annual Carthage International Festival (see Special Events in the main Tunis section earlier in this chapter for more details). It really has very little going for it.

The Roman villas are just east of the theatre, accessed from Rue Arnobe. Most of the site is heavily overgrown. The centrepiece is the reconstructed Villa de la Volière.

Antonine Baths Built in the middle of the 2nd century, these baths were once the third largest in the Roman Empire. They were destroyed by the Vandals in AD 439. The stone was later reused by the Arabs during the construction of Tunis.

The Antonine Baths are down on the waterfront and are impressive more for their size and location than for anything else. Bear in mind that the massive pillars that stand today represent only the sub-floor level of this huge complex.

Magon Quarter The Magon Quarter is a few blocks south of the Antonine Baths along Rue Septime Sévère (the street opposite the entrance to the baths). Excavations have uncovered a small area of Roman workshops superimposed on the ruins of an earlier Punic residential area.

Palaeo-Christian Museum This small museum would barely warrant a mention were it not for that the fact that it's featured on the list of sites covered by the Carthage multiple-entry ticket. It houses minor finds from Carthage's early Christian history.

The museum grounds include the ruins of the city's most important Byzantine church, the 6th century **Basilica of Carthagenna**. Only the foundations remain.

The museum is located on Ave Habib Bourguiba, between the Byrsa Hill and the Punic ports.

Punic Ports These two ports were the basis of Carthage's power and prosperity. The northern basin was the navy base, while the southern harbour was for commercial shipping. The two harbours were linked, and the entrance was by a channel to the sea south of the commercial port. It was filled in by Scipio after the destruction of Carthage in 146 BC.

The site referred to on the multiple-entry ticket is the **Îlot de l'Amiraute**, at the centre of the naval basin. It has a small museum which houses a reconstruction of the circular Punic naval dockyards that once occupied the island – then completely surrounded by water. The Romans built an equally impressive port complex here at the end of the 2nd century, as well as two small temples.

The small **Oceanographic Museum**, between the ports, is not covered by the multiple-entry ticket.

Sanctuary of Tophet The Tophet (sacrificial area), on Rue Hannibal just east of Carthage Salammbô TGM station, created a great deal of excitement when it was first excavated in 1921. The amateur French archaeologists responsible for the dig were curious about the source of a number of ancient grave stelae that were being offered for sale. Their excavations uncovered a sacrificial site and associated burial ground where the children of Carthaginian nobles were sacrificed to the deities Baal Hammon and Tanit.

More than 20,000 urns have been discovered at the site, each containing the ashes of a child and marked with a stele. The majority of them have been dated to the period between the 4th and 2nd centuries BC when Carthage was embroiled in numerous wars and rebellions – and the need to appease the gods was at its greatest.

Among their discoveries was the famous priest stele, now in the Bardo Museum, showing a priest holding an infant who is presumably about to be sacrificed. Most of the victims were newborns, but some are thought to have been as old as four.

US War Cemetery The cemetery is north of Carthage on Rue Roosevelt. It contains row upon row of neat tombstones marking the graves of 2840 Americans who died in North Africa during WWII.

TUNIS

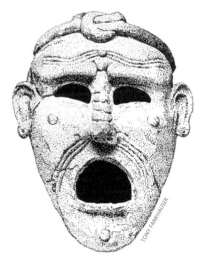

One of the Punic clay masks on display at the Musée de Carthage.

The names of 3724 others are listed on a remembrance wall.

Places to Stay & Eat

The *Hôtel Residence Carthage* (☎/fax 734 318, 16 Rue Hannibal) is a quiet place 100m from the Tophet. Singles/ doubles cost TD37.500/60 in summer, falling to TD25/35 in winter. The hotel's highly rated *Restaurant Le Punique* specialises in Moroccan food.

The *Hôtel Reine Elyssa Didon*, superbly located atop the Byrsa Hill, was closed at the time of research. This former three-star hotel was in the middle of a complete refit that should see it re-open as a five-star hotel in 2001.

Getting There & Away

There is no need to consider any options other than the train. The journey from Tunis Marine to any of the six Carthage TGM stations costs 930 mills in 1st class and takes about 30 minutes. See the Tunis Getting Around section and the Métro Léger & TGM Routes map earlier in this chapter for more details.

SIDI BOU SAÏD

☎ 01

is a picturesque little whitewashed village set high on a cliff overlooking the Gulf of Tunis, about 17km north-east of Tunis. Its maze of narrow, cobbled streets with old stone steps make it a delightful place to go for a stroll. Gleaming white-washed walls are dotted with the ornate, curved window grills that are a local trademark, all painted the same deep blue, and colourful arched doorways that open onto small courtyards filled with geraniums and bougainvillea. The style is so reminiscent of the Greek Islands that you could be forgiven for expecting to stumble upon a small Orthodox church or shrine. Instead you may come across the Mosque and Zaouia of Sidi Bou Saïd, the 13th-century Sufi saint after whom the place is named.

The lighthouse above the village stands on the site of an ancient *ribat* (fort), built at the beginning of the 9th century as part of a coastal early-warning system that included the ribats of Sousse and Monastir (see the Central Tunisia chapter).

The centre of activity is the small, cobbled main square, Place Sidi Bou Saïd, which is lined with cafes, sweet stalls and souvenir shops. To get here, follow the hotel signs. Watching the shopkeepers leap into action when the tour buses pull up can be fun; Sidi Bou Saïd is included with Carthage on a popular half-day tour.

The street heading off to the right at the top end of the main square takes you to the top of a steep path leading down through pine forest to the marina and a small beach. From here it is possible to follow the road around and back up the hill to emerge near Carthage Amilcar TGM station. The walk from Sidi Bou Saïd takes about one hour.

Places to Stay

The tiny *Hôtel Sidi Bou Fares* (☎ 740 091, fax 728 868, 15 Rue Sidi Bou Fares) is signposted up some cobbled stairs to the north of the main square. The rooms are small but clean and pleasant, set around a traditional courtyard full of flowering shrubs and vines. Singles/doubles with breakfast cost

TD20/40. This place is very popular and invariably full, so phone first.

The **Hôtel Dar Saïd** occupies a beautiful old palace just east of Place Sidi Bou Saïd, but was closed for renovations at the time of research – as it has been for years.

The upmarket option is the flash four star **Hôtel Sidi Bou Saïd** (☎ 740 711, fax 745 129) about 1km north of Sidi Bou Saïd off the road to La Marsa. Rooms cost from TD73/102 in winter up to TD99/147 in summer. Facilities include tennis courts and a swimming pool.

Places to Eat
The cheaper places to eat are around Place du 7 Novembre, near the TGM station. There are several small places here selling sandwiches and pizza by the slice, including **Pizza Bou Saïd** on Rue Bechir Sfar.

The **Restaurant Le Chargui**, at the southeastern end of the square, has a pleasant open-air courtyard and reasonable prices.

The **Restaurant Au Bon Vieux Temps** (☎ 744 733, 56 Rue Hedi Zarrouk) and the **Restaurant Le Pirate** (☎ 748 266), by the marina, both rate three forks – putting them at the top of the culinary ladder. Expect to pay around TD25 per person, plus wine.

Getting There & Away
The easiest way to travel is by TGM train from Tunis Marine (35 minutes, 930 mills). It's a 15-minute walk from the station up to the top of the hill and the centre of the old part of the village.

LA MARSA
La Marsa is an exclusive beachside suburb at the end of the TGM line from Tunis. There is no reason to come here other than to visit the beach, which is arguably the best on this stretch of coast. It stretches north around a great sweeping bay that finishes beneath the cliffs of the five-star resort village of Gammarth. The beach is

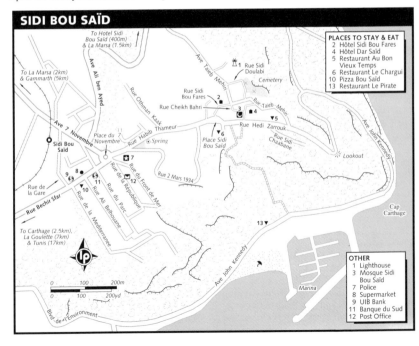

SIDI BOU SAÏD

To Hôtel Sidi Bou Saïd (400m) & La Marsa (1.5km)

To La Marsa (2km) & Gammarth (5km)

Ave Ali ben Ayed

Ave Taïeb Mehiri

Rue Sidi Doulabi

Cemetery

Rue Sidi Bou Fares

Rue Cheikh Bahri

Rue Othman Kaâk

Ave 7 Novembre

Place du 7 Novembre

Rue Habib Thameur

Spring

Sidi Bou Saïd

Rue Taïeb Mehiri

Rue Hedi Zarrouk

Place Sidi Bou Saïd

Rue Sidi Chaâbane

Lookout

Ave John Kennedy

Rue 2 Mars 1934

Rue de la Gare

Rue de la République

Rue du Front de Mer

Rue Bechir Sfar

Rue Ali Belhouane

Rue du Parc

Rue de la Méditerranée

To Carthage (2.5km), La Goulette (7km) & Tunis (17km)

Cap Carthage

Marina

Ave John Kennedy

Blvd de l'Environment

0   100   200m
0   100   200yd

PLACES TO STAY & EAT
2 Hôtel Sidi Bou Fares
4 Hôtel Dar Saïd
5 Restaurant Au Bon Vieux Temps
6 Restaurant Le Chargui
10 Pizza Bou Saïd
13 Restaurant Le Pirate

OTHER
1 Lighthouse
3 Mosque Sidi Bou Saïd
7 Police
8 Supermarket
9 UIB Bank
11 Banque du Sud
12 Post Office

relatively uncrowded during the week, but gets packed out at weekends when the wealthy set emerge to work on their suntans. There is a cluster of cafes and restaurants around the TGM station, and a couple of fish restaurants on the beach during summer.

GAMMARTH

Gammarth, 2km north of La Marsa, was once a pretty little seaside village nestled beneath the cliffs of Cap Gammarth. These days it has been transformed into a playground for the rich and famous and is packed solid with five-star hotels and expensive restaurants. The opulent *Hôtel Le Palace* (☎ *912 000, fax 911 971)* doubles as a casino. Room rates start at TD170 for a double.

Most people arrive here in their private limos. The less well-heeled can catch bus No 20B from Jardin Thameur, or walk around the bay from La Marsa. The walk takes about 45 minutes, unless you stop for a swim on the way.

Cap Bon Peninsula

This fertile peninsula stretches out into the Mediterranean Sea to the north-east of Tunis, forming the eastern shore of the Gulf of Tunis. The rugged hills that form the backbone of Cap Bon represent the eastern end of the Tunisian Dorsale, the country's main mountain range. Geologists speculate that the peninsula once extended all the way to Sicily, providing a land link between Europe and Africa that disappeared beneath the rising waters of the Mediterranean some 30,000 years ago.

The peninsula has been an important agricultural region since Carthaginian times. It was one of the main areas of European settlement during the French protectorate, and the countryside is dotted with the ruins of old, red-tiled farmhouses and their outbuildings. The French developed the vast citrus groves around Beni Khalled and Menzel Bou Zelfa in the central south of the peninsula, as well as the vineyards around Grombalia. The area's farms are still major suppliers of fruit and vegetables.

Today, Cap Bon – particularly the beaches around Hammamet and Nabeul – is Tunisia's number one destination for package tourists. The pace slowly slackens as you head north-east along the coast to Kelibia, with its small port overlooked by an ancient fortress. The area around the small town of El-Haouaria at the northern tip of the peninsula is also worth exploring. Much of the stone used in the construction of Roman Carthage was quarried from the caves on the coast just west of town. Halfway between Kelibia and El-Haouaria are the ruins of Kerkouane, the best preserved of Tunisia's Punic sites.

The west coast of Cap Bon is far more rugged and isolated. The main road runs about 2km inland for most of its length, leaving the coast virtually inaccessible. Settlement is confined to small, scattered villages. The only place of interest here is the small town of Korbous, which is famous for its hot springs.

Highlights

- Hanging out by the beach in cosmopolitan Hammamet
- Taking in the views from the ramparts of Kelibia's fabulous old fort
- Wandering around the remarkable Punic ruins at ancient Kerkouane
- Exploring the labyrinthine Roman cave complex at El-Haouaria

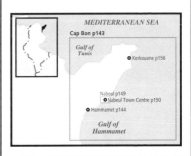

History

The hills of Cap Bon were clearly visible across the Gulf of Tunis from ancient Carthage, and the peninsula was firmly under Carthaginian control by the beginning of the 5th century BC.

It was both the market garden of the Punic capital and a key part of its defence system, which was centred on the fortress town of Aspis (Kelibia). In spite of its defences, Cap Bon was the route chosen by both Agathocles of Syracuse (in 310 BC) and the Roman general Regulus (in 256 BC) during their respective assaults on Carthage. Aspis was sacked both times, but survived. Ancient Kerkouane survived Agathocles, but was trashed by Regulus and abandoned forever.

Both visitors described the region as a veritable paradise, and Aspis went on to be-

CAP BON PENINSULA

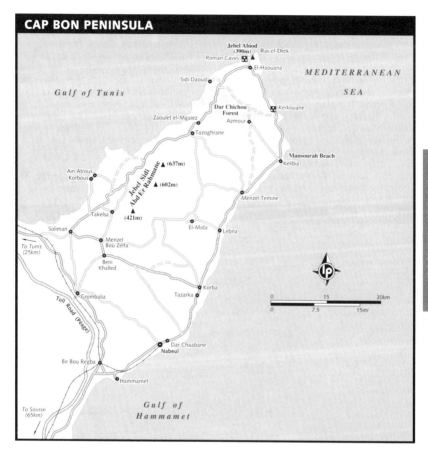

come the important Roman settlement of Clypea. Neapolis (Nabeul) was the other major population centre, and the country-side is today dotted with the relics of other unidentified, minor settlements.

Clypea later became a Byzantine strong-hold that held out against the Arabs until the end of the 7th century AD, long after the rest of Tunisia had fallen to the invaders. In the 16th century, Cap Bon was under con-stant threat from the Spanish, forcing many coastal communities to shift away from the sea. This is the reason why the centres of towns like Nabeul and Kelibia are located well away from the coast.

Axis forces retreated to Cap Bon in April 1943, establishing their headquarters at Ro-manian millionaire George Sebastian's lux-ury villa outside Hammamet, before the surrender that ended the North African phase of WWII.

HAMMAMET
☎ 02 • pop 20,000

The resort town of Hammamet, 70km south-east of Tunis, is widely regarded as the jewel in Tunisia's tourism crown, attracting more than 500,000 tourists a year.

It occupies a prime position at the north-ern end of the Gulf of Hammamet, with a cute, pocket-sized old medina overlooking a great expanse of sandy beach that curves away to the south-west as far as the eye can see. It's also a lively town, brimming with discos, restaurants and colourful souvenir shops – everything that a holiday-maker could want. It's also popular with local holiday-makers, especially as a weekend escape from the capital.

The transition from quiet fishing village to resort began in the 1920s when it was discovered by the European jet set, led by George Sebastian. Today, the coastline is fringed by dozens of giant hotels that stretch all the way to the custom-built tourist zone of Hammamet Sud, 5km to the south.

The hotels themselves are remarkably discreet – considerably more so than their guests! None of them are built above tree height; this is a remarkable piece of environmental awareness given that many of the hotels were built back in the 1960s and 1970s.

Sebastian's villa is now home to Hammamet's International Cultural Centre.

Orientation

Hammamet is an easy place to negotiate. The medina, at the heart of the town centre, over-

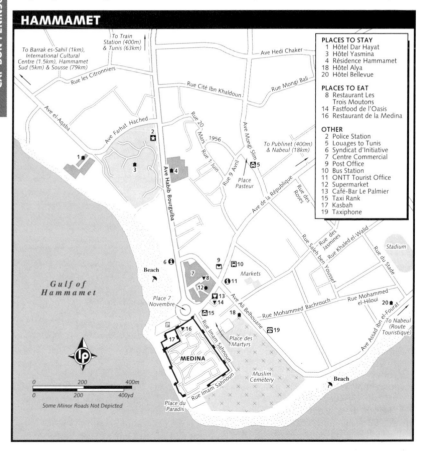

HAMMAMET

PLACES TO STAY
1 Hôtel Dar Hayat
3 Hôtel Yasmina
4 Résidence Hammamet
18 Hôtel Alya
20 Hôtel Bellevue

PLACES TO EAT
8 Restaurant Les Trois Moutons
14 Fastfood de l'Oasis
16 Restaurant de la Medina

OTHER
2 Police Station
5 Louages to Tunis
6 Syndicat d'Initiative
7 Centre Commercial
9 Post Office
10 Bus Station
11 ONTT Tourist Office
12 Supermarket
13 Café-Bar Le Palmier
15 Taxi Rank
17 Kasbah
19 Taxiphone

To Train Station (400m) & Tunis (63km)
To Barrak es-Sahil (1km), International Cultural Centre (1.5km), Hammamet Sud (5km) & Sousse (79km)
Ave Hedi Chaker
Rue les Citronniers
Rue Cité Ibn Khaldoun
Rue Mongi Bali
Ave el-Aqaba
Ave Farhat Hached
Rue 20 Mars
1956
Rue 1 Juin
Rue 9 Avril
Ave Mongi Slim
To Publinet (400m) & Nabeul (18km)
Place Pasteur
Ave Habib Bourguiba
Place 7 Novembre
Gulf of Hammamet
Beach
Ave de la République
Rue des Roses
Rue Saleh ben Youssef
Rue des Jasmines
Rue Khaled el-Walid
Rue du Stade
Stadium
Markets
Ave Ali Belhouane
Rue Mohammed Bachrouch
Rue Mohammed el-Hilou
Ave Assad Ibn el-Fourat
To Nabeul (Route Touristique)
MEDINA
Place des Martyrs
Rue Imam Sahnoun
Muslim Cemetery
Beach
Place du Paradis
Some Minor Roads Not Depicted
0   200   400m
0   200   400yd

looks the sea on a small spit of land jutting out into the Gulf of Hammamet. Most places of importance to travellers are located nearby on one of the two main streets, Ave Habib Bourguiba and Ave de la République. Ave Habib Bourguiba runs north from the medina and links up with the roads to the beach hotels, Sousse and Tunis, while Ave de la République heads north-east from the medina and becomes the main road to Nabeul.

Information

Tourist Office The ONTT tourist office (☎ 280 423) is in the centre of town at the junction of Ave de la République and Ave Ali Belhouane. It hands out a brochure with maps of Hammamet and Nabeul, and can supply you with a list of the latest accommodation prices – useful for finding special deals in winter. There's usually someone around who can speak enough English to answer questions.

The office is open from 8.30 am to 1 pm and 3 to 5.45 pm Monday to Thursday and to 1.30 pm Friday and Saturday. During July and August, it's open from 7.30 am to 7.30 pm Monday to Saturday.

There's also a small *syndicat d'initiative* 200m north of the medina on Ave Habib Bourguiba. It carries the same brochures and accommodation listings.

Money The banks are concentrated around the junction of Ave Habib Bourguiba and Ave de la République, opposite the medina. Each has an ATM permitting 24-hour cash withdrawals.

Additionally, all classified hotels and many shops can also change cash and travellers cheques.

Post & Communications The main post office is on Ave de la République, near the centre of town. There are Taxiphone offices everywhere, although it seems there are never enough phones to meet demand. The Taxiphone office at the south-eastern end of Ave Ali Belhouane is one place where you can normally avoid queuing.

Surprisingly for such a cosmopolitan town, there is only one place offering Internet access. Publinet Hammamet is 1km north-east of the medina at 117 Ave de la Liberation, which is the extension of Ave de la République.

Medina

Hammamet's pocket-sized medina was built by the Hafsids between 1463 and 1474 on the site of an earlier Aghlabid structure constructed at the end of the 9th century.

The main feature is the kasbah in the north-western corner. It's open from 8.30 am to 8.30 pm daily from May to September and to 6 pm for the rest of the year; admission is TD1. There are wonderful views over the coast from its ramparts.

The old souqs around the kasbah have been taken over by souvenir shops, but the residential district in the southern part of the medina remains surprisingly unspoiled.

International Cultural Centre

The celebrated villa built by millionaire George Sebastian in the 1920s was purchased by the state after independence and converted into the town's grandly titled International Cultural Centre, complete with the addition of a Roman-style open-air theatre. It is used during July and August to stage Hammamet's annual International Cultural Festival, which features everything from classical theatre to Arabic music. The events are heavily promoted around town, and you can get a copy of the program from the tourist office. Tickets are sold at the tourist office and at the door.

The centre is 3km north-west of the town centre, clearly signposted off Ave des Nations Unies – the main road to Hammamet Sud. The villa and grounds are open from 8 am to 6 pm in summer and from 9 am to 3 pm in winter. Admission is free.

Pupput

This very minor Roman site is located among the beach hotels at Hammamet Sud, 6.5km south-west of the town centre. It was once a staging post on the Roman road from Carthage to Hadrumetum (Sousse). There's not much to see except a couple of mosaics, and it's not worth the effort unless you're staying nearby. The name suggests it occupies the site of an earlier Punic settlement.

The site is open from 8.30 am to 5.30 pm daily in winter, and from 8 am to 1 pm and 3 to 7 pm daily in summer. Admission is TD1.

Beaches

Hammamet is primarilly a beach resort. The best beach is the main beach stretching north-west from the medina. It is prettier, and better maintained than the beach running north-east towards Nabeul.

Golf

Golf is big business in Hammamet, with two clubs to cater for the legions of enthusiastic European golfers who come here especially to play. Both clubs are west of town, accessed off the road to Sousse.

Golfing Citrus (☎ 226 500), beside the main Tunis-Sousse road, is a huge complex laid out among citrus and olive trees. Built in the early 1990s, it includes two demanding 18-hole courses and a nine-hole short course. Golfing Yasmine (☎ 227 665), about 2km to the north, has another 27 holes.

Neither club is for hackers – nor paupers. Both clubs demand proof of handicap, and Golfing Citrus insists the handicap be 36 or better. Green fees start at TD55.

Organised Tours

There are an enormous number of tour companies operating out of Hammamet, all offering very similar packages and prices. Popular local excursions include a half-day tour to the Berber villages of Takrouna, Zriba and Jeradou, west of Hammamet on the road to Zaghouan, and a one-day tour taking in Kerkouane and El-Haouaria.

Tour agencies include Visit Tunisia (☎ 280 860, fax 283 120), near the train station at 48 Ave de Kuweit, and Hammamet Travel Service (☎ 280 193, fax 291 936) on Rue Daag Hammarskjold in Hammamet Sud.

Places to Stay – Budget

Budget is not a word that features prominently in the vocabulary of Hammamet, where it's really a case of least expensive rather than cheap. Season is the main factor in determining prices, with some huge differences between winter and summer rates.

The best deal around is the three star *Résidence Hammamet* (☎ 280 406, fax 280 396), 600m north of the medina on Ave Habib Bourguiba. It has a range of comfortable studio apartments, with kitchen facilities, for up to four people. Singles/doubles cost TD44/73 in summer, dropping to a bargain TD14/22 in winter. Rates for four-person apartments drop from TD106 to just TD30 in winter. Breakfast costs an extra TD2.500 per person.

The two star *Hôtel Alya* (☎ 280 218, fax 282 365), in the middle of town on Ave Ali Belhouane, charges TD40/50 in summer, falling to TD13/20 in winter, including breakfast. The rooms are large and airy with generous balconies, and those away from the road have good views of the medina. You'll find a very similar deal at the *Hôtel Bellevue* (☎ 281 121, fax 283 156), overlooking the beach on Ave Assad ibn el-Fourat.

Places to Stay – Mid-Range & Top End

You're wasting your breath asking for a room at any of the big resort hotels in summer. They are all block-booked by package-tour companies and would be outrageously expensive for walk-up customers anyway. Prices plummet in winter, when you can take your pick from dozens of places offering singles/doubles with breakfast for around TD30/40. The tourist office can give you a list with all the prices. The rates quoted here all include breakfast, which is normally a generous buffet affair.

The main consideration is whether you want to stay in town, which has most of the restaurants and shops, or out at Hammamet Sud, which has most of the discos.

The *Hôtel Yasmina* (☎ 280 222, fax 280 593), opposite the Residence Hammamet, is an older three-star hotel on the beachfront. It has singles/doubles listed at TD62/104 in summer and TD26/40 in winter.

There are great winter deals to be found in Hammamet Sud. The four star *Hammamet Regency* (☎ 226 776, fax 227 200) slashes its summer prices of TD75/110 to a bargain TD28/40 in winter. The Regency is one of the smaller hotels around with only 60-odd rooms, and its right by the beach.

Hammamet also boasts a growing band of five-star hotels. Leading the way on price is the *Hôtel Oceana* (☎ 227 227, fax 227 003), which asks TD148/196 in summer and TD66/82 in winter. It's part of a complex of exclusive hotels surrounding the marina on the southern edge of Hammamet Sud.

The *Hôtel Dar Hayat* (☎ 283 399, fax 280 424), on the beach next to the Hôtel Yasmina, is an interesting place modelled on the traditional Tunisian courtyard home. It charges TD127/174 in summer and TD59/84 in winter.

Places to Eat

Restaurants If you're willing to splash out, there are lots of good restaurants to choose from. The *Restaurant Les Trois Moutons* (☎ 280 981), in the central commercial centre, is rated among the top dozen restaurants in the country. Expect to pay around TD35 for two, plus wine.

The main attraction at the *Restaurant de la Medina* is that seating is on the ramparts of the medina. Expect to pay around TD30 for two people, plus wine. The entrance to the restaurant is inside the medina, opposite the gateway to the kasbah.

Fast Food The seafront along Ave Habib Bourguiba is almost a solid wall of tourist restaurants, hamburger joints, pizza parlours, patisseries and ice-cream shops.

Cheap local food is hard to find, around the town centre at any rate. You'll find good sandwiches and simple dishes like *ojja* (spicy tomato sauce with eggs stirred in) at *Fastfood de l'Oasis*, east of the medina near Place des Martyrs. Otherwise, head out to the area around the train station, where there are several small restaurants.

Self-Catering Self-caterers can stock up on fresh fruit and vegetables at the *markets*, between Ave de la République and Rue des Jasmines. The small *supermarket* at the medina end of Ave de la République also sells a good range of local wines.

Entertainment

The entertainment season peaks during the International Cultural Festival in July and August.

For the rest of the year, the action is focussed on the discos in the resort hotels. Most of them are at the hotels along the main beach to the north-west of town, including the *Tropicana Club* at the Hôtel Regency and the *Boule d'Argent* at the Hôtel Les Charmes. Both are far enough out of town to warrant taking a taxi. There are no discos in the town centre.

The *Café-Bar Le Palmier*, opposite the supermarket on Ave de la République, is a lively local bar with beers for TD1.300.

Getting There & Away

Bus All buses leave from a small, vacant lot about 200m from the medina on Ave de la République. There are buses to Nabeul (530 mills, 30 minutes) every 30 minutes, hourly buses to Tunis (TD3, 1½ hours) and three buses a day to Sousse (TD3.150, 1½ hours).

Train Hammamet is on the Cap Bon branch line, which runs from Bir Bou Regba to Nabeul. There are 12 trains a day in each direction. The 20-minute journey to Nabeul costs 750 mills in 1st class and 490 mills in 2nd class.

It's only seven minutes by train from Hammamet to Bir Bou Regba, which is on the main line from Tunis to the south.

Services to Bir Bou Regba are timed to connect with main-line trains heading north to Tunis, or south to Sousse, Sfax and beyond.

There is also one through service a day to Tunis (TD3.900, 1½ hours), which starts from Nabeul. The station is about 1.5km from the centre of town at the northern end of Ave Habib Bourguiba.

Louage *Louages* to Tunis (TD3.250) leave from Place Pasteur, about 800m north-east of the medina. Louages to Sousse (TD4.500) and Kairouan (TD3.850) leave from Barrak es-Sahil, north of town off the road to Hammamet Sud.

CAP BON PENINSULA

Tunisian Wine

Wine has been produced in Tunisia since Phoenician times, although the modern industry is descended from French and Italian plantings made during the 19th and 20th centuries. In the 1950s Tunisia, along with Algeria and Morocco, accounted for two-thirds of international wine production, most of it flowing north across the Mediterranean to France.

Wine production has fallen steadily since independence, but still averages more than 15 million litres a year – most of it for domestic consumption. The industry is regulated by the Office du Vin, a state body that ranks Tunisia's wine regions in a quality designation system based on the one used in France, the *appellations controlées*.

The country's main wine producing area is the southern part of the Cap Bon Peninsula, around the town of Grombalia, which stages an annual wine festival in September. The region specialises in the production of consistent easy-drinking rosés such as Gris de Hammamet. The Mornag region, closer to Tunis, produces a popular light red called Haut Mornag, which is served chilled like a beaujolais. It's a favourite tipple in local bars.

Full-bodied acidic reds are the speciality of the Tebourba region, west of Tunis. Magon, named after a famous Carthaginian agronomist, is a good choice; better still is Vieux Magon, cellared seven years before release. Other possibilities include an interesting aged pinot – the 2000 release was bottled in 1989.

Most white wines come from the north-east, between Tunis and Bizerte, although production is based on the inferior quality muscat of Alexandria grape variety, which thrives in hot climates and produces a strong and very sweet *vin ordinaire*. It's better known as an eating grape. However, there are some drier whites on the market – look out for labels such as Sidi Rais, Domaine de Karim and the unusual Muscat Sec de Kelibia.

Car Agencies with offices in Hammamet include: Avis (☎ 280 303), Rue de la Gare; Europcar (☎ 280 146), Ave des Hôtels; Hertz (☎ 280 187), Ave des Hôtels; and Topcar (☎ 280 767), Ave du Koweit.

Getting Around

Taxis are the only alternative to walking. The main taxi rank is at the large roundabout just north of the medina. A taxi from here to Hammamet Sud costs around about TD3.500.

NABEUL

☎ 02 • pop 40,000

Nabeul, 18km north of Hammamet, is the main town and administrative centre of the Cap Bon Peninsula. It was an important town long before the advent of mass tourism and it continues to earn the bulk of its income from its traditional role as a service centre for the region.

Tourism has become a major player in recent years and in summer the streets are almost as packed with sunburnt Europeans as Hammamet. Most tourists stay at one of the beach resorts that stretch south along the coast towards Hammamet.

The biggest difference between Hammamet and Nabeul is that Nabeul has a good range of budget accommodation. Even in the middle of summer it is possible to find a room for a price that won't break the bank.

Orientation

Nabeul is spread out over a wide area. The town centre is about 1.5km inland – a legacy of the time during the 16th century when Christian forces terrorised the Cap Bon coast, forcing towns to relocate away from the sea. The town has slowly spread back towards the coast in modern times, but it's a fair hike between the beach hotels and the shops and services in the town centre.

The two areas are linked by the main street, Ave Habib Bourguiba, which runs roughly north-south through the middle of town. It comes into the north-west of town as the road from Tunis, and finishes down by the beach. The town centre is around the intersections of Ave Habib Bourguiba, Ave Habib Thameur and Souq de l'Artisanat. Ave Habib Thameur leads south-west past the main bus and louage stations and becomes the road to Hammamet, while Souq de l'Artisanat runs north-east through the old part of town and links up with the road to Kelibia.

Information

Tourist Office The ONTT tourist office (☎ 286 800) is on Ave Taieb Mehiri between the beach and the centre of town. It has a good brochure with maps of Nabeul and Hammamet and other information. Even when it's closed, bus, train and accommodation information is posted outside the office.

The office is open from 8.30 am to 1 pm and 3 to 5.45 pm Monday to Thursday and to 1.30 pm Friday and Saturday. During July and August it's open from 7.30 am to 7.30 pm Monday to Saturday.

Money There are plenty of banks; most are along Souq de l'Artisanat, Ave Habib Thameur and Ave Habib Bourguiba.

Post & Communications The main post office is on Ave Habib Bourguiba. There are lots of Taxiphone offices around town.

For Internet access, head to Publinet Nabeul, near the train station at the northern end of Rue des Palmiers.

Medical Services The huge regional hospital (☎ 286 633) occupies an entire block on the northern side of Ave Habib Thameur, just west of Ave Habib Bourguiba.

Market

Nabeul's Friday market has become one of the major tourist events in the country, although quite why is a bit of mystery. The crowds need to be seen to be believed. The tour buses descend from as far afield as Sousse and Monastir, disgorging thousands of day-trippers for a few hours of frantic souvenir shopping. Not surprisingly, prices are sky high; stall-holders are used to people paying top dollar, and have little time for people who want to haggle.

The town centre is chaotic on market day, when Souq de l'Artisanat is closed to traffic. The entire street is packed with tourists and traders. The market continues along

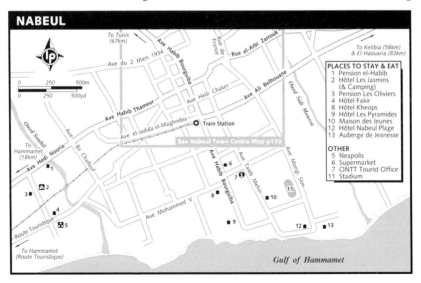

NABEUL

To Tunis (67km)
Ave du 2 Mars 1934
Ave Habib Bourguiba
Rue de France
Rue el-Arbi Zarrouk
To Kelibia (58km) & El-Haouaria (83km)
Ave Hedi Chaker
Ave Ali Belhouane
Oued Sidi Moussa
Ave Habib Thameur
Ave el-Jadida el-Maghrebia
Train Station
See Nabeul Town Centre Map p150
To Hammamet (18km)
Ave Hedi Nouria
Ave Bir Challouf
Ave Habib Bourguiba
Ave Taieb Mehiri
Ave Mongi Slim
To Hammamet (Route Touristique)
Route Touristique
Ave Mohammed V
Gulf of Hammamet

0   250   500m
0   250   500yd

PLACES TO STAY & EAT
1 Pension el-Habib
2 Hôtel Les Jasmins (& Camping)
3 Pension Les Oliviers
4 Hôtel Fakir
8 Hôtel Kheops
9 Hôtel Les Pyramides
10 Maison des Jeunes
12 Hôtel Nabeul Plage
13 Auberge de Jeanesse

OTHER
5 Neapolis
6 Supermarket
7 ONTT Tourist Office
11 Stadium

CAP BON PENINSULA

Rue el-Arbi Zarrouk. The markets are at their busiest between 9 am and noon. By 2 pm, life is slowly returning to normal.

Beaches

Most of Nabeul's beaches are in a disgraceful state, littered with all sorts of detritus (mainly rusting beer cans and plastic bottles). They are kept clean only in front of the resort hotels, so it makes sense to take advantage of this and make discreet use of the beach umbrellas etc.

Museum

Opposite the train station on Ave Habib Bourguiba, Nabeul's small archaeological museum is only for the real enthusiast. It houses a few pieces of Punic pottery from a range of sites around Cap Bon and a couple of mosaics from Roman Neapolis. It's open from 8 am to 7 pm daily in summer and from 8.30 to 5.30 pm daily in winter. Admission is TD1.100, plus a further TD1 to take photos.

Neapolis

The site of ancient Neapolis is about 1.5km south-west of the town centre, opposite the

Hôtel Fakir on the *route touristique* that runs along the coast to Hammamet. The original Punic settlement, established in the 5th century BC, was destroyed by Roman forces in 148 BC during the closing stages of the Third Punic War. It was later re-established as a Roman town, best known as a producer of a prized delicacy called *garum* – made from putrefied fish guts. Several amphorae full of the stuff were unearthed when the site was excavated in the 1960s.

The site was closed at the time of research and looks like it's been that way for some time.

Places to Stay – Budget

Camping An excellent little camp site in the grounds of the Hôtel Les Jasmins, 2km south-west of town on the way to Hammamet, is *Camping Les Jasmins* (☎ 285 343, fax 285 073). The hotel is clearly signposted on the left, 200m beyond the Oued Souhil on Ave Hedi Nouria. The camping area has shady sites beneath some large old olive trees, and charges TD2.200 per person, TD1.500 for a tent, TD2 for caravans and camper vans, TD2 for electricity and TD2 for a hot shower. The place is a five-

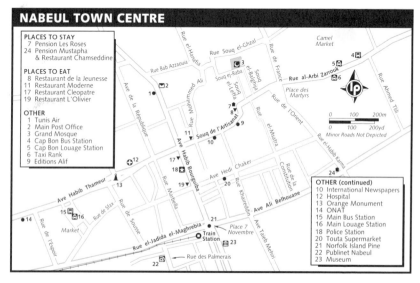

NABEUL TOWN CENTRE

PLACES TO STAY
7 Pension Les Roses
24 Pension Mustapha
   & Restaurant Chamseddine

PLACES TO EAT
8 Restaurant de la Jeunesse
11 Restaurant Moderne
17 Restaurant Cleopatre
19 Restaurant L'Olivier

OTHER
1 Tunis Air
2 Main Post Office
3 Grand Mosque
4 Cap Bon Bus Station
5 Cap Bon Louage Station
6 Taxi Rank
9 Editions Alif

OTHER (continued)
10 International Newspapers
12 Hospital
13 Orange Monument
14 ONAT
15 Main Bus Station
16 Main Louage Station
18 Police Station
20 Touta Supermarket
21 Norfolk Island Pine
22 Publinet Nabeul
23 Museum

minute walk from a relatively uncrowded stretch of beach.

Hostels Nabeul has both a *maison des jeunes* (a government run hostel) and an HI-affiliated *auberge de jeunesse*. The only things they have in common are that they are both cheap and they are both likely to be fully booked in summer.

The *Auberge de Jeunesse* (☎/fax 285 547) is on the beach at the end of Ave Mongi Slim. Accommodation is in a row of *ghorfas* (rooms), built in the traditional Berber style with high barrel-vaulted ceilings. They look a bit basic from the outside, but all is spic and span within following recent renovations. There are separate dorms for men and women, each with their own showers and toilets. It's good value at TD5 per person. Breakfast costs TD1, and additional meals are available at TD3 each.

The hostel also has an area set aside for camping, with a separate ablutions block. It charges TD5 per tent or campervan, and TD1 per person.

The no-frills *Maison des Jeunes* is towards the beach on Ave Taieb Mehiri. It has dorm beds for TD5.

Pensions There is a good choice of pensions, starting with the friendly *Pension Les Roses* (☎ 285 570) in the middle of town on Souq de l'Artisanat. It has clean, comfortable singles/doubles for TD9/16 in summer, falling to TD7/12 in winter. Cold showers are free and hot showers cost 500 mills. The pension can be hard to find; it's tucked away on the western side of the small open square where Souq de l'Artisanat makes a bend in the centre of town.

Another good place is the *Pension Mustapha* (☎ 222 262), on the corner of Rue Habib el-Karma and Ave Ali Belhouane. It charges TD12/21 in summer and TD9.500/16 in winter. The rooms have showers and hot water, and prices include breakfast. The *Pension el-Habib* (☎ 224 785), on Ave Hedi Nouria just beyond the Oued Souhil, has rooms with shared bathroom for TD7.500 per person, and rooms with private bathroom for TD10 per person.

Places to Stay – Mid-Range
There is a cluster of good places to the southwest of town between Ave Hedi Nouria and the route touristique to Hammamet.

The *Hôtel Les Jasmins* (☎ 285 343, fax 285 073), 2km south-west of town on the way to Hammamet, has singles/doubles with breakfast for TD28/50. In winter the rates drop to TD20/30. All rooms come with toilet and either shower or bath.

The friendly, family run *Pension Les Oliviers* (☎ 286 865) is signposted down a small lane opposite the entrance of the Hôtel Les Jasmins. It's a great place surrounded by olive and citrus groves. It charges TD33/40 in summer and TD17/22 in winter for immaculate rooms with shower, toilet and washbasin, plus breakfast. The owners are high-school teachers, and both husband and wife speak excellent English.

Between the Hôtel Les Jasmins and the beach is another possibility, the *Hôtel Fakir* (☎ 285 477, fax 287 616), which has a grand, spiral staircase and large, airy rooms costing TD32.500/48 in summer, dropping to TD23/30 in winter, including breakfast.

Places to Stay – Top End
The situation with the big resort hotels is much the same as in Hammamet: They are booked out by tour groups in summer, and offer some astonishingly cheap deals in winter. The giant three star *Hôtel Les Pyramides* (☎ 285 775, fax 285 679), by the beach at the southern end of Ave Habib Bourguiba, leads the way among the price-cutters. Singles/doubles that are listed at TD54/76 in summer are slashed to TD23/32 in winter, which includes a buffet breakfast. Facilities include tennis courts, a swimming pool and disco.

The smartest hotel in town is the four star *Hôtel Kheops* (☎ 286 555, fax 286 024), just north of the Hôtel Les Pyramides on Ave Habib Bourguiba. In summer, it charges a whopping TD96/126, dropping to TD36/44 in winter, including breakfast.

Places to Eat
There are lots of good, cheap restaurants around the town centre. The *Restaurant*

CAP BON PENINSULA

Chamssedine, attached to the Pension Mustapha, is as good as any. It has *briq à l'oeuf* (an egg deep-fried in a triangle of wafer-thin pastry, served with a wedge of lemon) for 800 mills, salads from TD1.200 and a variety of main dishes from TD2.500.

Other popular places include the tiny *Restaurant Cleopatre*, on Ave Habib Bourguiba south of the junction with Ave Habib Thameur, and the *Restaurant de la Jeunesse*, next the Pension Les Roses on Souq de l'Artisanat.

The *Restaurant Moderne*, at the western end of Souq de l'Artisanat, is something of a rarity: a cheap local restaurant that also serves alcohol.

If money is no object, Nabeul's top restaurant is the *Restaurant L'Olivier* (☎ 286 613), at the junction of Ave Hedi Chaker and Ave Habib Bourguiba. A meal for two costs about TD30, plus wine.

Self-caterers should head for the large *Touta supermarket* on Ave Hedi Chaker, which is also the place to buy wine. There is another *supermarket* on the southern reaches of Ave Habib Bourguiba, halfway between the town and the beach.

Shopping

Nabeul has long been famous for its pottery, and likes to think of itself as the national centre of the craft – a title it disputes with the town of Guellala, on Jerba. The potters of Nabeul turn out an amazing range of styles to meet the demands of the tourist trade. Traditionally, they were known for their fine Punic and Roman-influenced pots and vases, and for the ornate decoration introduced by Andalusian immigrants in the 17th century. There are some beautiful examples of traditional work in the shops around town. The interesting stuff, though, is outnumbered by the very tacky stuff – amphorae covered with tacky scenes of camels and palm trees, and gaudily decorated dinner sets that bear little relation to anything remotely Tunisian.

If you want to buy some pottery, but you're unsure of how much you should be paying, check out the prices at the ONAT emporium on Ave Habib Thameur first to get an idea. You'll find the biggest choice of pottery at the Friday market, but no bargains.

Books Local publisher Editions Alif has a retail outlet at 115 Souq de l'Artisanat. It stocks the full range of Alif publications: guides to ancient sites, pop-up books for children, posters and postcards.

Getting There & Away

Air The Tunis Air office (☎ 286 092) is at 178 Ave Habib Bourguiba, opposite the main post office. The nearest airport is at Tunis.

Bus There are two bus stations in Nabeul. The main bus station is near the centre of town on Ave Habib Thameur. It has departures to Hammamet (530 mills, 30 minutes) every 30 minutes from 5.30 am to 7 pm, and hourly buses to Tunis (TD2.800, 1½ hours). Other services include three buses a day to Zaghouan (TD2.810, two hours), Sousse (TD3.790, two hours) and to Kairouan (TD5.540, 2¼ hours).

Buses for Kelibia and the rest of Cap Bon leave from the site of the Friday market on Rue el-Arbi Zarrouk on the other side of town. On Friday, the buses move to a vacant lot just opposite. There are 16 services a day to Kelibia (TD2.250, 1¼ hours), the last bus leaving at 6.15 pm. The 10.30 am and 6.15 pm services continue to El-Haouaria (TD3.150, 1¾ hours); otherwise, catch any bus to Kelibia and change there.

Train Nabeul is the north-eastern terminus of the Cap Bon branch line, which connects to the main line from Tunis to Sousse at Bir Bou Regba.

There are at least 10 trains a day to Bir Bou Regba, stopping at Hammamet (750 mills in 1st class, 20 minutes). One train a day continues to Tunis (TD3.700, 1½ hours); otherwise change at Bir Bou Regba. There are also connections with services south to Sousse, Sfax and Gabès.

The station is conveniently central at the junction of Ave Ali Belhouane and Ave Habib Bourguiba.

Louage There are two louage stations, next to the respective bus stations. Regional services to other parts of Cap Bon, including Kelibia (TD2.500) and El-Haouaria (TD3.700), leave from next to the bus station on Rue el-Arbi Zarrouk. Services to the rest of the country leave from behind the bus station on Ave Habib Thameur. Tunis (TD3.100) is by far the most popular destination; other possibilities include Kairouan (TD5), Sousse (TD4.300) and Zaghouan (TD3.050).

Car Half a dozen agencies are represented in Nabeul, including Avis (☎ 286 555) at the Hôtel Kheops, Hertz (☎ 285 327) out towards Hammamet on Ave Habib Thameur and Nova Rent (☎ 222 072) at 54 Ave Habib Bourguiba.

Getting Around
Nabeul is reasonably spread out, and in summer it's a major effort to walk from the main street to the beach. A taxi costs about TD1 and can be a life-saver; otherwise you can take one of the many *calèches* (horse-drawn carriages), but bargain hard and agree on a price before setting off.

AROUND NABEUL
Dar Chaabane
The small village, 4km north-east of Nabeul on the road to Kelibia, is the stonework capital of Tunisia. Its main street is lined with workshops full of masons tapping away with chisels, carving out everything from ashtrays to replicas of famous statues. If you need a couple of monumental lions for the entrance to your country estate, this is the place to go shopping. There's no need to worry about exceeding your baggage allowance: The workshops can arrange delivery.

Any bus heading north can drop you at Dar Chaabane. A taxi costs about TD2 from Nabeul.

Korba Lagoon
This extended lagoon is one of the country's most important wetland areas, and a popular spot for bird-watchers.

It begins at the nondescript little town of Korba, 19km north-east of Nabeul, and extends some 15km up the coast, protected from the sea by a narrow spit of land. Common bird species include coots, curlews and plovers. In winter, there are often large flocks of pink flamingos; the juveniles can be seen all year.

The area around Korba closely resembles a rubbish dump, so it's better to head further north. The main road to Menzel Temine and Kelibia runs parallel to the lagoon, so any bus or louage travelling north can drop you off where you choose.

KELIBIA
☎ 02 • pop 18,000
By the time you get to Kelibia, 58km north of Nabeul, you'll have left the worst of the region's commercialism far behind. What you'll find instead is a small town that continues to survive mainly on the earnings of its fishing fleet and as a service centre for the surrounding farmland. The town centre is 2km inland and has nothing to recommend it. The attractions are all on the coast at the eastern edge of town, where you'll find a small, sheltered beach, the port and a few fairly low-key resort hotels – all overlooked by a picturesque old fort.

History
Kelibia was the main town of the Cap Bon Peninsula in ancient times, by virtue of its strategic position and sheltered harbour.

It began life as a Berber settlement, but little is known about the town until the arrival of the Carthaginians in the 5th century BC. The fort they built on the hill overlooking the port was a key part of the defensive shield protecting Carthage itself, and provided the town with its name – Aspis (shield). It proved ineffective against both Agathocles and Regulus, but the town survived to become the Roman town of Clypea, traces of which have been uncovered in the modern town beneath the fort.

Orientation & Information
Most travellers will arrive at the bus and louage station on Ave Ali Belhouane, which is the name of the main coast road during its run through town. The town centre is just

east of here around the junction of Rue Ibn Khaldoun and Ave Habib Bourguiba. To get there, head north along Ave Ali Belhouane (towards El-Haouaria) from the bus and louage station, and then turn right into Rue Ibn Khaldoun. There are a couple of banks and a supermarket on Rue Ibn Khaldoun, and the post office is on Ave Habib Bourguiba. There is no tourist office. The fort and port are 2km east of here along Ave des Martyrs.

Fort

Kelibia's main attraction is the fabulous old fort that overlooks the harbour. The foundations of this structure are still visible below the square tower in the south-western corner. The structure that stands today was built by the Byzantines in the 6th century AD, modified during a brief period of Spanish occupation in the middle of the 16th century AD and further modified by the Turks. The most recent additions are gun emplacements, which were built by German forces during WWII.

A road leads up to the fort from opposite the maison des jeuneson the Mansourah road, which runs north from just past the port. The fort is open from 8 am to 7 pm daily in summer, and from 8.30 am to 5.30 pm daily in winter. Admission is TD1.100. The caretaker and his extended family live on the site, and the entire area is something of a farmyard, with chickens and cows. It's still a restricted area of some sort, so it's advisable to ask permission before taking photos and to heed the *accès interdit* (no entry) signs. The views over the coastline from the ramparts are magnificent.

Beaches

Mansourah Beach, 2km to the north, is a glorious white-sand beach stretching north as far as the eye can see. It's almost deserted, even in summer. Its only drawback is that it's very exposed. The beach is clearly signposted on the road running north past the fort.

The beach at Kelibia itself is very small and not that flash.

Places to Stay

Hostel The *Maison des Jeunes* (☎ 296 105), down past the harbour on the Mansourah road, is the usual masterpiece of architectural innovation and excellence for the usual TD4 a night. The staff let people camp in the grounds.

Hotels Kelibia has limited hotel options, most are at the beach by the harbour. The one star *Hôtel Florida* (☎/fax 296 248), built in 1946, is an old favourite; it has a nice shaded terrace by the water's edge. Room rates range from TD12 per person in winter to TD18 in summer, including breakfast.

Next door to the Florida is the *Hôtel Palmarina* (☎ 274 062, fax 274 055), a smart new three-star place with a swimming pool and its own small patch of beach. It charges a hefty TD42/64 for singles/doubles in summer, dropping to a bargain TD27/44 in winter.

Location is the only black mark against the friendly *Pension Anis* (☎ 295 777), halfway between the beach and the town on Ave Erriadh. Spotless rooms cost TD22/32 in summer, dropping to TD16/24 in winter, including breakfast. Ave Erriadh forks south off Ave des Martyrs about 500m out of the town centre and also runs down to the coast. It emerges near the *Hôtel Mamounia* (☎ 296 088, fax 296 858), a big beach resort to the south-west of the port. Rates range from TD52/74 in summer to TD31/40 in winter.

Out at Mansourah Beach, the *Hôtel Mansourah* (☎ 295 992) is a village-style package resort that was touted as the first phase of a major development proposed for this stretch of coast when it opened in 1995. Nothing has happened since.

Places to Eat

The *Restaurant de la Jeunesse*, opposite the Hôtel Florida, is the main budget option. It serves up a generous turkey cutlet, chips and salad for TD3.500.

The best restaurant in town is at the *Pension Anis*, where two people can eat well for TD20, plus wine. It is well-worth a visit.

[Continued on page 159]

KERKOUANE

The remote Punic settlement of Kerkouane, 12km north of Kelibia, is one of Tunisia's most remarkable ancient sites. Abandoned in its prime in the middle of the 3rd century BC and never reoccupied, it offers a unique insight into the Punic world.

History

Very little is known about the town's history, not even its true name. It was named Kerkouane by French archaeologists, who stumbled on the site by accident in 1952.

Finds suggest it was already a well-established Berber town when the Phoenicians arrived in the area in the 8th century BC. It appears to have continued as a purely Berber town for some time before it began to adopt Phoenician ways. It then evolved into a classic example of a Punic town: a blending of Berber and Phoenician cultures. The ruins that await the modern visitor are those of a town laid out at the beginning of the 6th century BC.

Although ancient writers waxed lyrical about the fertility of the surrounding country, no evidence of agricultural activity has been found at the site. Kerkouane, it seems, was home to an urban elite of merchants and craftsmen. Excavations have uncovered numerous pottery workshops and kilns, as well as jewellery making, stone carving and glass making.

It was also a producer of a highly prized dye known as Tyrian purple (after the Phoenician capital, Tyre). It was extracted from *murex*, a species of shellfish once plentiful along the coast.

The town was plundered by Agathocles in 310 BC, but recovered – only to be put to the sword once more by the Roman general Regulus in 256 BC during the First Punic War. This time the site was abandoned, and the ruins reclaimed by the coastal sands until they were uncovered during excavations between 1957 and 1961. Kerkouane was added to the World Heritage List in 1982.

Information

Opening hours are from 8 am to 7 pm in summer (1 April to 15 September), and from 8.30 am to 5.30 pm in winter; it's open daily except Monday. Entry is TD2.100, plus another TD1 to take photos.

The site is clearly signposted off the road between Kelibia and El-Haouaria. Buses and louages can drop you at the turn-off, leaving a pleasant walk of 1.5km to the site.

Organised Tours

Companies in Hammamet and Nabeul offer one-day tours which couple Kerkouane with the Roman Caves at nearby El-Haouaria (from TD40).

Inset: The sign of Tanit, the main Carthaginian female deity. (Illustration by Tony Fankhauser)

Punic Architecture

Virtually nothing was known about Punic architecture before the discovery of Kerkouane. Previous knowledge was restricted to the little that could be gleaned from Carthage and other sites that had been re-modelled and rebuilt by a succession of subsequent civilisations.

Kerkouane showed that Punic town planning had achieved a high level of sophistication. It must have been a very comfortable place to live by the standards of the time, with well-appointed houses spread back from the sea along wide streets dotted with small squares.

The houses represent the oldest known examples of the modern Tunisian courtyard home. Most were laid out with rooms arranged around a small central courtyard, with a corridor leading to the street. They were single storey houses, with steps leading to a rooftop terrace.

Punic builders employed a wide variety of techniques, ranging from *pisé* (rammed earth) to precision masonry. One of the most common

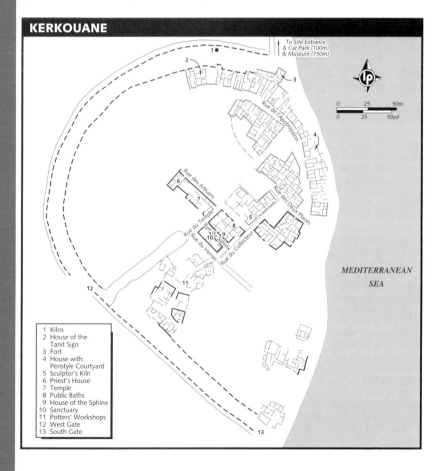

KERKOUANE

To Site Entrance & Car Park (100m) & Museum (150m)

Rue de l'Apotropaion
Rue des Artisans
Rue du Temple
Rue des Deux Places
Rue du Sphinx
Rue du Verrier
Rue du Collecteur

MEDITERRANEAN SEA

0   25   50m
0   25   50yd

1 Kilns
2 House of the Tanit Sign
3 Fort
4 House with Peristyle Courtyard
5 Sculptor's Kiln
6 Priest's House
7 Temple
8 Public Baths
9 House of the Sphinx
10 Sanctuary
11 Potters' Workshops
12 West Gate
13 South Gate

is the style known as *opus Africanum*, which features rubble walls strengthened at intervals with solid stone stabs and uprights. This Punic technique was later adapted by Roman and Byzantine builders, and is seen at its finest in the walls of the Capitol of Dougga.

Internal decoraion was an important feature. The houses had fine red paved floors decorated with inset fragments of white stone, an early form of mosaic known as *opus signinum*, while walls and ceilings were adorned with ornate plaster friezes and carvings.

Kerkouane's residents obviously placed a high value on personal hygiene. Most of the houses were once equipped with the hip baths for which the site is famous.

Highlights

The excavations uncovered a neatly laid-out small town within a semi-circular double outer wall. The inner wall was all that existed when Agathocles captured Kerkouane in 310 BC. After this disaster, the town's defences were rebuilt on a grander scale, adding a second, outer wall bolstered by various forts and towers. The small square **fort** by the coast on the northern side was built at this time, as were the fortifications around the south gate. It was all to no avail when Regulus arrived in 256 BC.

The town's main entrance was through the distinctive **west gate**, also known as the Port du Couchant (Sunset Gate). The gate is built into an overlap between the walls, an unusual Levantine style seldom found in the western Mediterranean.

The town itself has no great monuments. In fact, there's nothing standing above waist high. The names on the site plan were given by archaeologists in the course of the excavations.

It is the houses that are the main attraction, particularly those of the wealthy north-eastern quarter. There are some wonderful exam-

TONY FANKHAUSER

ples of *opus signinum* flooring around the place. Check out 3 Rue de l'Apotropaïon, better known as the **House of Tanit**, which features a beautiful white Tanit sign set into the floor.

It's easy to imagine the real-estate ads for 35 Rue de l'Apotropaïon. Absolute sea-front would be in there somewhere, along with mention of the delightful peristyle court-yard. This address also boasts one of the finest of the amazingly well-preserved **hip baths** for which the site is famous.

Right: A stele bearing an inscription of Tanit. The sign is common at Kerkouane – the House of Tanit has a particularly beautiful example set into its floor.

DAVID WILLETT

Left: The citizens of Kerkouane were obviously fastidious. Very modern-looking hip baths, finished with cement render, are common.

The town also had **public baths**, on Rue des Artisans, presumably so that the workers could also clean up.

At the centre of the site are the remains of the town's principal **temple**, running west from Rue du Temple. The temple was the scene of one of the most perplexing finds unearthed at Kerkouane: a small cache of Roman lamps and bowls dating from the 3rd century AD – 500 years after the town was abandoned. West of the temple is the **Priest's House**. The bread oven found here is an early example of the *tabouna* oven still widely used in Tunisia.

Rue du Sphinx is named after the ceremonial **sphinx** found at No 23. A small private **sanctuary** has been identified on the southern side of the street.

Pottery production seems to have been concentrated in the area just south of here, judging by the large number of kilns. The kiln on Rue du Verrier was for glass making, while the kilns to the north of the site date to the time before the construction of the outer wall.

Museum

The site museum houses finds uncovered during excavation. Its star attraction is the 'Princess of Kerkouane', a wooden sarcophagus cover carved in the shape of the goddess Astarte. There are also some beautiful pieces of jewellery and delicate funerary statues discovered at grave sites around Kerkouane.

[Continued from page 154]

The ***Restaurant el-Mansourah*** has a magnificent setting on a small headland at the southern end of Mansourah Beach. It's worth the trip for the view alone. Prices reflect this, with meals from TD15, plus wine. To get there, follow the road that leads out to Mansourah Beach from the port.

Getting There & Away

Buses and louages leave from Ave Ali Belhouane. There are 16 buses a day south to Nabeul (TD2.250, 1¼ hours), the last bus leaving at 6.45 pm, and 10 a day north to El-Haouaria (950 mills, 40 minutes) between 6 am and 2.45 pm. There are also regular louages to both destinations.

Getting Around

The bus station is 2.5km from the harbour and beach. A taxi to the bus station costs about TD1.500.

EL-HAOUARIA

☎ 02 ● pop 2500

This small town is tucked beneath the mountainous tip of Cap Bon. It's a quiet spot with a couple of good beaches, especially at **Ras el-Drek** on the southern side of the point. The main attraction, though, are the **Roman caves** on the coast 3km north-west of town. There are also some good walks from the town up to nearby Jebel Abiod.

The town has a choice of hotels and restaurants, and there are a couple of banks on the main street. There is no tourist office.

Roman Caves

Much of the stone used for the building of ancient Carthage and other towns of the region was cut from the remarkable complex of caves on the coast west of El-Haouaria. The cliffs along here are formed of a beautiful, easily worked yellow sandstone that was highly prized by the builders of the ancient world. Although signs on the way to the caves refer to them as the Grottes Romaines (Roman caves), they were in fact begun by the Carthaginians in the 6th century BC.

Murex

The famous purple dye so highly prized in ancient times by the Carthaginians and Romans came from two kinds of mollusc: the Murex and the Buccinum. They both have a long sac or vein filled with a yellowish fluid that turns purple when exposed to light.

A myth surrounds the origin of the discovery of the dye in Phoenicia, and goes as follows: Melkart, a Phoenician god, was walking on the beach one day with his lover, a nymph called Tyrus, and his dog. The dog bit into one of the murex shells and its muzzle became stained with a purple dye. When she saw the beautiful colour, Tyrus demanded that Melkart make her a garment of purple. So Melkart gathered a quantity of the shellfish to dye a gown which he presented to her.

This romantic tale hides the fact that production of the dye was a smelly, messy business, which involved a great deal of hard work. The molluscs were gathered in deep water by dropping narrow-necked baskets baited with mussels and frog meat. Once harvested the shellfish were hauled off to dye pits where their sacs were removed, pulped and heated in huge lead vessels. All the extraneous matter was skimmed off and the resulting dye fixed.

The dye pits were placed downwind of the residential areas to avoid the noxious smell. With practice the dyers could produce a variety of colours from pale pink to deep violet by mixing the Murex and Buccinum fluids in different quantities. The dye industry was on such a large scale that the farming of the molluscs caused them to become almost extinct.

Ann Jousiffe

The Murex shell: Extracting dye from the mollusc was a smelly and messy business.

The quarriers discovered that the quality of the stone was much better at the base of the cliff than on the surface, and opted to tunnel into the cliffs rather than to cut down. The end result after almost 1000 years of quarrying was an extraordinary network of caves stretching almost 1km along the coast. It was a highly sophisticated operation, with frequent light wells to the surface from the roofs of the pyramid-shaped caves. The cut stone was dragged out through the caves and loaded onto ships for transportation.

The caves are open from 8 am to 7 pm daily in summer, and from 8.30 am to 5.30 pm daily in winter. Admission is TD1.100, plus TD1 to take photos. The official guide, complete with brass nameplate, is keen to show people around.

The caves are clearly signposted 3km west of town. It takes about 45 minutes to walk there, but there's plenty of passing traffic as the caves are a popular attraction. The road ends at the Restaurant Fruits de Mer, next to the entrance to the site.

Bird-Watching

Jebel Abiod (390m), just north of town, is another prime bird-watching spot. The mountain represents the north-eastern tip of the Tunisian Dorsale, which is a prime migration route for thousands of raptors travelling between Africa and Europe. In May and June, the skies can be thick with birds waiting for the thermals that will carry them across the Straits of Sicily.

Access to the mountain is by an unsealed road that leads north of Rue Ali Belhouane in the centre of town. The road finishes at a telecommunications tower at the summit. The first few kilometres, finishing at a scenic lookout, are easily passable by normal car. The final leg is for 4WDs only.

You can find more information on local species at Les Amis des Oiseaux (☎ 269 200), signposted off the northern end of the main street.

Festivals

El-Haouaria has a tradition of falconry, and it stages an annual festival in mid-June.

Places to Stay

The **Pension Dar Toubib** (☎ 297 163) promises much with its blue-tiled entrance, but the rooms are no more than pokey little boxes. Singles/doubles are TD14/20 in summer, or TD8/12 in winter; breakfast is an additional TD2.500. To get there, follow the 'Hotel' signs from the main square out towards the mountain. It's a 10-minute walk.

The two star **Hôtel L'Epervier** (☎ 297 017, fax 297 258) is a comfortable, if overpriced, modern place on the main street in the middle of town. Rooms with breakfast are TD38/60, falling to a more manageable TD26/36 in winter.

The **Pension Les Grottes** (☎ 297 296, fax 269 070), on the road down to the caves, has rooms with breakfast for TD28/44 and TD19/28 in winter.

Places to Eat

The tiny **Restaurant de la Jeunesse**, opposite the Hôtel L'Epervier, is the only budget option in town. Tour groups use the restaurants at either the **Hôtel L'Epervier** or the **Pension Les Grottes**.

The **Restaurant Fruits de Mer**, out by the caves, has a lovely position overlooking the sea. It's a good place to sit and linger over a bowl of fish *chorba* (a type of fish soup; TD3).

Getting There & Away

El-Haouaria is well served by public transport. There are seven buses a day travelling along the north coast to Tunis (TD4.200, two hours), and 10 a day north to Kelibia (950 mills, 40 minutes). There are regular louages to Kelibia, and less-frequent ones to Nabeul (TD3.700) and Tunis (TD4.900).

KORBOUS

The small resort of Korbous, 51km west of Tunis, is a much-touted beauty spot and favourite destination for day-trippers from the capital. Squeezed into a narrow ravine and surrounded by steep cliffs on all sides, the place is famous for its hot springs, which supply a small band of hotels specialising in hot water and steam treatments – much loved by elderly Tunisians. The approach to Korbous from Soliman is spectacular, especially the final 6km along the coast when the road hugs the cliff-face. On a clear day, there are glorious views across the Gulf of Tunis to Carthage and Sidi Bou Saïd.

Most day-trippers continue to Aïn Atrous, about 1.5km north of Korbous, where a hot spring empties almost directly into the sea, providing a small batch of heated ocean where children love to frolic. Next to the spring there are half a dozen small restaurants specialising in grilled fish priced from around TD4.

Getting There & Away

It's much easier to get to Korbous from Tunis than from the resorts on the southern side of Cap Bon. There are frequent buses to Korbous (TD1.950, one hour) from the southern bus station in Tunis, as well as regular louages (TD2.300).

Services between Korbous and Nabeul operate via Soliman, 10km south-west of Korbous on the road to Tunis.

Northern Tunisia

Most visitors to Tunisia head for the Sahara and the beach resorts south of Tunis, leaving the north virtually undiscovered.

The beaches at Raf Raf and Sidi Ali el-Mekki, between Tunis and Bizerte, are among the best in the country. They are a favourite summer destination for Tunisian holiday-makers and scores of weekend-trippers from Tunis, but foreign tourists are relatively rare. There are more good beaches along the north coast, at Cap Serrat and around the small resort town of Tabarka.

Inland from Tabarka, perched high in the forests of the Kroumirie Mountains, the town of Ain Draham is high enough to receive snow in winter – and to remain pleasantly cool in summer while the rest of the country swelters.

The north's most-visited attractions are the Roman sites of Bulla Regia and Dougga. Less heralded, but equally worth visiting, is the ancient fortress city of Le Kef.

BIZERTE
☎ 02 • pop 110,000

The port city of Bizerte, 66km north of Tunis, is the largest city in Northern Tunisia. It's not the most glamorous destination, but there are a few reasonable beaches north and east of town and some fine examples of Islamic architecture in the unspoiled traditional quarter around the old port.

History

Just a few kilometres south of Cap Blanc (the northernmost tip of the African continent), Bizerte's strategic location has assured it an eventful history.

It was founded by the Phoenicians in the 8th century BC as Hippo Zarytus, one of their chain of ports along the North African coast. It was further developed by the Carthaginians, who built the first canal connecting Lake Bizerte to the sea – opening up one of the finest harbours in the western Mediterranean. This city was destroyed by

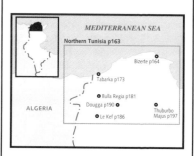

Highlights

- Walking in the beautiful cork forests around Ain Draham
- Lazing on Tabarka's sandy beaches
- Exploring the famous underground Roman villas at Bulla Regia
- Enjoying a Roman bath at Hammam Mellegue
- Soaking up the ancient history at the magnificent Capitol of Dougga

MEDITERRANEAN SEA

Northern Tunisia p163

Bizerte p164

Tabarka p173

Bulla Regia p181

ALGERIA

Dougga p190

Le Kef p186

Thuburbo Majus p197

the Romans in 146 BC in reprisal for supporting Carthage in the Punic Wars. It was rebuilt 100 years later as the Roman town of Hippo Diarrhytus, and later occupied by the Vandals and the Byzantines.

The name stuck until AD 678 when the town was captured by the Arabs and renamed Bizerte. The Spanish occupied the town from 1535 to 1570, when it fell to the Ottomans and became the principal port for the Muslim corsairs who preyed on Christian shipping in the Mediterranean. (See also the boxed text 'Pirates of the Barbary Coast' under Around Bizerte later in this chapter.)

The French transformed the town, and developed a major naval base at nearby Menzel Bourguiba, on the south-western edge of Lake Bizerte. They dug a new canal, completed in 1895, to handle modern

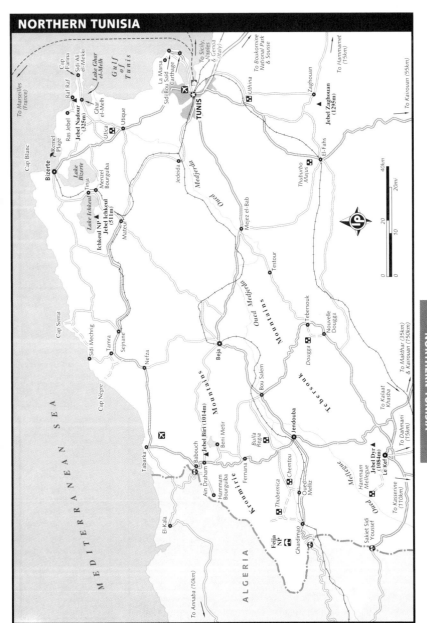

NORTHERN TUNISIA

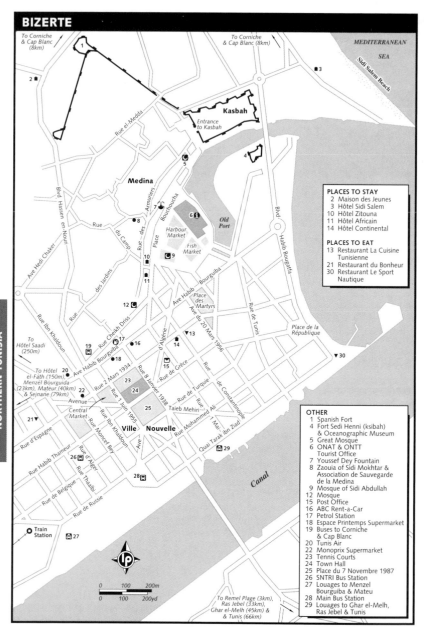

BIZERTE

PLACES TO STAY
2 Maison des Jeunes
3 Hôtel Sidi Salem
10 Hôtel Zitouna
11 Hôtel Africain
14 Hôtel Continental

PLACES TO EAT
13 Restaurant La Cuisine
   Tunisienne
21 Restaurant du Bonheur
30 Restaurant Le Sport
   Nautique

OTHER
1 Spanish Fort
4 Fort Sedi Henni (ksibah)
   & Oceanographic Museum
5 Great Mosque
6 ONAT & ONTT
   Tourist Office
7 Youssef Dey Fountain
8 Zaouia of Sidi Mokhtar &
   Association de Sauvegarde
   de la Medina
9 Mosque of Sidi Abdullah
12 Mosque
15 Post Office
16 ABC Rent-a-Car
17 Petrol Station
18 Espace Printemps Supermarket
19 Buses to Corniche
   & Cap Blanc
20 Tunis Air
22 Monoprix Supermarket
23 Tennis Courts
24 Town Hall
25 Place du 7 Novembre 1987
26 SNTRI Bus Station
27 Louages to Menzel
   Bourguiba & Mateu
28 Main Bus Station
29 Louages to Ghar el-Melh,
   Ras Jebel & Tunis

shipping and filled in the old canal, dug by the Carthaginians, to build their Ville Nouvelle (new town).

Such was the French attachment to Bizerte and its harbour facilities that they refused to abandon it after granting independence to the rest of the country in 1956. More than 1000 Tunisian lives were lost in the attempt to oust the French before they finally withdrew on 15 October 1963.

Orientation

The centre of the modern city is the French Ville Nouvelle, built on reclaimed land north of the shipping canal. The town planners broke away from the standard grid system used everywhere else in Tunisia, adding a couple of diagonal streets for good measure. These diagonal streets can be very disorienting. A new problem for visitors is that the latest batch of street signs are in Arabic only.

The old Arab quarter, which is almost signless, is immediately north of the Ville Nouvelle and borders the old port – which is all that remains of the original canal built by the Carthaginians.

Blvd Hassen en-Nouri runs north from the Ville Nouvelle to the beaches of the Corniche.

The shipping canal is spanned by a modern bridge with a central section that can be raised to allow larger vessels to pass through. The main road south to Tunis crosses the bridge.

Information

Most facilities of importance to tourists are in the Ville Nouvelle.

Tourist Office Finding the tourist office (☎ 432 897) can be hard work, especially if you try following any of the many signs around town. They point just about everywhere except the tourist office, which is above the ONAT building opposite the old port. It had just moved there at the time of research, but the signs still point to the old office by the canal on the corner of Quai Tarak ibn Ziad and Ave Taieb Mehiri. Some signs point to an old *syndicat d'initiative*, which closed many years ago.

It's not really worth the effort anyway: Their hand-out map was drawn in the days before the canal bridge was built, and shows traffic being ferried across on punts. However, you may be able to get your hands on a copy of the latest accommodation prices for selected places in the northern region. Opening hours are from 8.30 am to 1 pm and 3 to 5.45 pm Monday to Thursday and from 8.30 am to 1.30 pm Friday and Saturday.

Money There are branches of all the major banks around Place du 7 Novembre 1987 and along Ave Habib Bourguiba.

Post & Communications The main post office is on Ave d'Algérie. There are lots of Taxiphone offices in the Ville Nouvelle. The Internet is much harder to access: The only Publinet office is at the *maison des jeunes* (☎ 431 608), and you'll need to reserve a timeslot because the place is always packed.

Kasbah

The enormous kasbah is the most impressive structure in the old town, with its massive walls towering over the northern side of the entrance to the old harbour. It was originally a Byzantine fort, built in the 6th century AD to guard the port in conjunction with the smaller *ksibah* (small fort) on the southern side. The structure that stands today was built by the Ottomans in the 17th century.

The walls are 10m high in places and up to 11m thick – built to withstand artillery bombardment. They enclose a small town of narrow, winding streets surrounding the kasbah mosque. The only entrance is through the gateway at the western end.

Ksibah & Oceanographic Museum

The ksibah forms the southern bastion of the harbour defences built by the Byzantines. It comprises a small round tower linked to a larger rectangular fort. The fort was modified by the Aghlabids, who added the attractive arched *skifa* (gate) and a courtyard with a set of cells – not for prisoners but for silent study of the Quran. The

Ottomans later strengthened the walls to withstand artillery bombardment.

The fort, also known as Fort Sidi Henni, now houses a small Oceanographic Museum, which is a rather grand description for a small collection of sea beasties. It's open from 9 am to 12.30 pm and 2.30 to 6.30 pm Tuesday to Sunday, and admission is 500 mills (250 mills for children).

Place Bouchoucha

Flanked by the old port to the east and the medina to the west, this extended square connects the old and new towns.

The best place to start a tour of the area is the **Zaouia of Sidi Mokhtar**, tucked away in the narrow streets of the medina through the archway opposite the markets. The zaouia now houses the Association de Sauvegarde de la Medina, the group responsible for the preservation of the medina. You'll need to speak French or Arabic to extract much information from the staff, but they do have a fascinating map that shows how the town looked in 1881 when the French arrived.

In 1881, Place Bouchoucha was the western channel of the canal system connecting Lake Bizerte with the sea. It rejoined the eastern channel at Ave Habib Bourguiba, creating an island where the European merchants and town elite lived. This area now houses the lively **markets**.

The medina's most important buildings are close together on the edge of Place Bouchoucha and include the **Great Mosque**, built in 1652. Its striking octagonal minaret is best viewed from Rue des Armuriers.

Just south of the mosque is the **Youssef Dey fountain**, built in 1642. It has a typically Andalusian inlaid arch around an inscription, inviting users to avail themselves until the waters of paradise become available.

Spanish Fort

The so-called Spanish Fort overlooks the town from the hill north of the medina. It's actually Turkish and was built between AD 1570 and 1573 by Ulj Ali, the military ruler of Algiers, after he had kicked out the Spanish. It was built to reinforce the town's outer defensive wall, which had existed in one

form or another since Roman times. All that remains of the wall are two sections on either side of the fort.

Beaches

There are some reasonable beaches north of town. Hotels have a monopoly on the first few kilometres of sand, a stretch known as the Corniche, but it's not too difficult for westerners to slip in.

The coast road finishes about 8km north of town at **Les Grottes**, a small beach protected to the west by the white cliffs of Cap Blanc, the northern tip of the African continent. It's hard to get to without a car. If you catch the No 2 bus from town, you will have to walk – or hitch – the last 2km or so.

Remel Plage, 3km from east of Bizerte off the road, is the best beach in the area. Any bus heading east can drop you off at the turn-off, from where it's a 15-minute walk.

Places to Stay – Budget

Camping The *Centre de la Jeunesse de Remel Plage* (☎ 440 819) is a good camp site and hostel 3km east of Bizerte on Remel Plage. It's signposted at the turn-off to Remel Plage. The hostel facilities are basic, but there are good shady sites beneath the pine trees and the beach is only a five-minute walk away. It charges TD2 per person for camping, and TD5 for dorm beds. Buses to Ghar el-Melh, Ras Jebel or Raf Raf can drop you at the Remel Plage turn-off, but it's easier to spend TD3.500 on a taxi. If you're visiting outside the summer months, phone first to check that it's open.

Hostels The *Maison des Jeunes* (☎ 431 608) is just north of the town centre, signposted off Blvd Hassen en-Nouri near the Spanish Fort. As usual, it's more like a prison block than a hotel.

Hotels The budget hotels are all in and around the city centre. They are a fairly grim lot, best avoided if you can afford it.

The best is the *Hôtel Saadi* (☎ 422 528), opposite the soccer stadium on Rue Salah ben Ali, 400m from the centre of town. It has singles/doubles with shared bathroom for TD7.500/13.

After that, the *Hôtel Africain* (☎ *434 412, 59 Rue Sassi Bahri*) gets the vote ahead of its neighbour, the *Hôtel Zitouna* (☎ *438 760, 9 Place Bouchoucha*), a few doors to the north. The Africain has singles/doubles/triples with shared bathroom for TD7/9/12, doubles with shower for TD15 and a four-bed family room for TD20. The Zitouna has very basic singles/doubles for TD5/8. Neither hotel is for light sleepers – the markets are right outside and the action starts early.

The *Hôtel El-Fath* (☎ *430 596, 136 Ave Habib Bourguiba*) is worth considering in summer when prices are sky high on the coast. This small hotel charges the same all year – TD18/24 for singles/doubles with bathroom. It's just west of the town centre on the way to Mateur.

Places to Stay – Mid-Range

The resort hotels are spread along the coast to the north of town. Most of them offer good value if you stay away from peak season in July and August, when they tend to be booked out by tour groups anyway. Prices in this section include breakfast.

The line-up starts with the popular two star *Hôtel Sidi Salem* (☎ *420 365, fax 420 380,* e *ctss.bejaoui@planet.tn*), which has a great location just 200m east of the kasbah. The large bungalow-style rooms face out to a wide expanse of sandy beach, and facilities include tennis courts and a pool. In summer, singles/doubles go for a hefty TD70/110, but the price drops to just TD25/40 in winter – and TD35/60 in the middle season.

There are several possibilities further north along the Corniche. The two star *Hôtel Jalta* (☎ *420 350, fax 420 395*), 3km north of town, has singles/doubles for TD22/34 in winter and TD50/70 in summer. The best patch of beach is the preserve of the *Hôtel Corniche* (☎ *431 844, fax 431 830*), where rates are TD27/39 in winter and TD64/106 in summer.

The *Hôtel Le Petit Mousse* (☎ *432 185, fax 437 595*), 4km from the city centre, is better known for its restaurant than its rooms. It charges TD33.500/49 in winter and TD47/77 in summer.

Places to Stay – Top End

The best address in town is the four star *Bizerta Resort* (☎ *436 966, fax 422 955*), 500m north of the Hôtel Sidi Salem. Although it dropped its rates following deregulation, prices are still over the top for Bizerte: TD67/74 in winter, rising to TD103/114 in summer.

Places to Eat

The *Restaurant La Cuisine Tunisienne*, on the corner of Rue 2 Mars 1934 and Rue de Constantinople, is a popular spot with a good choice of traditional dishes. *Briqs* are priced from 450 mills and salads from TD1. Main courses include couscous with lamb (TD2.200) and grilled fish with chips and salad (TD3).

For a splurge, head north to the restaurant at the *Hôtel Le Petit Mousse* (☎ *432 185*). An excellent three-course meal with wine will set you back about TD25. The *Restaurant Eden* (☎ *439 023*), opposite the Hôtel Corniche, specialises in seafood and comes highly recommended.

The setting is the star feature at the *Restaurant Le Sport Nautique* (☎ *431 495*), at the entrance of the shipping canal on the edge of town.

Self-caterers should check out the *markets* on Place Bouchoucha. The fish markets are in a separate building behind the produce markets. There are several *supermarkets* in the Ville Nouvelle.

Getting There & Away

Air Tunis Air (☎ *432 201*) has an office at 76 Ave Habib Bourguiba. The nearest airport is Tunis-Carthage.

Bus There are buses to Tunis (TD3.070, 1¾ hours) every 30 minutes from 5 am from the main bus station near the canal at the end of Ave d'Algérie.

Local company SRT Bizerte has regular buses to Ras Jebel (TD1.350, one hour), the connecting point to Raf Raf, and a 6 am departure to Ain Draham (TD6.080, 4¼ hours) via Tabarka (TD5.200, 3½ hours). Buses to Ras Jebel can drop you at the Remel Plage turn-off for the beach and camp site.

NORTHERN TUNISIA

Train There are up to four trains a day to Tunis (TD3.950 in 1st class, 1½ hours). The train station is by the shipping canal at the south-western end of Rue de Russie.

Louage *Louages* to Tunis (TD3), Ras Jebel (TD1.550) and Ghar el-Melh (TD1.700) leave from near the bridge over the shipping canal. Louages to Menzel Bourguiba and Mateur depart from opposite the entrance to the train station. There are no louages to Tabarka.

Car The following agencies have offices in Bizerte: ABC Rent-a-Car (☎ 434 624), 33 Ave Habib Bourguiba; Avis (☎ 433 076), 7 Rue d'Alger; Hertz (☎ 438 388), Place des Martyrs; and Europcar (☎ 431 455), 19 Rue Rejiba, Place des Martyrs.

Getting Around
Buses to the Corniche (260 mills) stop at the corner of Blvd Hassen en Nouri and Ave Habib Bourguiba. The bus numbers to look out for are Nos 2 and 29. Bus No 2 can drop you at the turn-off to Les Grottes beach. There are plenty of taxis. As elsewhere, they're cheap if the driver uses the meter.

AROUND BIZERTE
Raf Raf
Few travellers make it to Raf Raf, but it is a favourite summer spot with holidaying Tunisians, particularly at weekends. There are numerous restaurants as well as a hotel.

The attraction is the beach, which ranks among the best in the country – a long stretch of white sand fringed by pine trees. It has a beautiful setting, tucked beneath the rugged escarpment that runs east from Jebel Nadour (325m) for about 2km to Cap Farina. Unfortunately, the white sand is overlaid with more than its fair share of both garbage and people. You can escape the people by walking along the beach a bit, but there's no escape from the rubbish.

Raf Raf town is about 1km inland and contains little of interest to the traveller. The main road from Ras Jebel bypasses the town centre and heads straight for the beach.

Places to Stay & Eat The only place to stay is the tiny *Hôtel Dalia* (☎ 02-441 688) to the left of the main road leading down to the sea. Summer rates are TD28/42 for singles/doubles with bathroom, or TD31.500/47 with a sea view. Winter rates are about 25% lower.

The *Café Restaurant Andalous*, closer to the sea on the main street, serves good fish.

Getting There & Away Public transport operates via Ras Jebel, a small agricultural service town 6km west of Raf Raf. Buses to Ras Jebel leave from the bus stop on the main street 50m before the beach. Louages to Ras Jebel leave from outside the Banque de l'Habitat in town. There are regular buses and louages from Ras Jebel to Bizerte.

Ghar el-Melh
The sleepy little village of Ghar el-Melh is situated on the southern side of Jebel Nadour, sandwiched between the hillside and a silted-up lagoon known as Lake Ghar el-Melh. It's only a few kilometres south of Raf Raf as the crow flies but it's almost 20km by road.

It is a place with quite a history. It was founded during the reign of Osta Murad Dey (1637–40) as the pirate base of Porto Farina, which stood on the edge of a deep lagoon at the mouth of the Oued Medjerda. Its notoriety was such that in 1654 it was attacked and temporarily knocked out of action by the celebrated English admiral Sir Francis Drake. The compact, early Ottoman-style **Borj Osta Murad Dey**, built in 1638, is the only reminder of this period. It overlooks the lagoon on the western edge of town. It was in the middle of a major restoration job at the time of research.

After privateering was abolished at the beginning of the 19th century, the Husseinite beys attempted to turn the port into a major naval base. During his reign, Ahmed Bey (1837–55) ordered the construction of two new forts, a surrounding defensive wall and a new port flanked by armouries. His efforts were soon defeated by the silt-laden waters of the Oued Medjerda, which began to fill the lagoon about this time. Attempts to dredge the lagoon failed, and the port was abandoned

The imposing Licinian Baths, built at the height of Roman Dougga's prosperity in the 3rd century AD

One of Tunisia's most romantic ruins, the Capitol of Dougga (AD 166), was dedicated to the Roman gods Jupiter, Juno and Minerva. Its frieze depicts Emperor Antonius Pius being carried off by an eagle.

Bizerte's unspoiled old port was once a base for Muslim corsairs.

The Roman bath complex at Le Kef

The colonnades of a Roman villa at Bulla Regia

The Portico of the Petronii (AD 225), at Thuburbo Majus, was once part of a Roman gymnasium.

Pirates of the Barbary Coast

Early in the 16th century the coast of Tunisia was threatened by naval raids from the newly resurgent Spain. Khair ed-Din Barbarossa, a Turk from the Aegean island of Lesbos, stepped into the breach and began an age of piracy along the Barbary Coast (the Mediterranean coast of North Africa), which lasted until the 19th century.

Together with his brother Aruj, Barbarossa hoped to carve out a domain in North Africa with the help of Muslim refugees expelled from Andalusia in Spain. Fearing defeat by the Spanish, he paid homage to the Ottoman sultan and in 1518 he was granted a title and sent military reinforcements. With his increased forces Barbarossa was able to capture Algiers in 1529, and soon after became the admiral-in-chief of the Turkish navy.

In 1534 Barbarossa captured Tunis and turned it into a secure base from which to attack coastal towns in Europe and to raid merchant vessels in the Mediterranean. By the time he died in 1546 his legend was secure. Khair ed-Din's associate Dragut, who had been captured by the Spanish and ransomed by Barbarossa, continued the fight against the Spanish – after one clash on Jerba, Dragut built a pyramid of skulls on the beach that remained there until 1849.

The corsairs used a number of ports around the Tunisian coast, including La Goulette (Tunis), Bizerte, Tabarka and Ghar el-Melh – then known as Porto Farina. They commanded cruisers fitted out by wealthy backers, who in turn received 10% of captured loot. The crews often had a European element – Christian sailors were said to have 'taken the turban' or converted to Islam when they entered the employ of the Barbary captains. Nevertheless, the legendary drunkenness of English pirates at their Tunis base of La Goulette indicates they kept some of their old customs.

The gradual decline of the Ottoman Empire after the 17th century resulted in the Barbary Coast becoming increasingly independent, and Tunis became so tolerant of piracy that it was known as a pirate state. The beys of Tunis received a considerable amount of protection money from sea-going nations wishing to ensure their security.

The pirates lived on into the 19th century, with naval conflicts between Tripolitania (now western Libya) and the USA starting in 1804, the first time the USA sent forces into the Middle East. Tunis was attacked by the US Navy in 1815, and by 1830 the French had finally rid the Mediterranean of pirates.

Richard Plunkett

in favour of La Goulette (Tunis). Today the lagoon is more like a coastal swamp, and only tiny fishing boats can use the narrow channel connecting the port to the sea.

Places to Stay & Eat There was once talk of major tourist development for the town and the nearby beach at Sidi Ali el-Mekki, but nothing has happened and it remains a charming little backwater. There are no hotels, and there's nowhere to eat other than a seasonal *restaurant* at Sidi Ali el-Mekki.

Getting There & Away You can get to Ghar el-Melh by public transport from Bizerte. There are two buses a day (TD1.350,

one hour) and occasional louages (TD1.700). There is no public transport making the trip to Sidi Ali el-Mekki.

Sidi Ali el-Mekki

The beach at Sidi Ali el-Mekki, 6km east of Ghar el-Melh on the southern side of Cap Farina, is every bit as good as Raf Raf – but nowhere near as crowded.

There is no accommodation, but camping out is OK. The small *cafe/restaurant* on the beach operates only in summer; at other times of the year you will have to bring your own supplies.

The problem is getting here without your own transport. There is no public transport and little transport of any kind heads this way except on summer weekends. There is nothing at Sidi Ali el-Mekki other than the beach and a small fishing port – built to replace the silted-up port at Ghar el-Melh.

Utica

Once upon a time, Utica was a thriving port at the mouth of the Oued Medjerda. It was founded by the Phoenicians in about 1100 BC, about 300 years before Carthage, and remained a major port and strategic city for more than 1000 years. Although long subservient to Carthage, it defected to the Roman camp before the Third Punic War and became the capital of the Roman province of Africa after the destruction of Carthage in 146 BC.

Its days were numbered, though, by the waters of the Oued Medjerda. Silt levels in the river rose dramatically in Roman times as a result of the huge increase in wheat cultivation upstream in the Medjerda Valley and surrounding hills. By the beginning of the 2nd century AD, the port had been rendered virtually useless, and the river itself was no longer navigable. Carthage by now was back in favour and had become the capital once more, while Utica was left to decline into an insignificant farming village.

These days, the site occupies a low hill overlooking a vast expanse of rich farmland. The coast is now some 8km to the east, where the port of Ghar el-Melh is now experiencing a similar fate.

The **ruins** make a pleasant detour if you have your own transport. The turn-off is signposted to the east from the small, modern village of Utique, 33km north of Tunis on the road to Bizerte. You'll come to the **museum** first on the left, 2km from the main road. It houses an extensive collection of bits and pieces found on the site. The site itself is a further 500m along the road, at the bottom of the slope. The main attraction is the **House of the Cascade**, named after the fountains that used to decorate this mansion.

Both the museum and site are open from 9 am to 7 pm daily in summer, and from 8.30 am to 5.30 pm daily in winter. Admission is TD2.100, plus TD1 to take photos.

Getting There & Away Any bus or louage travelling between Tunis and Bizerte can drop you at the turn-off to the ruins. There is no public transport to the site itself.

NORTH COAST

The rugged stretch of coastline between Bizerte and Tabarka, dotted with isolated bays, is virtually uninhabited and is inaccessible for most of its length. The main road runs a fair way inland, and much of the country between the road and the sea is covered with plantation forest. There are a couple of secluded coastal settlements, but they are very hard to get to unless you have a vehicle. If you do have a vehicle, this is a good area to get right off the beaten track in.

Mateur

Mateur is a dull regional town 40km south of Bizerte. It is worth mentioning only because it is large enough to have useful transport links. Trains travelling on the Bizerte-Tunis line stop here, and there are regular buses and louages to Bizerte, Sejnane and Tabarka. The town is best known for its cheese.

Ichkeul National Park

This World Heritage–listed national park, 30km south-west of Bizerte, covers Lake Ichkeul and adjoining Jebel Ichkeul (511m). It is an important bird sanctuary, particularly in winter when the waters of Lake Ichkeul and the surrounding marshes are home to more than 200,000 migratory waterfowl from all over Europe. (See the accompanying boxed text 'Lake Ichkeul Bird Life' for information about bird species found here.)

Ichkeul is the only national park in Tunisia with facilities for visitors. As well as an information centre, on a ridge above the car park, there are picnic tables and a network of paths. The information centre at the park has a display area with details on the park's fauna and flora. Animals include mongooses, porcupines, jackals, wild boars and a herd of water buffaloes – descendants of a pair given to Ahmed Bey in 1840. They live in the marshes around the lake.

There is no accommodation in the park, and camping is not permitted. The park is open from 7 am to 6 pm daily. Admission is free.

Getting There & Away There is no public transport to the park, making it difficult to visit without your own car. Access is from the south-eastern side of the lake, 10km north of Mateur. Coming from Bizerte, follow the main road south to Menzel Bourguiba for 21km, continue to the village of Tinja and fork right onto the Mateur road. The turn-off to the park is signposted on the right after 9km. This road runs dead straight along a causeway for 7km to the base of Jebel Ichkeul and the park entrance. Officials will check you in (and out later) 3km before the car park and information centre.

Buses and louages between Bizerte and Mateur can drop you at the park turn-off, but you will have to walk or hitch from there. There is very little traffic, except at weekends.

Sejnane

The small town of Sejnane, halfway between Mateur and Tabarka, is famous for the primitive, moulded **pottery** known as Sejnane ware.

The techniques used by the potters of the Berber villages around here date back to Neolithic times. Clay is hand-moulded into an assortment of unusual animal figurines, as well as bowls of all shapes and sizes, and open-fired on mounds of glowing coals before being decorated with traditional Berber motifs in rusty reds and deep browns. You'll

Lake Ichkeul Birdlife

Lake Ichkeul is a haven for water birds of all types. Different groups of birds use the lake in different ways: Some hunt along the shoreline or probe the soft mud at the water's edge; others stride on long legs into deeper water to seek prey. The brightly coloured kingfisher is a living jewel that dives for prey, while warblers, finches and rails dart about the dense vegetation surrounding the lake.

Ichkeul's shores are thronged with stilts, sandpipers and stints. Aptly named wagtails strut about; and grey herons and little egrets stalk the shallows for fish and frogs. In spring, thousands of 'passage migrants' arrive from south of the Sahara, stopping briefly to replenish their energy before flying on to fan out across Europe.

The resident species are joined by migrants, such as squacco herons, white storks and cattle egrets. Skulking in the reed beds, the bittern, a well-camouflaged relative of the heron, is more often heard than seen, and Cettis, great reed warblers and moustached warblers make a riot of sound as they proclaim their territories. The purple gallinule pokes among the vegetation on long, splayed toes; its bright blue plumage and red bill make it virtually unmistakable, especially when the sun picks out its beautiful colours.

The greater flamingo is a large and graceful – if bizarre – bird that often concentrates in large flocks in shallow lakes. Although flamingos are nomadic and may not always be present in large numbers, one of the ornithological highlights of Tunisia is the sight of a mass of pink birds sifting for food through shimmering waters.

As summer wanes and autumn draws on, the summer 'shift' of migrants disperses south again to be replaced by birds escaping the northern winter. Chief among these are the ducks and geese. For sheer numbers of these, Lake Ichkeul has few rivals in the region. Up to 100,000 waterfowls are sustained by the lake, which at this time of year is replenished by winter rains. Observers should see good numbers of ducks, such as wigeons, teals, gadwalls, pintails and, further out, pochards. As many as 15,000 greylag geese have been reported over-wintering at Ichkeul. Other waterfowl specialities include white-headed ducks and marbled teals, and coots may be present in great numbers.

find the figurines and bowls on sale at tourist shops throughout the country.

Unfortunately, one place where you won't find any for sale is Sejnane itself. The pottery is produced in the surrounding villages, and sold at roadside stalls. There are lots of them about 6km north-east of town on the road to Bizerte, and others on the road to Mateur.

Sejnane itself is no more than a small service town built around the junction of the roads to Bizerte, Mateur and Tabarka. The main attraction is its large population of **storks**. Their nests are everywhere – check out the number adorning the roof of the train station, towards Tabarka on the western side of town. There are dozens more nests on the abandoned mining rig behind the station.

There are a couple of basic *restaurants* on the Mateur side of the main junction, but no accommodation.

The main junction also serves as the bus and louage station. SNTRI buses travelling the northern route (via Mateur) between Tabarka and Tunis can drop you at Sejnane. There are regular local buses and louages between Mateur and Sejnane. The train station is for freight services only.

Cap Serrat

Cap Serrat, 27km north of Sejnane, is one of Tunisia's gems – a remote peninsula flanked to the east by an unspoiled sandy bay. You will probably come across a few campers in summer, but for much of the year the place is completely deserted.

The access road to Cap Serrat is signposted 11km north of Sejnane along the back road to Bizerte (which skirts around the northern edge of Lake Ichkeul). From the turn-off, the road winds through large stands of eucalyptus plantation forest before emerging in a small valley dotted with a few scattered farmhouses. The road continues north to a tiny settlement at the base of the peninsula, and ends at a parking area behind the beach 200m further on. Cap Serrat itself looms large to the west, while a glorious white-sand beach curves away to the east.

There is a small *cafe/restaurant* behind the beach that caters for summer campers,

and fresh water is available from the fountain in the parking area.

The area is no longer undiscovered, but the absence of public transport keeps the numbers down. There's very little transport of any kind around here, so you need your own vehicle if you want to keep moving.

Cap Serrat to Sidi Mechrig

If you have your own transport, you can continue along the coast from Cap Serrat to Sidi Mechrig, some 20km to the west. The unsealed road is rough in places, but passable with caution in even the smallest car. The road hugs the coast all the way.

Sidi Mechrig

The small coastal settlement of Sidi Mechrig is usually approached from the village of Tamra, 9km west of Sejnane. It's another 17km from Tamra to the coast. The road, which is mostly sealed, twists across two ranges of low hills covered with large tracts of pine and eucalypt plantation before ending at a brand new fishing port.

There's not much at Sidi Mechrig other than a few houses and the very basic *Hôtel Sidi Mechrig* (no telephone), which is on the left as you approach the settlement. It has a great location overlooking a small sandy beach and a photogenic Roman arch – the only remains of an old bathhouse.

The location makes up for the rooms, which are dingy little boxes with a couple of saggy single beds. It charges TD10 per person with breakfast. The hotel is open all year because it happens to have the only bar between Tabarka and Mateur, guaranteeing a steady flow of customers. It also has a *restaurant*, open daily for lunch and dinner, with terrace seating overlooking the sea. It's a good spot to sit down to a large plate of grilled fish, chips and salad (TD7.500), washed down with a cold beer.

Getting There & Away Public transport out to Sidi Mechrig is very limited. In July and August, there are two buses (TD1) a day from Sejnane; there are no buses the rest of the year. There are also occasional *camionnettes* (pick-ups) – ask in Sejnane.

TABARKA

☎ 08 • pop 10,000

The small resort town of Tabarka is the last town on the north coast before the Algerian border, 22km to the west. It has one of the most picturesque settings in Tunisia, nestled below the densely forested slopes of the Kroumirie Mountains. The beautiful little bay on the northern edge of town is watched over by an impressive-looking Genoese fort on Tabarka Island (now linked by a causeway), while a long stretch of beach curves away eastwards towards Cap Nègre.

It's hard to believe that the package-tourism operators stayed away for so long, but they are now trying hard to make up for lost time. There is an expanding *zone touristique* (tourist strip) 4km to the east of town, complete with its own golf course, and an international airport opened here in July 1992. In spite of this, the town remains a relaxing place to spend a few days.

History

Like so many towns along the North African coast, Tabarka began life as a Phoenician settlement. Originally called

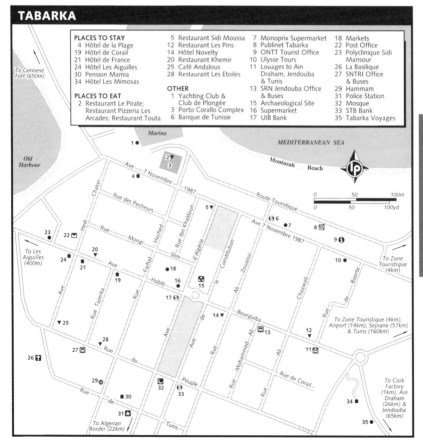

TABARKA

PLACES TO STAY
4 Hôtel de la Plage
19 Hôtel de Corail
21 Hôtel de France
24 Hôtel Les Aiguilles
30 Pension Mamia
34 Hôtel Les Mimosas

PLACES TO EAT
2 Restaurant Le Pirate;
  Restaurant Pizzeria Les
  Arcades; Restaurant Touta

5 Restaurant Sidi Moussa
12 Restaurant Les Pins
14 Hôtel Novelty
20 Restaurant Khemir
25 Café Andalous
28 Restaurant Les Etoiles

OTHER
1 Yachting Club &
  Club de Plongée
3 Porto Corallo Complex
6 Banque de Tunisie

7 Monoprix Supermarket
8 Publinet Tabarka
9 ONTT Tourist Office
10 Ulysse Tours
11 Louages to Ain
   Draham, Jendouba
   & Tunis
13 SRN Jendouba Office
   & Buses
15 Archaeological Site
16 Supermarket
17 UIB Bank

18 Markets
22 Post Office
23 Polyclinique Sidi
   Mansour
26 La Basilique
27 SNTRI Office
   & Buses
29 Hammam
31 Police Station
32 Mosque
33 STB Bank
35 Tabarka Voyages

NORTHERN TUNISIA

Thabraca, it remained a minor outpost until Roman times, when it was developed into a major port to handle the export of marble from the mines at Chemtou, 60km inland. It was also the exit point for many of the African big cats en route to the colosseums of Rome and elsewhere.

In the 16th and 17th centuries, Tabarka became one of a string of ports used by the Muslim corsairs (see the boxed text 'Pirates of the Barbary Coast' in the Around Bizerte section earlier). They included the notorious Khair ed-Din Barbarossa, who was obliged to hand over Tabarka Island to the Genoese in the 1540s as ransom for the release of his cohort Dragut. The castle the Genoese built on the island enabled them to hold out against the Ottomans until 1741, when it fell to the bey of Tunis.

The modern town was laid out by the French, who also built the causeway connecting the island to the mainland. Despite these developments, Tabarka was considered to be a backwater far enough removed from mainstream life to be a suitable place of exile for Habib Bourguiba in 1952. He spent a short time here, staying at the Hôtel Les Mimosas and the Hôtel de France.

Tourism is now the mainstay of the local economy, while the modern port is the main shipment point for the tonnes of cork harvested from the forests of the Kroumirie. The red coral, found just offshore, is still exploited for the jewellery trade.

Orientation

It's hard to get lost in Tabarka. The compact town centre is laid out on the traditional French grid, bisected by the main street, Ave Habib Bourguiba.

Ave Habib Bourguiba begins at the large roundabout at the south-eastern edge of town and ends at the old harbour. The causeway to Tabarka Island leads off from here, flanked to the west by a small beach and to the east by the marina and port facilities.

The roundabout south-east of town is at the junction of the roads south to Ain Draham and east to Sejnane. The zone touristique is 4km east of town, signposted off the road to Sejnane.

Information

Tourist Office The regional tourist office (☎ 643 496) occupies the old train station on Ave 7 Novembre 1987. It hasn't got much to offer apart from an ancient brochure. The office is open from 8.30 am to 1 pm and 3 to 5.45 pm Monday to Thursday and 8.30 am to 1.30 pm Friday and Saturday.

Money Most of the banks are on Ave Habib Bourguiba in the centre of town.

Post & Communications The post office is on Ave Hedi Chaker, diagonally opposite the Hôtel de France. There are plenty of Taxiphone offices around town. You can check email at Publinet Tabarka, near the tourist office on the new Route Touristique.

Emergency The Polyclinique Sidi Mansour (☎ 674 200), at the western end of Ave Habib Bourguiba, is open 24 hours for medical emergencies.

Beaches

Tabarka has two beaches. The building of the causeway linking Tabarka Island to the mainland created the sheltered bay known as **Old Harbour**, providing locals with a good, safe swimming beach just a couple of minutes walk from the town centre.

Montazah Beach is a great sweep of sand stretching east from the marina. The section near the marina is polluted and no good for swimming. The hotels of the zone touristique monopolise the best bit.

Genoese Fort

The magnificent Genoese fort, long occupied by the military, may be about to open its doors to the public at long last. Rumour has it that the army is moving out and the castle will become the new home for Tabarka's museum before the end of 2000.

Until then, the best views of the castle are from **Les Aiguilles** (The Needles), a line of dramatic, sheer pinnacles of rock opposite the fort on the western side of Old Harbour Bay. Les Aiguilles is signposted from the beach end of Ave Habib Bourguiba and is a popular place for an evening stroll. Head out there an hour before sunset when the light is at its best.

La Basilique

This small church was built by French missionaries at the end of the 19th century and occupies an old Roman cistern. It was the home of the town's museum until it closed for repairs several years ago, never to re-open.

It is still used as a venue for the Tabarka Jazz Festival.

Cork Museum

The Cork Museum is at the cork factory, 2km south of town on the road to Ain Draham. It has an information display on the local cork industry as well as lots of tacky cork souvenirs. It's open from 8 am to noon and 2 to 5 pm daily. Admission is free.

Diving

Tabarka has the best diving in the country with six excellent sites within 30 minutes of the port. They include the Roche Merou (grouper rock), where divers can swim among a school of large groupers, and Les Tunnels. Both are for more experienced divers, but there are also some good sites for beginners.

The Club de Plongée (☎ 671 478, e bessassi@planet.tn), which operates from the yachting club at the marina, organises trips, rents equipment and offers accreditation courses for beginners.

Golf

Tabarka Golf Club (☎ 671 031) is out at the zone touristique. Golfers will find the 18-hole layout hard to resist, although the cost

---

Cork

The villagers of the Kroumirie have been exploiting the amazingly versatile bark of the cork oak (quercus suber) for more than 2500 years.

Well aware of cork's insulating and water-resistant properties, local people built their houses of bricks made from cork and clay, and used bark slabs for roofing and guttering. These days, most of the crop is used for the production of wine corks and cork tiles, while the waste is mixed with linseed oil to create linoleum or used as a soil conditioner in potting mixes.

For such a versatile product, the tree itself is very fussy about where it grows. It's found only in coastal mountain areas exposed to moist westerly winds, requiring an annual rainfall of at least 600mm. It also needs light, well-drained sandy soils, boasting a powerful root system that is well suited to rocky ground. It can handle light frosts, but turns up its toes above 1000m.

The tree is a slow grower, and takes almost 30 years to produce its first useable crop. The first crop, taken after 20 years, is too open and fissured to be of commercial value. It's removed to encourage the development of more regular future layers, which can be harvested every 10 years. The quality improves each time, and the trees can live for 400 years – making them a solid long-term investment.

Decisions about harvesting are left in the hands of a cork master. It's a delicate operation, usually performed between May and August, requiring the removal of the outer bark without damaging the inner layer. Two horizontal cuts, about 2m apart, are made around the trunk and linked by vertical incisions, allowing the bark to be levered off in large slabs. Weather conditions are critical: Exposure to hot dry winds after harvest can kill the tree.

The freshly harvested trunk is a pale cork yellow, but soon turns a deep reddish-brown because of the copious quantities of tannin released by the tree. This phenomenon led to the virtual destruction of the cork forests of northern Italy in the 19th century, chopped down to supply the tanning vats of the leather industry.

The cork oak plays an important role in the ecosystem of the Kroumirie. Its acorns are an important food source for many forest animals, especially wild boars, while the bark is home to a host of insect species. Many small birds rely on the trees as a source of food during winter.

might help – reckon on close to TD50 by the time you've finished paying green fees and club hire. You'll need to start with plenty of balls. The fairways are carved out of dense coastal scrub that swallows up nearly every ball that strays from the straight and narrow.

It's one of the few clubs in the country that welcomes hackers; there's no need to show proof of handicap.

Horse Riding

Horse riding can be arranged through the Hôtel Paradise Golf (☎ 673 002), next to the golf course at the zone touristique. The hotel's stables are run by Fershishi Rahim, who charges TD20 for a two-hour ride. He also offers overnight treks into the forests of the Kroumirie Mountains. However, Fershishi deals only with groups – a minimum of six people are required for treks.

Organised Tours

Ulysse Tours (☎ 673 582, fax 673 622), 24 Ave 7 Novembre 1987, has a weekly program of tours that includes trips to Bulla Regia (TD25) and a combination of Dougga and Chemtou (TD46). It also has tours to Sidi Mechrig and Cap Serrat for TD45.

Tabarka Voyages (☎ 673 740, fax 673 726), near the roundabout on the Ain Draham road, combines Bulla Regia, Chemtou and Le Kef for TD45.

Places to Stay – Budget

The only real budget option is the run-down *Hôtel de Corail (☎ 673 082, 1 Rue Tazerka)*. It's by no means a great bargain at TD6 per person without breakfast, and this rises to TD7.500 in summer. However, a new paint job is an indication that the owners are making an effort to improve the place.

Pension Mamia (☎ 671 058, 3 Rue de Tunis) is a better bet. The rooms are basic but spotlessly clean, and are laid out around a small tiled courtyard. Facilities include hot showers or bath, kitchen and TV room. Singles/doubles are TD14.500/18 in winter, rising to TD22/30 in summer.

Places to Stay – Mid-Range

The *Hôtel de la Plage (☎ 670 039, 11 Ave 7 Novembre 1987)* has spent a lot of money upgrading its facilities in the last couple of years. It has singles/doubles with bathroom for TD25.500/35, and rooms with shared bathroom for TD23/30. Prices stay the same year-round, and include breakfast.

The friendly *Hôtel Les Aiguilles (☎ 673 789, fax 673 604, 18 Ave Habib Bourguiba)*, at the beach end of the main drag, is highly recommended. It's an old colonial building, originally a bank, which has been converted into a comfortable, modern two-star hotel. The rooms have air-con, satellite TV and bathroom. Singles/doubles with breakfast are TD20/30 in winter and TD40/60 in summer.

Opposite is the *Hôtel de France (☎ 670 752, 25 Ave Hedi Chaker)*. It looks OK from the outside, but suffers from serious plumbing problems inside. It needs a complete refit to justify the rates of TD28/40 in winter and TD37/58 in summer for singles/doubles with (nonfunctioning) bathroom. The hotel's moment of glory came way back in 1952 when former president Habib Bourguiba spent a couple of nights there, an event that is commemorated by a plaque at the head of the stairs.

Bourguiba spent most of his stint in Tabarka at the three star *Hôtel Les Mimosas (☎ 673 018, fax 673 276)*, signposted at the roundabout on the way into town. It has commanding views over the town to the sea; facilities include a swimming pool, tennis court and minigolf. Singles/doubles with bath are TD24/36 (low season) or TD48/72 (high season).

Places to Stay – Top End

Tabarka's top hotel is the four star *Iberotel Mehari (☎ 670 001, fax 673 943)*, overlooking the beach at the zone touristique. Rooms are TD32/48 in low season and TD63/98 in high season. The adjoining *Residence Mehari* has self-catering studio apartments. Rates for two people are TD70 in low season and TD110 in high season. Four-person apartments are TD110/TD160 in low/high season.

Other zone touristique hotels include the three star *Abou Nawas Montazah* (☎ *673 532, fax 673 530)*, the *Paradise Golf* (☎ *673 002, fax 673 918)* and the *Royal Golf* (☎ *673 625, fax 673 838)*. They are usually fully booked with package tour groups.

Places to Eat
Restaurants Fish features prominently on the menus, and not just at the smart tourist restaurants. There are lots of small places serving excellent grilled fish for about TD2.500 – look for the telltale charcoal grills, particularly around the junction of Rue du Peuple and Ave Farhat Hached. The *Restaurant Les Etoiles*, on Rue du Peuple, has daily specials like spicy beans with chicken (TD1.400) as well as grilled fish, and chicken.

The tiny *Restaurant Sidi Moussa*, on the corner of Ave 7 Novembre 1987 and Ave d'Algérie, has a choice of meals such as macaroni in spicy sauce (TD2.500) and *escallop de dinde* (TD3). All meals are served with side salad and fruit.

The restaurants at all the mid-range hotels are also excellent choices. Both the *Hôtel Les Aiguilles* and the *Hôtel Novelty* offer three-course deals for TD8. The *Hôtel Les Mimosas* charges TD9 – and eating there qualifies you to use the pool.

The *Restaurant Khemir*, opposite the Hôtel de France on Ave Habib Bourguiba, has a good range of seafood at prices that won't break the bank. There's a cluster of up-market tourist restaurants in the Porto Corallo complex by the marina, including *Restaurant Le Pirate* and *Restaurant Touta*. Both do meals for about TD20, plus wine.

Cafes For coffee, head for the *Café Andalous*, at the southern end of Ave Hedi Chaker. It has an amazing collection of old Ottoman-era bric-a-brac.

Self-Catering Self-caterers can stock up at the *Monoprix supermarket* on Ave 7 Novembre 1987. You'll find fruit and vegetables, as well as fresh local fish, at the *markets* behind the smaller *supermarket* by the roundabout in the middle of town.

Getting There & Away
Air Tabarka has an international airport, but it has very little in the way of action apart from the occasional charter flight from Europe. There are no domestic flights.

Bus The SNTRI office is on Rue du Peuple. It has nine services a day to Tunis: six via Mateur and three via Beja. For those who like to spend the shortest possible time on board, it's 15-minutes quicker via Mateur at 3¼ hours – and fractionally cheaper at TD7.140.

SRN Jendouba, on Ave Habib Bourguiba at the junction with Rue Mohammed Ali, has six buses a day to Jendouba (TD2.550, 1¾ hours) via Ain Draham (940 mills, 40 minutes). The 6.15 am service to Jendouba continues to Le Kef (TD5.500, 3½ hours). It also has a service to Bizerte (TD5.200, 3¼ hours) at 7 am.

SRT Bizerte has a daily service to Bizerte at 12.45 pm, leaving from outside the Monoprix supermarket on Ave 7 Novembre 1987.

Louage Louages for Ain Draham (TD1), Jendouba (TD2.900) and Tunis (TD7.050) leave from the south-eastern end of Ave Habib Bourguiba, near the roundabout.

Getting Around
The town is too small to warrant local buses, leaving taxis as the main form of transport. In summer, a 'Noddy' train shuttles back and forth between the Porto Corallo complex and the zone touristique.

To/From the Airport There is no public transport to the airport, which is 14km east of town on the road to Sejnane. It doesn't matter because all the passengers are charter customers who are whisked off to their hotels by private bus.

Car Hertz (☎ 670 670) has an office in the Porto Corallo complex.

TABARKA TO AIN DRAHAM
The road south from Tabarka to Ain Draham, 26km inland, passes through some beautiful countryside as it climbs from the

narrow coastal plain into the forests of the Kroumirie Mountains. The area is marketed by tourist authorities as 'Green Tunisia', and it's not hard to see why as you leave Tabarka along tree-lined roads flanked by contented dairy cows grazing in well-manicured fields. Even in late summer, the fields around here are remarkably green and lush.

The climb begins a few kilometres south of Tabarka, and the early stages offer some lovely **views** back over the coast. The road then starts to twist and turn its way up the valley of the Oued Kebir, and the paddocks gradually give way to forest. The predominant species is the cork oak; the deep red, tannin-stained trunks of freshly harvested trees are everywhere.

At the small village of **Babouch**, 21km from Tabarka, there is a turn-off to the Algerian border. The border is 3km to the west, and it's another 28km from there to the coastal town of El-Kala.

AIN DRAHAM
☎ 08 • pop 2500

Ain Draham is Tunisia's hill station. It's a pretty town of red-tiled houses that tumbles down the western flank of Jebel Biri (1014m), the highest peak of the Kroumirie Mountains. The elevation means that in summer it's a lot cooler than on the plains and on the coast, and snow is common in winter.

The town was popular with hunters in the days of the French administration – the last of Tunisia's lions and leopards were shot in the forests around here early last century. Hunting continues to be an attraction, with wild boars now the prime target, but most visitors come to relax and escape the summer heat.

The architecture here is quite unlike anything else in Tunisia, with steep tiled roofs designed to handle the winter snow. Locals, who obviously haven't been to Switzerland, reckon it looks just like a Swiss Alpine village.

Orientation & Information
The main road through town becomes the main street, Blvd de l'Environment. It dips into a small valley as you come into town from Tabarka, then climbs steeply through

---

Les Tapis de Kroumirie

Carpets and kilims (woven rugs) are produced in Ain Draham by a small women's co-operative called Les Tapis de Kroumirie. The project was launched in the early 1980s by two French doctors working in Ain Draham. Operated with the assistance of the Ain Draham Centre d'Action Sociale, its joint aims are to provide employment for local women and to revive local carpet-making traditions.

It's an interesting place to visit. The produce is sold directly from the workshop, where about a dozen looms are in operation. The appearance of a foreigner is likely to create a fair amount of interest. If you decide to buy a carpet, there's a good chance that you will get to meet the person who wove it.

The carpets are the thick-pile Berber type known as *alloucha*, produced in natural tones and decorated with simple, traditional Berber motifs. The wool is all spun by hand. Prices are fixed, but they're not high – a carpet measuring 140cm x 75cm costs TD85.

To get there, turn right at the bottom of the steps opposite the *syndicat d'initiative*. The cooperative is above the Ministère des Affaires Sociales, about 50m along on the right. The carpets are also sold in Tunis by Mains de Femmes, at 47 Ave Habib Bourguiba.

---

the centre of town and continues towards Jendouba.

The bus and louage stations are just west of the main street at the bottom of the hill, while everything else of importance is up the hill towards Jendouba: a couple of banks, a post office and Taxiphone offices.

Trekking
The forests around Ain Draham have great potential as a trekking destination. It remains largely unrealised, mainly because tourist operators have been slow to wake up to the possibilities.

The absence of decent maps makes it difficult to trek independently, although there are some good short walks close to town. One easy option is to walk out along the Tabarka road to the Hôtel Nour el-Ain and then take the well-trodden forest track that leads back to town. The circuit takes about two hours.

The Hôtel Rihana (☎ 655 391, fax 655 396), which has long specialised in organising wild-boar hunting parties in winter, uses the same guides to lead trekking groups in spring and autumn. It offers guided treks for small groups for about TD50 per person, per day.

Places to Stay

The *Maison des Jeunes* (☎ 647 087), at the top of the hill on the road to Jendouba, is the only budget option. It charges TD4.

There are two hotels in town. The long-running *Hôtel Beauséjour* (☎ 655 363, fax 655 527), 100m before the maison des jeunes, was once popular with hunting parties, and trophies line the walls. Singles/doubles cost TD23.500/36, with breakfast. Full or half board is available with a three-course meal costing TD4.

The *Hôtel Les Pins* (☎ 656 200) is a new pension right in the middle of town with singles/doubles for TD22.500/35, rising to TD27.500/45 in summer. It can be found just uphill from the bus station on the main street.

Ain Draham's smartest establishment is without doubt the three star *Hôtel Nour el-Ain* (☎ 655 000, fax 655 185), overlooking the town from the Col des Ruines, 2km to the north. It has rooms for TD30.500/48 and TD35.500/58 in low season and high season, respectively. Facilities include a *hammam* (bathhouse) fitness centre and indoor pool.

About 7km along the road to Jendouba is the two star *Hôtel Les Chênes* (☎ 655 315, fax 655 396), an old hunting lodge dating back to the 1920s. There are lots of hunting trophies, including an enormous stuffed boar, in the dining room. Rooms with bath and breakfast cost TD22/36 in winter and TD28.500/40 in summer. Unless you've got your own transport, you'll have to pay an extra TD14 per person for half board because there is nowhere else to eat in the area around the hotel.

The four star *Hôtel La Forêt* (☎ 655 302, fax 655 335) overlooks the national soccer centre, 8km south of Ain Draham.

Places to Eat

Ain Draham is a small town, and the possibilities for dining out are limited to a couple of basic places on the main street, like the *Restaurant du Grand Maghreb*.

The *Hôtel Beauséjour* has the best restaurant in town, as well as a choice of bars: one for residents and one for locals.

Getting There & Away

Bus SRN Jendouba operates frequent buses to Jendouba (TD1.620, one hour) and Tabarka (940 mills, 40 minutes), as well as a service to Le Kef (TD4.300, 2½ hours) at 7 am. There are two buses a day to Hammam Bourguiba (780 mills).

SNTRI has three services a day between Tunis and Ain Draham (TD7.280).

Louage Louages leave from outside the bus station. There are regular services to Tabarka (TD1) and Jendouba (TD1.800), and a few to Tunis (TD7.300). You'll need to be quick off the mark as demand often exceeds supply.

AROUND AIN DRAHAM
Hammam Bourguiba

The resort village of Hammam Bourguiba, 15km south-west of Ain Draham, is tucked away in a small valley near the Algerian border. The **hot springs** here have been developed into a health farm offering a range of steam-based treatments, popular with older Tunisians. It was once a favourite retreat of the country's former president, Habib Bourguiba.

Places to Stay & Eat The *resort* (☎ 08-632 552, fax 632 497) charges TD30/40 for singles/doubles, with breakfast, but there is no option but to take half board (TD33/46) because there is nowhere else to eat.

Getting There & Away To get there, take the road that leads to the Algerian border from Babouch and turn left after about 1km.

There are two buses a day from Ain Draham (780 mills).

Beni Metir

The village of Beni Metir, 10km south-east of Ain Draham, was built by the French in the 1950s to house the workers who constructed the dam that is the reason for the place's existence. Once the work was completed, the village was handed over to the locals.

The area is a much-touted beauty spot, popular with families at weekends. The large **lake** created by the dam is surrounded by forest and overlooked by the pretty red-roofed houses of Beni Metir.

The turn-off to Beni Metir is about 4km south of Ain Draham on the road to Jendouba, just beyond the brand new sports complex, custom-built to the requirements of the national soccer team. From the turn-off, the road winds down to the lake through dense forest of holm oak and myrtle.

Getting There & Away Your own transport is the best option. That way you can enjoy the 20-minute drive from Ain Draham at your leisure. Public transport is restricted to occasional camionnettes – ask around at the bus station in Ain Draham or outside the maison des jeunes in Beni Metir.

BULLA REGIA

Bulla Regia, 9km north of Jendouba, is famous as the place where the Romans went underground to escape the heat – they built their villas with one storey above ground and another below.

History

The dolmens (Neolithic tombs) that dot the hills around the site are evidence that the area was inhabited long before the Romans arrived. The town of Bulla emerged in about the 5th century BC as part of Carthage's move to develop the Medjerda Valley as a wheat-growing area. The 'Regia' was added later when it became the capital of one of the short-lived Numidian kingdoms tolerated by Rome following the destruction of Carthage.

The town flourished under subsequent Roman rule, its citizens growing rich on the income from wheat. It reached the peak of its prosperity in the 2nd and 3rd centuries AD, and most of the site's buildings belong to that era.

Bulla Regia was subsequently occupied by the Byzantines, who added their standard fort, but it was abandoned after the Arab conquest in the 7th century.

Things to See

The entrance to the site is opposite the museum and ticket office, just to the left of the Memmian Baths. Named after Julia Memmia, wife of Emperor Septimius Severus, the **Memmian Baths** are the most extensive of the remaining above-ground buildings and are a good orientation point.

The street in front of the baths leads east to a small but beautifully preserved **theatre** with a large mosaic of a bear adorning the stage. The seating is in particularly good condition. Note that the front three tiers are extra wide and separated from the rest by the remains of a low wall – dress-circle seating for VIPs. South-west of the theatre are the remains of a small **Temple of Isis**, in honour of the Egyptian goddess, who was a fashionable addition to the Roman pantheon at the time.

A path leads north from the temple past the old **market square** to the **forum**, which is surrounded by the ruins of two temples – the **capitol** to the west and the **Temple of Apollo** to the north. Excavation of the Temple of Apollo revealed a magnificent collection of statues, now housed in the Bardo Museum in Tunis.

The site's main attraction, however, are the underground villas of the city's wealthy quarter. Seven villas have been excavated so far, and several others remain unexplored. The villas vary in their level of sophistication, but are all built to the same basic plan. Above ground, they would have looked little different from any other Roman villa of the time. The surface structures were built around an excavated central courtyard, open to the sky, off which lay a second, subterranean level of rooms.

The villas are clustered together at the northern edge of the site, and are named according to the mosaics they contained. The

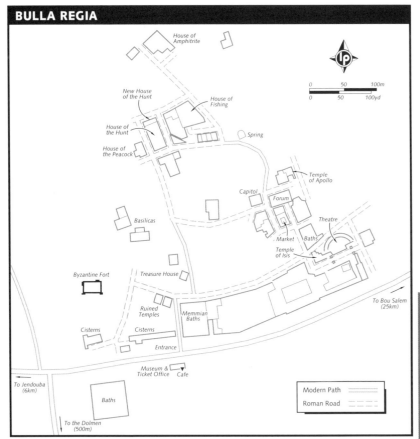

BULLA REGIA

House of
Amphitrite

New House
of the Hunt

House of
Fishing

House of
the Hunt

Spring

House of
the Peacock

0   50   100m
0   50   100yd

Temple
of Apollo

Capitol

Forum

Basilicas

Theatre

Market   Baths

Temple
of Isis

Byzantine Fort   Treasure House

To Bou Salem
(25km)

Ruined
Temples   Memmian
Baths

Cisterns   Cisterns

Entrance

Museum &   Cafe
Ticket Office

To Jendouba
(6km)

Baths

Modern Path
Roman Road

To the Dolmen
(500m)

NORTHERN TUNISIA

earliest of them is the **House of Fishing**, built during the reign of the Emperor Hadrian (AD 117–38). Most of the other villas were built during the reign of Hadrian's successor, Antoninus Pius (AD 138–61), and are a good deal more sophisticated – both in construction and in decoration. The most impressive of these later villas is the **House of the Hunt**. Although the mosaics have been removed, the elegant, colonnaded courtyard and large entertaining area are enough to give the visitor an insight into the lifestyle of its former occupants.

The hunting mosaic has been left in situ next door at the **New House of the Hunt**. Large chunks are missing, but there's still plenty left to view, including the obligatory lion hunt. The best of the mosaics is found at the **House of Amphitrite**, just north of the main cluster. Its beautifully preserved mosaic of Venus and a cupid riding dolphins is regarded by most as the site's *pièce de résistance*. Other villas to investigate are the **House of the Peacock**, where a peacock mosaic was found, and the **Treasure House**, so called because a horde of Byzantine coins was found during excavation.

The **spring** that once supplied the ancient city with water is just east of the main cluster of houses. It is now covered by a modern pump house, which delivers its cool waters to nearby Jendouba.

A visit to the small **museum** outside the site, across the road from the entrance, is included in the admission fee. There are a couple of mosaics from the site, a collection of chipped Roman busts, sundry old things and an interesting layout of the area in Numidian times.

The hill behind the museum is covered with Neolithic tombs and is worth a stroll if time permits.

The site is open from 8 am to 7 pm in summer and from 8.30 am to 5.30 pm in winter Tuesday to Sunday. Admission is TD2.100, plus TD1 to take photos.

Getting There & Away

The turn-off to Bulla Regia is 6km north of Jendouba on the road to Ain Draham. Any bus or louage travelling between the two towns can drop you there. It's another 3km from the turn-off to the site. Hitching along this stretch is easy enough, but it's also a pleasant walk if it's not too hot.

Most people visit the site from Jendouba. A taxi costs about TD3.500.

Organised Tours

Tour companies usually couple Bulla Regia with either Chemtou or Dougga. See the earlier Tabarka section for more information.

JENDOUBA

☎ 08 • pop 19,000

It's difficult to get enthusiastic about the dull regional centre of Jendouba, 153km west of Tunis. It exists to service the needs of the surrounding wheat-growing country rather than to titillate tourists, but it's hard to avoid the place if you want to visit Bulla Regia.

Orientation & Information

One thing the town does have going for it is that it's easy to negotiate. Most things of importance are around the central square, including the post office, banks, supermarket, the train station and the police station.

Look out for the impressive collection of storks' nests on the roof of the police station. It's arguably the most interesting feature of the town, although there is a minaret nearby with an even better collection.

The bus and louage stations are at the major roundabout on the western side of town. To get there, follow the main street (Ave Hedi Chaker) west from the central square for about 500m. The roundabout is the town's major traffic distribution point, situated at the intersection of the roads going north to Ain Draham, north-east to Tunis (bypassing the city centre), south to Le Kef and west to Ghardimao.

Places to Stay

The best advice is to time your comings and goings to eliminate the need to stay overnight in Jendouba. If you do get stuck here, try the *Hôtel Atlas* (☎ 603 217, fax 603 113, Rue 1 Juin 1955), just off the central square behind the police station. It has singles/doubles for TD18/25 with breakfast, or TD22/33 for half board. It also has a lively public bar, and a quieter residents' bar.

The town's premier establishment is the *Hôtel Simitthu* (☎ 634 043, fax 632 595), directly opposite the SRN Jendouba bus station at the roundabout. It's on Blvd 9 April 1938, which doubles as the main road west to Ghardimao. It's a clean, modern two-star hotel managed by an expat French woman and her husband. It charges TD29/42 for singles/doubles, with breakfast.

Places to Eat

There are a several small restaurants and *rôtisseries* around the central square, but most visitors seem to opt to eat at the hotel restaurants – where you can get a drink with your meal.

If you're heading out to Bulla Regia, you can pick up the makings of a picnic at the *supermarket* on the central square.

Getting There & Away

Jendouba is an important regional transport hub with good links to all the major centres of the north.

Bus SNTRI has five buses a day to Tunis (TD6, four hours) from the bus station at the roundabout on the western edge of town. The last bus to Tunis leaves at 4 pm.

The bus station is the home of regional company SRN Jendouba. Its services include six buses a day to Tabarka (TD2.550, 1¾ hours) via Ain Draham, six to Ghardimao (TD1.300, 40 minutes) and five to Le Kef (TD 2, 1½ hours). To get to Bulla Regia, take any bus going to Ain Draham and ask to be let out at the turn-off.

Train If you're travelling to Tunis, the train is the way to go. There are five departures a day to Tunis, the first at 6 am and the last at 5 pm. The journey takes 2¾ hours and the 1st-class fare is TD7.050.

Louage Louages leave from a range of locations around the roundabout at the western edge of town. The main destinations are Ain Draham (TD1.800), Ghardimao (TD1.400), Le Kef (TD2.550), Tabarka (TD2.900) and Tunis (TD6.650).

CHEMTOU
The ancient quarries at Chemtou, about 25km west of Jendouba, were once the source of an unusual pink-veined yellow marble that was prized throughout the Roman world.

History
The site, on the north bank of the Oued Medjerda near the village of Oued Melliz, was originally the Numidian settlement of Simitthu. Its marble was exploited from early times, and was used to construct the celebrated Monument of Micipsa at Cirta (modern Constantine in Algeria) in 130 BC.

The region came under Roman control after the battle of Thapsus in 46 BC, when Caesar defeated the combined forces of Pompey and the last Numidian king, Juba I. After Caesar's assassination, a 6m column of Chemtou marble was erected in his honour in Rome's forum.

The Roman settlement of Chemtou was founded during the reign of Augustus (27 BC to AD 16). Such was the demand for its marble that it quickly developed into an important town. The quarrying operation was said to be the most sophisticated in the Roman world. Each block carried the stamp of the emperor of the day, as well as that of the proconsul for Africa, the quarry supervisor and a reference mark.

Initially, the blocks were hauled to the Oued Medjerda on rollers and floated downstream to the port of Utica on barges. By the beginning of the 2nd century, rising levels of silt had all but closed the river to barge traffic, obliging the Romans to build a special road across the Kroumirie Mountains to link the quarries with the port of Thabraca (Tabarka).

The quarries were worked until Byzantine times, but were abandoned following the Arab invasion in the 7th century.

Things to See
The site sprawls over a wide area on the north bank of the Medjerda, sandwiched between the river and a band of low hills that were the source of the town's marble wealth.

Despite the town's proximity to the Medjerda, the river was not deemed to be a suitable water supply. Instead, water was brought to the town by **aqueduct** from a spring in the hills 30km to the north. If you arrive from the north, the first ruins you see are the remains of this aqueduct. The aqueduct ends at the ruins of the old **baths** on the right of the entrance road. The road continues past a somewhat better preserved Roman **theatre** and stops outside the **museum** and **ticket office**.

This excellent museum is the star attraction, and the best place to start a visit to the site. Built with German assistance, it displays finds unearthed by a German/Tunisian team, which has been excavating the site since 1992. As well as a comprehensive explanation of the site and the quarrying operation, it has re-creations of the Monument of Micipsa, a section on Numidian history and a working model of the ancient flour mill that once stood on the banks of the Medjerda.

The museum flanks a small excavated section of **Roman road**. Excavations elsewhere have concentrated on the nearby **forum**, and have revealed that it was built on the foundations of a Numidian temple.

The **quarries**, three in all, are opposite the museum. They are an impressive sight – the amount of work it must have taken to carve out these mighty holes by hand is daunting.

A path leads up to the ruins of a **temple** on top of the easternmost hill. It was originally a Numidian site *before* being converted first into a temple to Saturn by the Romans and then a Byzantine church.

Other features that are worth checking out are the remains of a **Roman bridge** over the Medjerda just downstream from the modern ford crossing. Judging by the massive pylons, the Romans took the river more seriously than locals do today. Downstream from the bridge are the ruins of a **mill**.

The site is open from 8 am to 7 pm in summer and from 8.30 am to 5.30 pm in winter Tuesday to Sunday. Admission is TD2.100, plus TD1 to take photos. Outside the museum, you will find guides waiting to show you around. They charge TD5 for a tour, which is a good investment.

Organised Tours
Tour companies usually couple Chemtou with either Bulla Regia or Dougga. See the earlier Tabarka section for more information.

Getting There & Away
There is no public transport to the site, which makes visiting hard work without your own vehicle. The easiest solution is to strike a deal with a taxi driver in either Jendouba or Ghardimao. Reckon on paying about TD30 to get there and back, with a couple of hours at the site.

If your budget doesn't stretch to such luxuries as chartered taxis, another possibility is to catch any bus or louage travelling between Jendouba and Ghardimao and ask to be dropped at the Chemtou turn-off, just east of the village of Oued Melliz. That will leave you with a 3km walk to the site. The only problem is that you will have to ford the Oued Medjerda. The flow is not much more than a trickle for most of the year, but it can become a mighty torrent after winter rains.

If you have your own vehicle, the approach is via the C59 loop road that runs north of the Oued Medjerda. This road begins at the Bulla Regia junction north of Jendouba and emerges just west of Ghardimao. Chemtou is clearly signposted from the Bulla Regia end, and the C59 is a good sealed road all the way to the site entrance. It switches to gravel west of Chemtou.

THUBERNICA
The minor Roman site of Thubernica is about 13km north of Ghardimao in the foothills of the Kroumirie.

It's not worth going to any great effort to get there, but it makes a pleasant diversion if you have your own vehicle. It is best visited in conjunction with Chemtou – the C59 loop road from Bulla Regia to Ghardimao goes past both sites. Thubernica is about 12km west of Chemtou on the C59, signposted at the village of Sidi Ali Belgassem. The ruins are scattered around the wooded hillside above the village. They are not enclosed, and there is no admission charge.

GHARDIMAO
☎ 08

If anything, Ghardimao is even more deadly boring than Jendouba. It really is the end of the line, especially since the suspension of the *Al-Maghreb al-Arabi* (Trans Maghreb Express) train service that once linked Tunisia with Morocco via Algeria.

The only reason to pass through here these days is as part of the circuit that takes in the Roman sites of Chemtou and Thubernica on the C59 loop road, which starts 2km west of town along the road to the Algerian border.

Places to Stay & Eat
There's no reason to stay the night in Ghardimao, but if you do get stuck the choice is at least a straightforward one. The only place in town is the depressing *Hôtel Tibournik* (☎ 660 043), opposite the train station in the middle of town. Half the letters on the hotel sign have fallen off, giving a fair indication of what's to be discovered inside. It charges TD18.500/22 for singles/doubles with breakfast, or TD22.50/30 with an evening meal as

well. The restaurant is surprisingly good given the place's general air of dereliction. The hotel also has the only bar in town.

Getting There & Away

There are usually five trains a day to Tunis (TD8.750, 3¼ hours) via Jendouba (25 minutes), departing between 5.30 am and 4.35 pm. Buses and louages leave from next to the railway line, about 200m towards Jendouba from the station. Jendouba is the main destination. There is one direct bus a day to Tunis (TD7.850, 3¾ hours).

LE KEF
☎ 08 • pop 30,000

The ancient fortress town of Le Kef (El-Kef in Arabic, meaning 'The Rock'), 170km south-west of Tunis, is a place not to be missed. Crowned by a mighty kasbah, the town tumbles down a rocky spur reaching out from the southern flank of Jebel Dyr (1084m), a solitary peak that rises dramatically from the surrounding wheat-growing plains.

Much of the appeal of the place lies in the fact that there is no single attraction important enough to warrant an invasion of tour buses – although the narrow streets of the old medina contain enough points of interest to keep you occupied for a day or so.

Foreigners remain something of a rarity, and you can expect a fair amount of polite curiosity. Locals are very proud of their town, and any conversation you strike up will soon require you to give your verdict.

One aspect of life in Le Kef is that it's easy to offer an immediate opinion on the climate. At an altitude of 800m, it's pleasantly cooler here than on the surrounding plains. Nights can be cool, even in summer, and it snows in winter.

History

Le Kef's strategic position means that it has experienced just about everything there is to experience in Tunisian history. People have lived around here since prehistoric times, drawn by the copious springs on this flank of Jebel Dyr. The first town, known as Sicca, was established in about 500 BC by

Carthage to protect the western fringe of its newly won empire. It was known for the temple prostitutes who hung out at its sanctuary to the goddess Astarte, whose portfolio included love. After the fall of Carthage, it became a stronghold of the Numidian king, Jugurtha, during his rebellion against Rome. In Roman times, the sanctuary to Astarte became a temple to Venus, and the town became known as Sicca Veneria.

The Vandals came and went, followed by the Byzantines and then by the Arabs – who captured the town in AD 688 and changed its name to Shaqbanaria. Locals rebelled against the central government at every opportunity before becoming autonomous after the Hilalian invasions of the 11th century. The town fell briefly to the Almohads in 1159, but soon returned to its independent ways. By the time the Ottomans arrived in the 16th century, the region had become the private fiefdom of the Beni Cherif tribe.

Le Kef prospered under the Ottomans, who put a lot of effort into rebuilding its fortifications. The town did nicely for itself under the beys, too. Hussein ben Ali, founder of the Husseinite line of beys (1705–1957), was born in Le Kef.

Orientation & Information

The kasbah can be seen from just about everywhere in town, which makes finding your bearings easy.

Most things of importance to travellers are found within a very short walk of Place de l'Indépendance, below the kasbah in the centre of town. The exceptions are the bus and louage stations, which are side by side on Ave Mongi Slim, approximately a 15-minute walk downhill from Place de l'Indépendance.

There is no tourist information centre, but the staff at the Association de Sauvegarde de la Medina (☎ 201 148), on Place de l'Indépendance, can handle most questions. The post office is nearby on Rue Hedi Chaker. There are plenty of banks around the town centre.

There is no Publinet in town, but visitors can access email at the Arij school (☎ 227 717), 22 Ave Mongi Slim, just south of the

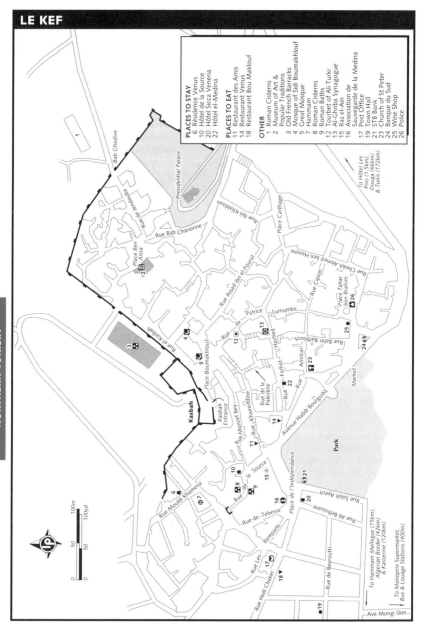

LE KEF

NORTHERN TUNISIA

bus and louage stations. It's on the 3rd floor of the Immeuble Barbouche, above the pharmacy.

Kasbah

Built on a rocky spur that overlooks the medina, the kasbah is the most impressive of the city's ancient monuments. A fort of some sort has existed on the site since about 500 BC, and the complex that stands today represents 2500 years of constant re-modelling by a succession of owners. The latest occupant was the Tunisian army, which was based here until 1992. It left its exercise equipment behind in the courtyard of the principle kasbah. This kasbah was built by the Byzantines in the 6th century, and reinforced by the Turks at the end of the 16th century.

A second, smaller kasbah was added within the outer walls of the main kasbah in 1679, during the time of Mohammed Bey. This second kasbah is now in very poor condition.

The kasbah is open from 8 am to 5 pm Tuesday to Sunday. Admission is free, but the elderly guardian appreciates a small consideration for accompanying you around the main points of interest – the Turkish mosque, prison cells, a bronze cannon left behind by the Dey of Algiers in 1705, several gates and walls of various vintages.

Museum of Art & Popular Traditions

The town's Museum of Art and Popular Traditions is housed in the Zaouia of Sidi Ali ben Aissa, 400m from the kasbah on Place Ben Aissa. The emphasis is on the culture of the region's Berber nomads and the exhibits include a tent, some crude utensils, jewellery and looms used to weave kilims (rugs). A new section in the rooms surrounding the zaouia's rear courtyard focuses on traditional trades and crafts. It includes an interesting display on herbal remedies.

The museum is open from 9 am to 1 pm and 4 to 7 pm in summer and 9.30 am to 4.30 pm in winter Tuesday to Sunday. Admission is TD1.100.

Medina

The principal monuments of the medina are located around Place Boumakhlouf, down the steps on the eastern side of the kasbah. The most unusual of them is the **Great Mosque**, although it ceased to operate as a mosque long ago. No-one seems to know what its original function was – or even when it was built. The cruciform design indicates that its role was connected with the church in some way. The current theory is that it was built by the Byzantines in the 6th century, and that it was either a monastery or some sort of social security centre. It was converted into a mosque in the 8th century, after the Arab invasion.

Next to the Great Mosque is the **Mosque of Sidi Boumakhlouf**, built in sharply contrasting style with gleaming white cupolas surrounding an octagonal Ottoman minaret. The mosque was built at the beginning of the 17th century and named after the town's patron saint, who is buried next to the mosque along with his family.

The **Tourbet of Ali Turki**, just off Place Boumakhlouf on Rue de Patrice Lumumba, houses the tomb of the father of Hussein ben Ali, founder of the Husseinite line of beys, who ruled Tunisia for 250 years (1705–1957) until independence.

The Al-Ghriba Synagogue This ancient synagogue is on Rue Farhat Hached at the heart of the medina's former Jewish quarter, the Harah. Information about the history of the Harah it hard to find. Early 19th-century travellers reported finding a thriving Jewish community, and there is a sizeable Jewish cemetery east of the Presidential Palace, with graves dating back to Roman times.

Recent renovations at the synagogue uncovered a collection of old manuscripts (as yet undated) and an ancient copy of the Torah (Jewish holy book).

Church of St Peter The remains of this 4th-century church, also known as the Dar el-Kous, are on Rue Amilcar just south of the synagogue. It contains a remarkably well-preserved apse that was added in Byzantine times.

Ras el-Ain

The town owes its very existence to this spring, located in the heart of town on Place de l'Indépendance. Its waters once supplied the huge Roman bath complex next door that was discovered during a recent archaeological dig. The spring also supplied the Roman cisterns, opposite the baths on the northern side of Rue de la Source.

Places to Stay – Budget

The *Hôtel el-Medina* (☎ *204 183, 18 Rue Farhat Hached)* is a safe choice, with clean singles/doubles for TD10/12. There are good views from the rooms at the back, which are also much quieter. Hot showers cost 500 mills.

The *Hôtel de la Source* (☎ *224 397)*, on Rue de la Source, improves once you make it past the mustard-yellow lobby. It has basic singles/doubles for TD8/10, and a four-bed family room for TD20. The incredibly ornate stucco ceiling of the family room is the owner's pride and joy.

Places to Stay – Mid-Range

The best place in town is the friendly *Résidence Venus* (☎/*fax 204 695)*, nestled beneath the outer walls of the old kasbah on Rue Mouldi Khamessi. It's a small, family run pension with comfortable singles/doubles for TD23/32, including breakfast. All rooms come with private bathroom and central heating – important in winter.

Another possibility is the *Hôtel Sicca Veneria* (☎/*fax 202 389)*, on the southern side of Place de l'Indépendance. Once the smartest place in town, the Sicca has finally re-opened after an extensive refit and is good value at TD18/30 for singles/doubles, with breakfast.

The two star *Hôtel Les Pins* (☎ *204 021, fax 202 411)*, about 1.5km east of town on the road to Tunis, charges TD36/54 for B&B.

Places to Eat

The town is not overflowing with restaurants, but there are a couple of good ones. The *Restaurant Bou Maklouf*, west of the post office on Rue Hedi Chaker, is recommended as a cheap, reliable restaurant.

There's no menu, just a choice of daily specials for around TD2, as well as salads.

You'll find similar fare at similar prices at the *Restaurant des Amis*, up the steps next to the Hôtel de l'Auberge. Both places are popular with locals.

The *Restaurant Venus*, on Rue Farhat Hached, is operated by the owners of the Résidence Venus and is the best restaurant in town. It has a set menu for TD8 as well as an extensive a la carte selection.

Self-caterers can stock up at the *Monoprix supermarket* next to the bus station.

Getting There & Away

Bus Transport is centred on the bus station, a 15-minute walk downhill from Place de l'Indépendance. SNTRI has eight daily buses to Tunis (TD7.230, three hours), travelling via Tebersouk (TD3.100, 1¼ hours; change here for Dougga).

There are regular local buses to Jendouba, and occasional services to Kairouan (via Makthar), Kasserine and Tabarka.

Louage The louage station is next to the bus station. There are frequent louages to Tunis (TD7). Other destinations include Jendouba, Kasserine and Makthar. There are no louages to Tebersouk.

AROUND LE KEF
Hammam Mellegue

The Roman baths at Hammam Mellegue, 15km west of Le Kef, must be one of the best-kept secrets in Tunisia. The setting alone is spectacular enough to justify the trip: the baths are hidden away at the base of a dramatic, sheer escarpment overlooking a broad sweep of the Oued Mellegue.

The attraction though is the opportunity to have a real Roman bath. While much of the 2nd-century complex now lies in ruins, the **caldarium** (hot room) is still used as a hammam. It's an extraordinary place that remains almost unchanged after almost 1800 years. A large timber door opens onto a cavernous, steam filled, subterranean chamber, lit by skylights set into the arched

[Continued on page 196]

DOUGGA

Perched on the edge of the Tebersouk Mountains overlooking the fertile wheat-growing valley of the Oued Kalled, the ancient hilltop city of Dougga, 106km south-west of Tunis, is the most spectacular of the country's many magnificent Roman sites.

It is also the most intriguing. The magnificent Capitol of Dougga may well be the most-photographed Roman monument in Tunisia, but Dougga is much more than just a Roman site. The Romans generally favoured flat, open sites – such as Sbeitla – where towns could be laid out on the neat grids of *insulae* (town blocks) so favoured by planners of the time. Dougga, in contrast, is a most un-Roman tangle of streets that weave around the contours rather than conforming to any pattern.

The Romans built their town on the site of ancient Thugga, a Numidian settlement that was already well established in Carthaginian times. The Libyo-Punic Mausoleum, built in the 2nd century BC, is the country's finest pre-Roman monument.

A curiosity of the site is the disproportionate number of temples. No less than 21 temples have been identified, which has prompted speculation that the area had some special religious significance. It's more likely though that the abundance of temples was related to the number of wealthy Roman citizens thanking the gods for their good fortune.

History

The dolmen graves that dot the ridge above the ruins suggest the site has been occupied since the end of the 2nd millennium BC. No doubt these early settlers were drawn to the site by its ample springs.

It was already a substantial settlement by the time Carthage made its move into the interior in the 4th century BC. The Greek historian Diodorus, writing at the time of Agathocles' assault on Carthage in 310 BC, described Thugga as an important town. The town stayed under Carthaginian control throughout the 3rd century BC, but became part of the kingdom of the Numidian king Massinissa in 202 BC at the end of the Second Punic War.

Thugga lay outside the boundaries of the first Roman province of Africa, created after the destruction of Carthage in 146 BC, and remained a Numidian town until 46 BC – when the last Numidian king, Juba 1, backed Pompey in the Roman Civil War and was defeated at the Battle of Thapsus.

Thugga became Dougga, part of the expanded province of Africa Nova, and the slow process of Romanisation began. Dougga's prosperity peaked between the 2nd and 4th centuries when it was home to an estimated 5000 people. It became a municipality in AD 205, and an honorary colony in AD 261.

Inset: The facade of ancient Dougga's magnificent capitol temple. (Photo by Chris Wood)

The town slipped into decline during the Vandal occupation, and the population had all but disappeared by the time the Byzantines arrived in AD 533 and set about remodelling Dougga as a fort. The ruins of

DOUGGA

1 Temple of Minerva	15 Fountain	29 Temple of Concorde,
2 Cisterns of Ain Mizeb	16 Cisterns of Ain el-Hammam	Frugifer and Liber Pater
3 Farm Buildings	17 Arch of Alexander Severus	30 Small Theatre
4 Temple of Saturn	18 Temple of Caelestis	31 Unidentified Temple
5 Sanctuary of Neptune	19 Aghlabid Baths	32 Licinian Baths
6 Church of Victoria	20 Byzantine Fortifications	33 Temple of Tellus
7 Crypt	21 Forum	34 Temple of Carcalla's Victory
8 Ticket Office	22 Capitol	35 Temple of Carcalla's Victory
9 Theatre	23 Temple of Mercury	36 House of Venus
10 Temple of the Sun God	24 Square of the Winds	37 Dar el-Echab
11 Administration Office	25 Temple of Augustine Piety	38 House of Marsyas
12 Cafe and Shop	26 Mosque	39 House of Omnia tibi Felicia
13 Fountain	27 Agora	40 House of Dionysos
14 Unidentified Temple	28 House with Stairs	and Ulysses

41 Sanctuary of Minerva	
42 Cisterns of Ain Doura	
43 Latrines of Ain Doura	
44 Baths of Ain Doura	
45 Grand Nymphaeum	
46 House of the Labyrinth	
47 Trifolium House	
48 Cyclops Baths	
49 House of the Seasons	
50 Temple of Pluto	
51 Arch of Septimus Severus	
52 House of the Gorgon	
53 Unidentified Temple	
54 Libyo-Punic Mausoleum	

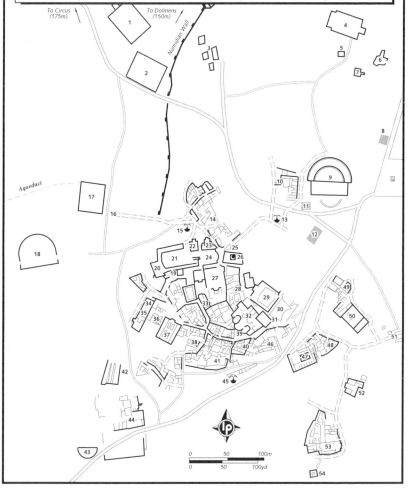

an Aghlabid bath house, east of the capitol, show that the site was still inhabited in the 10th century.

People continued to live among the ruins until the early 1950s when the inhabitants were moved to protect the ruins from further decay. They were relocated to the village of Nouvelle Dougga, below the ancient site on the Tunis-Le Kef road, and the archaeologists moved in.

Even now, the ruins are not totally deserted. There are still a few farm buildings to the north of the site, guarded by some very excitable dogs.

Practicalities

The site is 6km west of the small town of Tebersouk along a good bitumen road. If you're using public transport, the easiest approach is to catch a bus to Tebersouk, and then organise for a taxi to take you to the site and collect you again at a time of your choice. Reckon on paying about TD10 for two people.

If the weather is not too hot, you can walk up to the ruins from the village of Nouvelle Dougga, west of Tebersouk on the main Tunis–Le Kef road. The road up to the site is signposted in the middle of the village. It's a fairly gentle climb, but it still takes about 45 minutes to cover the 3km.

The site is open from 8.30 am to 5.30 pm daily in winter and from 8 am to 7 pm daily in summer. Admission is TD2.100, plus an extra TD1 to take photographs.

It's a good idea to arrive as early as possible so that you can enjoy the setting before the tour groups arrive. You'll need a good pair of walking shoes to handle the old Roman roads and rough paths that crisscross the site. Trainers, with a good tread and ankle support, are ideal.

There's not much shade around, so you'll need a hat and sunscreen in summer – as well as a bottle of water. Food is not essential because the cafe below the theatre sells snacks, but there are some great spots to enjoy a picnic lunch.

Exploring the Site

The following walking tour takes in all the highlights, beginning and ending at the car park at the site entrance. It takes from three to four hours, depending on how much time you spend investigating along the way. If time is short, you can skip the northern part of the site at the end of the tour – although it's a shame to pass up the glorious views from the Temple of Saturn.

The tour opens on a high note at the amazing old **theatre**, nestled into the hillside to the west of the car park. Built in AD 188 by one of the city's wealthy residents, Marcus Quadrutus, its 19 tiers could accommodate an audience of 3500. It's worth climbing to the top tiers to take in the views over the site to the patchwork of fields in the valley below.

The theatre has been extensively renovated, and makes a superb setting for floodlit performances of classical drama during the Dougga

Festival in July and August. Travel agents in Tunis and major resort areas organise special excursions during the festival.

From the theatre, head south and follow the Roman road that leads downhill towards the capitol, passing the ruins of a small **fountain** along the way. The road emerges at the **Square of the Winds**, named after the large circular engraving at its centre listing the names of the 12 winds. It is still possible to make out some of the names, including Africanus (the sirocco). The square's function is unclear, but it was probably used as a market in conjunction with the adjacent **agora** to the south.

The square is bounded by temples. First and foremost among them is the magnificent **capitol**. Raised on a large stone platform, this giant temple dominates the site. It was a gift to the city in AD 166 from two members of the wealthy Marcius family. The massive walls, which stand almost 10m, remain in remarkably good condition. They are the finest known example of a construction technique known as *opus africanum*, which uses large vertical key stones to strengthen walls built of smaller rubble stone.

The walls enclose the temple's inner sanctum. The three large niches on the north wall once housed a giant statue of Jupiter flanked by smaller statues of Juno and Minerva. Six enormous, fluted columns support the suitably oversized portico. You'll need good eyesight to make out the extraordinarily fine detail of the carved frieze. The centrepiece is a carving depicting the emperor Antonius Pius being carried off in an eagle's claws. The inscription below records that the temple was dedicated to the gods Jupiter, Juno and Minerva.

The Byzantines were responsible for the fortifications that enclose the capitol and the **forum**. They were built on the orders of the general Solomon, and were constructed using stones filched from surrounding Roman buildings. Look out for the stones bearing the dedication script from the **Temple of Mercury**, which have wound up at knee height on the eastern wall, facing the Square of the Winds.

The meagre remains of the Temple of Mercury can be found to the north of the square. To the east are four square pillars belonging to the tiny **Temple of Augustine Piety**, built at the beginning of the 2nd century. The tiny stone **mosque** next door stands on the rectangular base of a former Temple of Venus.

The tour heads south from here along the path that runs past the **House with Stairs**, so called because of the many sets of stairs that connect the various levels, to a large but poorly preserved temple complex dedicated to **Concorde**, **Frugifer** and **Liber Pater**. Beyond the temple complex is a **small theatre** facing south-east towards the valley. Scramble down the theatre's tiered seating, and turn right onto the Roman road that curves around the hillside to the west.

To the south of this road is a jumble of houses, all named after the mosaics discovered there. Most now reside at the Bardo Museum in Tunis. To the north is the **Licinian Baths**, built at the height of the town's prosperity in the 3rd century. The walls of this extensive complex remain largely intact, particularly those surrounding the grand central *frigidarium* (cold room).

Head east from the baths, and straight ahead over the staggered crossroads, until you come across an unusual square stone door frame to the south. It marks the entrance to an unidentified temple normally referred to as **Dar el-Echab** after the family that once occupied the site.

Turn south after the Dar el-Echab, and follow the rough path that winds downhill past the ruins of the **Cisterns of Ain Doura** to the **Baths of Ain Doura**, which were the city's main summer baths.

Head back uphill from here along the dirt road that traverses the site, passing the **grand nymphaeum** on the left. This huge, partly restored fountain is thought to have been supplied with water by an underground conduit from the Cisterns of Ain el-Hammam, 300m to the north-west.

Continue along the road for another 75m, then turn right, descending the steps leading to the courtyard of **Trifolium House**. This was once the town brothel, named after the clover-leaf shape of the small room in the north-western corner.

Next door to Trifolium House are the **Cyclops Baths**, named after the remarkable mosaic found here (now in the Bardo Museum in Tunis). The baths themselves are largely in ruins, except for the horseshoe-shaped

Right: Dougga's capitol – a gift presented to the city in 166 by members of the wealthy Marcius family. Its walls are the finest example of the building technique known as *opus africanum*.

CHRIS WOOD

row of latrines just inside the entrance. The Romans obviously thought that using the latrine should be a communal experience!

Head east from the baths along the paved Roman road that leads downhill to the ruins of the Arch of Septimius Severus, built in AD 205 to honour Rome's first African-born emperor.

Turn right before the arch and follow the path that winds south past the **House of the Gorgon** to the **Libyo-Punic Mausoleum**. This triple-tiered monument stands an impressive 21m high, crowned by a small pyramid with a seated lion at the pinnacle. It was built during the reign of Massinissa at the beginning of the 2nd century BC, and is the country's finest surviving example of pre-Roman architecture. It is dedicated, according to a bilingual (Libyan and Punic) inscription, to 'Ateban, son of Ypmatat, son of Palu'. The inscription once occupied the vacant window at the base. It was removed by the British consul to Tunis in 1842, de-

TONY FANKHAUSER

stroying the rest of the monument in the process. The stone was taken to England (where it is now the property of the British Museum), while the monument was rebuilt by a team of French archaeologists in 1910.

Retrace your steps towards the Arch of Septimius Severus and then head north past the **Temple of Pluto** and the **House of the Seasons**, neither worth more than a passing glance. Cross the dirt road and climb the steps leading to a cafe and shop. It's a good time to pause before continuing to the western and northern reaches of the site.

After refreshments, cut across the site to the well-preserved **Arch of Alexander Severus**, built between AD 222 and 235 to mark the western entrance to the city. A rough path leads south-west from here through olive trees to the **Temple of Caelestis**, built at roughly the same time. It was dedicated to the cult of Juno Caelestis, who was the Roman version of the Carthaginian god Tanit. Its construction was funded by a resident, who was made a *flamen* (a Roman priest) in AD 222.

Immediately west of the Arch of Alexander Severus are the cavernous ruins of the **Cisterns of Ain el-Hammam**, added during the reign of Commodius (AD 180–192) to handle the city's growing demand for water. The cisterns were supplied by **aqueduct** from springs in the hills 12km to the south-west. Sections are visible among the olive trees west of the cisterns.

Top: The Libyo-Punic Mausoleum, Tunisia's finest example of pre-Roman architecture.

A rough path leads north through the trees from here, emerging after 150m in front of the **Cisterns of Ain Mizeb**. These nine cisterns were the city's main water supply, fed by a spring some 200m to the west. They remain in good condition and are used for storage by the site authorities.

Follow the dirt road that leads north-west from the cisterns, and then cut across the fields to the ruins of the **Temple of Minerva**. North-west of here it's possible to discern the outline of the **circus**, now an elongated wheat field nestled in a saddle between two hills.

Turn right here and aim for the rocky ridge to the north-east, which is dotted with dozens of primitive **dolmen graves**. These are just north of the so-called **Numidian Wall**, which protected the city in pre-Roman days. The farm outbuildings south of the wall are guarded by dogs, so give them a wide berth as you cross the wall and follow the paths that curve across the hill towards the **Temple of Saturn**.

This great temple must have been a magnificent sight after its completion in AD 195, but only six stunted columns remain to remind visitors of its former glory. Built on a platform facing east over the valley of the Oued Kalled, it would have dominated the northern approach to the ancient city. The temple stands on the site of an earlier temple to Baal-Hammon, the chief deity of the Punic pantheon adopted by the Numidians. Baal Hammon became Saturn in Roman times, and was the favoured god of Roman Africa's native citizens.

The reconstructed apse south of the temple is all that remained of the **Sanctuary of Neptune**.

The ruins of the Vandal **Church of Victoria**, on the slope east of the sanctuary, are the only evidence of Christianity at Dougga. The church was built at the beginning of the 5th century using stone pinched from the surrounding temples. The small **crypt**, next to the church, is packed with large stone sarcophagi.

From here, follow the path that leads south to the theatre – and take a last look over the site to finish the tour.

Right: Built in 188, Dougga's theatre could once seat 3500 people.

CHRIS WOOD

[Continued from page 188]

ceiling. Stone steps lead down to a large pool fed by hot springs, with its slightly saline waters emerging from the ground at 50°C. It's open for men until noon, and for women in the afternoon. Entry is TD1.

Getting There & Away The turn-off to Hammam Mellegue is about 3km south-west of Le Kef, near the junction of the main roads to Tunis, Dahmani and Sakiet Sidi Youssef. If you're coming from Le Kef, follow the signs to Sakiet Sidi Youssef. The turn-off is opposite a military base on the edge of town. Look for a sign to the Forêts du Kef, above a distance marker to Hammam Mellegue (12km).

It's the only indication you're on the right track as the gravel road heads west across rolling wheat country. The first 10km is in good condition; the final 2km is dodgy as the road descends an escarpment to the Oued Mellegue. At the time of research, the road was passable (cautiously) in the smallest car.

TEBERSOUK
☎ 08 • pop 2500

This small town receives its fair share of tourists, but no-one actually seems to stop; they are all in a hurry to get to Dougga and on to the next place. Not a bad plan really, as there is nothing to do here.

Places to Stay & Eat
The sole reason you might want to stay overnight is to get to the ruins at Dougga before the crowds arrive. The only place to stay is the two star *Hôtel Thugga* (☎ 466 647, fax 466 721), which has singles/doubles for TD27/38, with breakfast. Half-board costs an extra TD3.500 per person. The hotel *restaurant* does a roaring trade, catering to tour groups at lunch time. *Sanglier* (wild boar) and *marcassin* (baby wild boar) are popular menu additions between November and April.

The hotel is about 2km out of town, down by the main Tunis-Le Kef road.

Getting There & Away
Bus is by far the easiest way to travel. All SNTRI services operating between Tunis and Le Kef call in at Tebersouk, meaning that there are services in each direction roughly every hour. The fare to Le Kef is TD3.100, and the fare to Tunis is TD3.900.

THUBURBO MAJUS
The remains of the Roman city of Thuburbo Majus are about 60km south-west of Tunis, near the small town of El-Fahs.

History
The ancient Berber settlement of Thuburbo Majus was one of the first towns to come under Carthaginian control during Carthage's drive to build an African empire in the 5th century BC. It remained loyal to Carthage until the bitter end that followed the Punic city's conflict with Rome.

Forced to pay tribute after the fall of Carthage in 146 BC, it became something of a backwater until it was declared a municipality following a visit by the Emperor Hadrian in AD 128. The town soon developed into an important trading centre for the region's agricultural produce – oil, wheat and wine. Most of the buildings date from the second half of the 2nd century, although there was a second phase of construction at the end of the 4th century.

Things to See
Capitol The capitol dominates the site, raised high above the surrounding residential ruins on a giant stone platform. Built in AD 168, it is reached by a wide flight of stairs leading up from the forum to the south-east. At the top of the steps stand four giant pillars of pink limestone marking the entrance to the temple. The capitol was dedicated to two emperors, Marcus Aurelius and Commodus, and was under the protection of the ancient trinity of Jupiter, Juno and Minerva. The giant sandalled foot and head of an enormous statue of Jupiter, estimated to have stood 7.5m high, were found here. The oversized fragments now reside at the Bardo Museum in Tunis.

The ruins of an **olive press** occupy the space beneath the capitol. It was built in Byzantine times, when the town had declined to a mere village. As elsewhere,

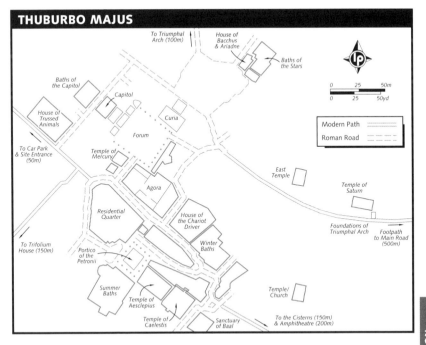

THUBURBO MAJUS

(Map labels:) To Triumphal Arch (100m); House of Bacchus & Ariadne; Baths of the Stars; Baths of the Capitol; Capitol; House of Trussed Animals; Curia; Forum; To Car Park & Site Entrance (50m); Temple of Mercury; East Temple; Temple of Saturn; Agora; Residential Quarter; House of the Chariot Driver; Foundations of Triumphal Arch; Footpath to Main Road (500m); To Trifolium House (150m); Portico of the Petronii; Winter Baths; Summer Baths; Temple of Aesclepius; Temple/Church; Temple of Caelestis; Sanctuary of Baal; To the Cisterns (150m) & Amphitheatre (200m)

(Legend:) Modern Path; Roman Road

(Scale:) 0   25   50m / 0   25   50yd

Byzantine builders showed themselves willing to adapt any available structure – in this case, the capitol.

Forum The forum was built in AD 161 and predates the capitol. It is colonnaded on three sides; the columns were erected in 182 BC.

Temple of Mercury & Market The Temple of Mercury, on the south-western side of the forum, abuts the market, naturally enough, as Mercury was the god of trade. The stalls of the market can be discerned on three sides of the courtyard below the temple. Directly behind the market is a very un-Roman tangle of residential streets, which were obviously in existence before the Romans arrived.

Portico of the Petronii The Portico of the Petronii is named after the family of Petronius Felix, who paid for the construction of this gymnasium complex in AD 225.

The columns are built of an unusual yellow-veined grey marble.

Baths The citizens of Thuburbo Majus had no reason to go short of a bath, with no less than five bath complexes to choose from.

The biggest were the **Summer Baths**, south of the Portico of the Petronii. Check out the Roman-style communal latrine in the north-western corner. The **Winter Baths**, 150m to the east, features a grand entrance flanked by four veined marble columns. Both bath complexes were full of mosaics, now on display in the Bardo Museum in Tunis.

The smaller **Baths of the Labyrinth**, south-east of the agora, and **Baths of the Stars**, north-east of the capitol, are named after their mosaics. Lastly, there are the **Baths of the Capitol**, just west of the capitol.

Sanctuary of Baal This small square temple is easily identified by the two pillars at the top of its steps. Baal was the chief god of the

Punic pantheon, but his cult survived (in Romanised form) long after the fall of Carthage.

Other Sites A rough path leads south-east from the Sanctuary of Baal towards the ruins of the massive **cisterns** which once supplied the town with water. The mound beyond the cisterns marks the site of a small **amphitheatre**. Another rough path leads north from here to a low hill topped by the remains of a **Temple of Saturn**.

Opening Hours The site is open from 8 am to 7 pm daily in summer and from 8.30 am to 5.30 pm daily in winter. Admission is TD2.100.

Getting There & Away
Thuburbo Majus is just west of the Tunis-Kairouan road, 3km north of El-Fahs. There is no public transport to the site, but any bus operating between Tunis and Kairouan can drop you at the turn-off, leaving a 15-minute walk to the site entrance and car park. The sight of a triumphal arch, which marks the northern edge of the city, is an indication that you're getting close.

There are regular louages to El-Fahs from the Cap Bon louage station in Tunis, and buses from the southern bus station.

ZAGHOUAN
☎ 02 • pop 10,000
This sleepy town, tucked beneath the foot of the rugged Jebel Zaghouan (1295m) used to supply ancient Carthage with fresh water. In those days a 70km-long aqueduct was built to carry the water, and parts of it (in remarkably good condition) can still be seen along the Tunis-Zaghouan road, about 20km from Tunis. The springs are still used today by local residents; there are a couple of gushing outlets on strategic corners in the town.

There are some fairly unremarkable Roman ruins in the form of the rather clumsily renovated Temple des Eaux, a once grand fountain surrounded by 12 niches that used to hold statues depicting each month.

Places to Stay & Eat
The only hotel is the *Hôtel Les Nymphes* (☎ 277 094). It has a great setting high above the town, nestled amid pine forests at the foot of the mountain. It was closed for renovation at the time of research, but was scheduled to re-open in late 2000. Expect to pay about TD30/45 for singles/doubles. Take care if walking in the forests around the hotel; there are lots of wild boars. The hotel doubles as the only bar in town, and also has a *restaurant*.

Getting There & Away
Public transport leaves from the middle of town, near the junction with the road leading uphill to the Hôtel Les Nymphes. There are regular buses to El-Fahs (920 mills) and Tunis (TD2.370), and daily buses to Nabeul (TD2.810) and Sousse (TD3.620).

Louages to Zaghouan leave from the Cap Bon station in Tunis.

UTHINA
Ancient Uthina is situated about 30km south of Tunis, just east of the aqueduct that once supplied fresh water from Zaghouan to Carthage. Long ignored by archaeologists, heritage authorities and tourists alike, Uthina is suddenly flavour of the moment. At the time of research, the site was in the middle of a major upgrade – presumably with a view to developing Uthina as a tourist attraction.

The site is open from 8 am to 6 pm daily in summer and from 8 am to 5 pm daily in winter. Admission is TD1.600.

History
The Roman historian Pliny lists Uthina among the oldest towns in Africa. It was originally the Berber settlement of Adys, site of a major battle between Carthage and the Roman general Regulus during the first Punic War in 255 BC. Regulus reported that it was an important walled town, although no evidence for this exists today.

The Roman town was founded by the emperor Augustus at the beginning of the 1st century AD, and settled with army veterans. These soldiers had little clue how to work the land, and Uthina struggled to survive until the land was bought up by real farmers. Like many Roman towns in Africa, its prosperity peaked in the 2nd and 3rd centuries. It slipped into decline after the Vandal conquest, but survived until Byzantine times.

The site was a munitions dump during WWII, which damaged several monuments.

Things to See

The site is spread over a large area, most of it unexcavated. The access road stops at a low hill at the centre of the site topped by an old colonial farmhouse. Known locally as El-Kalaa (the fortress), this was once the **capitol**. These days, there's such a jumble of buildings that it takes a while to figure out what's what.

The farmhouse, still occupied at the time of research, stands on the site of the Capitoline temple. The **forum**, identifiable to the south, is now a farmyard surrounded by outbuildings. Traces of the steps leading to the capitol can be found on the rocky slope between the farmyard and the farmhouse.

Beneath the capitol is a magnificent rectangular vaulted room, built in Byzantine times and recently restored to almost mint condition. The northern slope of the capitol hill is covered with the ruins of a fortress, presumably Byzantine.

South of the forum are the remains of a **reservoir**, standing at the end of an **aqueduct** that supplied water from springs at nearby Jebel Rassas. Most of the water was delivered to a network of enormous **cisterns** 200m south of the reservoir. Some of these cisterns have collapsed while others remain in remarkably good condition.

The sections of collapsed masonry east of the capitol mark the site of the main **public baths**. In contrast to the chaos above ground, the subterranean level is in good condition.

North of here, beside the access road, are the **Baths of the Laberii**. They stand beside the remains of the celebrated **House of the Laberii**, a sumptuous 40-room villa with its finest mosaics now on display at the Bardo Museum in Tunis.

The **amphitheatre**, west of the access road, could cater for crowds of more than 10,000 and is a good indication of the stature of the Roman town. It was being excavated and restored at the time of research.

Getting There & Away

There is no public transport to the site. It's clearly signposted 28km south of Tunis on the road to El-Fahs and Kairouan. It's another 2km to the site, which is close to the modern village of Oudna. The station here is for freight trains only.

Central Tunisia

Central Tunisia can be divided into two main regions. The flat eastern one-third, known as the Sahel, occupies the large coastal bulge between the Gulf of Hammamet and the Gulf of Gabès and includes the booming resort towns of the east coast. The port cities of Sousse, in the north, and Sfax, in the south, are the largest in the country after Tunis; Kairouan, the fourth-holiest city in the Islamic world, is situated on the plains an hour's drive west of Sousse. The western two-thirds, known as the Tell, cover the high plains of the Tunisian Dorsale, which are an extension of Algeria's Tell Atlas Mountains.

The Sahel has long been one of Tunisia's most important regions, both economically and politically. Its prosperity was founded on agriculture. The Romans turned the area into a vast olive grove, and the wealth generated through the trade in olives and olive oil financed spectacular construction projects such as the enormous amphitheatre at Thysdrus (El-Jem). Huge areas of olive groves remain, notably around Sfax. Market gardening is also big business on the more fertile soils south of Sousse, supplying winter salad vegetables to northern Europe as well as to local markets.

Tourism has emerged as the mainstay of the modern economy. The beautiful, sandy beaches around Sousse and Monastir are flanked by countless big hotels. A constant flow of charter flights from northern Europe to the international airport at Monastir keeps them topped up with package tourists. Tourist development becomes steadily more low-key as you head south along the coast.

Mahdia, custom-built capital of the Fatimids (AD 909–69), is a delightful old town that remains relatively unaffected by mass tourism. Few tourists make it to Sfax – which is good news for those who do. Sfax is also the departure point for ferries to the Kerkennah Islands, which offer an opportunity to escape the crowds altogether.

The Tell was also an important agricultural region in Roman times. The Roman Empire's ever-increasing demand for wheat meant that new land had to be found to grow it, and most of the region's once extensive forest cover disappeared in the process – destroying the ecology of the high plains forever.

Wheat is still grown in some places, but much of the land is badly degraded and has reverted to marginal grazing country. This desolate terrain comes to life briefly in spring, when there are spectacular displays of wildflowers, but for the rest of the year it's difficult to work out how even goats can survive. The summers are impossibly hot, while the winters are cold and bleak.

Roman ruins, in particular the remarkably well-preserved temple complex at Sufetula

Highlights

- Admiring Monastir's magnificent *ribat* – military architecture at its most photogenic
- Browsing through Mahdia's ancient medina – a maze of vine-shaded squares and narrow cobbled streets
- Marvelling at El-Jem's colosseum, one of the most impressive Roman monuments in Africa
- Shopping in the medina at Sfax
- Exploring the Roman temples at Sbeitla – magical in the early morning light

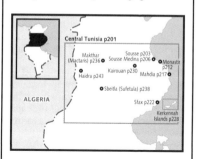

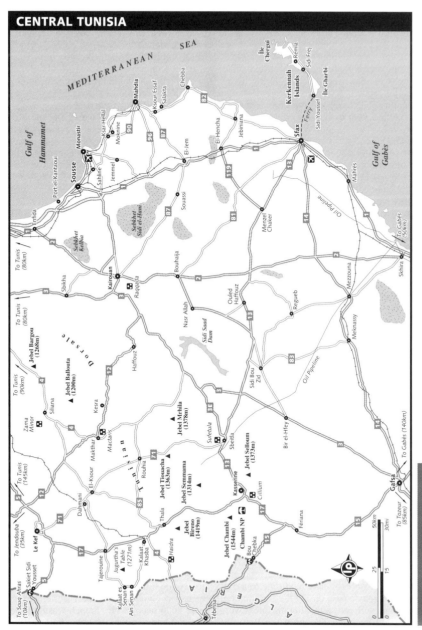

CENTRAL TUNISIA

(modern Sbeitla), are the main attraction of the Tell region. The Roman sites at Haidra and Makthar are more difficult to get to and are consequently much less visited.

Jugurtha's Table, legendary stronghold of the Numidian king Jugurtha during his rebellion against Rome at the end of the 2nd century BC, makes an interesting side trip if you have your own transport.

SOUSSE
☎ 03 • pop 230,000

The cosmopolitan coastal city of Sousse has been the premier city of the Sahel region since the days of ancient Carthage. An impressive old medina is evidence of its long history as a commercial centre. Favoured by the French, Sousse has continued to thrive post-independence. It is officially the country's third-largest city behind Tunis and Sfax.

Much of the growth in modern times has been fuelled by tourism. For most visitors, the main attraction is the beach, a long curve of golden sand stretching all the way to Port el-Kantaoui, 14km to the north. This coastline is flanked by a long line of hotels catering for a range of nationalities and budgets.

Sousse is also an important centre for light industry and a major port. It has a large student population, making it a lively town.

Independent travellers will find a good range of budget and mid-range accommodation around the medina and city centre.

History

Sousse was founded in the 9th century BC as the Phoenician outpost of Hadrumète, and fell under the sway of Carthage from the middle of the 6th century BC. The famous Carthaginian general Hannibal used the town as his base against the Romans in the final stages of the Second Punic War in 202 BC.

The town was saved from the fate that befell Carthage (see the History section in the Facts about Tunisia chapter) because it allied itself with Rome during the Third and final Punic War. Hadrumètum, as it became known, wasn't so lucky next time round. It was Pompey's base during the Roman civil war, and suffered badly after his forces were defeated by Julius Caesar at the Battle of Thapsus in AD 46. Caesar, incidentally, was based just down the coast at Ruspina (Monastir).

Eventually, though, the city prospered under Roman rule. Emperor Diocletian made it the capital of the Byzacèe Province, which covered the southern half of Tunisia.

When the Vandals arrived in the 5th century AD, Hadrumètum was a city of sufficient stature to be renamed Hunericopolis in honour of the son of the Vandal chief. When the Byzantines dislodged the Vandals 100 years later, the name was changed to Justinianopolis in honour of the ruling emperor. True to their obsession with fortification, the Byzantines were the first to surround the city with a defensive wall.

Justinianopolis was levelled, wall and all, by Okba bin Nafaa al-Fihri after it fell to the Arabs in the late 7th century. It was eventually rebuilt as the Arab town of Soussa, and became the main port of the 9th century Aghlabid dynasty based in Kairouan. Following the Hilalian invasions in the 11th century, it was briefly the centre of a small independent fiefdom before it was captured by the Normans. The Normans ruled for almost a century before the arrival of the Almohads in 1160.

Subsequent Hafsid rule resulted in the city enjoying almost 400 years of peace and relative prosperity. This was rudely interrupted in the mid-16th century, when Soussa became a hotly contested prize in the power struggle between the Ottoman Turks and Spain. The Spanish captured the city from the Turks in 1535, and held it for more than 20 years.

Back under Ottoman control, it became notorious as a base for the corsair pirates who preyed on Christian shipping in the Mediterranean; a role which resulted in it suffering severe reprisals when Christian forces gained the ascendancy in the late 18th century. A period of steady decline was hastened in 1864 when the city aligned itself with rebel forces in a failed revolt against Mohamed Sadok Bey.

By the time the French arrived in 1881, it had declined to a modest settlement of just 8000 people. The French wasted little time in transforming the town, building the

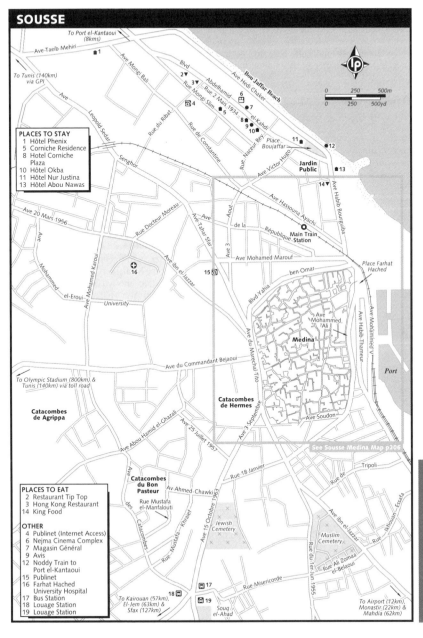

SOUSSE

To Port el-Kantaoui
(8kms)

Ave Taeib Mehiri

To Tunis (140km)
via GPI

Ave Mongi Bali

Leopold Sedar

Senghor

Blvd

Rue 2 Mars 1934

Rue Mongi Slim

Abdelhamid

Ave Hedi Chaker

Bou Jaffar Beach

el-Kahdi

Rue Naceur Bey

Place
Boujaffar

Ave Victor Hugo

Jardin
Public

Ave Habib Bourguiba

Rue du Ribat

Rue de Constantine

Ave 20 Mars 1956

Rue Docteur Moreau

Ave Tahar Sfar

Ave Ibn el-Jazzar

Ave

Aout

de la

République

Ave Hassouna Ayachi

Main Train
Station

Place Farhat
Hached

Ave
Mohammed

el-Eroui

University

Ave Mohamed Karoui

Ave Mohamed Marouf

ben Omar

Blvd Yahia

Ave
Mohammed
Ali

Medina

Ave Habib Thameur

Ave Mohammed V

Port

To Olympic Stadium (800km) &
Tunis (140km) via toll road

Catacombes
de Agrippa

Ave du Marechal Tito

Ave du Commandant Bejaoui

Catacombes
de Hermes

Ave 3 Septembre

Ave Soudon

See Sousse Medina Map p206

Catacombes
du Bon
Pasteur

Ave Abou Hamid el-Ghazali

Ave 25 Juillet 1957

Rue Mustafa
el-Manfalouti

des Catacombes

Rue Mustafa Khznaji

Av-Ahmed-Chawki

Ave 15 Octobre 1985

Rue 18 Janvier

Jewish
Cemetery

Rue du 1er Jun 1955

Rue de

Tripoli

Ave Ibn el-Jazzar

Rue Khouan - Essafa

Muslim
Cemetery

Rue Ali Zomaa
el-Belaoui

Rue Misericorde

To Kairouan (57km),
El-Jem (63km) &
Sfax (127km)

Souq
el-Ahad

To Airport (12km),
Monastir (22km) &
Mahdia (62km)

0   250   500m
0   250   500yd

PLACES TO STAY
1 Hôtel Phenix
5 Corniche Residence
8 Hotel Corniche
   Plaza
10 Hôtel Okba
11 Hôtel Nur Justina
13 Hôtel Abou Nawas

PLACES TO EAT
2 Restaurant Tip Top
3 Hong Kong Restaurant
14 King Food

OTHER
4 Publinet (Internet Access)
6 Nejma Cinema Complex
7 Magasin Général
9 Avis
12 Noddy Train to
   Port el-Kantaoui
15 Publinet
16 Farhat Hached
   University Hospital
17 Bus Station
18 Louage Station
19 Louage Station

customary Ville Nouvelle and establishing the infrastructure for the thriving city it is today.

The town, especially the area around the port, was badly damaged by Allied bombing during WWII.

Orientation

Life in Sousse revolves around its huge central square, Place Farhat Hached. The medina is to the south-west of the square, the port to the east and Ave Habib Bourguiba runs north from the square to the beach and the hotels of the *zone touristique* (tourist strip). Ave Habib Bourguiba forks when it reaches the coast at Place Boujaffar: Ave Hedi Chaker runs north-west along the beachfront, while Blvd Abdelhamid el-Kahdi runs parallel to it, one block inland.

All the city's major thoroughfares converge on Place Farhat Hached, including the main Tunis-Sfax railway line, which runs through the middle of the square. There has been lots of talk about rerouting the line, but it remains in the too-hard basket. The sight of a giant locomotive, lights flashing and bells ringing, edging through the traffic in the square will be around for a while to come.

Information

Tourist Offices There is an unusually efficient branch of the national tourist office (☎ 225 157, fax 224 262) at 1 Ave Habib Bourguiba, on the north side of Place Farhat Hached. It has a notice board with all sorts of useful information, including up-to-date timetables for buses and trains and details of local attractions. The staff speak English, French and German. They can give you a list of hotels with all the latest prices as well as a map of the city and surrounding area.

Opening hours vary with the season. For most of the year, the office is open from 8.30 am to 1 pm and 3 to 5.45 pm Monday to Thursday and to 1.30 pm Friday and Saturday. During July and August it is open from 7.30 am to 7 pm Monday to Saturday, and 9 am to noon Monday to Saturday.

The local *syndicat d'initiative* (municipal tourist office; ☎ 220 431) occupies the nearby Zaouia of Sidi Yahia – the small,

white-domed building on the western side of Place Farhat Hached, near the entrance to the medina.

Money There are plenty of banks along Ave Habib Bourguiba and by the beach.

Post & Communications The main post office is in the thick of things, on Ave de la République just off Place Farhat Hached. There are lots of Taxiphone offices around the city centre and along Blvd Abdelhamid el-Kahdi. The office just inside the medina is open long hours: from 7 am to 11 pm.

Sousse has more places to access the Internet than any city in Tunisia. There are three in the city centre alone. Infonet, 3 Rue Bechir Sfar, is open from 8 am to 8 pm daily and charges TD2.500 per hour. There are two Publinet offices nearby. Cyber Centre Publinet Sousse is in the arcade next to the UIB Bank on Ave Mohamed Maarouf, and there's another office on Ave Tahar Sfar, near the junction with Ave Mohamed Maarouf. Both charge TD3, as does a third Publinet office inland from the beach hotels on Rue de Ribat.

Bookshops Cité de Livre, at 3 Ave Habib Bourguiba, just north of the tourist office, stocks a small range of novels in English, and a larger range of similar books in French and German.

International Newspapers Cité de Livre stocks a large selection of international newspapers and magazines. You'll also find international newspapers for sale at the train station and in the lobbies of the bigger hotels.

Medical Services The city's main hospital is the Farhat Hached University Hospital (☎ 221 411), north-west of the medina on Ave Ibn el-Jazzar. The Clinique Les Oliviers (☎ 242 711), near the Hôtel Orient Palace on the tourist strip north of town, is more used to dealing with insurance forms etc.

Dangers & Annoyances Petty theft seems to have become a problem on Boujaffar Beach, so don't leave valuables lying around unattended.

Medina

Most of the city's attractions are to be found within the walls of its fine old medina. The walls themselves are an impressive sight, stretching 2.25km at a height of 8m and fortified with a series of solid square turrets. They were built by the Aghlabids in AD 859 on the foundations of the city's original Byzantine walls.

It's hardly surprising, given the scale of package tourism in the area, that the medina is overrun with tourists, tourist shops and over-enthusiastic shopkeepers. The situation is particularly bad around the two best-known monuments, the *ribat* (fortified Islamic monastery) and the Great Mosque, which are both in the north-eastern corner of the medina. You can escape the worst of the crowds by starting early, or by wandering off on your own into the medina's quieter streets.

Walking Tour

This tour visits all the major sites of the medina, except the museums, which are covered later in this section. It can take anywhere from two to four hours, depending on how much time you spend exploring the main attractions.

The tour starts at the north-eastern corner of the medina at Place des Martyrs. The area was created when Allied bombs blew away this section of the wall in 1943. The resulting hole, now lined with smart shops, forms the main access point to the medina.

It leads directly to the **Great Mosque**, first stop of the tour. It's a typically austere Aghlabid affair. It was built, according to a kufic (early Arabic) inscription in the courtyard, in the year AD 851 by a freed slave called Mudam on the instructions of the Aghlabid ruler Abul Abbas. If you think it looks more like a fort than a mosque with its turrets and crenellated wall, it's because Mudam adapted an earlier kasbah, built to protect the town in conjunction with the nearby ribat. This explains the mosque's unusual location; the great mosque is usually sited in the centre of a medina, not at the fringe. The structure has since undergone 17th-century modifications and 20th-century restoration. Non-Muslims aren't allowed beyond the courtyard, and so won't get to see inside Mudam's grand barrel-vaulted prayer hall. The courtyard is open from 9 am to 1 pm daily, and entry is TD1.100. Modest dress is essential. If your garb fails to meet the standard, you can rent a gown (500 mills) from one of the shops opposite the entrance.

The best views of the mosque are to be found at the nearby **ribat**. This small square fort is just to the north-west of the mosque, and is easily identifiable thanks to its round **nador** (watch tower) protruding above the surrounding rooftops. It is the oldest monument in the medina, built in the final years of the 8th century AD. The tower was added by the Aghlabids in AD 821.

The entrance to the ribat is through a narrow arched doorway flanked by columns salvaged from the ruins of Roman Hadrumètum. A long vaulted passage then opens out into a courtyard surrounded by porticos. The ribat was designed principally as a fort, intended to guard the frontiers of Islam against Christian marauders. It was garrisoned by devout Islamic warriors, who would divide their time between fighting and silent study of the Quran in the tiny, cell-like rooms built into the walls. Steps lead up to the roof, and give access to the nador. Scramble up the narrow spiral staircase and you'll emerge onto a small balcony with excellent views over the city and into the courtyard of the Great Mosque below.

It's open from 8 am to 7 pm in summer and 8 am to 6 pm in winter daily, except Friday. Admission is TD2.100.

The ribat stands on a lower level than the surrounding streets to the north and west, cut off by a 3m-high stone embankment. Continuing the tour west along Rue Dar Abid therefore means heading back towards the Great Mosque before turning right and doubling back on the high side of the embankment. The splendid octagonal stone minaret at the junction of Rue Dar Said and Rue de Tazerka belongs to the 17th century **Zaouia Zakkak**, the medina's leading example of Ottoman architecture. Non-Muslims can do no more than admire the minaret and gleaming white cupola from the street. The complex includes a mosque, a *medersa* (Quranic

SOUSSE MEDINA

PLACES TO STAY
8 Hôtel Claridge
12 Hôtel Hadrumete
18 Hôtel de Paris
21 Hôtel Ahla
27 Hôtel Medina
28 Hôtel Gabès
33 Hôtel Ezzouhour

PLACES TO EAT
1 Restaurant el-Ons
2 Restaurant Marmite
11 Restaurant/Bar de Tunisie

OTHER
3 Tunis Air
4 Cinema
5 Cité de Livre
   (International Newspapers)
6 OTC
7 ONTT Tourist Office
9 Monoprix Supermarket
10 Magasin Général
13 Syndicat d'Initiative
14 Post Office
15 Infonet
16 Cyber Centre Publinet
   Sousse
17 Buses to Mahdia &
   Monastir; Local Buses
19 Taxi Rank
20 Taxiphone Office
22 Ribat
23 Museum Dar Essid
24 Zaouia Zakkak
25 Great Mosque
26 Municipalité (Town Hall)
29 Hammam of Sidi Bouraoui
30 Red Light District
31 Café de la Medina
32 Kalaout el-Koubba
34 Sofra Cistern
35 Prison
36 Kasbah & Sousse
   Archaeological Museum

To Boujaffar Beach, Hôtel
Sousse Azur, Hôtel Abou
Nawas &
Zone Touristique

MEDITERRANEAN SEA

Rue d'Alger
Rue Remada
Ave Habib Bourguiba
Rue de
Rue Laroussi Haddad

Place
Teyes

Rue Palestine

Place de la
République

Ave Hasouna Ayachi

Rue Pasteur

Rue Cairo

Train
Station

Rue de l'Indépendance

Rue Aveceune

Rue Bechir Sfar

Ave de la République

Rue Ali Belhaouane

Rue 22 Janvier 1952

Ave Mohamed Maarouf

Place
Farhat
Hached

Place
du Port

Blvd Yahia ben Omar

Rue du Rempart Nord

Place des
Martyrs

Start\
Finish

Rue Nadjar

Rue Dar Abid

Rue Othene Osmane

Port

Rue Saida Nejma

Rue Sultan Dar

Rue de Malte

Rue d'Angleterre

Rue el-Aglhaba

Rue Sidi
Bouraoui

Rue Zarouk

Avenue - Mohammed - Ali

Ave Habib Thameur

Avenue Mohammed V

To
Tunis

Rue Abou Nawas

Rue Sidi Said

Sbat Dalma

Medina

Rue el-Caid

Souq er-Ribaa

Bab el-Jedid

Rue de France

Rue el-Araoui

Bab el-Finga

Rue Souq el-Caid

Rue Rajah Ibrahim

Market

Train
Station

To Monastir
& Mahdia

Medina Walking Tour

Bab el-Gharbi

Steps

Rue de la Kasbah

Rue el-Maar

Rue Kogbar

Rue el-Hajra

Rue Salem ben Hmida

To Catacombs
(500m)

Ave du Commandant Bjaoui

Ave Maréchal Tito

Rue el-Ghazali

Ave 25 Juillet 1957

Steps

Rue Ibn Rachik

Rue Bazira

Rue Didi

Rue du Rempart Sud

Ave Soudan

Bab el-Kebli

Place
Jebenet
el-Ghourba

Ave du 18 Janvier 1952

Rue de Sakka

To Louage Station,
Kairouan & Sfax

school) and a mausoleum. The original structure was built in Aghlabid times.

Turn left onto Rue de Tazerka at the minaret, and take time to study the floral scrolls of the *zaouia*'s elaborately carved doorway before turning right into Rue el-Aghlaba. This is one of the medina's main east-west thoroughfares, climbing steadily away from the Great Mosque towards Bab el-Finga. Look for the small **stone archway** after about 50m, just beyond Rue Sidi Bouraoui. A pathway above the arch was once used by a donkey, which would trudge around all day drawing water for the **hammam of Sidi Bouraoui**. The entrance to the hammam, which has now switched to town water, is on Rue Sidi Bouraoui – opposite the mosque of the same name.

Keep heading west along Rue el-Aghlaba until you reach **Bab el-Finga**. Its name *(finga* means 'blade' in Arabic) refers to the days when the French set up their guillotine outside the gate. The area is still notorious, but these days the notoriety stems from its **red-light district** – a special cordoned-off area just north of Bab el-Finga on Rue Abou Nawas. Hence the unusually attired clientele at the Café de la Medina, just inside the gate.

The tour, however, turns left at Bab el-Finga and follows the medina walls south along Rue Abou Nawas to **Bab el-Gharbi**. This is the main (and more respectable!) of the two western gates. Rue Souq el-Caid connects Bab el-Gharbi with the central souq district, and makes a useful shortcut if time is limited.

The main tour keeps heading south, now along Rue ibn Rachik, to the gates of a **civil prison**. The prison occupies the northern wing of the ancient **kasbah**. The remainder of the kasbah is home to Sousse's excellent archaeological museum. There is no access to the museum from within the medina: The entrance is on Ave du Maréchal Tito. See the following Archaeological Museum section for details.

Standing at the high point of the medina, the kasbah was built on to the city walls in the 11th century. It incorporates the central **Khalef tower**, constructed by the Aghlabids in AD 859 at the same time as the city walls.

This imposing square tower superseded the ribat as the city's watchtower. It's now a lighthouse.

At the entrance to the prison, turn left and head down the steps of Rue de la Kasbah. It passes through a quiet residential area as it twists and turns back into the heart of the medina. The modest doorways indicate that this was not a wealthy quarter, but there are some fine old Hand of Fatimah door knockers along the way. Rue de la Kasbah is poorly signposted; keep heading downhill following the newly laid rectangular stone paving. After 350m, turn left into Rue Sidi Slimene.

You'll soon find yourself flanked by a low, white, rendered wall on the right. It belongs to the **Sofra Cistern**, once the medina's principle water supply. This great underground cistern was created in the 11th century by enclosing a large Byzantine church. It's an eerie place, viewed by torchlight, with the columns of the church rising from the still black waters. The entrance is on the northeastern side, but the battered old metal door was locked at the time of research – and destined to stay that way until something is done to make the cisterns more visitor friendly. Skirt around the edge of the cisterns and exit north-east along Rue Ahmad Magroun until you hit the Souq er-Ribaa.

Suddenly the tranquillity of the southern medina is left far behind. Souq er-Ribaa lies at the centre of the atmospheric **covered souqs** that form the commercial heart of the medina. The place is a riot of colour, packed with haggling merchants, browsing tourists and barrow boys trying to squeeze through with their improbably overloaded carts. This central area is closed off at night.

Turn right onto Souq er-Ribaa, and then take the first turn left onto Rue Zarrouk. You'll be following a sign pointing to the **Kalaout el-Koubba**. The Koubba rates as the most unusual building in the medina. Its origins and purpose remain unclear. It is thought to have been built in the late 11th or early 12th century AD; the dimensions suggest it may have been some sort of palace reception area. The most striking feature is the cupola with its remarkable zigzag ribbing. The fluted interior is just as impressive. The

Koubba is now a museum, open daily except Friday. Admission is TD2.

Double back to Souq er-Ribaa, turn left and follow it east until it emerges on Rue de Paris, which is part of the medina's main north-south thoroughfare. Turn left, and browse your way north through the souvenir shops until you reach the Great Mosque, which is where the tour ends.

Sousse Archaeological Museum

Sousse's excellent archaeological museum occupies the southern section of the old kasbah at the south-western corner of the medina. The kasbah is impressive enough in itself, and is described in the earlier Walking Tour.

The displays are housed in the rooms around the kasbah's two main courtyards. They include the best collection of mosaics in the country outside the Bardo Museum in Tunis. The star exhibit is the **Triumph of Bacchus**, in Room 3, which depicts the Roman god of wine riding in a chariot at the head of a parade of satyrs. The triumph in question is that of wine over beer. Room 6 contains a collection of funerary objects from a Punic grave uncovered when the museum was created.

The museum is open from 8 am to noon and 3 to 7 pm in summer and 9 am to 12.30 pm and 2 to 6 pm in winter daily, except Friday. Admission is TD2.100, plus TD1 to take photos. The entrance is on Ave du Maréchal Tito.

Dar Essid Museum

This small, private museum is another place not to be missed. It occupies a beautiful old home at 65 Rue du Remparts Nord, furnished in the style of a well-to-do 19th-century Sousse official and family. The dimensions of the elaborately decorated, arched golden door are the first indication that the occupants weren't short of cash. It opens into a small anteroom for meeting strangers, and then into a tiled courtyard surrounded by the family rooms. A plaque in the courtyard reveals that the house was built in AD 928, making it one of the oldest homes in the medina. There are lots of nice touches. Check out the Roman lamp with the graphic

decoration of a copulating couple. It's by the master bed, and is accompanied by an amusing explanation of its function.

The museum is open from 10 am to 7 pm daily in summer and 10 am to 6 pm daily in winter. Admission is TD2.

Catacombs

The catacombs are something of a letdown, especially if you go along with expectations raised by the guff contained in some brochures – which enthuse about a network of tunnels extending for almost 5.5km, in better condition than the catacombs of Rome.

Reality is somewhat different, although there are indeed an estimated 5.5km of tunnels containing the graves of more than 15,000 local Christians, mostly from the 4th and 5th centuries AD. They are divided into four main areas, three of which have been excavated: the Catacombes du Bon Pasteur, the Catacombes de Hermes, the Catacombes de Severus and the Catacombes d'Agrippa.

Unfortunately, the only section open to the public is a small stretch (about 100m) of the Catacombes du Bon Pasteur, which are named after an engraving of the *bon pasteur* (good shepherd) found inside. There's not much to see, except a copy of the engraving. Most of the graves have been bricked in; a couple have glass fronts, revealing a few skeletal remains. The site is about 500m north of the bus and louage stations on Ave des Catacombes.

The catacombs are open from 9 am to 5 pm in winter and to 6 pm in summer daily, except Friday. Admission is TD1.100. There's a small display of finds from the catacombs in Room 8 at the archaeological museum.

Boujaffar Beach

Sousse's main tourist drawcard is Boujaffar Beach (named after a local *marabout* or Muslim holy man), which stretches north from the northern end of Ave Habib Bourguiba, a 1km walk from the city centre. It is quite a decent strip of white sand, but it's backed by a line of high-rise hotels and apartments and can get ridiculously crowded in summer.

You'll find all sorts of water-sports equipment for hire along the beach, as well as activities like water-skiing and parasailing.

Jardin Public

This small shady park stretches south from Place Boujaffar, and was laid out in 1895, at the same time as the Ville Nouvelle. It's home to a small collection of caged birds, and there's an admission charge of 200 mills. The entrance is on Place Boujaffar.

Markets

Sousse's weekly market is held on Sunday in the Souq el-Ahad compound just south of the bus and louage stations. It's a chaotic affair, with stalls spilling out into the surrounding streets. You'll find everything from handicrafts to livestock – and an astonishing amount of cheap plastic junk.

Places to Stay – Budget

All the cheap hotels are to be found in the medina. They are all fairly primitive, but worth considering if you're on a tight budget. The most presentable is the *Hôtel Ahla* (☎ 220 570), just north of the Great Mosque on Place de la Grand Mosquée. It charges TD6 per person in winter, and TD7.500 in summer. Other possibilities in this price range are the *Hôtel Gabès* (☎ 226 977, 12 Rue de Paris) and the *Hôtel Ezzouhour* (☎ 228 729, 48 Rue de Paris), south of the Great Mosque.

You can do a lot better for a few dollars more.

Places to Stay – Mid-Range

Most travellers head for the spotless *Hôtel de Paris* (☎ 220 564, fax 219 038, 15 Rue du Rempart Nord), just inside the medina's north wall. It has singles/doubles for TD14/20, rising to TD16/22 in summer, when you can also sleep on the roof (TD7). There are free hot showers and laundry facilities.

Another popular option is the *Hôtel Medina* (☎ 221 722, fax 221 794, 1 Rue Othene Osmane), a one-star place on the southern side of the Great Mosque, on the corner of Rue de Paris. It has rooms with bathroom for TD14/19 in winter. In summer, it has doubles for TD32, but no singles. You'll need to get

in early in summer, because a lot of tour groups use the hotel as an overnight stop.

The *Hôtel Hadrumete* (☎ 226 291, fax 226 863), on the northern side of Place Farhat Hached, is a former two-star hotel that no longer cuts the mustard with the tourist authorities. The hot water is erratic, but there are great views from the upper floors and TD25/40 is good value in summer for rooms with a bathroom. This falls to TD15/20 in winter.

There are several more possibilities along the Corniche. The *Hôtel Corniche* (☎ 226 697, fax 225 676, 18 Rue 32 Mars 1934) is a quiet place tucked away behind the main drag. It charges TD20/32 in summer. The *Hotel Corniche Plaza* (☎ 226 763, fax 226 433), next to the Hôtel Africa Beach on Blvd Abdelhamid el-Kahdi, charges TD28/38 in summer and TD19/24 in winter.

Places to Stay – Top End

The beachfront north of Sousse has been transformed into a row of big hotels that stretches as far as the eye can see. Most of them are booked out in summer, so they aren't an option anyway. There are some very cheap deals to be found in winter.

The line-up starts immediately north of Ave Habib Bourguiba with a few relatively low-key three-star places like the *Hôtel Nur Justina* (☎ 226 381, fax 225 993). Singles/doubles here range from a bargain TD19/28 in winter up to TD41/72 in summer. The hotels get steadily bigger and smarter as you head up the beach, culminating in the five star *Hôtel Orient Palace* (☎ 242 888, fax 243 345), 4km north of town. Facilities here include no less than three swimming pools, tennis courts, a fitness centre and disco. Rates are TD57/84 in winter, soaring to TD110/160 in summer.

Closer to town, the four star *Hôtel Abou Nawas Boujaffar* (☎ 226 030, fax 226 574) offers top winter value with singles/doubles for TD33/46. This rises to TD90/128 in summer.

Places to Stay – Apartments

Sousse also has a selection of apartment hotels, offering serviced studio apartments. A good place to check out is the *Hôtel Phenix* (☎ *224 288, fax 224 539)* on Ave Taieb Mehiri. It has a range of apartments for up to five people. Winter prices start at TD24 for two people and TD38 for four, rising to TD62/90 in summer.

Places to Eat

Restaurants Rue Remada, between the train station and Ave Habib Bourguiba, is the place to go for a good cheap feed. You'll find half a dozen small restaurants bunched together, all advertising very similar menus at similar prices. Places like the *Restaurant el-Ons* offer a range of salads for TD1 and main courses from TD2.200: It has good, no-nonsense traditional food at great prices.

If you want a glass of wine with your meal, and a touch more refinement, head to the popular *Restaurant/Bar de Tunisie* on Rue Ali Belhaouane. You'll find dishes like spicy *ojja aux fruits de mer* (TD3) as well as grilled fish (TD5).

There are dozens of upmarket restaurants along the northern section of Ave Habib Bourguiba and on Blvd Abdelhamid el-Kahdi. You'll find menus in three or four languages and waiters who can speak all of them.

The *Restaurant Tip Top* (☎ *226 158, 73 Blvd Abdelhamid el-Kahdi)* is one place that gets consistently good reports. Seafood is a prominent feature of the menu (as it is everywhere in Sousse), and it's possible to eat very well for about TD20 per person. The waiters here double as entertainers, making it a top place to take children.

Prices are more reasonable away from the main drag. The *Restaurant Marmite* (☎ *226 728, 8 Rue Remada)* is a cosy place where you can eat well for TD15 per person, plus wine. The name, incidentally, has nothing to do with the popular English savoury sandwich spread; a *marmite* in Tunisia is a large urn-shaped cooking pot.

The *Hong Kong* (☎ *221 366, 4 Rue de Rabat)* is one of but a handful of Chinese restaurants in the country. It has an extensive menu, including a full range of pork dishes. Reckon on TD25 for two, plus wine.

Fast Food The streets of Sousse are lined with countless fast-food outlets. *King Food*, diagonally opposite the Hôtel Abou Nawas on Rue Amilcar, has virtually the whole range under one roof with burgers from 950 mills, pasta from TD1.800, pizzas from TD2.250 and salads.

Self-Catering The *Magasin Général* in the Complex Touristique Nejma on Blvd Abdelhamid el-Kahdi is the best supermarket around. It has a good selection of Tunisian wine. There's also a *Monoprix supermarket* in town at the junction of Ave Habib Bourguiba and Rue Ali Belhaouane, and a *Magasin Général* nearby on Rue de l'Indépendance. Both stock wine and beer.

The main *produce markets* are in the medina, just inside the Bab el-Jedid.

Getting There & Away

Air Sousse is served by Monastir's airport (Habib Bourguiba International), which is 12km south of town on the main road to Monastir. See the Monastir Getting There & Away section later in this chapter for more details of flights to and from the airport. The Tunis Air office (☎ 225 232) is at 5 Ave Habib Bourguiba.

See the following Getting Around section for information on transport to and from the airport.

Bus All intercity buses, except those to Monastir and Mahdia, leave from the new bus station at Souq el-Ahad, 800m southwest of the medina. National line SNTRI is the biggest operator. See the list on the following page for details.

There are also local buses to Kairouan (TD2.700) every 30 minutes from 6 am to 7 pm.

SRTG Nabeul operates three services a day to Hammamet (TD3.150, 1½ hours) and Nabeul (TD3.650, two hours).

Monastir and Mahdia are classified as local destinations, and services leave from Blvd Yahia ben Oma, north of the medina. There are buses to Monastir (950 mills, 40 minutes) every 30 minutes, and to Mahdia (TD2.250, 1½ hours) every hour.

Bus Fares

destination	frequency (per day)	duration (hours)	fare (TD)
Bizerte	2	3¾	8.35
Douz	2	6½	15.69
El-Jem	11	1¼	2.90
Gabès	11	4¼	10.50
Jerba	2	7	15.67
Kairouan	2	1½	2.98
Kebili	3	6	14.65
Matmata	1	5½	11.99
Medenine	5	5¼	13.13
Nefta	1	6	15 00
Sfax	11	2½	5.66
Tataouine	2	6½	15.41
Tozeur	1	5¾	14.20
Tunis	10	2¼	6.22

Train Train is the best way to travel. The mainline station is conveniently central, 500m west of Place Farhat Hached on Ave Hasouna Ayachi.

There are eight trains a day north to Tunis (2¼ hours), and five south to Sfax (two hours). Three of these continue south from Sfax to Gabès, and one goes south-west to Gafsa and Metlaoui.

There are also frequent services on the branch line to Monastir and Mahdia. They leave from Bab el-Jedid station, which can be found by the port near the south-eastern corner of the medina. There are usually 15 trains a day to Monastir (35 minutes), leaving almost hourly between 6 am and 7.15 pm. Seven of these continue on to Mahdia (1½ hours). It takes 30 minutes to reach Monastir, and then another hour to Mahdia.

Train Fares (TD)

destination	2nd class	1st class	confort
El-Jem	3.10	4.10	4.35
Gabès	8.75	11.75	12.55
Mahdia	2.10	2.96	–
Monastir	0.82	1.12	–
Sfax	4.85	6.50	6.90
Tunis	5.35	7.20	7.65

Louage The louage station is opposite the bus station at Souq el-Ahad. Major destinations include El-Jem (TD3.050), Kairouan (TD3.150), Mahdia (TD2.650), Monastir (TD1.250), Sfax (TD5.550) and Tunis (TD6.300).

Getting Around
To/From the Airport The airport is 12km south of town, TD6 by taxi from the town centre. You can also get there by train; the airport has its own station (L'Aeroport) on the branch line from Sousse to Monastir. The station is about 200m from the airport terminal.

Bus The city has an extensive local bus network operating from the terminal just north of the medina on Blvd Yahia ben Omar. Useful services include Nos 8, 21, 22, which all travel past the bus and louage stations at Souq el-Ahad (280 mills). There are also buses to Port el-Kantaoui (480 mills) every 30 minutes.

Train There is a 'Noddy' train that runs up and down the main road of the tourist strip. It goes from the northern end of Ave Habib Bourguiba to Port el-Kantaoui, 9km to the north. It leaves Ave Habib Bourguiba hourly on the hour, returning on the half-hour. The fare is TD3.500 one way and TD5 return. It operates from 9 am to 11 pm in summer and to 6 pm in winter.

Taxi There are lots of taxis, particularly in the main tourist areas, and you'll struggle to run up a fare of more than TD3 around the city.

AROUND SOUSSE
Port el-Kantaoui
Touted as 'the pleasure port of the Mediterranean', Port el-Kantaoui, 14km north of Sousse, represents the luxury end of the package-tourism market. The focal point is a large marina complex surrounded by flash hotels, expensive restaurants and souvenir shops full of stuffed camels.

Many people come to Port el-Kantaoui specifically to play golf. The beautifully manicured 27-hole championship layout is spread through the olive groves opposite the marina. If you want to play, you'll need to book a tee-off time with the club (☎ 241 756). The experience will set you back about TD60 by the time you've finished paying for green fees, club hire, balls etc. Hackers are not allowed on the course – you will need to show proof of your handicap before you can play.

The beach is the other big attraction, but it's monopolised by huge five-star hotels, which emphasise their level of luxury by tacking palace onto their names (eg, El-Hana Palace and Hannibal Palace).

MONASTIR
☎ 03 • pop 40,000

Situated on a headland some 20km south of Sousse, Monastir must once have been a pleasant little fishing village. Today it has been transformed into a monument to the package tourism industry, its beaches lined with giant hotel complexes and its medina filled with souvenir shops. It has also become a monument to the family of the country's first president, Habib Bourguiba, who was born here and lived on the outskirts of town until his death in April 2000.

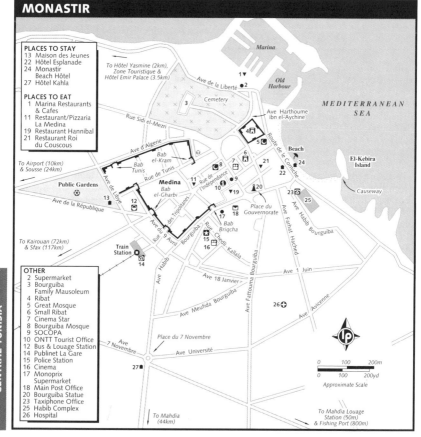

MONASTIR

PLACES TO STAY
13 Maison des Jeunes
22 Hôtel Esplanade
24 Monastir
   Beach Hôtel
27 Hôtel Kahla

PLACES TO EAT
1 Marina Restaurants
   & Cafes
11 Restaurant/Pizzaria
   La Medina
19 Restaurant Hannibal
21 Restaurant Roi
   du Couscous

OTHER
2 Supermarket
3 Bourguiba
   Family Mausoleum
4 Ribat
5 Great Mosque
6 Small Ribat
7 Cinema Star
8 Bourguiba Mosque
9 SOCOPA
10 ONTT Tourist Office
12 Bus & Louage Station
14 Publinet La Gare
15 Police Station
16 Cinema
17 Monoprix
   Supermarket
18 Main Post Office
20 Bourguiba Statue
23 Taxiphone Office
25 Habib Complex
26 Hospital

*To Hôtel Yasmine (2km),
Zone Touristique &
Hôtel Emir Palace (3.5km)*

Marina

Old Harbour

MEDITERRANEAN SEA

Ave de la Liberté

Cemetery

Ave Harthoume ibn el-Aychine

Rue Sidi el-Mezri

Route de la Corniche

Beach

El-Kebira Island

Ave d'Algerie

Bab el-Kram

Bab Tunis

Rue de Tunis

Medina

Bab el-Gharbi

Rue de l'Independance

*To Airport (10km)
& Sousse (24km)*

Public Gardens

Ave de Libye

Ave de la République

Causeway

Place du Gouvernorate

Ave Farhat Hached

Ave Habib Bourguiba

des Trpolitanes

*To Kairouan (72km)
& Sfax (117km)*

Bab Briqcha

Rue du 9 Avril

Rue Chedli Kallala

Bourguiba

Train Station

Ave Habib Bourguiba

Ave 18 Janvier

Ave 1 Juin

Ave Fattouma Bourguiba

Ave Meufida Bourguiba

Ave Avicenne

Place du 7 Novembre

Ave 7 Novembre

Ave Université

*To Mahdia
(44km)*

*To Mahdia Louage
Station (50m)
& Fishing Port (800m)*

0   100   200m
0   100   200yd
Approximate Scale

He was buried in the grand Bourguiba family mausoleum, which dominates the cemetery on the northern edge of town. The Bourguiba name is everywhere, with streets named after just about every member of the household except the cat. Place du Gouvernorate, in the middle of town, sports a bronze statue of a *chechia*-clad Bourguiba as a young man. There's even a mosque named in his honour, although Bourguiba spent his time in power doing battle with the country's religious authorities. The Bourguiba Mosque is at the eastern entrance to the medina on Rue de l'Indépendance.

The well-developed zone touristique runs all the way from Monastir to Skanes, 8km to the west. Most independent travellers leave Monastir to the package tourists, although there's enough to see to warrant a day trip from Sousse.

History

Monastir was founded as the Phoenician trading settlement of Rous, living (as now) in the shadow of its larger and more illustrious neighbour, Hadrumete (Sousse).

It briefly took the limelight in AD 46 when Julius Caesar based himself here before defeating Sousse-based Pompey at the Battle of Thapsus, the decisive moment of the Roman civil war, and suffered badly. His forces were trounced by Julius Caesar. It subsequently became the Roman town of Ruspina.

Information

Tourist Offices The ONTT tourist office (☎ 461 960) is on Rue de l'Indépendance in the medina, opposite the Bourguiba Mosque. It's open from 8.30 am to 1 pm and 3 to 5.45 pm Monday to Thursday and to 1.30 pm Friday and Saturday. It's closed Sunday.

There's also an ONTT office (☎ 521 016) at the airport. It's open – in theory – 24 hours a day, seven days a week, which seems a remarkable waste of effort since it has nothing to offer except a fairly useless map and a few hotel brochures.

Money There are branches of all the major banks on and around Place du 3 Septembre 1934 in the medina.

Post & Communications The main post office is on Ave Habib Bourguiba, just south of the medina. There are Taxiphone offices all around the town centre.

Email & Internet Access Publinet La Gare, at the train station, is open from 8 am to 8 pm daily.

Medina

Much of the medina was demolished after independence in an ill-considered rush to modernise the town in keeping with its status as birthplace of the president.

It was the eastern section, which dated back to the 9th century, that felt the full weight of the wrecker's ball. It was virtually levelled, leaving only the Great Mosque, the ribat and the nearby small ribat. The bulk of the town's medieval buildings thus disappeared in one fell swoop. The old sea wall was knocked down to create Route de la Corniche.

The renovators also went to work in the newer western reaches of the medina, but stopped short of pulling the walls down. These walls are comparatively modest alongside those at Sousse and Sfax, but they are dotted with some interesting old gates. The finest is Bab el-Gharbi, at the centre of the western wall. It was built by the Hafsids in the 15th century. Bab Tunis, in the northwest corner, was built in 1780 when the medina was expanded to incorporate the area north of Rue de Tunis. The main southern gate, Bab Briqcha, was built by the Ottomans at the end of the 17th century.

The **Great Mosque** stands just south of the ribat. It was built in the 9th century during the same burst of activity that produced the medina walls and the beginnings of the kasbah surrounding the ribat. It's a typically severe-looking Aghlabid creation, apart from the graceful horseshoe arches at the northern end. The Roman columns that support these arches were salvaged from the ruins of ancient Ruspina, the minor Roman settlement that once stood on the site of the medina. More columns were used to support the roof of the prayer room, which is closed to non-Muslims.

Ribat

Monastir's star attraction is its immaculately preserved *ribat* complex, regarded as the country's finest example of Islamic military architecture.

The original ribat, known as the Ribat de Harthama, was built in AD 796 as part of a chain of look-out posts along the Tunisian coast. Its layout was very similar to that of the ribat in nearby Sousse – a small, square fort surrounded by four round towers. The majority of this structure was demolished after the addition of the surrounding kasbah walls, leaving only the prayer hall and the circular *nador* (watch tower).

These walls were begun by the Aghlabids at the end of the 9th century and completed in the 11th century, and feature built-in accommodation for defenders. They have been remodelled many times since, notably in the 17th century when the octagonal corner towers were added. The entrance is through a massive L-shaped *skifa* (gate), which leads to a large central courtyard.

Assorted ramps and steps provide access to the ramparts. There are excellent views of the town and the coastline all the way back to Sousse from the top of the nador.

The ribat's prayer room houses a Museum of Islamic Art. The collection includes an assortment of early Arab coins, pottery and Ottoman pipes as well as an interesting map of Monastir's medina before independence and early photos of the town.

The small courtyard behind the prayer hall is known as the women's ribat, with its own prayer room and accommodation.

The complex is a great favourite with film directors in search of authentic Islamic architecture. Zeffirelli came here to shoot scenes for his *Life of Christ*, and the Monty Python team used it for *Life of Brian*.

The ribat complex is open from 8 am to 7 pm daily in summer and 8.30 am to 5.30 pm daily in winter. Admission is TD1.100, plus TD1 to take photographs.

The **Costume Museum** is just around the corner from the tourist office on the eastern side of the medina, and is worth a quick look. Opening hours are from 9 am to 1 pm and 3 to 7 pm in summer and 9.30 am to 4.30 pm daily in winter; it's closed Sunday. Entrance is TD1.100.

Beaches
Conveniently enough, the best beach is the main town beach just across Route de la Corniche from the ribat and the Great Mosque. The beach curves around a small bay, protected by the marina wall at its northern end and the island of El-Kebira to the south. The island is linked to the mainland by a causeway. The beaches west of town are dominated by the resort hotels of the zone touristique.

Markets
Saturday is market day in Monastir and the area around the bus station is jam-packed with stalls and people. The markets are sur-

prisingly untouristy, selling mainly bric-a-brac, second-hand clothes and cheap plastic goods.

Places to Stay – Budget
Monastir is not a budget destination. The only cheap accommodation is at the *Maison des Jeunes*, which is opposite the bus station – set in the corner of the public gardens off Ave de la République. As usual, it offers all the comforts of an army barracks.

Places to Stay – Mid-Range
The choice includes one of the more unusual hotels in the country, the *Monastir Beach Hôtel* (☎ 464 766, fax 463 594). It runs virtually the length of the main town beach, set beneath the massive footpath of Route de la Corniche. It's invisible from the street – the entrance is via the steps on the beach side of Route de la Corniche, in front of the Habib Complex. The rooms are basic but clean, and come with toilet and hot shower. Every room has huge French doors opening onto

the beach. The views are great, although opening the doors doesn't do much for your privacy. Single/double rooms, including breakfast, cost TD27/40 in summer, falling to TD18/25 in winter. That's good value for this part of the world.

Another good choice is the *Hôtel Yasmine* (☎ *501 546*), 2km west of town on Route de la Falaise – the coast road west of Ave de la Liberté. It's a small family run pension with rooms, with breakfast, for TD40/60, dropping to TD24/36 in winter.

Places to Stay – Top End

Most of the three- and four-star resort hotels are located along the beaches of the zone touristique, which runs all the way from Monastir to Skanes, 8km to the west. These places are geared towards charter groups, not casual drop-ins.

There are a few upmarket places by the beach in town. The three star *Hôtel Esplanade* (☎ *460 148, fax 460 050*), south of the Great Mosque on Route de la Corniche, has singles/doubles for TD76/102 in summer and TD36/48 in winter.

Monastir's finest is the swish *Hôtel Emir Palace* (☎ *520 900, fax 521 823*), 4km west of town, where the full five-star treatment costs TD57/84, which rises to TD110/160 in summer.

Places to Eat

The *Restaurant/Pizzaria La Medina*, in the centre of the medina, is a popular place with bargain *briqs* (500 mills), salads from TD1.200 and main courses from TD3. It also has a choice of pizzas from TD2. The *Roi du Couscous*, on the beach side of Place du Gouvernorate, has couscous of the day for TD3 and a good general selection.

The *Restaurant Hannibal*, tucked away in the south-eastern corner of the medina, is a popular spot with a rooftop terrace overlooking the medina. You can eat well here for TD15 per person.

The best restaurants are clustered together out at the marina, just north of town. They include *Le Grill* (☎ *462 136*) and the *Restaurant Marina* (☎ *461 449*). Reckon on TD30 per person, plus wine, at these places.

Self-caterers can head for the well-stocked *Monoprix supermarket*, next to the post office just south of the medina.

Getting There & Away

Air Monastir's airport handles a lot of international traffic, but no domestic flights. Most of the international flights are charters from Europe. Tunis Air also has weekly flights to 12 European cities, including Amsterdam, Frankfurt, Marseilles, Munich, Paris and Rome. See the main Getting There & Away chapter earlier for more information on international flights to and from Monastir.

The Tunis Air office (☎ 468 189) in Monastir is in the Habib Complex on Route de la Corniche.

Bus The bus station is at the western edge of the medina. There are services to Sousse (TD1.150, 30 minutes) every 30 minutes, and to Mahdia (TD1.550, one hour) every hour. Buses to Mahdia leave from the same bus station as buses to Sousse.

Train There are at least 15 trains a day to Sousse (taking 30 minutes), stopping at all stations, including L'Aeroport for the airport, and there are eight a day to Mahdia (one hour). The fares in 2nd/1st class cost 820 mills/TD1.120 to Sousse, and TD1.540/2.140 to Mahdia.

There are also two trains a day to Tunis (TD8.650, 2¾ hours).

Louage Louages to Sousse (TD1), Kairouan (TD4) and Tunis (TD7) leave from next to the bus station. Louages to Mahdia leave from their own louage station, which is on the south-eastern side of town on the road leading to the fishing port.

Car Rental Avis (☎ 521 031), Europcar (☎ 521 314) and Hertz (☎ 521 300) are all based at Monastir's airport.

Getting Around

Monastir is not big enough to support a local bus network, so taxis are your only transport option here.

To/From the Airport Monastir's airport is actually at Skanes, 10km west of town on the road to Sousse. The trip costs about TD4.500 by taxi from the town centre. You can also get to the airport on any of the trains between Monastir and Sousse. L'Aeroport station is 200m from the airport terminal.

MAHDIA
☎ 03 • pop 30,000
Mahdia is one of the few towns on this section of coast that has managed to escape being turned into a tourist trap. It remains a surprisingly relaxed place, set on a small peninsula 64km south-east of Sousse.

History
The town was founded in AD 916 by the first Fatimid caliph, Obeid Allah, known as El-Mahdi, the Saviour of the World. Fresh from his conquest of the Maghreb, Obeid Allah wanted a coastal base from which to plan his attack on his ultimate goal, Cairo. He also needed an easily defensible position to act as a safe refuge for his minority Shiite followers against the possibility of attack by the Sunni majority (see Religion in the Facts about Tunisia chapter). The narrow, rugged peninsula at Mahdia fitted the bill perfectly on both counts.

The original Fatimid city was protected by a massive wall, up to 10m thick, that cut across the peninsula at its narrowest point. Entry was through a single gate, the imposing Skifa el-Kahla. A smaller wall encircled the remainder of the peninsula, creating an enormous kasbah. The area within these walls was a royal compound, reserved for the Mahdi and his entourage. It contained palaces and their outbuildings, a mosque and a port. The Mahdi's subjects lived outside the walls in the suburb of Zawila.

The Fatimids abandoned Mahdia in AD 947 for a new palace compound at Sabra Mansouriya, near Kairouan, and the inhabitants of Zawila moved inside the walls. The population grew rapidly during the 11th century as Mahdia became a place of refuge for people fleeing the Hilalian invasions. In 1052, the Zirid ruler El-Moez retreated briefly to Mahdia.

The present medina was well established by the time the famous historian Ibn Khaldun visited in the 14th century and reported that Mahdia had become the wealthiest city on the Barbary Coast.

Its fortunes took a dive during the struggle between the Spanish and the Turks for control of the Tunisian coast in the 16th century. It was captured by Spanish troops in 1550, who blew up the walls when they abandoned the city to the Turks four years later – destroying the original Fatimid mosque in the process.

In the 19th century, Mahdia emerged as the major port for the agricultural produce, in particular olive oil, of the Sahel. It was superseded by the ports of Sfax and Sousse after WWI. Fishing, mainly for sardines, and tourism are now the town's main income earners. There's a growing band of big hotels along the beach to the north-west of town.

The medina remains alive and well as a residential area, but the majority of the town's 30,000 inhabitants live in the modern suburbs that spread west from Skifa el-Kahla.

Information
There is a small tourist office (☎ 681 098) just inside the medina, through the Skifa el-Kahla. As usual, there's not much information available apart from an ancient brochure with a useless map. If pushed, staff can come up with some bus times.

All other services are found in the Ville Nouvelle. The post office is about 650m west of the medina along Ave Habib Bourguiba, while most of the banks are on the southern side of the peninsula. They include a branch of the Banque de Tunisie by the market, and the Banque du Sud on Ave Farhat Hached.

Medina Walking Tour
Mahdia's main attraction is its fascinating old medina, which stretches out along the peninsula from the Skifa el-Kahla to the lighthouse on Cap d'Afrique, 1.5km to the east.

The main attractions are described in the following walking tour. It should take about two hours, depending how much time you spend exploring – or sitting in cafes.

MAHDIA

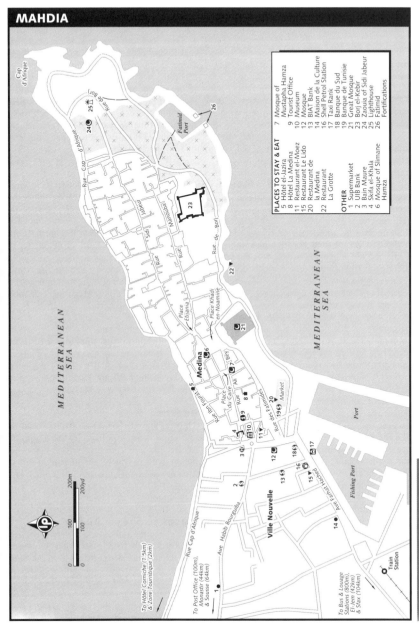

CENTRAL TUNISIA

The tour starts at the **Skifa el-Kahla**, a massive fortified gate, all that survives of the original Fatimid city. 'Gate' is a bit of a misnomer; entry is through a narrow, vaulted passageway, almost 50m long, that was once protected by a series of gates – one of them a suitably oversized iron portcullis. Once inside the medina, there are steps leading up to the top of the gate, from where there are great views over the town.

The Skifa el-Kahla opens onto the medina's narrow, cobbled main street, **Rue Ali Bey**. It was once the souq, and is now occupied by a growing band of souvenir shops. Follow Rue Ali Bey east to **Place du Caire**, which is a delightful small square, complete with shady trees, vines and cafes. The ornate arched doorway and octagonal minaret on the southern side of the square belong to the **Mosque of Mustapha Hamza**, built in 1772 when the square was the centre of the town's wealthy Turkish quarter. The mosque was in the middle of a major facelift at the time of research.

Continuing east, Rue Ali Bey emerges after a short distance at **Place Khadi en-Noamine**, on the northern side of the **Great Mosque**. The mosque that stands today is a modern replica of the original Fatimid mosque, built by Obeid Allah in AD 921, which was destroyed when retreating Spanish troops blew up the city walls in 1554. The replica was completed in 1965, and involved razing another mosque that had been built in the interim. The houses surrounding the mosque were pulled down at the same time. Non-Muslims are allowed into the courtyard outside prayer times.

The small minaret at the north-western side of Place Khadi en-Noamine marks the **Mosque of Slimane Hamza**, built by another member of the well-to-do Hamza family. A road, which provides vehicle access to the inner reaches of the medina, leads north-east from here to tiny Place Etijania and then forks to form the two main residential streets, Rue Sidi Jabeur and Rue Manouba. They run parallel, about 50m apart, and emerge at the large cemetery on the eastern side of the medina. Both streets are lined with dozens of short, zigzagging

cul-de-sacs, each of which represents a small neighbourhood of five or six houses.

Take the southern fork, Rue Manouba, and follow it east for about 500m until you come to a side street leading up to the **Borj el-Kebir**, a large fortress standing on the highest point of the peninsula. It was built in the 16th century on the ruins of an earlier Fatimid structure. There is not much to see inside, but the views from the ramparts are worth the TD1 entry fee. It's open from 9 am to noon and 2 to 6 pm in summer and 9.30 am to 4.30 pm in winter daily, except Friday.

From the fort, walk down to the coast road, Rue de Borj, and follow it as it winds through the cemetery towards the lighthouse. On the right are the remains of the **Fatimid port**, now largely silted up. The crumbling pillars flanking the entrance are all that remain of the harbour defences.

Keep following Rue de Borj as it loops around the lighthouse. The small, white-domed building west of the lighthouse is the **Zaouia of Sidi Jabeur**. Head back to town along Rue Cap d'Afrique, which hugs the coastline all the way. The water along here is amazingly clear and blue.

The museum is just south of the Skifa el-Kahla. It houses an assortment of minor finds from the area. It's open Tuesday to Sunday from 8.30 am to 5.30 pm, closed Monday. Admission is TD1.100.

Beaches

Mahdia's main beach is north-west of town and is monopolised by the big hotels of the zone touristique; you can use the beach even if you're not staying at one of the hotels. Local kids make do with swimming off the rocks that run along Rue Cap d'Afrique.

Places to Stay – Budget

Budget accommodation is in very short supply. Fortunately there's not much demand either, and it's usually possible to find a room at the small, family run *Hôtel el-Jazira* (☎ *681 629, fax 680 274, 36 Rue Ibn Fourat*), on the seafront on the northern side of the peninsula. Some of the rooms look out over the water. It's good value at TD8.500/13 for singles/doubles, including breakfast and hot showers, rising to TD10.500/17 in summer. There's a table and chairs on the roof, where you can sit and enjoy the view.

An alternative is the brand new *Hôtel Medina* (☎ 694 664), off Rue Ali Bey in the centre of the medina. It charges TD12/24 for rooms with breakfast.

The friendly *Hôtel Corniche* (☎ 694 201) is a stone's throw from the beach on Route de la Corniche, about 1.5km north-west of town. It charges TD11/16 in winter and TD17/28 in summer, including breakfast and hot shower. Route de la Corniche is the north-west extension of Rue Cap d'Afrique.

Places to Stay – Mid-Range & Top End

Mahdia's hotels are spread along the beaches to the north-west of town. As elsewhere, they are packed in summer and dead in winter. All prices in this section include breakfast. The line-up starts with relatively low-key places like the one star *Le Corail* (☎ 696 431, fax 695 433), which charges TD18/26 for singles/doubles in winter and TD40/60 in summer.

Mahdia's top hotel is the five star *Mahdia Palace* (☎ 696 777, fax 696 810). It charges TD50/70 in winter and TD103/166 in summer.

Places to Eat

Beware of thin chefs, or so the saying goes. Well, there's nothing to be afraid of at the excellent *Restaurant el-Moez*, tucked away on a small side street between the Skifa el-Kahla and the markets. It's run by a big man who obviously enjoys his food. He specialises in traditional dishes like *mloukhia* (lamb in thick sauce made from ground herbs) and *kammounia* (a spicy stew made with lots of cumin). The choice is limited to three or four daily specials, one of which will be fish. Most meals are priced under TD2.500. Lunch is the best time to visit as the choice of dishes shrinks by the evening.

Another good place is the *Restaurant de la Medina*, situated at the rear of the market building by the port. It's next to the fish markets, and fish features prominently on the

menu. A plate of *rouget* (red mullet), chips and salad costs TD5.

Most tourists head for the restaurants facing the port along Ave Farhat Hached, where you can enjoy a glass of wine with your meal. The *Restaurant Le Lido* offers three-course menus for TD9, not including drinks. An alternative is the *Restaurant La Grotte*, which has a wonderful setting overlooking the sea off Rue de Borj.

The produce section of the *market* building is the best bet for self-caterers. The only *supermarket* is about 400m west of the Skifa el-Kahla on Ave Habib Bourguiba.

Getting There & Away

Bus The bus station is on the road to Sfax, about 800m south-west of the train station. There are hourly departures to Sousse (TD2.450, 1½ hours) and five a day to El-Jem (TD1.850, one hour). There are no direct services to Sfax or Tunis; change at El-Jem for Sfax and at Sousse for Tunis.

Train The train station is conveniently central, just west of the port on Ave Farhat Hached, making train the recommended way to travel. There are at least eight trains a day to Monastir (one hour), seven of which continue to Sousse. Fares in 2nd/1st class to Monastir are TD1.540/2.140 and to Sousse it's TD2.100/2.960.

There is also a daily service to Tunis (four hours). The fare is TD7.350 in 2nd class or TD9.800 in 1st class.

Louage The louage station is also on the south-western side of town, one block inland from the bus station. It has noticeboards listing fares to all the available destinations. The most popular is Sousse (TD2.650). Other regular services are to El-Jem (TD1.760), Kairouan (TD4.100), Monastir (TD1.830), Sfax (TD4.350) and Tunis (TD8).

EL-JEM
☎ 03 • pop 10,000

There can be few more remarkable sights in Tunisia than the first glimpse of El-Jem, the ancient colosseum dwarfing the matchbox buildings of the modern town. Built on a low plateau halfway between Sousse and Sfax, the colosseum rates as one of the most impressive Roman monuments in Africa.

It was once the crowning glory of ancient Thysdrus, a thriving market town that grew up at the junction of the Sahel's main trade routes during the 1st century AD. They must have been valuable trade routes, because the site didn't have much else going for it. In the absence of suitable local building material, stone for construction had to be hauled all the way from the quarries at Sullectum (modern Salakta), 30km away on the coast, and water had to be brought 15km by underground aqueduct from the hills north-west of town.

The town continued to flourish in spite of these logistical problems, and reached the peak of its prosperity in the 2nd and 3rd centuries AD. By this time it had become the hub of a network of Roman roads that distributed goods between the interior and the cities on the coast.

In contrast to the drab buildings of modern El-Jem, Thysdrus was a town of sumptuous villas. The mosaics uncovered here include some of the finest in Tunisia – they're now distributed between the Bardo Museum in Tunis and the town's own museum.

El-Jem is situated almost exactly halfway between Sousse and Sfax on the main road between the two towns.

Orientation & Information

It's hard to get lost in a place as small as El-Jem, especially when there's a landmark as big as the colosseum standing in the middle of town.

The main street is Ave Habib Bourguiba, which runs from the colosseum to the train

---

The Colosseum of El-Jem

El-Jem's well preserved amphitheatre is almost as big as its counterpart in Rome. It rises spectacularly from the flat surrounding plains and completely dominates the town.

Its vital statistics are impressive – 138m long by 114m wide, with three tiers of seating 30m high. Its seating capacity has been estimated at 30,000, which is considerably more than the population of the town itself – indicating that people came from far and wide to watch events here.

The structure is believed to have been built between AD 230 and 238, and is generally attributed to the African pro-consul Gordian, a local landowner and patron. In AD 238, at the age of 80, Gordian was declared emperor of Rome here during an ill-fated rebellion against oppressive taxes imposed by Emperor Maximus. Gordian reportedly committed suicide in the amphitheatre when it became obvious that the rebellion was doomed.

The colosseum has been used as a defensive position many times in its history. Byzantine troops regrouped here after their defeat at Sbeitla in AD 647, and the Berber princess Al-Kahina was besieged here by Arab forces 50 years later. According to legend, the colosseum was linked by tunnel to the coastal town of Salakta, enabling Al-Kahina to torment her besiegers by waving fresh fish from the top of the walls (see also the boxed text 'The Berbers' under Population & People in the Facts about Tunisia chapter).

It suffered badly in the 17th century when the troops of Mohammed Bey blasted a hole in the western wall to flush out local tribesmen who had rebelled against taxation demands. The breach was further widened during another rebellion in 1850. The emphasis is now on preservation, and the site has been added to the United Nation's World Heritage List.

You can still climb up to the top tiers of seating and gaze down on the arena; it's also possible to explore the two long underground passageways that were used to hold animals, gladiators and other unfortunates before they were thrust into the arena to provide entertainment for the masses.

The colosseum is open from 7 am to 7 pm daily in summer and from 8 am to 5 pm daily in winter. Admission is TD4.200, plus TD1 to take photographs.

station on the southern edge of town. The post office and only bank are south-west of here on Ave Fahdel ben Achour, signposted as the road to Sfax. There is a left luggage office at the train station.

Museum

El-Jem's museum is about 1km south of the amphitheatre on the road to Sfax. It houses some beautiful mosaics, all found in the site behind the museum building – an area containing some particularly luxurious villas. Some of the mosaics have been left *in situ* while the best have been moved into the museum. Highlights include a dramatic depiction of Dionysios astride a tiger and the delightful Genius of the Year – a title everyone must aspire to! Admission is included in the price of the ticket to the colosseum. Opening times are the same.

Other Sites

The colosseum was not the first amphitheatre to be built at Thysdrus. Opposite the museum are the ruins of an earlier **amphitheatre**, dug into a low hill just east of the railway line. The site is not enclosed and is worth a look if you've got time to burn. There is also a second area of **Roman villas** to the north of the colosseum, signposted off Ave Farhat Hached, the road to Sousse.

Special Events

In late July and early August, the colosseum is transformed into a splendid floodlit venue for the El-Jem International Symphonic Music Festival. You'll find a program of events at the tourist office in Sousse.

Places to Stay & Eat

Although it's easy to visit El-Jem on a day trip, it's well worth considering staying the night so that you can get up early and visit the colosseum before the tour groups arrive.

The only accommodation is at the one star *Hôtel Julius* (☎ 690 044), next to the train station. It has singles/doubles with breakfast for TD13/18, rising to TD20.500/30 in summer. The rooms fill up fast in summer, so it's a good idea to book first if you're planning on arriving late in the day. The hotel also has

the only bar in town, and a *restaurant* with a set menu for TD5.

The nearby *Restaurant Le Bonheur*, on the road to Sfax, offers a small selection of traditional dishes like spicy couscous with chicken (TD3).

Getting There & Away

El-Jem is on the main road and rail route between Sousse and Sfax and is well served for public transport. Everything happens at the train station, 500m south of the colosseum at the end of the main street, Ave Habib Bourguiba.

Bus Buses leave from outside the train station. A lot of SNTRI buses pass through town on the way north and south, but they are often already full and you can't rely on getting a seat. There are 11 buses a day to Sousse (TD2.900, 1¼ hours) and 11 to Sfax (TD2.810, 1¼ hours), as well as local buses to Mahdia (TD1.850, one hour).

Train There are five trains a day north to Sousse (TD4.100 in 1st class, one hour) and Tunis (TD9.800, three hours), and five a day south to Sfax (TD3.900, one hour) and beyond. Unfortunately, most of these services are either very late at night or very early in the morning, leaving only a couple of trains in each direction that are of any use to colosseum visitors.

Louage Louages leave from opposite the train station. There are frequent departures to Mahdia (TD1.760) and occasional services to Sousse and Sfax (both TD3.250).

SFAX

☎ 04 ● pop 275,000

Sfax, 266km south of Tunis, is the second-largest city in the country. This rather unglamorous place is largely bypassed by Tunisia's otherwise all-pervasive package-tourism industry. Sfaxiens are famous for their business acumen, a fact that makes them the butt of jokes told by Tunisians from other areas, jealous of this reputation. You'll probably be mocked, too, if you announce that you're going to Sfax.

CENTRAL TUNISIA

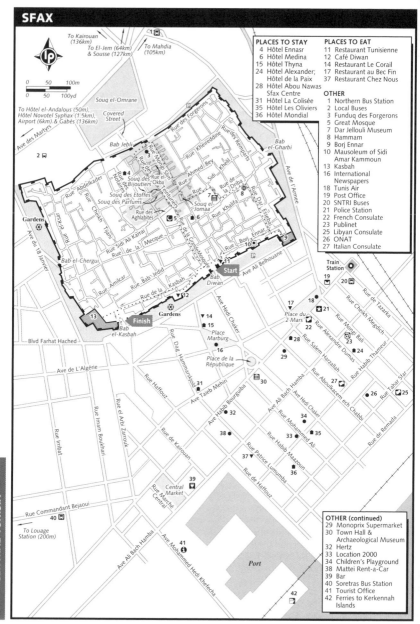

SFAX

PLACES TO STAY
4 Hôtel Ennasr
6 Hôtel Medina
15 Hôtel Thyna
24 Hôtel Alexander; Hôtel de la Paix
28 Hôtel Abou Nawas Sfax Centre
31 Hôtel La Colisée
35 Hôtel Les Oliviers
36 Hôtel Mondial

PLACES TO EAT
11 Restaurant Tunisienne
12 Café Diwan
14 Restaurant Le Corail
17 Restaurant au Bec Fin
37 Restaurant Chez Nous

OTHER
1 Northern Bus Station
2 Local Buses
3 Funduq des Forgerons
5 Great Mosque
7 Dar Jellouli Museum
8 Hammam
9 Borj Ennar
10 Mausoleum of Sidi Amar Kammoun
13 Kasbah
16 International Newspapers
18 Tunis Air
19 Post Office
20 SNTRI Buses
21 Police Station
22 French Consulate
23 Publinet
25 Libyan Consulate
26 ONAT
27 Italian Consulate

OTHER (continued)
29 Monoprix Supermarket
30 Town Hall & Archaeological Museum
32 Hertz
33 Location 2000
34 Children's Playground
38 Mattei Rent-a-Car
39 Bar
40 Soretras Bus Station
41 Tourist Office
42 Ferries to Kerkennah Islands

CENTRAL TUNISIA

All the more reason for going there, reckoned writer Paul Theroux, who records his impressions of Sfax in *The Pillars of Hercules*. Like others before him, Theroux came away pleasantly surprised by the laid-back city he found. The only attraction is the unspoiled old medina, used as a location in the film *The English Patient*, but the general absence of hype makes it a pleasant place to spend a couple of days. Sfax is also the departure point for ferries to the nearby Kerkennah Islands.

History

The coast around Sfax has been settled since Phoenician times, but none of the towns amounted to very much until Sfax was established by the Arabs at the beginning of the 8th century AD. It is thought to occupy the site of the minor Roman town of Taparura, no trace of which remains. The closest Roman town of any consequence was Thaenae, the meagre remains of which are on the coast 12km to the south-west.

The city's ramparts were built by the Aghlabids in the middle of 9th century AD. They proved effective enough for the city to hold out against the Hilalian invasions in the 11th century, and Sfax emerged as the major city in the south of Tunisia. In the 14th century, it controlled a stretch of coastline reaching as far as Tripoli, in Libya. It remained largely independent of the central government in Tunis until the beginning of the 17th century.

The modern city was shaped by the French in the late 19th century. They built the customary Ville Nouvelle on reclaimed land to the south of the medina, and developed the port to handle the export of phosphate from the mines at Gafsa.

Two of the heroes of the country's independence movement, trade union leaders Hedi Chaker and Farhat Hached, were from Sfax. Their names feature on streets signs throughout the country.

Orientation

While the modern city of Sfax fans out over a wide area, the city centre is compact and easy to negotiate. Most services of importance to travellers are located around the streets of the Ville Nouvelle, which is laid out in the traditional French grid pattern between the medina and the port. The main street is Ave Habib Bourguiba, which runs south-east through the town centre from the train station.

Information

Tourist Office The tourist office (☎ 211 040) is out by the port on Ave Mohammed Hedi Khefecha. There is more information here than is first apparent, including bus, train and ferry timetables, all kept in the folder on the desk. It's open from 9 am to 1 pm and 3 to 5.30 pm Monday to Thursday and to 1.30 pm Friday and Saturday; it's closed Sunday.

Money All the Tunisian banks here have branches in the Ville Nouvelle, either on Ave Habib Bourguiba or on Ave Hedi Chaker. Most have several branches. The post office has a separate foreign-exchange counter.

Post & Communications The post office is the enormous edifice on Ave Habib Bourguiba, which occupies the entire block just west of the train station. It is open from 8 am to 6 pm Monday to Saturday and 9 to 11 am Sunday.

Email & Internet Access The Publinet office is at 7 Rue Ali Bach Hamba; it's open from 9 am to 6 pm daily.

International Newspapers Foreign newspapers are sold at the kiosk on the northern side of Place Marburg.

Hammam The Hammam Sultan is near the Dar Jellouli Museum on Rue de la Driba in the heart of the medina. It costs TD1.5 and is open to women from noon to 4 pm, and to men from 4 pm to midnight.

Medina Walking Tour

The medina is the reason people come to Sfax. It's arguably the finest in the country, conforming perfectly to the fundamentals of Islamic architecture outlined in the Islamic Architecture special section in the Facts about Tunisia chapter at the beginning of this book. Apart from the small cluster of souvenir shops around Bab Diwan, the medina is remarkably untouched by tourism and remains a good example of a working medina.

The highlights have been incorporated into the following walking tour, which is marked on the accompanying Sfax map. The walk takes about two hours.

It begins outside the medina's main southern gate, the triple-arched **Bab Diwan**. This gate was added in 1306, and it stands in the middle of the most impressive section of the mighty **ramparts**. These massive stone walls were built by the Aghlabids in the 9th century, replacing an earlier 8th-century earthen wall. They have been remodelled many times since, but they retain some of the original features.

Enter through Bab Diwan, veer left across the small square and head north along Rue de la Grande Mosquée. This is one of the medina's principle north-south thoroughfares, although you'd never guess from the size of the street.

After 120m, the street emerges alongside the ornate eastern wall of the **Great Mosque**, founded by the Aghlabids in the middle of the 9th century AD, around the same time that the medina walls were constructed. The mosque is closed to non-Muslims. The eastern wall is the only section that's visible; the other three sides are hidden by souqs. The elaborate **minaret**, a smaller replica of the three-tiered square minaret at Kairouan, was added by the Fatimids in AD 988. It's best viewed from Rue des Aghlabites, to the north of the mosque.

The tour continues north across Rue des Aghlabites and enters the wonderful world of the **covered souqs**. The main souq heading north is the celebrated **Souq des Etoffes**, which was used to such good effect as the setting for the Cairo markets in the film *The English Patient*. Check out the intricate herring-bone brickwork of the vaulted ceilings, particularly around the junction with the **Souq des Parfums**. The shops around here are as good a place as any to do your souvenir shopping.

Browse your way north until Souq des Etoffes finally emerges on Rue des Tein-turiers. This is where the dyers once carried on their business – at a suitable distance from the Great Mosque. Keep going until you hit Rue Abdelkader, which runs inside the medina's northern wall. In front of you is the delightful **Bab Jebli**, one of the original Aghlabid gates. Beyond the Bab Jebli is the **Souq el-Omrane**, which houses the city's main markets.

The tour turns right onto Rue Abdelkader. On the right after about 50m is an archway leading to the old **Funduq des Forgerons**. It no longer functions as a funduq, but it still serves as a base for the city's *forgerons* (blacksmiths). It's like walking back a century in time, into a world of blackened faces, smoking fires, red-hot metal and constant hammering.

Continue past the Souq des Forgerons and turn right onto Rue Mongi Slim. This is another of the medina's major thoroughfares, running all the way south to Bab Diwan. Follow Rue Mongi Slim south for about 150m and turn left onto Rue Sidi Khelil immediately after the Souq el-Jomaa, the second of two small covered souqs. The street signs around here are often hidden by merchandise and can be hard to spot.

Head east along Rue Sidi Khelil and take the second right into Rue Sidi Ali Ennouri, home of the **Dar Jellouli Museum**. It occupies a classic courtyard house filled with beautiful carved wood panels and ornate stuccowork. It was built by the wealthy Jellouli merchant family in the 17th century. The displays include a good collection of traditional costumes and jewellery, and some unusual pieces of painted glass. The museum is open from 9.30 am to 4.30 pm daily, except Monday. Admission is TD1.100, plus TD1 to take photos.

The museum is at the southern end of Rue Sidi Ali Ennouri. From here, follow Rue de la Driba east and take the second right into Rue Dar Essebai. It runs south to the **Borj Ennar**, a small fort added in the 17th century to protect the south-eastern corner of the medina. It is now the headquarters of the Association de Sauvegarde de la Medina, the group responsible for preserving the medina. It has a good map of the medina, showing all

El-Jem's colosseum, Africa's finest Roman antiquity (top): preparations for an annual international symphonic music festival (bottom left); an internal passageway (bottom right)

Monastir's most popular beach is conveniently located right in the centre of town.

The superbly preserved kasbah and ribat at Monastir served as backdrops for the Monty Python movie, *The Life of Brian.*

69 mosques, as well as the souqs and other points of historical interest.

From here the tour heads back to the Bab Diwan along Rue Borj Ennar. The minaret on the left after 50m belongs to the **Mausoleum of Sidi Amar Kammoun**, built at the start of the 14th century.

Continue west across the extended square inside Bab Diwan and link up with Rue de la Kasbah, which runs all the way to the kasbah at the south-western corner of the medina. Before you get there, no tour of the medina would be complete without a stop for coffee at the **Café Diwan**, built into the medina's southern wall off Rue de la Kasbah, 100m west of Bab Diwan.

Suitably fortified, continue west to the **kasbah**. It began life as a watch tower, built by the Aghlabids as part of the ramparts, and was steadily expanded into a kasbah over the centuries. Part of the building now houses a museum of Islamic architecture; another part is used for art exhibitions.

Ville Nouvelle

The focal point is the very formal main square, **Place de la République**, at the junction of Ave Hedi Chaker and Ave Habib Bourguiba.

The grand building with the dome and clock tower on the southern side of the square is the **town hall**. As well as housing the city's bureaucrats, it is also the home of the **archaeological museum**. It houses finds from the nearby Roman sites of Acholla, Lariscus, Taparura and Thaenae. The highlight is a large mosaic from Thaenae of the poet Ennuis surrounded by nine Muses. The museum is open from 8.30 am to 1 pm and 3 to 6 pm Monday to Saturday. Admission is TD1.100.

Architectural highlights of the Ville Nouvelle include the fine **French consulate** at 13 Ave Habib Bourguiba, and the **police station** at No 11 – no photos, though. The magnificent facade of the **Hôtel Les Oliviers** has fallen into a sad state of disrepair following the hotel's closure. There's a **children's playground** in the park north of the hotel.

Places to Stay – Budget

As is the case in all the major cities, the cheapest places are found in the medina. The pick of them is the **Hôtel Ennasr** (☎ 211 037, 100 Rue des Notaires), near Bab Jebli on the northern edge of the medina. It's a tiny place with clean rooms for TD7 per person and has good views from the rooftop terrace. The best of the rest is the **Hôtel Medina** (☎ 220 354, 51 Rue Mongi Slim), which charges TD4 per person.

Most travellers prefer to stay in the Ville Nouvelle, where the **Hôtel de la Paix** (☎ 296 437, 15 Rue Alexandre Dumas) has singles/doubles with shower for TD10/12. Breakfast is an extra TD1.

Places to Stay – Mid-Range

The best value in town is the **Hôtel Alexander** (☎ 221 613, 21 Rue Alexandre Dumas), an old-style one-star place a few doors from of the Hôtel de la Paix. It has large, comfortable singles/doubles with bathroom for TD15/20, including breakfast. The baths are enormous, and there's plenty of hot water. The only catch here is that on Saturday night a folk band plays in the restaurant. The action doesn't quieten down until 2 am, making sleep all but impossible.

The **Hôtel Thyna** (☎ 225 317, fax 225 773, 37 Rue Habib Maazoun), on the corner of Place Marburg, is a small two-star hotel that is popular with travellers. It has rooms with breakfast for TD18/30. Other options include the one star **Hôtel La Colisée** (☎ 227 800, fax 299 350, 32 Ave Taieb Mehiri) and the **Hôtel Mondial** (☎ 226 620, 46 Rue Habib Maazoun). Both have rooms for around TD20/30, including breakfast. The Mondial is an outstandingly dull example of functional concrete architecture.

Places to Stay – Top End

The top hotel in town is the four star **Hôtel Novotel Syphax** (☎ 243 333, fax 245 226), 1.5km west of the medina on the way to the airport. It has singles/doubles for TD75/86. The **Hôtel Abou Nawas Sfax Centre** (☎ 225 700, fax 225 521, **e** abounawas .sfax@abounawas.com.tn, 15 Ave Habib Bourguiba) is right in the middle of town and much more convenient. It has doubles for TD82.

The **Hôtel el-Andalous** (☎ 405 406, fax 406 425, Ave des Martyrs), north-west of the medina, is a relative bargain at TD44/60.

Places to Eat

The **Restaurant Tunisienne**, on the right just inside the medina's Bab Diwan, is a popular place that is always full of locals tucking into dishes like beans in spicy sauce with chicken (TD2.200) or couscous with lamb (TD2.500).

The **Restaurant au Bec Fin** (Place du 2 Mars) is many steps up from this in style – but not in price. Waiters clad in snappy bow ties dole out a delicious fish *chorba* (TD1.200). Follow up with a plate of *spaghetti aux fruits de mer* (TD4) or *ojja aux crevettes* (TD3.500).

The **Hôtel Alexander** has one of the better restaurants around. A huge plate of spaghetti aux fruits de mer loaded with plump prawns will set you back TD4.200 – and you can wash it down with a cold beer (TD1.600).

The stylish **Restaurant Chez Nous** (☎ 227 128, 28 Rue Patrice Lumumba) does a set menu for TD9, or an extensive a la carte menu featuring loads of seafood for about TD20 per person, plus wine.

The best restaurant in town is the **Restaurant Le Corail** (☎ 227 301, 39 Rue Habib Maazoun) next to the Hôtel Thyna.

The city's main **markets** are in the Souq el-Omrane building just north of the medina. The meat section is not for the squeamish. As elsewhere, the butchers hang up the heads of the day's victims to show what they've got. There are more markets at the so-called **central market**, opposite the port on Ave Ali Bach Hamba.

There is a **Monoprix supermarket** on Rue Aboulkacem ech Chabbi, near Ave Habib Bourguiba. It's open from 8.30 am to 7 pm daily.

Entertainment

The restaurant at the **Hôtel Alexander** has a folk band on Saturday night. This is the real thing, not a stunt laid on for tourists. The music starts at about 8 pm and continues until the small hours. Proceedings get increasingly raucous as the night wears on.

Shopping

The medina is a good place to go souvenir shopping, provided you stay away from the shops inside the Bab Diwan. The shops in the Souq des Etoffes stock a good range of Berber rugs, blankets and other handicrafts from the villages of the Gafsa region. The shop owners here seem to take the view that they're more likely to secure a sale if they don't scare tourists away with absurdly high first prices – and it works! ONAT has a crafts shop on the southern part of Rue Salem Harzallah, which is open from 9.30 am to noon and 3 to 7 pm Monday to Saturday.

Getting There & Away

Air Tuninter has four flights a week between Tunis and Sfax (TD43.200/84.200, 45 minutes). It runs to a strange timetable, with daily flights Monday to Thursday, and none Friday to Sunday. The Tunis Air office (☎ 228 028) is at 4 Ave de l'Armée. Air France (☎ 224 847), which has a Saturday flight to Paris, has an office at 15 Ave Taieb Mehiri.

Bus The SNTRI bus station is opposite the train station on Rue Tazarka, although at the time of research there were plans to move to a new bus complex on Rue Commandant Bejaoui, presently the base of local company Soretras.

SNTRI also operates a daily international bus service to Tripoli, in Libya (TD16.130,

Bus Services

destination	frequency (per day)	duration (hours)	fare (TD)
Douz	1	5	11.19
El-Jem	10	1¼	2.81
Gabès	10	2	5.87
Jerba	3	5	9.84
Medenine	5	3	8.63
Sousse	11	2	5.66
Tatouine	2	4	10.91
Tunis	11	4¼	10.81

seven hours). It leaves at 8.30 pm weekdays and 5 pm Saturday and Sunday.

Local company Soretras also operates a busy intercity schedule from its depot on Rue Commandant Bejaoui. It offers a number of destinations not covered by SNTRI, including hourly services to Mahdia (TD2.450) and three buses a day to Kairouan (TD5.100). Unfortunately, most Soretras buses are old bone-shakers: You're better off catching a louage.

Train The trains are the most comfortable way to travel, although the choice of destinations is limited. The station is at the eastern end of Ave Habib Bourguiba.

Heading south, there are three trains a day to Gabès (three hours) and two to Gafsa (3½ hours) and Metlaoui (4¼ hours). Heading north, there are five trains a day to El-Jem (one hour), Sousse (two hours) and Tunis (four hours).

Train Services (TD)

destination	2nd class	1st class	confort
El-Jem	3.10	4.10	4.35
Gabès	5.25	7.20	7.90
Gafsa	7	9.35	10.05
Sousse	4.85	6.50	6.90
Tunis	8.75	11.75	12.55

Louage Louages leave from the large walled compound at the junction of Rue Commandant Bejaoui and Rue de Maurianie, 200m west of the Soretras bus station. There are frequent departures to Gabès (TD5.650), Sousse (TD5.550) and Tunis (TD10.500). Other destinations include El-Jem (TD2.900), Mahdia (TD4.350) and Jerba (10.700).

There are also regular louages to Tripoli (TD30). These vehicles are yellow and white, and often have Libyan markings.

Car There are lots of car-hire companies in town, which means prices are competitive. The big multinationals all have representatives, but you're more likely to find good deals at smaller local companies like Mattei (☎ 296 404), 18 Rue Patrice Lumumba, or Location 2000 (☎ 221 763) on

Ave Habib Thameur. Hertz (☎ 228 626) is at 47 Ave Habib Bourguiba.

Boat Ferries for the Kerkennah Islands leave from the south-western corner of the port off Ave Mohammed Hedi Khefecha. Timetables change seasonally, the frequency ranging from eight crossings a day in summer to four a day in winter. Current timetables are displayed at the port and at the tourist office. The trip costs 570 mills for passengers and TD4 for a car. The crossing takes about 1¼ hours in good weather. There can be long queues to take a vehicle across in summer. There is no reservation system, so you'll need to join the queue early to get a place.

Getting Around
To/From the Airport The airport (☎ 278 000) is 6km from town on the Gafsa road at Thyna – about TD3.500 by taxi. There's no public transport to the airport.

KERKENNAH ISLANDS
☎ 04 • pop 16,000
There are few quieter places in Tunisia than the Kerkennah Islands, a cluster of nine islands 25km east of Sfax.

Once used as a place of exile, the islands have a rather desolate air about them. They are flat and featureless – the highest point is only 13m above sea level – and nothing appears to relish growing in the arid conditions.

Fishing is the island's main activity. The islanders still use traditional fish traps made from palm fronds. Lines of fronds are stuck in the sea bed in a 'V' shape, and the fish are then driven into this large funnel and into a small trap at the end.

The islands remain almost untouched by tourism. There's a small cluster of resort hotels at Sidi Frej, but little else in the way of development. The islanders would prefer to keep it that way, and recently voted against a multimillion dinar Kuwaiti proposal to build a massive hotel complex north-east of Sidi Frej.

Orientation
The two main islands, Île **Gharbi** and Île **Chergui**, are connected by a small causeway

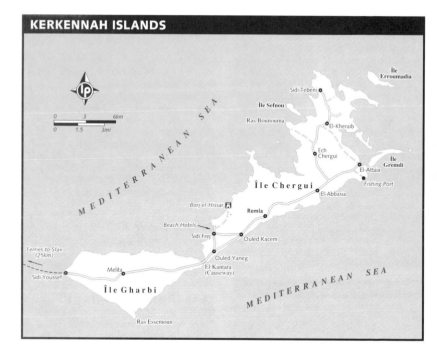

KERKENNAH ISLANDS

dating back to Roman times. Île Gharbi has little more than the ferry port at Sidi Youssef, from where it's a 16km drive to the causeway.

Most of the population lives on Chergui. The only place of any consequence is the small town of **Remla** on the south coast, which is the administrative and service 'capital' of the islands. Tourist development is restricted to a few very low-key resort hotels on the north coast around the small village of **Sidi Frej**.

Information
There is a branch of the UIB bank in Remla, on the road leading down to the sea next to the Hôtel el-Jazira. It's much easier to change money at one of the hotels, which all offer facilities.

Borj el-Hissar
Borj el-Hissar is an old fort on the coast about 3km north of the hotels at Sidi Frej.

It is well worth the 40-minute walk; it's clearly signposted from near the Hôtel Le Grand. The small fort itself was built by the Spanish in the 16th century, but the most interesting aspect of the site is the Roman ruins that surround the fort. You get the feeling that you are stumbling across something previously undiscovered, with mosaics covered by sand and ruins disappearing into the sea. The guardian is very happy to talk about the site – for a small consideration.

Beaches
The beaches are not good enough to promote as an attraction. The sea is very shallow around here and no good for swimming – you can walk out 100m before your knees get wet. The best beach is supposedly at Ras Bounouma, north-east of Sidi Frej on the large bay that cuts into the north coast of Chergui, but it's a long, hot haul to get there and there is no public transport.

Places to Stay & Eat

Remla The only hotel in Remla is the very basic *Hôtel el-Jazira* (☎ 481 058), opposite the bus station on the main street through town. It charges TD8 per person, with breakfast. The hotel also has a restaurant and the only public bar on the islands.

The *Restaurant La Sirène* has a prime location on the waterfront at the end of the road next to the Hôtel el-Jazira. It has a shady terrace overlooking the sea and does meals for around TD15, plus wine.

Sidi Frej Most tourists stick to the beach hotels at Sidi Frej, 8km from Remla. There's nothing else at Sidi Frej, so if you decide to stay in one of these hotels you're pretty much committed to eating there as well. All prices quoted here include breakfast.

The *Hôtel Cercina* (☎ 489 953, fax 489 878), 200m from the bus stop at the junction of the road to Remla, is the most convenient place to stay if you are on foot. It's OK if you can get one of the bungalows overlooking the sea, but most of the accommodation is in depressing little cylindrical concrete huts. Singles/doubles are TD23/32 in winter, rising to TD28/42.

The closure of the *Hôtel Farhat* leaves the two star *Hôtel Le Grand* (☎ 489 864, fax 489 866), about 800m east of the bus stop, as the undisputed top address on the islands. It is booked out by the charter trade in summer, but in the low season you can enjoy the facilities (including tennis courts and a swimming pool) for TD27/45.

The best restaurant in the resort strip is at the *Hôtel Cercina*. Ask for the local speciality, a thick, spicy octopus soup called *tchich* (TD2).

Getting There & Away

See the Getting There & Away section under Sfax for details of ferries between Sfax and Sidi Youssef.

Getting Around

Bus There is a small network of buses connecting the villages of the islands. There are always at least two or three to meet each ferry. All buses go to Remla. One has a 'hotel' sign in the window and goes via Sidi Frej (950 mills). There are buses from Remla and the Sidi Frej junction to Sidi Youssef departing about an hour before the ferry. Times are posted in the bus-station window in Remla.

The Remla bus station is opposite the Hôtel el-Jazira. There are a couple of buses daily to El-Attaia (700 mills), a small fishing village at the eastern end of Chergui. Be careful that you don't get stranded there, because the last bus returns about 3 pm and there's not much local traffic.

Bicycle The flat terrain is ideal for cycling. All the resort hotels rent out bicycles. Rates start at TD1.500 per hour, or TD8 per day.

KAIROUAN

☎ 07 • pop 110,000

Kairouan, 57km west of Sousse, is Tunisia's holy city. It was here that Islam gained its first foothold in the Maghreb, and the city ranks behind only Mecca, Medina and Jerusalem among Islam's holy places.

The main attraction is the Great Mosque, but it is just one of many fine buildings lining the streets of the old medina. Kairouan is well known for its carpet making; it also lies at the centre of a major fruit-growing region.

History

Although legend indicates otherwise (see the boxed text 'The Founding of Kairouan'), Kairouan was most likely founded on the site of an earlier Roman settlement. The first Arab settlement lasted a few years only before it was destroyed by a Berber rebellion. It was re-established in AD 694 by Hassan ibn Nooman.

The city's golden age began when it became the capital of the Aghlabid dynasty at the beginning of the 9th century. Although they preferred to rule from their palace at Raqqada, 9km south of Kairouan, it was the Aghlabids who endowed the city with its most important historic buildings.

Kairouan fell to the Fatimids in AD 909, and the city fell into decline after the capital was moved to Mahdia. Its fortunes hit rock bottom when it was sacked in 1057

KAIROUAN

PLACES TO STAY
3 Hôtel Continental
6 Hôtel el-Menema
7 Hôtel Les Aghlabites
8 Hôtel de la Kasbah
21 Hôtel Sabra
23 Hôtel Splendid
25 Tunisia Hôtel

PLACES TO EAT
17 Le Meilleur Makhroud
26 Restaurant Sabra
27 Restaurant Olympique
30 Restaurant Roi de Couscous

OTHER
1 Entrance to Aghlabid Basins
2 Syndicat d'Initiative
4 Hospital

5 Zaouia of Sidi Sahab
9 Great Mosque
10 Mosque of the Three Doors
11 Centre des Traditions et des
   Métiers d'Art de Kairouan
12 Police Kiosk
13 Zaouia of Sidi Amor
   Abbada
14 Cyber Centre Kairouan
15 Agil Petrol Station
16 Bir Barouta
18 Zaouia of Sidi Abid
   el-Ghariani
19 Giant Anchors
20 ONTT Tourist Office
22 ONAT Museum
24 Supermarket
28 Taxiphone Office
29 Post Office

during the Hilalian invasions. Although Kairouan was rebuilt in the 13th century, it never regained its position of political pre-eminence. It remains, however, the most important religious centre in the country.

Orientation

Life in Kairouan revolves around the medina at the centre of town. The French built a Ville Nouvelle to the south. The two meet at the large open space outside the medina's main southern gate, the Bab ech Chouhada, where the tour buses gather. The medina's principal street, Ave Ali Belhouane, runs north-west from here to the main northern gate, the Bab Tunis. Ave Ibn el-Jazzar continues north from the Bab Tunis past the large regional hospital to link up with Ave Ibn el-Aghlab opposite the Aghlabid Basins. This leads to the main road to Tunis and Sousse.

The biggest problem for travellers is negotiating the way to the medina from the bus and louage stations, which are about 1.5km to the north-west on the road to Sbeitla. The streets of the outer suburbs can be very confusing – it's a good idea to start off by catching a taxi into town.

Street Names Street names in Kairouan seem to change so often that the street signs can't keep up. It's hard to find two people who agree on a name. The names of the monuments and hotels don't change, however, so ask for them rather than for the street they're in.

Information

Tourist Offices The ONTT tourist office (☎ 221 797) is south of the medina on Place des Martyrs. Don't expect to come away from here much the wiser. The only offerings are a glossy brochure (available anywhere) with an out-of-date map.

There is also a syndicat d'initiative next to the Aghlabid Basins on the northern edge of town, at the junction of Ave Ibn el-Jazzar and Ave Ibn el-Aghlab. It sells multiple-entry tickets (TD4.200) for the six major attractions in town – the Great Mosque, the Aghlabid Basins, the Zaouia of Sidi Sahab, the Zaouia of Sidi Amor Abbada, the Bir

The Founding of Kairouan

Kairouan was founded in AD 670 by the Arab general Uqba bin Nafi al-Fihri and takes its name from the Arabic word qayrawan, meaning 'military camp'. According to legend, the site for the city was chosen after Uqba's horse stumbled on a golden goblet that lay buried in the sands. The goblet turned out to be one that had mysteriously disappeared from Mecca some years previously. When it was picked up, water sprang from the ground – supplied, it was concluded, by the same source that supplied the holy well of Zem-Zem in Mecca.

Barouta and the Zaouia of Sidi Abid el-Ghariani as well as the Islamic Art Museum at Raqqada, on the road to Sfax. Tickets can also be bought at the Great Mosque and the Zaouia of Sidi Sahab. The syndicat d'initiative is open from 8 am to 6 pm daily in summer and to 5.30 pm daily in winter.

If you want a guide to show you around, you'll usually find several hanging around outside the syndicat d'initiative. These guys carry accreditation, with photos, and they know their stuff. They charge TD13 for a tour of all the major sites. They all speak Arabic and French; some also speak English and/or German.

Money There are branches of all the major banks on the streets south of Place des Martyrs.

Post & Communications The main post office is about 600m south-west of Bab ech Chouhada at the large roundabout on the southern edge of town, between Ave de la République and Rue Habib Thameur. It is open from 8 am to 6 pm in winter and from 7.30 am to 12.30 pm in summer, Monday to Saturday.

Taxiphone offices are everywhere – just look for the signs.

Email & Internet Access The Cyber Centre Kairouan is opposite the Agil petrol station on Ave Zama el-Belaoui.

Medina

Most of the attractions are found within the walls of the medina. The first walls were built towards the end of the 8th century, but they have been razed and rebuilt many times since then. The walls that stand today date mainly from the 18th century.

Kairouan gets an enormous number of tourists, mostly day-trippers from the resorts of Sousse and Monastir. You can set your clock by the wave of tourist buses that rolls up outside the medina at 9 am every day, so you'll have to set out early if you want to avoid the worst of the crowds.

The **Great Mosque** occupies a large portion of the north-eastern corner of the medina. It is also known as the Sidi Okba Mosque, after the founder of Kairouan who built the first mosque to stand on this site back in AD 670. The original version was completely destroyed, and most of what stands today was built by the Aghlabids in the 9th century.

The outside has a typically austere Aghlabid design, lacking in decoration of any kind. With its buttressed walls, it looks more like a fort than the country's most hallowed mosque. Entry is through the main gate on Rue Okba ibn Nafâa. The other eight gates are closed to non-Muslims.

Impressions change once you step into the huge marble-paved courtyard, surrounded by an arched colonnade made up of columns salvaged from various Roman and Byzantine sites. The courtyard was designed for water catchment, and the paving slopes towards an intricately decorated central drainage hole which delivers the collected rainwater into the 9th century cisterns below. The decorations were designed to filter dust from the water. The marble rims of the two wells in the courtyard both have deep rope grooves worn by centuries of hauling water up from the depths.

The northern end of the courtyard is dominated by a square three-tiered minaret. The lowest level was built in AD 728.

The prayer hall is at the southern end of the courtyard. The enormous, studded wooden doors were a gift from Hassan Bey in 1829; the carved panel above the doors is particularly fine. Non-Muslims are not allowed inside the prayer hall, but the doors are normally open enough to allow a glimpse of the interior. The 400 or so pillars that hold up the roof were filched from various Roman sites throughout the country, including Carthage and Hadrumètum (Sousse). At the far end of the hall, it's just possible to make out the precious 9th-century tiles behind the mihrab (prayer niche in the mosque wall which indicates the direction of Mecca), which were imported from Baghdad along with the wood for the minbar (pulpit) next to it.

The mosque is open from 7.30 am to noon daily in summer and from 8 am to noon daily in winter. Visitors must be appropriately dressed; robes are available at the entrance for those whose dress is deemed inappropriate. Admission is covered by the multiple-entry ticket.

Rue Okba ibn Nafâa runs south-east through the medina from the Great Mosque and emerges at a small square just inside the **Bab el-Khoukha**, the oldest of the medina's many gates. Featuring a horseshoe arch supported by columns, it was built by Hussein ben Ali in 1706.

Just inside the Bab ech Chouhada, on Rue Sidi el-Ghariani, the **Zaouia of Sidi Abid el-Ghariani** is another of the monuments featured on the multiple-entry ticket. Recently restored, the building dates from the 14th century and contains some fine woodcarving and stuccowork. The custodian here is a very willing talker and will guide you around pointing out the finer points (in French). The zaouia also houses the tomb of the Hafsid sultan Moulay Hassan who ruled from 1525 to 1543.

The biggest tourist trap in the city is the building known as the **Bir Barouta**, just north of Ave Ali Belhouane. It was built by the Ottoman ruler Mohammed Bey in 1676 to surround the well that features in the city's foundation legend. This means that its waters are supposedly linked to those of the well of Zem-Zem in Mecca.

The main attraction is a poor, blindfolded camel that trudges around all day, drawing water from the well for people to taste, while a long line of tourists files through, taking the obligatory photo and leaving the obligatory tip. Architecturally, the main point of interest is the fancy open brickwork on the inside of the cupola roof. Admission is covered by the multiple-entry ticket.

The **Mosque of the Three Doors** was founded in AD 866 by Mohammed bin Kairoun el-Maafri, a holy man from the Spanish city of Cordoba. The interior is closed to non-Muslims, but that's not a problem because the main feature is the elaborate facade. The mosque's three arched doorways are topped by three friezes of kufic (early Arabic) script interspersed with floral reliefs and finally crowned with a carved cornice. The mosque is about 250m north-east of the Bir Barouta along Rue de la Mosquée des Trois Portes.

Aghlabid Basins

These two cisterns were built by the Aghlabids in the 9th century to hold the city's water supply. Water was delivered by aqueduct from the hills 36km west of Kairouan and flowed first into the smaller settling basin. From there it flowed on into the enormous main holding basin, which was 5m deep and 128m in diameter. In the centre of the main pool are the remains of pillars which once supported a pavilion where the rulers could come to relax on summer evenings.

The site is open from 7.30 am to 6.30 pm daily in summer and from 8.30 to 6 pm daily in winter. Admission is covered by the multiple-entry ticket.

Zaouia of Sidi Sahab

This extensive zaouia is about 1.5km by road north-west of the medina on Ave Zama el-Belaoui, just north of the road leading to the bus and louage stations. It houses the tomb of Abu Zama el-Belaoui, a *sahab* (companion) of the Prophet Mohammed. He was known as the barber because he always carried three hairs from the Prophet's beard around with him, and the zaouia is sometimes referred to as the Mosque of the Barber. While the original mausoleum dates back to the 7th century AD, most of what stands today was added at the end of the 17th century. The additions include a *funduq* (caravanserai or inn) to house pilgrims, a medersa and a mosque.

The entrance to the zaouia is along an unusually decorative marble passageway that leads to a stunning white central courtyard. Sidi Sahab's mausoleum is in the north-western corner, topped by a cupola added in 1629. Non-Muslims are not permitted to enter. The small room on the opposite side of the courtyard contains the tomb of the architect of the Great Mosque.

The zaouia is open from 7.30 am to 6 pm daily all year, and admission is covered by the multiple-entry ticket. As at the Great Mosque, robes are available at the entrance for those who are not suitably dressed.

Zaouia of Sidi Amor Abbada

This zaouia was built in 1860 around the tomb of Sidi Amor Abbada, a local blacksmith with a gift for prophecy. He specialised in the production of oversized things, like a set of giant anchors that were supposed to secure Kairouan to the earth. These anchors now stand in the middle of the roundabout outside the medina's Bab Jedid, north of Place des Martyrs.

The zaouia is just to the west of the medina off Rue Sidi Gaid, identifiable by its seven gleaming white cupolas. Admission is covered by the multiple-entry ticket.

Raqqada Islamic Art Museum

The museum occupies a former presidential palace at Raqqada, 9km south of Kairouan on the road to Sfax. Exhibits include a model of the Great Mosque of Kairouan, a faithfully reproduced plaster copy of the mihrab and lots and lots of calligraphy.

Unless you have your own transport and happen to be driving past, it's not worth the effort involved in getting there by bus. The museum is open from 9.30 am to 4.30 pm daily, except Monday.

ONAT Museum

The ONAT Museum (free admission) on Ave Ali Zouaoui houses a collection of rugs and other artefacts ancient and not so ancient.

Places to Stay – Budget

Hostels The city's *Maison des Jeunes* (☎ 228 239) is about 1km south-east of the medina on Ave de Fes. It's very uninviting, even by the organisation's low standards. It charges the standard TD4 per person.

Hotels Most travellers head for the *Hôtel Sabra* (☎ *230 263*), conveniently located opposite the Bab ech Chouhada on the southern side of the medina. The staff are used to dealing with budget travellers, and the rooms are good value at TD10/16 for singles/doubles with breakfast and free hot showers. It has very few singles, so individuals often end up enjoying a double to themselves for the price of a single.

An interesting alternative is the *Hôtel Les Aghlabites* (☎ *230 880*), a converted funduq off Place de Tunis to the north of the medina. The rooms here open out onto a splendid tiled courtyard. It charges TD8/12 with hot showers. The hotel is next to the fruit and vegetable markets, so ask for a quiet room away from the street.

The *Hôtel el-Menema* (☎ *225 003, fax 226 182*) is a small, modern hotel north of the medina on Ave el-Moez ibn Badis. Rooms cost TD10/20 with bathroom, and including breakfast.

Places to Stay – Mid-Range

The place to head for is the two star *Tunisia Hôtel* (☎ *231 775, fax 231 597*), a good older-style hotel about 400m south of the medina on Ave de la République. It has large singles/doubles with bathroom for TD22/36, including breakfast. The rooms are centrally heated in winter.

The *Hôtel Continental* (☎ *221 135, fax 229 900*) is a quiet three-star hotel on the northern edge of town opposite the syndicat d'initiative. Singles/doubles are TD28/44, rising to TD33/49.600 in summer. Facilities include a swimming pool.

Places to Stay – Top End

The best rooms in town are at the new *Hôtel de la Kasbah* (☎ *237 301, fax 237 302*), which occupies the old kasbah on Ave Ibn el-Jazzar – just north of the medina. It's a fantastic place to stay, with its large heated pool in the central courtyard. Singles/doubles cost TD55/80 in the low season, and then jump to TD80/120 for the rest of the year.

The *Hôtel Amina* (☎ *225 466, fax 225 411*), about 1km east of the syndicat d'initiative on the road to Tunis, is now the second-best hotel in town. It's a comfortable, modern three-star hotel with rooms for TD45/66 in the low season and TD48/70 for the rest of the year. It also has a swimming pool.

Places to Eat

The streets south of the medina are the place to go looking for a cheap meal.

The friendly *Restaurant Sabra*, next to the Tunisia Hôtel on Ave de la République, is a good place to start. It has salads for TD1.200, and main dishes priced from TD2.500. It also has a selection of three-course menus priced from TD6.

The *Restaurant Olympique*, one block south of the Sabra, has almost identical prices. It also offers pizza from TD2.

If you want a glass of wine with your meal, try the *Roi Roi du Couscous*, near the post office on Place du 7 Novembre. Alcohol is the main attraction here; liquor licences are hard to come by in Kairouan.

Kairouan is famous for its sticky sweets, especially a date-filled semolina cake soaked in honey called *makhroud*, which can be found everywhere. A good place to sample this and other specialities is *Le Meilleur Makhroud*, in the middle of the medina on Ave 7 Novembre.

Self-caterers can head for the *supermarket* on Ave de Mahdia. Lots of fruit is grown around Kairouan, especially cherries and other stone fruit. You'll find whatever's in season at the *stalls* around Place de Tunis, just north of the medina.

Shopping

Kairouan is one of Tunisia's major carpet centres, producing classical knotted carpets as well as the woven *mergoum*. If you are on the market for a carpet, this is as good a place as any to do your shopping.

It is important, however, to do your homework first. Initial prices can be ridiculously high, often as much as three times the true price.

A good place to go looking for souvenirs is the Centre des Traditions et des Métiers d'Art de Kairouan, just to the north of the Bir Barouta on a side street leading to the souqs. It was set up by ONAT to promote local handicrafts. The ground floor acts as a sales outlet, while the rooms upstairs are set up to demonstrate traditional techniques for weaving, embroidery and carpet making etc.

Getting There & Away
The bus and louage stations are next to each other about 300m west of the Zaouia of Sidi Sahab. It's a long way to walk in summer, especially if you're staying at one of the hotels to the south of the medina. A taxi from here costs about TD1.200.

Note that there is no direct public transport from Kairouan to El-Jem; you'll have to go via Sousse.

Bus The bus station is one of the busiest in the country. Kairouan is situated on the shortest route between Tunis and the cities of the south and south-west, and there is a constant stream of long-distance traffic 24 hours a day. Most of the services are operated by the national line, SNTRI, which has its own booking office in the terminal, together with an information board with destinations and departure times clearly indicated.

Bus Services

destination	frequency (per day)	duration (hours)	fare (TD)
Douz	1	7	16.6
Gabès	6	4¼	8.54
Gafsa	10	3	8.58
Jerba	1	5	13.11
Kasserine	3	2½	6.95
Medenine	6	5¼	10.60
Nabeul	3	2¼	4.28
Nefta	2	7½	12.89
Sbeitla	3	1½	5.22
Tozeur	2	4½	11.83
Tunis	hourly	2¼	6.80

Other destinations are served by regional companies with separate booking offices at the other side of the terminal. There are buses to Sousse (TD2.700, 1½ hours) every 30 minutes from 6.30 am to 7.30 pm, three buses a day to Sfax (TD5.280, two hours) and two to Makthar (TD4.200, 1¾ hours).

Louage There are frequent departures to Sousse (TD3.150), Sfax (TD5.500) and Tunis (TD6.800), and occasional services to Makthar (TD4.500) and Sbeitla (TD5.200).

MAKTHAR (MACTARIS)
☎ 08 • pop 8000
The bleak little town of Makthar is situated on the high plains of the Tunisian Dorsale 114km west of Kairouan on the road to Le Kef. The only reason to stop here is to visit the ruins of ancient Mactaris, which are on the south-eastern edge of town. The modern town has nothing going for it, but it's easy enough to visit the ruins en route from Kairouan to Le Kef, a further 69km to the north-west.

History
Ancient Mactaris was another of the many native towns to be incorporated into the Carthaginian Empire at the end of the 5th century BC as part of Carthage's push to control the hinterland. It was captured by the Numidian king Massinissa, an ally of the Romans, before the Third and final Punic War, and remained in Numidian hands until the beginning of the 1st century AD, when Rome began to take the settlement of Africa seriously.

The Roman town reached the peak of its prosperity in the 2nd century, and most of the buildings at the site date from this time. The Vandals and the Byzantines both left their mark at the site in subsequent centuries, and the town continued to be occupied until the 11th century, when it was destroyed during the Hilalian invasions.

Orientation & Information
The site is on the south-eastern edge of town at the junction of the main roads running south-east to Kairouan and north to Le Kef and Tunis. It is opposite a large triumphal arch that once marked the entrance

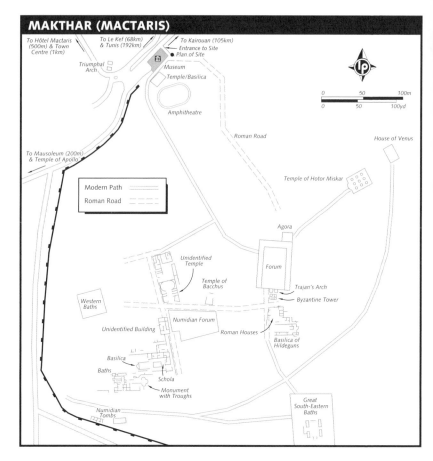

MAKTHAR (MACTARIS)

To Hôtel Mactaris (500m) & Town Centre (1km)

To Le Kef (68km) & Tunis (192km)

To Kairouan (105km)
Entrance to Site
Plan of Site

Triumphal Arch

Museum

Temple/Basilica

Amphitheatre

Roman Road

House of Venus

To Mausoleum (200m) & Temple of Apollo

Temple of Hotor Miskar

Modern Path ···········
Roman Road ── ── ──

Agora

Forum

Unidentified Temple

Temple of Bacchus

Trajan's Arch

Byzantine Tower

Western Baths

Numidian Forum

Unidentified Building

Roman Houses

Basilica of Hildeguns

Basilica

Baths

Schola

Monument with Troughs

Numidian Tombs

Great South-Eastern Baths

0   50   100m
0   50   100yd

---

to the town. It's open from 8 am to 6 pm in summer and 8.30 am to 5.30 pm in winter daily, except Monday. Admission to the site, including the museum, is TD2.100, plus TD1 if you want to take photographs.

If you're visiting the site in winter, come suitably dressed. At an altitude of more than 1000m, the winds that blow off the surrounding hills can be bitterly cold.

Museum
The entrance to the site is through the museum. It houses some interesting old gravestones found at the site as well as the obligatory collection of chipped Roman busts, lamps and old coins.

Amphitheatre
Immediately south of the museum are the remains of the town's small amphitheatre, built in the 2nd century AD and looking in remarkably good condition after recent restoration.

Trajan's Arch
The site's main path runs south from the amphitheatre towards the crumbling remains of an enormous triumphal arch, built

in AD 116 and dedicated to Emperor Trajan. The arch overlooks the Roman forum, built at the same time. The four columns at the north-eastern corner of the forum mark the location of the town's market. The foundations south of the arch belong to a Byzantine tower built in the 6th century AD.

Temple of Hotor Miskar
A path leads north-east from the forum to the scanty remains of an early temple dedicated to the Carthaginian god Hotor Miskar. Nearby are the remains of a Roman villa known as the House of Venus named after the mosaic of Venus found there, now in the museum.

Basilica of Hildeguns
The group of columns south of Trajan's Arch belong to a small Vandal church, built in the 5th century AD and named after the fellow who is buried by the entrance on the western side. The baptistery font, hidden behind the apse at the eastern end, still has traces of the original mosaics.

Schola
The jumble of arches and columns standing at the south-western corner of the site was once the home of the town's *schola juvenum*, a sort of youth club where local boys learned how to be good Romans. It was converted into a church in the 3rd century AD. It's a very pleasant, shady spot to sit and contemplate.

The area just south of the schola was the town's cemetery and is dotted with **Numidian tombs**.

Great South-Eastern Baths
The massive walls of this enormous bath complex dominate the southern part of the site. Built at the peak of the town's prosperity in the 2nd century AD, it was later converted into a fortress by the Byzantines in the 6th century. In spite of this, the baths are among the best preserved in Tunisia and the layout is still quite easy to follow. The star feature is the extraordinary blue and green mosaic floor of the central room.

Temple of Apollo
If you have time, it's an interesting walk out to the ruins of the Temple of Apollo, about 800m south-west of town and signposted from the museum. It was the town's principal temple in Roman times and was built on the site of an earlier Carthaginian temple to the god Baal Hammon. Adjoining the site are the crumbling remains of the Roman aqueduct that once supplied water to the town.

Places to Stay & Eat
You'd need to be desperate to consider spending a night at Makthar's only hotel, the tiny *Hôtel Mactaris* (☎ 876 465), about 500m from the ancient site on the road into town. Location is about all it has going for it. The three very basic rooms are above the only bar in town, and you'd need to drink a skinful before you even considered lying down on one of the saggy old iron beds. For the record, the rooms cost TD10 and can sleep up to three people.

It also has a cheap *restaurant* serving grilled food and salads. There's no sign, but everybody knows the place. It's a much better idea to hop on a bus and keep going to either Le Kef or Kairouan.

Getting There & Away
Bus Buses leave from the T-junction 100m north of the Hôtel Mactaris. There are five buses a day to Le Kef (TD2.600, 1¼ hours) and two to Kairouan (TD4.200, 1¾ hours). SNTRI operates three buses a day to Tunis (TD7.040, three hours).

Louage You can also get to Tunis, Le Kef and Kairouan by louage. They leave from the main street in the middle of town.

SBEITLA (SUFETULA)
☎ 07 • pop 6000
Stuck out in the middle of nowhere on the plains 107km south-west of Kairouan, Sbeitla merits a mention only because it is the site of the ancient town of Sufetula, famous for its remarkably well-preserved Roman temples.

The modern town has very little going for it, although it does at least have a couple of

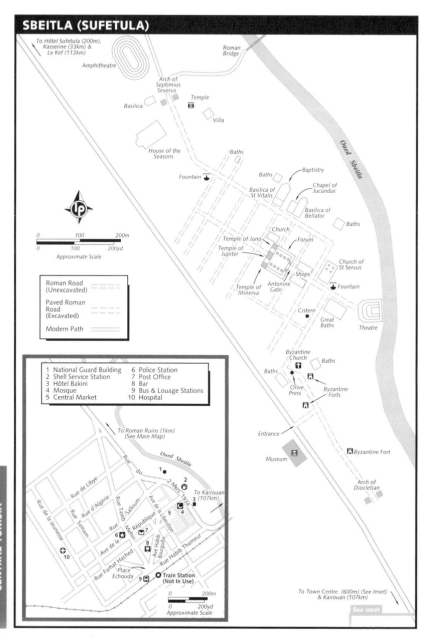

SBEITLA (SUFETULA)

To Hôtel Sufetula (200m),
Kasserine (33km) &
Le Kef (112km)

Roman Bridge

Amphitheatre

Arch of Septimius Severus

Basilica

Temple

Villa

House of the Seasons

Baths

Fountain

Baths

Baptistry

Basilica of St Vitalis

Chapel of Jucundus

Basilica of Bellator

Baths

Oued Sbeitla

Church

Temple of Juno

Forum

Temple of Jupiter

Shops

Church of St Servus

Temple of Minerva

Antonine Gate

Fountain

Cistern

Great Baths

Byzantine Church

Theatre

Baths

Baths

Olive Press

Byzantine Forts

Entrance

Museum

Byzantine Fort

Arch of Diocletian

Roman Road (Unexcavated)

Paved Roman Road (Excavated)

Modern Path

| 0 | 100 | 200m |
| 0 | 100 | 200yd |

Approximate Scale

1 National Guard Building
2 Shell Service Station
3 Hôtel Bakini
4 Mosque
5 Central Market
6 Police Station
7 Post Office
8 Bar
9 Bus & Louage Stations
10 Hospital

To Roman Ruins (1km)
(See Main Map)

Oued Sbeitla

Rue du

Ave 2 Mars 1934

To Kairouan
(107km)

Rue de Libye

Rue d'Algérie

Rue Taïeb Salloum

Rue Semam

Ave de la Libération

Ave de la République

Rue de la Jeunesse

Rue Tahar Mehiri

Rue Farhat Hached

Ave de le

Ave Habib Bourguiba

Rue Habib Thameur

Place Echouda

Train Station
(Not In Use)

| 0 | 200m |
| 0 | 200yd |

Approximate Scale

To Town Centre (600m) (See Inset)
& Kairouan (107km)

See Inset

CENTRAL TUNISIA

decent hotels to cater for the steady flow of tourists lured by the ruins.

History

Given the importance of Roman Sufetula, surprisingly little is known about its early history. It is assumed that it followed an evolutionary path similar to other Roman towns in the region, such as Ammaedara and Mactaris, and was established at the beginning of the 1st century AD on the site of an early Numidian settlement.

The surrounding countryside proved ideal for olive growing, and Sufetula quickly developed into a wealthy town. The temples were built when Sufetula was at the height of its prosperity in the 2nd century. Its olive groves ensured that the town continued to prosper long after other Roman towns slipped into decline, and it became an important centre of Christianity in the 4th century.

The Byzantines made Sufetula their regional capital, transforming it into a military stronghold from which to tackle the area's rebellious local tribes. It was here in AD 647 that Prefect Gregory declared himself independent of Constantinople. His moment of glory lasted only a few months before he was defeated and killed by the Arabs, who at the same time destroyed much of the town. The Arab victory is celebrated at the Festival of the Seven Abdullahs, held in the last week of July.

Orientation & Information

The ruins of Sufetula are about 1km north of the modern town centre, on the road to Kasserine. The first sign that you are approaching the site is the massive Arch of Diocletian. This arch once stood at the southern entrance to the ancient town. The site entrance is 200m further north, opposite the museum. The site and museum are both open from 7 am to 7 pm daily in summer and 8.30 am to 5.30 pm daily in winter. The admission fee of TD2.100 covers the site and the museum. There is an additional charge of TD1 to take photographs.

The best time to visit the site is very early in the morning, which means spending the night at one of the nearby hotels. It's well worth it, though, for the spectacular sight of the temples glowing orange in the early morning sun.

Temples

The celebrated temples hold centre stage. Built on a low rise in the middle of town, they tower over the surrounding ruins.

The wall that surrounds the temples was not part of the original scheme. It was built by the Byzantines in the 6th century AD. They used the temples as one wall of a fortress surrounding the old forum.

The entrance is on the south-eastern side of the complex through the magnificent triple-arched **Antonine Gate**, built in AD 139 and dedicated to Emperor Antoninus Pius and his adopted sons Marcus Aurelius and Lucius Verus. It opens onto a large paved forum flanked by two rows of columns which lead up to the temples. There are three temples, each dedicated to one of the three main gods of the Roman pantheon. The **Temple of Jupiter**, in the centre, is flanked by slightly smaller temples to his sister deities Juno and Minerva.

Great Baths

The ruins of these extensive baths are to the south-east of the temples, on the road leading down towards the Oued Sbeitla. They are remarkable mainly for the complex under-floor **heating system** used in the hot rooms, easily distinguishable now that the floors themselves have collapsed.

Theatre

The ancient theatre, just east of the Great Baths, has a prime position overlooking the Oued Sbeitla. Built in the 3rd century AD, not much remains except for the orchestra pit and a few scattered columns, but it's worth visiting for the **views** along the Oued Sbeitla – especially picturesque in spring.

Church of St Servus

The four precarious-looking pillars of stone on the left as you walk between the temples and the Great Baths mark the site of the Church of St Servus, built in the 4th century

AD on the foundations of an unidentified pre-Roman temple.

Basilica of Bellator

The Basilica of Bellator is the first of a row of ruined churches about 100m east of the temples on the main path leading north-west towards the Arch of Septimius Severus. Built at the beginning of the 4th century AD, its unusual name derives from an inscription found at the site. Like the Church of St Servus, it was built on the foundations of an unidentified pre-Roman temple. The tiny adjoining **chapel** was the basilica's baptistery until the 5th century, when it was converted into a chapel in honour of the Catholic bishop Jucundus, who is thought to have been martyred by the Vandals.

Basilica of St Vitalis

The nearby Basilica of St Vitalis was built in the 6th century AD as a bigger and grander replacement for the Basilica of Bellator. The basilica itself doesn't amount to much now, but hidden away in the baptistery at the back is a beautiful **baptismal basin** that has been left *in situ* in the ground. The rim is decorated with an intricate floral mosaic in brilliant reds and greens.

Other Sites

The path running north-west from the churches crosses a neat grid of unexcavated streets before arriving at the remains of Sufetula's second monumental gate, the **Arch of Septimius Severus**. To the west before you reach the arch are the meagre remains of the **House of the Seasons**, named for a mosaic now in the Bardo Museum in Tunis.

A rough path continues north from the arch, past the ruins of a small **basilica**, to the site of the town's **amphitheatre**, which has yet to be excavated and is so overgrown that you have to look hard to find the outline. Another path leads east from the arch down to a restored **Roman bridge** over the Oued Sbeitla.

Museum

You start to wonder about the value of a museum when the guy at the door tells you it's not worth visiting! He's not far wrong. The only exhibits worth seeking out are the statue of Bacchus reclining on a panther, which was discovered at the site's theatre, and the mosaics.

Places to Stay & Eat

The two star *Hôtel Sufetula (☎ 465 074, fax 465 582)* overlooks the ancient site from its hilltop location 1.5km north of town on the road to Kasserine. It's a comfortable, modern hotel charging TD35/50 for large singles/ doubles with breakfast. If you're staying here, you're pretty much obliged to eat here as well. The restaurant does a perfectly adequate three-course menu for an extra TD5 per person. The hotel also has a swimming pool.

The alternative is the uninspiring *Hôtel Bakini (☎ 465 244)*, at the eastern edge of town on Rue du 2 Mars 1934. It has rooms with breakfast for TD28/40.

The *bar/restaurant* on Ave Habib Bourguiba is more bar than restaurant, but it does serve basic grilled food like *brochettes* (kebabs), salad and chips for TD2.800.

Self-caterers can stock up at the *markets* on Ave de la Liberation.

Getting There & Away

Buses and louages leave from a dusty vacant lot on the southern edge of town off Rue Habib Thameur. The old train station is nearby, but the trains stopped running long ago.

SNTRI has three buses a day to Tunis (TD9.850, 3¾ hours) via Kairouan (TD-5.220, 1½ hours). Regional services include frequent buses to Kasserine (TD1.200, 45 minutes). There's a direct bus to Le Kef (TD6.350, three hours) at 8 am daily, otherwise change at Kasserine.

There are regular louages to Kasserine and Kairouan.

KASSERINE

☎ 07 • pop 30,000

Kasserine, 38km south-west of Sbeitla, would be a strong contender in any poll to nominate the dullest town in Tunisia. It is, however, an important regional centre with

The crenellated walls of the Sfax Medina, built by the Aghlabites in the 9th century AD

Sufetula's (Sbeitla) temples, built at the height of Roman influence in the 2nd century AD

The ribat at Monastir, part of a chain of lookout posts built to defend the Tunisian coast

A merchant's house, Kairouan

Inside the medina at Kairouan

The fortifications and medina at Sousse testify to the town's past commercial strength.

Esparto Grass

One of the few plants that thrives in the harsh conditions of the Tunisian interior is a wiry, narrow-bladed native grass known as esparto (*stipa tenacissima*).

Left to its own devices, it grows into dense clumps topped by graceful, feathered seed heads – making it a popular garden plant in some parts of the world. In Tunisia, it's too valuable just to be admired.

In ancient times, it was gathered and woven into a host of household items, such as matting and baskets. It was tough enough to produce crude ropes, animal harnesses and saddle bags.

These days, esparto is exploited primarily for the production of high-quality paper. Large areas of the countryside around Kasserine and Sbeitla are devoted to its cultivation. Traditionally, the harvest was regarded as women's work, and you'll see long rows of women working their way across fields of esparto armed with small sickles. The cut esparto is bailed up and trucked off to a modern paper factory in Kasserine.

useful transport connections and a reasonable choice of accommodation, and it makes a useful base for exploring the remote western reaches of the country.

Kasserine's main industry is the production of high-quality paper from esparto grass, which grows abundantly on the surrounding plains. You'll see a mountain of the stuff, piled up waiting to be processed, at the factory in the centre of town (see the boxed text 'Esparto Grass').

If you come to Kasserine in winter, come suitably dressed. The town is just east of Tunisia's highest mountain, Jebel Chambi (1544m), and gets desperately cold in winter. The wind fairly howls off the surrounding hills, and snow falls are not uncommon.

Orientation & Information

Everything of importance is found somewhere along the extended main street, Blvd

de l'Environment, which is also the main road through town.

The bus and louage stations are just north of Blvd de l'Environment on the Sbeitla side of town. The town centre is about 1.5km to the west around the main square, Place de l'Independence. This large, open square is commonly known as Place de l'Ancienne Gare, because of the disused train station on the southern side. The post office is nearby and there are several banks around the square.

Blvd de l'Environment continues west for a further 2km before finishing at a major roundabout, where there are roads north to Le Kef and south to Gafsa.

Things to See

The only attraction is the minor Roman site of **Cillium**. Like Kasserine today, Cillium was an important regional centre. The ruins are spread over a wide area, but are centred on a low hill overlooking the broad bed of the Oued Dhrib on the south-western edge of town.

This area is enclosed and watched over by a guardian, although there is no admission fee. The guardian spends most of his time with nothing but a flock of goats for company, and seems delighted to have the opportunity to show people around. The main features are a well-preserved **triumphal arch** and a large **theatre**, which is carved into the hillside overlooking the Oued Dhrib. Both date from the 3rd century, when Cillium was at the peak of its prosperity. The **capitol** and **forum** are also identifiable, as are the main **baths**. The site is signposted to the east of the road to Gafsa, about 250m south of the Hôtel Cillium.

Cillium's most famous monument is the **Mausoleum of the Flavii**. This triple-tiered monument to Flavius Secundus and his family stands by the roadside at the western end of Blvd de l'Environment. It looks stunning at night when spotlights highlight the remarkable condition of the 110 lines of poetry inscribed on the bottom tier.

Places to Stay & Eat

The place to head for is the friendly *Hôtel de la Paix* (☎ *471 465*), on the main street 50m east of the central square. It has singles/doubles with shared bathroom for TD9/16, including breakfast, or TD11.500/21 with dinner as well at the popular downstairs restaurant/bar. Nonresidents will find tasty meals from TD2.500.

The *Hôtel Pinus* (☎ *470 164*), 700m further out towards Sbeitla, isn't worth the TD20/30 it charges for singles/doubles with breakfast.

The upmarket option is the *Hôtel Cillium* (☎ *474 406, fax 473 682*), just south of the roundabout on the western side of town. This circular 1960s building rates as the most interesting structure in town. It has rooms for TD35/50, or TD40/60 with dinner as well. In winter there's a chance that you'll end up sitting at the bar with a bunch of elderly European men dressed up in paramilitary costumes; they're hunters who come here to go pig-hunting in the surrounding forests.

Getting There & Away
The bus and louage stations are side by side about 1km east of the town centre on the road to Sbeitla.

Bus SNTRI has four buses a day to Tunis (TD10.900, 4½ hours), via Kairouan. Regional services include frequent buses to Sbeitla (TD1.200, 45 minutes), six buses a day to Gafsa (TD4.200, 1¾ hours), and four buses a day north to Le Kef (TD4.950, 2½ hours) via Kalaat Khasba (TD2.550, 1¼ hours).

Louage Travelling by louage around here involves lots of short journeys and frequent vehicle changes. There are frequent services to Sbeitla (TD1.400), but travelling south to Gafsa involves changing louage at Fériana – and travelling north to Kalaat Khasba or Le Kef involves a change at Thala.

HAIDRA
The remote border village of Haidra, 69km north-west of Kasserine, is the site of ancient Ammaedara, one of the oldest Roman towns in Africa. It's a wonderfully evocative site, spread along the northern bank of the

Oued Haidra. The problem is that it's a difficult place to get to without your own transport, especially if you want to stick around for the fabulous sunsets. The sun sets slowly behind the mountains of Algeria to the west, bathing the site in a rich orange light.

Modern Haidra is little more than a customs post on the road to the Algerian town of Tébessa, just 41km south-west of here. There are shops and a cafe, but no restaurants and no hotels. The closest accommodation is in Kasserine – or in Le Kef, 78km to the north. The Algerian border is 10km west of Haidra.

History
Ammaedara is a Berber name, which indicates that the Romans weren't the first to occupy the site. The only evidence of pre-Roman occupation are the foundations of a Carthaginian temple to the god Baal Hammon, overlooking the Oued Haidra to the south-east of the site.

The first Roman settlement here was established by the troops of the Augustine Third Legion at the beginning of the 1st century AD as a base during their campaign to suppress a rebellion by the Numidian chief Tacfinares. Nothing from this period survived apart from a cemetery near the Arch of Septimius Severus. After Tacfinares was defeated, the legion moved its camp west to Theveste (Tébessa), and Ammaedara was repopulated with retired soldiers.

Ammaedara developed into a prosperous trading town at the junction of the Roman roads west to Theveste, north-east to Carthage, and south to Thelepte and Gafsa. The disproportionate number of churches – Roman, Vandal and Byzantine – indicate that it continued to be an important town until the arrival of the Arabs in the 7th century AD.

Things to See
The road from Kalaat Khasba passes through the middle of the site, which is not enclosed and can be visited at any time. Admission is free, but the amiable custodian appreciates a tip. Few tourists pass this way and he enjoys an opportunity to point out the highlights.

The site is dominated by the walls of an enormous **Byzantine fort**, built in AD 550. It

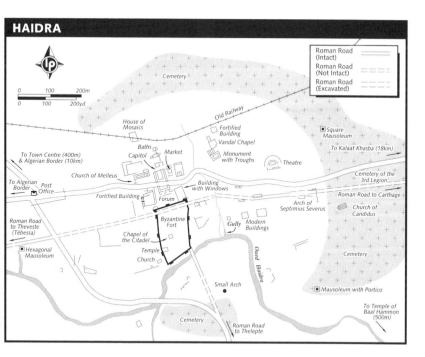

HAIDRA

Roman Road (Intact)
Roman Road (Not Intact)
Roman Road (Excavated)

Cemetery

0 100 200m
0 100 200yd

House of Mosaics

Old Railway

Fortified Building

Vandal Chapel

Square Mausoleum

To Kalaat Khasba (18km)

Baths

Capitol

Market

Monument with Troughs

Theatre

To Town Centre (400m) & Algerian Border (10km)

Church of Melleus

Cemetery of the 3rd Legion

To Algerian Border

Post Office

Building with Windows

Fortified Building

Forum

Roman Road to Carthage

Arch of Septimius Severus

Church of Candidus

Roman Road to Theveste (Tébessa)

Byzantine Fort

Gully

Modern Buildings

Hexagonal Mausoleum

Chapel of the Citadel

Temple

Church

Oued Haidra

Cemetery

Small Arch

Mausoleum with Portico

To Temple of Baal Hammon (500m)

Cemetery

Roman Road to Thelepte

straddles the old Roman road and runs down to the banks of the Oued Haidra. The ruins of an earlier **Roman temple** are incorporated into the south-western corner, while excavations have uncovered the small Byzantine **Chapel of the Citadel** at the centre of the fort.

Haidra's principal Roman monument is the extremely well preserved **Arch of Septimius Severus**, which stands on the Roman road at the eastern edge of the site. It was built in AD 195, and remains in good condition because it was protected for centuries by a surrounding Byzantine wall. About 300m south of here, the **mausoleum with portico** stands silhouetted on a small rise overlooking the oued.

Little else of the Roman town remains standing. The modern road passes over the old **forum**, while a single giant column marks the site of the great temple that once stood at the **capitol**. The rest of the columns lie scattered around. Around the capitol are the remains of the old **baths** and the **market**.

While the site is dotted with the ruins of numerous small churches, the only one that warrants serious inspection is the **Church of Melleus**, just west of the forum. Originally built in the 4th century, it was later expanded by the Byzantines and is named after a bishop who was buried here. The church was partly reconstructed in the 1960s.

Getting There & Away

Visiting Haidra without your own transport is a challenge, but can be achieved with a bit of determination. Access is via the small market town of Kalaat Khasba, 18km to the north-east.

You can get to Kalaat Khasba on any bus travelling between Kasserine and Le Kef, or by louage from Kasserine via Thala. There is a daily train from Tunis (TD9.150, five hours), which departs at 5.50 am, returning from Kalaat Khasba at 12.45 pm.

Buses and louages will deposit you on the main street of Kalaat Khasba, where you will find occasional louages out to Haidra (800 mills, 15 minutes). The alternative is to hitch from the roundabout on the main road at the southern side of town. Whatever you do, you will need to set out early, because public transport dries up by mid-afternoon.

JUGURTHA'S TABLE

Jugurtha's Table (1271m) is a spectacular flat-topped mountain that rises sheer from the surrounding plains close to the Algerian border near the small town of Kalaat es Senan, 85km north-west of Kasserine.

The mountain is named after the Numidian king Jugurtha, who used it as a base during his seven-year campaign against the Romans from 112–105 BC. Its sheer, impregnable walls make it a superb natural fortress. The only access to the summit is by a twisting set of steps hewn into the escarpment at the eastern end. The Byzantines added the small gate at the base of the steps, but there is no other indication that they used the site.

If you have your own vehicle, you can drive to the base of the steps. The turn-off is about 5km east of Kalaat es Senan on the road to Kalaat Khasba. The steps are steep, and awkward enough to require caution in places – although this hasn't stopped cows from scrambling up and down, judging from their deposits.

The reward for those who climb to the top is a spectacular view over the surrounding countryside. The hills you can see to the west are across the border in Algeria. There's little else to see apart from a small *marabout* (shrine), a network of low stone walls – and a few curious cows.

If you are in the mood for a longer walk, you can start your hike to the steps from the small village of Ain Senan, on the western side of the mountain 3km south-east of Kalaat es Senan.

A rough path leads uphill from the highest point of the village and skirts around the northern side of the mountain. There's only one path, and locals are used to pointing it out if you need reassurance. Keep following it around the base of the escarpment until you get to the eastern side of the mountain, when you will see the steps.

The return walk from Ain Senan takes about two hours. You'll need a decent pair of walking shoes to handle the rough terrain, and take sufficient water because there's none to be found along the way. Tourists are supposed to register at the National Guard office on the main street of Kalaat es Senan before they set out, and check back afterwards to announce their safe return.

Places to Stay & Eat

There's very basic accommodation at the *Hôtel Kalaat Senan (☎ 08-286 356)*, next to the National Guard office on the main street of town. It charges TD2.500 per person for a bed in a triple room, or TD7.500 if you want the room to yourself. The hotel also doubles as the only bar in town, and has a small restaurant where you can get a plate of grilled chicken, chips and salad for TD3. The closest decent rooms are in Le Kef.

Getting There & Around

There are good sealed roads connecting Kalaat es Senan with Kalaat Khasba, 28km to the south-east, and Tajerouine, 25km to the north-east. There are occasional louages from both towns.

Tajerouine is 35km south of Le Kef on the main road to Kasserine. All buses travelling between Le Kef and Kasserine stop there.

If you haven't got your own vehicle, you can save yourself a hot uphill walk by forking out TD1.500 for a taxi from Kalaat es Senan to Ain Senan.

Southern Tunisia

Tourism has boomed in the south in recent years as more people head inland in search of some of the country's most dramatic landscapes: the desert dunes of the Grand Erg Oriental south of Douz, ancient oasis towns, shimmering *chotts* (salt lakes), the spectacular Berber villages of the ksour district around Tataouine and the bizarre lunar landscapes surrounding the troglodyte (cave dweller) village of Matmata.

Spring and autumn are the best times to visit, although tour operators like to claim that the season lasts from late September to early May. Summer is the worst time. It's so hot, especially inland, that it can be a real effort to move. It's also the season of the sirocco, a hot, southerly wind that can blow for days on end, filling the air with fine, desert sand.

Gafsa Region

The Gafsa region occupies the transitional area between the wheat-growing and grazing lands of the Tell to the north and the Saharan regions to the south. It is one of the least-visited areas of Tunisia, mainly because it has steadily been turned into one giant mine since the French discovered that the hills west of Gafsa were made almost entirely of phosphate. The mines are the source of a large slice of the nation's export earnings – as well as being the source of the layer of fine, grey dust that coats everything in the region.

People have been living around here for 150,000-odd years. Prehistoric residents would have enjoyed a much wetter climate than today. As the climate became steadily drier, settlement began to concentrate around the oases of the region, particularly at Gafsa and at nearby El-Ksar and Lella.

GAFSA
☎ 06 • pop 60,000
Despite its long history, modern Gafsa is one of the least-inspiring towns in Tunisia. The

Highlights

- Trekking by camel through the dunes of the Grand Erg Oriental – the ultimate Saharan experience
- Exploring the mountain oasis villages of Chebika, Midès and Tamerza
- Admiring the intricate, traditional brick-work of Tozeur's old quarter
- Making early morning visits to the *ksour* (fortified granaries) around Tataouine
- Swimming in the hot springs at the oasis of Ksar Ghilane

town is, however, the hub of the region's transport network so there's a fair chance you'll pass through here sooner or later.

History
The oasis at Gafsa first grew to prominence as a staging post on the caravan route between the Sahara and the Tunisian coast. It became the town of Capsa, which was captured and destroyed by the Roman consul Marius in 107 BC as part of the campaign against the Numidian king Jugurtha (see the History section in the Facts about Tunisia chapter for more details). It went on to become an important Roman town – although a couple of pools and a few mosaics are the only surviving evidence.

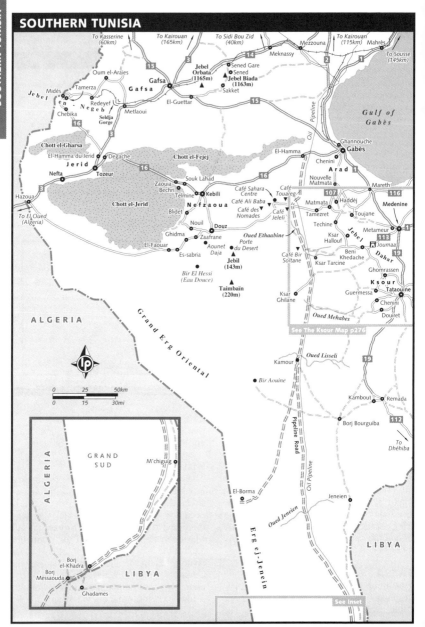

Information
There is a small tourist office (☎ 221 664) in the small, dusty square by the Roman Pools. It opens standard government hours.

The post office is on Ave Habib Bourguiba, 150m north of the kasbah. There are plenty of Taxiphone offices around the town centre. You can check email at the Publinet office at 19 Rue Khaddouma.

There are branches of all the major banks on the streets around Jardin du 7 Novembre in the centre of town.

Things to See & Do
The twin **Roman Pools** (Piscines Romaine) are easily located at the southern end of Ave Habib Bourguiba – turn left through the arch and then take the steps down to the right. There is little to see, but there is a pleasant cafe next to one of the pools, and it's easy to while away an hour or so watching the young boys jumping off the nearby roofs into the water.

Beside the entrance to the pools is a small **museum** which houses, among other things, a couple of large mosaics from ancient Capsa. It is worth a quick look; it's open from 8 am to noon and 2 to 5 pm Tuesday to Sunday. Admission is TD1.100.

Places to Stay – Budget
There are lots of cheap hotels in the area around the bus station but most of them are desperate dives. The only one worth giving any thought to is the *Hôtel de la République* (☎ 221 807), around the corner from the bus station on Rue Ali Belhaouane. Ask for a room away from the street if you want to sleep beyond 6 am. It charges TD5.500/7 for singles/doubles. Hot showers cost an extra TD1.500 per person.

Places to Stay – Mid-Range
The best hotel in town is the three star *Hôtel Maamoun* (☎ 226 701, fax 226 440), just south of the main market square on

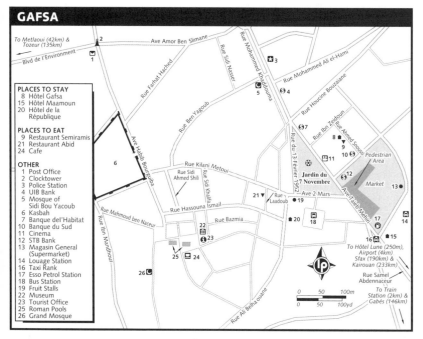

GAFSA

To Metlaoui (42km) &
Tozeur (135km)

Blvd de l'Environment

Ave Amor Ben Slimane

Rue Farhat Hached

Rue Sidi Nasser

Rue Mohammed Khaddouma

Rue Mohammed Ali el-Hami

Rue Houcine Bouzaiane

Rue Ben Yagoub

Rue Ahmed Snoussi

Rue Ibn Zeidoun

Ave Habib Bourguiba

Rue Kilani Metoui

Rue Sidi Ahmed Shili

Rue Sidi Khalifa

Rue du 13 Février 1952

Jardin du 7 Novembre

Pedestrian Area

Market

Rue Mahmoud ben Naceur

Rue Hassouna Ismail

Rue Laadou

Ave 2 Mars

Ave Tayeb Mehiri

Rue Bazmia

Rue Ibn Mandhour

Rue Ali Belhaouane

To Hôtel Lune (250m),
Airport (4km),
Sfax (190km) &
Kairouan (233km)

Rue Samel
Abdennaceur

To Train
Station (2km) &
Gabès (146km)

0   50   100m
0   50   100yd

PLACES TO STAY
8 Hôtel Gafsa
15 Hôtel Maamoun
20 Hôtel de la République

PLACES TO EAT
9 Restaurant Semiramis
21 Restaurant Abid
24 Cafe

OTHER
1 Post Office
2 Clocktower
3 Police Station
4 UIB Bank
5 Mosque of Sidi Bou Yacoub
6 Kasbah
7 Banque del'Habitat
10 Banque du Sud
11 Cinema
12 STB Bank
13 Magasin General (Supermarket)
14 Louage Station
16 Taxi Rank
17 Esso Petrol Station
18 Bus Station
19 Fruit Stalls
22 Museum
23 Tourist Office
25 Roman Pools
26 Grand Mosque

Ave Jamel Abdennaceur. Large, comfortable rooms with bathroom cost TD55/80 for singles/doubles. Full board, available for TD45/70, is not a bad idea given the lack of reasonable restaurants in town. The hotel also has a swimming pool.

Its main opposition is the *Hôtel Gafsa* (☎ *224 000, fax 224 747)*, nearby on Rue Ahmed Snoussi. It charges TD43/66 with breakfast. A third option is the *Hôtel Lune* (☎ *220 218, fax 220 980)*, a one-star place about 200m south of the Maamoun on Rue Jamel Abdennaceur. Singles/doubles with breakfast are TD26/36.

Places to Eat

There are lots of small restaurants around the bus station. The pick of them is the *Restaurant Abid*, one of three places on Rue Laadoub. It has an extensive menu of local dishes, including *chorba* (700 mills) and *kammounia* (TD2.200). The air-con is especially inviting on a hot day.

If you want to drink wine with your meal, try the *Restaurant Semiramis*, below the Hôtel Gafsa, or the restaurant at the *Hôtel Maamoun*.

The bar/restaurant at the *Hôtel Lune* doubles as the main nightspot in town, with entertainment every evening. It can get pretty lively on a Saturday night.

Getting There & Away

Air Tuninter flies to Tunis twice a week (TD42.700/85.200 one way/return). The airport is 4km north-east of town off the road to Kairouan, about TD2.500 by taxi.

Bus The bus station is in the centre of town. There are ticket windows for booking, and even boarding announcements.

SNTRI runs at least 10 buses a day to Tunis (TD14.170, 5½ hours) via Kairouan (TD8.580, three hours). One bus a day travels via Kasserine, stretching the trip to six hours and the fare to TD15. SNTRI also has a daily service to Sousse (TD10.900, four hours) at 11.20 am.

The buses run by the local company, Sotregafsa, are an amazing collection of wrecks that somehow keep running – minus

the odd panel etc. Six buses a day attempt the run to Tozeur (TD3.790) and Nefta (TD4.680, 2½ hours), with departures from 7.15 am to 6.15 pm. There are also six buses a day to Kasserine (TD4.200, 1¾ hours) and daily services to Gabés (TD5.590, 2½ hours) and Sfax (TD7.230, 3½ hours).

There are regular buses to Metlaoui (TD1.610, 45 minutes); three of these continue via Redeyef to Tamerza (TD3.650, 2½ hours).

Train The station is 3km to the south of town, about TD1.500 by taxi. The only departures are a night train to Tunis, and a morning service to Metlaoui – at 5 am.

Louage The louage station is near the Hôtel Maamoun. There are regular departures for Metlaoui (TD1.750) and Tozeur (TD3.950). Other possibilities include Tunis (TD14.500), Sfax (TD8.200) and Gabès (TD6.250). There are occasional direct services to Kasserine (TD4.600), otherwise change at Feriana.

AROUND GAFSA
Metlaoui & the Seldja Gorge
☎ 06

Metlaoui is a drab, dusty town 42km southwest of Gafsa that exists almost entirely because of phosphate mining. The only reason to come here is because it's the starting point for rides through the Seldja Gorge on the **Lezard Rouge** (Red Lizard) train.

Both are attractions in their own right. Built in 1910, the *Lezard Rouge* was once used by the bey of Tunis for journeys between Tunis and his summer palace at Hammam Lif. It was given a complete refit by the national railway company SNCFT in 1995, and put back to work transporting tourists in style.

The gorge features some weird and wonderful **rock formations** as it follows the path carved out by the Oued Seldja. The *oued* (riverbed) is dry most of the time, but there is enough moisture around to support small pockets of greenery.

The 1½-hour return journey through the gorge uses the line built in 1906 by the Gafsa

Phosphate and Railway Company to connect Metlaoui and Redeyef, 46km to the west. The *Lezard Rouge* leaves Metlaoui at 10.30 am on Monday, Tuesday, Thursday and Friday and at 11 am on Sunday. It's a good idea to contact the Bureau de Lezard Rouge in Metlaoui (☎ 241 469, fax 241 604) first to check that the train is running. The return fare is TD20.

Places to Stay Metlaoui has just one hotel, the incredibly shabby *Hôtel Ennacim (☎ 241 920)*, 1km or so from the centre of town on the road to Tozeur. You'd have to be desperate to fork out TD9/13 for a single/double. The place survives because it has the only bar in town – also somewhere to steer clear of.

Organised Tours Tour companies in Tozeur offer the trip on the Lezard Rouge as a half-day tour for TD35, which is good value when you consider the hassles involved in getting there and away by public transport.

Getting There & Away All buses between Gafsa and Tozeur pass through Metlaoui. There are also occasional buses from Metlaoui to Redeyef and Tamerza and there are regular louages to Gafsa and Tozeur.

Train services to Metlaoui are of little more than academic interest. There's one train a day from Tunis (8½ hours), which departs Tunis at 9.20 pm and deposits you on the streets of Metlaoui at 5.40 am. The only departure from Metlaoui is at 8 pm.

East of Gafsa

There are half a dozen **traditional Berber villages** east of Gafsa. They are spread along the mountain range that runs south of the Gafsa-Sfax road. Most of them are very difficult to get to unless you have a 4WD.

The most accessible of them is **Sened**. A reasonable dirt road leads up to it from the modern village of **Sened Gare**, an expanded train station 46km east of Gafsa on the road to Sfax. Old Sened is 10km to the south, spread along the banks of a river in the hills below Jebel Biada (1163m). Unlike the mud structures of the villages west of Gafsa, the houses at Sened are built of stone and are still in pretty good condition. People have

---

Compensation Dams

For centuries, the inhabitants of the mountain villages around Gafsa have scraped together a living from the arid landscape through a traditional dry-land farming technique known as compensation dams (*jesseur* in Arabic). The dams are rough stone walls built across watercourses and backfilled with soil, producing a pocket of land that gets the maximum benefit from any flow of water from seasonal rains. The water is held up by the wall of the dam, and soaks down through the soil before flowing on to the next dam further downstream.

The dams vary in size from tiny pockets of soil growing a patch of wheat to half-hectare plots with fruit trees and vegetable gardens. These dams are also a feature of the landscape in the hills around Matmata and in the ksour district further south.

---

lived around here for thousands of years – the escarpment behind the village is dotted with caves.

Depending on road conditions (check at Sened Gare), it may be possible to continue from Sened to **Sakket**, a smaller village 10km further south. The road improves again beyond Sakket and you can keep going south-west for another 24km to **El-Guettar**, a busy little oasis town 18km south-east of Gafsa on the road to Gabès.

The Jerid

The Jerid occupies the narrow strip of land between the region's two major salt lakes, the Chott el-Jerid and the Chott el-Gharsa. It has long been one of the most important agricultural districts in Tunisia. The oases at Degache, El-Hamma du Jerid, Nefta and Tozeur are famous for their high-quality dates. The harvest is in November, a good time to visit the area; the weather is cooling down and there's lots of activity. Many villagers work in other parts of the country but return home every year for the date harvest.

TOZEUR

☎ 06 • pop 22,000

Tozeur is one of the most popular travel destinations in Tunisia. It's an interesting old town with a great setting overlooking an enormous palmeraie (palm grove) on the northern edge of the Chott el-Jerid. Just getting there is half the attraction – the road from Kebili crosses the chott by causeway. Tozeur's main attractions are its enormous palmeraie; the labyrinthine old quarter, the Ouled el-Hadef; and the excellent Dar Charait Museum.

History

The oasis at Tozeur has been inhabited since Capsian (see under History in the Facts about Tunisia chapter for more information) times (from 8000 BC). It developed into the small town of Thuzuros, which became part of the Limes Tripolitanus – a defensive line which guarded the south-western boundaries of Roman Africa. This ancient town lay within the palmeraie, around the area now occupied by the district of Bled el-Hader. Tozeur's prosperity peaked during the age of the great trans-Saharan camel caravans, between the 14th and 19th centuries.

Orientation

Tozeur is fairly easy to find your way around because there are only three main streets: Ave Abdulkacem Chebbi, which runs along the edge of the palmeraie on the southern side of town; Ave Farhat Hached, which skirts the northern edge of town before becoming the Route de Nefta; and Ave Habib Bourguiba, which links the two.

Ave Habib Bourguiba is the main street. It is certainly the most attractive, with its carpet shops draped with brightly coloured Berber rugs. Ave Abdulkacem Chebbi has most of the accommodation. Its western extension is known as the Route Touristique, which is where you'll find the Dar Charait Museum and the hotels where tour groups stay.

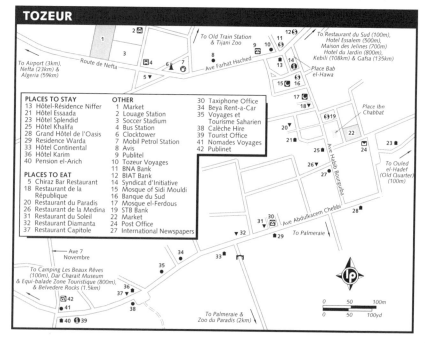

TOZEUR

PLACES TO STAY	OTHER	30 Taxiphone Office
13 Hôtel-Résidence Niffer	1 Market	34 Beya Rent-a-Car
21 Hôtel Essaada	2 Louage Station	35 Voyages et
23 Hôtel Splendid	3 Soccer Stadium	Tourisme Saharien
25 Hôtel Khalifa	4 Bus Station	38 Calèche Hire
28 Grand Hôtel de l'Oasis	6 Clocktower	39 Tourist Office
29 Residence Warda	7 Mobil Petrol Station	41 Nomades Voyages
33 Hôtel Continental	8 Avis	42 Publinet
36 Hôtel Karim	9 Publitel	
40 Pension el-Arich	10 Tozeur Voyages	
	11 BNA Bank	
PLACES TO EAT	12 BIAT Bank	
5 Chiraz Bar Restaurant	14 Syndicat d'Initiative	
18 Restaurant de la	15 Mosque of Sidi Mouldi	
République	16 Banque du Sud	
20 Restaurant du Paradis	17 Mosque el-Ferdous	
26 Restaurant de la Medina	19 STB Bank	
31 Restaurant du Soleil	22 Market	
32 Restaurant Diamanta	24 Post Office	
37 Restaurant Capitole	27 International Newspapers	

To Old Train Station & Tijani Zoo

To Airport (3km), Nefta (23km) & Algeria (59km)

Route de Nefta

Ave Farhat Hached

To Restaurant du Sud (100m), Hotel Essalem (500m), Maison des Jelines (700m), Hotel du Jardin (800m), Kebili (108km) & Gafsa (135km)

Place Bab el-Hawa

Place Ibn Chabbat

Ave Habib Bourguiba

To Ouled el-Hadef (Old Quarter) (100m)

Ave Abdulkacem Chebbi

To Palmeraie

To Palmeraie & Zoo du Paradis (2km)

Ave 7 Novembre

To Camping Les Beaux Rêves (100m), Dar Charait Museum & Equi-balade Zone Touristique (800m), & Belvedere Rocks (1.5km)

0   50   100m
0   50   100yd

Chott el-Jerid

The Chott el-Jerid is an immense salt lake covering an area of almost 5000 sq km, the bulk of it stretching away to the horizon south of the Kebili-Tozeur road. It's part of a system of salt lakes that stretches from the Gulf of Gabès to near the Algerian city of Biskra, 400km inland. The Chott el-Jerid is dry for the greater part of the year, when the surface becomes blistered and shimmers in the heat. The Kebili-Tozeur road crosses the northern reaches of the chott on a 2m-high causeway – it's a trip not to be missed. At times, the wind-driven salt piles up into great drifts by the roadside – creating the impression that you're driving through a snowfield. Mirages are a common occurrence, and if you've picked a sunny day to cross you're bound to see some stunning optical effects.

Your first glimpse of town will more than likely be Ave Farhat Hached. The roads into town from Gafsa and Kebili merge into Ave Farhat Hached at a roundabout at the northeastern edge of town. The bus and louage stations are on the other side of town, opposite each other in a couple of dusty lots north of Route de Nefta.

Information

Tourist Offices There is an ONTT office (☎ 454 088) at the western end of Ave Abdulkacem Chebbi. In July and August it's open from 7.30 am to 1.30 pm and 5 to 8 pm daily. For the rest of the year it's open from 8.30 am to 1 pm and 3 to 5.45 pm Monday to Thursday, and from 8.30 am to 1.30 pm Friday and Saturday. The staff are helpful and a couple of them speak English. There is also a *syndicat d'initiative* (☎ 462 034) on Place Bab el-Hawa in the centre of town.

Money You'll find branches of all the major Tunisian banks around the town centre. There are no ATMs.

Post & Communications The post office is on the main square by the market. There are telephone offices all over town, including an (allegedly) 24-hour Publitel office on Ave Farhat Hached opposite Place Bab el-Hawa.

Internet access is available at the Publinet office at 11 Ave de 7 Novembre. The office is open from 9 am to 10 pm daily. It charges TD3 per hour, with a TD1 minimum charge.

International Newspapers The kiosk on Ave Habib Bourguiba stocks many English-language and other international newspapers, usually two or three days after publication.

Dar Charait Museum

The museum is part of the burgeoning Dar Charait complex at the western end of Ave Abdulkacem Chebbi. It has a collection of pottery and antiques, as well as an art gallery, but the main feature is a series of replicas of scenes from Tunisian life, past and present. They include the bedroom of the last bey, a palace scene, a typical kitchen, a *hammam*, (bathhouse) wedding scenes and a Bedouin tent. The museum attendants, dressed as servants of the bey, set the tone. The museum is open from 8 am to midnight daily; admission is TD3, or TD1.500 for children under 10, plus TD1.500 to take photos.

The complex also includes attractions aimed at children. 'Dar Zaman – 3000 years of Tunisian History' features scenes from the nation's long history using some wonderfully tacky models. '1001 Nights' is a theme park full of cartoon characters. Both are open from 8 am to midnight daily, and both charge TD5 admission.

Palmeraie

Tozeur's palmeraie is the second largest in the country with around 200,000 palm trees spread over an area of more than 10 sq km. It is a classic example of tiered oasis agriculture. The system is watered by more than 200 springs that produce almost 60 million litres of water a day. It is distributed around the various holdings under a complex system devised by the mathematician Ibn Chabbat in the 13th century AD.

The best way to explore the palmeraie is on foot. Take the road that runs south off Ave Abdulkacem Chebbi next to the Hôtel

Continental and follow the signs to the Zoo du Paradis. After about 500m the road passes the old quarter of Bled el-Hader, thought to be the site of ancient Thuzuros. The mosque in the main square dates from the 11th century, while the minaret stands on the square base of an old Roman tower.

Further on is the village of Abbes, where the marabout (shrine) of Sidi Bou Lifa stands in the shade of an enormous jujube (Chinese date) tree. There are lots of paths leading off into the palmeraie along the irrigation canals. It's delightfully cool among all the vegetation – it must be at least 5°C cooler than in town.

If you want to see more of the oasis, you can hire bicycles from the Taxiphone office at the north-western end of the row of shops facing the Dar Charait Museum. Equipped with a bicycle, you can complete a loop through the palmeraie that emerges further west on Ave Abdulkacem Chebbi near the Grand Hôtel de l'Oasis.

Ouled el-Hadef

The town's delightful old quarter was built in the 14th century AD to house the El-Hadef clan, which had grown rich on the proceeds of the caravan trade. The area is a maze of narrow, covered alleys and small squares. It's famous for its amazing traditional brickwork, which uses protruding bricks to create intricate relief patterns. The style is found only here and in nearby Nefta.

The entrance to the Ouled el-Hadef is along the small road that runs east beyond the Hôtel Splendid. Follow the signs pointing to the small **Museum Archéologique et Traditionnel**, which occupies the old Kobba of Sidi Bou Aissa. It houses a small collection of local finds as well as costumes and displays on local culture. It's open from 8.30 am to noon and 3 to 5 pm Monday to Saturday; admission is TD1.100.

Belvedere Rocks

A sandy track running south off the Route Touristique near the Dar Charait Museum leads to a group of rocks known as the Belvedere Rocks. Steps have been cut into the highest rock, giving access to a spectacular view over the oasis and the chott. It's a

pleasant 20-minute walk; the best views are in the early morning and at sunset.

Zoos

For some reason, Tozeur has two zoos. The owners of the **Zoo du Paradis**, which is on the southern side of the palmeraie, must have a strange vision of paradise if the depressingly small cages are anything to go by. The star turn is a Coca Cola–drinking camel. Admission is TD1.

It looks good, however, when set against the **Tijani Zoo**, also known as the Zoo du Desert, which is north of town near the old train station. This place is worth a mention only as somewhere to avoid like the plague. It's a disgrace, complete with live scorpions housed in cigarette packets – 'just the thing for the mother-in-law' touts the attendant.

Ballooning

AerOasis (☎ 454 577) is a small French-run company that organises balloon rides at a range of locations around Tozeur. Flights are timed to catch either the sunrise or sunset and cost TD100 for one hour. They will travel as far as Douz in search of favourable conditions. The company's office at 138 Ave Abdulkacem Chebbi was closed at the time of research and was operating from the manager's home.

Horse Riding

Equi-Balade (☎/fax 452 613), based on the road leading out to the Belvedere Rocks, charges TD14 for a two-hour donkey ride, and TD20 for a two-hour horse ride.

Organised Tours

There are dozens of travel agencies around town, all offering very similar deals. They include half-day tours to the mountain oases of Chebika, Midès and Tamerza (TD30) and the Lezard Rouge (TD35) and evening outings to watch the sunset in the desert near Nefta (TD15).

Agencies include Tozeur Voyages (☎ 452 203), 58 Ave Farhat Hached; Voyages et Tourisme Saharien (☎ 460 300), Ave Abdulkacem Chebbi 128, and Nomades (☎ 453 423), Ave Abdulkacem Chebbi 196.

Places to Stay – Budget

Camping *Camping Les Beaux Rêves* (☎ *453 331, fax 454 208*), 250m west of the tourist office on Ave Abdulkacem Chebbi, is a good, shady site that backs onto the palmeraie. It charges TD4 per person to camp or to sleep in one of the communal nomad-style tents or palm-thatch huts. Hot showers are TD1.

Hostels Tozeur's *Maison des Jeunes* (☎ *452 335*) is only for the dedicated. It's opposite the police station on the Gafsa road, about 800m from the town centre. A bed in a dorm costs TD4.

Hotels The cheapest hotel in town is the grubby *Hôtel Essaada (no telephone)*, which is on a small street that runs behind the carpet shops on Ave Habib Bourguiba. It charges TD4.500 per person, plus an extra 500 mills for a cold shower. The nearby *Hôtel Khalifa* (☎ *454 858*), which is on the western side of the square at the middle of Ave Habib Bourguiba, isn't much better at TD7 per person, including breakfast. Hot showers are TD1. The only rooms with windows overlook busy Ave Habib Bourguiba.

Inconvenient, but much better than either of these, is the *Hôtel Essalem* (☎ *462 881*), 150m past the roundabout at the western end of Ave Farhat Hached. It's quiet and friendly and charges TD5 per person for rooms with outside bathroom and TD6 per person with private shower.

Places to Stay – Mid-Range

There are several good places on Ave Abdulkacem Chebbi. The *Residence Warda* (☎ *452 597, fax 452 744, 29 Ave Abdulkacem Chebbi*) has long been a favourite with travellers. It has clean singles/doubles with shared bathroom for TD12/18. Rates include breakfast – as they do for all places in this category.

Another good choice is the *Hôtel Karim* (☎/*fax 454 574, 150 Ave Abdulkacem Chebbi*), opposite the *calèche* (horse-drawn carriage) waiting area. It's a friendly, well-run place offering large, clean singles/doubles with bathroom for TD11/16.

The *Pension el-Arich* (☎ *462 644, fax 461 544,* e *arich@xoommail.com, 93 Ave Abdulkacem Chebbi*) is brand new and has lots of fancy brickwork. It has large, airy rooms for TD14/25 and three-room family apartments with TV for TD70.

The *Hôtel-Résidence Niffer* (☎ *460 610, fax 461 900, Place Bab el-Hawa*) is another new place. Rooms with private bathroom are TD13/20.

The best place in this category is the two star *Hôtel du Jardin* (☎ *454 196, fax 454 199*), about 1km east of town on Ave de l'Environment – the road to Kebili. It's a quiet place set among gardens with rooms for TD25/40.

Places to Stay – Top End

Tozeur has a stack of hotels claiming three stars or more – 25 at the last count, most of them out at the *zone touristique* beyond the Dar Charait Museum. They are used almost exclusively by tour groups, and aren't much fun for individuals – especially since you can be sure that the tour groups are paying a fraction of the official rates of around TD60/90 for singles/doubles.

The cheapest option is the *Hôtel Continental* (☎ *461 411, fax 452 109, 79 Ave Abdulkacem Chebbi*), an older three-star place set back from the road in shady gardens. There's a swimming pool next to the palmeraie; the rooms are looking a bit shabby these days. Singles/doubles are TD35.500/55. Full board is good value at TD39/62.

The *Grand Hôtel de l'Oasis* (☎ *452 300, fax 452 153, 1 Ave Abdulkacem Chebbi*), at the junction with Ave Habib Bourguiba, looks quite a sight at night with its illuminated, traditional-style brick facade. Most of the customers are small tour groups, who are probably getting a better deal than the listed rates of TD60/88 for singles/doubles with breakfast.

If money is no object, you can lash out around TD200 a night for a double room at the new *Palm Beach Palace* (☎ *453 211, fax 453 911*) or the *Dar Charait* (☎ *454 888, fax 454 472,* e *darcherait@tryp.tourism.tn*), which adjoins the museum. Both offer the full five-star treatment.

Places to Eat

Tozeur is better served by cheap restaurants than most places. The tiny *Restaurant du Paradis*, just a couple of doors along from the Hôtel Essaada, is a quaint place run by two very polite older guys, both sporting the traditional red *chechia* hat. The prices are old-fashioned, too, with chorba for 800 mills and couscous with sauce for TD2. The tables outside are a pleasant place to sit on a warm evening.

Ave Abdulkacem Chebbi has lots of restaurants as well as hotels. The pick of them is the *Restaurant du Soleil (58 Ave Abdulkacem Chebbi)*, opposite the Residence Warda. It's a bit smarter than the others and gets the lion's share of the tourist business as a result. It's one of the few restaurants in the country to acknowledge the existence of vegetarians, even if it is just one dish on an extensive menu that boasts some 30 items. Main dishes start at TD2.

Other good places are the *Restaurant Capitole (152 Ave Abdulkacem Chebbi)*, and the *Restaurant de la République (108 Ave Habib Bourguiba)*, tucked away in an arcade next to the Mosque el-Ferdous.

If you want a drink with your meal, the options start with the *Chiraz Bar Restaurant* at the western end of Ave Farhat Hached. It's a lively no-nonsense bar that also offers basic grilled meals like chicken and chips with salad for TD2.800.

For a splurge, head out to the *Restaurant Les Andalous* at the Hôtel du Jardin, on the road to Kebili. It's rated as the best restaurant in the south. Allow TD15 per person plus wine.

Getting There & Away

Air Tuninter runs five flights a week to Tunis (TD49.200/93.200 one way/return). The airport handles a growing number of international flights, mainly charters from Europe. Tunis Air also operates scheduled services from Tozeur to Brussels, Milan, Paris and Zurich.

The Tunis Air (☎ 450 038) office is out towards the airport along the Nefta road, opposite the Hertz car-rental agency.

Bus There are five air-con SNTRI buses a day to Tunis (TD17.420, seven hours), travelling via Gafsa (TD4.050, 1½ hours) and Kairouan (TD11.830, 4½ hours). SNTRI also has a service to Sousse (TD14.200, 5¾ hours) at 9.50 am. It's advisable to buy tickets the day before from the SNTRI office at the bus station.

Regional services include six buses a day to Gafsa (TD3.790) and six to Nefta (940 mills), and two to Tamerza (TD2.850). There are also daily buses to Douz (TD4.540, three hours) at 2.30 pm and to Gabès (TD7.660, 4½ hours) at 3.30 pm. The 9.30 am bus to Nefta goes all the way to Hazoua on the Algerian border.

Train Tozeur has a train station to the north of town but passenger services have long since been discontinued. Trains from Sfax now run only as far as Metlaoui, 50km to the north (see Getting There & Away under Metlaoui in the Around Gafsa section).

Louage The louage station has regular departures to Nefta (TD1), Gafsa (TD3.950) and Kebili (TD4.200). There are also occasional louages to Tunis (TD17.150), Tamerza (TD3) and Gabès (TD9.300).

Getting Around

To/From the Airport Tozeur's taxis don't have meters, which means that the fare depends on your bargaining skills – and how **wealthy** you look. Most charge around TD5 for the 4km trip, although some have been to ask as much as TD10 late at night.

Car There are half a dozen car-rental outlets in town. You'll find the best deals at local agencies like Lamia Rent a Car (☎ 462 433), opposite the Hôtel Palmaraie in the zone touristique, and Beya Rent a Car (☎ 462 211), Ave Abdulkacem Chebbi 146. Beya also has a range of quad (all terrain) excursions priced from TD25 for 1½ hours up to TD45 for half a day.

Other agencies include Avis (☎ 453 547), Ave Farhat Hached 96 and Hertz (☎ 450 214), out towards the airport on Route de Nefta.

Bicycle Bicycles can be hired from the Taxiphone office opposite the Dar Charait complex at the zone touristique. Rates start at TD2 per hour.

Calèche Calèches can be hired from opposite the Hôtel Karim for TD10 per hour.

AROUND TOZEUR
Mountain Oases
☎ 06

The beautiful old Berber villages of Tamerza, Midès and Chebika are situated close to the Algerian border in the rugged Jebel en-Negeb ranges, about 60km north of Tozeur. The three have existed since ancient times and were part of the Limes Tripolitanus defensive line developed by the Romans to keep out marauding Saharan tribes.

All three villages were abandoned after the region was hit by 22 days of torrential rain in 1969. The freak rains turned the earthen houses into mud, and the villagers moved to new settlements that were hastily constructed nearby. The original villages are now 'ghost villages', and they are fascinating places to explore.

Tamerza Nestled in a small valley in the heart of the mountains 75km north of Tozeur, Tamerza is the largest of the villages and the only one accessible by public transport. The shell of the old walled town is about 1km east of new Tamerza, on the southern bank of the Oued Horchane. Tamerza's water comes not from the *oued* (river) but from a spring that rises in the hills south of old Tamerza. The spring supplies water to the old town and then to an extensive palmeraie, which locals claim produces the finest dates in Tunisia. From this main palmeraie, the water flows on to a smaller palmeraie at new Tamerza. There are a couple of small waterfalls along the way. The new town is a characterless modern sprawl. There's a bank and a few small shops.

Midès Midès, 6km north of Tamerza, boasts the most stunning setting of all, perched high above a dramatic gorge that was previously employed strategically as the town's south-

The dates produced near the old walled town east of Tamerza are said to be Tunisia's best.

ern fortification. Midès is a few kilometres north-west of Tamerza as the crow flies, but it's 11km by road. The town is only 1km from the Algerian border. The gorge has been used a setting for many movies, including *The English Patient.*

Chebika This village, 16km south of Tamerza, is on the southern edge of the mountain range and overlooks the Chott el-Gharsa. The palmeraie is visible for miles – a great blob of green set against the barren mountains. Old Chebika is up the hill behind the palmeraie, next to a small spring-fed stream. You can trace the waters back upstream through a pretty little gorge.

Organised Tours There are plenty of tour companies in Tozeur offering day trips that call at all three villages, as well as pausing at a small waterfall between Chebika and Tamerza. They all charge about TD30 per person. See the previous Tozeur section for information about tour companies.

Places to Stay & Eat Tamerza has two hotels. The *Hôtel Les Cascades* (☎ 485 322) has a great setting, at the edge of the palmeraie, next to a small waterfall. However, rooms are uninviting palm-thatched boxes with bare concrete floors, costing over the odds at TD20/25 for singles/doubles with breakfast. The place is signposted in the middle of new Tamerza.

The well-heeled will probably prefer the four-star luxury of the *Hôtel Tamerza Palace* (☎ 453 722, fax 453 845), an unusual example of a big hotel attempting to blend in with its surroundings. B&B here will set you back TD89/130. It's worth visiting the hotel to take in the views of old Tamerza from the swimming pool terrace.

Tamerza has several restaurants, most of which cater to tour groups. The tiny *Restaurant de Tamerza*, on the right on the road leading down to the Hôtel Les Cascades, turns out a filling bowl of couscous with vegetables for TD2.800. The restaurant at the *Hôtel Tamerza Palace* does a three-course set menu for TD12.

There are two places at Midès calling themselves *camping grounds*. Neither have any set fees or facilities – just a patch of ground on which to pitch a tent. You need to take your own food, or you can buy meals from local families.

Getting There & Away Tamerza is the only place with public transport. There are at least two SNTRI buses a day from Tunis (TD18.360, eight hours), three buses a day from Gafsa (TD3.650, 2½ hours) and two from Tozeur (TD2.850, 1½ hours).

NEFTA
☎ 06 • pop 18,000
The oasis of Nefta, 23km west of Tozeur, is the last town before the Algerian border at Hazoua. In many ways, it is a smaller version of Tozeur. The architecture is similar, with some very good examples of the highly distinctive ornamental brickwork in the old sections of town. The oasis is of equal size and importance.

Nefta is also the home of Sufism in Tunisia (see the boxed text 'Sufism' in the Religion section in the Facts about Tunisia chapter) and there are a couple of important religious sites here, including the Zaouia of Sidi Brahim and the Mosque of Sidi M'Khareg.

Orientation
Nefta's main street, Ave Habib Bourguiba, is also the main Tozeur-Algeria road. The main feature of the town is the *corbeille* (literally 'basket'), a huge gully north of Ave Habib Bourguiba that cuts the town in two and funnels into the palmeraie proper on the southern side of town. The Route de

la Corbeille does a loop around the corbeille off Ave Habib Bourguiba, providing access to a couple of flash hotels that overlook the corbeille from the north.

Most of the tourist hotels are on the edge of the palmeraie at the western (Algerian) side of town.

Information
The small syndicat d'initiative office (☎ 430 236) is on the right as you come into town from Tozeur, just before the ring-road junction. The guys who staff the office are quite helpful, but are there primarily to promote their services as guides. One of them speaks some English.

The bus station is opposite the syndicat d'initiative, while louages hang around outside the restaurants about 100m further west on Ave Habib Bourguiba. The post office is another 250m along on the left, where the road descends to cross the corbeille. There is a branch of the UIB bank at the beginning of Route de la Corbeille, near the tourist office.

La Corbeille
The town's most obvious attraction is the corbeille, the deep palm-filled gully that takes up much of the northern part of town. It measures almost 1km across at its widest point and is about 40m deep, which makes it an impressively large hole. The best views are from the north-western side. Here you can take in the setting over a coffee at the Café de la Corbeille or Café Maure el-Khazen, which both have terraces overlooking the corbeille.

Below the cafes is a large spring-fed concrete pool, a popular swimming spot with local kids. The corbeille contracts to a narrow gorge which leads to the main **palmeraie** on the southern side of town. It is every bit as fascinating as the one at Tozeur.

El-Bayadha
The cafes at the north-western edge of the corbeille are a good starting point for a walk through the old El-Bayadha neighbourhood, which is south-west of the corbeille. Many of the houses here were badly damaged by heavy rain in early 1990, which also caused

NEFTA

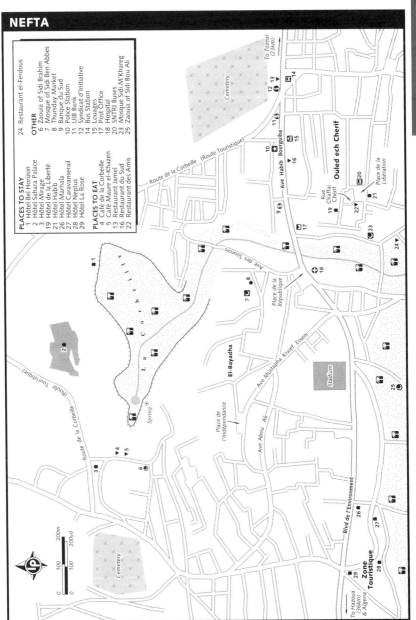

PLACES TO STAY
1 Hôtel Bel Horizon
2 Hôtel Sahara Palace
3 Hôtel Mirage
19 Hôtel de la Liberté
21 Hôtel Habib
26 Hôtel Marhala
27 Hôtel Caravanserail
28 Hôtel Neptus
29 Hôtel La Rose

PLACES TO EAT
4 Café de la Corbeille
5 Café Maure el-Khazen
13 Restaurant Jamel
16 Restaurant du Sud
22 Restaurant des Amis
24 Restaurant el-Ferdous

OTHER
6 Zaouia of Sidi Brahim
7 Mosque of Sidi Ben Abbes
8 Thursday Market
9 Banque du Sud
10 Police Station
11 UIB Bank
12 Syndicat d'Initiative
14 Bus Station
15 Louages
17 Post Office
18 Hospital
20 SNTRI Buses
23 Mosque Sidi M'Khareg
25 Zaouia of Sidi Bou Ali

several landslides around the edge of the corbeille. Just about every other building in El-Bayadha seems to have some level of religious significance. The most important of them is the **Zaouia of Sidi Brahim**, where the Sufi saint and some of his followers are buried. The *zaouia* (complex surrounding the tomb of a saint) is 100m south of the cafes, on the right. The open space opposite the Mosque of Sidi Ben Abbes, off Ave des Sources at the eastern edge of El-Bayadha, stages Nefta's Thursday market.

Ouled ech Cherif

The best preserved of Nefta's old districts is the Ouled ech Cherif, which occupies the south-eastern quarter of town below Ave Habib Bourguiba. To get there, follow the signs to the Hôtel Habib on the main road leading south next to the bus station. The hotel is on Place de la Libération, at the heart of the Ouled ech Cherif. The layout is very similar to the Ouled el-Hadef in Tozeur, with winding, vaulted alleyways and some stunning examples of traditional brick designs. Check out the street that runs west off Place de la Libération to the palmeraie, emerging next to the quarter's principal mosque, the Mosque of Sidi M'Khareg.

Organised Tours

The guides at the syndicat d'initiative offer a range of services. They charge TD15 for a two-hour tour of the town's highlights, or TD40 for a full day in and around Nefta. They say they know a spot between Nefta and the Algerian border where they guarantee you will see a mirage on a sunny day. The fees are only for their time – they don't provide transport, although they can organise it for you.

They can also organise **camel rides** in the surrounding desert. The most popular outing is a four-hour ride (TD24), leaving in the late afternoon so that you are out in the desert for the sunset.

Places to Stay – Budget

Nefta's cheapest hotel is the friendly *Hôtel de la Liberté* (☎ 430 643), off Place de la Libération among the winding alleys of the Ouled ech Cherif. Take Rue Chaffai Cherif, next to Restaurant des Amis on the north-western corner of the square, and look for the sign. It's not too hard to find, but if you need to ask directions locals call it the Hôtel Mahmoud after the former owner. It's now run by his daughter Khadouj. What awaits is a basic old hotel built around a vine-filled central courtyard. Beds are TD3.500 per person, with free cold shower.

The *Hôtel Habib* (☎ 430 497), on Place de la Libération, seems to have spent its decoration budget on signs directing people to the hotel. The rooms are gloomy, but the staff are friendly and the rates of TD7 per person include breakfast and hot showers.

Places to Stay – Mid-Range

The shabby one star *Hôtel Mirage* (☎ 430 622, fax 430 644), on the north-western side of the corbeille, has re-opened after being closed for years for 'renovation' – of which there is no evidence. The rates are TD17/26 for singles/doubles with breakfast.

Places to Stay – Top End

There is a small cluster of big hotels in the small zone touristique on the south-western side of town. All have private swimming pools, and prices include breakfast.

The latest addition is the two star *Hôtel Marhala* (☎ 430 027, fax 430 511), which has clean and comfortable singles/doubles for TD39/56. Sadly, the old *Hôtel Marhala*, which occupied a converted brick factory next door, has closed following the opening of the new model.

The Marhala is surrounded by a band of three-star hotels built on the edge of the palmeraie: The *Hôtel Caravanserail* (☎ 430 355, fax 430 344) leads the way on the price scale with singles/doubles for TD78/92 with breakfast. The nearby *Hôtel Neptus* (☎ 430 441, fax 430 647) and *Hôtel La Rose* (☎ 430 696/7, fax 430 385) aren't far behind.

The best hotel in town is the five star *Hôtel Sahara Palace* (☎ 432 005, fax 431 444) on the north-western side of the corbeille. It charges a whopping TD135/200. Check out its Web site (www.sangho.com). The prices are more modest at the three star *Hôtel Bel*

Horizon (☎ 430 328, fax 430 500), north of the corbeille TD50/64.

Places to Eat

The sum total of Nefta's eateries is a few basic restaurants on Ave Habib Bourguiba near the bus station and around Place de la Libération, plus the hotel restaurants. The best of the cheapies is the ***Restaurant Jamel***, next to the tourist office. It does a delicious chorba (TD1) and a range of daily specials like spicy beans with chicken (TD2). Next to the louage station, the ***Restaurant du Sud*** has couscous for TD2.

The ***Restaurant el-Ferdous*** is a popular bar/restaurant in the palmeraie. It's a quiet spot to have lunch, but it gets rowdy in the evenings.

Getting There & Away

Bus SNTRI has buses to Tunis (TD18.220, 7½ hours) at 10.30 am and midnight. The SNTRI office is on Place de la Libération, opposite the Hôtel Habib.

Regional services operate from the bus station on the southern side of Ave Habib Bourguiba on the way into town from Tozeur. There are six buses to Tozeur (940 mills, 30 minutes) and six a day to Gafsa (TD4.680, three hours).

There is also a daily bus to the Algerian border at Hazoua (TD1.400, one hour), 36km south-west of Nefta. Before the troubles in Algeria, this was a popular crossing – just 80km from the fascinating desert town of El-Oued by good bitumen road. There is 4km of neutral territory between the Tunisian and Algerian border crossings.

Louage Louages leave from outside the restaurants on Ave Habib Bourguiba. You won't have to wait long for a ride to Tozeur (TD1). There are also occasional departures for Hazoua (TD1.500).

The Nefzaoua

The Nefzaoua covers the area stretching east from the Chott el-Jerid to the edge of the Jebel Dahar ranges. It's bounded by the Chott el-Fejej in the north and the sands of the Grand Erg Oriental to the south.

Like the Jerid, the Nefzaoua is an important date-growing area, with a string of oases running south from Kebili around the edge of the Chott el-Jerid. The palmeraie at Douz is the largest in Tunisia with around 400,000 date palms. The settlements of the Nefzaoua, like those of the Jerid, once formed part of the Roman defensive system, the Limes Tripolitanus. The main Roman settlement was Turris Tamelleni (modern Telmine), a few kilometres west of Kebili.

Located at the edge of the Roman world, it became one of the first regions to be reclaimed by Berber nomads when the empire began to wane. Tribes began to move in from the south at the end of the 4th century AD, bringing with them the first camels to be seen in Tunisia. By the end of the 5th century, the area was under the control of the Nefzaoua confederation – a loose grouping of half a dozen Berber tribes. The descendants of these tribes continue to live a seminomadic existence in the south around Douz.

KEBILI
☎ 05 • pop 10,000

Kebili is the main town and administrative centre of the Nezaoua region. Few travellers pause any longer than it takes to catch the next bus or louage, which is a shame because there is more to the town than the dusty modern town centre.

Orientation & Information

The local authorities have been too busy with other projects to put up any street signs. The Gabès-Tozeur road crosses the northern half of town. Ave Habib Bourguiba runs south to Douz from the major junction on the eastern side of town. The main street, Ave 7 Novembre, runs parallel about 500m further west.

Facilities include a post office and bank (open for changing money from 9 am to noon only). Both are around the junction of the Gabès-Tozeur road and Ave Habib Bourguiba.

Ancienne Kebili

The main reason to stick around is the abandoned town of Ancienne Kebili, which crumbles away in obscurity in the palmaraie to the south of the modern town centre. To get there, head south towards Douz on Ave Bourguiba for about 10 minutes until you reach the **hot springs** on the left. The springs feed a hammam and pool complex.

Opposite the springs is a signposted track that winds through the palmaraie to the old town. The houses may be collapsing, but the gardens are neatly tended. The **mosque** is still in use, and an ancient **koubba** (shrine) has been given a fresh coat of blue paint.

Places to Stay

Few budget travellers stay overnight; the options are much better in nearby Douz. If you do get stuck, try the *Hôtel Ben Said* (☎ 491 573), 400m south of the Gabès-Tozeur road on Ave Habib Bourguiba. Clean singles/doubles with shared bathroom are TD5/8.

Stepping up a few notches, the *Hôtel Kitam* (☎ 491 338, fax 491 076) is a reasonable, modern two-star hotel on the road into town from Gabès. It has singles/doubles for TD34.500/39. A more interesting option is the *Hôtel Fort des Autruches* (☎ 490 233, fax 490 933), which occupies an old fort on the south-eastern side of town (signposted off the road to Douz). It's a pleasant spot with a swimming pool and terrace and rooms for TD37.500/42.

You'll see signs in town directing people to the *Hôtel Les Dunes de Nefzaoua* (☎ 480 675, fax 480 653), 22km west of town near the village of Bechri – which means that it's only really an option if you have your own transport. The turn-off south to Bechri is clearly signposted in the small village of Zaouia, which is the last village before the causeway on the Kebili-Tozeur road. You'll come to the hotel after about 2km. It has a fantastic setting on the edge of the Chott el-Jerid and an inviting swimming pool, but the calm is shattered at dusk when 4WD safari groups descend. At least you get to enjoy the displays of folk music and dancing that are put on for their benefit. Rooms are TD54/78, with breakfast.

Places to Eat

The *Restaurant Kheireddine*, between the louage stations, is the best bet for a cheap meal. You'll find briqs from 600 mills, chorba for TD1 and main courses from TD1.500.

Getting There & Away

Bus The bus station is no more than an office on the main street, near the junction with the Gabès-Tozeur road. There are frequent buses to Douz (TD1.130, 30 minutes) as well as regular departures for Tozeur and Gabès.

The SNTRI office, usually closed, is 100m away on the opposite side of the dusty square. There are three buses a day to Tunis (TD19.870, 8½ hours).

Louage Red-striped louages to Gabès (TD5) and Tozeur (TD4.200) leave from the street running between Place de l'Independence and Ave Habib Bourguiba. Blue-striped louages to Douz (TD1.400) leave from one street further south.

DOUZ

☎ 05 • pop 12,000

The town of Douz, 28km south of Kebili, touts itself as the gateway to the Sahara. It lies at the north-eastern edge of the Grand Erg Oriental, and you certainly get the feeling that you're driving out into the desert as you head south from Kebili. A long dune flanks the road, held back by a fence of palm fronds.

Douz remains fairly laid-back in spite of the huge numbers of 4WDs that pass through town. Most of them head straight for the hotels of the small zone touristique, 3.5km south-west of town, facing the desert on the edge of the enormous palmeraie. The town centre is probably the most backpacker friendly place in Tunisia, with some great budget accommodation and plenty of small restaurants.

The town's main attraction is the colourful Thursday market in the old souq. Douz also makes a good base from which to organise camel trekking (see the boxed text 'Camel Trekking' later in this section) and other desert activities.

Locals belong to the Marazig tribe, who all claim to be descended from one of two

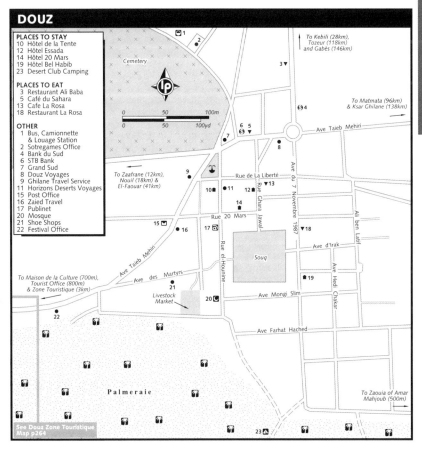

DOUZ

PLACES TO STAY
10 Hôtel de la Tente
12 Hôtel Essada
14 Hôtel 20 Mars
19 Hôtel Bel Habib
23 Desert Club Camping

PLACES TO EAT
3 Restaurant Ali Baba
5 Café du Sahara
13 Cafe La Rosa
18 Restaurant La Rosa

OTHER
1 Bus, Camionnette & Louage Station
2 Sotregames Office
4 Bank du Sud
6 STB Bank
7 Grand Sud
8 Douz Voyages
9 Ghilane Travel Service
11 Horizons Deserts Voyages
15 Post Office
16 Zaied Travel
17 Publinet
20 Mosque
21 Shoe Shops
22 Festival Office

Cemetery

To Kebili (28km), Tozeur (118km) and Gabès (146km)

To Matmata (96km) & Ksar Ghilane (138km)

Ave Taieb Mehiri

To Zaafrane (12km), Nouil (18km) & El-Faouar (41km)

Rue de la Liberté

Rue Ghara Jawal

Rue 20 Mars

Ave du 7 Novembre 1987

Ali ben Latif

Ave d'Irak

Souq

Ave Taieb Mehiri

Ave des Martyrs

Rue el-Hounine

Ave Hedi Chaker

Ave Mongi Slim

To Maison de la Culture (700m), Tourist Office (800m) & Zone Touristique (3km)

Livestock Market

Ave Farhat Hached

Palmeraie

To Zaouia of Amar Mahjoub (500m)

See Douz Zone Touristique Map p264

marabouts (holy men): Ahmed el-Gouth, whose shrine stands at the north-western edge of the cemetery, and Amar Mahjoub, whose shrine is next to the Great Mosque, on the south-eastern side of town.

Orientation & Information

Douz isn't big enough to get lost in. The town centre is laid out in a rough grid around the souq. Ave des Martyrs leads west from the town centre to Place des Martyrs, which is where you'll find both an ONTT tourist office (☎ 470 351) and a syndicat d'initiative (☎ 470 341), two doors

away. Roads lead south from here through the palmeraie to Place du Festival and to the zone touristique.

All important services are found around the town centre, including a branch of the STB bank on Ave Taieb Mehiri and the Banque du Sud by the roundabout on the road into town from Kebili. The post office is on Ave Taieb Mehiri, just west of the town centre.

Internet access is available at the Publinet office on Rue el-Hounine. It's often closed, although the advertised hours are from 8 am to 8 pm daily.

Musèe du Sahara

This small folk museum is on the western side of Place des Martyrs. As well as a good collection of regional costumes and a mock-up of a nomad tent, there is an interesting section explaining the tattoos worn by local women. There is also information on camel husbandry and a section on desert plants. The museum is open in summer (June to August) from 7 to 11 am and 4 to 7 pm, and from 9.30 am to 4.30 pm for the rest of the year. It's closed on Monday. Admission is TD1.100.

Palmeraie

The palmeraie is deceptively large – indeed, it is the largest of all the Tunisian desert oases, with more than 400,000 palm trees. It is a wonderfully productive place, turning out a remarkable assortment of fruit and vegetables – as well as prized *deglat ennour* dates.

The best way to explore it is to walk out along one of the two roads leading south through the palmaraie from the western end of Ave des Martyrs. The roads link up at the zone touristique.

Desert Activities

The desert south of the zone touristique has been turned into something of a desert playground for tour groups.

The action centres around the much-touted **great dune**; its convenient location opposite the tourist hotels, combined with the absence of any other large dunes, has led some to suggest that this phenomenon might not be entirely natural. It is, however, a good spot for those all-important 'been there, done that' Sahara photos. There are countless people offering short **camel rides**. If that's too sedate, you can also rent **quad bikes** for TD25 per hour.

The small **fort** to the east of the dune was a film set, built for Alberto Negrin's 1998 production, *Le Ciel sous le Desert*. Admission is TD1.

Desert Biking

Grand Sud (☎ 471 777, fax 470 269, [e] sahara king@voila.fr), on Ave Taieb Mehiri, specialises in off-road cycling tours. It charges TD600 for a seven-day tour starting in Tozeur. The tour crosses the Chott el-Jerid to Douz and continues to Matmata.

Organised Tours

There are nine tour operators in town, all offering a very similar range of desert excursions for about TD45 per day. Some include Douz Voyages (☎ 495 315), 3 Ave Taieb Mehiri; Ghilane Travel Services

---

The Dependable Date

Until recent times, life in the Sahara was almost entirely dependent on one remarkable plant, the date palm *(phoenix dactylifera)*.

So important was the plant to desert life that the traditional way of assessing the size of an oasis was in terms of the number of palm trees it could support, rather than the number of people. The largest in Tunisia is Douz, with almost 400,000 palms.

As well as producing dates for food, its trunk can be used for building, or hollowed out to channel water. It's branches are used for roofs and fences, while the tough leaf fibres can be woven into mats and ropes and the woody fruiting stems make good brooms. Nothing goes to waste. Even the date pits are used: in the old days, they were roasted and ground to make an ersatz coffee; today they are ground up as animal fodder.

The very presence of the date palm is an indicator of the desert's most precious resource, water.

The date palm is very specific in its climatic requirements. There is an old Arab saying that it likes 'its feet in heaven and its head in hell', a reference to the tree's need for very high summer temperatures and lots of water – about 500L a day in summer.

There are more than 100 varieties of date. The finest is known as the *deglat ennour* (finger of light), so called because the flesh is almost translucent. It constitutes 50% of all plantings in Tunisia.

Camel Trekking

Most people come to Douz to go camel trekking. It isn't difficult to organise: Camel trekking is big business around here.

The possibilities start with one-hour rides, available any time at the zone touristique. You'll probably have to bargain hard to get the official rate of TD2.500 per hour – unless you arrange your ride through the ONTT tourist office. If you've never been on a camel before, it's a good idea to try a short ride before signing up for a longer trek.

Camel riding is not for everyone, and many people decide that one hour is enough!

Overnight treks are also equally easy to organise, and longer treks require only 24-hours notice – sometimes less. The biggest problem is choosing between the range of treks on offer. The tourist office advises travellers to stay clear of the many unlicensed guides who tout their services around town, pointing out that they are uninsured and unaccountable if problems arise. It recommends using one of the tour companies in town, listed under the previous Organised Tours section.

In practice, many independent travellers end up using unlicensed guides operating through one of the budget hotels in town. Most charge TD30 for overnight treks. These treks leave Douz in the afternoon, and involve about four hours riding before pitching camp at sunset. Guides prepare an evening meal of damper bread, cooked in the ashes of a camp fire, and stew, before bedding down beneath the stars (blankets provided on request). An early breakfast of damper and jam is then followed by the return ride, arriving in Douz mid-morning.

The main complaint about these treks is that the desert immediately south of Douz isn't very interesting. The real desert, the Grand Erg Oriental, is a long way further south (see The Sahara section later in this chapter for details). Tour companies use 4WDs to transfer clients from Douz to trekking bases in the desert. Some of these bases are quite sophisticated, with accommodation on camp beds in large Berber-style goat-hair tents, kitchens and pit toilets. Overnight treks cost from TD45, with longer treks for TD45 per day.

You'll need to be properly equipped to go trekking. Essential items include a sensible hat which you can secure to your head, sunscreen and sunglasses (preferably wraparound). Sunglasses keep the sand as well as the sun out of your eyes. Long trousers are a good idea to prevent your legs getting chafed. Cameras and watches should be kept wrapped in a plastic bag to protect them from the very fine Saharan sand that gets into everything.

(☎ 470 692, fax 470 682, e gts@planet.tn), 38 Ave Taieb Mehiri; Horizons Deserts Voyages (☎/fax 470 088, e h.desert@planet.tn), 8 Rue el-Hounine; and Zaied Travel (☎ 491 918, fax 470 584), Ave Taieb Mehiri.

Special Events

The main event on the Douz calendar is the **Sahara Festival**, which is normally held at the beginning of November – although the dates can be hard to track down. It's one of the few genuine festivals in the country, and draws large numbers of domestic tourists as well as foreign visitors.

Most of the action takes place around the Place du Festival, where a special grandstand has been erected to handle the big crowds who come to watch the displays of traditional desert sports, such as camel racing and hunting with Saluki dogs – an animal built like a greyhound.

The festivities also include colourful parades and music in the town centre, and evening poetry readings and concerts at the **Maison du Culture**.

Places to Stay – Budget

Camping The *Desert Club* (☎/fax 470 575) camping ground is set among the palm trees to the right at the end of Ave du 7 Novembre 1987. Rates are TD4 per person in tents, or TD10 per person with breakfast staying in their nomad-style tents. There's hot water and the site has its own restaurant and bar.

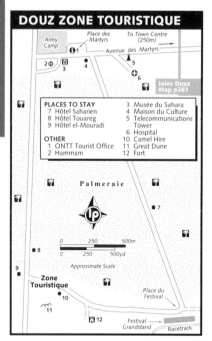

DOUZ ZONE TOURISTIQUE

Army Camp

Place des Martyrs

To Town Centre (250m)

Avenue des Martyrs

Joins Douz Map p261

PLACES TO STAY
7 Hôtel Saharien
8 Hôtel Touareg
9 Hôtel el-Mouradi

OTHER
1 ONTT Tourist Office
2 Hammam

3 Musèe du Sahara
4 Maison du Culture
5 Telecommunications Tower
6 Hospital
10 Camel Hire
11 Great Dune
12 Fort

Palmeraie

0   250   500m
0   250   500yd
Approximate Scale

Zone Touristique

Place du Festival

Festival Grandstand

Racetrack

Hotels All the cheapies are in the town centre.

Management doesn't come any friendlier than at the *Hôtel 20 Mars (☎/fax 470 269)* on the street of the same name, just north of the souq. Rooms are set around a small tree-filled courtyard and cost from TD5 per person, or TD7 with private bathroom. Breakfast is TD1.500, and other meals are available for TD3.500. If it's full, try the *Hôtel de la Tente (☎ 471 468)*, just around the corner on Rue El-Hounine. It charges similar prices.

Other budget possibilities include the *Hôtel Essada (☎ 470 824)*, which charges TD5 per person. Breakfast costs an extra TD1.

Places to Stay – Mid-Range

The two star *Hôtel Saharien (☎ 471 337, fax 470 339)* is in the middle of the palmaraie on the road to Place du Festival. Ask for a room in the new southern wing, which

has comfortable, modern singles/doubles for TD31/46. Some of the older rooms are looking a little tatty. Facilities include a swimming pool.

Places to Stay – Top End

All the upmarket hotels are in the zone touristique on the southern side of the palmeraie, facing the desert. They start with the three star *Hôtel Touareg (☎ 470 057, fax 470 313)*, which is built in the image of an old-style kasbah, complete with crenellations. There's a palm-covered island in the middle of the swimming pool. Singles/doubles are TD51/72.

Theoretically, the best of them is the four star *Hôtel el-Mouradi (☎ 470 303, fax 470 905)*, which charges TD60/90.

Places to Eat

Douz has plenty of budget restaurants, including the very popular *Restaurant La Rosa*, near the souq on Ave du 7 Novembre 1987. It's well set up for and popular with travellers and has a good range of dishes for less than TD3.

Restaurant Ali Baba, about 100m north of the roundabout on the Kebili road, is another traveller-friendly place. It has good outdoor seating in a courtyard garden at the back, and very similar prices. Couscous with spicy sauce (TD2.500) is the house speciality.

The *Café Rendez-Vous* and *Café du Sahara*, almost side-by-side on Ave Taieb Mehiri, are the favourite meeting places for the men of Douz and good spots to check out the comings and goings. The *Café La Rosa*, on Rue Ghara Jawal, has a quiet courtyard at the back where you can enjoy a coffee away from the crowds.

Shopping

There are three shops along Ave des Martyrs, just west of the souq, selling Saharan sandals (comfortable slip-on shoes made from camel skin). The tourist versions normally come decorated with palm motifs etc. The prices vary from TD14 to TD20, depending on the level of decoration and quality.

Getting There & Away

All forms of public transport operate from the new public transport centre just beyond the cemetery on the northern edge of town.

Bus SNTRI has two air-con services a day to Tunis (TD20.670, nine hours). The 6 am service goes via Tozeur, Gafsa and Kairouan (TD16.400, seven hours), and the 9 pm service goes via Gabès (TD6.470, 2½ hours), Sfax (TD10.910, five hours) and Sousse (TD15.690, 6½ hours).

Regional company Sotregames has regular buses to Kebili (TD1.130, 30 minutes), as well as buses to Tozeur (TD4.540, three hours) at 8 am and to Gabès (TD5.400, three hours) at 6.45 am and 9 pm. There are buses to Zaafrane (450 mils), Sabria (TD1.300) and El-Faouar (TD1.450) at 7, 9 and 11 am and 1 and 2.30 pm.

Louage There are regular departures to Kebili (TD1. 400) and Gabès (TD6.250), but none to Tozeur – change at Kebili.

Camionnette There are also regular *camionnettes* (small pick-ups) to Zaafrane (500 mills) and the other oases south of Douz.

Car & Motorcycle There is no public transport from Douz to Matmata, 110km to the east, but a lot of money has been spent on upgrading this route in recent years, and there is now an excellent sealed road as far as Tamezret. The final 13km from Tamezret to Matmata was under construction at the time of research. There are several small cafes along the way.

The pipeline road to Ksar Ghilane and points south intersects the Douz-Matmata road 66km east of Douz. See the Sahara section later in this chapter for more information about this road.

AROUND DOUZ
☎ 05

A sealed road runs south-west from Douz to a string of smaller oases, which are bases for the region's seminomadic tribes who prefer life in the desert to the concrete-block settlements provided by the government.

Zaafrane

The small oasis town of Zaafrane, about 12km south-west of Douz, has emerged as the camel-trekking capital of Tunisia in the past few years. The town is home to the Adhara tribe, which has found tourism to be a good way of turning desert skills into an income.

The town itself is not particularly attractive – a collection of utilitarian block houses, but it's on the edge of some interesting country.

Places to Stay & Eat The only hotel, the *Hôtel Zaafrane (☎/fax 491 720)*, charges TD23/32 for singles/doubles with breakfast. Half board costs an extra TD4 per person. There are no other restaurants in Zaafrane. The hotel also has the only bar in town.

Getting There & Away There are regular buses from Douz, as well as frequent camionnettes. They all charge 500 mills. The flow of traffic dries up around 4 pm and there is never anything much on Friday afternoons.

Beyond Zaafrane

The road continues from Zaafrane to El-Faouar, 41km south-west of Douz. This is the region's second-largest oasis after Douz, with a population approaching 6000. It is also the source of the bulk of the 'sand roses' (see Shopping in the Facts for the Visitor chapter) sold at souvenir stalls throughout the country; they are dug from the desert south-west of El-Faouar. The best day to visit is Friday, when the market comes to town.

There is accommodation at the three star *Hôtel Faouar (☎ 460 531, fax 460 576)*, signposted to the left on the road into town from Zaafrane. As well as the standard swimming pool, the hotels also offers **dune skiing** (TD10) on nearby dunes. Rates are TD40/60 for singles/doubles with breakfast, or TD50/80 with all meals.

A turn-off about 5km before El-Faouar leads to the smaller settlement of **Sabria**, occupied by the tribe of the same name. Buses from Douz to Zaafrane continue to both El-Faouar and Sabria, and there are regular camionnettes.

There is a back road that loops north from Zaafrane to Kebili via the oasis villages of **Nouil** and **Blidet**. The turn-off is just west of Zaafrane on the road to El-Faouar. Nouil is nothing much, but Blidet has a great setting on the edge of the Chott el-Jerid. Blidet can be reached by bus and camionnette from Kebili. The ***Campement Touristique Saharien*** (☎ *494 714, fax 491 918*) at Nouil charges TD12 per person for half board, with accommodation in nomad-style tents.

The Sahara

Tunisia's portion of the world's greatest desert occupies a swathe of territory stretching from Douz to the tiny settlement of Borj el-Khadra, more than 350km to the south.

Much this area is covered by the Grand Erg Oriental, one of the Sahara's two great sand seas. The erg begins about 50km south of Douz and extends almost 500km southwest into neighbouring Algeria.

The Tunisian Sahara can be broken into three main regions: the area south of Douz; the area around Ksar Ghilane in the west; and the far south, often referred to as Grand Sud.

Douz may be the gateway to the Sahara, but the region is administered from Tataouine – some 150km to the south-east as the crow flies. See The Ksour section later in this chapter for information about Tataouine.

Getting There & Away

Unless you have your own transport, access to the Sahara is via Douz.

The main road into the desert is the pipeline road. This unsealed road runs south from El-Hamma, on the Gabès-Kebili road, all the way to Borj el-Khadra. If you're heading for the Grand Sud, the best access is from Remada, 70km south of Tataouine.

Getting Around

Getting around is a problem. The only place it's possible to get to by conventional vehicle is Ksar Ghilane, and even that depends on the condition of the pipeline road. Other roads are passable only by 4WD. Even if you have a 4WD, you still have to find the roads, which are often obliterated by drifting sand. Adding to the confusion is the fact that the desert is crisscrossed by all sorts of tracks, left over from the days of oil prospecting, which don't appear on any commercially available map. Much more useful than a map is a local guide.

Organised Tours

Most people visit the Sahara on arranged tours, which makes a lot of sense. The best place to arrange tours is Douz, where the agencies specialise in desert travel. They use 4WDs to transfer people to desert camps for camel treks through the most interesting areas. Given adequate warning they can organise any itinerary you care to nominate. If your time is limited, stick to the area south of Douz.

SOUTH OF DOUZ

The country immediately south of Douz is flat and fairly featureless; low dunes interspersed with small chotts (salt lakes). The first point of interest is the abandoned village of **Aounet Rajah**, about 15km southwest of Douz, which has all but disappeared beneath a large dune. A small domed marabout at the crest is the only building that remains intact; elsewhere all that remains are the tops of old walls poking from the sand.

Officially, the desert begins at **La Porte du Desert**, about 20km south of Douz. This gleaming white crenellated arch is visible from miles around. Hunting is supposedly banned south of the fence-line running east-west from the arch.

Tour companies refer to this area as **Jebil** (small mountain), which is the low hill nearby. It is the starting point for trips to **Taimbaïn** (pronounced *Tembayine*), 5km further south. Taimbaïn itself is large, crescent-shaped outcrop of rock that offers magnificent views from its summit (220m), but the main attraction is the journey. It passes through some magnificent dune country, crossing three great walls of gleaming white sand that the wind has thrown up like defensive ramparts around Taimbaïn.

KSAR GHILANE

☎ 05

The once remote oasis of Ksar Ghilane, 147km south-east of Douz, has been transformed into the desert headquarters of the 4WD brigade in the last few years. In spite of the number of people passing through, it is still an amazing spot.

The *ksar* (a Berber stronghold consisting of many *ghorfas* or grain-storage cells) in question is the ancient Roman fort of Tisavar, once a desert outpost on the Limes Tripolitanus defensive line. It was modified and renamed by the local Berber tribespeople in the 16th century. The ksar now lies abandoned on a low hill about 2km west of a magic little oasis where hot springs feed a small swimming hole shaded by graceful tamarisk trees. There are some impressive dunes between the oasis and Tisavar, particularly once you get among them.

Three camp sites around the oasis cater for tour groups which use the place as an overnight stop on desert safari tours of the south. There are cafes around the swimming hole, but no shops or other facilities. There are no telephones in Ksar Ghilane. The numbers listed here are contact numbers elsewhere in Tunisia.

Camel Rides

Locals charge TD15 for the 1½-hour return journey from the oasis to the fort. Evening is the best time, when the setting sun produces some stunning optical effects across the dunes.

Places to Stay – Budget

Freelance camping is tolerated around the fringe of the oasis, but most visitors use one of the camp sites. All offer beds in large nomad-style tents as well as providing areas for pitching tents. All also have restaurants.

The pick of them is *Camping Ghilane* (☎ 470 750), ideally located next to the hot springs on the northern edge of the oasis. It charges TD7 person with breakfast, whether you use your own tent or use their accommodation. A three-course evening meal costs an extra TD6.

Other options include *Camping Paradise* (☎ 620 570), in the middle of the palmaraie, and *Camping L'Erg* (☎ 01-860 799), in the desert to the south.

Places to Stay – Top End

The extraordinary *Hôtel Pansea* (☎ 01-893 275, fax 846 129) is the deluxe alternative for people who can't do without their creature comforts. It offers in air-con tents, complete with private bathrooms. Singles/doubles are TD95/115 with breakfast.

Getting There & Away

There is no public transport to Ksar Ghilane. Most traffic uses the pipeline road. If you're driving a conventional vehicle, check conditions at the Café Jelili at the junction of the Douz-Matmata road. The turn-off to Ksar Ghilane is clearly signposted 66km further south. The final 13km from the pipeline road to Ksar Ghilane is sealed.

If you have a 4WD, there are several other possibilities, including the roads from Beni Kheddache, Guermessa and Douiret (see the entries on these two towns in The Ksour section later in this chapter).

AROUND KSAR GHILANE

There are a couple of interesting diversions off the pipeline road between Ksar Ghilane and the Douz-Matmata road.

Every passing tour group stops to take photos of **Bir Soltane**, where a small stone dome surrounds an ancient well. Centuries of use has cut deep rope grooves into the well-head. The only other building here is the nearby National Guard post, which uses a windmill to draw its water. Bir Soltane is about 2km west of the pipeline road, reached by signposted tracks both north and south of the **Café Bir Soltane**, 32km south of the Douz-Matmata road. Both are easily passable by conventional vehicle.

Hardly anyone heads out to **Ksar Tarcine**, about 12km south-east of Bir Soltane. Like Ksar Ghilane, this remote outpost began life as part of the Roman Limes Tripolitanes – when it was called Centenarium Tibubuci. Like Ksar Ghilane, it was later modified by local Berber tribes – and is now in ruins. It stands on a rise overlooking the broad bed of the Oued Ethaabine, which stretches away towards the Jebel Dahar range, silhouetted to the east. There's a well on the bank of the oued, as well as some cisterns.

Access is from the road to Beni Kheddache, which is signposted to the east off the pipeline road 500m south of the Café Bir Soltane. Keep going along here for 8km until you reach a small settlement with a well and a few struggling saplings. The turn-off to Ksar Tarcine is signposted to the south just beyond the settlement. You need a 4WD, especially for the final section.

GRAND SUD

This covers the vast expanse of desert south and west of Ksar Ghilane. Most of it – and all the points of interest – lie within a military zone. You need a permit to continue beyond **Kamour**, on the pipeline road 110km south of the Douz-Matmata road, and **Kambout**, about 10km east of Remada. Unless you are travelling as part of a group, you will need to apply in person to the governorate in Tataouine. The permit takes two days to process.

The pipeline road is the region's lifeline. From Kamour, it's a further 292km to **Borj el-Khadra**, the country's southernmost settlement. The road curves around the edge of the Grand Erg Oriental, across barren steppe country dotted with great outcrops of weathered rock and crisscrossed by the boulder-strewn beds of oueds that may flow only once in a 100 years. There's very little along the way save the odd military post. Borj el-Khadra itself comprises no more than a small military garrison and airfield. Sadly, it's impossible to continue to the legendary Libyan oasis of Ghadames, just across the border.

Dunes – seriously large ones – are the main reason tourists come to this part of world. Some of the best examples are found between **Bir Aouine** and **El-Borma**, and this trek is very popular with the tour operators in Douz. El-Borma, 84km southeast of Kamour, once produced the bulk of the nation's oil.

Gabès Region

GABÈS
☎ 05 • pop 90,000
The sprawling industrial city of Gabès lies on the coast 137km south-west of Sfax. It suffers from a sorry reputation as the most polluted town in Tunisia, which is a shame because the palmeraie is well worth a visit and there are more than enough things to see to warrant an overnight stop.

History
Gabès is the largest of a cluster of oases occupying the narrow strip of land between the Chott el-Fejej and the Gulf of Gabès. The oases have been inhabited since prehistoric times, and the settlement at Gabès grew into the Roman town of Tacapae.

The town grew rich in the 14th century AD as the principal Tunisian destination for the great camel caravans that brought gold from West Africa and slaves from Sudan. After the French invasion of the Sahara in the 19th century killed off the caravans, Gabès slipped back into a humbler role as the main town of the Arad, the coastal plain that flanks the Gulf of Gabès. It boomed again following the discovery of offshore oil in the gulf and the subsequent construction of a huge petrochemical complex on the coast just north of town.

Orientation
Although Gabès is a coastal city, the coast barely features in the layout of the town. The town centre is located about 2km inland, skirted by the Oued Gabès to the north and the disgustingly polluted Gabès Canal to the south.

If you arrive in Gabès by bus or louage, you will be dropped at the terminal next to a large roundabout on the north-western edge of town. The main road to Sfax heads north from here, across a bridge over the Oued Gabès, while Ave de la République leads south across the canal to Medenine and Matmata. Ave Farhat Hached runs south-east through the modern town centre to the port and beach, becoming Ave Habib Thameur for the final stretch.

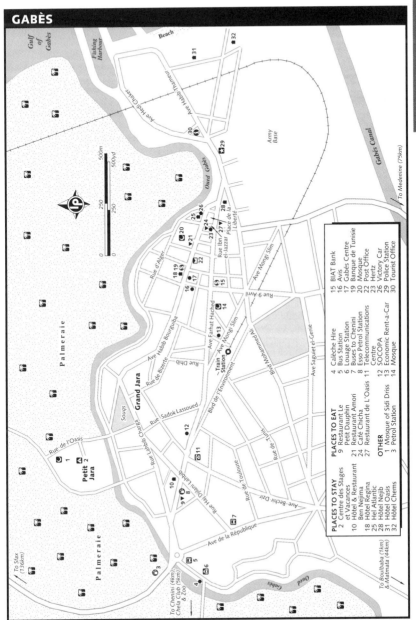

GABÈS

Gulf of Gabès

Beach

Fishing Harbour

Ave Hédi Chaker

Ave Habib Thameur

Ave Habib Thameur

■ 31

■ 32

Army Base

To Medenine (75km)

Gabès Canal

Oued Gabès

30

★ 29

Palmeraie

0   250   500m
0   250   500yd

Rue d'Alger

■ 20
■ 21
■ 18 19
■ 16 17
■ 22

25 26
24
23 27
Rue Ibn
el-Jazzar   28
Place de la
Liberté

Ave Mongi Slim

■ 15

Rue 9 Avril

Ave Farhat Hached

■ 13
■ 14

Ave Habib Bourguiba

Palmeraie

Ave Saguiet el-Genie

Rue de Bizerte

Rue Dhib

Grand Jara

Train
Station

Ave Mongi Slim

Boulevard Mohamed Ali

Souqs

Rue Sadok Lassoued

Blvd de l'Environnement

Rue de Tunis

■ 12

Petit Jara

■ 1
■ 2

Rue Lahbib Chaïeb

■ 11

Rue de Toulouse

Palmeraie

Rue Bechir Dzir

■ 10
■ 9 6
■ 8

Rue Hal Djilani Lahbib

■ 7

Ave de la République

To Sfax
(136km)

To Chenini (4km)
Chela Club (5km)

To Boultaba (1km)
& Matmata (44km)

■ 3

■ 4
■ 5
■ 6

Oued Gabès

PLACES TO STAY
2   Centre des Stages
     et Vacances
     Hôtel & Restaurant
     Ben Nejima
18   Hôtel Regina
19   Hel Atlantic
28   Hôtel Nejib
31   Hôtel Oasis
32   Hôtel Chems

PLACES TO EAT
9   Restaurant Le
     Petit Dauphin
21   Restaurant Amori
24   Café Chicha
27   Restaurant de L'Oasis

OTHER
1   Mosque of Sidi Driss
3   Petrol Station
4   Calèche Hire
5   Bus Station
6   Louage Station
7   Buses to Chenini
8   Esso Petrol Station
11   Telecommunications
     Centre
13   SOCOPA
14   Mosque

15   BIAT Bank
16   Avis
17   Gabès Centre
20   Banque de Tunisie
22   Mosque
23   Post Office
25   Hertz
26   Victory Car
29   Economic Rent-a-Car
30   Police Station
30   Tourist Office

Henna

Gabès is well known for its high-quality henna, which is made by grinding the dried leaves of the henna tree (laussonia inermis), a small evergreen native to the region. Gabès' henna produces a deep red-brown dye. Berber women use it to decorate their hands and feet, as well as to colour and condition their hair. You'll see henna powder for sale in the souqs and in the shops at the western end of Ave Farhat Hached, piled up in colourful green pyramids. Henna costs about TD1.500 for 100g.

Finding your way around town is made more difficult by the virtual absence of street signs. The huge telecommunications tower on Ave Farhat Hached makes a useful orientation point.

Information

Tourist Office The tourist office (☎ 270 254) occupies the small building in the middle of the intersection of Ave Habib Thameur and Ave Hedi Chaker, out towards the waterfront. They don't see many tourists and are keen to offer whatever help they can. There is a complete list of bus departures posted on the door.

Money There is a cluster of banks on Ave Habib Bourguiba, including branches of the Banque du Sud and STB in the Gabès Centre and the Banque de Tunisie opposite. BIAT has a branch on Ave Farhat Hached.

Post & Communications The post office is on Ave Habib Bourguiba. There are telephones here or use one of the Taxiphone offices around town. Internet access is available at the Publinet office on the mezzanine floor of the Gabès Centre on Ave Habib Bourguiba. It's open from 8 am to 10 pm daily.

Palmeraie

The palmeraie stretches inland along the Oued Gabès, mostly on the north bank. It begins on the coast at **Ghannouche**, now the site of a giant petrochemical plant, and ends more than 4km west of Gabès at the village of **Chenini** (not to be confused with the village of Chenini in the ksour district – see The Ksour section later in this chapter). This western section is the most interesting (and least polluted) part of the palmeraie, but it's also where all the tour groups head. There are numerous ways of getting there. The turn-off to Chenini is signposted off the road to Sfax, about 300m north of the oued. You can get there on the No 7 bus from Rue Haj Djilani Lahbib or pay around TD2.500 for a taxi. Most people opt for a tour (TD10) on one of the calèches that wait for the tour buses behind the bus station.

If the weather's not too hot, there's no reason not to walk. You can follow the shortcut used by the calèches, crossing the oued by the bridge behind the bus station and turning left onto the Chenini road. The road then twists and turns through the palmeraie to El-Aouadid, where a left turn leads down to Chenini. It's a pleasant walk of about one hour. The palmeraie looks its best during the pomegranate season in November and December, when the trees are weighed down with huge ruby-red fruit.

Chenini itself has not much more to offer than a depressing crocodile farm and zoo and a small, partly reconstructed Roman dam on the Oued Gabès. It also has lots of souvenir stalls selling all sorts of junk at inflated prices – this is where the tour buses come to pick up their passengers after their calèche ride through the palmeraie. Don't waste your money on the zoo.

A path (negotiable by bicycle) heads off around the back of the dam and winds around through the palmeraie to the Chela Club, a rather run-down resort hotel tucked away in the palms (see also Places to Stay in this section). It's about a 20-minute walk and you can continue on along the oued to the end of the valley. Climb up the small escarpment for a view of the surrounding area. From the Chela Club, the road leads back to Chenini.

Beach

It's hard to work out why anyone would come to Gabès for a beach holiday. Some people do though, and there are a couple of resort hotels just to prove it. Doubtless their brochures don't show the belching smokestacks of the nearby petrochemical complex, nor the film of black slime that coats the once-golden sand, nor the toxic waters of the Oued Gabès, nor the enormous rubbish dump behind the beach!

Jara
The Jara is the old district that straddles the oued on the northern edge of town. The **Petit Jara**, amid the palm trees north of the oued, is the oldest part of town. The **Mosque of Sidi Driss**, at the far end of Rue de l'Oasis, dates back to the 11th century. The old market, where the slaves once were sold, is in **Grand Jara**, south of the oued.

The best way to approach the Jara district is along Rue Sadok Lassoued, which runs north from Ave Farhat Hached in the middle of town. It leads to Rue de l'Oasis, which continues across the oued to Petit Jara.

Zaouia of Sidi Boulbaba
The city's most important religious monument, the Zaouia of Sidi Boulbaba, is situated about 2km south of town in the district of Boulbaba. It houses the 7th-century tomb of the man said to have been both the Prophet's barber and the founder of Gabès. The zaouia, with its ornate arched colonnades, is a modern copy; the original was destroyed by shelling in WWII. It is on the left off Rue 6 Octobre, which is the road to Matmata. There are buses out to Boulbaba, but you're better off forking out TD1.500 for a taxi.

Museum
The small Museum of Art and Popular Traditions is housed in a former medersa next to the Zaouia of Sidi Boulbaba. It's open from 8 am to noon and 4 to 7 pm in summer and from 9.30 am to 4.30 pm in winter daily, except Monday. Admission is TD1.100.

Places to Stay – Budget
Camping & Hostels Gabès has a *Centre des Stages et Vacances* (☎ 270 271) in the palmeraie in the old district of Petit Jara. It's clearly signposted north of the oued off Rue

de l'Oasis. It's a holiday camp version of a maison des jeunes. It has the usual spartan dorms for TD5, but it also has good shady camp sites for TD2, plus 500 mills per person. Power and hot showers cost extra.

Hotels Budget accommodation is centred around the junction of Ave Farhat Hached and Rue Haj Djilani Lahbib, close to the bus and louage stations on the western side of town. The *Hôtel Ben Nejima* (☎ 271 591), at the junction, is the pick of them. It charges TD7 per person, with free hot showers.

Places to Stay – Mid-Range
Most of the hotels in this category are found on the eastern (coastal) side of town, about a 15-minute walk from the bus and louage stations. Prices quoted here include breakfast.

The *Hôtel Regina* (☎ 272 095), opposite the Gabès Centre on Ave Habib Bourguiba, is where most travellers head. It's a quiet place with rooms arranged around a pleasant courtyard. All come with private bathroom and cost TD11.500/15 for singles/doubles. Breakfast is available at the co-owned cafe next door. You can ask for it to be served in the courtyard.

The one star *Hôtel Atlantic* (☎ 220 034, fax 221 358), at the eastern end of Ave Habib Bourguiba, is an old French place with a fine colonial facade for TD14.500/23.

The next step up from here is the *Hôtel Nejib* (☎ 271 686, fax 271 587), a big, modern two-star place on the corner of Ave Farhat Hached and Blvd Mohammed Ali. It charges TD27/40, rising to TD34.500/52 in July and August.

Places to Stay – Top End
The *Hôtel Chems* (☎ 270 547, fax 274 485) and the *Hôtel Oasis* (☎ 270 884, fax 271 749) are a couple of three-star resort hotels overlooking the beach off the end of Ave Habib Thameur. The Chems is an enormous bungalow complex with singles/doubles for TD35/50, rising to TD48/70 in high season. The Oasis is slightly cheaper and slightly more discreet.

Places to Eat

The **Restaurant Le Petit Dauphin**, on Ave Farhat Hached near the junction with Rue Haj Djilani Lahbib, is a tiny place with a small selection of specials like chorba (TD1) and couscous with vegetables TD1.500) or lamb (TD3). Owner Fathi loves to sit and chat to travellers when he can escape from the kitchen.

The **Restaurant Amori** is a popular place at the eastern end of Ave Habib Bourguiba with a selection of three-course menus priced from TD5.

If you feel like a splurge, the best food in town is at the **Restaurant de l'Oasis** (☎ 270 098), at the beach end of Ave Farhat Hached. A meal here will set you back TD15 or more, plus wine.

For a coffee, try the **Café Chicha** on Place de la Liberté, which is at the junction of Ave Habib Bourguiba and Ave Farhat Hached. It's up the stairs next to the Hertz office. The setting, with its intricate tiling, is a cut above the rest.

Shopping

There is a large government-run SOCOPA showroom on Ave Farhat Hached. It has the usual range of quality carpets and other handicrafts.

Gabès is a major centre for the production of straw goods – baskets, hats, fans and mats – and the souqs here are a good place to buy things.

Getting There & Away

Bus The bus station is next to the louage station at the western end of Ave Farhat Hached, a solid 15-minute walk from the hotels on Ave Habib Bourguiba. All three bus companies operating from Gabès are based here. Each has its own ticket office. If you can't find the service you want at one counter, keep asking. They never know each other's schedules.

The most popular destination is Matmata (TD1.500, one hour), with 10 buses a day between 6.15 am and 6.30 pm. There are also frequent buses to Jerba (TD5.700, three hours). Make sure that you catch one of the services that takes the shortcut via the Jorf-

Ajim ferry. Some services go via Medenine and Zarzis, adding 80km and more than one hour to the journey. There are two direct buses a day to Tataouine (TD6.150, two hours), otherwise you will have to take one of the many buses to Medenine (TD3.380, 1¼ hours) and change there.

Heading north, SNTRI has at least five buses a day to Tunis (TD14.480, six hours). They travel via Sfax (TD5.850, two hours) and either Kairouan or Sousse. Most of these buses originate from points further south and in summer they are often full by the time they reach Gabès. Heading west, SNTRI has three buses a day to Kebili (TD5.180, two hours), two of which continue to Douz (TD6.470, 2½ hours).

Local company Sotregames also operates three services a day to Kebili (TD4.350, 2½ hours). The 9 am service continues to Tozeur (TD7.660, 4½ hours) and Nefta, while the noon and 6.30 pm services continue to Douz (TD5.400, three hours).

Train The train station is just off Ave Mongi Slim, about a five-minute walk from Ave Habib Bourguiba. There are two trains daily to Tunis (TD15.200, seven hours) at 3.42 and 11 pm. Gabès is the southernmost point that can be reached by train.

Louage The louage station adjoins the bus station, with departures for Kebili (TD5), Jerba (TD4.900), Medenine (TD3.300), Sfax (TD5.650) and Tunis. Things quieten down considerably as the afternoon wears on. Change at Kebili for Tozeur and Douz.

Car Avis (☎ 270 210), on Rue 9 Avril, and Hertz (☎ 270 525), 30 Rue Ibn el-Jazzar, have offices in town. It's worth hunting around for deals at local companies like Economic Rent-a-Car (☎ 271 755), near the train station on Ave Farhat Hached, and Victory Car (☎ 221 222), next to the Hôtel Atlantic on Ave Habib Bourguiba.

MATMATA
☎ 05 • pop 1000

It's easy to work out why the makers of *Star Wars* picked Matmata, 45km south-west of

ADRIEN VADROT

DAMIEN SIMONIS

The Berbers developed the *ksar* as a means of storing and protecting their precious grain supplies in the face of Arab incursions. Some of the best examples can be found around Tataouine (top). Many have been converted into comfortable hotel accommodation (below).

A mosque crowns a hill below Chenini

Chenini's lofty outlook

A dazzling, whitewashed mosque at Guermessa

For over a thousand years the Berbers of Matmata have built troglodyte houses to escape the savage desert heat.

Gabès, as the home planet of Luke Skywalker. Set amid a bizarre lunar landscape, the Berbers of Matmata went underground centuries ago to escape the summer heat.

Although conventional modern buildings are now in the majority, the town still boasts dozens of the troglodyte pit homes that are its main attraction. Each of the many mounds that dot the landscape represents a home. They are all built along the same lines: A large central courtyard, usually circular, is dug out of the soft sandstone, and the rooms are then tunnelled off the perimeter.

Fascinating though Matmata might be, it's hard not to feel sorry for the long-suffering residents. The first tour buses roll up at 9 am every day, and they just keep on coming – day after day. Some of the children are very up-front about suggesting where tourists should go. They have picked up some very colourful language!

Orientation & Information

The road from Gabès descends into Matmata from the north and continues through town to the east as the back road to Medenine. Buses and louages stop at the square in the centre of town. The small syndicat d'initiative (☎ 230 114) is just uphill from the bus station, opposite the turn-off to Tamezret. The staff can help with information on getting to surrounding villages. There is also an ONTT office (☎ 230 075) on the road into town from Gabès.

There is a post office up on the hill to the left as you come into Matmata from Gabès. The closest bank is the Banque Nationale Agricole in Matmata Nouvelle, 15km away.

Things to See & Do

If you want to see Matmata for yourself, a good approach is to arrive late in the afternoon after the tour buses have gone. It will then be cool enough to go for a walk out beyond the Hôtel Ksar Amazigh (formerly Les Troglodytes) on the road to Tamezret. There are good **views** back over Matmata and north to the valley of the Oued Barrak, especially around sunset. You can then walk back to town and quench your thirst with a cold drink at the Hôtel **Sidi Driss**, used as a setting for

Star Wars, and you will have seen just about everything worth seeing in Matmata.

You'll see signs along the Tamezret road indicating houses that are open for inspection, and you will frequently be asked if you want to visit homes. Before you enter, be aware that these places all double as souvenir shops, and you will find yourself feeling obliged to buy junk at inflated prices.

Organised Tours

There are licensed guides who charge TD7 for a guided tour of the village or TD13 for tours of both Matmata and Tamezret. You will have to provide the transport to Tamezret. The six guides speak a range of languages between them, including English, French, German and Italian. You'll normally find them at the syndicat d'initiative, or hanging out around the hotels.

Places to Stay

The accommodation is the best feature of Matmata. Three of the town's hotels are traditional troglodyte dwellings. They're all well signposted and within a few minutes' walk of the bus stop.

The best of them is the *Hôtel Sidi Driss (☎ 230 005)*, along the road opposite the bus station. It was in the bar here that the disco scene from *Star Wars* was filmed. It charges TD8 per person with breakfast and hot shower. Unfortunately there are only a couple of double rooms – some rooms have as many as eight beds. The place once won a mention in a list of the world's loopiest hotels compiled by an airline in-flight magazine.

The *Hôtel Marhala (☎ 230 015, fax 230 109)* is one in a chain run by the Touring Club de Tunisie. The rooms are clean and pleasant, but the 'friendly' service is way short of normal Marhala standards. Singles/doubles with breakfast are TD12.500/18.

The final troglodyte option is the *Hôtel Les Berbères (☎ 230 024, fax 230 097)*. The sleeping quarters here are recent additions and are not of traditional construction; the walls are so thin that you can hear a mosquito buzzing next door. It charges TD8.800/13.600 with breakfast.

There's not much to recommend at the modern *Hôtel Matmata* (☎ *230 066, fax 230 177*) except for a swimming pool. Rooms cost TD267/436 with breakfast. Regular folk nights are laid on for the tour groups that use the hotel.

The *Hôtel Kouseila* (☎ *230 303, fax 230 265*) is a comfortable new three-star place in the middle of town opposite the bus station. Large singles/doubles with breakfast cost TD38/54. You'll find virtually identical prices at the *Hôtel Ksar Amazigh* (☎ *230 088, fax 230 173*), 1km out of town on the Tamezret road. It has a great position looking north over the Oued Barrak.

Places to Eat

Matmata's restaurants are nothing to get excited about. Sullen service is the order of the day at the *restaurant* adjoining the Café Ouled Azaiz, opposite the syndicat d'initiative, which does meals for TD6. The nameless *restaurant* next to the Café de la Victoire by the bus station does omelette, chips and salad for TD2.

If you're staying the night, you're better off taking a room with half board – available at all the hotels.

Getting There & Away

The bus station is in the centre of town next to the market. The syndicat d'initiative has a list of departure times.

There are 10 buses a day to Gabès (TD1.500) between 6.30 am and 8.30 pm, as well as buses to Tamezret (800 mills) at 1.30 and 5 pm and to Techine (800 mills) at 12.30 and 5 pm. There is one SNTRI bus a day to Tunis at 8.30 pm (TD16.970, 5½ hours). At the time of writing, SRT Medenine was about to launch a new daily service linking Matmata and Jerba, leaving Matmata at 10 am and Houmt Souq at 4.30 pm.

When coming from Gabès, make sure the bus you catch is actually going all the way to Matmata – some terminate at Nouvelle Matmata, on the plains 15km north of Matmata. There are louages (600 mills) between the two Matmatas, if you get stuck.

AROUND MATMATA
Haddèj

The village of Haddèj, 3km north-east of Matmata, is much less developed than Matmata. There are no hotels or restaurants, and the most substantial building in town is the school.

Although many pit homes were abandoned after severe floods in 1969, there are still plenty of people around – and no shortage of would-be guides. The main attraction is an underground olive press, where big millstones are turned by a camel in an impossibly small space. There is also a press operated by weights and levers, which is used to extract the oil from the olives once they have been crushed.

Getting There & Away The road to Haddèj is signposted to the east at the village of Tijma, 4km north of Matmata on the road to Gabès. There is no public transport from old Matmata, but there are occasional buses and camionnettes between Nouvelle Matmata and Haddèj. Check with the Matmata tourist office for bus times. Otherwise, you can catch a bus as far as Tijma and walk the remaining 3km to Haddèj. It's a pleasant walk as the road winds up a small valley following the course of a wide, boulder-strewn oued.

If the weather is favourable, there is an excellent walk back to Matmata along the mule track which cuts directly through the hills. It takes about 1½ hours at a steady pace. Just ask the locals in Haddèj to point it out to you, as it's not obvious where it starts. Once you are on it, it's well trodden and easy to follow.

Tamezret

Few tourists make it out to the quiet little village of Tamezret, which overlooks the Nefzaoua plains from its commanding hilltop position 13km west of Matmata.

The houses here are built above ground, using the abundant local rock. The old quarter, above the bus stop, is a maze of little alleyways that wind around the hillside. There are buses from Matmata at 1.30 and 5.30 pm, returning an hour later.

An excellent new sealed road continues from Tamezret to Douz, 97km further west.

East of Matmata

There is some dramatic country east of Matmata on the back road to Medenine.

It's a good sealed road as far as the turnoff to **Techine**, 12km to the south-east of Matmata. Techine is a smaller version of Matmata, minus the tour buses. The road into the village does a loop through the unattractive modern part of the village. You'll find plenty of volunteers for the job of leading the way to the pit homes, which are unusual for their built-in furniture. There are buses to Techine (800 mills) from Matmata at 12.30 and 5 pm, returning an hour later.

You'll need your own transport if you want to continue further east through the hills. The road was in very poor condition at the time of research following recent heavy rain, but still just passable in a 2WD. It runs through some pretty wild hill country, much of it covered by esparto grass, which the locals gather and use for making all sorts of things, from mats to mule harnesses.

It finally emerges at the village of **Toujane**, 23km south-east of Matmata. It's an extraordinary place with stone houses spread around a hillside beneath the ruins of an old kasbah. The village is cut by a gorge that leads down to the coastal plain. It's very photogenic, particularly in the early-morning light.

At the time of research, a 4WD was necessary to continue on the back road from Toujane to Medenine, 38km to the south-east. The worst section is the 9km through the hills between Toujane and **Souq Eddkhila**.

It doesn't really matter because there is a good sealed road north-east from Toujane to the town of **Mareth**, on the main road from Gabès to Medenine.

An alternative is to turn north-west at **Ain Tounine**, 4km north of Toujane, and head back to Matmata. This road follows the course of Oued Ghir, passing the charming stone village of **Ben Zeiten** on the way. It's 27km from Ain Tounine to Matmata Nouvelle, all of it on a good sealed road.

MARETH

The small market town of Mareth, 36km south of Gabès, was the scene of the most

The Mareth Line

The Battle of the Mareth Line pitted Allied forces led by Montgomery, advancing from victories at El-Alamein and Tobruk in late 1942, against retreating German and Italian forces dug in along the Mareth Line.

Dubbed the desert Maginot Line, the Mareth Line was originally built by the French in the lead-up to WWII to defend Tunisia against Italian forces in Libya, but was de-commissioned after the fall of France in 1940. After El-Alamein, the line was re-armed and re-inforced by the Germans to create a formidable defensive line along the north bank of the Oued Zigzaou. It stretched more than 25km from the coast to the Jebel Dahar ranges, and comprised a network of bunkers, barbed wire, minefields and antitank defences.

The battle lasted 12 days, from 16 to 28 March 1943, before the Axis positions were outflanked by an Allied forced which crossed the Jebel Dahar further inland.

You can check out battlefield plans, and other memorabilia at the Museum of the Mareth Line, 2km south of town on the road to Medenine. The museum is open from 8.30 am to 4 pm daily except Monday. The TD1.100 admission includes a guided tour, in French, by one of the Tunisian soldiers who staff the museum. If you have transport, they will accompany you to the German command bunker, 10 km inland off the road to Toujane.

important battle fought on Tunisian soil during WWII.

Any bus travelling between Gabès and Medenine can drop you at the museum.

The Ksour

The ksour district is centred on the rugged hills of the Jebel Dahar Range, which begins about 30km south of Gabès and runs south-east beyond Tataouine towards the Libyan border. It also includes the sweeping Jeffara Plains that stretch east from the hills.

It's best known for its ksour (singular ksar), the wonderfully idiosyncratic fortified granaries that are the region's trademark. Equally spectacular are the ancient hilltop villages west of Tataouine. (See the Berber Architecture special section for details.)

The Dahar has long been a stronghold of Berber culture – ever since the semi-nomadic Berber tribes who inhabited the Jeffara were driven into the hills by the Hilalian invasions of the 11th century. The range is broken into three main areas: the Matmata Hills in the north, which are accessed from Gabès; the Jebel Demmer in the centre;

and the Jebel Abiodh, south-east of Tataouine.

The main town and transport hub of the region is Medenine, on the plains 76km south-east of Gabès. Most travellers prefer to base themselves further south in Tataouine, which is closer to the best sites.

The only problem is getting around. Public transport is very limited around the hills. This is the perfect place to have your own transport. Equipped with your own vehicle, you can complete a fascinating circuit on the back road from Medenine to Tataouine via Beni Kheddache and Ghomrassen.

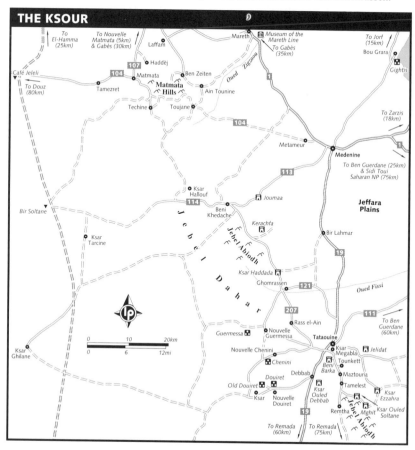

The villages around here are among the last places where the local Berber language, Chelha, can be heard. With the deaths of elderly speakers, the language too is dying out.

MEDENINE

☎ 05 • pop 20,000

The regional centre of Medenine, 76km south-east of Gabès, is a dull, modern town that would barely merit a mention were it not an important transport hub and useful starting point for trips to the villages of the Jebel Demmer to the south-east.

The skyline is dominated by the gigantic regional hospital, which seems totally out of proportion to the rest of the town.

Orientation & Information

The main street is Ave Habib Bourguiba, which runs north-south through the centre of town. It dips in the middle of town to cross the Oued Medenine. About 50m south of the oued is the town's major intersection, adjoining Place des Martyrs. Ave 2 Mai runs south-west from here and becomes the road to Tataouine, while Ave Abdel Hamid el-Kahdi leads south-east to Zarzis, Ben Guerdane and the Libyan border.

The post office is on Place des Martyrs. Most other things of importance – banks, hotels and restaurants – are north of the oued.

Ksar Medenine

Medenine's only tourist attraction is its old ksar, north of the oued on Ave 7 Novembre. It was built by the Ouergherma Federation in the 17th century following its decision to leave its mountain stronghold of Ghomrassen and assert authority over the plains. The ksar that stands today was once one of three. It is in fine condition, and the *ghorfas* (cells built to store grain that make up a ksar) surrounding the central courtyard house a flourishing band of souvenir shops catering to tour buses from Jerba.

The scene is very colourful, with the ghorfas draped in bright Berber rugs, but it's hard to classify the place as anything other than a tourist trap.

The ruins of the other two ksour are immediately north of here. The small section of ghorfas on Rue Darghoulia rises three storeys, but it is in very poor condition.

Places to Stay

There's no reason to stay overnight, but there are options if you do get stuck. The best budget option is the basic *Hôtel Essaada* (☎ 640 300), opposite the Esso station on Ave Habib Bourguiba. The rooms are around a courtyard set back from the street. Single/double rooms cost TD3.500/6. Hot showers cost TD1. The alternative is the *Hôtel el-Hana* (☎ 640 690), further north on Ave Habin Bourguiba.

The poshest place in town is the *Hôtel Ibis* (☎ 643 878, fax 640 550), a smart two-star hotel on Place 7 Novembre. It looks a bit out of place in the middle of Medenine. It charges TD34/52 with breakfast, rising to TD39/62 in July and August.

Places to Eat

The *Restaurant Paris*, just downhill from the Hôtel Essaada on Ave Habib Bourguiba, is a popular place with a small selection of daily specials for around TD2. It also does a tasty chorba (TD1) and a selection salads. The *Hôtel Ibis* has the only upmarket restaurant in town – and the only cold beer.

Self-caterers can stock up on supplies at the *Grand Magasin* supermarket just north of the oued on Ave Habib Bourguiba. You'll find fresh fruit and vegetables in the *market* building opposite the Hôtel el-Hana on Ave Habib Bourguiba.

Getting There & Away

Bus All services leave from the new bus station 1.5km north of town on the Gabès road.

SNTRI has six buses daily to Tunis. The buses via Kairouan are quicker and cheaper (TD16.760, 7½ hours) than those via Sfax, El-Jem and Sousse. Getting a seat in summer can be difficult because only one service originates in Medenine; the others start further south and are often full when they arrive.

There are frequent local buses to Jerba; services via the ferries at Jorf are faster and cheaper (TD2.850, 1½ hours) than those via Zarzis and the causeway (TD4.300, 2½ hours). There are four buses daily to Tataouine

SOUTHERN TUNISIA

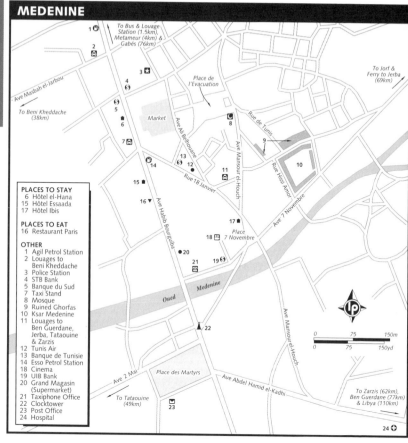

MEDENINE

To Bus & Louage Station (1.5km), Metameur (4km) & Gabès (76km)

To Jorf & Ferry to Jerba (69km)

Ave Masbah el-Jarbou
To Beni Kheddache (38km)

Place de l'Evacuation

Market

Ave Ali Belhouane

Rue de Tunis

Ave Mansour el-Houch

Rue 7 Novembre

Rue Hssi Amor

Rue 18 Janvier

Ave Habib Bourguiba

Place 7 Novembre

Oued   Medenine

Ave 2 Mai

Place des Martyrs

To Tataouine (49km)

Ave Abdel Hamid el-Kadhi

Ave Mansour el-Houch

To Zarzis (62km), Ben Guerdane (77km) & Libya (110km)

0   75   150m
0   75   150yd

PLACES TO STAY
6   Hôtel el-Hana
15 Hôtel Essaada
17 Hôtel Ibis

PLACES TO EAT
16 Restaurant Paris

OTHER
1   Agil Petrol Station
2   Louages to
    Beni Kheddache
3   Police Station
4   STB Bank
5   Banque du Sud
7   Taxi Stand
8   Mosque
9   Ruined Ghorfas
10 Ksar Medenine
11 Louages to
    Ben Guerdane,
    Jerba, Tataouine
    & Zarzis
12 Tunis Air
13 Banque de Tunisie
14 Esso Petrol Station
18 Cinema
19 UIB Bank
20 Grand Magasin
    (Supermarket)
21 Taxiphone Office
22 Clocktower
23 Post Office
24 Hospital

between 7.30 am and 4.30 pm (one hour, TD1.950), and Gabès (1¼ hours, TD3.380).

Local services include buses to Metameur (15 minutes, 400 mills) and Beni Kheddache (45 minutes, TD1.400) at 10 am and 3 pm.

Louage Louages to the north leave from next to the bus station. Gabès (TD3.300) is the main destination. Louages to points south leave from the centre of town – the small street linking Rue 18 Janvier and Ave Mansour el-Houch. Destinations include Ben Guerdane (TD3.300); Jerba (TD4) and Tataouine (TD2).

Louages for Beni Kheddache (TD1.500) leave from the Beni Kheddache turn-off on the northern edge of town.

AROUND MEDENINE
Metameur
☎ 05

At the small village of Metameur, 6km west of Medenine, you can stay overnight in the 17th-century ksar. It is clearly visible from the Gabès-Medenine road, 1km to the east, on a low hill above the modern village.

[Continued on page 281]

BERBER ARCHITECTURE

The dramatic architecture of the Berber villages of the south is one of the highlights of any visit to Tunisia. The architecture that evolved reflects the ability of Berber people to adapt to the extraordinarily harsh environment, eking out an existence from the barest of resources.

Ksour

The structure that typifies Berber architecture is the *ksar* (plural *ksour*), the traditional fortified granary built by the region's tribes. Its design reflects the main priority of its builders – to preserve and protect the precious grain crops produced in good seasons. Ksour were usually built on natural defensive positions, and occupy some spectacular ridge and hilltop locations.

A single ksar consists of many *ghorfas* – long, narrow, barrel-vaulted rooms built of stone and finished with a mud render. They were constructed in rows and arranged to form a stockade surrounding a central courtyard. These ghorfas were stacked three- or four-stories high to create a formidable defensive wall. Entry to the courtyard was by a single fortified gate.

The ghorfas themselves were like caves, with a single tiny door opening onto the courtyard. Access to the upper levels was by precarious exterior steps. They were designed for grain storage – the very low humidity of this arid region, combined with the cool conditions inside the ksar, meant that grain could be kept for years without deteriorating.

The oldest examples of ksour are to be found occupying the highest peaks of ancient hill-top villages like Chenini and Douiret, but these are in very poor condition. Most of the best examples are more recent constructions dating from the 15th and 16th centuries, built by Arab settlers who had adopted Berber traditions. They include Ksar Ouled Soltane, where the ghorfas rise a dizzying four stories, Ksar Joumaa and Ksar Haddada – used as a setting for the film *Star Wars*.

Inset: Steps leading from the courtyard to ground level in a typical underground Berber house – Ksar al-Hadada. (Photo by Damien Simonis)

Right: The distinctive remains of Ksar Megabla, Tataouine.

GEOFF STRINGER

Sadly, most of the ksour are falling into ruin. However, the ksour at Metameur and Ksar Hallouf have been converted into budget hotels, while the ksar at Medenine has been restored and converted into a tourist market.

Hilltop Villages

The region's oldest surviving settlements are the spectacular hilltop villages to the west of Tataouine, built to take advantage of the region's dramatic rocky outcrops. The outcrops are formed by alternate layers of soft and hard rock, which have weathered into a series of natural terraces.

They are dotted with natural caves, which became a place of a refuge for Berber tribes who were forced to flee the plains by the Hilalian invasions of the 11th century. The caves were extended into houses by tunnelling rooms into the soft rock, and further expanded by the addition of walled courtyards at the front. The highpoint of the village was occupied by a *ksar*, while the village itself stretched out along the terraces below.

The best-known of these villages is Chenini, 18km west of Tataouine, but nearby Douiret and Guermessa are every bit as spectacular and much less visited.

Troglodyte Villages

The Berbers of the Matmata region opted to go underground. Their homes are all built along the same lines: A central (usually circular) courtyard is dug about 6m deep into the very irregular terrain, and the rooms are then tunnelled out from the sides. The main entrance is usually through a narrow tunnel leading from the courtyard to ground level. The larger houses have two or three connected courtyards.

The best examples to check out in Matmata are three troglodyte hotels, the Marhala, the Sidi Driss and Les Berbères, although some of the rooms at Les Berbères were built by the more modern method of excavating with a hoe and backfilling over the roof at the end.

SCOTT DARSNEY

Left: Going underground. The whitewashed entrance and courtyard of the Hôtel Sidi Driss, Matmata.

[Continued from page 278]

Places to Stay & Eat The *Hôtel Les Ghorfas* (☎ 640 294/128) occupies a section of renovated ghorfas at the far end of the enormous main courtyard. Quite a few tour groups come through here during the day, stopping for lunch at the hotel restaurant. At night, hotel guests have the place pretty much to themselves – and there are only six rooms. Rates are TD12 per person for DB&B. The showers are a bit erratic (the water sprays up and bounces back off the ceiling), but who cares when you can wake up in surroundings like this.

The place goes into a sort of hibernation when tourist numbers drop away in winter, so it's a good idea to phone first if you're going to arrive after dark.

Getting There & Away The easiest way to get to Metameur is on one of the regular buses from Medenine. If you face a wait, hitching the 6km from Medenine to the turn-off to Metameur on the Gabès road is pretty simple. The turn-off is well signposted off to the left and you can see the village, about 1km from the main road. A taxi from Medenine costs about TD3.

Ksar Joumaa

Joumaa, 30km south-west of Medenine, is as good an example of a ksar as you could hope to find, and it's also one of the few that's easily accessible by public transport.

The ksar is best viewed from the nondescript modern village of Joumaa, which is the first place you come to after climbing the escarpment on the road to Beni Kheddache. The ksar is situated to the east, stretched out along a narrow spur. The best approach is via a rough track signposted off to the left about 1km before Joumaa on the road from Medenine. It's easy to spend an hour or so exploring the many ghorfas. Look out for the unusual motifs on the ceilings of some. An archway leads an inner courtyard and the ruins of the old *kalaa* (fort).

Buses and louages between Medenine and Beni Kheddache stop at Joumaa on the way.

Beni Kheddache

Beni Kheddache, 36km south-west of Medenine, is the main town of the northern Jebel Demmer. The run-down remnants of the town's old ksar are signposted on the way into the village, but there's little reason to stop here. There are two buses a day to Medenine (TD1.400, 45 minutes) and more frequent louages (TD1.500).

The road south-west to Ksar Ghilane is best left to 4WDs, but there are good roads north-west to Ksar Hallouf and south to Ksar Haddada and Ghomrassen.

Ksar Hallouf
☎ 05

Ksar Hallouf, 14km north-west of Beni Kheddache, presents a great opportunity for travellers to escape from the modern world for a few days.

The ksar, which overlooks a small modern village, has been converted into the wonderful *Relais Touristique de Ksar Hallouf* (☎ 637 148, fax 637 320) with accommodation in a small restored section of ghorfas. It's run by a very friendly local family which still seems genuinely thrilled that people like the place. DB&B costs TD12 and full board is TD17. The conditions are very basic: mattresses on the floor, cold showers and squat toilets – but worth it for the opportunity to wake up in such superb surroundings.

It's easy to spend a few days here exploring the area. The operators of the Relais can suggest some good walks.

Getting There & Away The road to Ksar Hallouf is clearly signposted from the centre of Beni Kheddache. There are a couple of unsignposted forks in the road along the way; take the right fork both times. The first 10km is a good sealed road, which finishes at an army base; the final 4km of dirt road presents no problems for conventional vehicles. A taxi from Beni Kheddache costs TD5.

TATAOUINE
☎ 05 • pop 8,000

Tataouine, 49km south of Medenine, is the best base for visiting the ksour. It's a modern administrative town with few attractions of its own, but it is well set up for travellers, with hotels, restaurants and useful transport connections to outlying ksour.

Orientation & Information

Everything of importance is found within the compact town centre.

The ONTT tourist office (☎ 850 686) is at the northern end of the main street, Ave Habib Bourguiba. There's also a small syndicat d'initiative on Ave Hedi Chaker.

The post office is at the southern end of Ave Habib Bourguiba – look for the radio tower. You can check email at the Publinet office on Ave Ahmed Tlili.

Most major banks have branches in town.

Ksar Megabla

The ksar is 2km from the town centre, signposted to the right off the Remada road. It takes about one hour to walk up to it from the main road. There are good views of the

town and surrounding area. The ksar itself is not in the best condition – in fact you need to be a bit careful when poking about in the courtyard. The villagers still keep their livestock in the cells.

Markets

If you're in town on Monday or Thursday, don't miss the lively markets held in the souq at the southern end of Ave Habib Mestaoui.

Places to Stay

The best budget place is the **Hôtel Residence Hamza** (☎ 863 506), just along from the Hôtel La Gazelle on Ave Hedi Chaker. It's more of a residence than a hotel, with just four rooms. It charges TD8.500 per person for B&B.

If the Hamza is full, try the **Hôtel Essour** (☎ 860 104), very close to the centre of town at the southern end of Rue 18 Janvier. The owners seem to delight in name changes, with three in the last four years, so just look

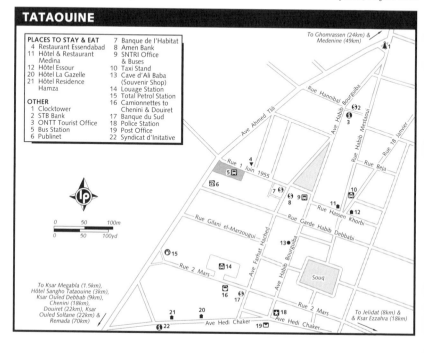

TATAOUINE

PLACES TO STAY & EAT
4   Restaurant Essendabad
11 Hôtel & Restaurant
    Medina
12 Hôtel Essour
20 Hôtel La Gazelle
21 Hôtel Residence
    Hamza

OTHER
1   Clocktower
2   STB Bank
3   ONTT Tourist Office
5   Bus Station
6   Publinet

7   Banque de l'Habitat
8   Amen Bank
9   SNTRI Office
    & Buses
10 Taxi Stand
13 Cave d'Ali Baba
    (Souvenir Shop)
14 Louage Station
15 Total Petrol Station
16 Camionnettes to
    Chenini & Douiret
17 Banque du Sud
18 Police Station
19 Post Office
22 Syndicat d'Initative

To Ghomrassen (24km) &
Medine (49km)

Rue Hannibal Bourguiba

Ave Ahmed Tlili

Rue Habib Bourguiba

Ave Habib Mestaoui

Rue 18 Janvier

Rue 1er Juin 1955

Rue Beja

Rue Hassen Khorbi

Rue Gilani el-Marzougui

Rue Garde Habib Debbabi

Ave Farhat Hached

Rue 2 Mars

Souq

Ave Habib Bourguiba

Rue 2 Mars

Ave Hedi Chaker

Ave Hedi Chaker

To Jelidat (8km) &
Ksar Ezzahra (18km)

To Ksar Megabla (1.5km),
Hôtel Sangho Tataouine (3km),
Ksar Ouled Debbab (9km),
Chenini (18km),
Douiret (22km), Ksar
Ouled Soltane (22km) &
Remada (70km)

0   50   100m
0   50   100yd

out for the colourful cartoon mural that covers the front of the building. The place itself hasn't changed. It has beds for TD4, or TD6 with hot shower and breakfast.

The *Hôtel Medina* (☎ 860 999) is opposite on Rue Habib Mestaoui. It charges TD5 a night, plus TD1.500 for breakfast. The rooms are OK, but the plumbing is a disaster.

The two star *Hôtel La Gazelle* (☎ 860 009), 150m from the post office on Ave Hedi Chaker, is the only upmarket choice in town. It has been feeling the pinch since the opening of the flash Sangho resort southeast of town, and is quick to offer discounts on its advertised rates of TD23.500/35 for singles/doubles with private bath, hot water and breakfast.

The stylish three star *Hôtel Sangho Tataouine* (☎ 860 124, fax 862 177) is 3km from town on the road to Chenini. It occupies a large, walled compound spreading up the hill south of the road, its name emblazoned in white on the rocky slope behind. In contrast, the rooms are tastefully decorated in traditional style, with lots of antique oddments and old photos. Singles/doubles with breakfast are TD59/88.

Places to Eat

The restaurant at the *Hôtel Medina* is smarter than its budget rivals with red tablecloths and neat table settings. The service is equally cheery, and the prices are much the same as you'll find elsewhere – TD1 for salads, and TD3.500 for a large turkey cutlet and chips.

The *Restaurant Essendabad*, on Rue 2 Mars, has a range of daily specials that normally includes a delicious, thick chorba (soup) for 800 mills.

The restaurant at the *Hôtel La Gazelle* does a three-course meal for TD6. The hotel also has the only bar in town, with cold beers for TD1.900.

All Tataouine's many patisseries sell the local speciality, *corne de gazelle* (350 mills) – a pastry case, shaped like a gazelle's horn, filled with chopped nuts and soaked in honey.

Getting There & Away

Bus The bus station occupies the large compound at the western end of Rue 1 Juin 1955.

There are buses to Medenine (TD1.950, one hour) at 6.30, 8 and 10 am and 2.30 pm. The 10 am bus continues to Zarzis and Houmt Souq (TD6.100, 2½ hours).

Remada, the southernmost point in the country served by the bus network, can be reached by a daily bus at 2.30 pm (TD3.150, 1¼ hours). There are six buses a day to Ghomrassen (800 mills, 30 minutes) between 8.30 am and 5.30 pm. The last bus back from Ghomrassen leaves at 4.30 pm. There's a daily bus south-east to Beni Barka, Maztouria and Ksar Ouled Soltane (850 mills, 45 minutes), leaving town at 6 am, and returning at 6 pm.

SNTRI runs air-con buses to Tunis (TD20.390, 8½ hours) at 7.30 am and 7.45 pm. These buses travel via Gabès (TD6.150, two hours), Sfax (TD10.910, four hours) and Sousse (TD15.410, 6½ hours). They leave from the SNTRI office on Ave Habib Bourguiba.

Louage Louages leave from a compound on the northern side of Rue 2 Mars. The entrance is through a small archway, which is easy to miss. There are regular departures for Medenine (TD2) and Remada (TD3.500), and occasional services to Ghomrassen (TD1). Seats to Tunis (TD22) can be reserved at the louage office (☎ 862 874) on Rue 1 Juin 1955.

Camionnette Camionnettes leave from near the Banque du Sud on Rue 2 Mars. There are fairly regular departures for Chenini (850 mills), Douiret (TD1.200) and Maztouria (800 mills), while some continue to Ksar Ouled Soltane (TD1.250). The earlier you set off the better. The system starts to slow down around noon and is virtually nonexistent after 3 pm.

Getting Around

While you can get to most of the larger ksour by public transport, there are lots of other places that you can't get to without your own vehicle. However, there are no rental cars in town. The nearest car rental agencies are on Jerba – see the Jerba & the South-East Coast chapter for more details.

You can charter taxis to take you out to the ksour from the taxi stand opposite the Hôtel Medina on Rue Habib Mestaoui. Typical rates include TD20 to Chenini and TD25 to Douiret.

WEST OF TATAOUINE
Ghomrassen

Ghomrassen, 24km north-west of Tataouine, is the main town of the Jebel Demmer. It was once the stronghold of the powerful Ouergherma federation, which ruled from here until it moved to Medenine in the 17th century.

The modern town is large enough to warrant a bank, a high school, shops and a couple of restaurants – but no hotels. The old part of town is to the south, on the way to Guermessa. It was spread along a gorge carved out by a broad oued, and protected by kalaa on both sides.

Getting There & Away Ghomrassen is something of a regional transport centre. There are six buses a day to Tataouine (800 mills, 30 minutes), and five to Medenine (TD1.850, one hour), as well as services to Guermessa (350 mills, 15 minutes) and Ksar Haddada.

Ksar Haddada

The fate of Ksar Haddada, 5km north of Ghomrassen, is little short of scandalous. Until recently, a restored section of the ksar was occupied by the fabulous Hôtel Ksar Haddada. It became a place of pilgrimage for *Star Wars* fans following its appearance in *Stars Wars IV – A New Hope*. The orange door jams were part of the set.

Sadly, the hotel has now closed and the place is slowly falling apart; apparently the maintenance bill was too much for the operators, and there were no other funds available. Despite this, it's still an amazing place and it continues to draw a steady stream of visitors – who continue to marvel at the maze of small alleyways and courtyards. It's best to ignore the disgusting toilets and concentrate on the many delightful features, such as the old palm doors. It was a memorable place to spend the night.

Getting There & Away There are occasional buses from Ghomrassen, but it's quicker to stand by the road and flag down whatever comes your way.

Guermessa

Guermessa, 8km south-west of Ghomrassen, is another spectacular Berber site in the same league as Chenini and Douiret. Like its southern neighbours, the old hilltop village has now been abandoned in favour of a modern village on the plains below. Unlike them, however, Guermessa remains almost undiscovered by the mass tourist trade. It's spread across two peaks, linked by a narrow causeway. The larger peak is topped by a ruined kalaa.

You need a 4WD to drive up to the site, which can be reached via the road to Ksar Ghilane and Douz, signposted to the east 1km north of the modern village. The turn-off to the site is 3km along this road, and loops back to Guermessa. This approach provides a great view of the twin peaks, linked by a narrow ridge. There are still people around, but no guides.

Getting There & Away The school buses that operate between Ghomrassen and Guermessa are useless for tourists. It costs about TD25 to charter a taxi there and back from Tataouine.

The road from Guermessa to Chenini is 4WD only.

Chenini

Chenini, 18km west of Tataouine, is the best known of the ksour hill villages. It's also the most visited and you will need to arrive early to appreciate the setting before the tour buses descend.

The ruins of the original kalaa, dating from the 12th century AD, stand at the junction of two ridges. The settlement extends down and out from here, built into the rock along a series of small terraces that lead around the steep hillside. The houses consist of a cave room, which has a fenced front courtyard containing one or two more rooms. Some of the doorways here are so small that you'd need to go on a diet to squeeze through.

The ksar is still used to store grain. The village still has a few occupants, but most have moved to the modern settlement of Nouvelle Chenini, several kilometres before old Chenini on the road to Tatouine.

A path leads up to a beautiful white mosque situated in a saddle between the two ridges.

Beyond here, a 20-minute walk leads to a mosque and the **graves of the Seven Sleepers**. A local legend has evolved to explain the existence of these strange 5m-long grave mounds: Seven Christians (and a dog) went into hiding in a nearby cave to escape persecution by the Romans; when they awoke 400 years later, they found that their bodies had continued to grow until they were 4m tall – whereupon they all promptly died. The cave in question has been closed off and can be viewed only on postcards.

There are many other extended graves in adjoining parts of the cemetery.

Places to Eat The *Relais Restaurant* is at the bottom of the hill by the car park. It specialises in set-menu lunches for tour groups. It also sells coffee and cold drinks, including beer.

Getting There & Away Camionnettes from Tatouine stop at Nouvelle Chenini; sometimes it's possible to persuade the driver to continue the last 2km to the site.

There's a good sealed road south to Douiret, looping around through the hills along the course of an oued. It passes the ruins of Ksar Ayaat and links up with the road to Douiret at Nouvelle Douiret. The road north from Chenini to Guermessa is best tackled by 4WD.

Douiret

This place is really something, with its crumbling ksar perched high on the spur of a hill above a dazzling white-washed mosque. As at Chenini, the houses are built into the rock along terraces that follow the contour lines around the hill. The main terrace leads south for 1km to more houses, some of which are still occupied. The rest of old Douiret is abandoned, and you can ex-

plore the ruins at your leisure. Look out for some of the ornate carved doorways and Berber designs painted on the walls. There are several camel-powered olive presses – just look for the telltale black streaks down the hillsides. You can get a coffee or an expensive cave-temperature soft drink (soda) from the small *buvette* (refreshment stall) below the mosque.

For some reason, Douiret doesn't suffer from tour group overkill in the way that Chenini does. Most of the time you'll have the place to yourself.

Getting There & Away Douiret is 22km south-west of Tatouine. The road is signposted from Debbab, 9km south of Tatouine on the road to Remada. As usual in this neck of the woods, transport is a bit of a hit-and-miss affair. Early morning is the best time to catch a camionnette out from Tatouine, but they normally go only as far as Nouvelle Douiret, 1.5km before old Douiret. You may be able to persuade the driver to take you the rest of the way, but you will certainly have to walk back afterwards to find a ride to Tatouine.

The easy solution is to spend TD25 to get a taxi to take you out and wait while you look around. Allow at least two hours.

If you have your own vehicle, you can drive to Chenini on the road that leads off to the south-west at Nouvelle Douiret. Don't be put off by the initial direction – the road loops back to the north after a few kilometres. Another road keeps going east to Ksar Ghilane, but it's strictly for 4WDs.

SOUTH OF TATAOUINE

There are plenty more good sites in the low hills of the Jebel Abiodh, as the southern tail of the Dahar range is known. These hills begin just south of Tatouine and curve away to the south-east towards the Libyan border.

Most are accessed via the loop road that begins about 1km south of Tatouine and follows a narrow valley south-west to Ksar Ouled Soltane via Beni Barka, Maztouria and Tamelest. The ridges either side of the road are dotted with the remains of several ksour, the most impressive being those above Beni Barka and Tamelest.

Ksar Ouled Soltane

Ksar Ouled Soltane, 22km south-east of Tataouine, has the best set of ghorfas in the south, rising a dizzying four storeys around two small courtyards. The upper levels are reached by a network of precarious, narrow, external steps. The lower courtyard is used as a stage for traditional dance and other performances during the Festival of the Ksour in late November, and the ghorfas here have been given the full renovation treatment.

Getting There & Away The only bus to Ksar Ouled Soltane (850 mills, 40 minutes, 6 pm) leaves Tataouine at 6 am. Camionnettes are a better bet. There are occasional services to Ksar Ouled Soltane, but plenty to Maztouria. There's quite a lot of traffic along this road, so hitching should not be a problem.

If you have your own transport, you can complete the loop by continuing south-east to Mghit and then returning to Tataouine via Ksar Ezzahra and Jelidat. The small section of dirt road between Mghit and Ksar Ezzahra is easily passable by conventional vehicle.

Ksar Ouled Debbab

This huge ksar sits on a low hill just east of the modern village of Debbab, 9km south of Tataouine on the Remada road. It was occupied until quite recently, if the electric cables are anything to go by. Most of the buildings are still in good condition. There's a sealed road leading up to the entrance gate from Debbab. The walk takes about 20 minutes.

Remada

There's 70km of very little between Tataouine and Remada, the southernmost point in Tunisia that can be reached by bus. There's no reason to come here unless you're heading on to the Sahara (see the previous The Sahara section for details).

Jerba & South-East Coast

Jerba

The resort island of Jerba has long been a popular spot, luring holiday-makers with its claim to be the legendary Land of the Lotus-Eaters. Its southerly location gives it a climate that is the envy of Northern Europe. Even in the middle of winter, temperatures seldom fail to drop below 15°C, guaranteeing that the tourist dinars keep flowing all year.

Jerba is situated about 50km north of Medenine, perched between the Jorf and Zarzis Peninsulas to create the virtually landlocked Gulf of Bou Grara. Jerba has been linked to the mainland since Roman times, when a causeway was built between the south-eastern corner of the island and the Zarzis Peninsula.

The island covers an area of approximately 500 sq km. The highest point is less than 30m above sea level, which makes it ideal for exploration by bicycle or, better still, by motorcycle. Both can be hired in the main town of Houmt Souq (see Car & Motorcycle under Getting Around in the Houmt Souq section).

The tourist season peaks in July and August, although it's too hot then to do much more than stagger to the beach. Winter and spring are the best times to visit – accommodation is cheaper, facilities are less in demand and the weather is ideal for getting out and exploring.

History
Local Berber tribes were well established when the Phoenicians arrived on the scene about 2700 years ago. Among them were the Gerbitani, whose settlement of Gerba (near modern Houmt Souq) provided the island with its name.

The Phoenicians were attracted by the safe anchorage provided by the Gulf of Bou Grara, and they established settlements at Meninx (modern El-Kantara) on Jerba and at Gightis on the mainland. Both grew in importance in Carthaginian times and continued

Highlights

- Staying at one of Houmt Souq's enchanting old funduqs
- Jerba's dazzling traditional architecture
- Lazing on the sands of Sidi Mahres Beach

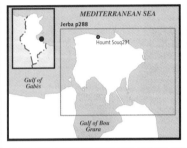

to prosper after the Roman conquest. During Roman times, Meninx was a town of sufficient stature to warrant the building of a 7km-long causeway linking it to the mainland.

Jerba was one of the first places to fall to the Arabs on their march into Tunisia, but it later became a stronghold of the Kharijites in the wake of the Kharijite rebellion that erupted across North Africa in AD 740. While the rebellion was suppressed elsewhere, the Kharijites held on in Jerba.

Their numbers were reinforced in AD 911 after the Fatimids overran the Kharijite Rustamid state based at Tahart in Algeria. Many refugees from Tahart wound up in Jerba. They belonged to the Ibadite sect of Kharijism, a faith still practised in the villages of southern Jerba. The Ibadites are found only here and in the villages of the M'Zab Valley in central Algeria. It is the Kharijites who are largely responsible for the huge number of mosques on the island – 213 in all.

Jerba spent most of the following 500 years outside the control of the region's central government, but it remained at the

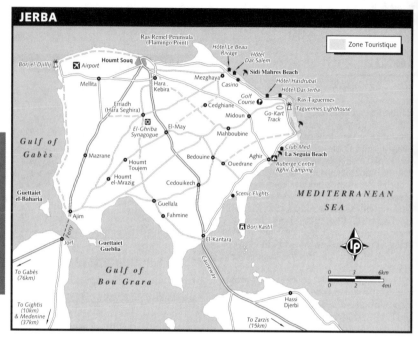

JERBA

Ras Remel Peninsula
(Flamingo Point)

Hôtel Le Beau
Rivage
Hôtel
Dar Salem

Zone Touristique

Borj el-Djillij

Airport

Houmt Souq

Sidi Mahres Beach

Mezghaya

Casino

Hôtel Hasdrubal
Hôtel Dar Jerba

Mellita

Hara
Kebira

Golf
Course

Ras Taguermes
Taguermes Lighthouse

Efriadh
(Hara Seghira)

Cedghiane

Midoun

Go-Kart
Track

El-Ghriba
Synagogue

El-May

Mahboubine

*Gulf of
Gabès*

Mazrane

Bedouine

Aghir
Ouedrane

Club Med
La Seguia Beach

Auberge Centre
Aghir Camping

Houmt
Toujem

Houmt
el-Mrazig

Cedouikech

*MEDITERRANEAN
SEA*

Guettaiet
el-Baharia

Guellala

Scenic Flights

Ajim

Fahmine

Jorf

Guettaiet
Gueblia

Borj Kastil

El-Kantara

To Gabès
(76km)

*Gulf of
Bou Grara*

Causeway

0   3   6km
0   2   4mi

To Gightis
(10km)
& Medenine
(37km)

Hassi
Djerbi

To Zarzis
(15km)

heart of the intrigues that affected the region. It was conquered by the Normans under Roger II of Sicily in 1135, briefly captured by the Almohads in 1159 and then occupied by the Aragonese.

In the early 16th century, the island became a battleground for Spanish and the Muslim corsairs, whose activities paved the way for Ottoman rule in North Africa. It was used as a base by the Barbarossa brothers, and then by their offsider Dragut – later to become Dargouth Pasha, ruler of Tripoli.

Dragut's renown was enhanced by a famous escape from the Spanish. In 1551 his fleet was trapped in the Gulf of Bou Grara, but he escaped at night by hauling the ships across a breach in the causeway. Returning in 1560, he massacred Spanish forces the following year, leaving the Tower of Skulls standing on the coast near Houmt Souq. (See the boxed text 'Pirates of the Barbary Coast' in the Northern Tunisia chapter.)

Jerba did well under the Ottomans, and earned a reputation for stability that resulted in it developing into an important trading post. The French left the Jerbans largely to their own devices.

The tourist boom, which began in the late 1960s, has brought a lot of money to the island, but has done more damage to traditional society than all the other invaders put together. Traditional ways survive in the Berber-speaking Ibadite villages of the south, like Guellala and Cedouikech, but they are fading as young people are drawn away to jobs in the tourist business.

Jerba once had a large Jewish community but, following the formation of the state of Israel, this has now shrunk to about 700. The El-Ghriba Synagogue, one of 14 on the island, is the oldest in North Africa.

See the boxed text 'The Jews of Jerba' in the Around Jerba section later in this chapter.

[Continued on page 290]

DAVID WILLETT

DAVID WILLETT

JON DAVISON

Top: Tribesmen show off their equestrian acumen at the Sahara Festival at Douz.
Bottom: Camels take time-out from the trekking circuit, Douz.

The ruins of an ancient kiln, Jerba

A defiant minaret surveys the Jerban coast

Borj Ghazi Mustapha, Jerba

A stronghold of the puritanical Kharijite sect, Jerba has over 213 imposing mosques. This well-buttressed example was built to stand the test of time.

JERBAN ARCHITECTURE

Jerba's highly distinctive fortress architecture reflects the island's long history as a stronghold of the fiercely autonomous Ibadite sect (see the History section at the beginning of this chapter). The constant fear of attack encouraged the development of a bunker mentality, and the landscape is dotted with what look like fortresses and air-raid shelters.

Defence, however, was not the sole concern: The architecture also reflects the islanders' pre-occupation with water conservation, and with keeping cool during the long, hot summers. Rooftops and courtyards were designed to channel rainwater into underground *impluviums* (tanks), providing both a water supply and a cool foundation. Thick rendered walls built of mud and stone provided further insulation. Finally, buildings were painted a brilliant white to deflect the summer sun.

Mosques

Nothing typifies Jerban architecture quite like the mosque. These squat, square buildings positively bristle with defiance. With their heavily buttressed walls and minimalist decoration, they look more like forts than places of worship. The finest example is the mosque at El-May, in the centre of the island. It stands in the middle of a large paved compound, dotted with hatches where you can check out the water level in the tanks below. The two principal mosques in Houmt Souq, the Mosque of the Turks and the Mosque of the Strangers, are Ottoman interpretations of the local style – built in the 17th century for orthodox Sunni worshippers.

Menzels

Menzels are traditional fortified homesteads. The island once boasted hundreds of them, but most have now been abandoned. There are still some good examples to be seen beside the main road between Ajim and Houmt Souq, and around El-May in the centre of the island.

They were all built to a standard design, with a defensive wall enclosing a large rectangular central compound entered by a single gate. Rooms were built around the inside of the walls. Square towers at the corners add to the fortress image. The top storeys of these towers were used as summer bedrooms, with window grates to let in the evening breezes and slatted floors for extra ventilation. The boundaries of the land belonging to each menzel are marked by low earth levees known as *tabia*.

Workshops

Known as *harout*, these traditional weaver's workshops could easily be mistaken for air-raid shelters. The design is simplicity itself, a long, barrel-vaulted *ghorfa* (room) built half below ground for insulation. They are characterised by a triangular front, extending well beyond the walls of the ghorfa, and buttressing along the outer walls.

Inset: A typically austere Jerban minaret. (Photo by David Willett)

Like menzels, most harout have now been abandoned. There's a good example to be found in the grounds of the Museum of Popular Arts and Traditions, in Houmt Souq.

[Continued from page 288]

Land of the Lotus-Eaters

According to legend, Jerba is the Land of the Lotus-Eaters, where Ulysses paused in the course of the *Odyssey* and had a lot of trouble persuading his crew to get back on board. Today's islanders are said to be descendants of these people, who lived 'in indolent forgetfulness, drugged by the legendary honeyed fruit'. It makes a good story for the tourists, and it is capitalised upon by hotels with names like the Lotos *(sic)* and Ulysses.

HOUMT SOUQ
☎ 05 • pop 65,000

The island's main town, Houmt Souq, is situated at the centre of the north coast. Its residents depend fairly heavily on tourism for their livelihood; the other, more traditional, source of income is the fishing industry.

Orientation
The town centre is about 800m inland. The main streets are Ave Habib Bourguiba and Ave Abdelhamid el-Kadhi. Ave Habib Bourguiba runs north through the town centre from the bus and *louage* stations and finishes near the port, while Ave Abdelhamid el-Kadhi skirts the eastern edge of town. The souqs and most of the town's hotels and restaurants are found within the large V formed by these streets. This is the old part of town, a maze of narrow, winding streets dotted with small squares.

Information
Tourist Offices The local *syndicat d'initiative* (☎ 650 915) is set back from the main street (Ave Habib Bourguiba), behind the two large maps of the island opposite Place Mongi Bali. The office is open from 9 am to 1 pm and 3.30 to 6 pm Monday to Saturday.

The ONTT tourist office (☎ 650 016) is out on the beach road, Blvd de l'Environment, about a 15-minute walk from the centre. It's not really worth the effort. Opening hours are from 8.30 am to 1 pm and 3 to 5.45 pm Monday to Thursday and 8.30 am to 1.30 pm Friday and Saturday.

Money All the major banks have branches somewhere around the town centre. Most have ATMs for MasterCard and Visa. There is always one bank rostered to be open on Saturday and Sunday. The syndicat d'initiative can tell you which, and where to find it.

Post & Communications The main post office is on Ave Habib Bourguiba. There are plenty of Taxiphone offices, including one opposite the post office on Place Mongi Bali. The office just north of the Mosque of the Strangers on Ave Abdelhamid el-Kadhi is much quieter and has more phones. It's open from 7.30 am to 10 pm or later, daily.

Email & Internet Access Djerba Cyber Espace, 135 Ave Habib Bourguiba, is open from 8.30 am to 1 pm and 3 to 6 pm Monday to Saturday, and from 8.30 am to 1 pm Sunday. It charges TD3 per hour, with a TD1 minimum. The office is on the 1st floor, accessed by the stairs in the courtyard. The courtyard is entered through the large arch at No 135.

Bookshops The bookshop just north of the post office on Ave Habib Bourguiba stocks international newspapers. It also has a small collection of novels in French.

Medical Services The large regional hospital (☎ 650 018) is about 500m southeast of the town centre on the road to Midoun. There's also the private Clinique Dar ech-Chifa (☎ 650 441, fax 652 215), which is north-east of town, off Ave Abdelhamid el-Kadhi.

Emergency The main police station is on Ave Abdelhamid el-Kadhi.

Souq
Houmt Souq is compact enough to be explored easily on foot. The **old souq district** is the centre of things and consists of a tangle of narrow alleys and a few open squares with cafes. The place is full of souvenir

HOUMT SOUQ

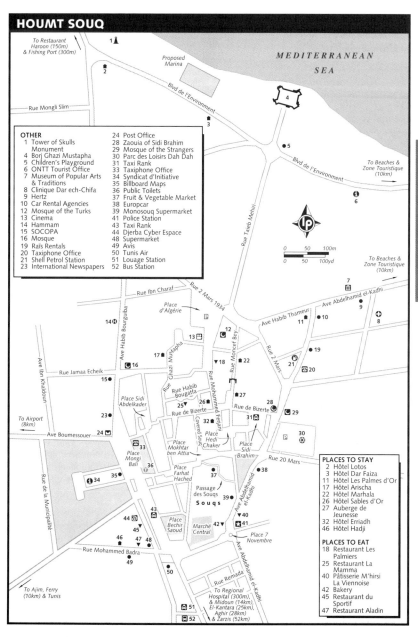

OTHER
1 Tower of Skulls Monument
4 Borj Ghazi Mustapha
5 Children's Playground
6 ONTT Tourist Office
7 Museum of Popular Arts & Traditions
8 Clinique Dar ech-Chifa
9 Hertz
10 Car Rental Agencies
12 Mosque of the Turks
13 Cinema
14 Hammam
15 SOCOPA
16 Mosque
19 Raïs Rentals
20 Taxiphone Office
21 Shell Petrol Station
23 International Newspapers

24 Post Office
28 Zaouia of Sidi Brahim
29 Mosque of the Strangers
30 Parc des Loisirs Dah Dah
31 Taxi Rank
33 Taxiphone Office
34 Syndicat d'Initiative
35 Billboard Maps
36 Public Toilets
37 Fruit & Vegetable Market
38 Europcar
39 Monosouq Supermarket
41 Police Station
43 Taxi Rank
44 Djerba Cyber Espace
48 Supermarket
49 Avis
50 Tunis Air
51 Louage Station
52 Bus Station

PLACES TO STAY
2 Hôtel Lotos
3 Hôtel Dar Faiza
11 Hôtel Les Palmes d'Or
17 Hôtel Arischa
22 Hôtel Marhala
26 Hôtel Sables d'Or
27 Auberge de Jeunesse
32 Hôtel Erriadh
46 Hôtel Hadji

PLACES TO EAT
18 Restaurant Les Palmiers
25 Restaurant La Mamma
40 Pâtisserie M'hirsi La Viennoise
42 Bakery
45 Restaurant du Sportif
47 Restaurant Aladin

To Restaurant Haroon (150m) & Fishing Port (300m)
Proposed Marina
MEDITERRANEAN SEA
Rue Mongli Slim
Blvd de l'Environment
Blvd de l'Environment
To Beaches & Zone Touristique (10km)
To Beaches & Zone Touristique (10km)
Rue Taïeb Mehiri
Rue Ibn Charaf
Rue 2 Mars 1934
Place d'Algérie
Ave Abdelhamid el-Kadhi
Ave Habib Thameur
Rue 2 Mars
Rue Moncef Bey
Rue Jamaa Echeik
Ave Habib Bourguiba
Ghazi Mustapha
Ave Ibn Khaldoun
Rue Habib Bougatfa
Place Sidi Abdelkader
Rue Mohammed Ferjani
To Airport (8km)
Ave Boumessouer
Rue de Bizerte
Covered Souq
Place Hedi Chaker
Place Sidi Brahim
Rue 20 Mars
Place Mokhtar ben Attia
Place Mongi Bali
Place Farhat Hached
Passage des Souqs
Souqs
Ave Abdelhamid el-Kadhi
Place Bechir Saoud
Marché Central
Place 7 Novembre
Rue de la Municipalité
Rue Mohammed Badra
To Ajim, Ferry (10km) & Tunis
Rue Remada
To Regional Hospital (300m), & Midoun (14km), El-Kantara (25km), Aghir (28km) & Zarzis (52km)
Ave Abdelhamid el-Kadhi
0 50 100m
0 50 100yd

shops. The owners are used to dealing with package tourists who don't bargain too hard, so prices are high.

A feature of the old town are the *funduqs* (caravanserais), former lodging houses for the travelling merchants of the camel caravans that stopped here in Ottoman times. They were built on two floors surrounding a central courtyard; the top floor had rooms for the merchants, while their animals were housed below. Some of these funduqs have been turned into excellent budget hotels (see Places to Stay later in this section).

Islamic Monuments

There are some interesting Islamic monuments around the town. Just on the edge of the souq is the , which contains the tomb of the 17th-century saint. On the other side of the road is the multidomed **Mosque of the Strangers**. The 18th-century **Mosque of the Turks** is north of the souq on Place d'Algérie. Built in the same fortress style as the island's traditional mosques, the only clue to its Turkish origins is the distinctive Ottoman minaret. All these monuments are closed to non-Muslims.

Museum of Popular Arts & Traditions

This fine little museum occupies the Zaouia of Sidi Zitouni, about 200m from the town centre along the north-eastern arm of Ave Abdelhamid el-Kadhi. It houses a good range of local costumes as well as other bits and pieces. One room still has the original terracotta tile ceiling. The museum is open from 9.30 am to 4.30 pm Saturday to Thursday; admission is TD2.100, plus an extra TD1 if you want to take photos. The ticket office is the small traditional weaver's hut near the entrance.

Borj Ghazi Mustapha

The town's old fort is on the coast 500m north of the Mosque of the Turks at the end of the tree-lined Rue Taieb Mehiri. Known as the Borj Ghazi Mustapha (and occasionally as the Borj el-Kebir), the fort, built by the Aragonese in the 13th century, was extended early in the 16th century by the Spanish.

The fort was the scene of a famous massacre in 1560 when a Turkish fleet under Dragut (see also under History earlier in this chapter) captured the fort and put the Spanish garrison to the sword. The skulls of the victims were stacked up on the shoreline 500m west of the fort (opposite the Hôtel Lotos) as a grim reminder to others not to try any funny business. This macabre Tower of Skulls stood for almost 300 years until it was dismantled on the order of the bey of Tunis in 1848. A simple monument now stands in its place.

The fort itself is worth a wander around and there are good views along the coast. Look for the mounds of cannonballs, both stone and rusting iron, that have been found in the course of recent renovations. The fort has the same opening hours as the museum. Entry is TD1.100, plus TD1 to take photos.

Fishing Port

Houmt Souq's busy fishing port is at the northern end of Ave Habib Bourguiba, a pleasant 10-minute walk from town. Check out the huge stacks of terracotta pots that are used by local octopus fishermen in a traditional technique known as *gargoulette*. The pots are tied together and cast out on long lines; they sink to the bottom and are left there for the octopus to discover. Octopus like to hide in rocky nooks and crannies, and they obligingly crawl into the pots only to be caught when they are hauled to the surface.

Beach

The beach north of Houmt Souq isn't worth checking out. The shoreline is rocky and covered in rubbish, and the sea is too shallow for swimming.

Scenic Flights

Air Tropic (☎ 606 996) charges TD30 for a 30-minute ride in one of its tiny Petrel hydroplanes. It operates from the sand flats 5km south of Aghir on the east coast.

Special Events

The Ulysses Festival is held in August. This is strictly for tourists and includes events like a Miss Ulysses beauty contest.

Places to Stay

Houmt Souq has an excellent range of accommodation, with some interesting options in every category. No hotel in town rates more than two stars; the big hotels are all out at the *zone touristique* (see the Around Jerba section).

Unless otherwise stated, the prices listed here are for the high season and include breakfast. There tends to be very little difference (a dinar or so) between seasons – unlike at the zone touristique where there can be huge differences between high and low season.

Places to Stay – Budget

Camping The island's only *camp site* is on the beach at Aghir, about 28km east of Houmt Souq. The *Auberge Centre Aghir* (☎ 657 366), at the junction of the Midoun road, is run by the Centre des Stages et Vacances organisation – the resort version of a *maison des jeunes*. It charges TD2 per person, plus TD1 for each tent. It also has dorm accommodation for TD5. To get there from Houmt Souq, catch the bus (900 mills, 40 minutes) to Club Med via Midoun.

Hostels Houmt Souq's excellent *Auberge de Jeunesse* (☎ 650 619) occupies an old funduq next to the Hôtel Marhala on Rue Moncef Bey. It's as good as hostels get. The staff are friendly, and the hostel is open throughout the day. Beds (in dorms only) cost TD3.500. Breakfast is available for TD1, and lunch and dinner for TD3. There is a three-day limit on stays in high season.

Hotels The most interesting places to stay are the old funduqs. The pick of them is the *Hôtel Arischa* (☎ 650 384), just north of the souq on Rue Ghazi Mustapha. It's a place to explore as well as a place to stay. The courtyard is filled with flowers and the large singles/doubles are good value at TD9/14.

Another good choice is the *Hôtel Marhala* (☎ 650 146, fax 653 317), on Rue Moncef Bey, one of a small chain of hotels owned by the Touring Club de Tunisie. As usual, the standard is excellent, although some people find the authentic, barrel-vaulted rooms claustrophobic. Rooms cost TD10.500/16 with breakfast, and additional meals are available for TD5 each.

An alternative to the funduqs is the *Hôtel Sables d'Or* (☎ 650 423), an old house on Rue Mohammed Ferjani that has been converted into a stylish little hotel. The two brothers who run it keep the 12 rooms absolutely spotless. They charge TD12/22.

Places to Stay – Mid-Range

The *Hôtel Erriadh* (☎ 650 756, fax 650 487), just north of the souq on Rue Mohammed Ferjani, is the most upmarket of the old funduqs. It's a beautiful place with large air-con double rooms with private bathroom around a cool vine-covered courtyard. It charges TD17.500/26 for singles/doubles.

The one star *Hôtel Hadji* (☎ 650 630, fax 652 221), 44 Rue Mohammed Badra, hasn't got a lot going for it apart from the cheapest air-con rooms in town. Rooms are TD16/25, plus TD4 for air-con.

The best rooms in town are at the two star *Hôtel Les Palmes d'Or* (☎ 653 369, fax 653 368, [e] palmes.dor@gnet.tn). The rooms are bright and airy, and all come equipped with reverse-cycle air-con and satellite TV. The place is brand new, and the staff eager to please. Rooms are TD37/58, falling to TD20/28 in winter.

If you want to get out of town, there are two good places facing the beach on Blvd de l'Environment to the west of the fort. The *Hôtel Dar Faiza* (☎ 650 083, fax 651 763) is a quiet retreat with accommodation spread through gardens at the rear of the hotel. It also has a small pool and a tennis court, albeit in desperate need of repair. It charges TD32/50, dropping to TD17.500/26 in winter. The hotel has one of the better restaurants on the island, so it's worth considering half or full board.

The *Hôtel Lotos* (☎ 650 026), 200m west of the Dar Faiza, opposite the Tower of Skulls monument, charges TD23/37. This was the original tourist hotel on the island. The rooms are huge, with correspondingly large balconies, and most offer excellent views of the coast. In winter, the Lotos is a bargain at TD14/20.

Places to Stay – Top End

The island's top hotels are all located out on the beaches of the *zone touristique* (see the following Around Jerba section for more details).

Places to Eat

The streets of Houmt Souq are filled with cafes and restaurants to suit every budget.

The tiny *Restaurant La Mamma* is a rough and ready place on Rue Habib Bougatfa that is worth checking out. It does a roaring trade at lunch time, with local workers tucking into such staples as *lablabi* (chickpea broth) and *chorba* (soup; both 800 mills). It also has daily specials like spicy, Tunisian-style macaroni for TD1.500.

The *Restaurant Les Palmiers*, on Place d'Algérie, is a good deal more refined, but not a lot more expensive. The extensive menu includes *briqs* from 700 mills, salads from TD1.500 and main courses from TD2.500. A hearty bowl of couscous with fish costs TD3.500. You'll find a similar range at the *Restaurant du Sportif*, centrally located on Ave Habib Bourguiba.

The *Restaurant Aladin* is a cheery little place on Ave Mohammed Badra that specialises in fish. Prices are much lower here than at the tourist restaurants. The menu includes some interesting seafood dishes such as octopus cooked in its own ink for TD3.500.

The *Patisserie M'hirsi La Viennoise* has an amazing range of cakes and pastries.

If you want to enjoy a glass of wine with your meal, you'll need to allow your budget belt out a notch or two. Most of the licensed restaurants are grouped together around Place Hedi Chaker and Place Sidi Brahim, and offer very similar menus – all well endowed with seafood. Most of the feedback about these places is less than positive. Several travellers have reported being stung by huge bills after being persuaded to have 'special meals'. Be aware that fish is priced by weight – and be specific about your order.

The *Restaurant Baccar*, on Place Hedi Chaker, gets good reports.

Locals with something to celebrate prefer to head elsewhere. One of the most popular is the seafood restaurant downstairs at the *Hôtel Arischa*. It's not a cheap alternative, with most main courses priced around TD10, but it's good food backed up by friendly service – and a very reasonably priced wine list. The restaurant at the *Hôtel Dar Faiza* is another favourite. The tourist menu is good value at TD8 for three courses, and it also has a good selection of local wines.

The best restaurant on the island is the *Restaurant Haroon* (☎ 650 488). Allow TD25 plus wine, or opt for the three-course menu (TD14).

Entertainment

Apart from restaurants, Houmt Souq has no nightlife to speak of, which is why there are some very big kids to be found on the bumper cars and other rides at *Parc des Loisirs Bah Bah* on Rue 20 Mars. It's open from 5 to 11 pm daily.

Getting There & Away

Air Jerba's airport, near the village of Mellita in the north-west of the island, handles a busy schedule of international flights. There's a constant flow of charter flights from Europe. Tunis Air operates four scheduled flights a week to Paris and weekly flights to Brussels, Frankfurt, Geneva, İstanbul, Lyon, Marseille, Munich, Rome, Vienna and Zurich.

There are seven flights a day to Tunis (TD50.500 one way, one hour). The first flight leaves at 6 am and the last at 8.15 pm. Four flights a week stop at Sfax (TD26 one way) on the way.

Bus The bus station is at the southern end of Ave Habib Bourguiba. Scheduled departures are listed on a board above the ticket windows.

SNTRI runs four air-con services a day to Tunis (TD17.760). The 8 am and 7.30 pm services travel via Kairouan (TD13.180, six hours) and take eight hours, while the 7 pm service goes via Sfax (TD10.520, five hours) and Sousse (TD15.670, seven hours) and take one hour longer. There is an additional earlybird special at 6 am to Sfax and Sousse. Fares are about a dinar less to compensate for getting up so early. All SNTRI services stop at Gabès (TD5.690, 2½ hours).

The regional company, Sotregames, has five buses a day to Medenine. Make sure you catch one of the services that travels *par bac* (by the Ajim-Jorf ferry). These services cost TD2.850 and take 1½ hours; services via Zarzis an hour longer and cost TD4.300. Two of these buses continue to Tataouine (TD4.750, 2½ hours). The afternoon service travels via Zarzis, stretching the journey time to 3½ hours and the fare is TD6.100.

There are also three buses a day to Gabès (TD5.700, three hours). The 4.30pm service continues to Matmata (TD6, three hours).

Louage Louages leave from opposite the entrance to the bus station. There are frequent departures for Gabès (TD4.900) and Medenine (TD4), and some services to Tataouine (TD6). Louages to Tunis (TD19.500) leave at 6 am and 6 pm and can be booked at the small office (☎ 652 164) at the side of the bus station. Ask at the office about occasional services to Sfax and Sousse.

Car & Motorcycle The main road from Houmt Souq to Zarzis travels along the old Roman causeway linking El-Kantara and the mainland. This route is only worth taking if you are heading south to Zarzis or Ben Guerdane. If you're heading for Medenine or Gabès, it's much quicker to use the car ferries between Ajim and Jorf (see the Ajim section later in this chapter for details).

Getting Around
To/From the Airport The airport is 8km west of Houmt Souq, past the village of Mellita. There are four buses (520 mills) a day from the central bus station, which makes it unlikely that a bus will suit your departure time.

If the buses don't suit, you'll have to catch a taxi. It'll cost about TD3 from Houmt Souq, or TD8 from the Hôtel Dar Jerba in the zone touristique.

Bus There is a fairly comprehensive local bus network connecting Houmt Souq with the main villages around the island.

There is a timetable and a colour-coded route map of the services around the island above the ticket windows in the bus station in Houmt Souq.

Car Houmt Souq is a popular place to hire cars for trips around the island and to sights around the south of the country. All the companies have offices both in town and out at the airport where the phone number for them all is ☎ 650 233.

The offices in town include Avis (☎ 650 151), on Ave Mohammed Badra; Europcar (☎ 650 357), on Ave Abdelhamid el-Kadhi; and Hertz (☎ 650 196), on Ave Abdelhamid el-Kadhi. It's worth hunting around for deals at the cluster of local companies at the northern end of Ave Abdelhamid el-Kadhi.

Taxi There are two taxi ranks in Houmt Souq – one is on Ave Habib Bourguiba in the centre of town and the other is at Place Sidi Brahim. Sample fares include Houmt Souq to Midoun for TD4.500 and Houmt Souq to Aghir for TD6. Fares are 50% higher after 10 pm.

Taxis are forever cruising the zone touristique for fares into Houmt Souq. The big hotels, such as the Dar Jerba, have their own taxi ranks.

In summer, demand for taxis far exceeds supply and it can be difficult to get hold of one in Houmt Souq, especially in the early afternoon when shops and businesses close for a couple of hours.

Taxis can also be hired for the day for trips around the island. A daily charter costs between TD40 and TD50, depending on your bargaining skills.

Bicycle & Moped Raïs Rentals (☎ 650 303), north of the Mosque of the Strangers on Ave Abdelhamid el-Kadhi in Houmt Souq, has a good selection of machines. It has basic bicycles for TD10 per day, mountain bikes for TD14, 50cc mopeds for TD30 and 80cc scooters for TD45.

When riding a moped you are unlikely to be covered by your insurance policy. Be extremely careful, especially out in the smaller inland villages where young children, wayward cyclists and suicidal dogs can be a real hazard. No licence is needed for machines less than 50cc.

AROUND JERBA
Zone Touristique
☎ 05

The island's tourist strip covers the entire north-eastern corner of the island – 20km of uninterrupted hotels that monopolise the only decent beaches, Sidi Mahres on the north coast and La Seguia on the east coast.

Sidi Mahres is a magnificent sweep of golden sand. It begins east of the low-lying Ras Remel Peninsula, which protrudes from the middle of the north coast 10km east of Houmt Souq. The peninsula is known as **Flamingo Point** because of the large number of flamingos that gather there in winter. Sidi Mahres beach then continues east all the way to **Ras Taguermes**, the cape at Jerba's north-eastern tip. It's marked by a bold red and black lighthouse by the roadside. A long sand spit extends south from the cape, enclosing a large lagoon.

South of here on the east coast is **La Seguia**. The hotels are further apart here, and the beaches less crowded.

Things to Do Most of the tourists who use the resort hotels do little more than cook themselves on the beach. Those who feel more energetic will find a wide range of **water-sports** equipment for hire, including windsurfers (TD4 per hour), pedalos (TD5) and catamarans (TD20).

Golf is a major attraction. Jerba Golf Club (☎ 659 055, fax 659 051, e djerba .golfclub@planet.tn) is 17km east of Houmt Souq. Golfers can create the course of their choice from three nine-hole layouts of varying degrees of difficulty. Green fees are TD48 for 18 holes, or TD28 for nine. Club hire costs an additional TD12. Tee-off times must be booked in advance.

The small **go-kart track** opposite the Ras Taguermes lighthouse costs TD6 for 10 laps.

If you're suffering from an overloaded wallet, the croupiers at Jerba's **casino** will be happy to help out. It's open from 6 pm to 5 am daily. Only foreign currency is accepted.

Places to Stay & Eat Accommodation options along the beach are dominated by a string of massive resort hotels. They include such monsters as the **Hôtel Dar Jerba**, a conglomeration of four hotels catering mainly for German tourists. More than 2700 sun seekers can enjoy the umpteen restaurants, bars, Bavarian folk nights, disco etc.

One place that's a little bit different is the **Hôtel Dar Salem** (☎/fax 757 667), a small three-star place 11km east of Houmt Souq that is pitched towards families rather than tour groups. Singles/doubles cost TD46/75, falling to TD25/40 in low season.

Another possibility is the nearby **Hôtel Le Beau Rivage** (☎ 757 130, fax 758 123), 10km east of Houmt Souq at the beginning of Sidi Mahres beach. It's a small pension-style place with singles/doubles for TD30/40, including breakfast. The rates fall to TD15/24 in winter.

The smartest place around is the five star **Hôtel Hasdrubal** (☎ 657 650, fax 657 730), which is 16km east of Houmt Souq on Sidi Mahres beach. It has singles/doubles with breakfast for TD115/170, and facilities that include two swimming pools and a disco.

Getting There & Away See the Getting Around section under Houmt Souq earlier for details of transport options around the zone touristique.

Midoun
☎ 05

This is the island's second major town and is best known for its busy Friday market. Most of the items on sale are really just tourist rubbish, with only a few stalls set up to sell fruit and vegetables.

The town also stages a traditional Jerban wedding ceremony for the benefit of tourists every Tuesday at noon.

Places to Stay & Eat There is no reason to stay in Midoun; the accommodation in Houmt Souq is better – and cheaper. Midoun's only option is the **Hôtel Jawhara** (☎ 600 467), on Rue Echabi, a small street off the main market square. It's basic and not great value at TD11/17 for singles/doubles.

For local food, try the **Restaurant de l'Orient**, which has couscous for TD2. It's next to the post office on the southern edge of town. The **Restaurant Le Khalife** (☎ 657 860), on Ave Salah ben Youssef, is an upmarket fish restaurant.

Getting There & Away There are eight bus services a day between Midoun and Houmt Souq (800 mills).

Cedghiane

The oasis of Cedghiane is situated about halfway between Houmt Souq and Midoun. It's in the most fertile part of the island, with an ample supply of sweet artesian water, which has allowed the development of traditional, tiered desert oasis agriculture. Tall palms provide shade for citrus and pomegranate trees, which in turn protect vegetable crops. The huge *menzels* (Jerban dwellings) of the area are evidence that this was once an important settlement, but most are in ruins and the landowners live elsewhere.

Erriadh (Hara Seghira)

Once exclusively a Jewish settlement, Erriadh (or Hara Seghira) is just off the main Houmt Souq-Zarzis road. With the mass migration of Jews to Israel, the population is now predominantly Muslim, but a number of synagogues still remain.

The most important Jewish synagogue is El-Ghriba (the Stranger), signposted 1km south of the town. It is a major place of pilgrimage during the Passover Festival, when Jews come to pay tribute to the grand master of the Talmud, Shimon Bar Yashai, who died more than 400 years ago.

The site dates back to 586 BC, although the present building was constructed early in the 20th century. The inner sanctuary is said to contain one of the oldest Torahs (Jewish holy book) in the world.

The Jews of Jerba

The Jewish community dates its arrival in Jerba either from 586 BC, following Nebuchadnezzar's conquest of Jerusalem, or from the Roman sacking of the same city in AD 71; either way this makes it one of the oldest Jewish communities in the world. Some historians, however, argue that many Jerban Jews are descended from Berbers who converted to Judaism. Over the centuries the community also received several influxes of Jews fleeing from persecution in Spain, Italy and Palestine.

In the times of the beys in the 19th century, Jews in Jerba were required to wear distinctive clothes: black pantaloons, black skull cap and sleeveless blue shirts. Discrimination ended with the arrival of the French in 1881. The community was known for being staunchly traditional, like their neighbours the Kharijite Muslims, and it rejected financial and educational aid from the rest of the Jewish world. Communities of Jerban Jews settled all over southern Tunisia, usually working as blacksmiths or shopkeepers, but returned to the island for the summer and for religious festivals.

Most Jerban Jews emigrated to Israel after the 1956 and 1967 wars; after centuries of relative peace, the clash between Arab and Israeli nationalism made their position untenable. The community also suffered during WWII, when the Germans extorted 50kg of gold as a communal fine.

The two main Jewish settlements on Jerba were Hara Kebira (Big Ghetto), just south of Houmt Souq, and Hara Seghira (Little Ghetto), in the centre of the island. While Hara Kebira has a dozen or so synagogues and a kosher restaurant, Hara Seghira features the main Jewish site on the island, the El-Ghriba Synagogue. This synagogue was thought to have been founded in about AD 600, after a holy stone fell from heaven at the site and a mysterious woman appeared to direct the construction of the synagogue. Although the present brightly decorated building dates only from the 1920s, it is home to one of the oldest Torahs in the world and numerous silver plaques from pilgrims can be seen. Today the synagogue remains an important pilgrimage site, although the Jewish community on Jerba numbers only a few hundred.

Richard Plunkett

The site was apparently chosen after a stone fell from heaven; it is also said that an unknown woman turned up and performed a miracle or two to assist the builders.

It is open to the public daily except Saturday; modest dress is required, and men have to don *yarmulkes* (skullcaps) on entering. Small donations are compulsory.

Buses from Houmt Souq to Guellala go past the synagogue (400 mills).

Guellala

This tiny village on the south coast is known for its pottery. In the past the pottery was sold on the mainland, but these days almost all of it is sold on site. A dozen or so workshops and galleries line the main road, all selling much the same stuff.

Be sure to check out the amazing Cave d'Ali Berbere, on the eastern edge of town – towards El-Kantara. Ali claims that the cave, supported by a series of stone arches, dates back to Roman times. It houses an ancient olive press.

There are seven buses a day between Guellala and Houmt Souq (800 mills, 30 minutes).

Ajim

Ajim is a busy fishing port and the departure point for car ferries to Jorf on the mainland. There's nothing much to do other than watch the fishermen. If you have to wait a while for a ferry, there are a few restaurants on the main street.

Getting There & Away Car ferries operate 24 hours a day between the Jerban port of Ajim and Jorf on the mainland. They leave every 30 minutes from 6.30 am to 9.30 pm; hourly from 9.30 to 11.30 pm; two hourly from 11.30 pm to 4.30 am and hourly again from 4.30 to 6.30 am. The trip takes 15 minutes and the fare is 600 mills for a car. Passengers travel free.

West Coast

There is very little along the entire western coastline. There's just one dirt track, which hugs the coast all the way, and a few scattered houses.

The lighthouse at the north-western corner of the island occupies an 18th-century Turkish fort, the Borj el-Djillij. It's closed to the public and there's no reason to come here other than curiosity.

South-East Coast

The flat coastal plain on the mainland south of Jerba has little of interest other than the minor Roman site of Gightis and some reasonable beaches around Zarzis. Tourism is very low-key, although there are a few resorts on the coast just north of Zarzis. Fishing and olive-growing are the main income earners.

GIGHTIS

The Roman port of Gightis, 20km south of Jorf on the back road to Medenine, is one of Tunisia's least-visited ancient sites.

Established by the Phoenicians, Gightis became a busy port during Roman times – exporting gold, ivory and slaves delivered by trans-Saharan caravans. Most of the buildings date from the 2nd century AD and are spread around the ancient capitol and forum. The site lay buried until the early 20th century and is relatively undeveloped. It's a lovely spot for a stroll, with clumps of palms and acacia trees dotting the coast above the gleaming waters of the Gulf of Bou Grara.

The site is open from 8 am to noon and 3 to 7 pm daily in summer and from 8.30 am to 5.30 pm daily in winter. Don't worry if the site appears closed – the guardian lives opposite and will emerge. Admission is TD1.100, plus TD1 to take photos.

Getting There & Away

Buses and louages between Houmt Souq and Medenine can drop you at the site, which is just south of the tiny modern village of Bou Grara. You will have to pay the full fare for Houmt Souq to Medenine if you catch a louage. Getting away is more difficult; you may have a long wait for a bus, and the louages are likely to be full. The local practice is to flag down whatever comes by.

ZARZIS

- **pop 15,000**

Zarzis is one of the least exciting towns in the country. It's worth a mention only because the coast to the north of town is home to Tunisia's newest tourist strip, an area that tourism authorities are promoting with glossy brochures filled with photos of golden beaches backed by olive groves.

In reality, Zarzis is a dull, dusty, modern, single-storey concrete town with little to see or do. The nearby beach that features in the brochures is OK, but is dominated by half a dozen huge resort hotels like Club Sangho and Club Oamarit.

BEN GUERDANE

- **pop 3000**

The town of Ben Guerdane, 33km west of the Libyan border, was once pretty much the end of the road in Tunisia. The international air embargo imposed on Libya in 1992 (for refusing to hand over suspects in the Lockerbie jumbo-jet bombing) briefly transformed it into a boom town on Libya's road lifeline to the outside world. All land traffic between the two countries passes through here.

Things have quietened since the lifting of the embargo. The main feature of the town is a large market selling cheap Libyan-produced clothing and domestic goods.

Getting There & Away

There are frequent buses and louages to Medenine, as well as services to Zarzis. There is a daily bus to Tunis (TD19.900, nine hours) at 10.30 pm.

If you're heading for Libya, the border formalities are conducted at the Ras Ajdir crossing point. Almost everybody needs a visa to enter Libya. They can't be issued on the spot, and are difficult for individuals to obtain.

Language

ARABIC

Tunisian Arabic belongs to a dialect known as Western Colloquial Arabic. There is no dictionary or phrasebook specifically for Tunisian Arabic, but this language guide includes some of the most common words and phrases. For a more comprehensive guide to Arabic, get hold of Lonely Planet's *Egyptian Arabic phrasebook*.

More specialised or educated language tends to be much the same across the Arab world, although pronunciation varies considerably. The spread of radio and television have increased all Arabs' exposure to and understanding of what is commonly known as Modern Standard Arabic (MSA). MSA, which has grown from the classical language of the Quran and poetry, is the written and spoken lingua franca of the Arab world. It's the language of radio, television and the press, and also the majority of modern Arabic literature.

Foreign students of the language constantly face the dilemma of whether to learn MSA first (which could mean waiting a while before being able to talk with the locals) and then a chosen dialect, or simply to acquire spoken competence in the latter. Dialects supposedly have no written form (the argument goes it would be like writing in Cockney or Strine), although there's no reason why they could not avail themselves of the same script used for the standard language. If this leaves you with a headache, you'll have some idea of why so few non-Arabs or non-Muslims embark on the study of this complex tongue!

Pronunciation

Pronunciation of Arabic can be tongue-tying for someone unfamiliar with the intonation and combination of sounds. Pronounce the transliterated words slowly and clearly.

This language guide should help, but bear in mind that the myriad rules governing pronunciation and vowel use are too extensive to be covered here.

Vowels

Technically, there are three long and three short vowels in Arabic. The reality is a little different, with local dialect and varying consonant combinations affecting pronunciation. This is the case throughout the Arabic-speaking world – generally, five short and five long vowels can be identified:

a	as in 'had' (sometimes very short)
e	as in 'bet' (sometimes very short)
i	as in 'hit'
o	as in 'hot'
u	as in 'book'

The dash (macron) above the vowel indicates that it is long:

ā	as the 'a' in 'father'
ē	as the 'e' in 'heir'
ī	like the 'e' in 'ear', only softer
ō	as the 'o' in 'for'
ū	as the 'u' in 'rude'

You may also see long vowels transliterated as double vowels, eg, 'aa' (ā), 'ee' (ī), 'oo' (ū).

Consonants

Pronunciation for all Arabic consonants is covered in the alphabet table on the following page. Note that when double consonants occur in transliterations, both are pronounced. For example, *al-hammam* (toilet), is pronounced 'al-ham-mam'.

Other Sounds

Arabic has two sounds that are very tricky for non-Arabs to produce, the 'ayn and the glottal stop. The letter 'ayn represents a sound with no English equivalent that comes even close. It is similar to the glottal stop (which is not actually represented in the alphabet), but the muscles at the back of the throat are gagged more forcefully – it has been described as the sound of someone

The Arabic Alphabet

Final	Medial	Initial	Alone	Transliteration	Pronunciation
‍ا			ا	ā	as the 'a' in 'father'
ب	ب	ب	ب	b	as in 'bet'
ت	ت	ت	ت	t	as in 'ten' (but the tongue touches the teeth)
ث	ث	ث	ث	th	as in 'thin'; also as 's' or 't'
ج	ج	ج	ج	j	as in 'jet'; often also as the 's' in 'measure'
ح	ح	ح	ح	H	a strongly whispered 'h', almost like a sigh of relief
خ	خ	خ	خ	kh	a rougher sound than the 'ch' in Scottish *loch*
د			د	d	as in 'den' (but the tongue touches the teeth)
ذ			ذ	dh	as the 'th' in 'this'; also as 'd' or 'z'
ر			ر	r	a rolled 'r', as in the Spanish word *caro*
ز			ز	z	as in 'zip'
س	س	س	س	s	as in 'so', never as in 'wisdom'
ش	ش	ش	ش	sh	as in 'ship'
ص	ص	ص	ص	ş	emphatic 's'
ض	ض	ض	ض	ḍ	emphatic 'd'
ط	ط	ط	ط	ţ	emphatic 't'
ظ	ظ	ظ	ظ	z̧	emphatic 'z'
ع	ع	ع	ع	'	the Arabic letter 'ayn; pronounce as a glottal stop – like the closing of the throat before saying 'Oh oh!' (see Other Sounds on p.300)
غ	غ	غ	غ	gh	a guttural sound like Parisian 'r'
ف	ف	ف	ف	f	as in 'far'
ق	ق	ق	ق	q	a strongly guttural 'k' sound; often pronounced as a glottal stop
ك	ك	ك	ك	k	as in 'king'
ل	ل	ل	ل	l	as in 'lamb'
م	م	م	م	m	as in 'me'
ن	ن	ن	ن	n	as in 'name'
ه	ه	ه	ه	h	as in 'ham'
و			و	w	as in 'wet'; or
				ū	long, as the 'oo' on 'food'; or
				aw	as the 'ow' in 'how'
ي	ي	ي	ي	y	as in 'yes'; or
				ī	as the 'e' in 'ear', only softer; or
				ay	as the 'y' in 'by' or as the 'ay' in 'way'

Vowels Not all Arabic vowel sounds are represented in the alphabet. See Pronunciation on p.300.

Emphatic Consonants To simplify the transliteration system used in this book, the emphatic consonants have not been included.

being strangled. In many transliteration systems 'ayn is represented by an opening quotation mark, and the glottal stop by a closing quotation mark. To make the transliterations in this language guide easier to use, we have not distinguished between the glottal stop and the 'ayn, using the closing quotation mark to represent both sounds. You should find that Arabic speakers will still understand you.

Transliteration

It's worth noting here that transliteration from the Arabic script into English – or any other language for that matter – is at best an approximate science.

The presence of sounds unknown in European languages and the fact that the script is 'defective' (most vowels are not written) combine to make it nearly impossible to settle on one universally accepted method of transliteration. A wide variety of spellings is therefore possible for words when they appear in Latin script – and that goes for places and people's names as well.

The whole thing is further complicated by the wide variety of dialects and the imaginative ideas Arabs themselves often have on appropriate spelling in, say, English (words spelt one way in Jordan may look very different again in Lebanon, with strong French influences); not even the most venerable of western Arabists have been able to come up with a satisfactory solution.

While striving to reflect the language as closely as possible and aiming at consistency,

The Transliteration Dilemma

TE Lawrence, when asked by his publishers to clarify 'inconsistencies in the spelling of proper names' in *Seven Pillars of Wisdom* – his account of the Arab Revolt in WWI – wrote back:

Arabic names won't go into English. There are some "scientific systems" of transliteration, helpful to people who know enough Arabic not to need helping, but a washout for the world. I spell my names anyhow, to show what rot the systems are.

this book generally spells place, street and hotel names and the like as the locals have done. Don't be surprised if you come across several versions of the same thing.

FRENCH

Almost everybody in Tunisia speaks French, so if the thought of getting your mind around Arabic is too much, it'd be a good investment to learn a little French instead.

In French, an important distinction is made between *tu* and *vous*, which both mean 'you', although in general younger people insist less on this distinction. *Tu* is only used when addressing people you know well, or children. When addressing an adult who is not a personal friend, *vous* should be used unless the person invites you to use *tu*.

USEFUL WORDS & PHRASES

The following words and phrases should help you communicate on a basic level in either Arabic or French. For a more detailed list of food terms, see the food section at the end of the Facts for the Visitor chapter.

Pronouns

I	*ana*	je
you (sing)	*inta/inti* (m/f)	tu (informal)/ vous (pol)
he/she	*huwa/hīya*	il/elle
we	*eHna*	nous
you (pl)	*intum*	vous
they	*huma*	ils/elles (m/f)

Greetings & Civilities

Hello.
   as-salām 'alaykum (literally: 'peace be upon you')
   Bonjour.
Hello. (in response – 'and upon you be peace')
   wa 'alaykum as-salām
Goodbye. ('go in safety')
   ma' as-salāma
   Au revoir/Salut.
Good morning.
   sabaH al-khēr
   Bonjour.
Good morning. (in response)
   sabaH an-nūr

Good evening.
masa' al-khēr
Bonsoir.
Good evening. (in response)
masa' an-nūr
Welcome.
marhaba
How are you?
kayf Hālek?
Comment allez-vous/ça va?
Fine, thank you.
bikhēr al-Hamdu lillah (thanks be to
God)
Bien, merci.

Basics
Yes.	*īyeh/na'am*	Oui.
No.	*la*	Non.
No, thank you.	*la, shukran*	Non, merci.
Please.	*men fadhlek*	S'il vous plaît.

Thank you (very much).
shukran (jazilan)
Merci (beaucoup).
You're welcome. (ie, don't mention it)
la shukran 'ala wajib
De rien/Je vous en prie.
Excuse me.
sa'mahni
Excusez-moi/Pardon.
Why?
laysh?
Pourquoi?
Is there ...?
hal hou ...?
Il y a ...?
Who is that?
mīn hadha?
C'est qui, celui/celle? (m/f)
Go ahead/Move it/Come on!
hay bina!
Allons-y!

Language Difficulties
Do you speak ...?
tatakallem ...?
Parlez-vous ...?

English	*inglīz*	anglais
French	*farans*	français
German	*almāni*	allemand

I understand.
fhemt
Je comprend.
I don't understand.
ma fhemtesh
Je ne comprend pas.

Small Talk
What's your name?
ma'howa ismok?
Comment vous appelez-vous?
My name is ...
ismī howa ...
Je m'appelle ...
How old are you?
ma' howa'amrak?
Quel âge avez-vous?
I'm 25.
'āndī khamsa wa 'ashrīn
J'ai vingt-cinq ans.
Where are you from?
min īn inta/inti/intum? (m/f/pl)
D'où êtes-vous?

I'm/We're from ...
ana/eHna min ...
Je viens/Nous venons ...

America	*amrīka*	de l'Amérique
Australia	*ustralya*	de l'Australie
Canada	*kanada*	du Canada
England	*inglaterra*	de l'Angleterre
France	*firansa*	de la France
Germany	*almanya*	de l'Allemagne
Italy	*itāliyya*	de l'Italie
Japan	*al-yaban*	du Japon
Netherlands	*holanda*	des Pays Bas
Spain	*isbanya*	de l'Espagne
Sweden	*as-swīd*	du Suède

Getting Around
I want to go to ...
urīd an adhaba ila ...
Je veux aller à ...
What is the fare to ...?
mahowa assir ila ...?
Combien coûte le billet pour ...?

When does the ... leave/arrive?
emta qiyam/wusūl ...?
À quelle heure part/arrive ...?

bus	*al-otobīs*	l'autobus
train	*al-qitar*	le train
boat	*as-safīna*	le bateau

Where is (the) ...?
   fein ...?
   Où est ...?
bus station for ...
   maHattat al-otobīs li ...
   la gare routière pour ...
bus stop
   mawqif al-otobīs
   l'arrêt d'autobus
train station
   maHattat al-qitar
   la gare
ticket office
   maktab at-tazkara
   la billeterie/le guichet

street	*az-zanqa*	la rue
city	*al-medīna*	la ville
village	*al-qarya*	le village

Which bus goes to ...?
   ey kar yamshī ila ...?
   Quel autobus part pour ...?
Does this bus go to ...?
   yamshī had al-kar ila ...?
   Cet autobus-là va-t-il à ...?
How many buses per day go to ...?
   kam kar kul yūmchi ila ...?
   Il y a combien d'autobus chaque
   jour pour ...?
Please tell me when we arrive.
   emta nassil men fadhlek
   Dîtes-moi quand on arrive, s'il vous plaît.
Stop here, please.
   qif honamen fadhlek
   Arrêtez ici, s'il vous plaît.
Please wait for me.
   intadhirnē men fadhlek
   Attendez-moi, s'il vous plaît.
May I/we sit here?
   (wash) yimkin ajlis/najlis hona?
   Puis-je m'asseoir ici?
Where can I rent a bicycle?
   fein yimkin ana akri beshklīta?
   Où est-ce que je peux louer une bicyclette?

address	*'anwān*	adresse
airport	*matār*	aéroport
camel	*jamal*	chameau
car	*sayara*	voiture
crowded	*zHam*	plein
daily	*kull yūm*	chaque jour
donkey	*Humār*	âne
horse	*Husān*	cheval
number	*raqm*	numéro
ticket	*tazkara*	billet
Wait!	*intadhirnī!*	Attendez!

Directions

How far is ...?
   kam kilo li ...?
   Combien de kilomètres à ...?
Which direction?
   aya ittijah?
   Quelle direction?

Where?	*fein?*	Où?
left/right	*yasar/yamīn*	gauche/droite
here/there	*huna/hunak*	ici/là
next to	*bi-janib*	à côté de
opposite	*muqabbal*	en face de
north	*shamal*	nord
south	*janūb*	sud
east	*sharq*	est
west	*gharb*	ouest

Around Town

Where is (the) ...?
   fein ...?
   Où est ...?

bank	*al-banka*	la banque
barber	*al-Hallaq*	le coiffeur
beach	*ash-shātta'*	la plage
embassy	*as-sifāra*	l'ambassade
market	*as-sūq*	le marché
mosque	*al-jām*	la mosqué
museum	*al-matHaf*	le musée
old city	*al-medīna*	la médina
palace/castle	*al-qasr*	le palais/château
pharmacy	*farmasyan*	la pharmacie
police station	*al-bolīs*	la police
post office	*al-bōsta/*	la poste
	maktab al-barīd	
restaurant	*al-mat'am*	le restaurant
university	*al-jami'a*	l'université

Signs

ENTRY	مدخل
EXIT	خروج
TOILETS (Men)	حمام للرجال
TOILETS (Women)	حمام للنساء
HOSPITAL	مستشفى
POLICE	الشرطة
PROHIBITED	ممنوع

I want to change ...
urīd/an asrif ...
Je voudrais changer ...
money
fulūs
de l'argent
travellers cheques
shīkāt siyaHiyya
des chèques de voyage

Accommodation

Where is the hotel?
fein (mawjoud) al-otēl?
Où est l'hôtel?
Can I see the room?
(wash) yimkin lī nshūf al-ghorfa?
Peux-je voir la chambre?
How much is this room per night?
kamel ghorfa ellaylar?
Combien est cette chambre pour une nuit?
That's too expensive.
ghālī khatiran
C'est trop cher.
Do you have any cheaper rooms?
hal indakum ghorfa arkhas?
Avez-vous des chambres moins chères?
This is fine.
hada bahi
Ça va bien.

air-con	*klīmafīzasīyon*	climatisation
bed	*firash*	lit
blanket	*batanīya*	couverture
camp site	*mukhaym*	camping

full	*malyen*	complet
hot water	*ma skhūn*	eau chaude
key	*meftaH*	clef (or clé)
room	*ghorfa*	chambre
shower	*dūsh*	douche
toilet	*bayt al-ma/ mirHad*	les toilettes
youth hostel	*oberž dar shabbab*	auberge de jeunesse

Shopping

Where can I buy ...?
fein yimkin ashterī ...?
Où est-ce que je peux acheter ...?
Do you have...?
wash 'andkum ...?
Avez-vous ...?

How much?	*bi-kam?*	Combien?
too much	*ghalī awī*	trop cher
cheap	*rakhīs*	bon marché
expensive	*ghalī*	cher
big	*kbīr*	grand
small	*sghīr*	petit
open	*meHlool*	ouvert
stamps	*tawāba*	des timbres
newspaper	*al-jarida*	un journal

Time

When?	*emta?*	Quand?
now	*allān/nak*	maintenant
today	*al-yūm*	aujourd'hui
tomorrow	*ghaddan*	demain
yesterday	*al-bareh*	hier
morning	*fis-sabaH*	matin
afternoon	*fil-ashīya*	après-midi
evening	*masa'*	soir
day/night	*nahar/layl*	jour/nuit
week	*usbu'*	semaine
month	*shahr*	mois
year	*'am*	an

What time is it?
sa'a kam?
Quelle heure est-il?
At what time?
fī sa'a kam?
À quelle heure?

after	*min ba'd*	après
on time	*fil-waqt*	à l'heure

| early | *bakrī* | tôt |
| late | *mu'attāguiz* | tard |

Days of the Week

Monday	*(nhar) al-itnēn*	lundi
Tuesday	*(nhar) at-talata*	mardi
Wednesday	*(nhar) al-arba*	mercredi
Thursday	*(nhar) al-khamīs*	jeudi
Friday	*(nhar) al-juma*	vendredi
Saturday	*(nhar) as-sabt*	samedi
Sunday	*(nhar) al-ahad*	dimanche

Months of the Year

In Tunisia, the names for the months of the Gregorian calendar are virtually the same as in English and are easily recognisable:

January	*yanāyir*	janvier
February	*fibrāyir*	février
March	*māris*	mars
April	*abrīl*	avril
May	*māyu*	mai
June	*yunyu*	juin
July	*yulyu*	juillet
August	*aghustus*	août
September	*sibtimbir*	septembre
October	*uktoobir*	octobre
November	*nufimbir*	novembre
December	*disimbir*	décembre

The Islamic year has 12 lunar months and is 11 days shorter than the Gregorian calendar, so important Muslim dates fall about 10 days earlier each (Western) year. It's impossible to predict exactly when they will fall, as this depends on when the new moon is sighted. The Islamic, or Hijra, calendar months are:

1st	*Moharram*
2nd	*Safar*
3rd	*Rabi' al-Awal*
4th	*Rabi' al-Akhir* or *Rabi' at-Tani*
5th	*Jumada al-Awal*
6th	*Jumada al-Akhir* or *Jumada at-Taniyya*
7th	*Rajab*
8th	*Sha'aban*
9th	*Ramadan*
10th	*Shawwal*
11th	*Zūl Qe'da*
12th	*Zūl Hijja*

Numbers

While numerals in Arabic script are simple enough to learn, you won't have to worry about them because Tunisia uses the Western system.

0	*sifr*	zéro
1	*wāHid*	un
2	*itnīn*	deux
3	*talata*	trois
4	*arba'a*	quatre
5	*khamsa*	cinq
6	*sitta*	six
7	*saba'a*	sept
8	*tamanya*	huit
9	*tissa'*	neuf
10	*'ashara*	dix
11	*wāHidash*	onze
12	*itna'ash*	douze
13	*talattash*	treize
14	*arba'atash*	quatorze
15	*khamastash*	quinze
16	*sitt'ash*	seize
17	*saba'atash*	dix-sept
18	*tamantash*	dix-huit
19	*tissa'atash*	dix-neuf
20	*'ashrīn*	vingt
21	*wāHid wa 'ashrīn*	vingt-et-un
22	*itnīn wa 'ashrīn*	vingt-deux
30	*talatīn*	trente
40	*arba'īn*	quarante
50	*khamsīn*	cinquante
60	*sittīn*	soixante
70	*saba'īn*	soixante-dix
80	*tamanīn*	quatre-vingts
90	*tissa'īn*	quatre-vingt-dix
100	*miyya*	cent
101	*miyya wa wāHid*	cent-un
200	*miyyatīn*	deux cents
300	*talata mia*	trois cents
400	*arba'a mia*	quatre cents
1000	*alf*	mille

Ordinal Numbers

first	*'awwal*	premier
second	*tānḍ*	deuxième
third	*tālit*	troisième
fourth	*rābi'*	quatrième
fifth	*khāmis*	cinquième

Glossary

This glossary includes terms and abbreviations you may come across during your travels in Tunisia. Where appropriate, the capital letter in brackets indicates whether the terms are French (F) or Arabic (A).

Abbasids – Baghdad-based ruling dynasty (AD 749–1258) of the Arab/Islamic Empire
Africa Proconsularis – Roman province of Africa
agha – a military commander or a title of respect (in the Ottoman Empire)
Aghlabids – Arab dynasty based in Kairouan who ruled Tunisia (AD 800–909)
ain (A) – water source or spring
Allah (A) – God
Almohads – Berber rulers of Spain and North Africa (1130–1269)
Almoravids – dynasty of Berbers from the Sahara, reigned from 1061 to 1106 in Morocco and the Maghreb, and later in Andalusia, after 1086.
assaba (A) – headband worn by Berber women
ASM – Association de Sauvegarde de la Medina; group charged with preserving the medinas of a number of Tunisian towns
auberge de jeunesse (F) – youth hostel affiliated to Hostelling International

bab (A) – city gate
bakhnoug (A) – traditional shawl worn by Berber women
Barbary Coast – European term for the Mediterranean coast of North Africa in the 16th to 19th centuries
basilica – Roman building used for public administration; early Christian church
Berbers – indigenous (non-Arab) people of North Africa
bey – provincial governor in the Ottoman Empire; rulers of Tunisia from the 17th century until independence in 1957
boissons gazeuses (F) – carbonated drinks
borj (A) – fort (literally 'tower')
boukha (A) – local spirit made from figs
brochette (F) – kebab

burnous (A) – hooded winter cape worn by men
buvette (F) – refreshment room or stall

calèche (F) – horse-drawn carriage
caliph – Islamic ruler, originally referred to the successors of the Prophet Mohammed
camionnette (F) – small pick-up used as a taxi
capitol – main temple of a Roman town, usually situated in the forum
caravanserai – see *funduq*
casse-croûte (F) – Tunisian fast food; a sandwich made from half a French loaf stuffed with a variety of fillings
centre des stages et des vacances (F) – holiday camps
chechia (A) – red felt hat
chicha (A) – water pipe used to smoke tobacco
chorba (A) – soup
chott (A) – salt lake or marsh
confort (F) – class above 1st class on passenger trains
corniche (F) – coastal road
corsairs – pirates, especially those who operated on the North African coast from the 16th to the 19th century
couscous – semolina granules, the staple food of Tunisia

dar (A) – town house or palace
deglat ennour (A) – a type of date (literally 'finger of light')
dey – the Ottoman army's equivalent of a sergeant; rulers of Tunisia in the 16th century
diwan – assembly (in the Ottoman Empire)

eid (A) – feast
Eid al-Adha (A) – feast of Sacrifice marking the pilgrimage to Mecca. Sometimes called Eid al-Kebir.
Eid al-Fitr (A) – feast of the Breaking of the Fast, celebrated at the end of Ramadan
emir – military commander or governor
erg – sand sea; desert

Fatimids – Muslim dynasty (AD 909–1171) who defeated the *Aghlabids* and ruled Tunisia from Mahdia from AD 909 to 969

forum – open space at the centre of Roman towns

fouta (A) – cotton bath towel provided in a *hammam*

funduq (A) – former lodging houses or inns for the travelling merchants of the camel caravans, also known as *caravanserai*; Arab word for hotel

gare routière (F) – bus station

gargotte (F) – cheap restaurant that serves basic food

ghar (A) – cave

ghorfa (A) – literally, room; especially a long, barrel-vaulted room built to store grain

guetiffa – a thick-pile, knotted Berber carpet

Hafsids – rulers of *Ifriqiyya* from the 13th to the 16th century

hajj (A) – the pilgrimage to the holy sites in and around Mecca, the pinnacle of a devout Muslim's life

hammam (A) – public bathhouse

harissa (A) – spicy chilli paste

harout (A) – traditional Jerban weaver's workshop

hedeyed (A) – finely engraved, wide bracelets made of gold or silver

hijab (A) – woman's veil or headscarf

hijra (A) – Mohammed's flight from Mecca in AD 622; also the name of the Muslim calendar

Hilalian tribes – tribes of Upper Egypt who invaded the Maghreb in the 11th century, causing great destruction

Hizb al-Nahda – Renaissance Party, the main Islamic opposition party

Husseinites – dynasty of *beys* who ruled Tunisia from 1705 to 1957

Ibadites – an offshoot of the *Kharajite* sect found only on Jerba and in the villages of the M'Zab valley in Algeria

ibn (A) – son of

Ifriqiyya – Arab province of North Africa, including Tunisia and parts of Libya

iftar (A) – (also spelt 'ftur') the breaking of the day's fast during *Ramadan*

imam (A) – Islamic equivalent of a priest

jami (A) – the main district mosque

janissary – infantryman in the Ottoman army

jebel (A) – hill or mountain

jihad (A) – holy war

kalaa (A) – Berber hill fort

kasbah (A) – fort or citadel

kassa (A) – a coarse mitten used in the steam room of a *hammam*

Kharijites – puritanical Islamic sect, which broke away from the mainstream *Sunnis* in AD 657 and inspired Berber rebellions from the 8th to the 10th century

kholkal (A) – gold or silver anklets

khomsa – hand-of-Fatima motif

khutba (A) – weekly sermon in the mosque

kilim (A) – woven rug decorated with typical Berber motifs

koubba (A) – domed roof

kouttab (A) – Quranic primary school

ksar (A) – (plural *ksour)* a fortified Berber stronghold consisting of many *ghorfas*

ksibah (A) – small fort

Limes Tripolitanus – the defensive line developed by the Romans in southern Tunisia

louage (F) – shared long-distance taxi

Maghreb – term used to describe north-west Africa, including Morocco, Algeria and Tunisia

maison des jeunes (F) – government-run youth hostel

malouf (A) – traditional Tunisian music

marabout (A) – Muslim holy man or saint

masjid (A) – small local mosque

medersa (A) – Quranic school

medina (A) – city; the old quarter of Tunisian towns and cities

menzel (A) – fortified family dwelling found on Jerba

mergoum (A) – woven carpet with geometric designs

mihrab (A) – vaulted niche in a mosque, which indicates the direction of Mecca

minaret – tower of a mosque from which the *muezzin* calls the faithful to prayer

minbar (A) – the pulpit in a mosque

mouloud (A) – *Maghreb* term for the Mawlid an-Nabi, the feast celebrating the birth of the Prophet Mohammed

moussem (A) – pilgrimage to a *marabout* or shrine

muezzin (A) – mosque official who calls the faithful to prayer

Muradites – line of Tunisian *beys*, ruling from the 17th to 18th century

nador (A) – watch tower

Numidians – tribe from present-day Algeria, once controlled Northern Tunisia; founders of the cities of Bulla Regia, Sicca (El-Kef) and Thugga (Dougga)

ONAT – the Office National de l'Artisanat Tunisien; government-run fixed-price craft shops

ONTT – Office National du Tourisme Tunisien; government-run national tourist office

Ottoman Empire – former Turkish Empire, of which Tunisia was part; based in Constantinople from the late 13th century to the end of WWI

oued (A) – river; also dry riverbed

palmeraie (F) – palm grove; the area around an oasis where date palms, vegetables and fruit are grown

pasha – provincial governor or high official in the Ottoman Empire

patisserie (F) – cake and pastry shop

pension (F) – guesthouse

Phoenicians – a great sea-faring nation, based in modern Lebanon, which dominated trade in the Mediterranean in the 1st millennium BC; founders of Carthage

PSD – Parti Socialiste Destourien (called the Neo-Destour Party before 1964); the first nationalist party in Tunisia

Punic – The Phoenician culture that evolved in North Africa

Punic Wars – three wars waged between Rome and Carthage in the 3rd and 2nd centuries BC, resulting in the destruction of Carthage by the Romans in 146 BC

qibla (A) – the direction of Mecca in a mosque, indicated by the *mihrab*

Quran (A) – the holy book of Islam

Ramadan – ninth month of the Muslim year, a time of fasting

razzegoui (A) – a large white grape that ripens to a pink blush

RCD – Rassemblement Constitutionel Democratique; President Ben Ali's ruling party

ribat (A) – fortified Islamic monastery

rôtisserie (F) – basic restaurant serving roast chicken

Sahel – eastern part of central Tunisia occupying the large, fertile coastal bulge between the Gulf of Hammamet and the Gulf of Gabès

sebkha (A) – salt flat or coastal marshland

sharia'a (F) – Quranic law

Shiites – one of two main Islamic sects (see also *Sunnis);* followers believe that the true imams are descended from Ali

sidi (A) – saint

skifa (A) – gate

SNCFT – Société Nationale des Chemins de Fer Tunisiens; the national railway company

SNTRI – the Société Nationale du Transport Interurbain; the national bus company

souq (A) – market

stele – grave stone

Sufi – follower of any of the Islamic mystical orders that emphasise dancing, chanting and trances to attain unity with God

Sunnis – the main Islamic sect (see also *Shiites)* derived from followers of the *Ummayyad* caliphate

syndicat d'initiative (F) – municipal tourist office

Taxiphone – public telephone

Tell – the high plains of the Tunisian Dorsale, in central Tunisia

thibarine – a local spirit from the village of Thibar near Dougga

tophet – sacrificial site

tourbet (A) – mausoleum

Ummayyads – first great dynasty of Arab Muslim rulers (AD 661–750), based in Damascus

zaouia (A) – a complex surrounding the tomb of a saint

zone touristique (F) – tourist strip

Lonely Planet Guides by Region

Lonely Planet is known worldwide for publishing practical, reliable and no-nonsense travel information in our guides and on our Web site. The Lonely Planet list covers just about every accessible part of the world. Currently there are 16 series: Travel guides, Shoestring guides, Condensed guides, Phrasebooks, Read This First, Healthy Travel, Walking guides, Cycling guides, Watching Wildlife guides, Pisces Diving & Snorkeling guides, City Maps, Road Atlases, Out to Eat, World Food, Journeys travel literature and Pictorials.

AFRICA Africa on a shoestring • Botswana • Cairo • Cairo City Map • Cape Town • Cape Town City Map • East Africa • Egypt • Egyptian Arabic phrasebook • Ethiopia, Eritrea & Djibouti • Ethiopian Amharic phrasebook • The Gambia & Senegal • Healthy Travel Africa • Kenya • Malawi • Morocco • Moroccan Arabic phrasebook • Mozambique • Namibia • Read This First: Africa • South Africa, Lesotho & Swaziland • Southern Africa • Southern Africa Road Atlas • Swahili phrasebook • Tanzania, Zanzibar & Pemba • Trekking in East Africa • Tunisia • Watching Wildlife East Africa • Watching Wildlife Southern Africa • West Africa • World Food Morocco • Zambia • Zimbabwe, Botswana & Namibia
Travel Literature: Mali Blues: Traveling to an African Beat • The Rainbird: A Central African Journey • Songs to an African Sunset: A Zimbabwean Story

AUSTRALIA & THE PACIFIC Aboriginal Australia & the Torres Strait Islands •Auckland • Australia • Australian phrasebook • Australia Road Atlas • Cycling Australia • Cycling New Zealand • Fiji • Fijian phrasebook • Healthy Travel Australia, NZ & the Pacific • Islands of Australia's Great Barrier Reef • Melbourne • Melbourne City Map • Micronesia • New Caledonia • New South Wales • New Zealand • Northern Territory • Outback Australia • Out to Eat – Melbourne • Out to Eat – Sydney • Papua New Guinea • Pidgin phrasebook • Queensland • Rarotonga & the Cook Islands • Samoa • Solomon Islands • South Australia • South Pacific • South Pacific phrasebook • Sydney • Sydney City Map • Sydney Condensed • Tahiti & French Polynesia • Tasmania • Tonga • Tramping in New Zealand • Vanuatu • Victoria • Walking in Australia • Watching Wildlife Australia • Western Australia
Travel Literature: Islands in the Clouds: Travels in the Highlands of New Guinea • Kiwi Tracks: A New Zealand Journey • Sean & David's Long Drive

CENTRAL AMERICA & THE CARIBBEAN Bahamas, Turks & Caicos • Baja California • Belize, Guatemala & Yucatán • Bermuda • Central America on a shoestring • Costa Rica • Costa Rica Spanish phrasebook • Cuba • Cycling Cuba • Dominican Republic & Haiti • Eastern Caribbean • Guatemala • Havana • Healthy Travel Central & South America • Jamaica • Mexico • Mexico City • Panama • Puerto Rico • Read This First: Central & South America • Virgin Islands • World Food Caribbean • World Food Mexico • Yucatán
Travel Literature: Green Dreams: Travels in Central America

EUROPE Amsterdam • Amsterdam City Map • Amsterdam Condensed • Andalucía • Athens • Austria • Baltic States phrasebook • Barcelona • Barcelona City Map • Belgium & Luxembourg • Berlin • Berlin City Map • Britain • British phrasebook • Brussels, Bruges & Antwerp • Brussels City Map • Budapest • Budapest City Map • Canary Islands • Catalunya & the Costa Brava • Central Europe • Central Europe phrasebook • Copenhagen • Corfu & the Ionians • Corsica • Crete • Crete Condensed • Croatia • Cycling Britain • Cycling France • Cyprus • Czech & Slovak Republics • Czech phrasebook • Denmark • Dublin • Dublin City Map • Dublin Condensed • Eastern Europe • Eastern Europe phrasebook • Edinburgh • Edinburgh City Map • England • Estonia, Latvia & Lithuania • Europe on a shoestring • Europe phrasebook • Finland • Florence • Florence City Map • France • Frankfurt City Map • Frankfurt Condensed • French phrasebook • Georgia, Armenia & Azerbaijan • Germany • German phrasebook • Greece • Greek Islands • Greek phrasebook • Hungary • Iceland, Greenland & the Faroe Islands • Ireland • Italian phrasebook • Italy • Kraków • Lisbon • The Loire • London • London City Map • London Condensed • Madrid • Madrid City Map • Malta • Mediterranean Europe • Milan, Turin & Genoa • Moscow • Munich • Netherlands • Normandy • Norway • Out to Eat – London • Out to Eat – Paris • Paris • Paris City Map • Paris Condensed • Poland • Polish phrasebook • Portugal • Portuguese phrasebook • Prague • Prague City Map • Provence & the Côte d'Azur • Read This First: Europe • Rhodes & the Dodecanese • Romania & Moldova • Rome • Rome City Map • Rome Condensed • Russia, Ukraine & Belarus • Russian phrasebook • Scandinavian & Baltic Europe • Scandinavian phrasebook • Scotland • Sicily • Slovenia • South-West France • Spain • Spanish phrasebook • Stockholm • St Petersburg • St Petersburg City Map • Sweden • Switzerland • Tuscany • Ukrainian phrasebook • Venice • Vienna • Wales • Walking in Britain • Walking in France • Walking in Ireland • Walking in Italy • Walking in Scotland • Walking in Spain • Walking in Switzerland • Western Europe • World Food France • World Food Greece • World Food Ireland • World Food Italy • World Food Spain **Travel Literature:** After Yugoslavia • Love and War in the Apennines • The Olive Grove: Travels in Greece • On the Shores of the Mediterranean • Round Ireland in Low Gear • A Small Place in Italy

Lonely Planet Mail Order

onely Planet products are distributed worldwide. They are also available by mail order from Lonely Planet, so if you have difficulty finding a title please write to us. North and South American residents should write to 150 Linden St, Oakland, CA 94607, USA; European and African residents should write to 10a Spring Place, London NW5 3BH, UK; and residents of other countries to Locked Bag 1, Footscray, Victoria 3011, Australia.

INDIAN SUBCONTINENT & THE INDIAN OCEAN Bangladesh • Bengali phrasebook • Bhutan • Delhi • Goa • Healthy Travel Asia & India • Hindi & Urdu phrasebook • India • India & Bangladesh City Map • Indian Himalaya • Karakoram Highway • Kathmandu City Map • Kerala • Madagascar • Maldives • Mauritius, Réunion & Seychelles • Mumbai (Bombay) • Nepal • Nepali phrasebook • North India • Pakistan • Rajasthan • Read This First: Asia & India • South India • Sri Lanka • Sri Lanka phrasebook • Tibet • Tibetan phrasebook • Trekking in the Indian Himalaya • Trekking in the Karakoram & Hindukush • Trekking in the Nepal Himalaya • World Food India **Travel Literature:** The Age of Kali: Indian Travels and Encounters • Hello Goodnight: A Life of Goa • In Rajasthan • Maverick in Madagascar • A Season in Heaven: True Tales from the Road to Kathmandu • Shopping for Buddhas • A Short Walk in the Hindu Kush • Slowly Down the Ganges

MIDDLE EAST & CENTRAL ASIA Bahrain, Kuwait & Qatar • Central Asia • Central Asia phrasebook • Dubai • Farsi (Persian) phrasebook • Hebrew phrasebook • Iran • Israel & the Palestinian Territories • Istanbul • Istanbul City Map • Istanbul to Cairo • Istanbul to Kathmandu • Jerusalem • Jerusalem City Map • Jordan • Lebanon • Middle East • Oman & the United Arab Emirates • Syria • Turkey • Turkish phrasebook • World Food Turkey • Yemen **Travel Literature:** Black on Black: Iran Revisited • Breaking Ranks: Turbulent Travels in the Promised Land • The Gates of Damascus • Kingdom of the Film Stars: Journey into Jordan

NORTH AMERICA Alaska • Boston • Boston City Map • Boston Condensed • British Columbia • California & Nevada • California Condensed • Canada • Chicago • Chicago City Map • Chicago Condensed • Florida • Georgia & the Carolinas • Great Lakes • Hawaii • Hiking in Alaska • Hiking in the USA • Honolulu & Oahu City Map • Las Vegas • Los Angeles • Los Angeles City Map • Louisiana & the Deep South • Miami • Miami City Map • Montreal • New England • New Orleans • New Orleans City Map • New York City • New York City City Map • New York City Condensed • New York, New Jersey & Pennsylvania • Oahu • Out to Eat – San Francisco • Pacific Northwest • Rocky Mountains • San Diego & Tijuana • San Francisco • San Francisco City Map • Seattle • Seattle City Map • Southwest • Texas • Toronto • USA • USA phrasebook • Vancouver • Vancouver City Map • Virginia & the Capital Region • Washington, DC • Washington, DC City Map • World Food New Orleans **Travel Literature**: Caught Inside: A Surfer's Year on the California Coast • Drive Thru America

NORTH-EAST ASIA Beijing • Beijing City Map • Cantonese phrasebook • China • Hiking in Japan • Hong Kong & Macau • Hong Kong City Map • Hong Kong Condensed • Japan • Japanese phrasebook • Korea • Korean phrasebook • Kyoto • Mandarin phrasebook • Mongolia • Mongolian phrasebook • Seoul • Shanghai • South-West China • Taiwan • Tokyo • Tokyo Condensed • World Food Hong Kong • World Food Japan **Travel Literature:** In Xanadu: A Quest • Lost Japan

SOUTH AMERICA Argentina, Uruguay & Paraguay • Bolivia • Brazil • Brazilian phrasebook • Buenos Aires • Buenos Aires City Map • Chile & Easter Island • Colombia • Ecuador & the Galapagos Islands • Healthy Travel Central & South America • Latin American Spanish phrasebook • Peru • Quechua phrasebook • Read This First: Central & South America • Rio de Janeiro • Rio de Janeiro City Map • Santiago de Chile • South America on a shoestring • Trekking in the Patagonian Andes • Venezuela **Travel Literature**: Full Circle: A South American Journey

SOUTH-EAST ASIA Bali & Lombok • Bangkok • Bangkok City Map • Burmese phrasebook • Cambodia • Cycling Vietnam, Laos & Cambodia • East Timor phrasebook • Hanoi • Healthy Travel Asia & India • Hill Tribes phrasebook • Ho Chi Minh City (Saigon) • Indonesia • Indonesian phrasebook • Indonesia's Eastern Islands • Java • Lao phrasebook • Laos • Malay phrasebook • Malaysia, Singapore & Brunei • Myanmar (Burma) • Philippines • Pilipino (Tagalog) phrasebook • Read This First: Asia & India • Singapore • Singapore City Map • South-East Asia on a shoestring • South-East Asia phrasebook • Thailand • Thailand's Islands & Beaches • Thailand, Vietnam, Laos & Cambodia Road Atlas • Thai phrasebook • Vietnam • Vietnamese phrasebook • World Food Indonesia • World Food Thailand • World Food Vietnam

ALSO AVAILABLE: Antarctica • The Arctic • The Blue Man: Tales of Travel, Love and Coffee • Brief Encounters: Stories of Love, Sex & Travel • Buddhist Stupas in Asia: The Shape of Perfection • Chasing Rickshaws • The Last Grain Race • Lonely Planet ... On the Edge: Adventurous Escapades from Around the World • Lonely Planet Unpacked • Lonely Planet Unpacked Again • Not the Only Planet: Science Fiction Travel Stories • Ports of Call: A Journey by Sea • Sacred India • Travel Photography: A Guide to Taking Better Pictures • Travel with Children • Tuvalu: Portrait of an Island Nation

LONELY PLANET

You already know that Lonely Planet produces more than this one guidebook, but you might not be aware of the other products we have on this region. Here is a selection of titles that you may want to check out as well:

Africa on a shoestring
ISBN 0 86442 663 1
US$29.99 • UK£17.99

French phrasebook
ISBN 0 86442 450 7
US$5.95 • UK£3.99

Read this First: Africa
ISBN 1 86450 066 2
US$14.95 • UK£8.99

Healthy Travel Africa
ISBN 1 86450 050 6
US$5.95 • UK£3.99

Mediterranean Europe
ISBN 1 86450 154 5
US$27.99 • UK£15.99

Egypt
ISBN 0 86442 677 1
US$19.95 • UK£12.99

Egyptian Arabic phrasebook
ISBN 0 86442 070 6
US$3.95 • UK£2.50

Morocco
ISBN 0 86442 762 X
US$19.99 • UK£12.99

Middle East
ISBN 0 86442 701 8
US$24.95 • UK£14.99

Cairo
ISBN 0 86442 548 1
US$14.95 • UK£8.99

Available wherever books are sold

Index

Text

Bold indicates maps.

Bold indicates maps.

Boxed Text & Special Sections

MAP LEGEND

CITY ROUTES

Freeway	Freeway
Highway	Primary Road
Road	Secondary Road
Street	Street
Lane	Lane
	On/Off Ramp
	Unsealed Road
	One Way Street
	Pedestrian Street
	Stepped Street
	Tunnel
	Footbridge

REGIONAL ROUTES

	Tollway, Freeway
	Primary Road
	Secondary Road
	Minor Road

BOUNDARIES

	International
	Fortified Wall

HYDROGRAPHY

	River, Creek
	Lake
	Dry Lake; Salt Lake
	Spring; Rapids

TRANSPORT ROUTES & STATIONS

	Train
	Underground Train
	Metro
	Tramway
	Ferry
	Walking Trail
	Walking Tour
	Pier or Jetty

AREA FEATURES

	Building
	Park, Gardens
	Market
	Sports Ground
	Beach
	Muslim Cemetery
	Palmeraie
	Plaza

POPULATION SYMBOLS

✪ CAPITAL	National Capital
◉ CAPITAL	State Capital
● CITY	City
● Town	Town
● Village	Village
	Urban Area

MAP SYMBOLS

▪ Place to Stay	▼ Place to Eat	● Point of Interest
✈ Airport	♨ Fountain	⚲ Monument
⌂ Archaeological Site	⌓ Gate	☪ Mosque
✿ Bank	Ⓗ Hammam	▲ Mountain
⊕ Border Crossing	✛ Hospital	🏛 Museum
▣ Bus Terminal	🖥 Internet Cafe	🏞 National Park
▤ Cafe	☾ Islamic Monument	🏛 Palace
⛺ Camping	☆ Lighthouse	Ⓟ Parking
☩ Church	☀ Lookout	⊙ Petrol Station
▦ Cinema	🚖 Louage/Taxi	✚ Police Station
✉ Embassy		▭ Post Office
		Ⓟ Pub or Bar
		⊗ Shopping Centre
		✡ Synagogue
		☎ Telephone
		⊖ Toilet
		▪ Tomb
		❶ Tourist Information
		▭ Transport
		🔊 Zoo

Note: not all symbols displayed above appear in this book

LONELY PLANET OFFICES

Australia
Locked Bag 1, Footscray, Victoria 3011
☎ 03 8379 8000 fax 03 8379 8111
email: talk2us@lonelyplanet.com.au

USA
150 Linden St, Oakland, CA 94607
☎ 510 893 8555 TOLL FREE: 800 275 8555
fax 510 893 8572
email: info@lonelyplanet.com

UK
10a Spring Place, London NW5 3BH
☎ 020 7428 4800 fax 020 7428 4828
email: go@lonelyplanet.co.uk

France
1 rue du Dahomey, 75011 Paris
☎ 01 55 25 33 00 fax 01 55 25 33 01
email: bip@lonelyplanet.fr
www.lonelyplanet.fr

World Wide Web: www.lonelyplanet.com *or* AOL keyword: lp
Lonely Planet Images: lpi@lonelyplanet.com.au